In Pursuit of the PhD

In Pursuit of the PhD

William G. Bowen
and Neil L. Rudenstine

In collaboration with
Julie Ann Sosa, Graham Lord,
Marcia L. Witte, and Sarah E. Turner

PRINCETON UNIVERSITY PRESS
PRINCETON, NEW JERSEY

This book has been composed in Palatino.

Princeton University Press books are printed on acid-free paper and meet the
guidelines for permanence and durability of the Committee on Production Guidelines
for Book Longevity of the Council on Library Resources

Printed in Mexico

10 9 8 7 6 5 4 3

Library of Congress Cataloging-in-Publication Data

Bowen, William G.
    In pursuit of the PhD / William G. Bowen and Neil L. Rudenstine
        p.   cm.
    Includes bibliographical references and index.

    ISBN 0-691-04294-2

    1. Universities and colleges—United States—Graduate work.
    2. Doctor of philosophy degree—United States. 3. Educational
    surveys—United States.   I. Rudenstine, Neil L.   II. Title.
    LB2371.4.B68   1992
    378.1'553'0973—dc20   91-32321
                                                                      CIP

Contents

List of Figures

List of Tables

Preface

THIS study addresses questions that have been on our minds for many years as a result of our own experiences as graduate students, faculty members, and academic administrators. But it also has been prompted by more recent work. As is explained in Chapter One, a 1989 study (*Prospects for Faculty in the Arts and Sciences*) gave a new sense of urgency to our interest in seeking ways to improve the effectiveness of graduate programs. Doctoral education occupies a particularly critical place in the overall structure of higher education because it is the training ground for almost all those who become faculty members, as well as for many who pursue other vocations of broad import.

We also understand, however, why Derek Bok, president-emeritus of Harvard University, recently referred to graduate education as "the soft under-belly of the research university." It enjoys enormous prestige and yet is relatively unexamined and not carefully monitored. Undergraduate education is generally more visible, course evaluations are more common, students are members of a graduating "class," and commencement provides an occasion for annual stock-taking. Parents, alumni/ae, and student newspapers scrutinize education at the undergraduate level much more carefully than at the graduate level. Undergraduate studies are generally more comprehensible and have been experienced directly by more people. Faculty research is also subject to more scrutiny—when funding is sought, when manuscripts are submitted for publication, when articles and books are criticized by professional peers, and when faculty members submit resumes in connection with salary reviews and recommendations for promotion.

We were well aware earlier, and are even more aware now, of how hard it has been to obtain answers to even the most elementary questions concerning graduate education. For example, no one has been able to say with confidence what proportion of students who enter doctoral programs eventually earn doctorates. The long and uncertain duration of doctoral study makes it much more difficult to assess outcomes than would be the case if the entire process were usually completed within some specified period, such as four years. Another relevant consideration is the simple fact that graduate education is departmentally based. The decentralization of activities and responsibilities (with further de facto delegations to groups of faculty in subfields and even to individual faculty members) complicates enormously the task of even describing the process in anything like general terms, quite apart from collecting the most basic data. The relevant "units" are often small and very different from one another. Centralized record-keeping is a rarity, and when records do exist, they are often incompatible.

Doctoral education in the arts and sciences would benefit, we concluded, from intensive study, and we embarked on the present project in the summer of 1989. Like most studies of this kind, it resisted efforts to confine its scope and developed a voracious appetite for data. It has grown far beyond our original conception.

Still, we are extremely conscious of all the ground that we have failed to cover (see the discussion of scope in Chapter One). Since many of the data had to be collected at the level of the individual graduate program in highly labor-intensive ways, there was no escaping the need to be extremely selective, and somewhat arbitrary, in defining our institutional universe. Considerations of practicality and convenience (and the capacity of others to assist us) had to be given considerable weight.

A consequence is that many of the results reported here pertain to only a small number of fields of graduate study and to only a small number of graduate programs, most of them highly ranked. This is, by conscious design, a study focused on the top echelon of graduate programs, with special attention given to core fields of study within the humanities and related social sciences. It would be hazardous to generalize too readily to other fields and other programs.

An additional limitation is that we were unable to make any thorough study of the factors responsible for differences in outcomes for separate demographic groups. To cite an important example, we provide relatively little analysis of factors that have had particularly strong effects on the experiences of women in graduate school. We provide evidence indicating that many basic relationships hold for men and women alike (for example, the relationship between field of study and time-to-degree), and we also discuss some of the ways in which completion rates and time-to-degree have changed over time for women as compared with men. But these aspects of our research touch key issues associated with gender in only a glancing way, and there is clearly a need for more research addressed specifically to these questions.

Data limitations, and the extremely small numbers of individuals enrolled in particular programs of study, have made it even more difficult to say anything of consequence about minority groups. An obvious point is that far too few receive doctorates in the arts and sciences. It is equally evident that the factors responsible for such small numbers extend through the entire educational system and operate at all levels.

The kinds of questions that we could address also had to be limited. Not infrequently, we encountered intriguing findings that were sufficiently off our main path that we could not explore their meaning or significance. Our general approach has been to call attention to such observations, in the hope that others may wish to pursue the larger questions that they pose. (One example is differences between cohorts of students in their propensities to earn BAs versus PhDs in various fields, during different periods.) The appendix tables contain detailed data that may be relevant to a wide range of ancillary questions. Similarly, the methods that we have followed (for example, in aggregating data) are explained in some detail so that others may elect other approaches, if they wish to do so.

In contemplating again the mass of information contained in this book (and the even greater masses of numbers residing in computer files), we are reminded of a quotation concerning the intrusiveness of facts from one of J. M. Barrie's dramas: "He acquired them with reluctance and relinquished them with relief."

And we also recall a line from another play by Barrie, which may well be the response of tired readers who struggle through the prose that follows: "I loathe explanations."

We understand the sentiments expressed.

We now wish to thank the extraordinary group of colleagues and friends who have participated in this research project. Without attempting to mention everyone who has helped, we find that we still have an exceptionally long list of debts to acknowledge—which is itself a commentary on the collaborative nature of the process that has resulted in this book.

First, we wish to acknowledge the contributions of our four principal collaborators, whose names are listed on the title page in the chronological order of their involvement with the project:

- Julie Ann Sosa, a co-author of the previous study, *Prospects for Faculty in the Arts and Sciences*, played a critical role in the design of this study, worked closely with the participating universities and foundations in organizing the collection of data, and then made many valuable editorial suggestions in the last few months—while pursuing her medical education at Johns Hopkins University.
- Graham Lord, Manager, Financial Services, Mathtech Inc., took particular responsibility for certain technical aspects of the analysis, including the construction of data sets, decisions concerning significance tests, the fitting of functions to data, and the unraveling of the puzzle concerning methods of grouping graduate students described in Appendix D.
- Marcia L. Witte, an engineer-turned-history-major as an undergraduate, started as a part-time collector of data and then, as a full-time staff member in the Foundation's Princeton office, performed every conceivable task, from organizing and checking data to questioning key assumptions, drafting chapters, and improving our prose.
- Sarah E. Turner, Research Associate in our New York office, became actively involved with this project in the fall of 1990, and deserves special credit for relentlessly pressing analytical questions that otherwise might have been pushed aside, for doing the basic analysis underlying the results reported in Chapters Three and Nine, and for helping in innumerable ways with the preparation of the final manuscript.

Many others associated with the Mellon Foundation also made critical contributions. Kamla Motihar, the Foundation's librarian, prepared the index with a sensitivity to the purposes of the study that will be evident to users and also assembled needed library materials from an astonishing variety of sources. Sharon Brucker, who oversees the Foundation's Princeton office, took particular responsibility for searching the literature, suggesting references, and preparing the list of sources cited. Ms. Brucker succeeded Kate Ryan, who was a mainstay of early efforts to get the project organized and moving. Pamela McNeil undertook the task of preparing figures and tables. Thomas Nygren, who joined us near the end of the study, proved highly adept at working with the copy-edited manuscript, correcting errors, and going over all tables and figures with meticulous care. Ulrica Konvalin, Margaret McKenna, Laura Nadworny, and Martha Sullivan were unfailingly helpful in keeping track of wayward materials and working with innumerable drafts of the manuscript.

Richard Ekman, who has just joined our staff as Secretary after distinguished service as Director of Research at the National Endowment for the Humanities, made helpful suggestions on Chapter Fourteen. Professor Harriet Zuckerman, a widely respected sociologist at Columbia University who now serves as Vice President of the Foundation, was a constant source of good advice on both substance and methods. Carolyn Makinson, Program Associate for Population, drafted the questionnaire distributed to all Mellon Fellows in the Humanities. William Robertson, Program Director for Conservation and Ecology, managed quietly and effectively to see that all necessary computer resources were harnessed to the task. Others on the Mellon staff entered long lists of data, proofread the final text, and helped in countless other ways. Still others contributed ideas and listened patiently to too many expositions of partially understood concepts. No one could ask for more supportive colleagues.

At earlier stages in the process, Paul Murphy, Archana Pradhan, Mark Slavonia, and Kei Sochi (all undergraduates) helped assemble data of various kinds. Dexter Chu, an economics graduate student, wrote the original SAS programs used to evaluate our data sets. Donna Sulak, a graduate student in sociology, then assumed responsibility for the data sets and spent long, and often arduous, hours utilizing Princeton University's mainframe. David Quackenbush compiled many of the original summary tabulations. Seth Shepetin, a multitalented economist now at McKinsey and Company, did much of the original analysis for Chapter Four while awaiting calls to jury duty. Thomas Martine of Princeton University's Firestone Library was responsible for making the initial matches of winners of national fellowships with dissertation records via Dialog. Doug Mills of the Princeton University Computer Center was also unfailingly helpful.

As has been said, we were utterly dependent for original data on the cooperation of individuals at participating universities, and (grouped by university) we wish to express particular thanks to:

- Joseph Cerny, Joseph Duggan, Judi Sui, and Maresi Nerad (University of California at Berkeley);
- Gerhard Caspar and Allen Sanderson (University of Chicago);
- Jonathan Cole, Roger Bagnall, and Patricia Burch (Columbia University);
- Alison Casarett (Cornell University);
- Michael Spence, Brendan Maher, John Fox, and Vod Hatch (Harvard University);
- John D'Arms and Maia Bergman (University of Michigan);
- Denis O'Connor, Garland Hershey, Myrna Bower, Edison McIntyre, and the late John Blanton (University of North Carolina at Chapel Hill);
- Harold T. Shapiro, Theodore Ziolkowski, David Redman, and Anthony Broh (Princeton University);
- Elizabeth Traugott and Karlene Dickey (Stanford University); and
- Jerome J. Pollitt, Frank Turner, and Rena Cheskis-Gold (Yale University).

We should add that Deans D'Arms and Ziolkowski also provided much general advice in their capacity as leaders of the Association of Graduate Schools, as well as steady support and encouragement throughout the period of the study. President Harold Shapiro was similarly generous with his time and his ideas. Robert Rosenzweig and John Vaughn of the Association of American

Universities were also most helpful, particularly in discussing the federal role in graduate education.

Among those involved with national fellowship programs sponsored by foundations, we obtained essential help in obtaining background information and the names of award winners from:

- William Danforth, Gene Schwialck, Diana Kirby, Lillie Mae Rose Marquis, and Patricia Kendall (Danforth Foundation);
- George Boyce and Masi Compagnerci (National Science Foundation);
- Robert Pennoyer, Champion Ward, and Beth McCabe (Whiting Foundation); and
- Robert F. Goheen and Judith Pinch (Woodrow Wilson National Fellowship Foundation, which administered the Woodrow Wilson portable fellowships in the 1950s and 1960s and now administers the Mellon Fellowships in the Humanities).

Robert Goheen, who has been a teacher, colleague, and friend of both authors for over 20 years, deserves a special word of appreciation for his counsel on all matters, his unflagging interest in the most important questions, and his consistent good sense. Dr. Goheen reviewed a draft of the text of Chapter Eleven, which is concerned directly with several fellowship programs with which he has been closely associated. "Champ" Ward was also a source of general advice, as well as information, on both the earlier Ford Foundation program of institutional grants and the current program of dissertation grants sponsored by the Whiting Foundation.

The third principal source of data for this study was the National Research Council (NRC) in Washington, D.C., which supplied special tabulations from the Doctorate Records File, made available other unpublished information that we needed, and made heroic efforts to match the names of winners of national fellowships against names of recipients of PhDs recorded in the Doctorate Records File. Without the constant cooperation and high technical competence of the staff of the NRC, many of the most useful parts of this study could never have been done. More personally, we want to thank Alan Fechter, Pamela Flattau, Jo Ann Weinman, Lori Thurgood, Daniel Pasquini, and Andrew Flannery for their help. The Doctorate Records File is *the* invaluable resource for those interested in graduate education, and it is fortunate that access to it is in the hands of individuals with high standards and a clear appreciation of the nature of research.

Among the individual scholars who have worked in this general field, we would like to single out David Breneman, now at Harvard University, for special recognition. More than anyone else still active, he saw the importance of these questions years ago and made pioneering efforts to address them, severe limitations of data notwithstanding. We have learned much from his work (as citations in the text indicate), and we have also benefited from his specific comments on an earlier draft of a part of this manuscript. Special mention should also be made of Professor Ronald Ehrenberg of Cornell University, who is actively engaged with related issues, and who has contributed more to our work than he may suspect.

We have been fortunate to find a publisher, the Princeton University Press, that was willing to make special efforts to produce the book under tight time constraints. We are especially indebted to Jack Repcheck, Jane Low, and Kate

Ryan (now at the Press, after having worked with us at the Foundation). The copy editor has done an exceptionally conscientious and effective job of copy-editing a most difficult manuscript—while demonstrating remarkable patience with our stylistic idiosyncracies. Karen Fortgang, bookworks, has worked hard and effectively to assemble "all the pieces" into a finished product.

While all of the organizations and individuals listed above have played significant roles in this project, none of this work would have been possible had it not been for the overall support of the Andrew W. Mellon Foundation. The Trustees (including two remarkable individuals who are now retired, Dr. William O. Baker and Arjay Miller) appreciated from the first our strongly felt desire to understand this general subject as well as we could before being expected to define a grant-making program in which we could have confidence. The Trustees have been endlessly patient with the time and effort that this project has required. We hope that the results will justify, at least in part, their encouragement and support.

The highly collaborative nature of this project is evident from the preceding account of the contributions of many of those who worked on it. If we had not been reluctant to burden this preface still more, we could have produced a list that would have approximated the size of a small-town telephone book—by mentioning, for example, more of those who gave advice on specific sections, contributed written proposals, were interviewed, sent us letters, and found other ways to be useful. This is surely a project that required a wide range of talents and capabilities. No one person, or small group of people, could be expected to have the substantive knowledge of particular fields of study, computer skills, familiarity with at least basic statistical techniques, and the historical-institutional perspective that have seemed to us to be necessary. A blending of skills, tastes, and experiences has without question enriched the research process for us, and has, we hope, improved the product.

Of one thing we are certain. Our personal partnership, which has lasted for some 23 years, has survived yet another test! And that is the most extreme understatement. We have benefited once again by counting on each other to do those things that one of us could not do at all, or hardly at all. Writing this book has been a new and most rewarding experience for two very good friends who will always be grateful for the extraordinary opportunities that they have been given to work together.

WGB and NLR
August 1991

In Pursuit of the PhD

Introduction and Principal Findings

AT THE doctoral level, the preeminence of this country's programs of study, viewed in terms of both quality and scale, is widely accepted and perhaps even taken for granted. Incontrovertible evidence is provided by the large (and rising) number of students from other countries who elect to study for doctorates here. In 1989, 6,590 doctorates were awarded by U.S. universities to non-U.S. residents.[1]

Still, all of its accomplishments notwithstanding, graduate education in the United States is far from any ideal state. Nor would anyone claim that its prospects and future role are well understood or assured. The recent Hearings on the Reauthorization of the Higher Education Act, reports issued by the Association of American Universities (AAU), and numerous commentaries attest to wide-ranging debates that continue. Similar issues are also being discussed in other countries.[2]

While there have been a number of good studies of certain facets of graduate education (especially of the sciences, engineering, and professional education in fields such as medicine), it is surprising that so little systematic study has been devoted to doctoral education in general. Both its undisputed importance and its substantial cost would seem to justify considerably more attention. Not since the publication of Berelson's major study in 1960 has there been a comprehensive review of the overall system of graduate education. The humanities and the related social sciences have been especially neglected.[3]

---

[1] See Chapter Two for a brief discussion of U.S. investments in higher education vis-à-vis investments made by other countries and a much more extended discussion of trends in the number of doctoral degrees awarded to non-U.S. residents in various fields of study. Approximately *half* of all doctorates in mathematics awarded by U.S. universities in recent years were awarded to non-U.S. residents. Comparable percentages in fields such as English and history tend to be much lower (around 10 percent), but there is no denying the wide-ranging popularity of American doctoral programs in most fields of study.

[2] See U.S. Congress 1991; Association of American Universities 1990a, 1990b; and various issues of the *Chronicle of Higher Education* (for example, Hirschorn 1988; Evangelauf 1989; Magner 1989; and Mooney 1990b) and *Challenge* (Cude 1987). Much of the discussion outside the United States is summarized in a recent OECD publication (OECD 1989); also, there has been a particularly interesting debate in the United Kingdom (see, for example, Rudd 1985; and Young, Fogarty, and McRae 1987).

[3] See Berelson 1960. At about the same time, Carmichael (1961) wrote a general critique of graduate education with specific proposals for organizational change. Harmon (1978) prepared a most impressive statistical study of aspects of graduate education, including extensive historical materials, but he did not discuss at length questions of interpretation or of policy. The extensive publications of the Carnegie Commission contained only one Commission Report concerned primarily with graduate education in the arts and sciences (Carnegie Commission on Higher Education 1968). The series of sponsored research reports associated with the work of the Commission includes only one relevant study, entitled "Graduate and Professional Education, 1980: A Survey of Institutional Plans" (Mayhew 1970). For a subsequent discussion of general trends in graduate education, see Smith and Karlesky (1978). A useful collection of essays on graduate education was published in 1980, following an international conference held at the University of Michigan in 1978 (Frankena

There has been considerable speculation about the reasons for the relative lack of scholarly interest in graduate education. Possible explanations include a general tendency among academics in several social science disciplines (especially economics) to prefer to study other areas, as well as the particularly daunting conceptual and empirical problems that bedevil study of graduate education. The specialized nature of fields of knowledge at the graduate level makes it unusually difficult to generalize, and the decentralized administration of graduate programs means that the problems of collecting even the most rudimentary data can be monumental. One clinical psychologist has suggested that the traumas associated with pursuit of the PhD may even have discouraged many scholars from returning to such a personally painful subject![4]

The Context and Main Questions

Concern for the future staffing of colleges and universities has been one stimulus to the research reported here. For reasons described in detail in *Prospects for Faculty in the Arts and Sciences*,[5] we believe that many American colleges and universities are likely to face serious staffing problems by the end of the 1990s. Significant imbalances between demand and supply could result from a combination of expected retirement patterns, the demography of the college-age population, and declines over recent decades in the number of PhDs awarded to U.S. residents. A surprising (unanticipated) finding of the earlier research was that recruitment of faculty could prove to be as difficult in the humanities and related social sciences as in the sciences and engineering.

It is outside the scope of the present study to reexamine the projections made in 1989. We should reemphasize, however, the long-term, "other-things-equal" nature of those projections. Any projections based on simple, static assumptions will frequently be overtaken, at least in the short term, by external forces. At the present time (summer of 1991), the current recession and the accompanying fiscal problems of governments at all levels are creating difficult budgetary problems for colleges and universities. Many faculty vacancies are being left unfilled, and recruitment plans are being put on hold. If they continue for extended periods of time, financial constraints of this kind can have long-term effects on faculty staffing. But they are more likely to affect the timing of shifts in the pattern of faculty recruitment than eventual staffing levels.[6]

Since the main underlying trends in the age distribution of the present faculty and in the size of the college-age population are unchanged, we see no reason

---

1980). A former dean of the Yale Graduate School, Jaroslav Pelikan, published a general commentary on graduate education in the early 1980s (Pelikan 1983). There have been many other studies dealing with specific aspects of graduate education, which will be cited in their relevant contexts.

[4]Dr. Frederick Stern (personal conversation with one of the authors). Dr. Stern's own doctoral dissertation is an analysis of the effects of psychological factors on the length of time it takes students to complete their dissertations (Stern 1985).

[5]Bowen and Sosa 1989.

[6]The effects of cutbacks in funding in mathematics are described well in a recent article in *Science* (Cipra 1991). An added complication in this field is the sudden appearance in the job market of "an unexpected influx of mathematicians from the Soviet Union and Eastern Europe, as well as a large number of Chinese students now looking to remain in the United States" (ibid., 252). These developments are a good reminder of the potential impact of external events that no one can foresee.

The severe effects of recent financial problems on normally stable colleges and universities are illustrated poignantly by experiences with layoffs at Middlebury College at the end of the 1990–91 academic year, as recounted in the *Chronicle of Higher Education* (Grassmuck 1991).

to modify our sense that serious staffing problems should be anticipated by the late 1990s. We also continue to believe that policies affecting graduate education have more potential than any other set of actions to address potential staffing problems. Failing to make any provision for deeply rooted trends could be a most serious error—and an error very hard to correct subsequently because of the long time lags between changes in "inputs" and "outputs" that are inherent in graduate education.

If graduate education can be such an important lever of change, obvious questions arise: Is there sufficient capacity within existing graduate programs to meet the projected needs for additional faculty members? Should consideration be given to encouraging the creation of new programs? Can existing programs be expected to meet projected needs through the operation of more-or-less automatic adjustment mechanisms, or are some forms of external support/stimulation likely to be required?

In evaluating whether proposals for additional external support ought to be encouraged, consideration must be given to the effectiveness of current programs and patterns of support. How efficient are they? Do graduate programs appear to have become more or less effective over time? Are there lessons to be learned from the differential outcomes achieved when students are grouped by field of study and scale of graduate program? Is it possible to find ways to reduce attrition and time-to-degree, while simultaneously sustaining, and perhaps improving, quality? How well structured and well organized are existing programs? Is it true that much greater reliance has been placed on teaching assistantships (TAs) in recent years, and if so, what have been the consequences? What has been the record of national fellowship programs, both governmentally and privately funded?

The more we thought about such questions, the more convinced we became that many of them were of such intrinsic importance that they deserve the most careful consideration, regardless of what one believes about the likelihood of possible shortages of faculty by the end of the 1990s. Doctoral education is, after all, the apex of this country's system of higher education in the arts and sciences. The effectiveness of undergraduate teaching as well as the quality of scholarship and research depend to some considerable extent on how well graduate programs function. Talented, well-motivated, and well-trained graduate students—both as students and later as professionals, working in or out of academia—contribute critically to our collective ability to generate ideas and educate new generations of students. They are assets of incalculable value.

Present concern with the costliness of higher education at all levels reinforces the conviction that graduate programs deserve careful analysis. It is incumbent on those of us in universities, and those associated with organizations that support universities, to improve the effectiveness with which we deploy whatever resources are at our disposal. This obvious proposition surely applies to graduate education no less than to undergraduate programs and the conduct of research.

Recognition of the extraordinary amounts of time and effort (as well as money) that many of the brightest students are expected to invest in graduate study heightens still more the feeling that it is wrong simply to accept current rates of attrition and present assumptions about how long it should take to earn a doctorate. We need first to understand the factors responsible for current norms. Then we need to see if there are ways to do better.

SCOPE OF THIS STUDY

This book is intended to help fill part of what we perceive as a significant gap in knowledge. It is not, however, a comprehensive treatment of graduate education, and many important questions are not addressed. The scope of this study can be summarized as follows:

- The focus is on PhD programs within the arts and sciences. We do not discuss master's programs or professional programs at the doctoral level.
- Within the arts and sciences, we have elected to study most intensively a limited number of graduate programs in specific fields of study in particular universities. This "departmental approach" reflects our conviction that many of the most important issues facing graduate education can be understood and addressed most effectively at the level of the individual department or graduate program.
- Many of the most important findings reported here pertain to two measurable outcomes of graduate education—namely, completion rates (or, conversely, attrition) and time-to-degree. We analyze trends in these two measures over time, differences in them across fields of study and types of universities, and the effects on them of different forms of financial aid, as well as departmental structures, requirements, expectations, and conventions ("cultures").

    The attention given in this project to seemingly mundane numbers, such as the percentage of students in an entering graduate school cohort who complete their studies within various periods of time, does not reflect any lack of concern on our part for questions of *quality*, which are fundamental. Qualitative concerns are highly relevant both at the level of the individual graduate program and at the national level. But emphasizing the need to maintain and, if possible, improve quality, cannot be an excuse for failing to examine critically the more measurable outcomes of the process of graduate education that must be considered in assessing the effectiveness with which both time and financial resources are employed.
- We are concerned mainly with the experiences of U.S. residents enrolled in these programs. We make no effort to analyze differences in outcomes for U.S. residents compared with non-U.S. residents.
- While our primary interest is in outcomes for all U.S. residents enrolled in these graduate programs, we also examine differences in outcomes related to gender, as well as trends in the participation in graduate education of women and (to a lesser extent) members of ethnic and racial minorities.
- Finally, while specific findings often relate most immediately to individual graduate programs and particular universities, we also analyze the results achieved by various national fellowship programs and, where possible, include references to other national data as well.

DATA AND METHODS

Data

It was obvious from the outset of this project that the data needed to analyze many of the central questions did not exist in any manageable form. The lack of a comprehensive set of reasonably "hard" data has shaped both our initial approach to these issues and the final presentation of results. It would be difficult to exaggerate the importance of the collection of new sets of data. Many of the most important findings depend directly on data heretofore unavailable.

One irony is that the lack of certain essential information has been accompanied by a veritable treasure-trove of other kinds of national data, which have proved to be extremely valuable. The basic source is the Doctorate Records File (DRF), maintained by the National Research Council (NRC).[7] For about 70 years, records have been kept of the number of doctorate recipients each year, classified by field of study and by the institution granting the degree. From 1958 forward, far more detailed data are available.

This remarkable database (which is generated by reports on each individual receiving a doctorate, rather than by a sampling technique) is the source of the time series on degrees conferred and numbers and sizes of doctorate-granting programs that are presented and analyzed in Chapters Two, Three, and Four. It is also the source of estimates of median time-to-degree for specified populations of recipients that we present in later parts of the study.

From the standpoint of ability to answer many of the key questions posed above, the DRF has one fundamental limitation: It contains information only on those individuals who *receive* doctorates. It does not permit the calculation of completion rates because it is silent on the numbers and characteristics of students who enroll in PhD programs but do not earn degrees.

There is no substitute for longitudinal data that track each entering cohort or "class" of students as its members move (or fail to move) from one stage of graduate education to another. The only method that we could devise to assemble such data systematically, at the necessary level of detail, was by soliciting the cooperation of particular universities that had enrolled reasonably large entering cohorts over a number of years and were also willing and able to provide relevant statistics for individual students (without identifying them, of course).

Practical considerations—the time and expense involved in building such a database—dictated that we limit this data-collecting effort to a manageable number of fields of study and a reasonably small number of carefully selected graduate programs. Because we were interested in studying trends, we decided to request data going back to the early 1960s, even though we realized the formidable nature of such a data-gathering process.

Following considerable consultation with faculty members and administrators, we chose six fields of study for intensive analysis: English, history, political science, economics, mathematics, and physics. Each is a reasonably well-defined field that has enrolled significant numbers of students over many years. English and history represent important areas within the humanities, broadly defined; political science and economics illustrate somewhat different emphases within the social sciences; and mathematics and physics are central disciplines within the broad sphere of the physical sciences. These six fields together

---

[7]See *Summary Report 1989* for both an explanation of the characteristics of this database and an illustration of the summary tables that are published regularly. Harmon (1978) provides additional historical detail, as far back as the early 1920s.

covered, we thought, a reasonable cross-section of those graduate programs in the arts and sciences that often lead to academic careers.[8]

In much of our work, we have found it useful to group certain fields of study because of their common characteristics and the tendency for patterns of behavior to be quite consistent. For instance, English, history, and political science form a group referred to throughout this study as the "EHP" fields. Similarly, it is sometimes appropriate to group mathematics and physics (the "MP" fields), even though both basic characteristics and outcomes differ in some noteworthy respects between these two fields. Economics is in many respects a case all its own, but in terms of the measurable outcomes considered here, it behaves much more like the MP fields than the EHP fields.

We have not been even-handed in the attention we have given to these six fields. While the same statistical analysis of outcomes has been done for all fields (so that comparisons could be made), the EHP fields have been the focus of our detailed study of the content of graduate programs, their design, internal structure, and oversight. That part of the research required extensive interviews, an examination of institutional self-studies, and the perusal of related materials. It would have been impractical to extend such an analysis to more fields, and we felt that the most complicated (and troubling) issues facing graduate students and graduate programs were to be found in the humanities and related social sciences.

Choosing universities for concentrated analysis was even more difficult than choosing fields of study. We finally decided to seek permission to collect data at 10 major universities: the University of California at Berkeley, the University of Chicago, Columbia University, Cornell University, Harvard University, the University of Michigan, the University of North Carolina at Chapel Hill, Princeton University, Stanford University, and Yale University. All 10 agreed to participate in the project, and this is therefore referred to as the "Ten-University" data set. (The questions asked of these universities are described in detail in Appendix A, along with conventions adopted to achieve reasonably consistent reporting.) Understandably, not all 10 universities were able to provide the full array of information that was sought for all fields and time periods. Still, statistical records relating to over 36,000 individuals were collected, which gives some indication of why it was essential to limit the number of fields and universities included in this part of the study.

All 10 of these universities are widely recognized as strong centers of graduate education, and concentrating on them inevitably limits the generality of some findings (and also raises worries about "elitism"). But these are central institu-

---

[8]In presenting summary statistics, we sometimes refer to results for "Six-Fields," and the reference is, of course, to these six fields. It would have been interesting to include other sciences, such as biology, chemistry, and psychology, but the relationship of those fields to medical schools, the field of medicine, and industrial research would have introduced so many complications that it would have been difficult to complete the analysis. In the case of psychology, the importance of clinical work and the relationship to clinical practice are additional considerations. Within the humanities, we would have liked to devote more attention to art history, classics, and foreign languages, but each of these fields tends to enroll relatively small numbers of graduate students, and for that reason it would have been much harder to obtain statistically reliable results. (We do have some results for these fields, which we include wherever possible, but our attention to them is much more limited than the attention given to English and history.) Within the social sciences, anthropology is another particularly interesting field that we regretfully concluded had to be placed outside our range of subjects.

tions from the perspective of graduate education—especially when studying long-term historical trends as well as current conditions. It seemed better to accept the limitations imposed by selecting these universities than to seek to include so large and diverse a group that it would be nearly impossible to collect enough information (reaching back nearly 30 years) to permit reasonably reliable conclusions.

While this group of institutions has a number of attributes in common, there are pronounced differences in scale, patterns of financing, curricula, and policies. These differences—existing within an otherwise reasonably comparable group of graduate institutions and programs—lead to some of the most interesting findings. The apparent effects of some of these differences are nothing less than startling, considering the known similarities.

In addition to wanting to understand factors affecting outcomes within particular graduate programs, we also wanted to evaluate the effectiveness of national fellowship programs. This objective was important because of our interest in questions of policy that have to be confronted not only by universities, but by foundations and government agencies. Again, no national database existed, and it was necessary therefore to create a second database defined specifically by the requirements of this study (the National Fellowship database described in Appendix B).

The initial step in accomplishing this task was to obtain the names of recipients of Danforth, Woodrow Wilson, Whiting, and National Defense Education Act (NDEA) fellowships. This list of individuals—classified by field of study, gender, year of award, and university—was then matched with names in the Doctorate Records File to determine, for the first time, the actual completion rates achieved by these programs. The database created in this way includes 13,000 statistical records. The National Science Foundation (NSF) provided tabulations for its own fellowship program, which permitted comparisons with the results achieved by the other fellowship programs.

A third set of data collected specifically for this study consists of responses to questionnaires distributed to all recipients of Mellon Fellowships in the Humanities, starting with the first (1983) cohort of winners. The two questionnaires used in this survey are reproduced in Appendix C.

Methods

In seeking to describe and analyze outcomes, our approach has been to proceed as simply as possible. We have relied mainly on descriptive statistics and on tabulations designed to identify particular relationships. Liberal use has been made of figures and tables in an effort to make this highly quantitative analysis as accessible as possible. Formal tests of statistical significance have been used when it seemed appropriate to do so, and limited use has been made of rather sophisticated methods of fitting curves to data. But this is not an econometric study, and we decided not to use multivariate techniques.

We cannot promise, however, that all of the discussion that follows will be easily penetrable. One general characteristic of graduate education complicates all of the analysis and needs to be emphasized. The very long time that often elapses between completion of a BA program and eventual receipt of a PhD means that longitudinal data must cover extended periods. One of the most serious consequences is that the behavior of students (such as deciding whether to begin a PhD program, what field of study to elect, whether to persevere, and so on) cannot be analyzed solely in terms of conditions at the time when the doctorate was awarded. Conditions from a much earlier period, when the BA was awarded, are generally more relevant, even though everyone would presumably agree that an appropriate summation of conditions over a graduate student's entire period of study would be most relevant of all.

Implicit in these comments is a fundamental point about the ways in which observations are grouped. While it is often easier to work with data organized by the year in which individuals *received* their doctorates, results based on this PhD-year method of aggregation can be highly misleading. It is generally more useful to group observations by either the year in which students completed their undergraduate studies (BA-year cohorts) or the year in which they embarked on graduate study. This simple point about methods recurs throughout the study and is discussed in detail in the context of measurements of time-to-degree in Appendix D.

The extended duration of graduate study also means that little can be said about outcomes for recent entering cohorts. Most of these students are still enrolled, and it will be some time before anyone knows how many will eventually earn doctorates. Accordingly, estimates that can be calculated at the present time must be interpreted with great care because completion rates and median time-to-degree will change as more of these students complete their studies.

The heavily statistical materials that make up such a large part of this study are supplemented by references to the literature, statements from lengthy interviews, examination of institutional self-studies, proposals prepared for the Mellon Foundation, and other information of an impressionistic kind. Some of the most useful insights come from these sources.

ORGANIZATION OF THE STUDY

This is a long, detailed, and at times somewhat tedious book. We have felt an obligation to explain carefully what we have done and why, to describe our sources, to acknowledge the speculative character of some propositions, and to explore alternative interpretations of what is often new evidence. A brief "reader's guide" may be helpful.

The book consists of three parts. The first set of chapters describes the broad contours of graduate education. In this part, we have sought to:

- Place doctoral programs in the arts and sciences within the larger context of doctoral education in all fields and examine trends in recipients of PhDs over the last 35 years, with special emphasis on differences by field of study, changes in citizenship mix, and trends in the participation of women and members of racial and ethnic minorities (Chapter Two);
- Analyze the main forces (especially changing labor market conditions and draft-related events at the time of Vietnam) that were related to the rapid increase in the number of doctorates conferred in the expansionary years and then to the sudden, sharp contraction that lasted through the 1970s and into the 1980s (Chapter Three);
- Describe and assess the dramatic increases that have occurred over the last 35 years in the number of doctorate-granting programs and their distribu-

tion by quality tier, by size of program, and by success in achieving a critical mass (Chapter Four); and

- Report more generally on developments that together have shaped the evolution of leading graduate programs in the EHP fields—changes in courses offered, numbers of faculty, enrollments, patterns of financial aid, and the structure of teaching (Chapter Five).

The second part of the study focuses on measurable outcomes of graduate study in the arts and sciences. Individual chapters are intended to:

- Define and describe the key measures of outcomes that are used throughout this research, with particular attention paid to trends in completion rates and time-to-degree (Chapter Six);
- Analyze the associations between these measurable outcomes and fields of study, noting especially the persistence of patterns across universities and over time (Chapter Seven);
- Present evidence showing the major differences in completion rates and time-to-degree that are observed when we compare "Larger" and "Smaller" university programs (Chapter Eight); and
- Assemble all of the quantitative dimensions of the preceding analysis into a single measure of "Student-Year Cost of a PhD" (SYC), noting differences in this measure by field of study, type of graduate program, and time period (Chapter Nine).

In the third part of the book, the focus shifts to financial aid policies and questions of departmental structure, program design, and oversight. Individual chapters address:

- The effects on completion rates and time-to-degree of differing patterns of financial support, including the implications of relying on personal resources versus teaching assistantships versus fellowships (Chapter Ten);
- The results achieved by various national fellowship programs in different periods, with attention paid as well to differences in outcomes for men and women (Chapter Eleven);
- The major role played by changes in academic requirements and the content of fields of study within the EHP fields, including debates over the role of recent theoretical approaches and the development of new subfields (Chapter Twelve);
- Ways in which the structure, pacing, reward systems, supervisory practices, and organization of graduate programs affect completion rates and time-to-degree (Chapter Thirteen); and
- Recommendations for governmental policies, the role of foundations, and university policies and practices (Chapter Fourteen).

Summary of Principal Findings[9]

Broad Trends in Graduate Education

The years following World War II witnessed an unprecedented expansion in graduate education. During the 1960s alone, the number of doctorates conferred

---

[9]The chapters that follow contain additional detail, supporting evidence, caveats, necessary qualifications, and discussions of methods. To avoid misunderstandings, the findings summarized below need to be interpreted in that larger context.

annually by U.S. universities nearly tripled. An abrupt change in direction occurred in the early 1970s, when the overall number of doctorates conferred began to decline. In the humanities, the drop was precipitous—from 5,400 in 1973 to 3,600 in 1988.

An analysis of the expansion and subsequent contraction in graduate education in our six arts-and-sciences fields reveals that, contrary to what many of us have assumed, favorable academic labor markets played only a secondary role during the period of most rapid growth in the number of doctorates conferred. Large increases in the sizes of the underlying undergraduate pools of potential candidates for graduate study were much more important. The subsequent—very sudden—reversal of the upward trend in the number of PhDs conferred can be attributed primarily to draft-related events at the time of the Vietnam War. The severely depressed job markets for academics in the 1970s played a major role in the continuation of the contraction, as did the general flight from the arts and sciences at the undergraduate level. An important implication for policy is that the number of doctorates conferred cannot be expected to respond promptly to changes in labor market conditions. Long time lags must be anticipated.

During these same years, the number of PhDs awarded to non-U.S. residents rose dramatically, partially offsetting (especially in the sciences) a decline in the number of doctorates earned by U.S. residents. Women earned a rapidly increasing share of all doctorates, and by 1988 the "gender gap" had narrowed appreciably in many fields (and had closed entirely in some, such as English). The number of doctorates awarded to African-Americans declined in both absolute and relative terms between 1982 and 1988, and Hispanics made only modest gains.

The rapid growth in the number of doctorates conferred between 1958 and 1972 was not simply a consequence of larger enrollments in previously established PhD programs. The number of doctorate-granting programs in our six fields of study doubled during this period, in part as a response to the incentives created by the NDEA fellowship program. Institutions proved to be most reluctant to eliminate programs, even when the overall demand for PhDs declined significantly, and new doctoral programs continued to appear well after the subsequent contraction had begun. The share of doctorates awarded by the most highly ranked programs fell dramatically during this period.

Small graduate programs created during the 1960s and 1970s now represent a large proportion of all graduate programs, and many have never awarded enough doctorates over their life span to meet our rough definition of "critical mass" (an average of at least three doctorates conferred per year). It is reasonable to ask whether the large investments of resources required to sustain all of these programs can be justified in every instance. It is clear, in any case, that existing graduate programs have ample capacity to educate larger numbers of doctoral candidates—especially if their overall effectiveness can be improved.

Important changes also occurred within highly ranked graduate programs in the EHP fields. Our examination of a small number of these programs reveals that the number of graduate courses offered grew rapidly during the 1960s and early 1970s, declined somewhat during the latter half of the 1970s, and then remained approximately constant (with some growth in the late 1980s). Roughly speaking, trends in the number of faculty paralleled trends in courses offered (with slightly less oscillation). Patterns of financial support for graduate students in these programs changed markedly during these years. The relative number of graduate students supported primarily by fellowships in the EHP fields was much lower in the 1970s than in the 1960s because of a large drop in externally provided fellowships and the severe financial problems experienced by many universities. A sharp increase in reliance on teaching assistantships occurred in the 1970s and early 1980s, in part because of the need to find alternative ways of supporting graduate students and in part because of significant increases in undergraduate enrollments.

Factors Affecting Outcomes

Trends in two measurable outcomes of doctoral study—completion rates and median time-to-degree—need to be considered within this context. In general, completion rates for doctoral students in the arts and sciences have been much lower than completion rates for undergraduates at selective institutions and for graduate students in professional programs. Moreover, completion rates for more recent entering cohorts have been appreciably lower than completion rates for graduate students who began their studies in the early to mid-1960s. Significant amounts of attrition are found to have occurred both before and after achievement of ABD ("all-but-dissertation") status.

The increasing length of time that usually elapses between receipt of the BA and receipt of the PhD has been widely discussed. We find that time-to-degree has increased (especially in the humanities and social sciences), but not nearly as rapidly as governmental studies have suggested. The steepness of the apparent trend indicated by published national data is mainly a statistical artifact, resulting from the method used to group recipients. (The technical explanation in support of this conclusion may be found in Appendix D.) Still, there has been some lengthening of the time the typical recipient in the humanities and social sciences takes to earn a doctorate, and this is clearly cause for concern. Comparing cumulative completion rates (the percentage of an entering cohort that completes the doctorate within a specified number of years) for successive cohorts provides further evidence of an upward drift in the time cost of a doctorate.

Completion rates and time-to-degree vary systematically with field of study. These differences are, we believe, intrinsic to certain characteristics of graduate study in the sciences as compared with the humanities and related social sciences. Completion rates were higher in the sciences in all time periods and within all groups of universities for which we were able to obtain data. This persistent pattern cannot be attributed to differences by field in the proportions of men and women students or in the availability of financial aid.

One would expect to find (*ceteris paribus*) an inverse relationship between completion rates and time-to-degree, and results are generally consistent with this hypothesis. Students in the EHP fields who have completed their doctorates have taken much longer to do so, on average, than their counterparts in the MP fields and in economics. A differential of two to three years in median time-to-degree has been common, and the size of this gap appears to have widened somewhat in recent years.

A more surprising finding is that outcomes vary substantially between Smaller and Larger graduate programs (defined by sizes of entering cohorts). Graduate programs with relatively small entering cohorts have had consistently higher completion rates and lower time-to-degree than those with larger entering cohorts. Limiting the analysis to recipients of national fellowships demonstrates that associated differences in the selectivity of students and provision of financial aid do not eliminate these differentials. The inference is that scale per se matters greatly, especially in the EHP fields where completion rates have been nearly twice as high in the Smaller programs than in the Larger programs. Within these fields, time-to-degree was also appreciably shorter in the Smaller programs than in the Larger programs—a finding that, once again, holds even after controlling for differences in selectivity and the availability of financial aid by looking only at recipients of national fellowships who attended the two sets of universities.

When completion rates and time-to-degree are combined into a single measure of the average number of years invested by an entering cohort of students in earning one doctorate (called the Student-Year Cost, or SYC), we obtain figures of 12 years per doctorate in the EHP fields and 8 years per doctorate in the MP fields. Greater attrition in the EHP fields (much of it in the post-ABD stage) accounts for roughly three-quarters of this differential. Again, scale matters, especially within the EHP fields where the Student-Year Cost of a doctorate averaged more than 15 years in the Larger programs as compared with about 10 years in the Smaller programs. The overall level of SYC has risen substantially over time in programs of all sizes, but most of the increase occurred between the 1962–1966 and 1967–1971 cohorts. Projections for the 1977–1981 cohorts yield estimates that are very close to those for the 1972–1976 cohort.

Policies and Program Design

Financial aid policies clearly affect outcomes. In all of our data sets, students who had to rely primarily on their own resources had markedly higher attrition rates and longer time-to-degree than students who received various forms of financial aid. These differences were found to persist even after a crude attempt was made to control for associations between financial aid awards and the perceived merit of candidates. In short, as one would expect, money matters.

The form in which financial aid is provided also matters. Teaching assistantships offer both financial support and participation in a structured environment, which may help to explain why, within the EHP fields, completion rates tend to be somewhat higher for students with TAs than for students with fellowships. Regular interaction with faculty members and students in the context of teaching assignments may well be an important, perhaps even vital, factor in encouraging some graduate students in the EHP fields to complete doctorates. Holders of fellowships may do exceedingly well—but some may also feel "lost." In the sciences, research assistantships and the basic structure of laboratory work serve functions similar to those provided by the teaching assistantship in the EHP fields.

Reliance on teaching assistantships lengthens time-to-degree, however. This appears to have been especially true in recent years, and the limited data available to us probably understate the full extent of this effect. Testimony from faculty and students indicates that increasingly heavy dependence on teaching assistantships prolongs graduate study and, in some cases, leads to attrition as well. There is a serious danger that this valuable form of support will be overused.

Detailed examination of the experiences of national fellowship programs reveals a complex pattern of results (see Chapter Eleven). The Danforth program, which made determined efforts to maintain contact with its fellows and support them in ways beyond the provision of financial aid, achieved higher completion rates in the EHP fields than did the Woodrow Wilson fellowship program. However, neither of these prestigious national fellowship programs achieved completion rates appreciably higher than those recorded by other students who were enrolled in the same graduate programs. Time-to-degree was also comparable across groups. A third portable fellowship program, the Mellon fellowships in the Humanities, has not been in existence long enough to permit a full evaluation of outcomes, but completion rates and time-to-degree achieved to date have been somewhat disappointing.

Holders of National Science Foundation fellowships have had high completion rates, but of course these fellows have studied mainly in the sciences, where completion rates for other students also have been high. The NSF program appears to have had its greatest effect on outcomes by reducing time-to-degree. The NDEA fellowship program, which was institutionally based and not portable, had completion rates essentially the same as those for comparable students without NDEA awards.

The Ford Foundation's program of institutional awards had a different purpose. Instituted in 1967, it was designed to shorten time-to-degree. It did not succeed in achieving this objective, in part because its target of a four-year norm was unrealistic, and in part (we believe) because it failed to create the right incentives at the departmental level.

The Whiting fellowship program awards final-year dissertation fellowships, and its completion rates have been high (about 85 percent). However, the Whiting Fellows have taken longer to complete their degrees than had been anticipated, presumably for reasons imbedded in the structure of humanities graduate programs (see Chapters Twelve and Thirteen).

Analysis of national fellowship programs provides an especially good opportunity to study relationships between gender and outcomes. During the late 1950s and early 1960s, less than one-quarter of women Woodrow Wilson Fellows ever earned doctorates. Men in the same Woodrow Wilson cohorts had completion rates that were two to three times higher than the rates for women. When the Danforth Foundation reopened its program to women in the late 1960s, it achieved startlingly different results: a completion rate for women of 71 percent. However, this outcome needs to be considered in relation to factors that were unique to both the timing of the decision to include women and characteristics of the Danforth program.

More generally, the Ten-University data set indicates that the gender gap in completion rates in the EHP fields closed in the late 1970s, with women completing at especially high rates in the Smaller programs. In the case of time-to-degree, on the other hand, a distinct gender gap remains. Women in the EHP fields have tended to take, on average, about one-half year longer than their male counterparts to complete doctorates. Only in the NSF program has time-to-degree been comparable for men and women.

Of course, all of these national fellowship programs were designed to accomplish goals much broader than improvements in our two measurable outcomes of graduate study, and they succeeded admirably in many respects.

They attracted a great deal more attention to graduate study, encouraged more able students to enroll in PhD programs, and provided substantial amounts of tangible support when it was badly needed by students and institutions alike. At the same time, their limited success in reducing attrition and time-to-degree underscores the difficulties of trying to affect outcomes by working mainly *outside* the graduate programs themselves.

Our analysis of factors *internal* to graduate programs (which is limited largely to the EHP fields) yields one simple, overriding conclusion: The ways in which programs are defined, carried out, and monitored make a great deal of difference. This more institutionally oriented part of the study helps to explain the persistent differences in outcomes between Larger and Smaller programs and the great range in estimates of the Student-Year Cost of a doctorate (from 5.0 to 20.1 years), when consideration is given to both field of study and individual university.

Comparisons of catalogs over a 25-year span indicate that the number of subfields and interdisciplinary options has increased markedly, formally stated expectations concerning time-to-degree have slipped, and the overall structure of graduate education has become more loosely defined. Within the EHP fields, for example, there has been a movement toward greater concentration on the non-Western dimensions of fields, on the modern periods, and on the role of "theory" (defined broadly as methodology, criticism, and interpretation). These changes have inevitably complicated graduate study in many departments and, according to the testimony of a number of faculty members, created new sources of difficulty for students attempting to choose dissertation topics as well as appropriate theoretical approaches to their fields.

Certain stages of graduate study have become especially problematic. By virtually all accounts, the time between the end of course work and the moment of energetic engagement with a dissertation topic is an unusually vulnerable time for many graduate students in the EHP fields. Selection of a topic appears to have become an increasingly formidable task, at a time when the expectations of many faculty (and institutions) concerning the dissertation have become more demanding than ever.

Dissertation advising is mentioned frequently as a serious problem. In some instances, dissatisfaction with the traditional apprenticeship model has led to the substitution of committee systems. The isolated nature of doctoral research is an additional source of stress for many students, and some departments have instituted dissertation workshops to help combat it, as well as to provide the substantive benefit of criticism and advice from faculty members and other students.

We are persuaded that more structure is needed in graduate education, with clearly specified objectives, incentives, and time lines. These need to be accompanied by more rigorous enforcement of rules, goals, and guidelines (allowing always for the truly exceptional case). In addition, there seems to us to be a strong case for more careful record-keeping and monitoring of the entire process of graduate education, including the performance of faculty advisors. Students and institutions invest massive amounts of time and other resources, and it seems only reasonable that there be standards of collective accountability that are both explicit and consistently applied.

Recommendations

The recommendations presented in the concluding chapter of this study are tentative and, in some respects, implicit in what has been said already. We offer no fine-grained blueprint for graduate education in the arts and sciences. Particularly in the humanities and related social sciences, there is an inherent, and complicated, tension between the need for real independence of effort on the part of the graduate student (the image of the solitary scholar) and the need for support and encouragement. We would be strongly opposed to a system of regimentation that deprived the individual student of the opportunity to learn what is involved, for instance, in finding a viable research topic and developing the capacity to undertake genuine scholarship. Nor do we want to suggest that doctoral education in the arts and sciences should be so streamlined as to threaten qualitative standards.

There appears to be a great deal of distance, however, between present arrangements and any such model. In the last part of the book, we suggest what we regard as realistic goals and some ways of meeting them. We also urge more flexible patterns of financial support, with tailored forms of assistance available at key junctures when students have met prescribed standards in prescribed periods of time.

It is unrealistic, in our view, to expect universities to make the needed changes in graduate programs entirely on their own. Not even the most favorably situated institutions and programs can provide the flexible funds that must be combined with tighter structures. Universities are already carrying by far the largest share of the costs of graduate education in the humanities and social sciences. Yet even with current levels of institutional funding, doctoral candidates in these fields have to find substantial resources of their own (for example, through employment, borrowing, and the earnings of spouses). Thus, additional external funding from a variety of sources is an absolute prerequisite, in our view, for substantial improvement in graduate education.

National foundations may be able to be more helpful than in the past by working collaboratively with interested departments—the right location, we believe, for focused efforts to achieve systemic improvements in graduate programs. As in previous periods, foundations should be expected to be at least occasionally adventuresome, willing to place bets that might be inappropriate for governmental entities. They should also be capable of acknowledging disappointing results, learning from them, and then starting over. Corporations can play important roles in supporting graduate education (as a number do now), but most funding from this source should be expected to go to the sciences and engineering.

Governmental entities in this country, as in other countries, have important roles to play in supporting an activity that has profound implications for the national welfare—for economic progress, social progress, cultural and intellectual life, and even the capacity to provide political and moral leadership. The NSF fellowship program offers one useful model, although we would recommend certain modifications if it were applied to meet the needs of the humanities. (In particular, our study leads us to question the efficacy of multiyear fellowship awards in these fields, at least as graduate programs are now structured.)

Consideration should be given, in our view, to a governmental program of dissertation awards in the humanities that would encourage outstanding students to complete their doctorates. We also reiterate our belief in the value of programs (supported by corporations, foundations, universities, and government agencies) targeted at minority groups, where more direct assistance is essential at many stages in the educational process if greater progress is to be made in increasing their participation in graduate education.

We end this study more aware than before of the complexities of graduate education and of the difficulties besetting efforts to improve the process. Sustained efforts are required, and a willingness to learn along the way. Simple—and inexpensive—solutions are unlikely to be found. But we are also more persuaded than ever that real progress can be made. Interested parties need to assign a proper priority to graduate education, to work together to complement one another's efforts, and to approach a most complex task with the requisite combination of humility, determination, and a long time horizon.

PART ONE

Trends in Graduate Education

CHAPTER TWO

Recipients of Doctorates

FOR A combination of cultural, political, and economic reasons, the United States has always invested heavily in education at *pre*collegiate levels. While there were well regarded colleges in colonial America (usually affiliated with churches and religious organizations), higher education was not given as much emphasis here as in some European countries until the late nineteenth and twentieth centuries, when it became a premier "growth industry" in the United States.[1]

Today, the achievement of this country in providing postsecondary education for unusually large numbers of its citizens (and, especially in recent years, for citizens of other countries) is recognized throughout the world. UNESCO data indicate that the percentage of the population in the 25-and-over age range achieving a postsecondary level of education is higher in the United States than in any other country except Canada (see Table 2.1 for some illustrative figures).

There is less information available on the distribution of doctoral education among countries, in part because of problems in defining consistently what constitutes a "doctorate." The limited data available suggest that the United States awarded approximately two-thirds of all doctorates conferred within eight countries for which reasonably comparable data exist (Australia, Finland, France, Japan, the Netherlands, Sweden, the United Kingdom, and the United States). The rankings by number of doctorates conferred cannot be explained solely in terms of differences in national income. For example, the United States generated 47 percent of the combined GNP of these eight countries but awarded 66 percent of all doctorates conferred. At the other extreme, Japan contributed 28 percent of the combined GNP but conferred only 3 percent of the doctorates.[2]

Doctoral programs did not exist in the United States until 1876, when the first such program was established at Johns Hopkins University. When the Association of American Universities (AAU) was organized in 1900, fewer than 400 doctorates were conferred annually. In 1920, less than 600 doctorates were conferred by only 14 universities. From that time forward, however, the growth

---

[1]Puritanism is believed to have had a great deal to do with the early emphasis on basic education, since literacy was a necessity for reading the Bible. Other factors were immigration (and the need to educate and assimilate the waves of immigrants) and the importance attached to educating a democratic citizenry. See Pulliam 1976; and Cohen 1974. Higher education, on the other hand—especially at its "higher" levels—was more advanced in countries such as Britain, France, and Germany than in the United States until well into the twentieth century. See Ringer 1979; Veysey 1965; and Kohler 1990, 639ff.

[2]OECD 1989, 14–15. The lack of a close correlation between GNP and numbers of doctorates conferred is a warning not to oversimplify the relationship between national investment in advanced education and the economic status of a country; for an extended discussion of this topic, see Shapiro (1990). The case of Japan illustrates vividly that excellent economic performance can be achieved without large "at home" investments in graduate education. This is especially true under current circumstances, when there is so much mobility of students across national boundaries.

TABLE 2.1
Achievement of Postsecondary Level of Education, Various Countries, 1980–1981
(percent of age 25+ population)

Canada	37.4	Korea	8.9	Italy	3.7
U.S.	32.2	USSR	8.3	South Africa	3.6
Israel	23.1	Ireland	7.9	Turkey	3.4
Australia	21.5	Greece	7.6	Egypt	3.3
Switzerland	21.2	Chile	7.2	Austria	3.3
Germany (GDR)	17.3	Spain	7.1	India	2.5
Sweden	15.4	Hungary	7.0	Jamaica	2.0
Japan	14.3	Czechoslovakia	6.0	Tunisia	1.3
Norway	11.9	Argentina	5.8	China	1.0
United Kingdom	11.0	Mexico	5.3		

Source: UNESCO 1989, Table 1.4.

Notes: Data are available only for selected countries. Most of the data are for 1980 or 1981, but there are some differences in the years in which censuses were conducted and in the age groups used as the reference points for these calculations. Data are for the age 25+ population except in the case of the USSR where data are for the age 10+ population.

in doctoral education has been nothing short of phenomenal—in 1988, 33,456 doctorates were conferred by over 350 institutions.[3]

This chapter provides a summary of the pattern of growth in the number of recipients of doctorates from U.S. universities. Special attention is paid to differences associated with field of study, citizenship, gender, and race/ethnicity. This descriptive discussion is followed (in Chapter Three) by an analysis of the factors associated with the rapid expansion in graduate education during the 1960s and the subsequent contraction.

OVERALL TRENDS

Many in this country are accustomed to thinking of higher education primarily in terms of undergraduate studies, and the extraordinary expansion of undergraduate enrollment, especially since World War II, is well known. Approximately 1 million bachelor's degrees are awarded annually by American colleges and universities, as compared with about 300,000 master's degrees and about 34,000 doctorates.[4] It is less widely understood that growth in the number of

---

[3]For a general history of graduate education in the United States from its beginnings until the 1950s, see Berelson (1960, 6–43). Harmon (1978) provides more statistical detail and covers a slightly longer period. Data on doctorates conferred in 1988 are from the National Research Council (NRC) publication, *Summary Report 1988*, Appendix A, Table 1. At the time of this revision of the manuscript, published data for 1989 were available; however, substituting 1989 figures for 1988 figures would not have changed the main conclusions and would have introduced inconsistencies since other data (especially those provided by the NRC through special tabulations) extend only through 1988.

For convenience, and in order to maintain consistency with the terminology used by the National Research Council, we use the terms *doctorate* and *PhD* interchangeably. The large majority of doctorates awarded that are not PhDs are in the field of education. In 1988, for example, about 87 percent of the doctorates awarded were PhDs or DScs, 10 percent were EdDs, and the remainder were other specialized doctorates (*Summary Report 1988*, iii and 2).

[4]*Digest of Education Statistics*, 1990, Table 220.

TABLE 2.2
Number of Doctorates Conferred per Thousand BAs, 1920–1980

Year	PhDs per 1,000 BAs
1920	12.6
1930	18.8
1940	17.6
1950	14.9
1960	25.0
1970	37.7
1980	35.1

Source: Digest of Education Statistics, 1990, Table 220.

PhDs awarded has outpaced growth in the number of undergraduate degrees over most of this century. Indeed, over the entire period from 1920 to 1988, the number of PhDs grew nearly three times faster than the number of BAs.

A rough comparison of the changing relative scales of graduate and undergraduate education can be made by calculating the number of PhDs per thousand BAs awarded in various years. This ratio rose significantly during the 1920s, remained roughly constant during the Depression of the 1930s, and then declined in the immediate post–World War II years, as veterans returned to earn BAs in large numbers (Table 2.2).[5] It more than doubled over the next 20 years—rising from 15 PhDs per thousand BAs in 1950 to 38 per thousand in 1970—before declining modestly and then leveling off at about 35 PhDs per thousand BAs.

The dramatic year-by-year growth in the number of PhDs conferred between the early 1900s and 1970–1973 (the peak years for PhDs conferred in this country) was remarkable for both its pace and its steadiness (Figure 2.1). Apart from the World War II dip, the path upward has had a remarkably constant—and steep—slope. The number of doctorates conferred increased at an average annual rate of approximately 7 percent from 1920 through 1970.[6]

The 1960s were clearly the decade of most rapid growth (excluding only the 1920s, when the absolute number of doctorates conferred at the start of the decade was very low). Between 1960 and 1970, the number of doctorates awarded *tripled*, rising from under 10,000 in 1960 to nearly 30,000 just one

[5]Students receiving BAs and PhDs in a given year began their undergraduate studies at different times and consequently were subject to different influences when making educational decisions. Thus the ratios reported here are intended only to demonstrate broad trends in the relative magnitudes. See Chapter Three for an extended discussion of the more complex question of how changes in the number of BAs have influenced the number of PhDs conferred.

[6]See bottom panel of Figure 2.1. The straight line shown there is an ordinary least squares regression line, fit to the natural logarithms of the numbers of doctorates conferred each year from 1920 through 1970 (even though the data are plotted on Figure 2.1 for only even-numbered years). The actual compound growth rate obtained in this way is 6.7 percent per year, and the R^2 for the equation is 0.925. Harmon (1978, 6) first emphasized the steadiness of this average annual rate of increase, which he put at 7 percent. We stopped the regression in 1970 to determine the average annual rate of increase over the half-century of expansion. If we had included all years through 1988, the average rate of increase obviously would have been lower (6.2 percent). All of these data are from the Doctorate Records File. For the years 1920 through 1957, they have been taken from Harmon (1978); for the years 1958 through 1988, they are from special tabulations provided by the National Research Council.

Number of Doctorates

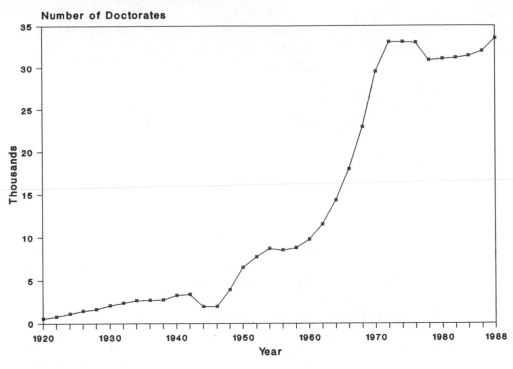

Rate of Change

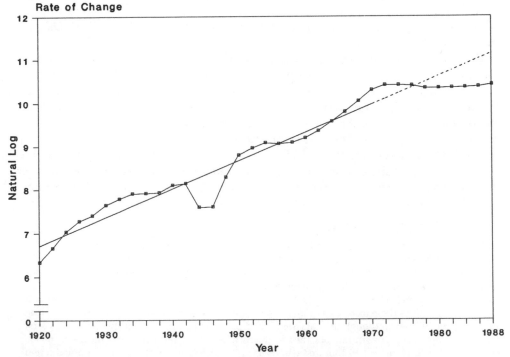

Figure 2.1
Doctorates Conferred, 1920–1988

Source: All data are from Doctorate Records File: for 1920–1957, from Harmon (1978), and for 1958–1988, from special tabulations.

Notes: In the bottom panel, the straight line is an ordinary least squares regression line, fit to the natural logarithms of the numbers of doctorates conferred from 1920 to 1970.

decade later. The abrupt halt in this upward progression that dates from 1973 was a major departure from the experience of the previous half-century.

The forces fueling the expansion of the 1960s are well known. Strong incentives to pursue graduate study were created by the extraordinary increase in the demand for college teachers in that decade and by the existence of draft deferments during much of the Vietnam War. Special mention should also be made of the sharp rise in federal support for higher education. Federal fellowships and traineeships increased dramatically, and higher education's share of GNP nearly doubled, rising from 1.4 percent in 1959 to 2.7 percent in 1970. Particularly heavy investments were made in those institutions and individuals associated with the awarding of PhDs, as the government increasingly saw graduate education as vital to national security.[7]

In the wake of this remarkable period of growth came a new set of circumstances that slowed and, in some cases, even stalled the heretofore steady increases in the number of doctorates conferred. Federal spending on research and development began to decline in real terms after 1967; the balance between demand and supply in the academic labor market swung dramatically, as the number of teaching positions began to decrease at the same time that record numbers of new PhDs were seeking jobs; and draft deferments for graduate study were withdrawn after the summer of 1968.

The subsequent decline in the number of PhDs conferred stimulated a growing concern that the ablest college graduates were shying away from graduate study in the arts and sciences in order to pursue careers in business, law, and medicine. Indeed, the number of first professional degrees awarded in these three fields rose at the same time that the number of PhDs conferred fell. Between 1973 and 1985, the number of MBAs more than doubled, from 31,007 to 67,527; the number of JDs and LLBs increased by more than a third, from 27,205 to 37,491; and the number of MDs increased by more than a half, from 10,307 to 16,041.[8] This movement towards professional and applied fields was evident at both BA and doctoral levels, and was seen as a general "flight from the arts and sciences."[9]

We conclude this discussion of overall trends by noting the inconclusive debate over whether the average "quality" of PhDs has deteriorated—along with the number of doctorates—in recent years. (The word "quality" is in quotation marks because no one knows how to measure this elusive attribute. Standardized test scores continue to be the most common measuring rod, even as all recognize the limitations of such measures.) Studies have shown that the percentage of the most outstanding college graduates electing to pursue PhD programs in the arts and sciences declined following the "golden" era of the 1960s. There is also some evidence of more broadly based declines in quality. For instance, there has been a national decline in GRE-Verbal scores, and admission to many graduate programs became somewhat less competitive during the

---

[7]The effects of the draft and of educational deferments are examined in detail in Chapter Three. For discussion of trends in federal funding and graduate student support, see National Board on Graduate Education 1974; National Commission on Student Financial Assistance (Brademas Report) 1983; Snyder 1985; and Wolfle 1978.

[8]*Digest of Education Statistics* 1987, Tables 206 and 212.

[9]Bowen and Sosa 1989, 47–51. A subsequent, and much more detailed, analysis of the factors behind this "flight" at the undergraduate level (and especially of differences associated with gender) may be found in Turner and Bowen (1990, 517–21).

1970s. However, careful examination of some of these data sets (especially the GRE data) raises questions about the extent of the changes that have occurred. Also, there is evidence of "recovery" in some of these measures in the 1980s.[10]

Our own research leads to two conclusions about quality that are discussed later but can be anticipated here. First, there has been a substantial shift in the institutional "mix" of doctorate-granting programs, with a much higher proportion of all doctorates now being conferred by programs that are both lower-rated and small in size (see Chapter Four). Second, within the universe of the most highly rated programs, the average quality of entrants shows no sign of having declined significantly during even the darkest days of the 1970s and appears to have risen somewhat in the latter half of the 1980s (see Chapter Five).

FIELDS OF STUDY

Differences by Broad Field

A main purpose of this chapter is to provide the context for the rest of this study, which focuses on a subset of fields within the arts and sciences: English, history, political science, economics, mathematics, and physics. In concentrating on these arts-and-sciences fields, it is easy to forget the large numbers of doctorates awarded in other broad areas (Table 2.3).

All the broad fields of doctoral study experienced extraordinary expansion in the 1960s (Figure 2.2). The peak years came a little earlier in the sciences and engineering than in the humanities, social sciences, and other fields, but rates of growth were broadly similar. Between 1960 and 1973 (the peak year for doctoral education overall), the number of doctorates awarded in most of these broad fields increased between 200 and 350 percent. Contrary to what many may have thought, the percentage increase in doctorates conferred within the humanities

TABLE 2.3
Number of Doctorates Conferred by Broad Field, 1988

Field	Doctorates Conferred
Physical sciences (including mathematics)	5,309
Life sciences	6,143
Engineering	4,190
Social sciences (including psychology)	5,769
Humanities (including history)	3,553
Business	1,039
Education	6,349
Other	1,104
Total	33,456

Source: *Summary Report 1988*, Appendix A, Table 1.

[10]The available literature is cited and summarized well in Ehrenberg (1991). Special mention should also be made of a study by Hartnett (1987) that makes interesting use of SAT data; however, as the author emphasizes, this study is already dated in that it contains information only on students who *began* graduate study in years up to about the early 1970s. For a detailed examination of the GRE data, see Adelman (1984). Interpretation of the GRE data is complicated by (among other things) the presence of growing numbers of foreign students in the test-taking population.

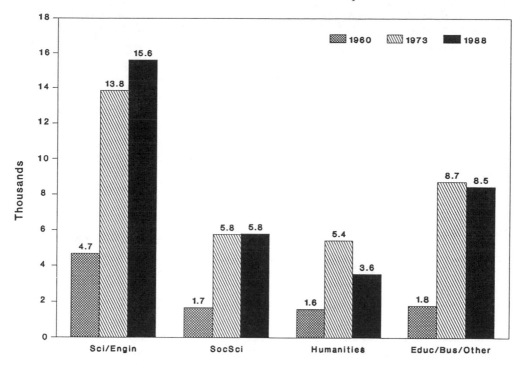

Figure 2.2
Number of Doctorates Conferred by Broad Field, 1960, 1973, and 1988
Source: Summary Report 1988, Table C.

over this period (238 percent) was slightly greater than the percentage increase in the science and engineering category (196 percent).[11]

Subsequently, patterns diverged much more noticeably. While the total number of doctorates conferred in 1988 was very close to the total number conferred in 1973 (33,456 versus 33,755), the near-constancy of these aggregate numbers conceals important shifts in composition. The "gainers" and "losers" were as follows:

- The science and engineering category was the largest gainer (an increase of 1,800 doctorates, or 13 percent).
- The number of doctorates awarded in the social sciences remained almost constant (an increase of 11 doctorates, or 0.2 percent).
- There was some decline in education and other professional fields (a decrease of 889 doctorates in education alone, but a net loss of only 249 doctorates for the education/business/other category when we offset gains in fields such as business and communications).
- The humanities were the principal losers (a decrease of 1,861 doctorates, or 34 percent). This "loss" in the humanities almost exactly offset the "gain" in the sciences and engineering.[12]

---

[11]*Summary Report 1988*, Table C.
[12]*Ibid.* Recently available data for 1989 indicate a continuation of the general trends noted here. However, both the science and engineering and the social science categories show unusually sharp increases in 1989 as compared with 1988 (approximately 4 percent and 3 percent, respectively).

More generally, there has been a pronounced movement along the continuum from basic to more applied studies over the last two decades. This generic shift has occurred within almost every one of the broad fields shown in Figure 2.2. For instance, the number of doctorates awarded in engineering increased much more rapidly between 1973 and 1988 (and, for that matter, between 1960 and 1973) than did the number of doctorates awarded in the sciences. Within the social sciences, psychology (especially clinical psychology) grew relative to fields such as anthropology. Business, communications, and "other professional" fields experienced high rates of growth. Even within the humanities, there was a shift away from many of the more traditional fields toward, for instance, music performance.[13]

Differences among Six Arts-and-Sciences Fields

This study focuses on six specific fields within the arts and sciences: economics, English and American literature, history, mathematics, political science, and physics. When trends in these six fields are examined separately, both commonalities and noteworthy differences appear.

It is useful to group English, history, and political science (EHP), since they share a number of characteristics.[14] English and history are most closely related in terms of academic attributes (both are generally regarded as falling within the humanities, are "reading" subjects, and usually require library and archival research). Perhaps for this reason, trends in doctorates conferred for these fields follow closely parallel paths, showing steady (and rapid) growth until about 1973, and then very sharp declines (top panel of Figure 2.3). In both English and history, the number of doctorates conferred in 1989 was only about half the number conferred just fifteen years earlier.

The third of the EHP fields, political science, while falling within the social sciences, has more in common with English and history than it does with economics. Some specialties within political science (political philosophy may be the clearest example) have many of the attributes of the humanities. The behavior of degrees conferred in political science tracks, in some degree, the trends in English and history. Even though it started out at an appreciably lower level of doctorates conferred, political science also grew rapidly during the 1960s, but subsequently did not experience nearly as fast a decline as either English or history. In 1988, the absolute levels of degrees conferred in the EHP fields had converged to a considerable extent (716 doctorates in English, 603 in history, and 634 in political science).[15]

---

[13] This shift toward more applied fields of study occurred concurrently with a shift in the citizenship mix of doctoral recipients. The percentage of all doctorates earned by non-U.S. residents rose rapidly during these years, and, as a group, the non-U.S. residents have tended to have an especially strong interest in applied fields of study. Thus, when we look only at trends in the number of doctorates received by U.S. residents, the picture changes somewhat. (See the next section for a detailed discussion of the effects of changes in citizenship mix.)

[14] In an early study of graduate education at Berkeley, Stark (1966) also chose to combine these same three fields, contrasting them with chemistry.

[15] These data and the annual data plotted on Figure 2.3 include both U.S. residents and non-U.S. residents. Appendix G, Table G.2–1, shows the actual figures for selected years. Chapter Five contains a detailed discussion of associated trends in courses offered, enrollments, and faculty staffing in these fields within a selected group of leading graduate programs.

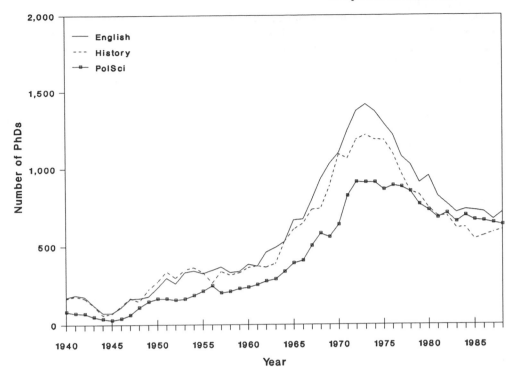

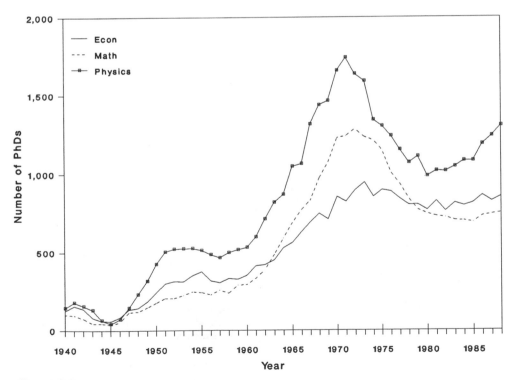

Figure 2.3
Number of Doctorates Conferred by Field, 1940–1988
Source: Special tabulations from Doctorate Records File.

The general pattern in mathematics and physics (MP) was broadly similar to that in the EHP cluster of fields during the years of expansion (bottom panel of Figure 2.3). As noted earlier, the postwar peak in doctorates conferred occurred slightly earlier in mathematics and physics (especially physics) than in the other fields. The rate of expansion between 1958 and 1972 was greatest in mathematics, where the average annual growth rate in doctorates conferred was 12.8 percent. An important difference between these more quantitative disciplines and the EHP cluster is the former's earlier and somewhat stronger recovery during the early 1980s from declining popularity in the 1970s. In physics (the clearest case in point), the number of doctorates conferred increased more than 30 percent between 1980 and 1988.

Economics has, in some respects, followed a pattern all its own. Like other fields, it experienced substantial growth in doctorates conferred during the 1950s and 1960s, but the rate of growth was not as spectacular as in mathematics and physics. However, the number of PhDs awarded in economics declined only minimally following the peak year for the field. By 1988, the number of doctorates conferred had almost returned to the highest level recorded. Perhaps economics was more successful than other fields in resisting the general "flight from the arts and sciences" because it was seen (rightly or wrongly) as having more of a practical aspect.

CITIZENSHIP

It is a well-known and widely reported fact that the proportion of doctoral degrees awarded by U.S. universities to residents of other countries has increased rapidly. An article in the *New York Times* observed that "American universities are being flooded by waves of foreign graduate students."[16] Only 772 non-U.S. residents received PhDs from American universities in 1958. Just 30 years later, the comparable number was 8,589.[17]

The simply extraordinary increase in the number of foreign recipients of doctorates, particularly in years since 1980, offset almost exactly the decline in the number of U.S. residents earning doctorates. Thus, the apparent stability in the *overall* number of doctorates awarded annually since the early 1980s is highly misleading. The number of doctorates awarded to U.S. residents in all fields continued to decline until at least 1986 (Figure 2.4).

Further distinctions are evident when separate consideration is given to the six fields within the arts and sciences on which this study concentrates (Figure 2.5). English and history have been relatively resistant to the influx of foreign students. There has been a modest absolute increase—though a large relative increase—in the percentage of PhDs awarded to non-U.S. residents in these two fields (from under 5 percent in 1958 to more than 10 percent in 1988). In general, these subjects are more intimately tied to local culture than are the sciences and

---

[16]DePalma 1990, 1.

[17]The data for 1958 and 1988 are from special tabulations of the Doctorate Records File. See Appendix G, Table G.2–1. "U.S. residents" include citizens and permanent residents; they are distinguished from "non-U.S. residents" (temporary residents). "Unknowns" are counted as non-U.S. residents. For most purposes, the resident versus nonresident distinction is the appropriate one, and we use it whenever possible; some data, however, are available only by citizenship status.

Lomperis (1992, forthcoming) has completed an extensive study entitled "The Demographic Transformation of American Doctoral Education," based on published and unpublished data from the Doctorate Records File. She considers citizenship, gender, and race/ethnicity.

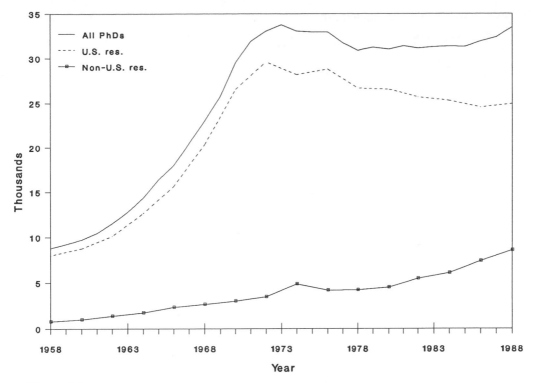

Figure 2.4
Number of Doctorates Conferred by Citizenship, 1958–1988
Source: Special tabulations from Doctorate Records File.
Notes: See footnote 17 for definitions of "U.S. residents" and "Non-U.S. residents."

social sciences, and that may be one reason why doctoral education offered by U.S. universities in these fields has had relatively limited appeal to foreign students.

The internationalization of American doctoral education has been much more pronounced in political science, especially in recent years. Whereas only 12 percent of PhDs in political science were awarded to non-U.S. residents in 1958, the comparable figure had increased to more than 30 percent by 1988. One explanation for the greater popularity of this field among foreign students is that it includes international relations and comparative politics, which are more accessible to foreign students than many other specialties in the humanities and social sciences. Indeed, intimate knowledge of their own countries and general familiarity with other parts of the world can be a decided advantage to foreign students in studying these subjects alongside U.S. students.

Still more far-reaching changes in citizenship mix have occurred in economics, mathematics, and physics, where language and cultural context are less forbidding barriers for foreign students. In 1958, only about 10 percent of degrees awarded in mathematics and physics went to non-U.S. residents (almost 20 percent in economics). Subsequently, however, the increase in the proportion of non-U.S. residents receiving PhDs in these three fields has been nothing short of phenomenal (bottom panel of Figure 2.5).

The trends for mathematics and physics were very similar until 1980, when they diverged. Although the relative number of foreign recipients of doctorates in physics continued to increase steadily (reaching 40 percent of all doctorates in

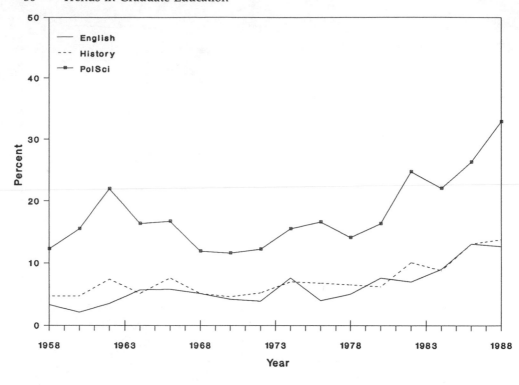

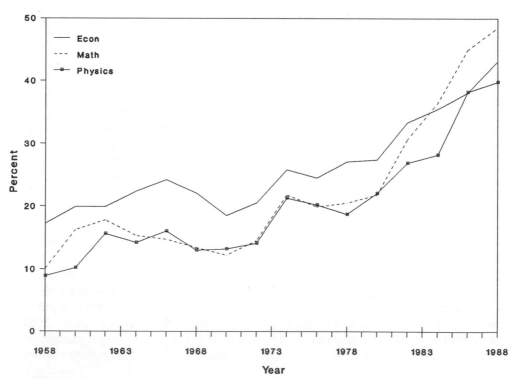

Figure 2.5
Doctorates Earned by Non-U.S. Residents as Share of Total, by Field, 1958–1988
Source: Special tabulations from Doctorate Records File.

TABLE 2.4
Changes in Number of Doctorates Conferred by Citizenship and Field, 1972–1988

Field	U.S. Res.	Non-U.S. Res.	Total
English	−690	+37	−653
History	−604	+21	−583
Political science	−374	+97	−277
Economics	−226	+185	−41
Mathematics	−709	+177	−532
Physics	−619	+287	−332

Source: Special tabulations from Doctorate Records File. See Appendix G, Table G.2–1.

1988), the number of foreign recipients of doctorates in mathematics increased even more rapidly. In just eight years, between 1980 and 1988, the proportion of foreign students receiving doctorates in mathematics roughly doubled. In 1988, almost 50 percent of all PhDs in mathematics in this country were awarded to non-U.S. residents. The proportion of foreign recipients of doctorates in economics also increased rapidly in these same years, rising from 27 percent in 1980 to 43 percent in 1988.

One way of examining the extent to which foreign recipients have substituted for U.S. residents is by examining absolute changes in degrees conferred between 1972 (the approximate peak year) and 1988 (Table 2.4). Outside of English and history, the influx of non-U.S. residents prevented a precipitous decline in the number of recipients of doctorates. The most extreme case is economics, where the large increase in foreign students has been the key factor in stabilizing the number of recipients of PhDs between 1972 and 1988.

The impact of foreign students has been especially strong in the most recent years. Between 1984 and 1988, the apparent recovery of "output" of doctorates in certain key fields has been entirely dependent on ever-rising numbers of foreign recipients (see especially mathematics and economics in Table 2.5). The recent large increase in the number of PhDs awarded in physics has been due entirely to an absolutely extraordinary jump in the number of non-U.S. recipients of doctorates.

In general, the most rapid increases in the number of foreign recipients of doctorates occurred in the same years that the number of U.S. recipients declined most rapidly. This raises important questions of cause and effect. Part of the rise in the proportion of foreign recipients was presumably due to the

TABLE 2.5
Changes in Number of Doctorates Conferred by Citizenship and Field, 1984–1988

Field	U.S. Res.	Non-U.S. Res.	Total
English	−41	+25	−16
History	−43	+29	−14
Political science	−116	+55	−61
Economics	−27	+86	+59
Mathematics	−57	+108	+51
Physics	+9	+213	+222

Source: Same as Table 2.4.

determination of graduate programs to maintain some critical mass of students at a time when there was severely diminished interest in graduate education on the part of U.S. residents. But we are skeptical as to whether this is the full explanation. The growing worldwide interest in advanced training, especially in technical subjects, combined with the appeal of graduate programs in this country, must surely have been a factor of great importance in its own right. Even if more U.S. residents again pursue PhDs in the arts and sciences, it seems unlikely that the flow of foreign students to U.S. graduate programs will suddenly abate.[18]

Major questions of policy are also raised by the changing citizenship composition of the pool of new PhDs. The implications of this shift for the faculty shortages anticipated in this country in the years ahead are one relevant concern. To what extent will far larger numbers of non-U.S. residents in the pool of doctorate holders affect the supply of candidates for faculty positions at U.S. colleges and universities? Obviously, relatively smaller numbers of foreign PhDs remain in this country after graduation, and their status is at times dependent on the vagaries of international relations between the United States and their home countries. However, over the past 20 years, increasing numbers of non-U.S. residents have chosen to stay on (at least temporarily) after graduation to continue their studies or research.[19]

GENDER

The rapidly increasing representation of women in graduate programs over the last two decades has been a major development, and the gender gap in doctoral education has closed significantly. In the 1920s and 1930s, about 15 percent of all doctorates were awarded to women. During the 1940s and the years following World War II, the share of doctorates awarded to women oscillated within the 11 to 20 percent range. As recently as the years between 1958 and 1966, the percentage of all doctorates awarded to women remained between 10 and 12 percent. This overall percentage then started to rise steadily and rapidly, more than tripling between 1966 and 1989.[20]

So far as we are aware, no field of study has failed to participate in this general upward movement, but the scale and timing of increases have varied considerably. Detailed data are available for U.S. residents in the six specific fields within the arts and sciences on which we concentrate. Within this universe, women have made the largest gains in the EHP fields (top panel of Figure 2.6).

---

[18]Unfortunately, detailed data on cross-flows of students from one country to another are available only for total foreign students, not for doctoral students alone. Still, aggregate data provide some sense of the extent of foreign interest in American education. In the mid-1980s, over 30 percent of all non-U.S. students studying abroad were in the United States. Countries with the largest proportions of their "exported" students in the United States were Canada (80.5 percent), India (79.4 percent), China (75.5 percent), Japan (74.2 percent), and Korea (67.7 percent). France continues to attract by far the highest proportion of African students. These data have been compiled from UNESCO sources by the Institute of International Education (1989, especially Tables 1.6 and 1.8).

[19]See *Summary Report 1989* (31–56) for an extended discussion of "non-U.S. citizen recipients of doctorates"; see also Carnegie Foundation 1987, 41–42.

[20]All of these data are from the Doctorate Records File, and have been reported in the various *Summary Reports* published by the NRC. For a general discussion of the sociocultural forces that have had such a major impact on the role of women within graduate education, see Rossi and Calderwood (1973) and Cole (1979).

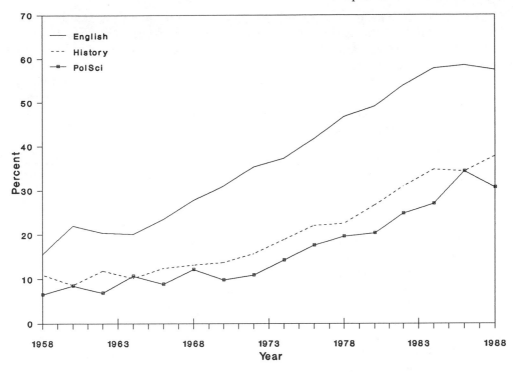

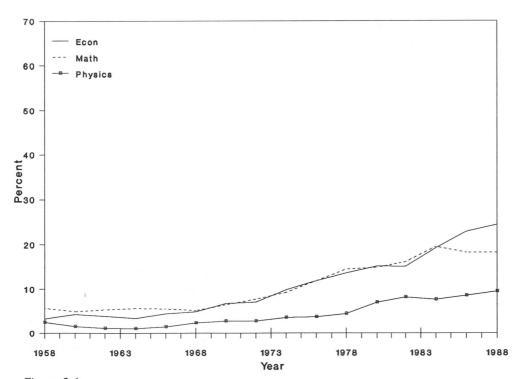

Figure 2.6
Doctorates Earned by Women as Share of Total, by Field, U.S. Residents Only, 1958–1988
Source: Special tabulations from Doctorate Records File.

The field of English and American language and literature stands out. Between 1958 and the early 1980s, a yawning gender gap was closed. The proportion of doctorates awarded to women increased nearly fourfold, rising from just over 15 percent to almost 60 percent. The gender gap in both history and political science has been shrinking as well, but men still outnumber women by considerable margins. About 30 percent of PhDs in each of these fields went to women in 1988, as contrasted with about 10 percent in 1958.

The trend in the sciences has been rather different (bottom panel of Figure 2.6). Again, one field—this time, physics—is especially noteworthy. While there has been a slight upward drift in the percentage of physics doctorates earned by women, the change has been less pronounced than in any of the other five fields; in 1988, less than 10 percent of all doctorates awarded to U.S. residents in this field were received by women. The percentages of PhDs awarded to women also remain quite low in economics (24 percent) and mathematics (18 percent), but there has been more movement in these fields.

The greatest changes in the share of doctorates earned by women occurred during precisely those years (since 1970) when graduate education in general was contracting. These women entered graduate school and worked toward their PhDs during years (primarily the 1960s) when the women's movement and other broad social and cultural forces were expanding opportunities for women. These developments took effect at a time when other forces (the weakening of the academic labor market, for instance) were pushing in the opposite direction, and it is interesting to speculate about what would have happened to graduate programs, and to the aggregate number of PhDs conferred, in their absence.

The remarkable rates of increase in percentage shares notwithstanding, the representation of women among doctoral recipients has remained substantially below the representation of women among BA recipients. The most recent data available indicate that women now earn over half (52 percent) of all bachelor's degrees, but just over 36 percent of all doctorates.[21]

The continuing disparity in the overall shares of BA and PhD degrees earned by women could lead to the conclusion that if more women are to earn doctorates, one must address whatever problems exist in the interval between receipt of the BA and receipt of the PhD. After all, since women now earn more than half of all BAs, it might be argued that barriers at that level have been overcome.

While this is a plausible line of thinking, it is only partly correct. A first step in disentangling the forces at work is to recognize that approximately 5 percentage points of the current disparity in overall shares of degrees earned by women at the BA and PhD levels can be explained simply by the presence of large numbers of non-U.S. residents among recipients of PhDs. Many more men than women from other countries earn doctorates at U.S. universities, and when the analysis of doctorates conferred is limited to U.S. residents, the share earned by women in 1988 rises to 40.2 percent from 35.2 percent (for all doctorates).[22]

An additional component can be attributed to differences in the undergraduate fields chosen most frequently by men and women. Historically, women have majored in disproportionately larger numbers in fields that have been relatively

---

[21]*Digest of Education Statistics* 1991, Table 224; the 52 percent figure is for 1987–1988.

[22]Data for all doctorates are from *Summary Report 1988*, Appendix A, Table 1; data for U.S. residents only are from special tabulations.

more popular at the undergraduate level than at the PhD level, such as communications. Men, in contrast, have been more heavily represented in fields in which relatively large numbers of undergraduate majors have continued on to earn PhDs, such as physics. We estimate that slightly less than half of the disparity in percentage shares of degrees earned by women at the BA and PhD levels can be explained by this BA distribution effect.[23]

The last factor to be noted is the greater tendency of men than women in specified fields to earn PhDs. The extent of these differences can be seen by comparing the representation of women at the BA and PhD levels on a field-by-field basis. Figure 2.7 shows these comparisons for the 1976 BA cohort. In every field, the percentage of degrees earned by women is at least slightly higher at the BA level than at the PhD level, which suggests that PhD programs have attracted somewhat fewer women than one might have expected on the basis of the sizes of the respective BA pools.

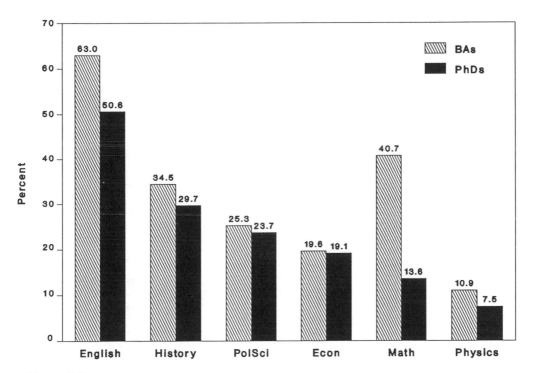

Figure 2.7
BAs and Doctorates Earned by Women as Share of Total, by Field, 1976 BA Cohort
Source: BA data are from the *Earned Degrees Conferred Survey* (U.S. Department of Education, various years). PhD data are from special tabulations of the Doctorate Records File.

---

[23]The calculations made to arrive at this estimate are rough and focus exclusively on recipients of BA degrees in 1976 (the 1976 BA cohort), and on members of this BA cohort who went on to earn PhDs. This approach avoids the problems of interpretation that arise when efforts are made to compare numbers of BAs and PhDs that were received in the same year, but by individuals who made decisions concerning fields of study and whether to pursue doctorates at very different points in time.

(continued)

Mathematics is the extreme case in point. In this field, there is a threefold difference: Women earned 40.7 percent of the BAs but just 13.6 percent of the PhDs. In the five fields other than mathematics, the differences were much smaller. In economics, for instance, 19.6 percent of all BAs went to women and 19.1 percent of all PhDs earned by this same BA cohort went to women. In physics, to take another example, 10.9 percent of the BAs went to women, as compared with 7.5 percent of the PhDs. In English and American literature, 63 percent of BAs were earned by women, as compared with 50.6 percent of PhDs.

In short, once the numbers of men and women in BA pools within a certain field are established, the (relative) numbers who go on to earn PhDs are not all that dissimilar—noting again that mathematics is a clear exception to this generalization. The tendency for women to be much more heavily represented at the doctoral level in some fields than in others is rooted primarily in decisions that were made much earlier concerning fields of study. This is clear justification for efforts to encourage women to develop interests in fields such as the sciences and the quantitative social sciences well before the choice of a field of specialization is made at the undergraduate level.[24]

A second interval in the educational process deserves attention. The further drop that occurs between receipt of the BA and receipt of the PhD can be attributed to some combination of lower participation by women within PhD programs and higher attrition at the PhD level. Women have been said to be more likely to "stop out at the MA level," and there are also scattered bits of evidence suggesting that those who have entered PhD programs have experienced above-average attrition.[25]

Of the total number of BAs earned in our six fields, 38.6 percent were earned by women. Of the total number of PhDs earned in these same six fields within twelve years by members of this BA cohort, 21.2 percent were earned by women. Thus, the BA-PhD disparity in women's shares was about 17 percentage points on an absolute basis.

To estimate the extent of the "BA distribution" effect, we first determined the number of BAs that would have been awarded to women in each of the six fields had the BA field shares for men (the percentage of all BAs awarded to men that were awarded in each field) applied to women as well. This hypothetical number is higher than the real number because men majored in these particular fields in larger relative numbers than women.

The second step was to multiply this hypothetical number of women BAs in each field by the known ratio of PhDs to BAs for women in each field. (This is called the "PhD-proclivity" in the analysis presented in Chapter Three, and the discussion there may clarify some of these procedures.) The result is a set of (hypothetical) numbers of women who would have earned PhDs in each field had the distribution of undergraduate majors for women been the same as it was for men.

The third step was to divide this hypothetical number of PhDs that would have been earned by women in each field by the sum of this number and the actual number of PhDs earned by men, thus obtaining a new hypothetical share of PhDs that would have been earned by women (36.0 percent). Similarly, we calculate a hypothetical share of Six-Field BAs that would have been earned by women under these assumptions (45.6 percent).

The BA-PhD disparity thus falls from 17 percentage points (38.6 minus 21.2) to 10 percentage points (45.6 minus 36.0). Because of the approximate nature of all of these calculations, we speak of this reduction in the disparity as constituting slightly less than half of the original disparity.

[24]This interpretation is consistent with the conclusions reached by a number of studies of women in science and engineering (Widnall 1988 and references cited therein to studies by Berryman, Vetter, and others, including those who served on commissions and working groups established by the National Science Foundation, the Office of Technology Assessment, and the National Academy of Science). Much less research has been done within the humanities and social sciences.

[25]Widnall 1988, especially 1741ff. The lack of reliable data on completion rates within PhD programs has handicapped these studies. Our Ten-University and National Fellowship data sets are helpful in this regard, and in later chapters we compare completion rates for men and women in different fields.

RACE AND ETHNICITY

It is a commonplace observation that most minority groups are poorly represented among doctoral recipients.[26] In 1988, blacks received 3.9 percent of all doctorates awarded to U.S. residents in all fields of study; Hispanics received 2.9 percent; Asians received 5.1 percent; and whites received the remaining 88.1 percent.[27]

Differences in representation by field are even more pronounced (Table 2.6). For instance, blacks are relatively heavily represented in professional fields, in education, and in the more policy-relevant social sciences; of the 951 doctorates received by blacks in 1988, over 400 were in education. In our six arts-and-sciences fields, the percentages of doctorates received by blacks ranged from a low of 0.8 percent in mathematics to 1.6 percent in physics, 1.8 percent in history, 3.2 percent in economics, 4.2 percent in English and American literature, and a high of 7.1 percent in political science and public policy.

Hispanics rank highest in the humanities, with (as one would expect) particularly large numbers of doctorates in Romance languages and literature and lower representation in English and American literature. Overall, the Hispanic representation by field is more evenly distributed across the arts-and-sciences fields than is the distribution for either blacks or Asians.

Asians are very heavily represented in all of the quantitative sciences; for example, Asians earned 16 percent of all doctorates conferred in engineering, as compared with under 3 percent in history, English, and psychology. The field-specific pattern of relatively heavy and relatively light representation for Asians is almost the mirror image of the pattern for blacks.

Interpretation is helped if there are benchmarks, and one obvious reference point is the number of BAs. In all fields of study combined, blacks received 6.7 percent of BAs, as compared with 3.9 percent of all doctorates; Hispanics received 2.4 percent of BAs, as compared with 2.9 percent of doctorates; and Asians received 2.1 percent of BAs, but 5.1 percent of doctorates. Disparities in BA-PhD relationships are even greater within the arts and sciences than within all fields (Appendix G, Table G.2–3).[28]

---

[26]Any discussion of differences among racial/ethnic groups is sensitive and subject to misinterpretation. One problem is the existence of important differences among diverse subgroups within broad racial/ethnic categories, which cannot be noted or considered in the following discussion. For example, "Hispanics" include Puerto Ricans, Mexican-Americans, and Cuban-Americans, as well as others of Hispanic origin. Similarly, in recent years the "Asian" category has included larger numbers of Vietnamese and Cambodians, whose circumstances often differ markedly from those of most Japanese, Chinese, and Koreans. In our discussion, we use the classification and the nomenclature employed by the NRC.

For recent discussions of minority representation at the PhD level, including an examination of some behavioral relationships, see Ehrenberg (1991) and Schapiro, O'Malley, and Litten (1991). See also Clewell (1987) and Blackwell (1990). Blackwell is concerned with inequalities at all levels of education. For a still more broadly based discussion of the status of African-Americans, including a discussion of educational patterns, see Jaynes and Williams (1989).

[27]All data in this section pertain only to U.S. residents who could be classified in one of the four racial/ethnic categories identified in the text. Excluded, in addition to non-U.S. residents, are American Indians (because of their small numbers) and a group called "other and unknown." The source of these data is *Summary Report 1988*, Appendix A, Table 1A. We have recombined and reorganized the figures most relevant to our own analysis in Appendix G, Table G.2–2.

[28]These comparisons relate PhDs received in 1988 (*Summary Report 1988*, Appendix A, Table 1A) to BAs awarded in 1980–1981 (*Digest of Education Statistics* 1986, 134–35). The BA-cohort method of analysis used elsewhere in this study is not used here because of data limitations.

Different classification systems are used by the respective governmental agencies at the BA and PhD levels, and judgments have to be made in seeking to reconcile them. Appendix G, Table G.2–3,

TABLE 2.6
Representation of Racial/Ethnic Groups among Recipients of Doctorates by Field, 1988
(percent of all doctorates in each field)

	Blacks		Hispanics		Asians	
Fields with Share >5%						
	Professional	8.2	Humanities/Other	5.1	Engineering	16.0
	Education	7.6			Computer Science	14.1
	PolSci/Policy	7.1			Economics	10.4
	SocialSci/Other	5.6			Business	9.6
					Mathematics	8.9
					Physics	7.0
					Chemistry	6.0
					Biological Sci	5.2
Fields with Share <5% and >2%						
	English/AmLit	4.2	SocialSci/Other	3.7	Health/AgrSci	4.6
	Health/AgrSci	4.1	Psychology	3.5	Professional	4.0
	Psychology	3.8	Chemistry	3.4	SocialSci/Other	3.8
	Economics	3.2	Engineering	3.0	PolSci/Policy	3.2
	Humanities/Other	3.0	Education	3.0	Earth Sciences	2.9
	Business	2.8	History	2.9	History	2.8
			Economics	2.5	Humanities/Other	2.4
			PolSci/Policy	2.4	Education	2.4
			Health/AgrSci	2.4	English/AmLit	2.0
			Biological Sci	2.3		
			Professional	2.0		
Fields with Share <2%						
	History	1.8	Physics	1.9	Psychology	1.8
	Physics	1.6	Earth Sciences	1.5		
	Chemistry	1.5	Business	1.3		
	Engineering	1.5	Mathematics	1.1		
	Biological Sci	1.5	English/AmLit	1.0		
	Mathematics	0.8	Computer Science	0.6		
	Computer Science	0.6				
	Earth Sciences	0.6				

Source: Special tabulations from Doctorate Records File. See Appendix G, Table G.2–2.
Notes: Values are for U.S. residents only. See text for explanation of racial/ethnic categories.

Differences in the numbers of BAs earned in various fields by racial/ethnic groups are far from sufficient to explain away the pronounced differences in the distribution of doctorates. This is the objective evidence that supports special efforts at the undergraduate level to encourage larger numbers of minority students to consider doctoral programs in the arts and sciences. It is also the reason why some funders have not believed it necessary to include Asians in programs of this kind, since it is difficult to see how this group could be

shows the way in which we have assembled the subtotals for groups of fields from the available data for BAs and PhDs to achieve as much consistency as possible. For example, history has to be assigned to the social sciences at the PhD level in this analysis because history is part of the aggregate social sciences total at the BA level.

considered "underrepresented" in many fields. While Asians are most heavily represented in the sciences, their proportion of doctorates also exceeds their proportion of the college-age population in fields within the humanities and social sciences.[29]

The unusual pattern for Hispanics can be understood only when pre-BA benchmarks are examined. In comparison with other racial/ethnic groups, far fewer Hispanics in the primary college-age population (age 18 to 21) attend college and earn BAs in this country. Hispanics comprised 7.3 percent of the entire age 18–21 population in 1980, whereas they earned only 2.4 percent of BAs.[30]

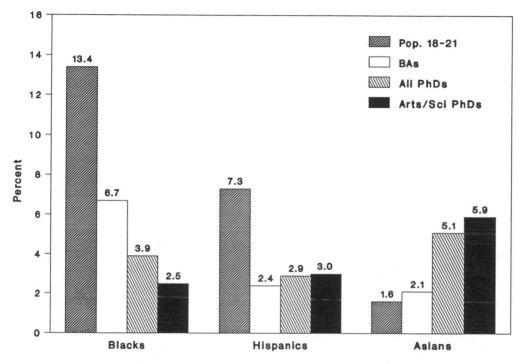

Figure 2.8
Representation of Racial/Ethnic Groups in Population and among Degree Recipients (percent of total)

Source: Population data are from tabulations of the 1980 census in which individuals of Hispanic origin are not counted in other racial/ethnic groups. Data for BAs and PhDs are from numbers presented in Appendix G, Table G.2–3. "All Arts/Sci" includes all doctorates except those in Education, Business, and Other (includes professional fields).

---

[29]See Figure 2.8 for population percentages and Table 2.6 for field-specific shares of doctorates.

[30]A low high school graduation rate is an important part of the explanation of the underrepresentation of Hispanics at the BA level. For a combination of reasons (related to language barriers, geographical location within the United States, as well as socioeconomic circumstances and educational attainments of parents), the high school completion rate for Hispanics was just 56 percent for all 18–24 year-olds (the only age cohort available), as compared with completion rates of 82 percent for whites and 68 percent for African-Americans (U.S. Bureau of the Census 1986). These graduation rates are for 1976, the most relevant year when considering BAs conferred in 1980 and PhDs conferred in 1988. The high school graduation rate for Hispanics includes individuals of any race.

These data show why it is misleading to take the number of BAs earned by Hispanics as the only benchmark in considering whether their number of doctorates seems relatively low or relatively high. Since relatively few Hispanics matriculate in (or complete) undergraduate programs, it is plausible to hypothesize that this smaller group might contain at least a somewhat larger proportion of undergraduates who would also wish to pursue doctoral degrees. Another possible explanation is that there is considerable in-migration of Hispanics who receive their BA-level education outside the country and then earn PhDs here and become U.S. residents.[31]

Much of the information presented in this section is summarized in Figure 2.8, which shows for each minority group its percentage share of (1) the age 18–21 population; (2) all BAs conferred; (3) all doctorates conferred; and (4) all doctorates conferred in the arts and sciences. Each minority group has a distinct profile. The percentages for blacks fall as we move from category to category. The percentages for Asians rise just as steadily. The Hispanics show the largest drop-off between population share and BA share, but their doctorate shares then rise slightly.

If we now ask what proportion of the age 18–21 population within each racial/ethnic group eventually earned doctorates in any field in 1988, the answers are quite similar for blacks and Hispanics. About 17 doctorates were earned by blacks per thousand of population, and about 22 doctorates were earned by Hispanics per thousand of population. The comparable ratios for whites and Asians were, respectively, 65 doctorates per thousand and 189 doctorates per thousand.[32] This is perhaps the most inclusive measure of "representation." It illustrates vividly why so many believe that greater efforts need to be made to enhance opportunities for disadvantaged minority groups at all levels of education.

Nor are recent trends encouraging, especially for the black population. Between 1982 and 1988, the number of doctorates awarded to blacks in all fields declined, from 1,133 to 951; the group's share of all doctorates fell from 4.6 percent to 3.9 percent. (Declines within the arts and sciences and within our six fields were, if anything, slightly greater on a relative basis.) Hispanics recorded modest increases, Asians had large increases, and whites had very modest decreases (Appendix G, Table G.2–4). Looking separately at numbers of black men and women recipients of doctorates confirms the general impression that degrees awarded to black men have declined faster than degrees awarded to black women.[33]

As important as it is to understand the diversity and shifting composition of the overall group of doctoral recipients, it is at least as important to examine carefully the forces that have shaped the larger trends in their numbers. This analysis—and its implications for planning and policymaking—is the subject of the next chapter.

---

[31]Ehrenberg (1991) credits Michael Olivas for having called attention to this point.

[32]In calculating these ratios, we divided the age 18–21 population group by four to obtain "annual" population values that could be compared with the numbers of degrees earned in a single year.

[33]Between 1982 and 1987, the percentage decline in doctorates awarded to black men was nearly three times greater than the corresponding percentage decline for black women. The overall drop in doctorates earned by blacks was greater between 1982 and 1987 than between 1982 and 1988, but we do not have data by gender for 1988. The source of these data is special tabulations prepared by the NRC.

CHAPTER THREE

The BA-PhD Nexus*

AGAINST THE descriptive backdrop of Chapter Two, we now consider a central analytical question: What combination of factors led to such sharp swings over the postwar years in the overall number of PhDs conferred within arts-and-sciences fields?[1] There has been surprisingly little analysis of the factors responsible for both the post–World War II expansion and the subsequent, unprecedented contraction. Careful analysis of the anatomy of these dramatic changes in the number of doctorates conferred is both interesting in its own right and helpful in assessing the responsiveness of graduate education to changing conditions in academic labor markets. This is a key issue in current debates over how rapidly we can expect potential imbalances between supply and demand to be self-correcting.

In brief, we find that favorable academic labor markets played a secondary role during the period of rapid growth in the number of PhDs conferred. Demographic factors, and especially large increases in the sizes of the underlying BA pools of potential candidates for graduate degrees, were more dominant. A second principal finding is that the abrupt reversal of this upward trend in PhD output is primarily attributable (at least in a proximate sense) to the end of draft deferments for graduate students during the Vietnam War. Finally, we find that the continuation of the contraction was due to the combination of a general "flight from the arts and sciences" at the undergraduate level and the effects of the severely depressed job markets for academics that were so much in evidence in the early 1970s.

METHOD AND DEFINITIONS

A key point pertaining to methods must be emphasized. The trends described in Chapter Two were based mainly on changes in the number of PhDs conferred as reported in the conventional way: by the year in which students *received their doctorates* (the PhD-cohort method of aggregation). As far as we are aware, this method has been used in all previous studies of changes over time in the number of doctorates conferred. The difficulty with this approach is that students who receive PhDs in any given year will have earned BAs, and commenced graduate study, in a wide variety of earlier years. For that reason, this PhD-cohort method of aggregation makes it difficult, if not impossible, to relate changes in the number of PhDs conferred to conditions at the time students actually made their decisions to begin graduate study.

---

*A very similar version of this chapter appears in William G. Bowen, Sarah E. Turner, and Marcia L. Witte, "The B.A.-Ph.D. Nexus," *Journal of Higher Education*, January–February 1992, 65–86.

[1]In this chapter we are not concerned, except incidentally, with the kinds of differences between fields and demographic groups discussed in the previous chapter. However, we make some comparisons by gender, mainly because they are useful in clarifying the role played by draft deferments in influencing the timing and magnitude of shifts in the number of PhDs conferred.

To overcome this problem, we reorganized the underlying data on individuals receiving doctorates by the years in which these recipients received their *BA degrees* (BA cohorts). This approach allows a more precise matching of numbers of doctoral recipients with conditions that prevailed at the time most of them began graduate study (and with conditions in subsequent years).[2]

Comparison of biannual data showing doctorates received by BA cohorts and PhD cohorts within six fields of study (Figure 3.1) indicates that the respective peaks are eight years apart (1964 versus 1972)—a plausible time lapse between receipt of the BA and completion of the PhD. Also, the curves are generally congruent when the data for BA cohorts are shifted eight years forward.[3]

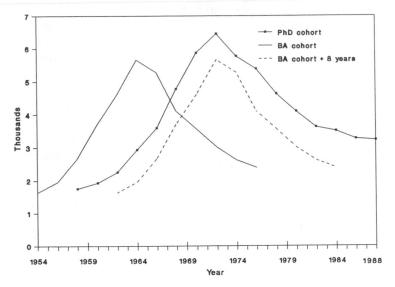

Figure 3.1
Number of Doctorates Conferred by BA- and PhD-Year Methods of Aggregation, Six-Field Total, 1954–1988

Source: Special tabulations from Doctorate Records File.
Notes: BA data have been truncated at 12 years (see footnote 3).

---

[2]The willingness of the National Research Council (NCR) to run special tabulations by BA cohorts made it possible to adopt this approach. The opportunity to specify the characteristics of these special runs also permitted us to limit our universe to U.S. residents (as defined in Chapter Two). This is an important restriction if the BA-PhD nexus is to be studied with any precision, since a very large majority of recipients of doctorates who are not U.S. residents earned their undergraduate degrees in other countries. Data from the Doctorate Records File organized by BA cohort have been used previously in studies of a very different question: the undergraduate origins of recipients of PhDs (see, for example, Tidball and Kistiakowsky 1976, Tidball 1980, and Tidball 1986).

[3]The points on the BA-cohort curve are consistently below the comparable points on the PhD-cohort curve because the BA-cohort data include only those members of the respective BA cohorts who earned doctorates in 12 years or less. The PhD-cohort data, on the other hand, include all recipients of doctorates in each year, some of whom took more than 12 years to earn the degree. In the 1958 BA cohort, for example, 27 percent of all PhD recipients in the six fields took more than 12 years to earn their doctorates.

Truncation of the BA-cohort data is necessary to avoid distorted comparisons of doctorates earned by different BA cohorts. Absent truncation, earlier BA cohorts would tend to be larger than later BA cohorts simply because their members would have had more years in which to complete their doctorates. Because data on doctorates conferred were available only through 1988, the last year for

The number of doctorates earned within these six fields of study by a particular BA cohort can be thought of as the product of three proximate determinants: the overall number of students earning BAs, the proportion of these undergraduates electing to concentrate in these six fields, and the proportion of these "majors" who go on to earn PhDs. These factors are defined as follows:

- B is the total number of BA degrees in all fields of study earned by members of each BA cohort—the base population relevant to this analysis, since we assume that a BA degree is almost always a prerequisite to a PhD. (Of course, one could follow the educational pipeline further back, taking account of sizes of population groups, high school enrollment and graduation rates, and college enrollment rates, but our focus is on the connections between BAs received and subsequent receipt of PhDs.)
- f_6 is the "Six-Field share" of all BAs conferred in a given year—that is, the percentage of all BAs who elected to major in these six fields. This variable, multiplied by the total number of BAs (B), equals the number of BAs awarded in the six fields ($B * f_6$), which we treat as a reasonable approximation of the pool of potential candidates for doctoral study in these same fields.[4]
- p is the "PhD-proclivity" of a given BA cohort—the percentage of those in each pool of BA majors who subsequently earned PhDs in these six fields. This measure can be thought of as a function of the number of students in each BA cohort who began study toward the PhD and the percentage of these "starters" who eventually earned degrees (the completion rate for the cohort, which is a principal subject of the next part of this study).

We have, then, the following identity[5] for the number of doctorates earned in the six fields (D_6) by each BA cohort:

$$D_6 = (B * f_6) * p.$$

---

which data for BA cohorts truncated at 12 years can be shown is 1976; subsequent BA cohorts would not have had the full 12 years in which to complete PhDs.

A fuller discussion of related questions, including the important issue of bias in measures of time-to-degree when the PhD-cohort method of aggregation is used, is presented in Chapter Six and Appendix D.

[4]A student earning a doctorate in one field may have majored in another field as an undergraduate, which is why the number of BAs in a particular field is only an approximation of the pool of potential candidates for graduate study in that field (or set of fields).

The BA data used in this paper are from the *Earned Degrees Conferred Survey* (U.S. Department of Education, various years). BAs in fields later classified as "first professional degrees" have been subtracted from the published data for total BAs awarded in each year between 1954 and 1962 to achieve reasonable consistency in the aggregate data over time. The published data are also affected by periodic changes in the definition of fields of study (caused primarily by the proliferation of subfields); we have attempted to maintain comparability in the composition of our six fields.

[5]The word *identity* denotes that this is a mechanical way of separating out the influences of proximate variables. Causation is more complex, and we will note some interactions among proximate variables and the underlying forces affecting these variables. This threefold categorization is, however, a useful method of focusing on relevant factors, and it may suggest a basis for developing more sophisticated behavioral models.

TRENDS IN PROXIMATE DETERMINANTS

During the two decades between 1954 and 1974, the total number of BAs awarded rose steadily and rapidly, increasing by a factor of 3.6 (Figure 3.2). This remarkable growth reflected both an increasing college-age population (attributable to the baby boom) and rising enrollment rates during most of this period. Only over the last two-year interval (1974 to 1976) did the total number of BAs decline.

Figure 3.2
Number of BAs Conferred, 1954–1976
Source: Earned Degrees Conferred Survey.

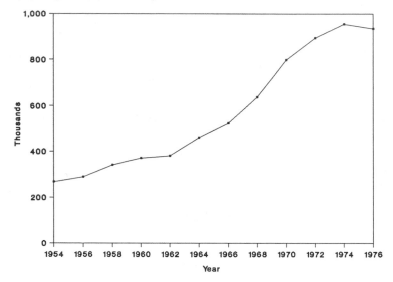

Figure 3.3
Six-Field Share of All BAs, 1954–1976
Source: Earned Degrees Conferred Survey.

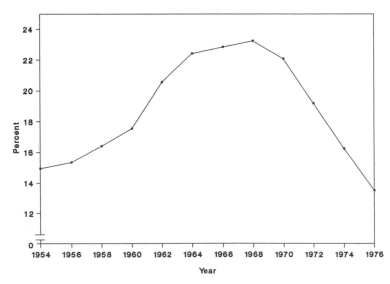

The Six-Field share (f_6) of all BAs followed a more varied path (Figure 3.3). It rose from 15 percent in 1954 to more than 22 percent in 1968. A flight from the arts and sciences then commenced. The Six-Field share of BAs conferred declined with great rapidity, and by 1976 it had fallen below the 1954 level—all the way to 13.5 percent.

Taken together, the trends in total BAs conferred and in the Six-Field share of BAs ($B * f_6$) determine the trend in the absolute number of BAs conferred in the six fields (Figure 3.4). The increase between 1954 and 1970 was extraordinary: The number of BAs in the six fields increased from about 40,000 in 1954 to over 175,000 in 1970. It was, of course, the reinforcing effects of simultaneous increases in both B and f_6 that produced this more than fourfold increase over a span of 16 years.

Between 1968 and 1970, the two variables (B and f_6) began to move in opposite directions, but over that two-year interval the continuing growth in the overall number of BAs more than compensated for the initial decline in the Six-Field share. The rapidly accelerating flight from the arts and sciences then became the dominant factor. The absolute number of BAs awarded in the six fields was lower in 1972 than in 1970, and it continued to decline through 1976.

The last of our three variables, the percentage of each Six-Field BA pool earning doctorates (the PhD-proclivity, p), also increased during the early years of the period, rising from 4 percent in 1954 to 4.4 percent in 1958, and then to a high of 5.9 percent in 1962—before plummeting to the very low level of 1.7 percent in 1974 (Figure 3.5).

The up-and-down movement of p is the most revealing factor in the analysis of the forces behind the expansion and subsequent contraction of graduate education. What led to the greater than expected tendency of students in the six fields to pursue PhDs between 1954 and 1962? What then accounted for the timing and the magnitude of the exceptionally sharp decline in PhD-procliv-

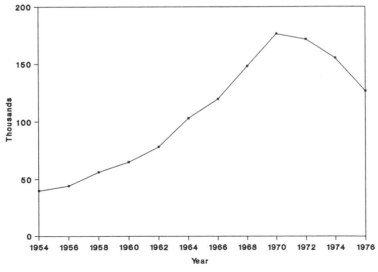

Figure 3.4
Number of BAs Conferred, Six-Field Total, 1954–1976
Source: Earned Degrees Conferred Survey.

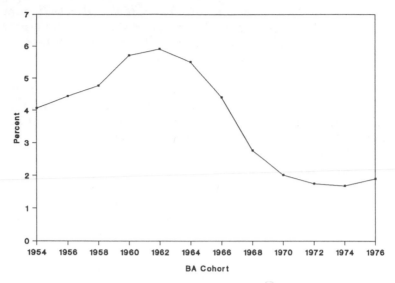

Figure 3.5
PhD-Proclivity, Six-Field Total, 1954–1976 BA Cohorts

Source: BA data are from the *Earned Degrees Conferred Survey*. PhD data are from special tabulations of the Doctorate Records File.

Notes: "PhD-Proclivity" is defined as the number of PhDs awarded to a BA cohort divided by the number of BAs in that cohort.

ity—a decline that set in well before there were any weaknesses in academic job markets?

INTERPRETATION

The 1954–1962 Period of Expansion

We attribute the increase in PhD-proclivity between the BA cohorts of 1954 and 1962 to the widely understood sense that there was a great need for faculty members, to the availability of generous financial aid for graduate students, and to the generally positive attitude toward higher education that then prevailed. The second half of the 1950s and the early 1960s were widely perceived as "golden years" for aspiring academics.[6]

The launching of Sputnik in 1957 and the accompanying wave of national support for advanced study in mathematics and science had a clear impact. Furthermore, undergraduates in all fields of study were encouraged to consider academic careers by their teachers and by major national fellowship programs such as those sponsored by the Danforth Foundation and the Woodrow Wilson National Fellowship Foundation. Governmental support for higher education at both federal and state levels was increasing rapidly, colleges and universities were successfully pursuing ambitious fund-raising campaigns of their own, and the outlook for higher education seemed bright in all respects.

The increase in PhD-proclivity that was stimulated by this confluence of forces is evidence that the output of PhDs will respond to consistently positive signals

---

[6]For documentation, see Bowen and Schuster (1986), Cartter (1976), and Katz and Hartnett (1976), as well as the references cited therein.

from the academic marketplace. This point has been understood and documented previously.[7]

Although the increase in PhD-proclivity did contribute to a rise in the number of doctorates conferred, this contribution was in fact much less significant quantitatively than the contributions of our other two variables. Indeed, about three-quarters of the total increase in doctorates conferred between the BA cohorts of 1954 and 1964 (the last BA cohort in the period of expansion) can be attributed to scale effects at the undergraduate level: specifically, to a combination of larger overall BA cohorts and increases in the Six-Field share of BAs.[8]

This is an important finding because it cautions against believing that the exceedingly favorable outlook for seekers of academic jobs over these years was mainly responsible for the rapid increase in PhD output that occurred. Labor market effects in the 1960s overlay powerful demographic forces. As greatly increased demand for academics by the end of the present decade is now anticipated, optimistic assumptions about the likely degree of automatic supply-side response should not be predicated on the experience of the 1960s.

It has also been suggested that part of the rise in PhD-proclivity for men that did take place during the expansion was caused not by favorable labor market conditions but by draft deferments. Largely because of the timing of events, we find this proposition unconvincing in the particular context of the expansion— even though we argue below that the ending of draft deferments had a great deal to do with the subsequent contraction. In the late 1950s and early 1960s—when p for men was rising most significantly—induction of draftees was at its lowest levels since the Korean War. The first large increase in inductions did not occur until 1965.[9] To be sure, p for men rose faster than p for women between the BA cohorts of 1958 and 1962 (as we show below), but we are inclined to attribute this difference mainly to other factors.[10]

The draft may well have increased graduate enrollments for post-1962 BA cohorts (as it surely increased undergraduate enrollments).[11] However, the

---

[7]See Freeman 1975a, 1975b; and Bowen and Sosa 1989, 166–67.

[8]See Appendix G, Tables G.3–1 and G.3–2, for the underlying data and an explanation of the method used to derive this result. The interaction between p and the pool of BA candidates also needs to be considered. If the number of places in doctoral programs in these six fields had been absolutely fixed, one would have expected an inverse relationship: As the Six-Field BA pool increased, p necessarily would have decreased, since p is defined as the number of PhDs divided by the Six-Field BA pool. This relationship obviously did not hold, and the reason is the great elasticity of places in PhD programs during these years. Capacity constraints simply were not a factor of any consequence, as we explain in Chapter Four.

[9]Large numbers of men were inducted in the early 1950s (551,806 in 1951; 438,479 in 1952; and 471,806 in 1953). Inductions then declined to 253,230 in 1954. They ranged from 152,777 in 1955 to 142,246 in 1958, before falling still more; the range between 1959 and 1964 was 96,153 to 112,386. Inductions more than doubled in 1965, rising to 230,991. They reached a peak of 382,010 in 1966 and stayed at high levels through 1970 (U.S. Selective Service System 1984, 74).

[10]There were a number of differences with regard to changes in field preferences at the undergraduate level during these years (Turner and Bowen 1990, 519–20). In general, men appear to have moved more rapidly than women from field to field as job opportunities shifted, a pattern that we think reflected greater responsiveness to changes in labor market conditions. Today, such differences in responsiveness may no longer exist, but in the late 1950s and early 1960s they were significant, and may help explain (in an analogous way) why PhD-proclivities for women were less sensitive to changes in job prospects than PhD-proclivities for men.

[11]Singer (1989) discusses increases in enrollments at the undergraduate level, as well as in professional and graduate programs. Angrist (1990) has demonstrated rigorously that draft lottery numbers affected enrollment rates after the lottery was introduced.

characteristics of these six fields (generally rigorous, "academic," and less applied), especially at the PhD level, made them less subject to draft-induced increases in enrollment than, say, many master's degree programs. This pattern can be seen clearly at the undergraduate level, where BAs in these six fields increased less rapidly relative to the age 18–21 population than did total BAs during the period when draft deferments were having their greatest effect. In any case, there appears to have been little, if any, impact on the number of PhD recipients in these six fields.

The Vietnam War Stage of Contraction

An abrupt reversal of direction in the trend in number of PhDs conferred took place between the BA cohorts of 1964 and 1966 (refer back to Figure 3.1)—with the subsequent effects on the supply of new PhDs entering the academic labor market first felt in the mid-1970s. Following a decade of steady increases, fewer doctorates were earned by the 1966 BA cohort than by the 1964 cohort, and fewer doctorates yet by each succeeding BA cohort through 1976. This sharp contraction in the output of doctorates can be divided into two stages, and the proximate cause of the first stage (which we date from 1964 through 1970) is clear.

Whereas the combined growth in the number of BA recipients and the proportion majoring in the six fields played the major role in the expansion of PhD output through 1964, an astonishingly sharp decline in PhD-proclivity was by far the dominant cause of the swing to contraction. As we saw earlier, the Six-Field BA pool continued to rise for another six years, through 1970, and in and of itself would have led to a further increase in the number of doctorates earned by successive BA cohorts had it not been for the much stronger effects of a veritable "free fall" in the percentage of BA recipients earning doctorates between the 1962 and 1970 cohorts. PhD-proclivity fell by a factor of almost three: from 5.9 percent to 2.0 percent.

This dramatic reversal of direction in the p variable was certainly not caused by poor job prospects, which remained favorable until the end of the 1960s. A simple supply-demand ratio derived from data collected originally by Allan Cartter (1976) reached its lowest point (the point most favorable from the perspective of potential job seekers) in 1965, and it remained below one candidate per position through 1969.[12] Moreover, national financial aid programs were still expanding. The NDEA Fellowships, for example, which had been inaugurated in 1958, doubled in number between 1964 and 1965 and reached a peak level of 6,000 awards in 1966–1967.[13]

We believe that changes in the availability of draft deferments played a major role in causing p to reverse course for BA cohorts in the mid-1960s. Persuasive evidence is provided by a direct comparison of PhD-proclivities for men and for women in the same BA cohorts (Figure 3.6), since the draft affected men but not

---

[12]Bowen and Sosa 1989, 162–63.

[13]The number of National Defense Education Act (NDEA) awards was 1,000 in 1959, 1,500 in 1960–1964, 3,000 in 1965, 6,000 in 1966–1967, and then 3,000 from 1968 through at least 1971 (Lindquist 1971, iii). The program ended in 1973. It is true that labor market conditions in general also improved following the tax cut of 1964, and better employment opportunities outside academia could have contributed to the decline in proclivity. However, Hansen's analysis of salary movements in various fields during the 1960s does not suggest that nonacademic opportunities improved significantly relative to opportunities in colleges and universities (Hansen 1986, 89).

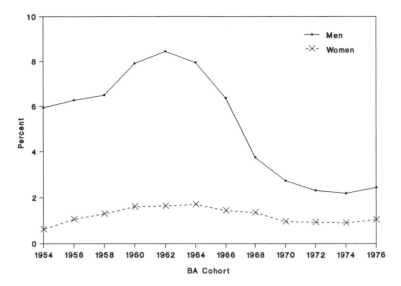

Figure 3.6
PhD-Proclivity by Gender, Six-Field Total, 1954–1976 BA Cohorts
Source and Notes: Same as Figure 3.5.

women during these years. Men and women alike completed doctorates in rising numbers (relative to the sizes of the underlying Six-Field BA pools) from the 1954 through 1962 BA cohorts. PhD-proclivity for men fell modestly between the 1962 and 1964 BA cohorts (while PhD-proclivity for women continued to rise). Between the 1964 and 1966 BA cohorts, men's PhD-proclivity fell steeply; women's PhD-proclivity also declined, but much less sharply. PhD-proclivity for men then fell precipitously between the 1966 and 1968 BA cohorts, while PhD-proclivity for women declined only modestly.

This was precisely the period when the draft law was changed to eliminate graduate school deferments.[14] The Selective Service Act of 1967 became effective June 30, 1967, and Executive Order 11360 contained provisions that meant that "after a one-year moratorium to end at the close of the 1967–1968 academic year, no more 2-S deferments would be granted to graduate students except those specifically written into the law" (essentially those for students in medicine and related fields).[15] Graduate students already enrolled in the fall of 1967 could complete only one more year, and undergraduates in the 1968 BA cohort would be ineligible for any graduate school deferments (except as specifically provided). Also, the law provided that among those eligible for the draft, "oldest eligibles" would be called first.[16]

Under these dramatically changed conditions, it is hardly surprising that the PhD-proclivity for men dropped from 6.4 percent for the BA cohort of 1966 all the way to 3.7 percent for the BA cohort of 1968. While draft deferments do not seem to us to have played the major role in increasing graduate enrollments, the continuation of deferments through 1967 clearly made it easier for graduate

---

[14]There are a number of histories of changes in draft legislation during the 1960s, including Baskir and Strauss (1978) and Marmion (1968).
[15]Marmion 1968, 164.
[16]*Ibid*.

students to plan their programs and their careers. When deferments were ended, expectations changed fundamentally. Men had to weigh carefully the possibility that their graduate study would be interrupted, and this uncertainty must have discouraged some from enrolling. Moreover, men from the 1968 BA cohort who might earlier have carried deferments with them into graduate school were now highly likely to be drafted. The comparison with women in the 1966 and 1968 BA cohorts is compelling evidence of the strength of these effects: The PhD-proclivity for women fell by less than one-tenth of one point (from 1.4 percent to 1.3 percent) between these two BA cohorts.

Since the values of p reflect the number of students in each BA cohort finishing PhDs, not just those enrolling initially in PhD programs, some men from earlier BA cohorts (1966 and 1964) who had already completed a few years of graduate study should also have been affected by the 1967 provisions of the draft code. As of 1968, members of these earlier BA cohorts were subject to the draft, and this explains (at least in part) why there were declines in PhD-proclivity for men between the 1962 and 1964 BA cohorts and larger declines between the 1964 and 1966 BA cohorts.

Data on completion rates reported later in this study (percentages of entering graduate school cohorts eventually earning doctorates) support this intuitively plausible line of reasoning. Completion rates for male recipients of Danforth Fellowships fell steadily between the 1964 and 1967 BA cohorts. Data for male graduate students in a set of five universities are generally consistent with the figures for the Danforth Fellows, although the drop in completion rates for this group did not begin until the 1966 BA cohort.

The strongest corroboration of this interpretation of events is provided by comparing the patterns of PhD-proclivities for men and women in each of the six fields of study (Figure 3.7). While there are any number of interesting variations in patterns across fields,[17] in every field there is a sizable drop in the PhD-proclivity for men in the 1968 BA cohort, as compared with the previous BA cohort—and a much smaller drop, if any drop at all, in the PhD-proclivity for women (Table 3.1). The consistency of this pattern leaves little room for doubt as to the impact on doctoral education of the 1967 change in the draft law.[18]

While the war and the end of draft deferments played the major role in reducing PhD-proclivity for men during this first stage of the contraction, it would be simplistic to suggest that no other forces were at work. The best evidence for the presence of other factors is the drop in PhD-proclivity for women between the BA cohorts of 1964 and 1970 (refer back to Figures 3.6 and 3.7). This drop was modest in comparison with the drop for men, but it was hardly insignificant: PhD-proclivity for women fell from 1.7 percent to 1.0 percent over these six years.

---

[17]The closing of the gaps in PhD-proclivities between men and women in all of these fields except mathematics is of independent interest, especially when considered with complementary changes in the number of BAs awarded to women in these same fields. These patterns were described in general terms in Chapter Two (Figure 2.7 and the accompanying discussion).

[18]The impact was foreseen by many at the time, even though they could not quantify it and, in fact, exaggerated the likely effect on enrollments. For example, a study published in March of 1968 projected that "the entering male enrollment in full-time graduate school next year (1968–69 academic year) will be down 70% from the current school year." Scientific Manpower Commission and Council of Graduate Schools 1989, 1.

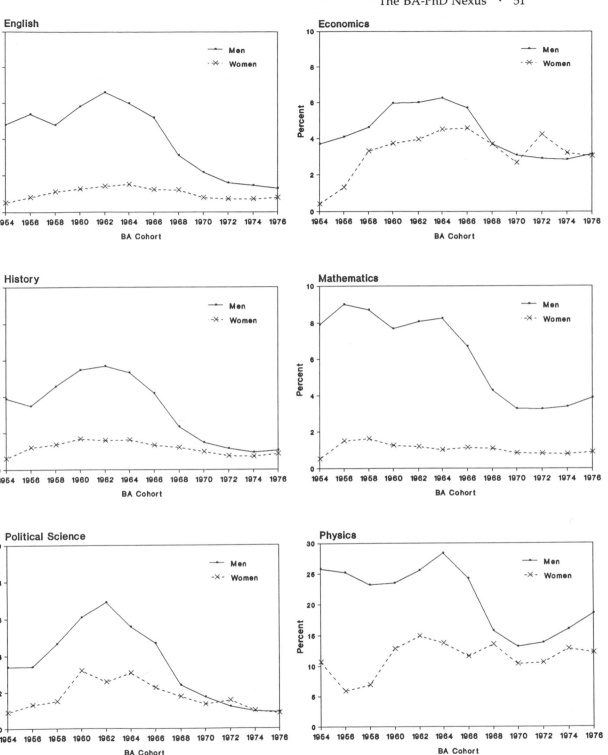

Figure 3.7
PhD-Proclivity by Field and Gender, 1954–1976 BA Cohorts
Source and Notes: Same as Figure 3.5.

TABLE 3.1
Field-Specific Changes in PhD-Proclivity by Gender, 1966–1968 BA Cohorts

	PhD-Proclivity (%)			
	Men		Women	
Field	1966 BA Cohort	1968 BA Cohort	1966 BA Cohort	1968 BA Cohort
English	5.2	3.1	1.2	1.2
History	4.2	2.3	1.6	1.3
Political science	4.7	2.4	2.2	1.8
Economics	5.7	3.7	4.6	3.7
Mathematics	6.7	4.3	1.1	1.1
Physics	24.2	15.7	11.6	13.5
Six-Fields	6.4	3.7	1.4	1.3

Source and notes: Same as Figure 3.5.

The extraordinary upsurge in undergraduate enrollment (and especially in BAs conferred in the six fields) that characterized the 1960s could well have had a considerable negative impact on PhD-proclivity. The number of BAs awarded increased by 74 percent between 1964 and 1970, and by 71 percent in these fields. (The corresponding increases for women alone were 75 percent and 78 percent, respectively.) A disproportionate part of this very rapid growth in the number of BAs conferred occurred outside those sectors of higher education (the Research I and Liberal Arts I institutions, in the terminology of the Carnegie Commission) that traditionally have graduated the most candidates for PhDs.[19] This distributional shift in the 1960s put downward pressure on PhD-proclivity, and it could have accounted for much of the drop in p for women between 1964 and 1970. This interpretation is supported by the fact that PhD-proclivity for women dropped faster in English (and, we suspect, in other fields offered by a wide array of institutions) than in mathematics and physics.

Both men and women were affected by this distributional shift, as well as by the labor market effects discussed above. A crude way of estimating the "pure" effect of all non–draft-related variables on the PhD-proclivity of men is by calculating the change in PhD-proclivity for men that would have occurred between the 1964 and 1968 BA cohorts had they been affected in the same way by the factors that affected women only. Under this hypothetical assumption, p for men would have fallen from 7.9 percent in 1964 to 6.0 percent in 1968—as compared with the actual decline, which was from 7.9 percent to 3.7 percent.[20] The conclusion seems clear: While other factors were also at work, the removal of draft deferments for graduate students was a dominant event in causing PhD-proclivity to fall so rapidly during this period.

[19]See Tidball and Kistiakowsky 1976. The sectors that grew especially rapidly during this period were the "Comprehensive" and "Other 4-Year" institutions. Turner and Bowen 1990, 518ff.

[20]PhD-proclivity for women in 1968 was 76 percent of PhD-proclivity for women in 1964. We simply multiplied this percentage by the PhD-proclivity for men in 1964 to obtain the (hypothetical) figure of 6.0 for 1968. Estimating the change in the PhD-proclivity for men by using the proportionate change for women places an upper bound on the "pure" effect of all non–draft-related variables; a more conservative approach would use the absolute change in the PhD-proclivity for women.

The Postdraft Stage of Contraction

Following the draft-related phase of the contraction—which we date as ending in 1970 with the institution of the draft lottery—the absolute number of PhDs earned by succeeding BA cohorts continued to fall steadily (from 3,557 in the six fields in the 1970 cohort to 2,394 in the 1976 cohort). However, the main causal forces in this second stage of the contraction were very different from those in the first stage.

The marked decline in f_6, as a consequence of the flight from the arts and sciences at the undergraduate level, was the most important proximate determinant. Between 1970 and 1976—in just six years—the percentage of all BAs awarded in the six fields fell from 22.1 percent to 13.5 percent (refer back to Figure 3.3). The result was a significant contraction in the absolute numbers of BA recipients in the six fields, in spite of continued increases in the overall number of BAs conferred. While there are many reasons why large numbers of students lost interest in the arts and sciences, the economic environment undoubtedly had a great deal to do with this shift in field preferences. A number of undergraduates responded to rising unemployment and difficulties in finding "good" jobs by moving to more vocationally related fields of study.[21]

The employment outlook in academia was deteriorating even more rapidly than opportunities in other job markets. This drastic change in prospects was surely the main reason why PhD-proclivities for men not only remained at the very low levels initially induced by the draft but continued to decline. PhD-proclivities for women (shown in Figure 3.6) also remained at low levels—again, presumably because of poor job prospects.

To recapitulate, we believe that the years from 1954 to 1976 can be divided into three quite distinct subperiods, each of which was dominated by different forces. Table 3.2 "parses out" quantitatively the overall change in the number of PhDs conferred during each of these periods among the three proximate determinants on which the previous discussion has focused.

This analysis indicates that:

- *The 1954–1964 expansion* was driven in roughly equal parts by increases in the overall number of BAs awarded and a rising proportion of BAs awarded to students in the six fields. The total increase in the number of PhDs conferred was 4,032, of which 3,228 can be attributed to these two factors. Rising PhD-proclivity also made a positive contribution, but accounted for only 588 doctorates.
- *The 1964–1970 stage of the contraction* reflected primarily a fall in PhD-proclivity that, in turn, was directly related to the end of draft deferments for graduate students. The number of PhDs conferred fell by 2,103 over this interval. The overall number of BAs awarded continued to increase and exerted a strong positive effect (in and of itself leading to a presumptive increase of 2,972 PhDs). However, the drop in PhD-proclivity was so steep (implying a decrease of 4,195 PhDs) that it overwhelmed the growth in the BA pool. The Six-Field share of all BAs awarded was essentially unchanged,

---

[21]See Freeman (1971) for a discussion of the market forces at work during this period. While Freeman's work focuses on undergraduate enrollments, the same factors surely affected field preferences as well.

TABLE 3.2

Factors Determining Changes in Number of Doctorates Conferred, Major Periods

| | Attributable Change | | |
| | | Contraction | |
Factor	Expansion 1954–1964	Phase 1 1964–1970	Phase 2 1970–1976
Total BAs	+1,773	+2,972	+576
Six-Field share	+1,455	−4	−1,367
Subtotal: Six-Field BAs	+3,228	+2,968	−791
PhD-proclivity	+588	−4,195	−257
Cross-effects	+216	−876	−115
Total change in PhDs conferred	+4,032	−2,103	−1,163

Source: See Appendix G, Tables G.3–1 and G.3–2.

Note: The cross-effects shown on the table are a residual category needed because of the use of discrete intervals and the fact that the three explanatory variables often change simultaneously.

having first risen and then fallen, and therefore had no net effect of consequence.

• *The 1970–1976 stage of the contraction* can be attributed mainly to a flight from the arts and sciences, combined with the discouraging effects of a very poor job market for academics. The overall number of PhDs conferred fell (decreasing by 1,163 PhDs), and the negative effects of the decline in the Six-Field share of BAs awarded were sufficiently powerful (a loss of 1,367 PhDs) to more than offset the positive effects of a continued, but much more modest, increase in the overall number of BAs awarded (a gain of 576 PhDs). PhD-proclivity not only failed to recover from the low levels of the Vietnam War period but even declined somewhat further (a loss of 257 PhDs).

CONCLUSION

An irony is that the war (and the end of draft deferments for graduate students) served, in retrospect, at least one positive purpose: It essentially halted what was clearly an overly rapid expansion in the number of PhDs conferred. If draft deferments for graduate students had not been eliminated by the Selective Service Act of 1967, the PhD glut of the 1970s and 1980s would have been worse. The magnitude of this "contribution" is by no means trivial. To illustrate, if the decline in PhD-proclivity for men between 1966 and 1968 had been only half as great as it was, nearly 2,000 more doctorates would have been added to the overall supply of PhDs in these six fields by that one BA cohort alone.

The shift of academic labor markets from excess demand for faculty to excess supply—beginning at the end of the 1960s and continuing into the 1970s—would have, in all likelihood, eventually reduced p to approximately the same levels induced much earlier by the end of draft deferments. Such a process, however, would have been far more protracted.

The general conclusion is that the course of graduate education, while susceptible to many influences, is not readily altered by *prospective* changes in academic labor markets. "Natural" market forces affect outcomes, but they are slow to take hold. This is in part because of the very long lags between the time students begin their graduate work, subsequently finish their studies, and then compete for positions. It is also because of institutional priorities (the desire to sustain graduate programs even under straitened conditions) and the difficulty of developing and communicating even rough projections of what lies ahead.

In the mid-1960s, Allan Cartter warned anyone who would listen (and almost no one did) that the halcyon days of the 1960s would not last indefinitely, and that there would be a serious oversupply of academics in the 1970s. But it was not Cartter's warnings that affected the scale of PhD output at that time—as he himself emphasized subsequently in reviewing the history of this period.[22] The end of draft deferments served as a kind of *deus ex machina*, which prevented a situation that already contained the seeds of future problems from leading to frustrations and disappointments for even more graduate students.

The implications of this lesson from the past should not be missed. The number of doctorates conferred did not respond promptly to changes in labor market conditions. It is also evident that capacity limitations of graduate programs were not of any great importance as a factor restricting the expansion of PhD output. The system of graduate education in this country has been readily expandable through most of the twentieth century (perhaps too readily expandable), and once graduate programs are established, they tend to take on lives of their own. The discussion in the next chapter will focus on this theme.

---

[22]Cartter 1974 and Cartter 1976.

CHAPTER FOUR

Graduate Programs: The Dual Questions of Quality and Scale

THE WIDE fluctuations during the postwar years in the number of doctorates conferred have been accompanied by a broader set of fundamental changes in the system of graduate education. In effect, a new structure has been created. This new structure reflects dramatic increases in the overall number of degree-granting programs, major reductions in the proportion of degrees conferred by highly rated programs, and especially rapid increases in the number of small programs.

From a national point of view, this transformation—in all its dimensions—raises inescapable questions concerning the nature of the system as a whole. How many strong centers of graduate education in the arts and sciences, with sufficient critical mass and quality, are needed to maintain the health of the overall enterprise? Is there an approximate minimal level of scale (in terms of the number of PhDs awarded each year) that can be related to the quality and effectiveness of graduate programs? Conversely, can programs become too large to be effective?[1]

In considering such questions (which certainly do not permit facile answers), one must bear in mind not only the broad national perspective, but also the dynamics of individual institutions. For any particular university, the presence of graduate programs adds to its standing and reputation, and consequently to its capacity to attract faculty with strong research interests and talents. The internal institutional drive to create graduate programs can therefore be powerful, and the need, from an institutional perspective, for some reasonable constellation of such programs across disciplines can lead to continued expansion. Faculty and students who are interested in graduate education and research rarely, if ever, wish to be in isolated units or departments. Rather, they want colleagues in neighboring disciplines, and they want to be members of a

---

[1] It should be emphasized that the focus here is on graduate *programs*, rather than on graduate *institutions*. Bowen and Sosa (1989, 112–17) examined trends in the distribution of degrees conferred by broad categories of institutions, using the Carnegie classification system (e.g., Research I, Research II, Doctorate I and Doctorate II). That analysis identified some of the major trends, but the system of institutional classification did not permit an examination of the related issues of quality and scale that must be carried out at the program level.

While there is clearly some correlation between the perceived quality of a graduate institution and the perceived quality of particular graduate programs, the correlation is far from perfect. Even the strongest institutions have some programs of only modest distinction, while some well-regarded graduate programs are located within institutions that are less distinguished overall.

For an earlier study of the relationship between program quality and scale of graduate program, see Breneman (1975). The approach used here is similar in many respects to the approach that Breneman used in studying developments between 1968 and 1973 in a variety of fields (with special emphasis on the sciences, engineering, and economics).

university that is firmly committed to strengthening graduate studies and research as a total enterprise.[2]

Consequently, once new programs have been created, and once a heavy financial investment has been made in them, there are compelling institutional reasons for wishing to sustain those programs, even if they fall below expectations with respect to quality or size. The implications of any effort to eliminate graduate programs in important fields of knowledge can be very considerable— whether measured in terms of possible faculty attrition, institutional reputation, or "lost" financial investments. As a consequence, judgments that may seem thoroughly reasonable, cost-effective, and conducive to higher quality for the graduate educational system as a whole are frequently at odds with the priorities of individual institutions as they assess their own needs and aspirations.

In this chapter, we explore some aspects of these large questions by focusing on doctoral programs in six fields of study: English, history, political science, economics, mathematics, and physics. We examine the numbers of programs that were created (or terminated), as well as the respective contributions of new and established programs to overall changes in the number of doctorates conferred during different time periods. We also analyze trends in the number of doctoral degrees conferred by sets of programs classified according to quality and size. Finally, we discuss some of the ways in which program scale interacts with quality, and the tendency for programs, once established, to continue in operation even when they appear to fall below "critical mass." Much of the last part of the chapter centers on the recently created small programs, since they now play a much more significant role in American graduate education than in earlier decades.

Trends in the Number of Programs

As we saw in previous chapters, there was nearly a fourfold increase in the number of doctorates conferred in our six fields between 1958 and 1972. This unprecedented increase in the output of PhD programs was the result of both significant increases in the number of degrees conferred by established programs and the creation of a number of new doctoral programs.

In these six arts-and-sciences fields, the number of doctoral programs more than doubled between 1958 and 1972. Percentage rates of increase varied from a low of about 90 percent in economics to a high of more than 130 percent in mathematics (Table 4.1). By 1972, new programs actually outnumbered established programs in three of our six fields. Put another way, roughly half of all programs that conferred doctorates in these fields in 1972 had conferred no doctoral degrees just fourteen years earlier.[3]

---

[2] These tendencies have been noted frequently. Berelson (1960, 35) used colorful language in citing forces that stimulate the creation of new doctoral programs: "the colonization of the underdeveloped institutions by ambitious products of the developed ones who then seek to make the colony a competitor of the mother university; the need to have graduate students as research and teaching assistants, partly in order to get and hold senior staff; the vanity, pride, and legitimate aspirations of the institutions."

[3] In our terminology, "new" programs are those that conferred degrees in some even-numbered year after 1958 but conferred no degrees in 1958, and "established" programs are those that conferred one or more degrees in 1958. These are imperfect definitions, since a new program might have been in operation in 1958 even though it conferred no degrees in that particular year, and an

TABLE 4.1

Changes in Number of Doctorate-Granting Programs by Field, 1958–1972

Field	Number of Programs		% Change
	1958	1972	
English	60	124	106.7
History	61	118	93.4
Political Science	47	91	93.6
Economics	57	108	89.5
Mathematics	60	139	131.7
Physics	70	145	107.1
Six Fields	355	725	104.2

Source: Special tabulations from Doctorate Records File. See Appendix G, Table G.4–1.

This demonstration of the capacity of the educational system to create new graduate programs is impressive by any standard. At the same time, it is important to recognize that the new system of graduate education created by the dynamics of this process of expansion was the result of several different factors. Market demand and energetic institutional initiative were important, but they were not the only forces at work.

Equally noteworthy were the explicit policy goals of some federal and state agencies that sought either to encourage or to mandate a broader distribution of funding for research and graduate education. In 1958, for example, the Title IV graduate fellowship program was created as part of the National Defense Education Act (NDEA) to "increase the number of college and university teachers." Another purpose of the program was to "promote a wider geographic distribution of doctoral programs of good quality"—a goal that stemmed from "expressions of fear that a large proportion of the 5,000 fellowships might go to a relatively few institutions in which there [was] a high concentration of students who are holders of fellowships." As a result, new programs (and some existing programs that were "underutilized") received between 70 and 80 percent of the NDEA fellowships awarded, consistent with the "impact preferred by the majority of the academic community." Only a small fraction of the fellowships were portable and went directly to students ("freedom of choice" awards) rather than to institutions; most fellowships were "awarded in a way to compensate for any imbalance to which the freedom of choice awards might lead." According to the Title IV guidelines, portability and choice tended to

established program might have conferred degrees for the first time in 1958. However, inspection of the patterns of degrees conferred over time indicates that such aberrations were rare, and that this simple dichotomy serves reasonably well to divide the universe of programs into the two broad categories of new and established.

All of the figures and tables in this chapter are based on a tabulation provided by the National Research Council (NRC) of the number of doctorates conferred in each even-numbered year between 1958 and 1988 by each doctorate-granting program in our six fields. The massive nature of this database precludes the presentation of much raw data. However, the Summary Reports published annually by the NRC demonstrate the level of detail (for example, Summary Report 1989, Appendix Table A–7). We have assembled some of the key statistics for groups of universities and selected years in Appendix G, Tables G.4–1 through G.4–6.

create "the kind of concentration at prestigious institutions concerning which fear has been expressed."[4]

During the subsequent period of widespread contraction in the scale of the graduate education enterprise, long-established programs that had expanded significantly in order to meet the demands of the previous two decades were compelled to confront the question of whether—and if so, by how much—to curtail their intake of PhD candidates. Given the substantial investment in tenured faculty members, research facilities, library materials, and all the other resources that the creation of a graduate program demands, such decisions were far from easy. Options were even more limited for recently created programs. Since they were small to begin with, they were in a position to reduce only slightly (if at all) the number of students they enrolled. For such programs, the choice was either to close down altogether or to continue at something close to the very modest scale previously achieved. For reasons already suggested, most programs were continued.

In fact, new doctoral programs continued to appear well after the period of substantial contraction had begun (Table 4.2). While the number of degrees conferred by all doctorate-granting institutions in the six fields declined by a third between 1972 and 1988, the number of doctorate-granting programs actually increased at least modestly in five of the six fields. And the sixth field, mathematics, which had experienced the sharpest increase in number of programs during the expansion, barely qualifies as an exception, since there was a net decrease of just two doctorate-granting programs between 1972 and 1988.

It should also be said, however, that many of the PhD programs that awarded their first doctorates after 1972 presumably were launched (in terms of admitting their first students) in the late 1960s, before it was as obvious as it later became that the prospects for academic employment had changed drastically. More precisely, growth in the number of programs lagged well behind increases in doctorates conferred during the rapid expansion of the 1960s, but then continued well after the number of doctorates conferred had started to decline.

TABLE 4.2
Changes in Number of Doctorate-Granting Programs by Field, 1972–1988

Field	Number of Programs		% Change
	1972	1988	
English	124	132	6.5
History	118	124	5.1
Political Science	91	115	26.4
Economics	108	119	10.2
Mathematics	139	137	−1.4
Physics	145	155	6.9
Six Fields	725	782	7.9

Source: Same as Table 4.1.

[4] Lindquist 1971, 56. Breneman (1975, 41) has noted that President Johnson's Executive Order of September 13, 1965, also "asserted that every region should be served by excellent graduate schools . . . ."

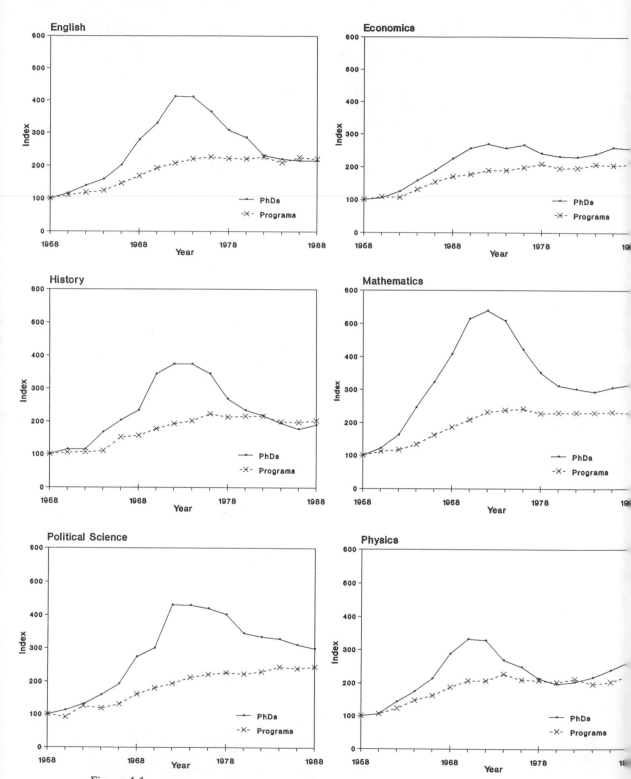

Figure 4.1
Number of Graduate Programs and Doctorates by Field, 1958–1988 (Index: 1958 = 100)
Source: Special tabulations from Doctorate Records File.

This pattern is evident in all six fields (Figure 4.1).[5] From the mid-1970s on, the number of PhD programs in most of these fields remained quite constant even though the number of degrees conferred continued to fall. Political science represents a more extreme case. In this field, the number of doctorate-granting programs continued to increase steadily—as the overall number of doctorates conferred decreased.

A useful way of summarizing these developments is by comparing the number of degrees conferred by new (post-1958) doctorate-granting programs to the number conferred by established programs (Figure 4.2). Both sets of programs contributed significantly to the overall increase in the number of PhDs conferred during the expansionist years. The incremental number of PhDs awarded by the established programs (3,500 degrees between 1958 and 1972) was roughly twice the incremental number awarded by the new programs (1,848 degrees). At the same time, the faster rate of increase characteristic of the new programs meant that by 1972, they were conferring about one-quarter of all doctorates awarded in these six fields.

The substantial overall contraction in the output of doctorates that followed the 1972 peak was highly differentiated, and the trajectories followed by the

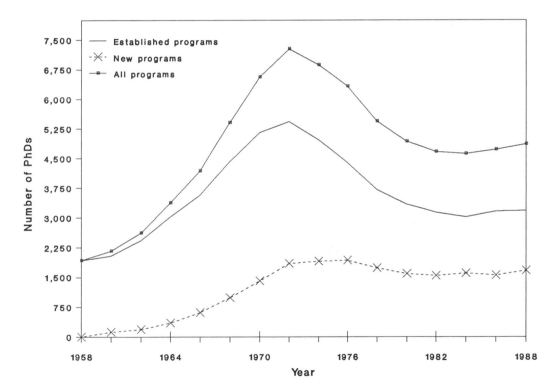

Figure 4.2
Number of Doctorates Conferred by New and Established Programs, Six-Field Total, 1958–1988
Source: Special tabulations from Doctorate Records File.
Notes: See footnote 3 for definitions of "New" and "Established."

---

[5]To facilitate comparison of relative rates of increase, the underlying numbers of degrees conferred and programs have been indexed (with both set equal to 100 in 1958).

established and the new programs diverged sharply. The number of doctorates awarded each year by the established programs fell steadily, as many of these programs elected to enroll fewer PhD students in the face of depressed job markets, and fewer of those who did begin graduate study eventually earned degrees (see Chapters Six–Eight). It was not until 1982–1986 that a new plateau in the number of doctorates awarded was reached by these programs—at a level approximately 40 percent below the 1972 peak. Institutions that had created new programs, on the other hand, saw less room for contraction, and in fact continued to award an increasing number of PhDs well into the 1970s (reaching a peak in 1976).

By 1988, the relative proportions of degrees awarded by these two sets of programs seemed to have stabilized. The new (post-1958) programs had raised their share to slightly more than one-third of all doctorates conferred, and the corresponding proportion was even higher in the English, history, and political science fields (41 percent in English, for example). In physics, the comparable figure was 29 percent, and this lower percentage may be linked to the greater financial commitment needed to create and sustain graduate programs in the sciences.[6]

What can be said about the broader aspects of the reconfiguration of the system of graduate education that took place between the mid-1950s and the late 1980s? While shifts in the number of students pursuing PhDs, in the conditions of academic job markets, and in patterns of financial support were certainly significant, developments of this kind are—by their very nature—associated with the inevitable ebbs and flows that occur in any system of education, especially one (like ours) that is highly decentralized, competitive, and "open" with respect to the wide latitude of choice that it offers individual students as well as institutions. Although such shifts were unusually pronounced during the postwar era, there was nothing unique about the phenomena themselves.

By contrast, the systemic changes just described appear to be fundamental and more likely to have long-lasting effects. The number of PhD-granting programs more than doubled in less than two decades. Even though that expansion was followed by a severe and protracted drop in the number of PhD candidates, combined with generally hard times for academic institutions, these adverse circumstances had comparatively little impact on the number of newly created doctoral programs. The contraction affected many aspects of graduate education, but not this most fundamental attribute. The new institutional structure for graduate education—far more distributed, more variegated, and more extensive in terms of participating institutions—survived under extremely exacting conditions, and that new structure has so far proven to be one of the most durable elements among the many postwar changes in graduate education.

TRENDS IN PERCEIVED QUALITY

An assessment of this new structure of graduate education should begin, in our view, with an analysis of its implications for the overall quality of doctorate-granting programs. This requires at least a rough sense of how "quality" is to be measured.

---

[6]See Appendix G, Table G.4–3, for detailed data on degrees conferred by new and established programs by field in all even-numbered years from 1958 through 1988.

Construction of Quality Tiers

Institutional quality is a notoriously elusive concept. Assessments of undergraduate education, for example, are frequent and often well publicized, but they are so imprecise and impressionistic that their utility is highly questionable. Efforts to evaluate graduate education are less frequent, and while such evaluations are certainly open to criticism, they have the great advantage of focusing on individual disciplines or departments at specific institutions, and of applying a limited set of criteria relevant to the more sharply defined purposes of doctoral training and advanced research in specific fields.[7]

For present purposes, we combined the ratings of Roose and Andersen (1970) with those of Jones, Lindzey, and Coggeshall (1982) to create a new set of four composite quality tiers. Using standard criteria, each program awarding a doctorate between 1958 and 1988 in English, history, political science, economics, mathematics, or physics was assigned to one of the four tiers, with Tier I representing the highest quality composite.[8]

Under this classification system, a program is assigned to a particular tier for all years; that is, programs were not "promoted" or "demoted" on the basis of changes in perceived quality during this period.[9] One objection often raised to such ratings is that there is a lag in judgments of departments that are moving up or down in quality, so that ratings may become out of date. We accept this

---

[7]There is a considerable history of efforts to rate graduate programs and institutions. See, for example, Hughes (1925), Keniston (1959), Berelson (1960), and Cartter (1966), as well as the two studies discussed more extensively below.

[8] For a detailed description of the two quality assessment systems that we used, see Roose and Andersen (1970) and Jones, Lindzey, and Coggeshall (1982). In brief, Roose and Andersen (RA) compiled ratings of more than 6,325 faculty members, covering 2,626 doctorate programs in 36 fields at 155 institutions. They asked participants to rank departments in terms of the effectiveness of the graduate program and the quality of the faculty (the particular set of ratings that we used). Programs were ranked according to the following classification system: "distinguished" (5); "strong" (4); "good" (3); "adequate plus" (2); "marginal" (1); and "not sufficient to provide doctoral training" (0). These rankings were generally regarded as the best available source of information on the quality and effectiveness of doctoral programs until the publication of the Jones, Lindzey, and Coggeshall (JLC) study in 1982. This study was based on four broad measures: program size, characteristics of graduates (such as fraction of program graduates receiving fellowship support and median elapsed time-to-degree), the reputation of the faculty and program based upon peer survey results, and university library size. The JLC study used standardized numbered rankings from 1 to 100, with 50 representing the mean and a change of 10 points representing one standard deviation.

We combined these ratings as follows in assigning programs to one of four quality tiers:

• Tier I includes those programs that received top (4 or 5) ratings from RA or high ratings from JLC (a minimum score of 52).

• Tier II includes those programs that received a rating of 3 from RA and a minimum JLC rating of 45. In addition, any program rated between 49 and 52 on the JLC scale but not included in Tier I was assigned to Tier II.

• Tier III includes those programs that received a rating of 2 from RA and between 40 and 48 from JLC, and thus did not appear in either Tier I or Tier II according to the criteria already described.

• Tier IV is the residual category and includes all programs that were either low-rated (that is, did not achieve scores high enough to be placed in Tiers I through III) or not rated at all. Generally speaking, these were programs that were either new or quite small. The not-rated group contains a small number of programs that were strong in their specialties but did not meet more general criteria used to determine whether a program was rated.

[9]In fact, the ranking of programs has been quite consistent across the different rating systems and over different periods. See Webster (1983) for a discussion of changes in rankings over time, with special emphasis on the top-rated programs.

reservation (as do the authors of the assessments in question), and we regard the system of tiers developed here as only a rough way of gauging broad ranges of quality, not as anything like a precise index of the present-day standing of particular universities or programs.

Combining two independently conducted assessments (which together span more than a decade) has permitted us to construct what is, in effect, a long-term "average" rating. By focusing on tiers of programs rather than on fine distinctions within tiers, we believe that we have been able to create categories that do not depend greatly on one's confidence (or lack of confidence) in the details of rating systems.

The distribution of programs by tier is roughly consistent across fields, with more programs in Tiers III and IV than in Tiers I and II. Tiers I and II contain an average of 25 graduate programs per field. Tier III contains an average of 36 programs, and in Tier IV, the average number is 74 (ranging from 65 programs in economics to 82 in history and physics).[10]

Of course, not all programs conferred degrees in all years, and we indicate (in the tables that follow) the number of programs in each tier that conferred degrees in 1958, 1972, and 1988. The overwhelming majority of the Tier I, II, and III programs did, however, confer degrees in each of these years. Many of the Tier IV programs did not exist in 1958 and thus awarded no degrees then; also, some of the Tier IV programs had either ceased to exist or conferred no degrees in 1988.

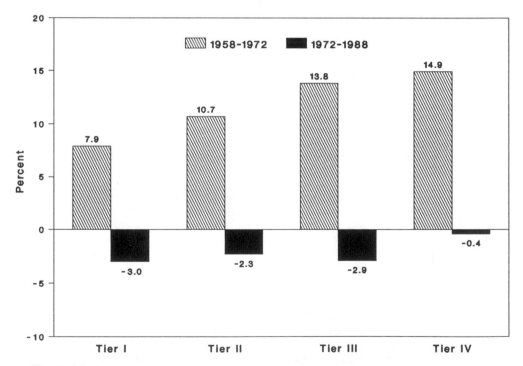

Figure 4.3
Annual Growth Rates in Doctorates Conferred by Quality Tier, Six-Field Total, 1958–1988
   Source: Special tabulations from Doctorate Records File. See Appendix G, Table G.4–2, for the underlying data used to compute annual growth rates.

---

[10] See Appendix G, Table G.4–1, for specific numbers of programs in each tier in each field.

Trends in the Distribution of Programs and Degrees Conferred by Quality Tier

Graduate programs in all four quality tiers contributed significantly to the unprecedented expansion in the number of doctorates conferred between 1958 and 1972, but the rates of increase were disparate. One interesting finding is the clear inverse correlation between quality tier and rate of increase in doctorates awarded (Figure 4.3). Tier I programs increased their number of doctorates (in the six fields combined) by 7.9 percent per year, but the number of PhDs conferred by both Tier III and Tier IV programs rose by nearly twice that much (at annual rates of 13.8 percent and 14.9 percent, respectively); Tier II programs also conformed to this pattern, increasing their doctorates awarded at an intermediate rate (10.7 percent per year).

The patterns for individual fields of study are generally similar (Table 4.3). The exceptionally robust growth rates in Tier IV for mathematics and physics were

Table 4.3
Annual Growth Rate of Doctorates Conferred by Field and Quality Tier, 1958–1988 (percent)

Field and Years	Quality Tier				Total
	I	II	III	IV	
English					
1958–1972	8.1	13.0	14.8	18.2	10.6
1972–1988	−5.2	−3.1	−5.2	0.1	−4.0
1958–1988	0.8	4.1	3.6	8.1	2.6
History					
1958–1972	7.3	15.5	14.3	11.2	9.9
1972–1988	−4.3	−4.8	−4.9	−1.6	−4.1
1958–1988	0.9	4.2	3.6	4.2	2.2
Political Science					
1958–1972	9.7	12.6	17.5	8.0	11.0
1972–1988	−4.0	−2.3	−2.7	2.4	−2.2
1958–1988	2.2	4.4	6.3	5.0	3.7
Economics					
1958–1972	5.6	6.1	10.0	14.3	7.3
1972–1988	−1.3	0.3	0.5	0.3	−0.3
1958–1988	1.8	3.0	4.8	6.6	3.2
Mathematics					
1958–1972	9.9	14.3	15.7	24.3	12.8
1972–1988	−3.3	−3.2	−3.6	−3.0	−3.3
1958–1988	2.6	4.6	5.0	8.9	3.9
Physics					
1958–1972	7.3	7.3	13.2	21.0	8.9
1972–1988	−1.3	−1.2	−2.4	−0.6	−1.4
1958–1988	2.6	2.7	4.6	9.0	3.3
Six Fields (Total)					
1958–1972	7.9	10.7	13.8	14.9	10.0
1972–1988	−3.0	−2.3	−2.9	−0.4	−2.5
1958–1988	1.9	3.6	4.6	6.5	3.1

Source: Special tabulations from Doctorate Records File. See Appendix G, Table G.4–2.
Note: These are compound annual growth rates.

almost certainly the result of national security concerns (following the launching of Sputnik in 1958), combined with efforts by governmental agencies to support work at a more broadly dispersed set of universities and a general upsurge of interest in science and technology. Developments in English and economics resemble those in mathematics and physics (although the growth rates are less dramatic), with the greatest increases in Tier IV programs. History and political science, on the other hand, experienced their greatest increases in Tiers II and III.

These varied rates of expansion between 1958 and 1972 combined to produce a definite negative shift in the share of doctorates awarded by Tier I programs (Figure 4.4). These programs conferred over 60 percent of all PhD degrees in these six fields in 1958, but less than half of all doctorates in 1972. Tier II programs, in contrast, modestly increased their share of doctorates conferred. Tier III programs recorded the largest absolute gain in share achieved by any tier, while Tier IV had the largest relative gain.[11]

During the period of contraction (1972–1988), there was a continued but more moderate falloff in the share of doctorates conferred by Tier I programs (from

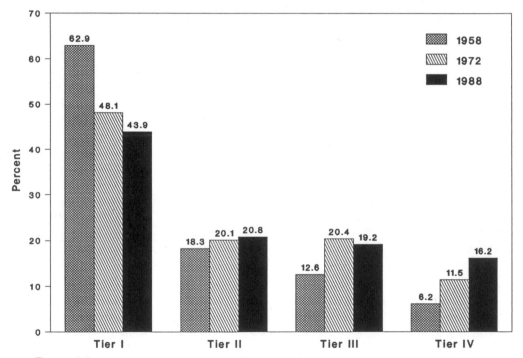

Figure 4.4
Distribution of Doctorates Conferred by Quality Tier, Six-Field Total, 1958, 1972, and 1988
Source: Special tabulations from Doctorate Records File. See Appendix G, Table G.4–2, for the underlying data used to compute the percentages.

---

[11]The greatest losses of share by Tier I programs were in the fields of English and history. Approximately 70 percent of all doctorates in each of these fields were awarded by Tier I programs in 1958, as contrasted with 50 percent in 1972. Percentage shares for all six individual fields for 1958, 1972, and 1988, can be calculated from the data in Appendix G, Table G.4–2.

48.1 percent to 43.9 percent). This is a most revealing result, and it may be somewhat counterintuitive. While it may have been natural to expect programs outside Tier I to grow more rapidly during a period of unprecedented expansion in graduate education, it is much less obvious that Tier I programs should have been expected to contract more rapidly than less prestigious programs when the entire system curtailed its production of doctorates. In the world at large, periods of general contraction often result in greater concentration of "output" in the best-established "firms"—exactly the opposite of the pattern observed in graduate education.[12]

The Tier II share was essentially constant over this period; there was a small decline for Tier III, and a fairly substantial increase in share for Tier IV (from 11.5 percent to 16.2 percent). In other words, losses in share from Tier I were no longer (as in 1958–1972) being "transferred" marginally to Tier II and significantly to Tier III. Rather, they were clearly absorbed by Tier IV programs. In fact, the Tier IV programs showed hardly any decrease at all in doctorates awarded during years when all other tiers contracted significantly.[13]

The cumulative effects of the shifts in shares of doctorates awarded that occurred during the periods of expansion and contraction have been considerable (Table 4.4). The percentage share of all doctorates conferred by the most highly ranked programs fell 19 percentage points, with more than half of this loss in share shifted to the Tier IV programs.

Underlying these major shifts in shares of degrees conferred were some equally significant changes in the number of degree-granting programs in each quality tier. Even during the period of rapid expansion, Tier I experienced only a modest growth in the number of new programs in the six fields. The number of Tier I programs rose from 133 programs in 1958 to 150 in 1972 (an increase of 13 percent), and there was no change in this number from 1972 to 1988. Far more dramatic increases occurred in Tiers III and IV. The number of graduate programs in these two tiers combined rose from 134 in 1958 to 429 in 1972 (a 223

TABLE 4.4

Share of Doctorates Conferred by Quality Tier, Six-Field Total, 1958 and 1988 (percent)

| | Quality Tier | | | |
Year	I	II	III	IV
1958	62.9	18.3	12.6	6.2
1988	43.9	20.8	19.2	16.2
Net change	−19.0	2.5	6.6	10.0

Source: Same as Table 4.3.

[12]There was a considerable furor during the early and mid-1970s centered on the questions of which departments should retrench and what role federal cutbacks were playing in affecting the pattern of retrenchment. Newman (U.S. Department of Health, Education, and Welfare 1973) argued that federal policy was producing a "Gresham's law of PhD enrollments." Breneman (1975) evaluated this proposition and concluded that it was overstated. The Association of Graduate Schools (AGS) issued a report in the mid-1970s that listed criteria to be considered in making decisions concerning retrenchment and addressed the issues of efficiency and cost in graduate education in a forthright way (Association of Graduate Schools 1976).

[13]See Figure 4.3 and Appendix G, Table G.4–2.

percent increase). Moreover, the number of graduate programs in Tier IV continued to rise even during the later contraction phase, with an additional 56 added between 1972 and 1988. The pattern in Tier II was again intermediate.[14]

It is hardly surprising, therefore, that the year-to-year changes in the number of doctorates awarded by new versus established programs were radically different in Tiers I and IV (Figure 4.5). In Tier I, established programs awarded such a high proportion of all PhDs over this entire period that increases and decreases in the output of these programs dominated the overall movements in doctorates conferred. For example, virtually all of the contraction in the number of degrees awarded by Tier I programs following the peak year of 1972 occurred within established programs. An opposite pattern has prevailed in Tier IV, where periods of both expansion and contraction have been dominated by the new programs. The number of doctorates conferred by new Tier IV programs continued to increase until 1976, and by 1988 new Tier IV programs awarded fully 86 percent of all doctorates conferred by programs within this tier. Over the entire period from 1958 to 1988, the growth in the number of PhDs conferred by Tier IV programs was due *entirely* to the development of new programs; established Tier IV programs actually awarded fewer degrees in 1988 than in 1958.[15]

SIZE OF PROGRAM

Determining the size of graduate programs is easier than estimating quality, though this concept, too, is subject to various interpretations. For the purposes of this chapter, we define size in terms of the number of doctorates conferred by a program in a particular year (an "output" measure), although we recognize that there are many other measures that could also be used (enrollments, number of faculty teaching graduate courses, and so on). The changing relationships among some of these different aspects of graduate education are discussed in the next chapter, and much of the rest of the book is devoted to an analysis of the effectiveness of graduate programs in transforming student "inputs" into doctoral "outputs."

Size and Quality

The size (or scale) of a graduate program is important because of its implications for educational quality, as well as for the effective use of the considerable resources required to sustain strong PhD programs. When we analyze the programs in the various quality tiers by average size (the number of doctorates conferred in a given year divided by the number of programs granting degrees in that year), we find an extraordinarily persistent positive relationship between quality ranking and program size. (The 1988 averages for two quite different fields, history and physics, are shown in Figure 4.6, along with the average values for all six fields.)

This relationship between quality and scale holds across fields and over time. Tier I programs have averaged more than twice as many doctorates per program as have Tier II programs, which in turn have operated at roughly twice the levels

---

[14]See Appendix G, Table G.4–1.
[15]See Appendix G, Table G.4–3.

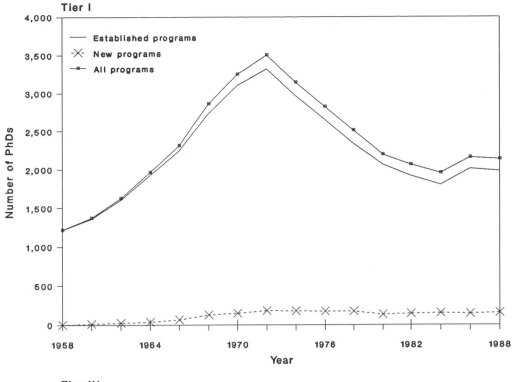

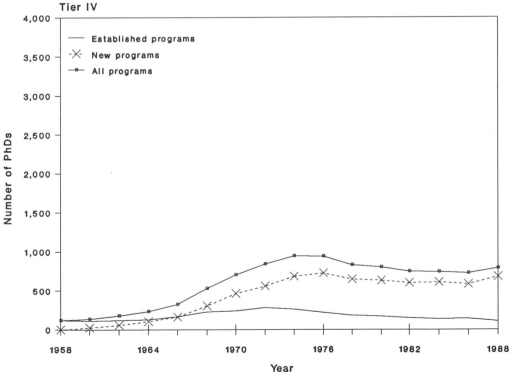

Figure 4.5
Number of Doctorates Conferred by New and Established Programs and Quality Tier, Six-Field Total, 1958–1988

Source: Special tabulations from Doctorate Records File. See Appendix G, Table G.4–3, for the underlying data.

Notes: See footnote 3 for definitions of "New" and "Established."

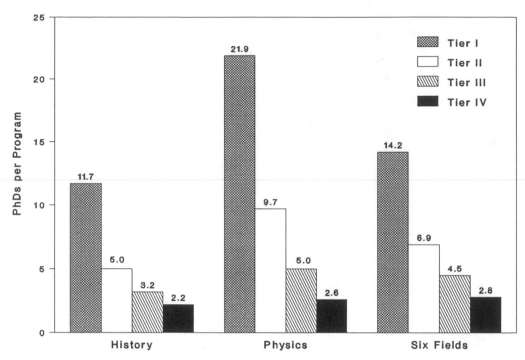

Figure 4.6
Average Size of Programs by Quality Tier, Selected Fields, 1988 (doctorates per program)
Source: Special tabulations from Doctorate Records File. See Appendix G, Tables G.4–1 and G.4–2, for the number of PhD programs and the number of PhDs conferred by quality tier.

of average output achieved by Tier III and Tier IV programs considered together. Tier IV programs have been noticeably smaller than Tier III programs. Although there are a few exceptions, this pattern prevails across all six fields in all three years for which we made detailed calculations (Table 4.5).

This finding is not surprising, especially since causation clearly flows in both directions. Relatively large numbers of students are attracted by the strongest programs; and most observers agree that doctoral programs ordinarily require a reasonably substantial "critical mass" in order to create the conditions for excellent graduate work. In larger programs, there is a sufficient number of graduate students to permit a lively exchange of ideas and to allow for seminars of at least modest size in the various subfields of a discipline.

Such opportunities for group discussion are valuable in all fields of study. In the sciences, a dependable influx of new students is especially important. Advanced research in most scientific fields demands a high degree of collaboration, and it is essentially impossible to address many of the most significant problems outside the context of a laboratory setting in which a team of graduate students, postdoctoral fellows, and faculty work together. These considerations help to explain why physics programs in all tiers tend to be larger than programs in our other five fields, and why the relationship between size and quality is especially strong in physics (refer back to Figure 4.6). A program of reasonable size, regardless of the particular discipline, ensures that there is likely to be a sufficiently large group of faculty to provide adequate coverage across several

TABLE 4.5

Average Size of Doctorate-Granting Programs by Field and Quality Tier, 1958, 1972, and 1988 (number of doctorates)

Field and Year	Quality Tier				Total
	I	II	III	IV	
English					
1958	9.4	3.5	2.9	1.7	5.6
1972	24.1	8.9	9.1	4.1	11.0
1988	10.3	5.6	4.0	3.3	5.4
History					
1958	8.8	2.7	2.5	2.8	5.2
1972	23.8	10.0	6.9	3.6	10.1
1988	11.7	5.0	3.2	2.2	4.9
Political Science					
1958	6.4	3.2	2.1	4.6	4.5
1972	20.0	10.0	7.4	4.2	10.0
1988	10.5	6.6	4.4	3.4	5.5
Economics					
1958	11.2	6.2	3.2	1.7	5.8
1972	20.1	9.2	5.9	3.6	8.3
1988	16.3	8.7	6.3	3.0	7.2
Mathematics					
1958	6.7	2.3	2.5	1.6	4.0
1972	22.0	9.8	6.4	3.9	9.2
1988	13.3	5.8	3.7	2.4	5.5
Physics					
1958	11.9	5.8	3.1	2.5	7.1
1972	27.7	11.8	7.6	3.4	11.3
1988	21.9	9.7	5.0	2.6	8.4
Six Fields (Total)					
1958	9.1	4.0	2.8	2.5	5.4
1972	23.3	10.0	7.2	3.8	10.0
1988	14.2	6.9	4.5	2.8	6.2

Source: Special tabulations from Doctorate Records File. See Appendix G, Table G.4–1 and G.4–2.

areas, and that faculty and students alike will be provided with necessary library materials, laboratory facilities, equipment, and other resources.

Trends in Average Size

Although the basic relationship between quality and scale has persisted, the average size of graduate programs has changed significantly. Once again, it is essential to differentiate between changes that occurred during the period of expansion and those that occurred during the period of contraction. During the growth years between 1958 and 1972, the average size of doctoral programs in the six fields nearly doubled, from 5.4 degrees per program to 10.0 (Figure 4.7). Later, when demand contracted, the size of programs diminished. By 1988, the average had fallen back to 6.2. This general pattern is consistent across the six

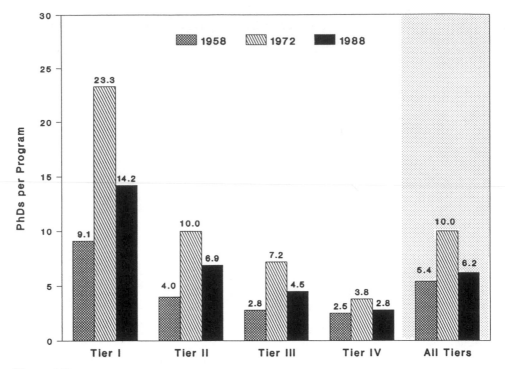

Figure 4.7
Trends in Average Size of Programs by Quality Tier, Six-Field Total, 1958, 1972, and 1988
(doctorates per program)

Source: Special tabulations from Doctorate Records File. See Appendix G, Tables G.4–1 and G.4–2,
for the number of PhD programs and the number of PhDs conferred by quality tier.

fields, with the slight qualification that English and history—alone among these
fields—had a slightly lower average size in 1988 than in 1958 (Table 4.5).

This pattern is also similar across the four quality tiers, but there are some
significant differences (Figure 4.7). During the period of expansion, the increase
in the absolute size of the typical graduate program was by far the greatest in
Tier I (which gained 14.2 degrees per program). The relative rates of increase,
however, were nearly identical for Tiers I, II, and III (with the average number
of doctorates per program in 1972 being roughly 2.5 times the average in 1958).
In contrast, the Tier IV programs increased only modestly (by less than a factor
of one) because, as noted above, growth in doctorates awarded within this tier
occurred almost exclusively through the establishment of new programs.

During the period of contraction, the Tier I programs declined more than the
others in absolute terms, falling from 23.3 PhDs per program to 14.2 PhDs per
program. However, the relative rates of decline were not so different across tiers
(−39 percent in Tier I, −31 percent in Tier II, −37.5 percent in Tier III, and −26
percent in Tier IV).

While averages (arithmetic means) provide a generally reliable picture of the
changing sizes of typical graduate programs, it should be recognized that the
distribution of programs around the means has been irregular. History is
illustrative. The left-hand panels of Figure 4.8 show the pattern for Tier I history

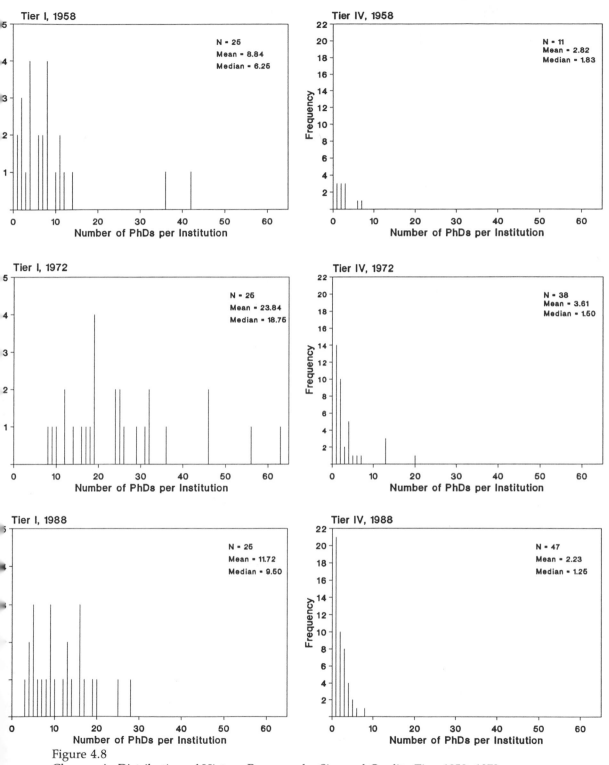

Figure 4.8
Changes in Distribution of History Programs by Size and Quality Tier, 1958, 1972, and 1988

Source: Special tabulations from Doctorate Records File.

programs. The mean in 1958 is exaggerated somewhat by the presence of two very large programs (which awarded 36 and 42 degrees). Otherwise, the Tier I programs clustered in the range of 1 to 15 degrees. The increase in average size between 1958 and 1972 can be seen to have been a consequence of a broadly based expansion in most Tier I programs, with no program awarding fewer than eight degrees in 1972. By 1988, following the subsequent contraction, there was a more uniform distribution of programs by size than existed in 1958; there were fewer small programs, and no individual program awarded more than 28 degrees. Median program size in 1988 was more than 50 percent larger than the same measure in 1958. One implication is that rapid expansion is harder to contemplate now than it was in 1958, largely because the number of small programs that stand to benefit educationally from enrolling more students has been reduced considerably.

The changes in the distribution of Tier IV programs in history are even more revealing (right-hand panels of Figure 4.8). In 1958, there were only 11 Tier IV programs, and the median program size was 1.8 degrees. By 1988, there were 47 Tier IV programs, but the median size had fallen to just 1.25 degrees per program. Nearly half of all Tier IV programs in history (21 of 47) conferred only one degree in 1988—a statistic that provides a good introduction to a more general discussion of programs of small size.

Small (and Very Small) Programs

The rest of this chapter focuses on the number of doctoral programs that we consider either small or very small in scale. We have (rather arbitrarily) drawn the definitional lines as follows: "Small" programs are those that conferred an average of fewer than four degrees per year during the 1980s, while "very small" programs are the subset of programs that conferred an average of fewer than two degrees per year.

Some small programs are, of course, excellent, particularly if they are in significant but highly specialized fields where the nature of the specialty—and the very modest number of academic or other jobs ordinarily available—tend to act as a natural limit on the flow of students pursuing PhDs. In larger and more central fields, however, the presence of a small program (and certainly of a very small program) often indicates that there are problems. For example, if only one or two doctoral degrees are awarded annually in English, history, economics, or physics at a given institution, that fact may well indicate that the department in question is having serious problems either in attracting students or in supporting and retaining them. Identifying the number of small programs (most of which are not highly rated) can, therefore, offer a useful perspective on the national structure and quality of graduate offerings.

One clear conclusion is that the small doctoral programs created during the 1960s and 1970s are a continuing presence. They constitute quite a large proportion of the universe of degree-granting programs in each of our six fields (Figure 4.9). Programs granting an average of less than four degrees per year over the decade of the 1980s comprise 50 percent of all doctorate-granting programs in the six fields. The range is from highs of 62 percent in history and 55 percent in mathematics to lows of 45 percent in English and 37 percent in economics. Fully 48 percent of all programs in physics granted less than four degrees per year, which is especially surprising because of the heavy investment

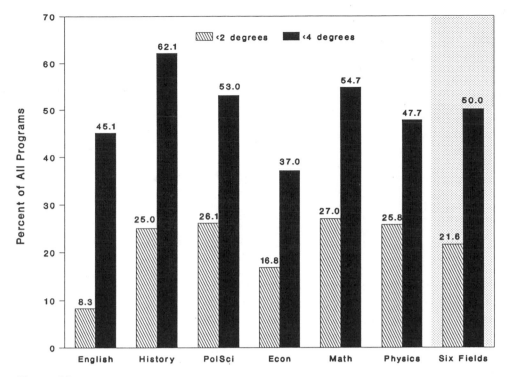

Figure 4.9
Small and Very Small Programs as Share of All Programs by Field, 1988
Source: Special tabulations from Doctorate Records File. See Appendix G, Table G.4–4. .

in laboratories and associated research activities normally associated with the sciences. The very small programs—granting an average of fewer than two degrees per year—represent 22 percent of all programs in the six fields. Moreover, this mode of analysis understates the true number of small programs that are still active. Because we excluded from the count all programs that did not give at least one degree in 1988, the stated number of small programs is clearly a most conservative estimate. Some programs that awarded no doctorates in 1988 undoubtedly gave one or more degrees in neighboring years and are still active.

While the data on degrees conferred do not permit a full assessment of the current "life signs" of programs (providing no information, for instance, on the number of new doctoral candidates being admitted), they do permit some inferences to be drawn. For instance, we have been able to determine that of all the programs that conferred no degrees in 1988, nearly one-third (32 percent) conferred degrees in 1986 and were presumably still reasonably active. Another 15 percent conferred degrees in 1984, leaving just over half (53 percent) in the category of having failed to confer degrees in 1986 and 1984 as well as in 1988.[16]

The importance of this way of analyzing the data is illustrated by looking even more intensively at the subset of very small programs—those that awarded

---

[16] See Appendix G, Table G.4–5, for a detailed analysis by field of study and quality tier of the years in which programs that did not award doctorates in 1988 awarded their last doctorate.

TABLE 4.6
Number of Programs Conferring Fewer Than Two Doctorates per Year by Field,
1984–1988

| | Year of Most Recent PhD | | | Sum of 1988, |
Field	1988	1986	1984	1986, 1984
English	11	6	2	19
History	31	7	7	45
Political Science	30	10	5	45
Economics	20	4	5	29
Mathematics	37	15	7	59
Physics	40	4	5	49
Six Fields (Total)	169	46	31	246

Source: Special tabulations from Doctorate Records File.
Note: These tabulations do not include degrees conferred in odd-numbered years.

fewer than two degrees per year during the 1980s (Table 4.6). If we treat as presumptively active all programs that conferred degrees in any even-numbered year from 1984 to 1988, the number of very small programs increases from 169 (the number that awarded at least one degree in 1988) to 246 in the six fields. The large absolute numbers in mathematics, history, political science, and physics are particularly striking. A stricter definition of continuing activity (which counts only those programs that conferred at least one doctorate in either 1986 or 1988) yields 215 programs. By either definition, we see that substantial numbers of doctorate programs are being sustained even when they have been conferring very few degrees. We are reminded again of how hard it is for institutions to eliminate doctoral programs once they have been established.

Because of their size, the number of doctorates conferred by these small (and very small) programs is necessarily modest. Still, the small programs together accounted for fully 20 percent of the 4,858 degrees conferred in the six fields in 1988. Very small programs alone accounted for 6 percent. These shares are hardly inconsequential.

The same analysis can be used to obtain an approximate answer to another question: Of all the programs in the six fields that conferred doctorates between 1958 and 1988, how many have been terminated? If we again adopt the convention that programs that awarded a degree in 1988, 1986, or 1984 should be regarded as still active, we find that 91 of 964 programs that were active at any time between 1958 and 1988 (about 9 percent), failed to satisfy this criterion. Stated the other way around, over 90 percent of all programs that conferred a doctorate in one of the six fields in any year between 1958 and 1988 still appear to be active.[17]

---

[17]See Appendix G, Table G.4–5, for the data on which these calculations are based (including data for specific fields). The format of the table permits other cutoffs to be used in defining when failure to confer doctorates is to be construed as placing a program in the inactive category. This kind of functional definition of the current status of a program may be more meaningful in many instances than more direct inquiries.

Number of Programs Reaching Critical Mass

If many of the small programs tend to operate at a level of effectiveness that is close to the margin in terms of critical mass and quality, then a significant proportion of the existing national system of graduate education may well need thoughtful reassessment. Of course, one reason for sustaining these small programs—apart from the complex internal dynamics and programmatic goals of individual institutions—is that they may ultimately grow, both in size and quality. This possibility is an important one, but it also needs to be tested.[18]

In this instance, past experience provides a helpful perspective. It is useful to remember that even in 1972—approximately the zenith of the postwar period of growth in doctorates conferred—the majority of lower-rated programs were awarding very few doctorates and must certainly have been below what one would normally view as critical mass. In the six fields, the mean number of doctorates awarded in 1972 for Tier IV programs of *any* size was approximately four degrees per year.

An even more precise sense of the postwar experience with relatively small programs can be obtained by introducing another method of assessing critical mass. This approach analyzes the average number of doctorates conferred over the life span of each program. Life span is defined as the time period bounded by the year in which a program awarded its first doctorate (either 1958 or a later year) and the year in which it awarded a doctorate most recently (1988, or an earlier year if no degree was awarded in 1988). We then ask how many programs achieved some degree of critical mass, defined somewhat arbitrarily, as an average of at least three doctorates awarded per year over the life span of the program. This approach has the advantage of relating the number of doctorates conferred to the period of time when the program was demonstrably active; it does not penalize a program for years when it was not conferring degrees (either because it started conferring doctorates after 1958 or because it stopped awarding degrees before 1988).

Only 57 percent of all doctoral programs in the six fields achieved critical mass by this definition over their life spans (top panel of Figure 4.10). Once again, scale and quality are seen to be strongly related, with only 24 percent of all Tier IV programs awarding more than three degrees per year over their life spans. Judged by this standard, the best results have been achieved by English and economics, and the worst results by history and physics, where only 16 to 17 percent of Tier IV programs reached critical mass. We suspect that the library and laboratory requirements, respectively, of these two subjects have made it

---

[18]Consideration should also be given to another reason for sustaining small programs—namely, to ensure a reasonable degree of geographic diversity in graduate education. However, analysis of the actual geographic distribution of large and small programs raises doubts about the persuasiveness of this argument. We divided the country into nine geographical regions (New England, Middle Atlantic, South Atlantic, East North Central, East South Central, West North Central, West South Central, Mountain, and Pacific). We then calculated the number of small programs (those that averaged less than four doctorates per year in the 1980s) in regions that did not include a larger program in the same field. Of the 964 programs that conferred doctorates in at least one year between 1958 and 1988, 571 were small; of these small programs, only 11 were in a "noncovered" region. (All 11 were history programs in the East South Central region.) When we repeated the analysis on a state-by-state basis, we found that 149 of the 571 small programs (26 percent) were in a "noncovered" state.

Roose (1971) performed a somewhat similar analysis near the end of the period of expansion and concluded that regions were adequately served by the most highly rated programs. However, his study did not analyze the distribution of programs by field of study.

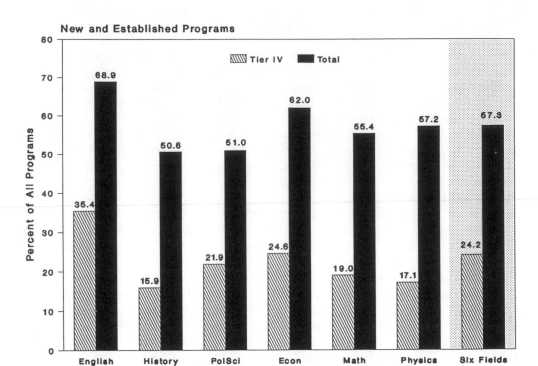

New and Established Programs

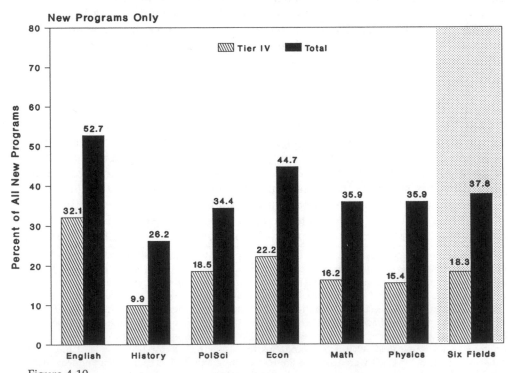

New Programs Only

Figure 4.10
Programs Reaching Critical Mass by Quality Tier and Field, New and Established
Programs, 1958–1988 (percent of all programs)

Source: Special tabulations from Doctorate Records File. See Appendix G, Table G.4–6.

Notes: Critical Mass is defined as conferring three or more degrees per year during the years the
program was active. See text and footnote 19.

especially difficult for aspiring but not yet established programs to reach a level of quality sufficient to sustain enrollment at a satisfactory level over the long run.

If we limit the universe of programs under consideration to those established after 1958, so that we can focus more directly on the experiences of new programs, we find that only 38 percent of them, whatever their quality tier, reached this specification of critical mass (bottom panel of Figure 4.10). Finally, if we look only at new Tier IV programs, we find that just 18 percent awarded three or more doctorates per year. The results by individual field of study are similar to those for all programs, except that history now stands alone as the field with the smallest percentage of new programs (in all tiers) reaching critical mass (26 percent).[19]

These and other statistics from the postwar period raise large warning flags. If the existing number of small and lower-ranked programs is now being sustained in the hope or expectation that they will in the future grow to full maturity, it is worthwhile asking whether the conditions for such a development in the next decade or two seem likely to be manifestly better (or even equal to) those which existed during the exceptionally favorable years between 1958 and the early 1970s. Such an analysis would provide at least one context for helping universities evaluate whether a continued substantial investment in so large a number of small programs is apt to be promising, either from the point of view of the universities and their students, or from the vantage point of the system of graduate education as a whole.

These are hard questions, for individual institutions and for the society at large, but they need to be asked more directly—and answered more candidly—than has often been the case in the past.[20]

---

[19]Defining critical mass as requiring an average of at least three degrees per year of program life is of course judgmental and arbitrary, and one could argue that some other boundary line would be more appropriate. The most appropriate measure of critical mass could well vary by field. In any event, while we view three degrees per year as a quite reasonable minimum, we have also made calculations using two degrees per year as the criterion. Substituting this new criterion naturally increases the number of programs said to have reached critical mass, but the number of programs still captured by this cutoff remains large. In all fields combined, 70 percent of all programs achieved an average of two degrees per year; the comparable figure is only 40 percent for Tier IV programs, 55 percent for all new programs, and 36 percent for all new Tier IV programs (Appendix G, Table G.4–6).

For an earlier discussion of critical mass, see Balderston (1974). Balderston's approach implies that to achieve critical mass, programs would need to confer more degrees than our measures suggest. A recent report by the California State Postsecondary Education Commission (1985) raises the question of critical mass explicitly but suggests a very low cutoff: "The assumption is . . . that an effective program requires a certain minimum number of faculty and students—a 'critical mass'—to interact, stimulate, challenge, and reinforce. While the number necessary for critical mass undoubtedly varies with circumstances, a program that awards only two or three doctorates over a five-year period probably lacks it" (p. 70).

[20]A recent article in *Science* discusses a still larger question raised by Paula Stephan—whether more PhDs implies a decrease in quality (Holden 1991). Various sources of evidence, including Stephan's own empirical work (Levin and Stephan 1991), are cited to suggest that there has been a dilution in the quality and productivity of scientists trained in the last few decades, perhaps because of increases in their numbers relative to demand in their fields. (Others cited in the *Science* article believe the evidence is inconclusive.) Stephan advocates simply allowing the demand for scientists to increase relative to the supply, as a way of improving quality (whatever the other consequences). Our approach is quite different. We focus more explicitly on the distribution of doctorates among doctorate-granting programs and favor measures that, at the minimum, might discourage a further reduction in the share of doctorates awarded by the strongest programs. It would be desirable, in our view, to raise the share of doctorates awarded by the strongest programs.

CHAPTER FIVE

The Evolution of Selected Tier I Programs in the EHP Fields

THIS CHAPTER, which concludes the discussion of broad trends in graduate education, is very different from its predecessors. The last three chapters explored aspects of the overall system of graduate education. In order to complement that analysis, we now shift the focus to internal developments that are generally visible only at the level of the individual graduate program.

The objective here is to provide a reasonably coherent sense of how selected graduate programs have evolved from the early 1960s through the 1980s. Attention is focused on changes in the number of courses offered, the number of faculty engaged in graduate teaching, the number of listed "masthead" faculty, the size and quality of graduate student cohorts, and patterns of financial aid, including the increasing reliance on teaching assistantships (TAs).

A "micro" analysis of this kind can be carried out on only a limited scale, and we have chosen to concentrate on eleven Tier I graduate programs in English, history, and political science (EHP) at five universities.[1] The decision to focus on the EHP fields is consistent with our general emphasis on these less-studied (but central) areas within the arts and sciences. Also, it is linked to a more complex presentation (in Chapter Twelve) of the ways in which these three fields have developed intellectually since the early 1960s. The analysis in Chapter Twelve traces major shifts in the content of course offerings, in the emergence of new methodologies, and in requirements for the doctoral degree. A textured discussion of that kind is useful only if it contains enough detail to characterize with some precision the development of particular programs (and fields of knowledge). Hence the need for considerable selectivity.

---

[1]These programs and universities are as follows: Cornell (English); Harvard (English, history, government); Yale (English, history, political science); Columbia (political science); Princeton (English, history, political science). One reason for selecting these particular programs is that all of them belong to the Ten-University data set, making it possible to integrate that data set with the other data presented here and in Chapter Twelve. (See Appendix A for a description of the Ten-University data set.)

These are all well-established programs, located within strong universities, and their experiences therefore may have differed in important respects from the experiences of a more diverse set of programs and institutions. However, this sampling of graduate programs does permit reasonably reliable inferences to be drawn about behavior within this subset of Tier I institutions. We are able to compare trends in degrees conferred, and we know that the pattern within these programs is generally consistent with the overall pattern for the Tier I programs in the EHP fields. The programs discussed in this chapter grew relatively less rapidly than did all Tier I programs between 1958 and 1972 (at roughly two-thirds the overall rate), but then contracted at almost precisely the same rate. For example, doctorates conferred in English fell 44 percent in this set of programs, as compared to 46 percent for all Tier I programs. The corresponding figures for history are 47 percent and 50 percent; for political science, they are 62 percent and 60 percent.

The first part of the chapter is essentially descriptive. It is intended to show the extent to which trends in other attributes of graduate programs mirrored the trends in PhDs conferred. The second half is more interpretive. Universities are unitary entities to a greater extent than is ordinarily appreciated, and their behavior can be understood best if each element is seen in relation to other elements. Particular attention is paid to two overlapping issues: the factors responsible for an increasing reliance on TAs and the more general set of institutional pressures that affected faculty staffing and the role of graduate education within the universities.

TRENDS AT THE PROGRAM LEVEL

Graduate Courses Offered

Trends in the number of graduate courses *offered* (not simply listed in the catalog) have been reasonably consistent across the EHP fields (Figure 5.1). In English, the number offered by the four programs included in this analysis rose by an average of 27 percent during the expansionary period from 1963–1965 to 1973–1975. During the contractionary years, courses offered by the same departments fell much of the way back toward the 1963–1965 level. There was

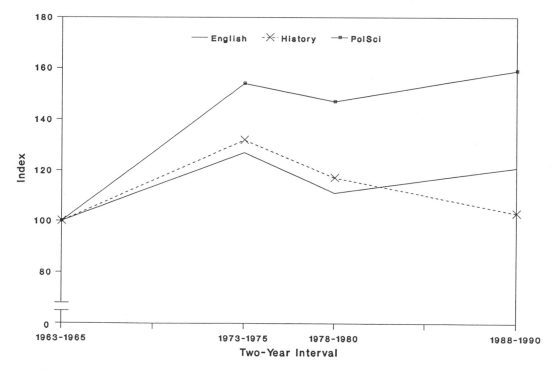

Figure 5.1
Number of Graduate Courses Offered by EHP Field, 1963–1990 (Index: 1963–1965 = 100)

   Source: Authors' tabulations. See footnotes 1 and 2 for method of tabulation and programs included, and Appendix G, Table G.5–1, for underlying data.

then a recovery in the mid- to late 1980s, but it was only partial. The number in 1988–1990 was still below the 1973–1975 peak.[2]

The pattern of course offerings in history was almost identical to that in English during the periods of expansion and contraction. However, contrary to the experience in English, the average number of courses offered by these history departments continued to decline in the 1980s, and the 1988–1990 figure was almost identical to the 1963–1965 figure.[3] Clearly, the common perception that universities have continuously added new programs and steadily proliferated course offerings is seriously at odds with these data for English and history.

Political science demonstrates a slightly different pattern, not only during the years of expansion (when course offerings grew very rapidly), but also afterward. The 1970s decline was less pronounced than in English and history, and the 1980s recovery was such that the total number of political science courses offered by these programs was greater in 1988–1990 than in any previous year for which detailed data are available. Several explanations seem plausible. First, although some political science programs were fairly sizable by the 1960s (as we saw in Chapter Two), the discipline as a whole—measured in such terms as the annual number of doctorates conferred nationwide—began from a lower base than did either English or history, and it remained in a developmental phase for some time. In addition, a greater interest in international affairs, in the law, in issues of race and ethnicity, and in the social and political dimensions of many contemporary problems may have combined to attract larger numbers of students to this field.

Number of Faculty

Faculty growth was naturally most rapid in all three fields during the boom years of the late 1960s and early 1970s (Figure 5.2). Between 1973–1975 and 1978–1980, changes in the number of faculty teaching graduate courses varied by field, growing slightly in history, continuing to expand significantly in political science, and dipping rather sharply in English. However, by the end of the 1980s, English had essentially regained its 1973–1975 staffing level.[4]

---

[2]Statistics concerning course offerings were obtained primarily by hand counts of lists in course catalogs and through other official publications. Interpretation and judgment were often required in an effort to impose as much consistency as possible on the somewhat disparate records under review, and some supplementary information had to be obtained from administrative and academic offices.

The resulting data have been organized in two-year clusters in order to smooth out the eccentricities of single-year fluctuations. The two-year clusters have been selected to serve as at least approximate boundary points for distinctive eras in the recent history of higher education: 1963–1965 to 1973–1975 (ten years generally characterized as a time of expansion); 1973–1975 to 1978–1980 (five years of quite sharp contraction); and 1978–1980 to 1988–1990 (the last ten years, characterized first by rough stability, albeit at contractionary levels, and then by a period of some recovery). The absolute numbers have been indexed, with 1963–1965 set equal to 100, in order to facilitate the comparison of rates of change. See Appendix G, Table G.5–1.

[3]We were surprised by the different directions of change in the numbers of courses offered in English and history between 1979–1980 and 1988–1990. The greater recovery in course offerings in English may have been due, at least in part, to the rapid change in ways of conceptualizing that field (especially the growth of theory). See the discussion of course content in Chapter Twelve.

[4]The statistics on faculty teaching graduate courses and on masthead faculty (discussed later in the text) were obtained in the same way as the statistics on courses offered—primarily by hand counts of lists in catalogs and other publications. The comments in note 2 concerning the need to make judgments and to cluster data apply here as well.

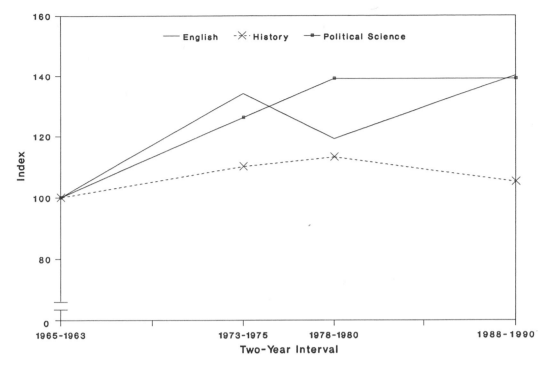

Figure 5.2
Number of Teaching Faculty by EHP Field, 1963–1990 (Index: 1963–1965 = 100)
Source: Authors' tabulations. See footnotes 1 and 2 for method of tabulation and programs included, and Appendix G, Table G.5–1, for underlying data.

The comparison with the general pattern for number of courses offered is clearest when we examine composite figures for the EHP fields (Figure 5.3). The index for graduate courses is more volatile, but the two indices end up at almost precisely the same place in 1988–1990 relative to their base values in 1963–1965 (both having increased about 25 percent). The main difference is that the 1988–1990 index for number of courses offered remains below the peak level reached in 1973–1975, whereas the 1988–1990 index for number of teaching faculty is slightly higher than the corresponding number for 1973–1975.

The indicated growth in the number of teaching faculty was not simply the product of internal resource reallocations (favoring graduate education, for example, at the expense of undergraduate teaching). This is suggested by examining a second measure of faculty numbers: the total number of faculty listed on the mastheads of these same programs, including those who teach undergraduates, those on leave, and so on.[5] While masthead listings are a comparatively crude index (since they include visitors, joint appointments, and part-time faculty), they nonetheless provide a reasonable guide to the overall size of the faculty in specific departments. Shifts in numbers of masthead faculty parallel very closely shifts in numbers of faculty teaching in graduate programs,

---

[5]See Appendix G, Table G.5–1, for the numbers of masthead faculty in the three EHP fields in various years.

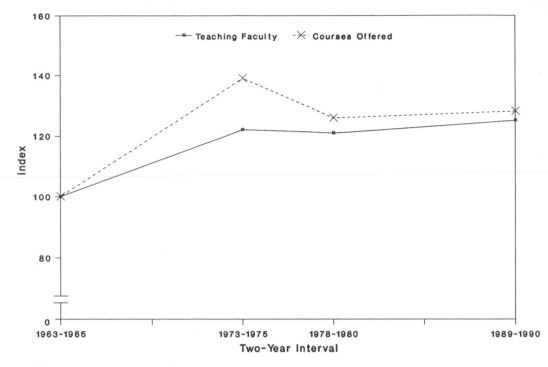

Figure 5.3
Number of Graduate Courses Offered and Number of Teaching Faculty, EHP Total, 1963–1990 (Index: 1963–1965 = 100)

Source: Authors' tabulations. See footnotes 1, 2, and 4 for method of tabulation and programs included, and Appendix G, Table G.5–1, for underlying data.

with the one caveat that the numbers of masthead faculty tend to be somewhat more variable.

Graduate Student Enrollment

Trends in both number of courses offered and number of faculty need to be seen in the context of trends in graduate enrollment. Because of the long time that it often takes to earn a doctorate, the data presented in earlier chapters on the number of doctorates conferred can be quite misleading if used as the sole index of the size of the student population. The numbers of students beginning graduate programs must also be taken into account.

Sizes of entering cohorts in individual graduate programs can swing quite sharply from one year to the next, in part because it is so difficult to predict how many students offered admission will in fact matriculate. Still, definite patterns exist (Figure 5.4). While the information in the Ten-University data set is limited for years before 1968, the figures that are available suggest that the number of entering students rose during the early 1960s.[6] A long period of decline began around 1969–1970, when the number of PhDs conferred was still rising steadily.

---

[6]The national data for all graduate students in EHP fields support strongly the contention that the graduate student population grew rapidly during the early 1960s: 1,965 PhDs were awarded to the 1958 BA cohort, and this number rose steadily through the early 1960s, reaching a peak of 3,454 for the 1964 BA cohort.

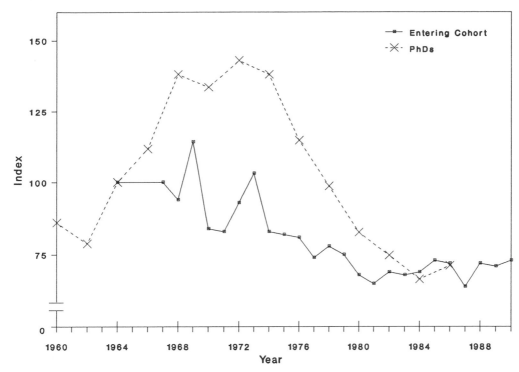

Figure 5.4
Number of Entering Graduate Students and Number of Doctorates Conferred, EHP Total, 1960–1990 (Index: 1964 = 100)

Source: Ten-University data set. Data are from Columbia, Cornell, Harvard, Princeton, and Yale. See Appendix G, Tables G.5–2 and G.5–3, for method of calculating indices.

(The unusually sharp fluctuations in entering cohorts between 1968 and the early 1970s were related in significant measure to the Vietnam War and to the changes in draft deferments discussed in Chapter Three.) By 1977, entering graduate classes were about 25 percent smaller than they had been in the late 1960s; and by the early 1980s, they were 35 percent below the 1960s level. A slow recovery in the sizes of entering cohorts then ensued, with a stronger recovery apparent in the late 1980s.[7]

The pronounced dip in the sizes of entering cohorts in the mid- to late 1970s and early 1980s was surely due in large part to the depressed conditions in

---

[7]The indices shown in Figure 5.4 are based on data in Appendix G, Tables G.5–2 and G.5–3. They are for all entering students, including non-U.S. residents, and differ, therefore, from data in the rest of this study, which generally pertain only to U.S. residents. From the standpoint of estimating pressures on faculty resources and implications for courses offered, it is of course the total student population, not U.S. residents only, that is relevant. Data available for entering cohorts prior to 1968 were so limited that we thought it wisest to set the value for 1964 equal to the value for 1967.

A comparison of the two lines in Figure 5.4 illustrates clearly the extent to which the long lag in the PhD "production process" permits numbers of doctorates conferred and numbers of entering students to move in divergent directions for a considerable number of years. However, once the number of doctorates conferred by these programs also began to fall (after 1974), they dropped rapidly, with the number of PhDs awarded in 1984 equal to just about 50 percent of the number of degrees awarded a decade earlier.

academic labor markets. Many faculty members and deans decided to reduce PhD "production" dramatically because they doubted that there would be a sufficient number of academic jobs available in the foreseeable future. At the same time, many prospective students were well aware of the unfavorable prospects in academia, and were discouraged from even considering doctoral education in the arts and sciences. Thus, students themselves were dubious about their future in the professoriate, and faculty often advised bright under-graduates not to pursue an academic career.[8]

The subsequent (albeit modest) recovery in the size of entering cohorts during the latter part of the 1980s was undoubtedly helped by perceptions of improving job prospects. Able undergraduates appear to have become more interested in considering graduate study in the arts and sciences, and applicant pools have grown (see discussion below). Leading departments, in turn, have been much more inclined to admit (and encourage) talented students.

A particularly relevant comparison is between changes in graduate enroll-ments and changes in the number of graduate courses offered. Clearly there is some congruence in the patterns (compare Figures 5.3 and 5.4). The number of courses offered fell about 10 percent between 1973–1975 and 1978–1980, which is the period when graduate enrollments contracted most rapidly. In the 1980s, the number of courses offered has remained essentially constant, while entering cohorts have increased roughly 12 percent.

A more complex question, of at least equal importance, concerns the effects of these trends on the quality of admitted students. While there has been much—generally inconclusive—discussion of broad shifts in levels of student quality over these years, little systematic information has been available on the particular experiences of highly rated programs. Did the declining interest of recipients of BAs in graduate education compel even these strong graduate programs to lower their standards and admit students whom they would not have chosen in earlier years?

Detailed information is available for the EHP fields at Cornell, where unusu-ally good records have been maintained. The applicant pool contracted sharply during the 1970s, and by 1980 it was half as large as it had been ten years earlier (Figure 5.5). The number of matriculants also declined, but not nearly as rapidly. The 1980s have been characterized by the obverse pattern: Both the size of the applicant pool and the number of matriculants have risen, but with the applicant pool rising much faster than the number of entering students.

Through all these ups and downs in numbers of applicants and matriculants, the average GRE-Verbal score of the entering students at Cornell remained remarkably constant, at about 700 (shown in Figure 5.5). Judged by this rough criterion, the Cornell departments appear to have succeeded in maintaining their traditional standard in admissions.[9]

Examination of average GRE-Verbal scores at five additional universities in the Ten-University data set (Chicago, Columbia, Michigan, Stanford, and the University of North Carolina) corroborates this central finding. The composite curve showing movements over time in the average GRE-Verbal score for EHP students at all of these universities is extraordinarily stable (Figure 5.6).

---

[8] See Breneman 1975, 67; and Hellstrom 1979, 95–97.

[9] This conclusion also holds when we substitute GRE-Subject scores in the fields in question (English, history, and political science) for the GRE-Verbal scores.

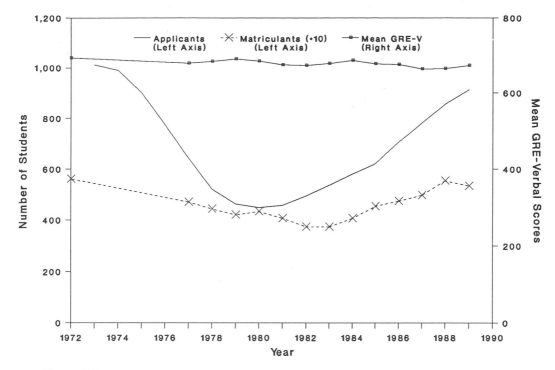

Figure 5.5
Number and Mean GRE-Verbal Scores of Applicants and Matriculants at Cornell, EHP Total, 1972–1989
  Source: Data provided by Alison Casarett, Dean, Cornell Graduate School of Arts and Sciences.
  Notes: The number of matriculants has been multiplied by 10 to facilitate comparison of trends between applicants and matriculants.

When we look at the tails of the distribution of these scores, we see that since 1982, there has been both an increase in the percentage of entering students scoring over 700 and a decrease in the percentage scoring below 550. Therefore, within this set of strong graduate programs, we conclude that the difficulties of the 1970s did not have a measurable impact on at least this crude measure of student quality. Also, in more recent years, there appears to have been at least a modest improvement in test scores.[10]

Graduate Student Financial Support

The changing pattern of financial support for graduate students is the last, and most complicated, aspect of graduate education to be considered in this part of the chapter. The rather extended discussion presented here is intended to

---

[10]Comparable data exist for mathematics, physics, and economics within the Ten-University data set. During the 1970s, neither applicant pools nor the number of entering cohorts in these fields declined nearly as rapidly as in the EHP fields. Average GRE-Math scores have been quite steady in these fields, and (as in the EHP fields) there has also been some modest improvement in the more recent years.

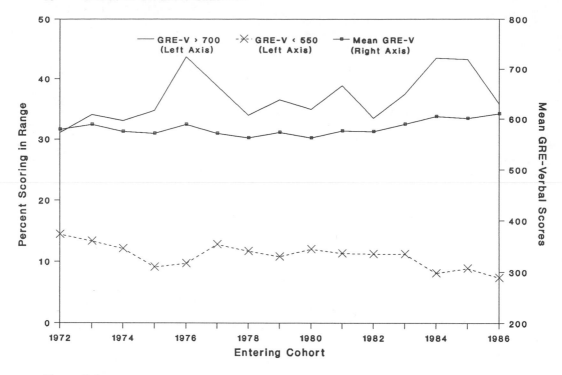

Figure 5.6

GRE-Verbal Scores of Entering Cohorts, EHP Total, 1972–1986

Source: Ten-University data set. Data are from Chicago, Columbia, Cornell, Michigan, Stanford, and UNC.

Notes: "Mean GRE-V" is the mean GRE-Verbal score.

provide background for the later examination (in Chapter Ten) of the relationship between forms of financial support and completion rates and time-to-degree, as well as material relevant to understanding interconnections among the factors that have shaped these graduate programs over the last 30 years.[11]

In the EHP fields, and in most of the rest of the humanities and social sciences, graduate students have long been supported primarily by some combination of: (1) fellowships, which offer stipends over and above tuition and fees; (2) teaching assistantships (TAs); and (3) their "own resources" (including personal savings, loan funds, academic or nonacademic employment other than a TA provided by the institution, and contributions by the student's family). Research assistantships, which are a major source of support in the sciences, are of negligible significance in these fields.

Patterns of financial support are often exceedingly complex within a single department, with students frequently receiving support from a variety of sources in any one year, with different financial aid packages made available to different students within the same entering cohort, and with the possibility of pronounced differences in support from one year of graduate study to the next. Differences in patterns of support among departments in a single university, across universities, and over time add additional layers of complexity.

---

[11]Unfortunately, there is little national data available on patterns of graduate student support in the humanities. In contrast, there is a great deal of published information on financial support in the sciences and engineering. See, for example, National Science Foundation 1965–1971, 1977.

The graduate programs in the universities on which this chapter focuses exhibit marked differences in the amounts and forms of financial aid offered to graduate students. Princeton and Yale, for instance, have had relatively small entering cohorts and relatively large amounts of fellowship funds. Columbia has had larger entering cohorts and fewer fellowships to award than almost any of the other universities in this set. As a result, more than half of its students have had to rely primarily on their own resources, in spite of the fact that Columbia has also made considerable use of TAs. Cornell is an intermediate case, in that it has had relatively small entering cohorts and has used a more balanced mix of fellowships and TAs than have most of the other universities. (We have no data on patterns of financial support at the fifth university, Harvard.)

It is also instructive to examine financial aid patterns at several other universities that are included in later parts of this study. The University of Chicago has made little use of TAs because of the relatively small size of its undergraduate college and its traditional methods of instruction. At the same time, it has had fewer funds available for fellowships than, say, Princeton or Yale, and therefore has had to expect relatively large numbers of its graduate students to provide their own resources. The three public institutions in the Ten-University data set (the University of California at Berkeley, the University of North Carolina and the University of Michigan) define yet another general case: All have relied heavily on TAs and also have comparatively large numbers of students dependent on their own resources.

Broad differences in what one might call the institutional structure of graduate student financial support can be summarized by showing the relative numbers of entering students in each university (in the 1977–1981 entering cohorts) who relied primarily on each of the three main types of financial support (Table 5.1).[12]

TABLE 5.1
Distribution of Primary Source of Support by University, EHP Total, 1977–1981 Entering Cohort (percent)

| University | Primary Source of Support | | | |
	Fellowships	TAs	Own Support	Unknown
Berkeley (1978–1981)	9.6	24.9	65.5	—
Chicago	33.9	0.0	60.1	5.6
Columbia	25.9	12.4	61.8	—
Cornell	49.3	42.7	8.0	—
Michigan (1978–1981)	32.4	30.8	34.8	1.6
Princeton	72.9	5.3	21.8	—
UNC	2.9	54.0	35.6	7.9
Yale	78.4	0.0	16.3	5.3

Source: Ten-University data set.

Notes: The figures for Berkeley and Michigan are for students in the 1978–1981 cohorts only. See Appendix A for the definition of primary support and a discussion of related aspects of the Ten-University data set.

---

[12]Because of attrition, classifying forms of financial support by primary source may overweight somewhat forms of support received disproportionately in the early years of graduate study. However, financial support data organized by stage of graduate study exhibit roughly similar patterns.

Despite these variations—which correlate with such variables as the sizes of graduate and undergraduate programs and financial resources—the patterns of financial support at all of these universities have been affected by broadly similar forces over time. Figure 5.7 shows the shifts in the relative importance of each of the three primary sources of financial support at the three universities for which we have the best data spanning some reasonable number of years (Chicago, Cornell, and Princeton).

FELLOWSHIPS

During the expansionary years of the 1960s, the number of fellowships increased both absolutely and relative to the sizes of entering cohorts of graduate students in the EHP fields. Beginning roughly with the entering cohort of 1970, there was a precipitous drop in this critically important source of funding. At Chicago, Cornell, and Princeton, the aggregate percentage of all students who were able to rely primarily on fellowship aid fell from 65 percent in the 1969 entering cohort to just under 40 percent in the mid-1970s.[13]

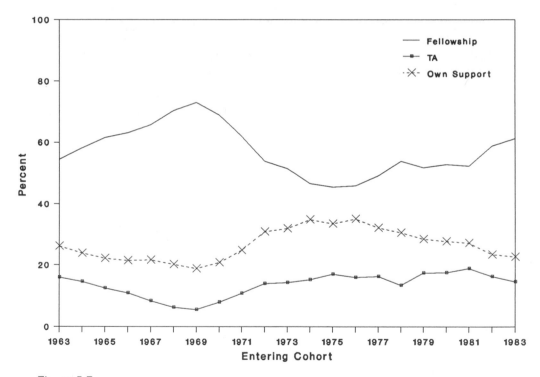

Figure 5.7
Distribution of Support by Primary Source, EHP Total, 1963–1983 Entering Cohorts (three-year moving averages)
Source: Ten-University data set. Data are from Chicago, Cornell, and Princeton.

---

[13]The changes across these three quite different universities (with different structural levels of fellowship support, as shown in Table 5.1) were remarkably uniform. At Chicago, the percentage of students relying primarily on fellowship aid fell from 51 percent in the 1969 cohort to roughly 30 percent for the 1974–1975 cohorts; at Cornell, the corresponding percentage fell from 81 percent to 51 percent; at Princeton, the drop was from 88 percent to 60 percent. Three-year moving averages have been used to smooth out idiosyncratic movements from one year to the next.

The birth and subsequent demise of large, externally funded fellowship programs was the dominant factor shaping this roller-coaster pattern. During the late 1950s and 1960s, major national fellowship programs benefiting students in the humanities and social sciences were sponsored by the federal government under the National Defense Education Act (NDEA) and by the Woodrow Wilson National Fellowship Foundation, the Ford Foundation, and the Danforth Foundation—to mention only some of the most prominent efforts. By the mid-1970s, virtually all of these programs had terminated. Even though the number of enrolled graduate students had also declined, the magnitude of lost funding was so substantial that universities were faced with an enormous shortfall as they projected the costs of sustaining high-quality graduate education. Moreover, these were years of general budgetary stringency for all of higher education.[14]

At least a partial recovery in fellowship assistance occurred in the early 1980s. This was not the result of any general resurgence in external support from either the private sector or government. Rather, it was due primarily to increased internal commitments to fellowship assistance, made possible in some instances by successful fund-raising campaigns and by concurrent decisions to allocate more institutional resources to graduate education.

When we examine patterns of financial support during separate stages of graduate study, we find exactly the same trends in fellowship support. We also find that fellowship support has been consistently more common during the first and second years than during the dissertation stage of graduate study (Figure 5.8).[15]

TEACHING ASSISTANTSHIPS

The data shown in Figure 5.7 indicate that TAs have not been a *primary* source of support for many students at Chicago, Cornell, and Princeton during any recent period. This result, while accurate as stated, is misleading, since TAs have become an important source of financial support for graduate students in the EHP fields—and an important source of teaching for most universities. The relatively small number of students shown in Figure 5.7 as depending primarily on TAs is partly attributable to the fact that two of the three universities represented on that figure (Chicago and Princeton) have made less use of TAs than almost any of the other major universities included in our study. (The following discussion covers a broader set of universities, including some that make more use of TAs.) Moreover, a considerable number of students at many universities may have held TAs even though they did not rely on TAs as their primary source of support.

The changing role played by TAs can be understood best by looking closely at support provided to students in individual universities and considering the number of students who held TAs (whether or not TAs were the primary source of support). In the 1960s, when more and more fellowships were becoming

---

[14]See Cheit 1971.

[15]In collecting data on financial support at separate stages of the graduate education process, a different question was asked—namely, whether the student received *any* fellowship support: (a) during the first or second year of graduate study, and (b) during the ABD or dissertation stage. All entering students were used as the base in calculating the percentage of students receiving any fellowship support during the first or second year of study, while only those students who had reached ABD status were included in the base used to calculate the dissertation-stage percentages.

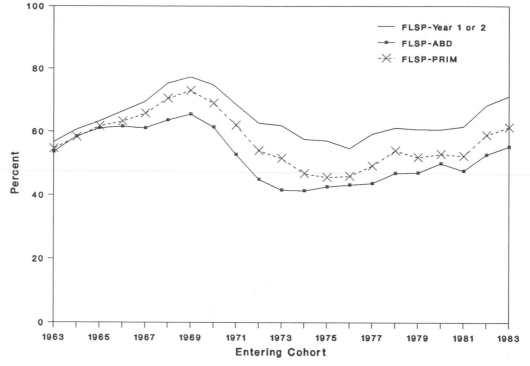

Figure 5.8

Distribution of Fellowships by Stage of Graduate Study, EHP Total, 1963–1983 Entering Cohorts (three-year moving averages)

Source: Ten-University data set. Data are from Chicago, Cornell, and Princeton.

Notes: "FLSP-PRIM" is the percentage of the entering cohort relying primarily on fellowship support throughout graduate study; "FLSP-Year 1 or 2" is the percentage of the entering cohort receiving any fellowship support during either the first or second year of graduate study; "FLSP-ABD" is the percentage of students reaching the ABD stage receiving any fellowship support during the dissertation stage.

available, the percentage of entering students who held TAs during their first or second years actually declined at Cornell (the only university for which good data exist for those years), reaching a low of 19 percent for the 1969 entering cohort.

It was in the 1970s, when fellowship support decreased precipitously, that universities became much more dependent on TAs to support both entering graduate students and those working on their dissertations (Figure 5.9). By 1980 at Cornell, for instance, TAs were held by over 60 percent of all EHP students during *both* the early years of graduate study and the dissertation writing stage. The rate of increase in the prevalence of TAs was at least as great at Yale, and a roughly similar pattern is also evident for Columbia. Data for three major public universities reflect this same general pattern, even though the figures for two of them (Berkeley and Michigan) cover limited periods of time.

By the early to mid-1980s, this increasing dependence on TAs appears to have run its course.[16] Still, there is no evidence of a return to the levels characteristic

[16]In fact, at a number of institutions, the percentage of students holding TAs actually declined. At Yale, for example, the percentage of all graduate students in the humanities holding TAs fell from a high of 55 percent in 1979–1980 to just about 50 percent in 1987–1988; similarly, the comparable

(continued)

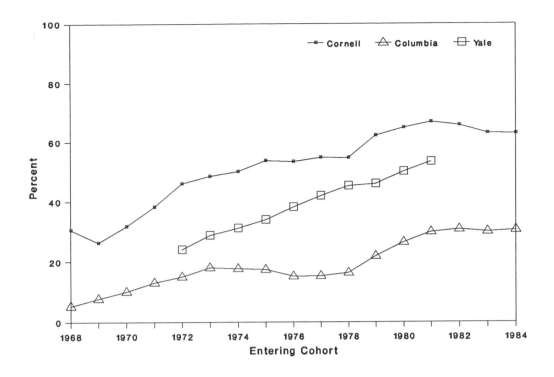

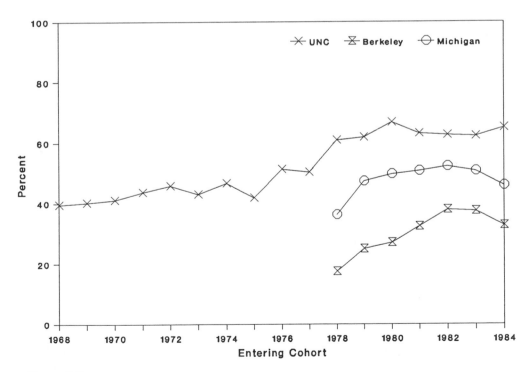

Figure 5.9
Distribution of Teaching Assistantships by University, EHP Total, 1968–1984 Entering
Cohorts

Source: Ten-University data set. These data are averages of two underlying percentages: (1) the percentage of the entering cohort holding a teaching assistantship during either the first or second year of graduate study; and (2) the percentage of students reaching the ABD stage who held a teaching assistantship during this stage.

of the 1960s and early 1970s. Increased reliance on TAs is one of the most important changes in patterns of graduate student support over the last two decades.[17]

OWN SUPPORT

As shown in Figure 5.7, the relative importance of graduate students' own support naturally tends to be a mirror image of support provided through fellowships and TAs. This pattern holds regardless of whether the self-support is primary or total and regardless of the stage of graduate study. Figure 5.10 shows the 1963–1983 percentages of students depending primarily on their own support across all stages of graduate study, the percentages depending entirely on their own support (that is, holding neither a fellowship nor a TA) during the first two years of graduate study, and the percentages depending entirely on their own support while writing their dissertations. The paths traced by the three graphs are virtually congruent.

Students entering graduate school in the mid-1970s were particularly dependent on their own resources, and special efforts were made in those years to spread the limited institutional resources available for graduate students as equitably as possible. Some universities experimented with a modified form of a financial means test,[18] and some also were more willing to admit students who had a demonstrated capacity to pay their own way. The financial situation for graduate students then began to ease at least somewhat, first because of the increasing use of TAs, and then because of new infusions of fellowship funds in the early and mid-1980s.

One final point should be made concerning all graduate students in the EHP fields. As a group, they receive much less financial support, and much less assurance of financial support, than students in, say, science or engineering. Among all recipients of doctorates in the humanities in 1989, personal resources (loans, earnings, family contributions) accounted for 52 percent of primary support. The comparable percentage in the physical sciences was 18 percent.[19]

For large numbers of students in the EHP fields, there has been (and is) real uncertainty about the amount or form of financial aid that may be available. For

---

percentage at Cornell fell from 53 percent in 1980–1981 to 45 percent in 1988–1989. These percentages differ from the data presented earlier in that they cover all students enrolled during the years in question, rather than being organized by entering cohort. Also, they include students holding TAs in pre-ABD years other than the first and second years. The Yale data are from an internal report published by the Ad Hoc Committee on Teaching in Yale College on April 25, 1989 (the "Prown Report"). The Cornell data were kindly provided by Dean Alison Casarett.

[17]There are also some national data available from the Doctorate Records File, but these data provide information only for those students who completed PhDs and (in their published form) are organized by PhD cohorts. Still, they tell a story generally consistent with the one reported here. Among 1978 recipients of PhDs (the first group for which we have data consistent with later data), 61 percent of all recipients in the humanities had held a TA at some time during their graduate careers. This percentage rose steadily until about the mid-1980s, reaching levels of 68 percent to 69 percent; it then rose again to 72 percent for the 1989 PhD cohort. Since the overwhelming number of these 1989 recipients were in graduate school in the late 1970s and early 1980s, these data do not speak directly to patterns in recent years. See *Summary Report 1988*, Appendix A, Table 3.

[18]The Graduate and Professional School Financial Aid Service (GAPSFAS), administered by the Educational Testing Service (ETS), was (and is) the primary instrument used to assess the financial need of graduate students.

[19]*Summary Report 1990*, 26, Table 11. Tabulations of this kind are available from the Doctorate Records File only for the most recent years (after the survey questions were modified in 1987), and no time series can be constructed.

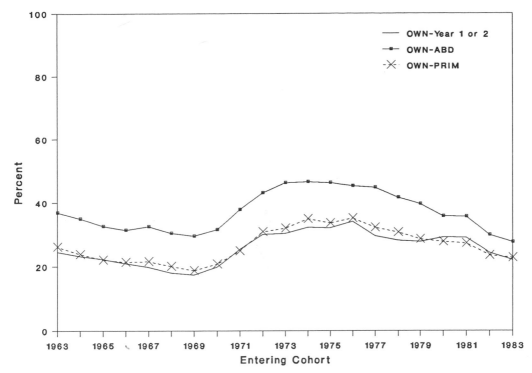

Figure 5.10
Distribution of Self-Support by Stage of Graduate Study, EHP Total, 1963–1983 Entering Cohorts (three-year moving averages)

Source: Ten-University data set. Data are from Chicago, Cornell, and Princeton.

Notes: "OWN–PRIM" is the percentage of the entering cohort relying primarily on personal resources throughout graduate study; "OWN–Year 1 or 2" is the percentage of the entering cohort receiving neither fellowship nor teaching assistantship support during either the first or second year of graduate study; "OWN–ABD" is the percentage of students reaching the ABD stage receiving neither fellowship nor teaching assistantship support during this stage.

many of these students, progress toward the PhD is not only an academic endeavor but also a pursuit of the resources necessary to continue their studies.

INTERPRETATION OF INSTITUTIONAL DEVELOPMENTS

The patterns just examined are more comprehensible if viewed in a broader institutional context. For example, it would be helpful to have a fuller sense of what led to the considerable growth in the number of graduate students serving as teaching assistants, beginning in about 1970 and continuing into the 1980s. Also, it is important to consider the broader array of factors that influenced faculty size and workload over this period.

Expansion of Undergraduate Enrollments: 1970–1985

An exceptionally important fact is that all five universities for which we conducted detailed analyses of graduate programs experienced a significant expansion in undergraduate enrollment after about 1970 (Appendix G, Table G.5–4). From 1972 on, the paths of undergraduate and graduate enrollment diverged dramatically (Figure 5.11).

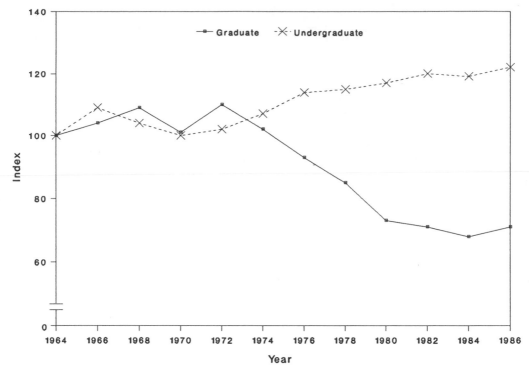

Figure 5.11
Undergraduate Enrollment and Graduate Enrollment, EHP Total, 1964–1986 (Index: 1964 = 100)
Source and Notes: See Appendix G, Tables G.5–3 and G.5–5.

At the same time that graduate enrollment was falling at an unprecedented rate, undergraduate enrollment continued to increase steadily. The total number of BAs conferred by these five institutions rose from 5,758 in 1970 to 7,200 in 1982, and by 1988 it had increased by more than 30 percent, to 7,565 (Appendix G, Table G.5–4).[20] Increases in absolute numbers of this magnitude are highly consequential, and since much of the growth occurred during just that period when universities were confronted by difficult financial conditions that often required major cuts in programs, the combination of circumstances frequently led to severe strains. The declining numbers of graduate students and graduate courses were at best only a slight help in alleviating these pressures, since the number of PhD candidates is far smaller than the number of undergraduates at nearly all research universities.

A further complication is that changes in scale at the undergraduate level usually create much more difficult teaching problems than comparable changes

[20]The reasons for such widespread expansion at the undergraduate level between about 1970 and the mid-1980s are too complex to discuss at length. Two all-male institutions in our Ten-University group (Princeton and Yale) became coeducational during this period, which alone produced a 30–40 percent expansion in their undergraduate enrollment. Others (such as Columbia and Chicago) had very small undergraduate colleges relative to their graduate schools, and decided to achieve a better balance by allowing their colleges to grow. (Chicago went from 468 undergraduate degrees conferred in 1970–1971 to 661 in 1984–1985, and Columbia went from a low point of 1,117 in 1976–1977 to 1,392 in 1984–1985.)

at the graduate level. For example, an academic department that gradually reduces its enrollment of entering graduate students from 40 to 20 (or expands it from 20 to 40) can take the time needed to redesign its graduate courses and plan its teaching assignments in ways that can be reasonably well calibrated. However, an institution that expands the size of its undergraduate entering class by even 10 percent in a relatively brief time (quite apart from the 45–60 percent increases characteristic of three of our five institutions over this period) may find, for example, that an additional 60–80 first-year students have suddenly chosen to enroll in introductory French, and that four to six more sections are needed in the course, with each section meeting three or more times a week. First-year courses in English composition, large survey courses with discussion groups, and science courses with laboratory components may experience similar problems.

Hence, even moderate relative changes in the size of an undergraduate student body can generate—precipitously—an immediate need for sizable numbers of additional teachers in various academic specialties, largely because undergraduates have great latitude in deciding which courses to take and which academic field to choose as a major. This relatively unfettered process of choice is of course utterly different from arrangements at the graduate level, where students are admitted into specific departments, and where each department controls admissions on an annual basis, with serious consideration given to the declared interests of students in different subfields.

In short, a pronounced expansion of the undergraduate student body can create a range of effects; some can be trivial in their impact, while others may be close to overwhelming—especially in popular departments where enrollments are high and teaching demands are already heavy. One obvious consequence can be a decline in the ratio of faculty members to undergraduates, and a concomitant need to identify sources of additional instructors to meet some portion of the increased teaching needs.

Increases in Teaching Assistants and Changes in Faculty Teaching Assignments

The dramatic and steady loss of externally funded fellowships in the humanities and social sciences undoubtedly played a central role in shaping graduate education over this period. This shortfall in external support, combined with rising undergraduate enrollments and tight financial constraints, led to a considerable growth in the number of graduate students who began to be employed as teaching assistants. Not only were many more graduate students used as teaching assistants, but the students so engaged tended to teach more semesters (or years) than their counterparts in previous decades, and they were sometimes asked to work more hours per week (or per semester). By the mid-1980s, teaching assistants constituted a large, identifiable cadre of prepro-fessionals who were now playing an integral role in the educational programs of many major research universities.

This structural shift—related both to the need to find new sources of financial support for graduate students and to the increased need for teachers of undergraduates—was extremely important. The expanded role of teaching assistants contributed to the creation of a significantly different teaching profile than that which had characterized most universities in earlier years, and it was one of the most significant legacies of the complex circumstances that prevailed in American higher education during the 1970s and much of the 1980s.

These years were also marked by a related shift in the pattern of faculty teaching assignments, which was initially stimulated by competition for the most able young academics in the early to mid-1960s. Since then, senior faculty have tended to play less of a role (except as lecturers) in many introductory undergraduate courses. Meanwhile, highly sought-after junior faculty have been given the opportunity to teach at least some courses that were "their own."

Shifts in the structure of teaching assignments often operated quite independently of shifts in overall faculty teaching loads, although they did eventually contribute to a more substantial use of teaching assistants. For example, an assistant professor who earlier might have taught four hours of sections in one or two introductory undergraduate courses might subsequently have been given the opportunity to teach a research seminar, a lecture course (more rarely), or both. Each of the new courses could involve two teaching hours per week, but potentially much more preparation time than for four hours of sections. The faculty member's total number of class hours would not have changed, but the university would have been faced with the need for other teachers to take on the introductory classes once taught by the assistant professor.

When resources were relatively plentiful and universities were still expanding (and hiring more faculty), most institutions were able to manage the new dynamics created by this changing pattern of teaching assignments. But financial constraints began to tighten quite significantly in the 1970s, and it became clear that new strategies would have to be adopted. Reversing (or at least modifying) recently established teaching assignments was one possible way of responding, but this proved difficult to accomplish except on the margin. Moreover, this approach alone would not have been sufficient to cope with the marked expansion in size of the undergraduate body that was then taking place. The need to serve these additional undergraduates and the need to provide graduate students with some fresh source of financial support in the face of declining external fellowship awards reinforced each other. Together, they gave strong impetus to the structural changes in teaching arrangements and patterns of graduate student support that we have been discussing.

Faculty Growth in the 1980s

The main impulses and underlying conditions that led to the eventual expansion of faculty numbers during the 1980s are implicit in what has been said thus far. First, the student population increased because of the rise in the aggregate number of undergraduates at these institutions. Although the creation of many more teaching assistantships met some of the increased undergraduate teaching demands, changes in the pattern of faculty teaching assignments were simultaneously creating additional staffing needs. Meanwhile, sustained financial problems required some reductions in faculty size during the 1970s.

Concurrent with these developments, new fields of knowledge and new approaches in established fields continued to evolve. A beginning was often made in some of the areas in question, such as neurobiology, materials science, molecular biology, computer science, comparative literature, modern linguistics, and a variety of related humanities and social science fields that were becoming more interdependent. But it was rare when much more than a beginning could be made, simply because the resources were not ordinarily available to provide the necessary faculty positions, facilities, sophisticated equipment, or library materials.

In other words, a protracted period of restraint with respect to the development of the formal curriculum, of new programs, and of many research efforts was one of the major by-products of the financial difficulties that characterized the 1970s and early 1980s. Consequently, when more funds became available again, most universities moved actively to undertake a great deal of academic rebuilding. One task was simply to recoup lost ground by improving faculty-student teaching ratios and redressing some of the teaching needs that had developed through expanded enrollments, especially in departments with large numbers of undergraduates. An equally important objective was to regain the initiative in exploring (and establishing on a more secure basis) those rapidly developing fields of knowledge that had, in effect, been placed "on hold" for many years.

Increases in faculty staffing levels within the EHP fields were in fact achieved in recent years (Figure 5.12), but the adjustments have been modest, especially when seen in the context of previous cuts in numbers of faculty and subsequent increases in undergraduate enrollment. The faculty index dropped about 10 percent between 1973–1975 and 1978–1980 (and faculty staffing in 1974 was almost certainly reduced from an earlier peak). By 1988–1990, the number of masthead faculty was 7 percent above the 1973–1975 level. Still, this increase was a good deal less substantial than the associated rise of 14 percent in the number

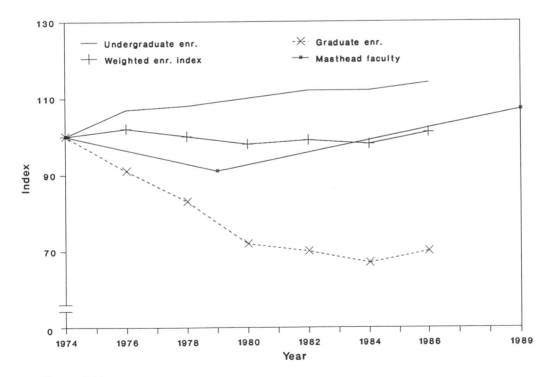

Figure 5.12
Enrollment and Number of Masthead Faculty, EHP Total, 1974–1989 (Index: 1974 = 100)
Source and Notes: See Appendix G, Table G.5–5.

of undergraduates. If simultaneous drops in the enrollment of graduate students are taken into account and given some reasonable weight (such as one graduate student equals two undergraduates, from the standpoint of demands on teaching time), the resulting weighted enrollment index reached a level close to that of the faculty index in the most recent years for which data are available.

The faculty masthead statistics, it should be emphasized, can only be viewed as a rough index of actual teaching strength measured in numbers of full-time equivalent (FTE) faculty. We suspect (but have no corroborating data) that the growing tendency to cross-list faculty, and to use visitors, may mean that increases in masthead faculty overstate the true increase in FTE faculty. On the other hand, growth in the number of TAs surely absorbed a considerable share of the added undergraduate teaching duties created during the 1970s and early 1980s (although teaching assistants were not normally in a position to help with graduate teaching or the development of new fields and programs). To know whether the net result of these various shifts represented an average decrease in faculty teaching loads would require a systematic examination of a large number of factors, and there is neither the space (nor the data) to attempt such an analysis in this study—which is, in any case, concerned primarily with graduate education rather than with faculty matters per se.

All that can be tentatively suggested here is that generalizations concerning faculty teaching loads during this period should be tested against the entire set of complex changes that have taken place in universities, not only over the last ten years but over the much fuller historical period reaching back to the late 1950s and early 1960s. It seems plausible, for example, that faculty teaching loads (especially in larger and more popular departments) underwent periodic oscillations. They may well have increased during the 1970s—despite added numbers of teaching assistants—as compared to the previous decade. If there were subsequent reductions in the 1980s, then one must decide which baseline to use as a point of comparison before arriving at far-reaching conclusions.

Finally, as we have seen, the distribution of teaching assignments (including the much greater role of teaching assistants) has had an extremely significant effect on the educational process. This development is at least as consequential as any other change related to pedagogy at major universities.

It may be helpful to underscore those points that bear most directly on issues to be addressed in later chapters. As we think about the effectiveness of graduate education today, some of the developments described above are especially relevant. These include the massive loss of external support for graduate fellowships, the much greater reliance on TAs (both to provide students with financial assistance and to increase undergraduate teaching capacity), and the weak job market in academia since the early 1970s.

Job market effects plainly had overarching consequences. The relative lack of attractive positions in colleges and universities discouraged many individuals from considering academic careers at all, and it caused these Tier I universities to scale back the size of their graduate programs. In addition, the depressing outlook for opportunities in academia had an understandably deleterious effect on those students who elected to pursue PhDs. There was no certainty of employment after a long and expensive apprenticeship. Consequently, there was much less inducement to move ahead expeditiously in order to finish the degree.

Both attrition and time-to-degree were undoubtedly affected by this difficult set of circumstances. The next four chapters consider in detail the changes that have occurred in these measurable outcomes of graduate programs, as they are associated with field of study, type (scale) of graduate program and university, and time period. Then, in Chapters Ten and Eleven, we analyze the effects of financial support and national fellowship programs on completion rates and time-to-degree before turning to a broader discussion of the critical roles played by departmental requirements, structures, and conventions.

PART TWO

Factors Affecting Outcomes

CHAPTER SIX

Completion Rates and Time-to-Degree: Concepts and General Patterns

GRADUATE EDUCATION has many "outcomes," and the decision to focus much of this study on completion rates and time-to-degree implies no lack of concern for the qualitative dimensions of teaching and learning at the graduate level. What graduate students learn is, of course, most important of all—with "learning" understood to encompass not just the substance of particular fields or disciplines, but also ways of forming questions, thinking about issues, and communicating ideas. The process by which students come to understand and master the essential material, methods, and practices of graduate study is by no means easily understood or described, and we would not want to strip all of the mystery from it even if we could.

At the same time, the subtleties of the process, and the impossibility of defining the full range of outcomes with precision, cannot be allowed to immobilize us. There are useful insights to be gained from detailed analysis, and in this chapter we define and illustrate two key concepts: completion rates and time-to-degree. Surprising—and significant—results emerge from this analysis.

One major finding is that only about *half* of all entering students in many PhD programs eventually obtain doctorates (frequently after pursuing degrees for anywhere from six to twelve years). In sharp contrast, it is common for completion rates in leading professional schools of business, law, and medicine to exceed 90 percent. And it is not just the plight of the ABDs (students who have completed "all but dissertation") that has caused completion rates in PhD programs to be low; attrition has been high at all stages of graduate study. Moreover, attrition appears to have increased over the last three decades.

A second major conclusion pertains to trends in time-to-degree. The time spent by the typical graduate student in earning a doctorate has risen in the last two decades, but much less dramatically than is generally believed. Comparing median time-to-degree values for students grouped by the year in which the PhD was conferred (which is the usual practice) produces a misleading picture of reality. We correct for the statistical bias introduced by this PhD-year approach and show that time-to-degree has increased relatively modestly. Properly measured, time-to-degree is seen to have increased by about 10 percent over the last 20 years, rather than by 30 percent as widely reported. Of course, any increase is cause for concern, simply because time-to-degree in the arts and sciences is already so long. But lengthy time-to-degree is a problem with old (and deep) roots; it is not a new phenomenon.

Taken together, relatively low completion rates, lengthy time-to-degree, and large commitments of time by many who start but do not finish doctoral programs mean that the average societal investment of student time in graduate study is high in relation to the number of PhDs conferred. The concepts introduced in this chapter allow us to pinpoint the stages in the process where disproportionately large amounts of student time are invested—sometimes without commensurate gain.

COMPLETION RATES

Concepts

The main complication in studying all aspects of the effectiveness of graduate education—and certainly in defining and measuring completion rates—is that students pursue doctorates, on and off, over many years. For a small number of students, pursuit of the PhD becomes almost a lifelong endeavor.[1] Since the percentage of each entering cohort who earn the doctorate rises as the number of years since entry increases, we have elected to work primarily with two kinds of completion rates: minimum completion rates (MCR) and truncated completion rates (TCR).[2]

Perhaps the easiest way to define these rates is by using a set of hypothetical numbers. Suppose that:

- 100 students enter graduate study in English in 1972;
- By 1978, 50 have earned doctorates, 25 have ceased pursuing the doctorate, and 25 are still enrolled;
- By 1982, 60 have earned the doctorate, 32 have ceased pursuing the doctorate, and 8 are still enrolled.

The minimum completion rate is the percentage of the entering cohort who have earned the doctorate *by a specified year*. In this example, the MCR was 50 percent in 1978 and 60 percent in 1982. Obviously, the MCR rises with the number of years that have elapsed between entry to graduate school and the year in which the measurement is made. Because of its simplicity and wide applicability, this is the completion rate that is used most frequently in this study, and whenever we refer simply to the completion rate (with no modifier), this is the concept that is being used. The MCR can be misleading, however, especially when time series comparisons are being made, and that is why we also use the concept of the truncated completion rate.

The truncated completion rate is the percentage of an entering cohort who earned the doctorate *within a specified number of years from entry to graduate study*. In this example, the TCR after six years was 50 percent in 1978, as well as in 1982 and all subsequent years, since it is impossible for more students to earn degrees within a time interval once the limit of that interval has been exceeded. If the cutoff number of years had been set at ten rather than at six, the TCR could not have been measured in 1978 and would have been 60 percent in 1982 and all subsequent years. Truncated completion rates are particularly useful when comparisons are being made between outcomes for recent cohorts (who will

---

[1] Almost all graduate schools can cite legendary cases. Lori Thurgood of the National Research Council (NRC) tells us that one recipient of a PhD in 1989 had earned a BA in the 1920s, and that three others had earned their BAs in the 1930s (personal communication).

[2] Mention should also be made of a third measure, the conditional completion rate, which assumes that students still enrolled will eventually complete their doctorates in the same proportions as those who have already finished (that is, either received doctorates or decided not to pursue the PhD any longer).

have had only a limited number of years in which to complete their studies) and outcomes for earlier cohorts.

A further complication in computing completion rates concerns transfers. The completion rates that we calculate on the basis of the Ten-University data set treat all students who left each university as having dropped out, even though some may have completed a PhD after transferring to another university (see Appendix A).[3] The National Fellowship data set, on the other hand, tracks individual students who moved from one university to another (see Appendix B), and the completion rates including transfers will, of course, be somewhat higher than the corresponding completion rates that do not allow for transfers.

General Patterns

While there have been a number of case studies, surprisingly little has been written about the general pattern of completion rates.[4] Harmon's classic study, *A Century of Doctorates*, which contains a wealth of information on many aspects of doctoral education, is entirely silent on this critically important measure of outcomes.[5] Nor do current government publications contain any data of this kind. A main reason for the lack of regularly published national data is presumably that completion rates can be calculated only if records are maintained for all students who begin doctoral study, whereas the practice has been (for understandable reasons) to concentrate on those students who actually earn doctorates, allowing those who drop out to disappear from sight.[6]

Berelson's (1960) major study of graduate education does not mention completion rates until two-thirds of the way through the book and then treats the subject briefly. The only data cited are very rough estimates derived from questionnaires distributed to graduate deans and graduate faculty members; the deans apparently put completion rates at about 60 percent, while the graduate faculty gave much higher estimates of about 80 percent. Berelson wrote: "If the estimates of the graduate faculty are more nearly right, then there is not much to the problem of attrition at all."[7] Berelson's conclusion that time-to-degree was

---

[3]"Internal" transfers also occur occasionally within universities. For instance, a student who enters a graduate program in history may shift fields and subsequently earn a doctorate in political science or anthropology. With rare exceptions, our completion rates allow internal transfers within the arts and sciences. However, if a student moves from pursuit of a doctorate in a field such as economics to a field outside the arts and sciences (such as business), that student is recorded as no longer pursuing a PhD even though the student may eventually earn a doctorate in business.

[4]There is, however, an early study by Tucker, Gottlieb, and Pease (1964). This was an ambitious effort to analyze completion rates at 24 universities using longitudinal data for students who were enrolled between 1950 and 1953. Mention should also be made of case studies at Northwestern by Goldberg (1984), at UCLA by Benkin (1984), and at Berkeley by Nerad and Cerny (1991). In addition, there is a more recent study of completion rates at three universities by Zwick (1991). Two other older case studies (Decker 1973; Pogrow 1978) found that within individual institutions, completion rates are affected by the amount of time (if any) taken off by students prior to beginning graduate study. The effects of part-time status on completion rates is considered by Ott, Markewich, and Ochsner (1984) in a case study at the University of Maryland and discussed more generally by Widnall (1988).

[5]Harmon 1978.

[6]The primary source of national data is the Doctorate Records File, which is based on questionnaires obtained from recipients of doctorates in the years in which the doctorates are conferred.

[7]Berelson 1960, 167–68. Berelson suspects that the faculty remember less well and have more selective recollections (recalling the "successes" among their graduate students most readily). Some

a much greater problem than attrition had a major effect on the shape of the Ford Foundation's program for support of doctoral education (see Chapter Eleven).

Breneman, on the other hand, evaluating the Ford Foundation Graduate Program, recognized the severity of the problem of attrition and felt that "the emphasis of the FFGP [Ford Foundation Graduate Program] had been misplaced." He noted the peculiar complacency with which this issue was approached: "Attrition rates of 50 percent or more would be a scandal in any professional school, but seem to be accepted in doctoral education as part of the natural order."[8] Given the paucity of data, there is no way of knowing whether completion rates were higher or lower prior to World War II than they are today. However, we now know a great deal about completion rates over the last 25 or 30 years, and these findings are discussed in detail in subsequent chapters. Here it is sufficient to note that at the nine universities for which we have reliable data for the cohort entering in 1972–1976, the minimum completion rate (in 1989) for all students in our six fields of study was 48.1 percent.[9]

These nine universities are by no means representative of the full range of institutions awarding doctorates. Moreover, there are significant differences in completion rates within this rather select group—particularly among fields of study (see Chapter Seven) and between "larger" and "smaller" graduate programs (see Chapter Eight). A key question is the extent to which these differences can be attributed to differences in selectivity, in resources available to support graduate students, and/or to programmatic aspects of graduate study that in turn are related to characteristics of various fields, to the scale of graduate departments, or to other aspects of the organization of graduate work (see Chapters Ten, Twelve, and Thirteen).

While no one would suggest that the patterns characteristic of professional schools could—or should—apply to PhD programs, it is important to note the magnitude of the differences in completion rates. Leading schools of law, medicine, and business consistently report completion rates higher than 95 percent, and a detailed examination of experiences at particular professional schools supports these claims.[10]

---

of the presidents and graduate deans quoted by Berelson regarded the attrition problem as much more serious than he did. President Benjamin Wright of Smith College described attrition as "inordinately high"; Jacques Barzun of Columbia is quoted as deploring "the appalling waste on both sides: of student energy, hope, and money, and of faculty time and effort"; and Dean Hugh Taylor of Princeton called on graduate schools to "make a thorough examination of conscience in this matter . . ." (p. 167).

[8] Breneman 1977, 54.

[9] The nine universities are University of California at Berkeley, Chicago, Columbia, Cornell, Harvard, Michigan, University of North Carolina at Chapel Hill (UNC), Princeton, and Stanford. (Yale, which is also included in the Ten-University data set, is excluded from this calculation because it did not provide data for economics, mathematics, or physics.) The overall completion rate reported in the text was obtained by pooling all the data for individual students. In effect, this procedure gives each student (rather than each department) an equal weight.

We present the data for the 1972–1976 cohort for two reasons. First, we have complete data for a reasonably large number of universities. Second, students who began their graduate studies in 1972–1976 had between 10 and 14 years to complete their work, and the minimum completion rate should therefore be a reasonably reliable measure of the ultimate completion rate.

[10] At Harvard Law School, for example, of the 2,214 students who entered the JD program between 1983 and 1986, all but 33 had received the JD degree by March of 1990—an overall completion rate of 98.5 percent (data supplied by Charlotte M. Robinson, Registrar). The Johns Hopkins University

A different perspective is obtained by looking at BA programs. Here, the picture is much more complex and, in its largest statistical dimensions, more like the pattern for doctoral candidates in the arts and sciences than like the one for students pursuing professional degrees. A recent study of 28,000 students in four-year colleges who graduated from high school in 1980 found that less than half (40.7 percent) had earned BA degrees within six years.[11] Plainly, there are monumental differences between PhD programs in the arts and sciences and BA programs in educational objectives, the range of student interests and aptitudes, pedagogy, and the expectations of the highly diverse set of institutions conferring BA degrees. Accordingly, the broad similarity in overall completion rates is probably best viewed as nothing more than an interesting coincidence.

A more apt comparison is with completion rates at highly selective undergraduate colleges. A recent study by the Consortium on Financing Higher Education (COFHE) shows median completion rates of about 90 percent five years after entry at the eleven universities included in their survey; 86 percent at the seven coeducational colleges; and 83 percent at the four women's colleges. These completion rates provide an interesting contrast to the 50 percent rate for PhD candidates at similarly selective universities.[12]

Trends in Completion Rates

The lack of comprehensive national data is a handicap in examining trends in completion rates. It is possible, however, to construct a time series based on completion rates for two specific groups of students: (1) those men who enrolled in PhD programs in our six fields between 1962 and 1976 within the Ten-University set of institutions; and (2) those men who won Danforth Fellowships between 1958 and 1976.[13]

The stories told by the university and fellowship data sets are remarkably consistent. In both cases, completion rates declined, especially for cohorts of students who started graduate study in the latter half of the 1960s (Figure 6.1). The same data, along with data for National Science Foundation (NSF) Fellows,

---

School of Medicine and the Yale University School of Medicine supplied comprehensive data for students entering between 1962 and 1982 (1972 and 1982 in the case of Yale), and completion rates were consistently in the 95 to 97 percent range (data supplied by Mary E. Foy, Assistant Dean and Registrar at Johns Hopkins and Judy Mayo, Registrar at Yale).

[11]Porter 1989, 3–4. As these figures are derived from surveys of students (not institutions), they presumably do permit transfers from one BA program to another.

[12]See Consortium on Financing Higher Education 1990, Table 1.2. These undergraduate completion rates are for classes entering between 1981 and 1983. Institutions participating in this study included, among others, Amherst College, Brown University, Bryn Mawr College, Carleton College, and Cornell University. A full list is presented in Appendix 1 of the COFHE report.

In a study that compares completion rates achieved at various levels of study within a single institution, the University of North Carolina, Naylor and Sanford (1982) found rates of 75.7 percent for undergraduates, 98.7 percent for professional schools, and 59.4 percent for doctoral candidates.

[13]We calculated separate completion rates for men in this instance because it seemed desirable to examine the question of trends in completion rates separately from the question of the relationship between gender and completion rates, which we consider in Chapter Seven and subsequent chapters (especially Chapter Eleven). The participation of women in graduate education and trends in their completion rates have been affected by additional factors beyond those affecting trends in completion rates for men.

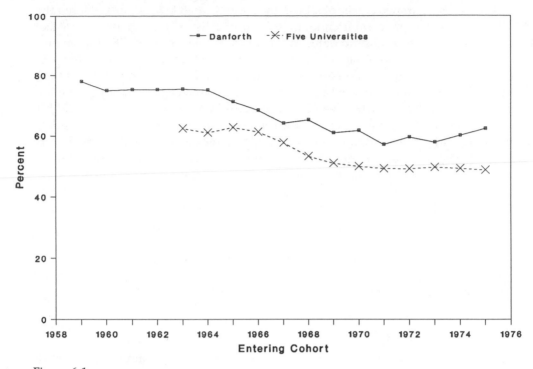

Figure 6.1
Trends in Men's Minimum Completion Rates, 1958–1976 (three-year moving averages)
Source: National Fellowship data set and Ten-University data set. University data are from Berkeley, Chicago, Cornell, Harvard, and Princeton.
Notes: The absolute levels of the completion rates for the university average have been adjusted (downward) to reflect the differing availability of data over these time periods, and it is only the trend that should be noted.

can be summarized for five-year cohorts (Table 6.1). The falloff in completion rates is again evident, with the most marked decline—about ten percentage points—between the 1962–1966 and 1967–1971 cohorts.[14] (Comparison of completion rates across data sets is left to later chapters.)

It is surely no coincidence that this rather abrupt drop in completion rates occurred at almost exactly the same time that labor market prospects for academics deteriorated markedly. As academic jobs became more difficult to obtain, some graduate students in the arts and sciences no doubt elected to change their career plans, thus increasing attrition rates. The movement at this time into fields such as business and law is evident in trends in enrollment, and it would be very surprising if the same considerations failed to affect the thinking of at least some students who had already entered graduate programs. Concurrent reductions in the availability of fellowship support presumably had reinforcing effects.[15]

---

[14]We do not plot NSF data on the time series figure because these data are unavailable on a year-by-year basis.

[15]The evidence persuades us that the end of draft deferments in 1967 precipitated a sharp fall in the proportion of BA recipients who later earned PhDs, but we are unable to distinguish between

TABLE 6.1

Trends in Minimum Completion Rates, Men Only, All Fields, 1958–1976 Entering Cohorts (percent)

Entering Cohorts	Danforth Fellows	University Average	NSF Fellows
1957–1961	76.7	—	—
1962–1966	73.2	62.9	82.0
1967–1971	63.0	51.6	75.2
1972–1976	59.8	48.9	78.1

Source: Ten-University and National Fellowship data sets.

Notes: Data for Danforth Fellows include transfers. The university average is for Berkeley, Cornell, Chicago, Harvard, and Princeton. The absolute levels of the completion rates for the university average have been adjusted to reflect the differing availability of data over these time periods, and it is only the trend that should be noted. NSF data are for Quality Group I (see Appendix B).

Stages of Attrition

Students leave programs of graduate study—either on their own volition or because of the decisions of others—at various stages along the path toward the PhD, and the personal, economic, and institutional consequences vary considerably depending on the point in the process at which attrition occurs. In collecting data from individual universities, an effort was made to determine how many students in each cohort left graduate school: (1) before starting the second year of study ("pre-2ndYr"); (2) after starting the second year, but before completing all requirements for the PhD other than the dissertation ("Other Pre-ABD"); and (3) after completing all requirements but the dissertation ("ABD").

The pattern of attrition is somewhat different from what might have been expected, since so much of the literature on attrition has focused on the ABD group.[16] The experiences of the 1972–1976 cohort at six universities (Berkeley, Chicago, Cornell, Princeton, Stanford, and the University of North Carolina) indicate that more than twice as many students left these PhD programs prior to achieving ABD status as left after achieving ABD status (Figure 6.2).[17]

The same data permit us to calculate conditional probabilities for these students—the likelihood that they will move to the next stage in the doctoral

---

effects on sizes of entering cohorts and effects on completion rates. (See the discussion in Chapter Three of the effects of both labor market conditions and the draft on changes in the number of PhDs conferred.) For discussions of changes in academic labor markets during these decades, see Cartter (1976), Freeman (1975b), and Hansen (1986). For discussions of changes in financial support available to graduate students, see the sources cited in Chapter Five.

[16]See, for example, Berelson 1960, especially 171–72; and Stern 1985.

[17] We present data for these six universities only (rather than for all ten universities in the data set) because of the limitations in the data for the other universities described in Appendix A. These data are for all six fields of study. The somewhat porous barrier between MA and PhD programs at some of these universities affects these calculations; however, efforts were made to exclude students registered in MA-only programs (see Appendix A).

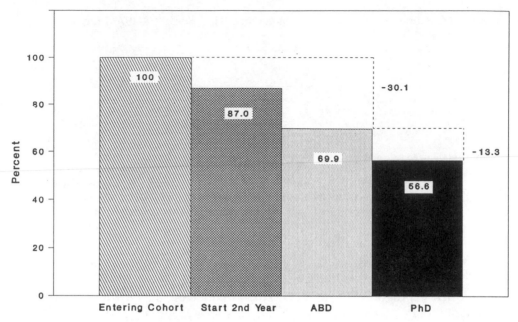

Figure 6.2
Attrition by Stage, Six-Field Total, 1972–1976 Entering Cohort (percent of entering cohort)
Source: Ten-University data set. Data are from Berkeley, Chicago, Cornell, Princeton, Stanford, and UNC.

education process, given their having reached the previous stage. These probabilities are as follows:

- Achieving second year—87.0 percent;
- Achieving ABD, given second-year status—80.3 percent; and
- Achieving PhD, given ABD status—81.0 percent.[18]

Students who had achieved ABD status had roughly an 80 percent chance of finishing a dissertation and receiving a PhD. While ways should be found to improve the likelihood of an individual's completing this final requirement for the PhD, it should be recognized that this stage of attrition was no more consuming than the prior stages, since only about eight out of ten students starting the second year achieved ABD status. In terms of "wastage" of both money and time, the attrition at later stages is, of course, more significant. Ideally, those who eventually drop out should do so as early in the process as possible in order to minimize this loss.[19] For this reason, attention focused on

---

[18]The product of the three conditional probabilities is the total completion rate, that is, 87.0 percent times 80.3 percent times 81.0 percent equals 56.6 percent.

[19]Surveying experience at Berkeley in the 1950s and 1960s, Stark commented: "It is possible to justify a relatively slow PhD program for those who complete it. Perhaps it takes 8 years to properly train scholars. But it seems difficult to justify such a slow process of weeding out those who fail to achieve a degree. . . . The fact that so many remain four, five, even 10 years before becoming academic casualties thus seems odd" (Stark 1966, 13).

the ABDs is understandable, but it should not obscure the large amount of attrition concentrated during the earlier stages of graduate study.[20]

There is no evidence of significant trends in the *relative* amounts of attrition that occurred at the various stages of graduate study. The general pattern described above has been quite consistent across cohorts from the late 1960s into the 1980s despite the overall drop in completion rates.

An entirely different way of thinking about attrition focuses on what some see as a distinction between "voluntary" and "involuntary" attrition. Obviously, there are extreme cases in which it is clear that a student leaves a graduate program because the student has decided, entirely voluntarily, that pursuit of the doctorate is not for him (her). There are also clear cases in which students who wish to continue fail to meet requirements and are dismissed.

In a great many cases, however (most cases, we suspect), it is impossible to invoke this simple dichotomy. Students having trouble with their studies wonder if they have done the right thing in going to graduate school and eventually decide to leave—is their departure voluntary or involuntary? Changing job prospects may affect both the views of students concerning the desirability of continuing in graduate school and the standards that the department thinks it appropriate to enforce. Decisions by students to withdraw may be influenced heavily by lack of financial aid, which in turn may reflect some (often unknown) combination of lack of resources available to the department and lack of confidence in a student's potential.

These are but a few examples of the complex interactions that often occur among the expression of personal preferences by the student for continuing in the program, judgments about the student's performance by the department, and external forces that affect both. What is "voluntary" and what is "involuntary" becomes murky indeed, and it is hard to see what criteria can be relied on to tell anyone where to draw the line. It is much more sensible, in our view, to focus on when attrition occurs, which can be determined objectively.

TIME-TO-DEGREE

Concepts

The time required to complete the doctorate can also be measured in a number of ways. The three principal measures are:

- Total time-to-degree (TTD);
- Elapsed time-to-degree (ETD); and
- Registered time-to-degree (RTD).

Total time-to-degree is the number of years between the awarding of the BA and the awarding of the PhD. It is the longest measure. Elapsed time-to-degree is the number of years between entry to graduate school and the awarding of the PhD. It does not count the years that a student took off between finishing undergraduate work and beginning graduate study. Registered time-to-degree is the number of years that a student was actually registered in graduate school before receiving the PhD. It excludes both the years that a student took off before

---

[20]For a discussion of attrition at different stages of graduate education, see Tucker, Gottlieb, and Pease (1964), Benkin (1984), and Tinto (1991).

beginning graduate study and the years that a student took off during graduate study.

The most reliable data are available for TTD and ETD, and these are the measures used in this study. In general, we calculate median TTD and ETD for groups of recipients of doctorates, not mean values. Means are less satisfactory measures of central tendency because they are influenced more heavily by extreme observations—such as the rare student who takes more than 20 years to earn the doctorate.

This study makes little use of registered time-to-degree. There has been, in any case, a relatively stable relationship between RTD and TTD over at least the last two decades. The limited data available suggest that RTD has accounted quite consistently for at least two-thirds of TTD. There is some evidence of a slight upward drift between 1967 and 1986 in time taken off between completion of the BA and entry to graduate school, as measured by the difference between TTD and ETD; but in most fields, there has been a more-than-offsetting decline in time not enrolled after the start of graduate studies. In short, differences over time and across fields in TTD and in ETD represent real differences in the time devoted to graduate study.[21]

General Patterns

In contrast to the lack of systematic study of completion rates, the time lapse between the BA degree and the PhD has been the subject of many studies over many decades. The richness of the Doctorate Records File allows examination of detailed figures at the national level going back to 1920, and both Berelson and Harmon discussed time-to-degree at great length.[22]

Berelson regarded the duration of graduate study as the third most important issue in graduate education (after preparation of college teachers and the national distribution of opportunities for graduate study). He reported that median TTD for students finishing their degrees in all fields in 1957 was eight years. This seemed an unusually long time to him then and it would seem very long to many of us today—if we had not been told that the comparable figure in 1989 was 10.5 years.[23]

This figure seems curiously high, and we first became concerned about its interpretation when we compared it with figures for the graduate students who attended the individual universities that we have studied in great detail. Median ETD was just 6.7 years for the 1972–1976 entering cohort of graduate students in the six-field, nine-university universe defined earlier. If we assume that these graduate students averaged one year off between completion of the BA and the start of their PhD programs (which seems an upper limit, given the national

---

[21]The most reliable data on RTD, and its relation to TTD, are reported in *Summary Report 1989*, Table I and Appendix Table 2. Comparable data for earlier years may be found in corresponding tables in the *Summary Reports* for those years. The numbers published in these reports are medians. A second source of data is Tuckman, Coyle, and Bae (1990, 13 and Appendix Tables 1, 2.1, 2.2, 2.3, and 2.4). Tuckman's data, which are also derived from the Doctorate Records File, are means, and they are presented for just two years (1967 and 1986), but they have the advantage over the first source of implicitly including ETD as well as RTD and TTD. RTD is an even higher proportion of TTD (more than 70 percent) in this second source of data. A compilation of data from these two sources is presented in Appendix G, Table G.6–1.

[22]Berelson 1960, 156ff.; and Harmon 1978, 54ff.

[23]Berelson 1960, 157; and *Summary Report 1989*, 1.

data, summarized in Appendix G, Table G.6–1), median TTD for this group of students would have been something like 7.7 years.

This is obviously a much lower number than the national figure of 10.5 years, and it is undoubtedly influenced by a combination of institutional, departmental, and other factors discussed in later chapters. However, at least part of this difference is attributable to a general problem of statistical bias, which we explain and quantify in the next section in the context of a discussion of trends in time-to-degree over the last two decades.

Trends in Time-To-Degree

Recently, a great deal of attention has been directed to what have been described as major increases in the time lapse between the BA and the PhD since 1970. For example, the NRC's *Summary Report 1988* stated that "time-to-degree has increased approximately 30 percent over the last 20 years . . . ."[24] The basis for this conclusion, and for accompanying expressions of concern, is readily apparent when the published median TTD figures for all recipients of doctorates (U.S. residents only) are graphed (Figure 6.3).

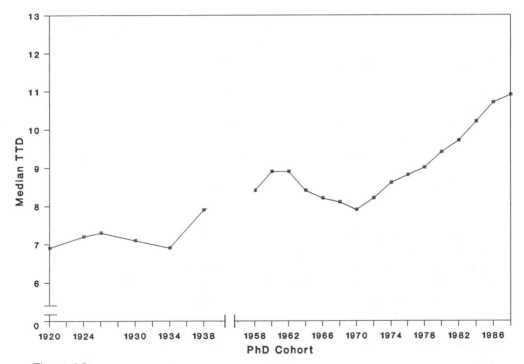

Figure 6.3
Median Total Time-to-Degree, All Fields, 1920–1988 PhD Cohorts

Source: All data are from *Doctorate Records File*: for 1920–1957, from Harmon (1978), and for 1958–1988, from special tabulations.

Notes: Data from 1940 to 1958 are not included because the output of PhDs was affected significantly by World War II.

---

[24]*Summary Report 1988*, 21. See also Tuckman, Coyle, and Bae (1990, 21). Commentators in the *New York Times* (Berger 1989, 1) and the *Chronicle of Higher Education* (Evangelauf 1989, 1) have seized on these findings to issue new calls for reform of graduate education.

Broadly speaking, three "eras" stand out: (1) the early years, extending through World War II and up to 1962, when TTD rose; (2) the expansionary years of the 1960s, extending up to about 1970, when TTD apparently fell back to earlier levels; and (3) the most recent period, dating from the early 1970s, when TTD seems to have risen steadily and significantly in essentially all fields of study.

We were skeptical about the steepness of the apparent trend in the recent period. A 30 percent increase in time-to-degree over a period of two decades is extraordinary—and decidedly at odds with the results obtained from our Ten-University data set. Median ETD for our six fields was not only at a lower level throughout the same period, but also appears to have risen much more modestly over approximately the same time interval.[25]

After much discussion with demographers, we determined that the steepness of the apparent trend indicated by the published national data is mainly a statistical artifact. It is neither real nor explainable in terms of differences between the two data sets. Rather, it is a direct consequence of a methodological decision concerning the way in which students are grouped for the purpose of calculating median time-to-degree. Under certain conditions, a substantial bias results from grouping graduate students by the year in which they *completed their PhDs*, rather than by the year in which they *entered graduate school*.

More specifically, the PhD-completion-year method of aggregation (hereafter called simply the PhD-cohort method) leads to a significant bias in any period when there have been fairly rapid and very pronounced swings in the sizes of entering cohorts. And we have seen in previous chapters that the postwar years were in fact marked by a great expansion in graduate education, followed by a sharp contraction during the 1970s, and then by a subsequent plateau. The apparently steep trend in median TTD shown by the published national data has been affected drastically by these unprecedented shifts in the size of entering cohorts. Neglect of this consideration has seriously distorted the reported trends in TTD.

The technical explanation in support of this significant conclusion, which has obvious implications for current discussions of doctoral education, is presented in Appendix D.[26] The discussion below is a more intuitive explanation of the problem of bias and an attempt to describe the "true" trend.

Each PhD cohort is comprised of members of various entering cohorts, who all completed their PhDs in the same year, but who certainly did not all *begin* their graduate studies at the same time. For example, some students will have completed their PhDs in four or five years, and others may have taken eight or nine (or more) years. If the cohorts of entering graduate students shrink over time (as they did, beginning in the early 1970s), successive PhD cohorts will contain fewer "fast" finishers and an increasing proportion of "slow" finishers. The progressively smaller entering cohorts yield smaller and smaller numbers of fast finishers to the relevant PhD cohorts. It also takes more years for the slow finishers in these smaller entering cohorts to affect the medians for the PhD cohorts.

---

[25]Median ETD at these universities in English, history, and political science rose somewhat more rapidly (about 15 percent during the 1970s) than median ETD for all six fields—but at nothing like the rate for the humanities shown by the national data (roughly 40 percent). A detailed analysis of the trend in TTD in the national data for the humanities can be found in Appendix D.

[26]See also Bowen, Lord, and Sosa (1991), where this material was published originally.

Thus, during a period when the size of entering cohorts is diminishing quite rapidly, the mix of students in any given graduate student population, and thus in successive PhD cohorts, necessarily drifts toward a longer median time-to-degree. In other words, the change in the relative proportions of slow finishers and fast finishers carries with it a built-in bias in the direction of the former group.[27]

The solution to this problem is to organize the data by entering-year cohorts (or by year of BA, which usually correlates quite closely with year of entrance to graduate school). Under the BA-cohort (or entering-cohort) method of grouping students, we track all of the individuals in each BA cohort as a single set, identifying precisely how long it takes every individual member of the cohort to earn a doctorate. Thus, median time-to-degree is no longer affected by shifts in the size of successive cohorts.

Each entering cohort of students, therefore, will have its own distribution of time-to-degree values and its own median. The absolute size of the cohort, in and of itself, has no effect on the distribution (or the median). Furthermore, each of these distributions organized by entering cohorts is independent of the sizes of neighboring entering cohorts. Once a cohort has matriculated, the distribution of time-to-degree values (and thus the median) is based on the experiences of its own defined population, and the characteristics of previous or subsequent entering cohorts cannot affect median time-to-degree.

Application of this entering cohort approach to the same set of national data grouped earlier by PhD cohorts shows that the true increase in TTD for all fields has been on the order of 10 percent, not 30 percent, over the last 15 to 20 years (Figure 6.4). While the absolute levels of time-to-degree for national data are still higher than comparable figures based on the Ten-University data set, the true increases in the median are now seen to have been modest in both sets of data.

This is the empirical basis for concluding that the published trends in TTD, based on data for PhD cohorts, are misleading. Any lengthening of the duration of graduate study is a serious matter and should be addressed, but we should be careful not to exaggerate either the newness of this problem or its magnitude.

A related technical point needs to be made. If the PhD-cohort method of aggregation is used and if there is a constant rate of change in the size of entering cohorts, an equilibrium will eventually be reached where the observed trend in median TTD (that is, the rate of increase or decrease) will be accurate.[28] This abstruse proposition has direct relevance to the interpretation of historical data, since the 1920s and 1930s were decades of steady and consistent growth in graduate student populations. Because of the relatively constant rate of change (about +7 percent per year),[29] rough judgments concerning trends in TTD can be based on these data even though they are grouped by the years in which students received PhDs.

Median TTD for all fields was 7.1 years in 1930, 6.9 years in 1934, and 7.9 years for students receiving their degrees in 1938. Thus, there appears to have been a

---

[27]This is a direct application of "Stable Population Theory" (Coale 1972). Special credit goes to Ansley Coale of the Office of Population Research at Princeton University, who saw immediately the relevance of this proposition from the field of demography to our problem and explained why the observed medians for PhD cohorts would be affected by the rate of change in the size of the entering cohorts. The tables in Appendix D illustrate in detail the process outlined in the text.

[28]See Appendix D. However, the overall levels of TTD still will be biased.

[29]Harmon 1978, 1.

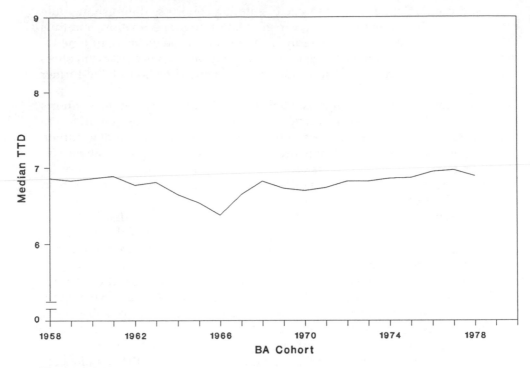

Figure 6.4

Truncated Median Time-to-Degree, All Fields, 1958–1980 BA Cohorts

Source: Special tabulations from Doctorate Records File.

Notes: The data have been truncated at 10 years for each BA cohort to permit consistent year-to-year comparisons. See discussion of truncation in Appendix D.

significant lengthening of TTD during the second half of the 1930s, following an earlier decade of rough stability (TTD was 6.9 years in 1920 and 7.2 years in 1924). The upward creep in TTD then seems to have continued, with the median TTD for recipients of PhDs in all fields reaching 8.4 years in 1958 and 8.8 years in 1960 and 1962 before beginning the descent that accompanied the expansion of the 1960s (refer to Figure 6.3).

This interpretation of the historical record is consistent with the conclusions reached by Harmon, who pinpointed the major source of this early increase in median TTD when he observed: "It is noteworthy . . . that the time required by the fastest 10 percent, or even 5 percent, has drifted gradually upward over almost the whole of the 1920–1974 period . . . ."[30] In other words, the percentage of all recipients of doctorates earning their degrees in four years or less fell slowly but steadily during the 1930s, from a high of fully 26 percent of all recipients in 1924 to 20 percent in 1938, before plummeting to 10 percent in 1958 (Table 6.2).

Some individuals in all time periods and all fields have completed their PhDs in three to four years (most commonly in fields such as mathematics). However, experience indicates that the actual norms in most of the arts and sciences have generally fallen within a six- to ten-year range at most institutions. It is difficult

---

[30]Harmon 1978, 55–56. For whatever reason, Berelson (1960) interpreted the same data differently. He apparently did not see the upward creep in time-to-degree in earlier decades, and wrote that "duration has remained essentially constant in the past twenty years . . ." (p. 157).

TABLE 6.2
Distribution of Total Time-to-Degree, All Fields and Universities, 1924–1958 (percent)

TTD	1924	1930	1938	1958
4 years or less	26.2	23.0	20.4	10.3
5–7 years	26.5	30.2	27.1	30.9
8–10 years	18.1	18.0	18.3	26.4
11–13 years	10.6	9.6	12.8	8.7
14–16 years	6.4	7.5	9.0	7.5
17 years or more	12.1	11.7	12.4	16.1
Median (years)	7.2	7.1	7.9	8.4

Source: Special tabulations from Doctorate Records File.

Notes: Data are for all doctorates (U.S. and non-U.S. residents) and are based on the years in which PhDs were received. "Unknowns" (which range from 0 to 4 percent of the overall total) have been removed from the bases in calculating these percentages.

to see how this evidence can be reconciled with the recurrent assertions that three to four years should be the stated norm for the PhD.[31] We return later to the policy question of what might constitute achievable objectives for students in various fields, and how doctoral programs might be modified to reach realistic goals.

CUMULATIVE COMPLETION RATES

Although we have discussed completion rates and time-to-degree as separate topics, they can be examined simultaneously by calculating cumulative completion rates (which show the percentage of each entering cohort that earned PhDs within three years, within four years, within five years, and so on). The cumulative completion rate rises toward the ultimate completion rate, and the more rapid the rise, the lower the median time-to-degree.

Figure 6.5 shows the cumulative completion rates for three successive entering cohorts at eight universities. The 1967–1971 cohort shows the relationship between completion rates and time-to-degree over the longest time interval. After rising steeply over the interval between 3 and 11 years of elapsed time, the curve plateaus at a completion rate of approximately 60 percent. Although a small number of students may complete the degree after more than 11 years have passed, the minimum completion rate at this number of years is a reasonably good approximation of the ultimate completion rate. Median TTD can be derived as the x value (approximately 5.5 years in this case) that

---

[31]See Ziolkowski (1990, 187ff), for a good discussion of the history of this idea. Ziolkowski notes that in 1916 the Association of American Universities proposed that "the period of post-graduate study should ideally be three years"; in 1964, the Association of Graduate Schools and the Council of Graduate Schools issued a joint statement suggesting that "the entire course of study [leading to a PhD] should normally involve no more than three or, at most, four years beyond the baccalaureate." Berelson's 1960 study also reaffirmed the three- to-four year norm for full-time study, and asserted that the longer TTD often reported resulted mainly from time spent after the BA outside of graduate study (pp. 158–162). However, recent survey data rebut Berelson's proposition by indicating that RTD is much greater than three to four years, and that it has increased in recent years (Appendix G, Table G.6–1).

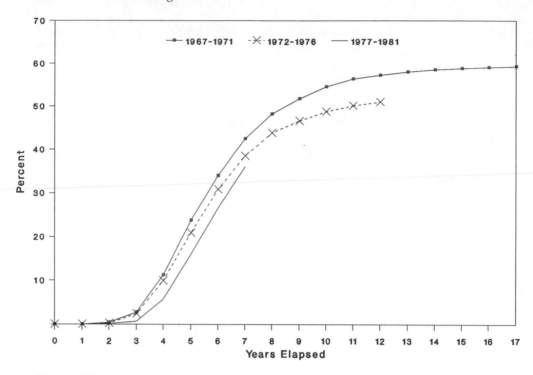

Figure 6.5
Cumulative Completion Rates, by Cohort Groups, Six-Field Total, 1967–1981 Entering Cohorts

. *Source*: Ten-University data set. Data are from Berkeley, Chicago, Columbia, Cornell, Harvard, Princeton, Stanford, and UNC.

corresponds with the point on the *y*-axis midway between 0 percent and the horizontal asymptote.

The concept of the cumulative completion rate is useful in projecting TTD and completion rates for more recent cohorts. In Figure 6.5, the completion rate for the 1972–1976 cohort appears to be plateauing at a level decidedly lower than the completion rate for the 1967–1971 cohort, and the median TTD is higher. For the 1977–1981 cohort, we can calculate cumulative completion rates with confidence for only seven years (since 1988 is the last year for which we have data). In general, the 1977–1981 curve is slightly below the level of the curve for the previous cohort, but the truncated completion rates in the seventh year are very similar for the two cohorts.

Detailed analysis of a large number of separate cumulative completion rate curves (for different fields of study, universities, and time periods) has led to a final, somewhat esoteric finding. All of them fit (very closely) a common functional form.[32] In other words, while the parameters (mean, standard

---

[32]The function found to fit the observed data for time to completion can be described by the equation $g(x) = c * f(x)$, where c is the proportion of doctoral candidates in a cohort who will eventually earn degrees and $f(x) = k * \exp [-a (x - d) - \exp \{-b(x - d)\}]$ is an extreme value probability density function. This model permits a succinct description of the time-to-degree process in terms of the ultimate completion rate, c, and the mean and standard deviation of the fitted time-to-degree distribution. The latter two statistics are derived from the parameters k, a, b, and d of the function $f(x)$. The model and the maximum likelihood procedure used to estimate these

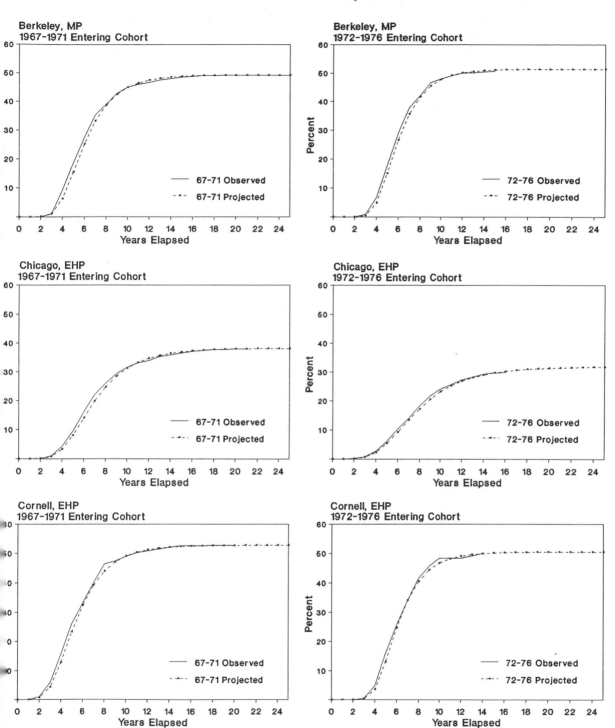

Figure 6.6

Projected and Observed Cumulative Completion Curves, Selected Universities and Cohorts

Source: Ten-University data set.

Notes: See text and footnote 32 for explanation of projection method.

deviation, and ultimate completion rate) differ, these curves have the same generic "shape." An analogy may help explain what is meant. While elephants come in various shapes and sizes, all have trunks and big ears, and look more or less alike. The fact that a common form of equation describes well so many cumulative completion curves (even though some have higher ultimate completion rates, some shorter median time-to-degree, and so on) means that all of them appear to be elephants. No zebras are in evidence.

These similarities in appearance can be illustrated by comparing the actual observations with the estimated values generated by the curves fitted to these observations (Figure 6.6). The closeness of the fits is visually evident.

An intriguing aspect of the function used to fit these data is that it suggests a possible behavioral interpretation of the shape of the cumulative completion rate distribution. The function can be thought of as combining a normal distribution of time-to-degree for those students who finish expeditiously with a series of three or four delays that may represent specific stumbling blocks that impede the progress of other students. In the absence of specific behavioral data, it is possible only to speculate on the nature of the delays. For example, the first delay might be problems encountered in achieving candidacy; the second, problems associated with finding a topic and getting dissertation research under way; the third, difficulties associated with gaining final approval of the dissertation and waiting for the next commencement.[33]

A more obvious use for these fitted curves is to project completion rates and time-to-degree for recent cohorts, thereby providing at least some sense of the direction and magnitude of changes in these measures over the last decade and a half. These projections are incorporated in subsequent chapters into broader discussions of trends (particularly with regard to the total time investment made by students, per doctorate received). There is some evidence of an upward drift in this measure of the "time cost" of a doctorate, but the patterns are so divergent that discussion of them is best postponed until after we consider other data related to fields of study and type of university attended. It is to differences in outcomes by field of study that we turn next.

---

parameters for a cohort effectively capture most of the information in the observed completion time distribution while taking account of the truncated nature of the data. The closeness of the fits is borne out by high P-values for the appropriate likelihood ratio and Pearson chi-square goodness-of-fit tests.

A special case of the above extreme value distribution was used by Ansley Coale in his study of age at first marriage and underlies what is known as his model nuptiality schedule (Coale and McNeil 1972).

[33]To illustrate how this kind of "decomposition" of the data would be estimated (using four exponential delays with the normal distribution), consider the entering cohorts in the EHP and MP fields at Berkeley in 1979. For the EHP fields, the imputed normal distribution has a mean of 5.44 years and a standard deviation of 0.58 years. The implication is that with no delays, the successful students took on average about 5.5 years to finish. The four exponential delays have means of 1.97, 0.75, 0.46, and 0.33 years, which together with the 5.44 normal mean build up to a total average time-to-degree of 8.94 years. For the MP grouping, the mean and standard deviation of the "normal" time-to-degree are 4.00 and 0.28, respectively, and the means of the exponential delays are 1.79, 0.68, 0.42, and 0.30 years. This comparison suggests that mathematicians and physicists who experience no significant delays finish 1.5 years sooner than comparable EHP students and that, in general, they do not prolong their studies (the MP standard deviation is 50 percent of that for the humanities).

CHAPTER SEVEN

Fields of Study

BOTH COMPLETION rates and time-to-degree vary more systematically with field of study than with any other variable. This simple statement has major implications for any study of graduate education, since it stimulates careful consideration of the reasons why these measurable outcomes are so dependent on a student's choice of subject. What are the key characteristics of various fields of study that affect completion rates and time-to-degree so markedly? Have relationships between fields of study and these measures of outcomes changed over time? Do they differ for men and women? Are fields of study serving mainly as proxies for the availability of financial aid?

A major conclusion of this chapter is that differences in completion rates and in time-to-degree are intrinsic to graduate study in these fields. They are present in all time periods and within all groups of universities for which we have data. They exist when we examine outcomes for men and women students separately and when we control for differences in the availability of financial aid (by looking only at winners of national fellowships).

The distinct patterns that emerge when we examine the extent and pervasiveness of field-specific differences in completion rates and time-to-degree are related, we believe, to such factors as the degree to which a field lends itself to abstract (theoretical) analysis, the prevalence of collaborative research, the extent to which unusual language skills are required, and the need to travel and work with archives in order to complete the research required for a dissertation. They may also be related to differences in assumptions, expectations, and other conventions that are less easily specified.

COMPLETION RATES

The lack of national data has inhibited efforts to compare completion rates systematically across fields of study. While our research has also been circumscribed by the absence of a national data base, longitudinal data collected for this project from individual universities in six specific fields of study and from national fellowship programs for even more fields (albeit with fewer students in each) together provide much more extensive information than has been available previously.[1]

---

[1] See Appendix A for a discussion of the Ten-University data set and Appendix B for a discussion of the National Fellowship data set. As noted in Appendix A, not all universities were able to provide full information for all time periods. In this chapter, we rely heavily on data provided by a subset referred to as the "eight-university" group: University of California at Berkeley, University of Chicago, Columbia, Cornell, Harvard, University of North Carolina at Chapel Hill (UNC), Princeton, and Stanford.

The completion rates presented here for specified fields are averages of the minimum completion rates at the individual universities (with each university weighted equally), rather than pooled data for all students. This procedure ensures that the overall eight-university completion rates for fields of study will not be dominated by the experiences of the largest programs.

(continued)

The Basic Pattern by Broad Field

Between 1967 and 1976, over 13,000 students enrolled in PhD programs in the six specific fields included in the university data set. English and history represent, at least roughly, the humanities; economics and political science, the social sciences; and mathematics and physics, the natural sciences. Completion rates for students grouped in this way provide a useful point of departure. They range from 50 percent in English and history to 55 percent in economics and political science to 65 percent in mathematics and physics.[2]

The persistent pattern of completion rates across broad fields of study is illustrated clearly in Figure 7.1.[3] The ordering of fields is entirely consistent, regardless of data set: Natural sciences always has the highest completion rate, followed by social sciences, and then humanities. Moreover, the extent of differences in completion rates is quite uniform across data sets. For example, the completion rates for the humanities are consistently from 22 to 28 percent lower than the corresponding rates for the natural sciences.

Financial aid has always been more readily available in the sciences than in the humanities and social sciences.[4] For that reason, it is particularly striking that the same pattern of completion rates that holds for all enrolled students in the eight-university group (reflecting differences in financial support across fields) also holds for the subgroup limited to recipients of awards given by national fellowship programs (each of which generally provided equivalent awards to winners in different fields of study). Holding the fellowship package constant in

---

In noting the lack of large-scale, national studies of differences in completion rates by field, we do not mean to imply that there is no literature on this subject. There have been several studies focused on an individual university, one on a small set of universities (Zwick 1991), and an early study of 24 universities (Tucker, Gottlieb, and Pease 1964). There have also been studies of particular fellowship programs (e.g., Mooney 1968).

[2]There is reason to believe that these three pairs of fields serve as reasonably good proxies for the broader sets of disciplines that they represent. The National Fellowship data set, while smaller than the university data set, covers more fields and permits relevant comparisons. In the Woodrow Wilson fellowship program (which was the largest and most comprehensive in its coverage, with 2,150 awards made in the arts and sciences for the 1962–1966 cohort), the completion rate for English and history was 50.1 percent, as compared with 49.0 percent for all of the humanities. The rate for economics and political science was 55.8 percent, as compared with 53.7 percent for all social sciences; and the mathematics and physics rate was 74.2 percent, as compared with 71.8 percent for all natural sciences. Corresponding differences for other national fellowship programs were comparable (averaging about one percentage point).

[3]To isolate differences by field of study, we have rescaled the completion rates for doctoral recipients in different data sets, with the completion rate for mathematics and physics (MP) in the eight-university group used as the (arbitrary) reference point. In other words, the completion rate for the natural sciences in each fellowship program was set equal to the completion rate for MP in the eight-university group, and the completion rates for other fields were adjusted proportionately. (For example, if the MP rate in the eight-university group was 65 percent, and the rate for the natural sciences in another data set was 60 percent, all of the completion rates in the second data set would have been multiplied by 65/60.) This procedure was followed to avoid introducing too many kinds of differences at once. It would have been distracting to analyze here differences in levels of completion rates across data sets at the same time that we want to concentrate on relative differences related to field of study. Differences in outcomes within various types of universities are analyzed in Chapter Eight, and differences in outcomes across fellowship programs are examined in Chapter Eleven.

The same general ordering of fields of study is found in case studies of attrition. See, for example, Benkin 1984; Stark 1966; Rosenhaupt 1958; Nerad and Cerny 1991; and Zwick 1991.

[4]See Chapter Five and the references cited therein.

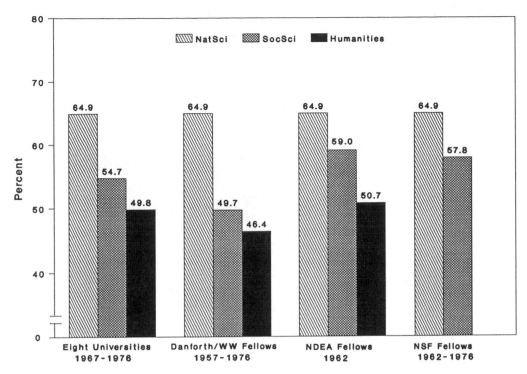

Figure 7.1
Minimum Completion Rates (Rescaled) by Broad Field, Selected Data Sets and Entering Cohorts

Source: National Fellowship data set and Ten-University data set. University data are from Berkeley, Chicago, Columbia, Cornell, Harvard, Princeton, Stanford, and UNC.

Notes: See footnote 3 for an explanation of rescaled minimum completion rates.

this way by no means eliminates field-specific differences in completion rates, which evidently reflect strong forces that go well beyond variations in financial support.

Gender is another variable that must be taken into account, since women historically have had generally lower completion rates than those of men and have been more heavily represented in the humanities and social sciences. The quantitative question is, to what degree are the generally lower completion rates in the humanities and social sciences due to the larger relative numbers of women students in these fields?

The evidence suggests that gender is only a very small part of the explanation for lower completion rates in the humanities and social sciences. Restricting the student population to men (top panel of Figure 7.2) reduces the difference in completion rates between the natural sciences and the humanities within the eight-university group from 23 percent (for men and women together) to 21 percent (for men only). A similar shift occurs in the cases of the Danforth/ Woodrow Wilson and NDEA Fellowships. Moreover, a similar pattern is found when the analysis is restricted to women (bottom panel of Figure 7.2). The inference is that the pronounced differences in completion rates across broad fields of study are, indeed, structural. They persist in almost precisely the same

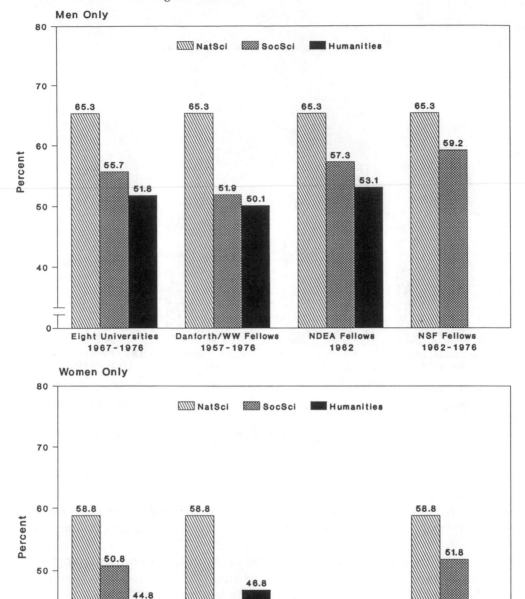

Figure 7.2
Minimum Completion Rates (Rescaled) by Broad Field and Gender, Selected Data Sets and Entering Cohorts

Source: National Fellowship data set and Ten-University data set. University data are from Berkeley, Chicago, Columbia, Cornell, Harvard, Princeton, Stanford, and UNC.
Notes: See footnote 3 for an explanation of rescaled minimum completion rates.

degree whether we look at men only, at women only, or at men and women together.[5]

These deep-seated differences in completion rates reflect, we believe, fundamental aspects of the content and organization of graduate work in the various fields of study. For example, graduate programs in physics tend to be more structured than graduate programs in history. Also, there is more agreement concerning appropriate methodologies in the sciences, and therefore less risk that a graduate student will become so perplexed that the PhD is never obtained. Much of the rest of this study explores such themes, sometimes in the context of findings pertinent to specific disciplines and sometimes in the context of university-wide patterns.

EHP Fields versus MP Fields

Examination of completion rates in specific fields illustrates again that political science seems to have much in common with English and history; thus it is often convenient to compare outcomes within the English/history/political science (EHP) cluster with outcomes in the mathematics/physics (MP) cluster.[6] As one would have expected, completion rates in the three EHP fields have been generally lower than completion rates in the MP fields (a proposition that holds for all data sets and cohorts available for scrutiny). The more intriguing finding is that the size of this gap widened appreciably between the entering cohorts of 1967–1971 and those of 1972–1976 (Table 7.1). While completion rates fell over this interval in both sets of fields, the drop was much more pronounced in the EHP fields.

The unusually large drop in completion rates in the EHP fields can be attributed to a variety of factors. The general deterioration in academic labor markets during the 1970s and early 1980s may have had a stronger impact on the morale of students in fields such as English and history, and caused more of them to leave graduate school, compared to the impact on students in the sciences, who had a wider range of employment options.[7] Also, the falloff in the availability of student aid was greatest in the humanities.

---

[5]No figures are shown for women in the NDEA program because the cell sizes were too small. For instance, the 1962 NDEA cohort included only nine women in mathematics and physics combined.

Two of the differences in completion rates by field of study shown in Figure 7.2 fail to pass the usual test of statistical significance at the 95 percent level of confidence. The exceptions are the differences in completion rates between the humanities and the social sciences (for men and for women) in the Danforth and Woodrow Wilson fellowship programs. The difference for the men yields a Z-score of just 1.18, and the difference for the women is in the wrong direction (a higher completion rate in the humanities than in the social sciences). The differences between the sciences and the humanities/social sciences are highly significant.

[6]A more detailed set of completion rates for individual fields of study is presented in Appendix G, Table G.7–1. We find, for example, that mathematicians have had appreciably lower completion rates than physicists (a relationship discussed below, when we also consider time-to-degree), that chemists have high completion rates, that economists have significantly higher completion rates than those of other social scientists, that there is no regular hierarchy of completion rates across the EHP fields, and that art history tends to have quite low completion rates.

The statistical significance of differences such as these could be determined by using multivariate logit regression analysis, with dummy variables for the data sets. We concluded, however, that the general tenor of the results seemed clear without these additional tests.

[7]Breneman (1970, 72) noted that students in the humanities and social sciences rely more heavily on academic placements than students in the sciences.

TABLE 7.1

Minimum Completion Rates in MP and EHP Fields,
1967–1976 Entering Cohorts (percent)

	Cohorts	
Fields	1967–1971	1972–1976
MP	66.8	62.7
EHP	55.1	45.0
Difference	11.7	17.7

Source: Ten-University data set. Data are from Berkeley, Chicago, Columbia, Cornell, Harvard, Princeton, Stanford, and UNC.

An entirely different kind of possible explanation concerns "internal" changes within the fields of study themselves. At a number of universities, departments of English, history, and political science had searching debates concerning the content and character of their fields, and both the debates themselves and the resulting curricular changes may have complicated graduate study for some doctoral candidates, while attracting and energizing others.[8]

Whatever the explanation for the disproportionately large drop in completion rates within the EHP fields, our analysis suggests that the relationship has now stabilized. The gap between completion rates in the MP and EHP fields remains very large, but it is not continuing to widen. This conclusion is based on a comparison of projected ultimate completion rates for the 1972–1976 and 1977–1981 entering cohorts. The projected rates for these two cohorts in the MP fields are the same (59.1 percent). In the EHP fields, the projected rate for the 1977–1981 entering cohort is actually slightly higher than the corresponding rate for the 1972–1976 cohort (47.2 percent versus 45.5 percent).[9]

Stages of Attrition

The major EHP-MP differential in attrition occurs at the dissertation stage, where losses were slightly more than twice as great in the EHP fields as in the MP fields. This relationship holds for both the 1967–1971 and 1972–1976 entering cohorts.[10] The underlying data, especially when expressed as conditional probabilities, provide further insight into the problem of "wastage." The conditional probability of completing a dissertation in mathematics or physics

---

[8]See Chapters Twelve and Thirteen for an extended discussion of this conjecture.

[9]The projected rates are the asymptotes of the curves fitted to the observations available for the 1972–1976 and 1977–1981 cohorts (see Chapter Six). In the case of the 1972–1976 cohorts, the projected ultimate completion rates are naturally quite close to the current minimum completion rates, since only a very small number of additional members of these cohorts are expected to earn doctorates in the future. In the case of the 1977–1981 cohorts, on the other hand, the projected ultimate completion rates are considerably higher than the current minimum completion rates. Projections were made separately for the MP and EHP fields within five universities for which satisfactory data were available (Berkeley, Chicago, Cornell, Princeton, and Michigan).

[10]Nerad and Cerny (1991) also find the differences in attrition by field to be greatest after advancement to candidacy; attrition at the ABD stage in sciences and engineering is roughly one-third as great as in the arts and other fields.

(once a student had achieved ABD status) was about 90 percent for both the 1967–1971 and the 1972–1976 cohorts. Among the EHP students, the corresponding conditional probability was 79 percent for the 1967–1971 cohort and just 75 percent for the 1972–1976 cohort.

These data also help to explain the particularly large decline in completion rates in the EHP fields (and the widening gap in completion rates between the MP fields and the EHP fields) between the 1967–1971 and the 1972–1976 entering cohorts. The stages of attrition at which the main shifts occurred can be pinpointed by comparing the top and bottom panels of Figure 7.3. Contrary to what one might have assumed, especially in the light of what has just been said about the magnitude of late attrition in the EHP fields, it was at the pre-ABD stage, not at the dissertation stage, that attrition increased most rapidly. Almost all of the wider gap in completion rates between MP and EHP was due to a large increase (from 26.9 percent to 33.1 percent) in the fraction of entering students in these three fields who failed to achieve ABD status. Over this same interval, attrition at the dissertation stage increased only modestly.

These results are consistent with several of the interpretations offered previously concerning factors responsible for the especially large drop in completion rates within the EHP fields during these years. Changes in the character and content of subjects such as English could have had their strongest impact on students during the early years of graduate study, when they were first fully immersed in debates over the direction of their field. Also, worries about jobs, and the appeal of alternative careers in fields such as business and law, may well have had more of an effect on students who had not yet made the personal investment of time and resources needed to reach the dissertation stage of graduate study.

TIME-TO-DEGREE

By Broad Field

The panoply of characteristics that define fields of study affects time-to-degree as consistently as it affects completion rates. National data for the 1962–1966 BA cohort indicate that at one extreme, students earning doctorates in education had a median total time-to-degree (TTD) of over twelve years. The typical PhD recipient in the physical sciences took half as long (just over six years). The comparable medians for the social sciences and humanities were roughly eight and nine years, respectively (Figure 7.4).[11]

---

[11]These data are presented for the 1962–1966 BA cohort because later cohorts are affected by truncation problems. Still, the general structure of medians by field for later cohorts is similar to the structure for the 1962–1966 cohort. For instance, the median TTD in the physical sciences for the 1972–1976 cohort is 6.4 years; in the social sciences, 7.8 years; in the humanities, 9.0 years; and in education, 9.9 years. The effect of truncation is evident in that the reported medians for recipients in the long-duration fields, such as the humanities and education, appear to have declined between the 1962–1966 and 1972–1976 BA cohorts (with the extent of the declines more or less proportionate to the duration of study in the various fields). Evidence presented in Chapter Six and later in this chapter suggests that the true trend has been slightly upward.

Other studies have found the same general ordering of time-to-degree in relation to field of study. See, for example, Wilson's study of recipients of doctorates at 24 southern universities between 1950 and 1958 (Wilson 1965), and the more recent analysis by Baird (1990).

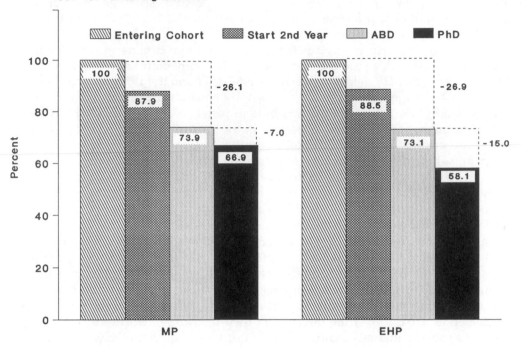

1967–1971 Entering Cohorts

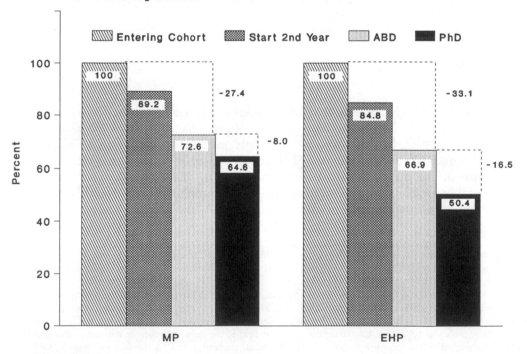

1972–76 Entering Cohorts

Figure 7.3
Attrition by Stage and Fields of Study, 1967–1971 and 1972–1976 Entering Cohorts
  Source: Ten-University data set. Data are from Berkeley, Chicago, Cornell, Princeton, Stanford, and UNC.

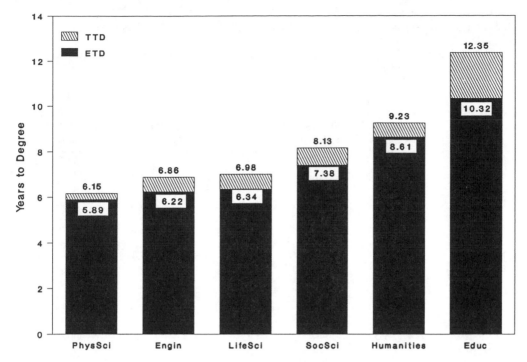

Figure 7.4
Median Total Time-to-Degree and Elapsed Time-to-Degree by Broad Field, All Doctorate-Granting Institutions, 1962–1966 BA Cohort
Source: Special tabulations from Doctorate Records File.

The relationship between TTD and elapsed time-to-degree (ETD), measured as year of doctorate minus year of entry to graduate school, rather than as year of doctorate minus year of BA, is also shown in Figure 7.4. The gap between the measures rises from less than one-third of a year in the physical sciences (where the majority of students begin graduate school immediately after completing their BAs) to two full years in education (where it is more common to gain experience, often in teaching or administration, before pursuing a doctorate). The pattern of field-by-field differences is essentially the same for the two measures, however, and ETD is used most commonly in the rest of this analysis.[12]

Within the Arts and Sciences

We are particularly interested in time-to-degree within the arts and sciences, and the consistency of the pattern by field is again striking (Table 7.2).[13] Graduate

---

[12]ETD is the only measure that is available for the Ten-University data set. The data for national fellowship programs measure year of doctorate minus year of award, and since the large majority of winners of these fellowships began graduate school right after receiving the awards (there were fewer deferrals in the 1960s than in recent years), this is close to a measure of ETD. It is slightly longer than the true measure of ETD, but shorter than TTD.

[13]One new source of data in this table is the records of 443 faculty promoted to tenure in the arts and sciences between the 1980–1981 and 1989–1990 academic years at seven colleges and universities

TABLE 7.2
Median Time-to-Degree by Field, Selected Groups and Entering Cohorts (number of years)

	Danforth and Woodrow Wilson Fellows, 1962–1971 Cohorts[a,b]	Whiting Fellows, 1967–1971 Cohorts[b]	NSF Fellows, 1967–1971 Cohorts[b]	Faculty Promoted to Tenure, 1965–1980 BA Cohorts	Eight Universities, 1967–1971 Cohorts[c]	All Universities, 1967–1971 Cohorts
All students						
English	6.4	7.3		5.4	6.4	7.9
History	7.1	7.4		8.2	7.2	8.3
Political Science	6.8	—		7.2	6.8	8.0
EHP	6.8	7.4			6.8	8.0
Math	5.3		4.6	4.3	5.1	5.9
Physics	5.5		5.4	6.1	6.2	6.4
MP	5.4	na	5.0	5.2	5.7	6.1
Women only						
English	6.5	—		6.3	6.7	8.6
History	8.0	—		9.5	7.7	9.1
Political Science	7.2	—		7.1	7.3	8.8
EHP	7.2	—			7.2	8.8
Math	—		—		5.4	6.4
Physics	—		—		6.8	6.9
MP	—		—		6.1	6.7

Sources: Danforth, Woodrow Wilson, Whiting, and NSF Fellows—National Fellowship data set; faculty promoted—special study, described in Appendix E; eight universities—Ten-University data set (Table 7.1); all universities—special tabulations from Doctorate Records File.

Notes: Time-to-degree is year of PhD minus year of award for fellowship programs (closer to ETD than to TTD), ETD for university data, and TTD for faculty promoted. MP and EHP are simple arithmetic averages of field-specific medians, where each field has equal weighting. Dash indicates that cell size is too small to permit meaningful comparisons.

[a]Median for data pooled from three cohorts (Woodrow Wilson, 1962–1966; Danforth, 1962–1966; Danforth, 1967–1971).

[b]Includes transfers.

[c]Unweighted average median ETD for Berkeley, Chicago, Columbia, Cornell, Harvard, Princeton, Stanford, and University of North Carolina.

---

with high standards for promotion (Columbia, Michigan, Princeton, Smith, Stanford, Swarthmore, and Williams). This data set was constructed to allow examination of time-to-degree by field, gender, time period, and type of employing institution for individuals who demonstrated one measure of achievement—having cleared the hurdle to promotion. The years on the tabulation indicate the years during which most of these faculty members earned their BAs. (See Appendix E for a fuller description of this study, which is referred to hereafter as FacPro.)

This table is also the first use of data from the Whiting fellowship program, which is described in Appendix B. The award cohorts are later for this program than for other programs because these fellowships were given to students who were already far along in graduate study and were expected to complete their dissertations within one or two years. For this reason, the calculation of median time-to-degree for these fellows is based on year of PhD minus year of entry to graduate school

students in English, history, and political science take appreciably longer, on average, to earn doctorates than do students in economics, mathematics, and physics. This conclusion holds when we analyze separately the data for all U.S. residents earning doctorates in this country, winners of prestigious national fellowships, and recipients of PhDs from universities represented in the Ten-University data set. Medians for students in the EHP fields have consistently exceeded medians for students in the MP fields by 1.3 to 2.0 years.

More can be learned by examining results for individual fields within these broad categories. In the case of time-to-degree, there is a highly regular pattern within the EHP fields. In five different data sets, English consistently displays the lowest ETD; history has the highest ETD; and political science occupies a middle position.[14] An obvious hypothesis is that history often requires more familiarity with foreign languages and more archival research than English. Political science is a more variegated field, with some subfields requiring much the same kind of study and research as history, while others are quite theoretical.

Precisely the same relationship between field and time-to-degree holds when we restrict the analysis to women only (bottom panel of Table 7.2).[15] The absolute length of time-to-degree for women has obviously been affected by many factors and is discussed later in this study (see Chapter Eleven). Here, it is sufficient to recognize that while the absolute length of time-to-degree is related to gender, the pattern across fields of study is not.

As in the case of completion rates, a comparison of mathematics and physics reveals a distinct pattern. Though completion rates were consistently lower in mathematics than in physics, those mathematicians who earned doctorates finished appreciably more rapidly (on average) than their counterparts in physics. In the case of the Quality Group I winners of NSF Fellowships (see Appendix B), for example, median ETD was 4.5 years in mathematics and 5.3 years in physics. The same pattern holds for the eight-university group of students, for faculty promoted to tenure at selective colleges and universities (see Appendix E), for Danforth and Woodrow Wilson Fellows (in more muted form), and in national data for all recipients of doctorates in these fields. It holds for women considered separately as well as for men and women together.

A more visually compelling picture of the differences between mathematics and physics is provided by the cumulative completion rates for the 1967–1971

(ETD, strictly defined), not on year of PhD minus year of award (the definition used for the other fellowship programs).

[14]These differences are, in the main, statistically significant at a 95 percent confidence level. We conducted a battery of statistical tests on the medians using distribution-free procedures, particularly the Mann-Whitney-Wilcoxon test adapted for discrete data, as well as a variant of Hettmansperger's (1984, 45–51) two-sample test based on interpolated order statistics. The tests showed that the difference between medians for English and history was significant at a 95 percent level of confidence for each of the fellowship or institutional groupings in Table 7.2; the difference between medians for English and political science was significant for all but the all-universities grouping. As for the comparison between history and political science, the difference between time-to-degree distributions was less pronounced, failing to attain statistical significance for the all-universities grouping. These are all tests of pairwise differences. Tests of the statistical significance of the over-all pattern of results could only be done by using much more elaborate techniques of robust regression.

[15]We have not included a separate set of numbers for men because the medians for men are all within 0.2 to 0.3 years of the medians for men and women together.

entering cohort within the eight-university group (Figure 7.5). In the early years following entry to graduate school, relatively more mathematicians than physicists obtain doctorates. By Year 4, for example, over 20 percent of the students entering graduate programs in mathematics had earned doctorates, as compared with only about 8 percent of the graduate students in physics. The mathematicians retain their lead in cumulative completion rates only through Year 6, however, as relatively more physicists continue to complete their degrees. The two curves cross between Years 6 and 7, and by Year 11 the cumulative completion rate for the entering group in physics has reached 71 percent, while the cumulative completion rate in mathematics has plateaued at about 60 percent.

Mathematicians may tend to finish faster than physicists in part because of the (generally) more theoretical nature of mathematics, which lacks the large experimental "wing" found in most physics departments. A mathematician who has a good idea presumably has a better chance to complete rather quickly all requirements for the PhD, including the dissertation, than does someone who must carry out an experimental project.

Exceptionally able mathematicians may benefit most from this possibility of early completion—a conjecture that is supported by the extremely low medians in mathematics for NSF Quality Group I Fellows and for mathematicians in our study of faculty promoted to tenure (described in Appendix E). Conversely, the difference in time-to-degree between mathematicians and physicists might be

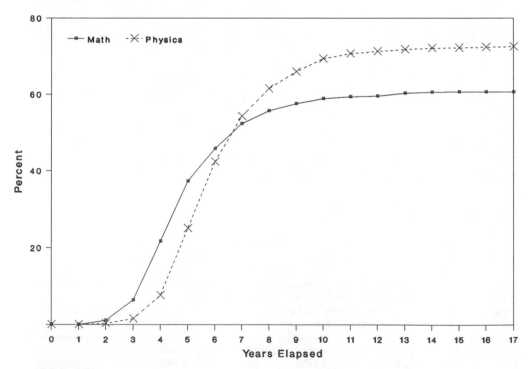

Figure 7.5
Cumulative Completion Rates by MP Field, 1967–1971 Entering Cohort
Source: Ten-University data set. Data are from Berkeley, Chicago, Columbia, Cornell, Harvard, Princeton, Stanford, and UNC.

expected to be smaller when the groups compared are larger and more inclusive—as is the case when ETD is calculated for all U.S. residents earning doctorates in this country ("all universities" data). Once again, the same pattern is found when the analysis is limited to women only.

Detailed data on time-to-degree in other individual fields of study are summarized in Appendix G, Table G.7–2. In general, chemists are found to have the lowest time-to-degree, perhaps because of the highly organized character of graduate education in the field, the close relationship to faculty research, and the strong link to employment opportunities in industry. Economics, the most mathematical and quantitative of the social sciences, has a duration of graduate study generally comparable to what one finds in the physical sciences.[16] Exceptionally high median ETDs are found in multidisciplinary fields within the humanities and related social sciences, such as religion and area studies.[17] These fields often involve additional course work and complicated supervisory arrangements.

Trends within the EHP and MP Fields

There has been a sizable (and reasonably stable) difference in duration of graduate study between the MP and EHP fields for as long as national data have been collected. Differences in median TTD of as much as two to three years were common in the 1920s and 1930s. Some narrowing of this large differential may have occurred between the pre–World War II and immediate postwar years, but it would be hazardous to be too confident about the exact dimensions of any such shift. Data for years since 1958 are more reliable, and they reveal at least a mild widening of the differential since the mid-1960s (Figure 7.6).[18]

The top panel of Figure 7.6 shows a trough in median TTD for students in the 1966 BA cohort in both the humanities and the physical sciences, which may

---

[16]This has not always been the case. In fact, a marked shift has occurred in the relation of time-to-degree in economics to time-to-degree in other fields over time. Prior to World War II, and in the immediate post–World War II years, much of the discipline was more historical and institutional than it is today. In those periods, time-to-degree in this field was similar to time-to-degree in fields such as history. It is only in the last few decades that the duration of graduate study in economics has become more like the duration of graduate study in mathematics and related sciences. In 1934–1938, median TTD in economics was only 0.4 years less than median TTD in history and 2.6 years more than median TTD in mathematics. By 1972–1974, however, median TTD in economics was 1.4 years less than median TTD in history and only 0.6 years more than median TTD in mathematics. (These figures are based on a special tabulation by the NRC of data in the Doctorate Records File for all U.S. residents.) This dramatic shift over time in relationships between fields of study illustrates particularly well the effect that the (changing) nature of subject matter can have on the duration of graduate study.

[17]In tabulations and listings, these multidisciplinary fields are frequently grouped under the headings of "other humanities" and "other social sciences" (Appendix G, Tables G.7–1 and G.7–2).

[18]The top panel of Figure 7.6 shows median TTD (by BA cohort) only for those students who obtained doctorates in 12 years or less at all U.S. universities. The eventual medians will, of course, be higher than those shown on the figure (once all students have completed graduate studies), but these truncated medians permit reasonably consistent comparisons over time. The data in the bottom panel of the figure for the eight-university group of institutions are more reliable because they are less affected by truncation. These universities do not have nearly as many students in the long-duration tails of the time-to-degree distributions as does the all-universities category.

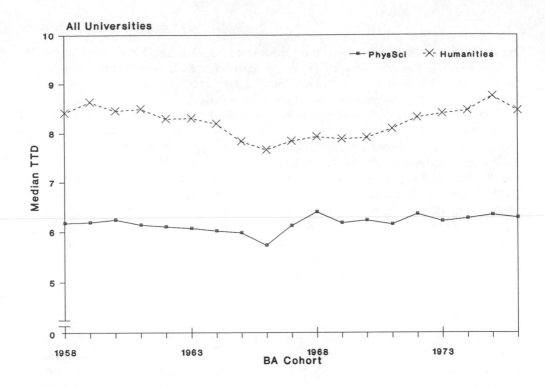

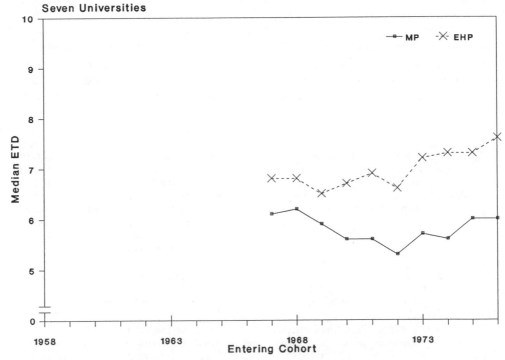

Figure 7.6
Truncated Median Time-to-Degree by Fields of Study, 1958–1976 BA Cohorts and 1967–1976 Entering Cohorts

Sources: Special tabulations from Doctorate Records File (top panel), and Ten-University data set (bottom panel). University data are from Berkeley, Chicago, Columbia, Cornell, Harvard, Princeton, Stanford, and UNC.

Notes: In the top panel, median TTD is truncated at 12 years; see footnote 18.

well have been related to the Vietnam War and associated events.[19] In any event, the years to focus on are those from the mid-1960s forward. The lack of any change in the truncated median for the physical sciences is noteworthy, as is the gentle, but rather steady, upward drift in median TTD within the humanities.

The year-to-year changes in median time-to-degree within the restricted universe of the Ten-University data set (bottom panel of Figure 7.6) confirm the widening of the differential between the MP and EHP fields. The even simpler comparison of median ETDs for successive five-year cohorts within these selective universities reinforces this conclusion (Appendix G, Table G.7–2). While median ETD for mathematicians and physicists was essentially unchanged between the 1967–1971 and 1972–1976 entering cohorts, median ETD within each of the three EHP fields rose, with the overall median increasing from 6.8 to 7.1 years.

It is difficult to determine with precision if this upward trend has continued in later cohorts because of the ever-present problem of truncation (with many graduate students, especially in the EHP fields, still pursuing their degrees). It is possible, however, to make some inferences by examining cumulative completion rates for members of successive cohorts. Figure 7.7 shows the cumulative completion rates for all entering EHP students in the three cohorts — covering 17 years for the 1967–1971 cohort, 12 years for the 1972–1976 cohort, and 7 years for the 1977–1981 cohort.[20]

The cumulative completion rate curve for the 1972–1976 entering cohort is well below the level of the one for the 1967–1971 cohort at every yearly interval, which reflects the large drop in completion rates already noted. The new information conveyed is the relative position of the curve for the 1977–1981 cohort. It is slightly below the level of the curve for the 1972–1976 cohort at each of the yearly intervals at which comparisons can be made, suggesting a further, but extremely modest, increase in time-to-degree. Even if the completion rate for this cohort should ultimately reach the level of the completion rate for the 1972–1976 cohort (as suggested by the projections of ultimate completion rates reported earlier), time-to-degree would have increased by some small amount.

The same (fitted-curve) technique used to project ultimate completion rates can also be used to project ultimate (untruncated) values for median time-to-degree. For the five universities for which this analysis is possible, the projected median in the EHP cluster of fields does show a very small increase. It rises from 7.65 years for the 1972–1976 cohort to 7.72 years for the 1977–1981 cohort. The corresponding projection for the MP fields rises from 6.13 years for the 1972–1976 cohort to 6.27 years for the 1977–1981 cohort. Perhaps the main

---

[19]Chapter Three contains an extended discussion of this period. The sharpness of the drop in median TTD for the 1966 BA cohort remains something of a mystery, but we suspect that one of the consequences of the sudden end of draft deferments (and of the widespread hostility toward the Vietnam War on campuses, combined with general antiestablishment feelings) was that a number of students in the 1966 BA cohort who otherwise might have been in the long-duration tail of the TTD distribution simply left graduate school altogether.

[20]We stop these calculations at the 17-year, 12-year, and 7-year points because later observations would be affected by truncation. For example, all students who began graduate studies in the 1967–1971 cohort had had 17 years to complete their studies by 1988 (when we obtained our data), and the cumulative completion rates for this cohort through Year 17 are therefore accurate—no subsequent developments can change these rates. Similarly, we can make reliable measurements for 12 years for the 1972–1976 cohort, and for 7 years for the 1977–1981 cohort.

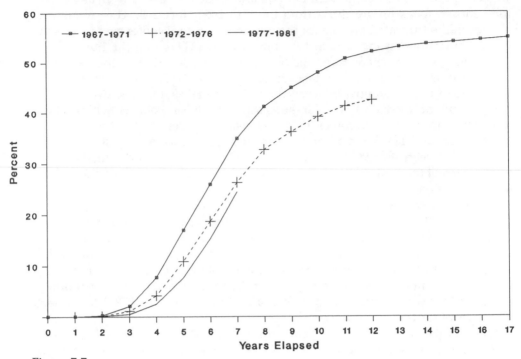

Figure 7.7
Cumulative Completion Rates, EHP Total, 1967–1981 Entering Cohorts
Source: Ten-University data set. Data are from Berkeley, Chicago, Columbia, Cornell, Harvard, Princeton, Stanford, and UNC.

conclusion to be drawn from this analysis is that the time-to-degree gap between the EHP and MP fields has now ceased to widen.[21]

Another trend deserves mention. There has been a general shift in the distribution of students across time-to-degree intervals that is masked by the modest changes in the medians. The number of "fast finishers" (students who complete their doctorates in four years or less) fell markedly after World War II, as did the number of "slow finishers" (students who take 13 years or more to complete their doctorates). Very similar changes in the shape of the distributions affected fields as different as history and mathematics (Figure 7.8). In the postwar years, much larger percentages of doctorates in both fields were earned in the middle time-to-degree intervals (five–ten years in history and five–eight years in mathematics).[22]

---

[21]Our inability (because of lack of data) to include all members of the eight-university group in this analysis may have reduced somewhat the size of the increase we found in the projected median in the EHP fields between the 1972–1976 and 1977–1981 cohorts. The truncated completion rates for the "missing" universities appear to have risen somewhat more rapidly over this interval than the truncated completion rates for the five universities for which data exist.

[22]The pre–World War II data are for the 1938 PhD cohort, whereas the post–World War II data are for the 1962–1966 BA cohort. (The Doctorate Records File is the original source of data in both cases.) We confirmed, however, that the shifts in the shapes of these distributions are not due to this difference in methods of aggregation. The distribution for the 1974 PhD cohort closely resembles the distribution for the 1962–1966 BA cohort.

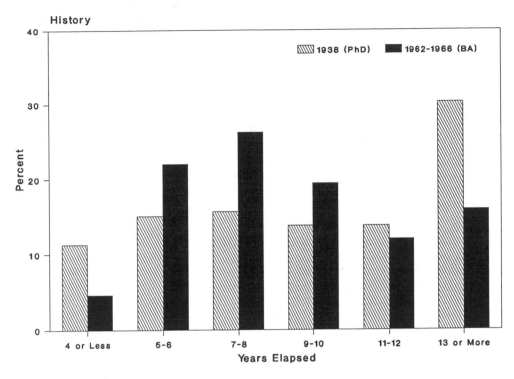

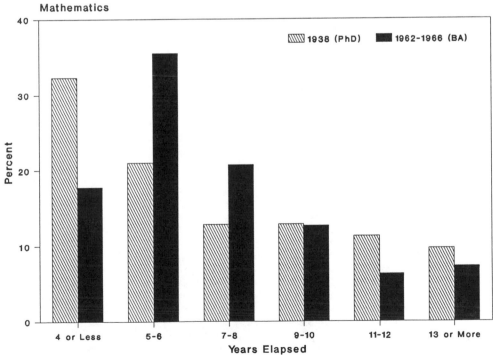

Figure 7.8 Distribution of Total Time-to-Degree, History and Mathematics, 1938 PhD Cohort and 1962–1966 BA Cohort

Source: Special tabulations from Doctorate Records File.

THE RELATIONSHIP BETWEEN COMPLETION RATES AND TIME-TO-DEGREE

An intriguing question concerns the relationship between completion rates and time-to-degree. In general, one would expect an inverse relationship. In any context in which average time-to-degree is relatively high, completion rates should be expected, other things being equal, to be relatively low. The longer it takes the typical student to finish a program of study, the greater the likelihood that something (personal or professional in character) will cause the student to cease pursuit of the degree.

On opportunity-cost grounds, one would also expect anticipation of long time-to-degree to deter students from entering graduate programs. This consideration should influence mainly the number of students who begin graduate study in various fields and need not alter completion rates for those who have elected to pursue PhDs. However, not all beginning students will have understood at the outset how much time it usually takes to earn a doctorate, and for students lacking this information initially, long time-to-degree should be expected to decrease completion rates when the full extent of the time commitment is understood.[23]

The findings reported in this chapter are generally consistent with this hypothesis. The expected inverse relationship between time-to-degree and completion rates holds at least roughly when we examine trends. Periods marked by increases in time-to-degree (for certain groups of fields and for fellowship programs) have tended to be marked as well by decreases in completion rates. Cross-sectional comparisons by field of study provide even stronger support. The physical sciences and some of the social sciences (primarily economics) tend to have both relatively low time-to-degree and relatively high completion rates, whereas the EHP fields have relatively high time-to-degree and relatively low completion rates. Also, within the sciences, we have seen that chemistry has exceptionally low time-to-degree and exceptionally high completion rates. Within the humanities, religion has unusually high time-to-degree and relatively low completion rates.[24]

The nature and strength of the relationship between time-to-degree and completion rates is very important from the standpoint of policy. Successful efforts to reduce time-to-degree may have the ancillary effect—perhaps as important as direct effects on the duration of graduate study—of raising completion rates that seem very low by almost any standard.

---

[23]One recent study (Gillingham, Seneca, and Taussig, 1991), using data for graduate students at Rutgers, focuses on *expected* time-to-degree. A central conclusion is that doctoral students underestimate actual time-to-degree. Also, expected time-to-degree is found to increase as students proceed through their graduate studies. The authors speculate that "the realization by students of the difference between actual and initial expected TTD . . . explains most of the attrition after the first several years of graduate work" (p. 452). While these findings and this line of argument are consistent with the propositions in the text, we would not go as far as the authors of this article in assigning primary responsibility for late attrition to a growing realization that obtaining a doctorate can be a very long process. In our view, the kinds of institutional and departmental practices discussed in Chapters 12 and 13 are likely to be even more fundamental; they may well lead to longer time-to-degree and (independently) to attrition.

[24]There are some finer-grained exceptions to this pattern of inverse relationships. Mathematics, for example, is characterized by both low time-to-degree and low completion rates (relative to other sciences). Graduate students who turn out to be well matched to PhD programs in mathematics often finish their doctorates reasonably promptly. Those less well matched (by abilities or interests) often possess skills and aptitudes that can be put to a wide variety of uses and thus may feel less trapped in a particular PhD program than students in fields that offer fewer alternatives.

Underlying influences, of course, may affect time-to-degree and completion rates concurrently, rather than operating on completion rates only through the mechanism of time-to-degree. We suspect, for instance, that the greater degree of structure and closer faculty supervision generally characteristic of graduate study in the sciences encourage both lower time-to-degree and higher completion rates. In the experimental sciences, in particular, the laboratory environment provides both support for students and a setting in which progress is monitored and help is (usually) available if problems arise.

In contrast, students doing library research are more independent, and more likely to pursue unproductive lines of thinking for considerable periods of time. As Jacob Viner, a former teacher of one of us, used to warn his graduate students, "There is no limit to the amount of nonsense one can think if one thinks too long alone." Prolonged periods of discouragement are also more likely in the absence of structured contacts with colleagues and faculty on a day-to-day basis.

Thus, the considerable variations in time-to-degree and completion rates among fields of study provide one useful way of thinking about the fundamental determinants of these measurable outcomes of graduate study. But there is also a great deal of variation in both time-to-degree and completion rates *within* fields of study. In the next chapter, we examine these differences as they relate to the scale of graduate programs (and to other institutional characteristics).

CHAPTER EIGHT

Scale of Graduate Program

WHEN WE undertook this study, we expected to find clear differences among fields of study in completion rates and time-to-degree, and the results reported in the previous chapter are surprising only in the extent and pervasiveness of such differences. We also planned from the beginning to compare outcomes for groups of graduate programs, but without nearly as clear a set of expectations concerning these relationships.

It was quite surprising, then, to discover that completion rates and time-to-degree vary as systematically by type of graduate program as they do by field of study. This simple finding—documented in detail in this chapter—provokes deeper questions concerning the effects of institutional settings on the outcomes of graduate study. These include the optimal scale of graduate programs and ways of operating more effectively at any given scale.

Graduate programs are far from one-dimensional, and at least five relevant attributes can be identified: (1) scale, as measured by the sizes of entering cohorts of students; (2) perceived quality of the faculty and the graduate education offered; (3) selectivity and admissions policies, as these affect both the qualifications of students and their other characteristics (distribution by gender, for example); (4) financial support of graduate students; and (5) curricular designs and degree requirements. The emphasis in this chapter is on the scale of universities and their graduate programs.

The evidence suggests that better-established graduate programs of recognized quality and reasonable size have somewhat higher completion rates and lower time-to-degree than the rest of the universe of graduate programs. A more significant finding is that within our restricted set of leading graduate institutions, the "Smaller" programs have much higher completion rates and lower time-to-degree than the "Larger" programs. These differences cannot be explained solely in terms of greater selectivity of students or more generous provision of financial aid. Scale alone appears to matter, especially in the EHP fields.

COMPLETION RATES

"Larger" versus "Smaller" Comparisons

Much of our analysis rests on comparisons between what we call Larger and Smaller graduate programs within our group of leading graduate institutions. These categories are based entirely on the sizes of entering cohorts of students, and the graduate programs for which we have consistent data can be grouped into two distinct sets. Three universities have had relatively large entering cohorts in almost all fields (Berkeley, Chicago, and Columbia), and four have had relatively small numbers of entering students (Cornell, Harvard, Princeton, and Stanford). These, then, are our three Larger and four Smaller universities, and the data presented are simple, unweighted arithmetic means of the values for the constituent graduate programs.[1]

In the case of the English, history, and political science (EHP), the differences in size are both particularly pronounced and particularly consistent, with the Larger programs enrolling roughly three times as many students as the Smaller programs. Taking the 1972–1976 entering cohorts in English as an example (Table 8.1), the Larger universities averaged over 60 entering students per year (328 over the entire 1972–1976 period), while the Smaller universities averaged 16 new students per year (80 between 1972 and 1976). In economics and mathematics/physics (MP), the Larger programs enrolled roughly twice as many students on average as the Smaller programs.[2]

TABLE 8.1
Size of Entering Cohorts by Field and Scale of Graduate Program, 1972–1976 Cohort

University	English	History	Political Science	Economics	Math	Physics	EHP Total	MP Total	Six-Field Total
Larger									
Berkeley	376	265	179	177	334	239	820	573	1,570
Chicago	220	321	220	182		117	761	234	1,060
Columbia	387	335	266	121	34	79	988	113	1,222
Average	328	307	222	160		145	856	307	1,284
Smaller									
Cornell	82	62	82	54	45	131	226	176	456
Harvard	98	127	110	120	35	77	335	112	567
Princeton	68	98	84	75	66	82	250	148	473
Stanford	73	100	46	81	55	100	219	155	455
Average	80	97	81	83	50	98	258	148	488

Source: Ten-University data set.

Notes: Averages are unweighted arithmetic means. In calculating MP averages for Chicago, we have used the physics figure for mathematics as well as for physics. Since the citizenship information for 1972–1974 is unreliable in EHP fields at Columbia, we estimate U.S. entrants as 87 percent of total entrants for those years (see Appendix A).

---

[1] The terms *Larger* and *Smaller* as used here are, of course, *relative* measures, which must be understood within our restricted universe of well-established programs. All of the programs classified as Smaller have had appreciably larger entering cohorts than most graduate programs in the United States. (See Chapter Three for a discussion of programs that are small in an absolute sense.) While our Larger and Smaller categories apply, strictly speaking, to graduate programs, rather than to universities, in every case but one (mentioned in footnote 2), all graduate programs in our six fields within a single university fall consistently into either the Smaller or Larger category; thus, for ease of exposition, we sometimes refer to Smaller and Larger universities, as well as to Smaller and Larger programs. The phrases "Smaller (Larger) program" and "Smaller (Larger) university" are used interchangeably.

[2] These substantial differences in scale have been quite consistent over the years for which we collected data (Appendix G, Table G.8–1). The clearest exception is physics, where the sizes of the entering cohorts at the Smaller universities have risen relative to the sizes of the entering cohorts at the Larger universities. The overall differences in the sizes of entering cohorts between the Larger and Smaller universities have been least pronounced in physics, and there is at least one case in which the dichotomy breaks down entirely (Cornell, a Smaller university, enrolled more students than did Chicago or Columbia).

In all of our fields of study, graduate students entering PhD programs at the Smaller universities have had much higher completion rates than their counterparts at the Larger universities (Figure 8.1). In the EHP fields, the probability of obtaining a PhD was nearly twice as high for graduate students who entered Smaller programs as for graduate students who entered Larger programs. In economics and the MP fields, the differentials were also pronounced: Completion rates at the Smaller universities were roughly 20 percentage points higher than completion rates at the Larger universities. The pattern is unmistakable. A key question is whether these sizable variations in completion rates are due to differences in scale per se (and other factors related closely to scale), or whether they are primarily attributable to variables of a quite different kind that happen to be associated with size of graduate programs.

Differences in the relative numbers of men and women in the various graduate student populations need to be considered, since women historically have had lower completion rates than men. Overall, the Larger universities have enrolled relatively more women graduate students than have the Smaller universities (31 percent versus 24 percent of all students in the six fields for entering cohorts between 1967 and 1986). However, the relatively greater numbers of women in the Larger universities do not explain any significant part of the overall differential in completion rates.

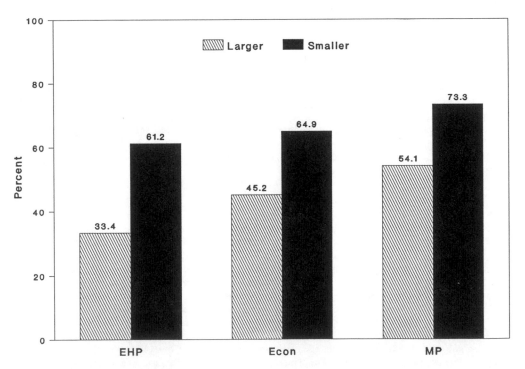

Figure 8.1
Minimum Completion Rates by Scale of Graduate Program and Fields of Study, 1967–1976 Entering Cohort

Source: Ten-University data set. Data are from Berkeley, Chicago, and Columbia (Larger programs), and Cornell, Harvard, Princeton, and Stanford (Smaller programs). See Appendix G, Table G.8–1.

Differences in male-only completion rates are generally within four percentage points of differences in completion rates for men and women together, and differences in female-only completion rates follow very much the same pattern (with lower absolute levels of completion rates). Two fields, English and history, enrolled enough students of both sexes to permit a reliable comparison of patterns, and the Larger/Smaller differential in completion rates was remarkably similar for women and men (Figure 8.2).[3]

Nor can these Larger/Smaller differentials be attributed to differences in the quality of the graduate programs. All of the graduate programs included in these Larger and Smaller groupings rank as Tier I (using the classification system described in Chapter Four). The Jones, Lindzey, and Coggeshall (1982) rating system is more fine-grained, and this system also fails to reveal any significant distinctions in quality between Larger and Smaller universities. If anything, the Larger universities were more highly rated in the EHP fields, while the Smaller universities were slightly ahead in economics and in the MP fields (Table 8.2).

The two sets of universities differ more in the provision of financial aid and, at least in the case of some departments, in their willingness to admit some

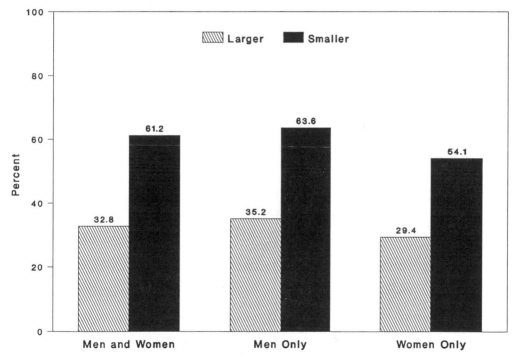

Figure 8.2
Minimum Completion Rates by Scale of Graduate Program and Gender, English and History, 1967–1976 Entering Cohort
Source: Ten-University data set. Data are from Berkeley, Chicago, and Columbia (Larger programs), and Cornell, Harvard, Princeton, and Stanford (Smaller programs). See Appendix G, Tables G.8–1 to G.8–3.

[3]See Appendix G, Tables G.8–2 and G.8–3, for detailed breakdowns by gender.

Table 8.2
Average Quality Ratings by Scale of Graduate Program and Field

Field	Larger	Smaller
English	69.0	67.3
History	69.3	67.3
Political Science	67.0	65.8
Economics	67.7	68.0
Mathematics	66.7	69.3
Physics	70.3	71.3

Source: Jones, Lindzey, and Coggeshall 1982.
Notes: See Chapter Four for a discussion of these rankings. Higher values represent higher ratings, and the mean for all graduate programs is set at 50.0 in each field.

students who are less highly regarded at the time of admission than the students at the very top of the department's preferential ranking list (where, we presume, the two sets of universities admit and enroll students of comparable quality). While we defer to Chapter Ten a general discussion of the effects of financial support and presumed merit of students on completion rates and time-to-degree, we can separate the effects of scale per se from some of these other influences by examining the completion rates of holders of prestigious national fellowships who attended the Larger and Smaller programs.

If associated differences in fellowship aid and in presumed merit of candidates were the key variables at work, overall differences in completion rates between Smaller and Larger programs should be reduced significantly (if not eliminated altogether) when the analysis is limited to winners of national fellowships. In fact, these differences change surprisingly little.

For Woodrow Wilson Fellows chosen between 1957 and 1966, the completion rate in the humanities (excluding transfers[4]) was 47 percent for those fellows who attended the Smaller graduate programs as compared with 27 percent for those who attended the Larger programs (top panel of Figure 8.3). The corresponding differential for the EHP fields is almost exactly the same (Appendix G, Table G.8–4). In the sciences, Woodrow Wilson Fellows who attended Smaller programs also had appreciably higher completion rates than their counterparts who enrolled in the Larger programs—64 percent versus 52 percent (top panel of Figure 8.3). The general pattern for Danforth Fellows in the

---

[4]"Excluding transfers" means that in calculating these completion rates, we counted as "completers" only those students who earned PhDs at the same universities that they entered as fellowship winners. This criterion was applied rigorously to students who entered the 16 major research universities listed on the coding form in Appendix B. However, Woodrow Wilson Fellows who entered "other universities" (most of which were other Research I universities) were included as completers if they finished their PhDs at any of the "other universities."

These transfers-excluded completion rates are consistent, therefore, with the completion rates for individual universities, which also exclude those students who moved to another university before completing their PhDs. More generally, it would hardly seem appropriate to give credit to the original university of entry for a degree conferred by a university to which the student transferred, and this is another reason for preferring (for present purposes) completion rates that exclude transfers. But there is also an argument for taking some account of transfers (especially when evaluating fellowship programs), since they do not represent attrition from "the system" in the same way that dropouts do. We discuss below, and again in Chapter Eleven, the results obtained when students who earned PhDs at any university are counted as completers.

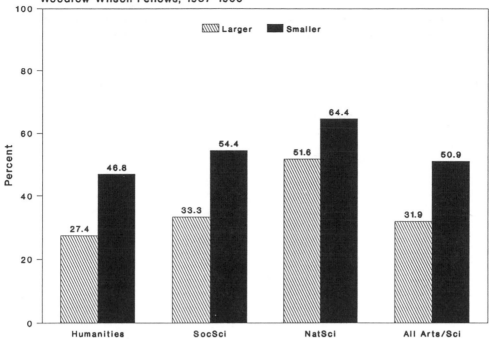

Woodrow Wilson Fellows, 1957-1966

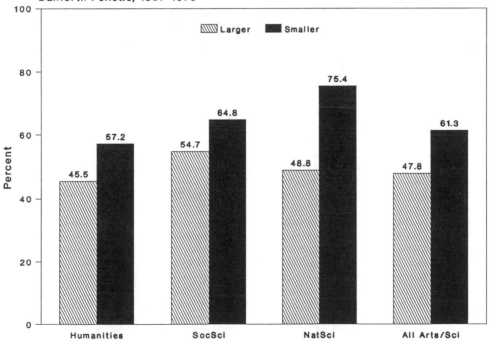

Danforth Fellows, 1957-1976

Figure 8.3
Minimum Completion Rates of Woodrow Wilson and Danforth Fellows by Scale of
Graduate Program and Broad Field, 1957–1976 Entering Cohorts

Source: National Fellowship data set. Data are from Berkeley, Chicago, and Columbia (Larger
programs), and Cornell, Harvard, Princeton, Stanford, and Yale (Smaller programs). See Appendix
G, Table G.8–4.

Notes: Data do not include transfers.

1957–1976 cohorts is very similar: Completion rates for fellows enrolled in Smaller programs were consistently higher than those for fellows enrolled in Larger programs (bottom panel of Figure 8.3).[5]

Including transfers in the calculation of completion rates for fellowship programs does not change the basic pattern shown here, but it does reduce some of the differences between Larger and Smaller universities. The proportion of entering students who transferred from their original institutions and then earned doctorates elsewhere was greater at the Larger universities than at the Smaller universities.[6]

As in the case of the university data, these sharply delineated differences in completion rates for fellowship winners are not a function of gender. The patterns hold for men and women alike. The most reliable comparisons can be made in the EHP fields and in the humanities, where cell sizes for women are largest. Fellowship winners in Smaller programs had consistently higher completion rates than did fellowship winners attending Larger programs, whether the comparison is restricted to men or to women (Appendix G, Tables G.8–5 and G.8–6).[7]

The experience to date with the Mellon Fellowships in the Humanities reveals the same pattern. This program has been in operation only since 1983, and it is too early to know what completion rates will be achieved. However, we do know that 474 of the fellows chosen between 1983 and 1988 enrolled at either one of the Larger or one of the Smaller universities. Of the 164 fellows who enrolled in one of the Larger programs, 13 percent have dropped out thus far (the rest are either still enrolled, are on leave, or have obtained their doctorates). Of the 310 who enrolled in one of the Smaller programs, 6 percent have left the program thus far. The consistency of the pattern merits mention: The percentage of Mellon Fellows who have already dropped out is higher in each of the three Larger programs than it is in any one of the five Smaller programs.

---

[5]Additional results for Indiana University and the University of Wisconsin (which fit the criteria for Larger programs) are entirely consistent with this pattern. When we pool data for Danforth and Woodrow Wilson Fellowships between 1962 and 1971, we obtain completion rates of 30 percent for Indiana and 35 percent for Wisconsin in the EHP fields. These rates compare with comparable completion rates of 36 percent for the Larger programs in our study and 55 percent for the Smaller programs.

See Appendix G, Table G.8–4, for more detailed data underlying Figure 8.3. That table also contains the results of the binomial proportions test of statistical significance. The field-by-field differences in completion rates between Larger and Smaller programs for Woodrow Wilson Fellows are all significant at the 99 percent level of confidence. Most of the differences for the Danforth Fellows, where cell sizes are smaller, also pass the test of statistical significance at the 95 percent level or better. There is no question, in any case, as to the significance of the overall pattern. These data also reveal substantial differences in the overall level of completion rates between the Woodrow Wilson and Danforth programs, which are examined in detail in Chapter Eleven.

[6]See Appendix G, Table G.8–4. The National Fellowship data set yields, as a by-product, a unique set of data on flows (in and out) of doctoral recipients between universities.

[7]Appendix G, Table G.8–6, shows the extraordinarily low completion rates for women who won Woodrow Wilson Fellowships between 1957 and 1966. Excluding transfers, the rates were 12.5 percent and 21 percent in the Larger and Smaller universities respectively. These astonishingly low completion rates are not an artifact due to small cell sizes, since 615 women winners of Woodrow Wilson Fellowships enrolled in the Larger universities and 766 enrolled in the Smaller universities. See Chapter Eleven for a more general discussion of gender in the context of a review of the effectiveness of various fellowship programs.

There is no escaping the central conclusion: The scale of graduate programs appears to have had a powerful effect on completion rates. Whatever restrictions are imposed on the comparisons (field of study, time period, gender, fellowship winners only), students enrolled in Smaller programs earned PhDs in appreciably higher proportions than students in Larger programs. We regard this as one of the most important findings of this study.[8]

It is less clear what explains this pervasive pattern. Differences in admission policies and in the structure of degree programs (with less distinction between terminal master's degree programs and doctoral programs in the Larger universities) are relevant. The Larger programs are in more urban areas, and one of our colleagues has suggested that the attractions (and distractions) of the city could have something to do with this pattern. Another set of possible explanations has to do with the greater anonymity of Larger programs, less favorable student/faculty ratios, and the attendant effects on the amount of faculty contact that is likely to be available.[9]

Other Institutional Comparisons

In addition to comparing Larger and Smaller programs within the highly selective confines of the Ten-University data set, it is possible to make some comparisons of completion rates across broader ranges of graduate institutions. One potentially interesting comparison is between graduate programs at Research I universities and at Other Research/Doctorate institutions (following the Carnegie classification).[10] The National Defense Education Act (NDEA) fellowship program focused specifically on expanding the geographical coverage of doctoral instruction and supporting new and expanding graduate programs (see Appendix B); as a consequence, sufficient numbers of NDEA Fellows attended universities outside the Research I category to permit meaningful comparisons. In fact, the split was almost exactly even: 49 percent of the recipients of NDEA awards (1962 cohort) were enrolled in Research I universities, and 51 percent were in the Other Research/Doctorate category.[11]

---

[8]Mooney (1968, 60), working with a more restricted set of observations (truncated completion rates for a subset of Woodrow Wilson Fellows who won awards between 1958 and 1960), came to essentially the same conclusion. He found a rank correlation coefficient of −.8 between size of graduate program and completion rates, which he interpreted as suggesting "a high inverse relationship between the size of the graduate school and its ability to produce PhDs."

Cartter (1976, 244–45), working with even more limited data, also found that "small departments were more efficient in the number of doctorates awarded as a percent of enrollment."

[9]We suspect—without direct evidence to support the supposition—that programs that are *very small* may also tend to have completion rates that are lower than those for programs of intermediate size. The comparisons presented below for graduate programs in different quality tiers provide some indirect support, since we know (see Chapter Four) that non–Tier I programs are appreciably smaller than the most highly rated programs.

[10]Strictly speaking, "Other Research/Doctorate" is not itself a Carnegie category. Rather, it is the combination of three Carnegie categories: Research II, Doctorate I, and Doctorate II.

[11]See Appendix G, Table G.8–7. The proportion of NDEA Fellows in Research I universities was appreciably higher in the humanities than in the natural sciences, where just 38 percent were enrolled in Research I universities. We do not have completion rates for individual graduate programs outside the Research I category, and the recipients of Danforth, Woodrow Wilson, and National Science Foundation (NSF) fellowships were so heavily concentrated in the Research I institutions that they provide no useful data. (In the portable NSF program, 96 percent of all Quality Group I Award winners between 1962 and 1976 attended Research I universities, according to a special tabulation provided by the NSF.)

(continued)

Completion rates for NDEA Fellows differed markedly by category. Whereas 60 percent of all recipients in Research I universities earned doctorates, only 44 percent of recipients outside this sector did so (Figure 8.4 and Appendix G, Table G.8–7).[12] The differences were most pronounced in the humanities and natural sciences, and part of the explanation could be that successful completion of a doctorate in these areas depends heavily on a relatively well-established infrastructure (research libraries in the humanities, and laboratories, equipment, and research assistants in the sciences). Graduate work in at least some of the social sciences may be less dependent on long-term institutional investments of these kinds.

When this analysis was rerun for women only (who made up just under 18 percent of all NDEA Fellows in 1962), we found the same general pattern, but markedly lower completion rates in all fields and sectors (bottom panel of Figure 8.4).[13]

Completion rates can also be compared across *quality tiers*, using data from both the NDEA program and the Woodrow Wilson fellowship program.[14] Recipients of awards in both of these fellowship programs who entered Tier I programs had higher completion rates than students who entered programs in other quality tiers (Table 8.3). The consistency of the results is again striking. The differences tend to be most pronounced in the sciences (especially for the NDEA Fellows), no doubt because of the special importance of costly research facilities and scale, but they are evident in all three clusters of fields.[15]

In addition to the two comparisons described below, we used the National Fellowship data set to compare completion rates for winners of these fellowships who attended one of our eight universities with completion rates for winners of Danforth and Woodrow Wilson fellowships enrolled at all universities outside the Ten-University group. No consistent patterns were found. This may reflect the excessively crude nature of this dichotomy, which does not control for type of university, perceived quality, or scale.

[12]These completion rates exclude students who transferred outside the given sector; that is, to be counted as a completer, a student had to earn a PhD from an institution in the same Carnegie category as the institution from which the student received his or her NDEA award. The effects of including such intercategory transfers are discussed below.

[13]We do not show rates for the social sciences because only seven women with NDEA awards in the social sciences enrolled in Other Research/Doctorate institutions, and only 24 enrolled in Research I universities. These small cell sizes do not permit reliable comparisons.

One surprise is that women recipients of NDEA awards in the natural sciences in both the Research I and Other Research/Doctorate sets of institutions had lower completion rates than their counterparts in the humanities. Outside the Research I universities, only 13.5 percent of this group of women scientists earned doctorates within the sector in which they enrolled.

[14]See Appendix G, Table G.8–8. Quality tiers are defined in Chapter Four. While only 14 percent to 16 percent of the Woodrow Wilson Fellows in the 1957–1961 and 1962–1966 cohorts attended graduate programs ranked outside Tier I, the cohorts were large enough to yield sizable absolute numbers of non–Tier I Woodrow Wilson Fellows (593 and 669, respectively, in the two cohorts). The number of 1962 NDEA Fellows enrolled in non–Tier I programs was only slightly greater (798), but they accounted for about 75 percent of all 1962 NDEA Fellows. The Danforth program was both too small and too concentrated in Tier I programs to permit meaningful comparisons across quality tiers.

[15]Tucker, Gottlieb, and Pease (1964, 40–51, especially Table 3.7) also found a definite relationship between completion rates (or attrition) and a measure of institutional quality. The 24 universities in their study included some that were not highly ranked, and the universities were placed in one of three strata on the basis of a combination of Keniston's rankings and the number of doctorates awarded. Stratum 1 was most prestigious, Stratum 2 was next, and Stratum 3 contained universities that were not in Keniston's top fifteen and that also awarded fewer than 300 PhDs between 1936 and

(continued)

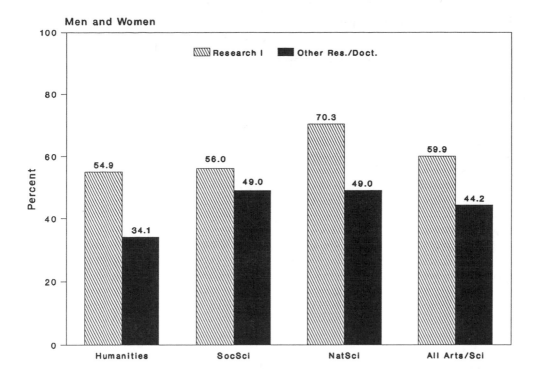

Men and Women

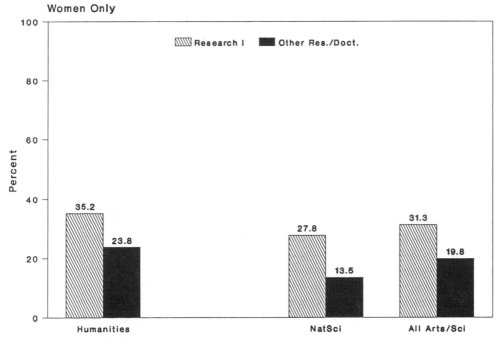

Women Only

Figure 8.4
Minimum Completion Rates of NDEA Fellows by Type of Institution, Broad Field, and Gender, 1962 Entering Cohort

Source: National Fellowship data set. See Appendix G, Table G.8–7.

Notes: Data do not include transfers (see footnote 12). There were too few women NDEA Fellows in the social sciences to permit reliable comparisons. "Research I" and "Other Res./Doct." are based on *A Classification of Institutions of Higher Learning* (Carnegie Foundation for the Advancement of Teaching 1987b). "Other Res./Doct." consists of institutions classified Research II, Doctorate I, and Doctorate II under the Carnegie system.

TABLE 8.3
Minimum Completion Rates of Woodrow Wilson and NDEA Fellows by Broad Field and Quality Tier, 1957–1966 Entering Cohorts (percent)

	No Transfers		With Transfers	
	Tier I	Other	Tier I	Other
Woodrow Wilson, 1957–1961				
Humanities	35.0	28.9	47.9	36.9
Social sciences	42.1	40.2	51.4	42.5
Natural sciences	58.0	51.2	70.1	54.4
Three-field average	45.0	40.1	56.5	44.6
Woodrow Wilson, 1962–1966				
Humanities	41.3	34.8	50.0	40.8
Social sciences	49.1	33.1	55.9	39.2
Natural sciences	62.7	52.7	73.8	59.3
Three-field average	51.0	40.2	59.9	46.4
NDEA, 1962				
Humanities	47.4	42.9	56.2	50.2
Social sciences	56.2	51.9	57.5	62.4
Natural sciences	71.4	50.0	74.6	65.9
Three-field average	58.3	48.3	62.8	59.5

Source: National Fellowship data set. Appendix G, Table G.8–8.

Notes: Quality tiers are defined in Chapter Four. "Other" is the total for Tiers II, III, and IV. "No transfers" means that a student had to finish the PhD at the university at which the student started to be counted as a "completer." (This definition differs slightly for each fellowship program, see text.) "With transfers" means that students were counted as "completers" regardless of where they finished graduate study; these students are grouped by entering institutions. "Three-field average" is the average completion rate for the three broad fields, with each field receiving an equal weight.

Another special word should be added about transfers. The "no transfers" columns in Table 8.3 contain the completion rates that we regard as most relevant to the issue at hand. However, the results in the columns that show completion rates inclusive of transfers are a useful check on the central finding and provide additional information relevant to the transfer phenomenon itself. Particularly noteworthy are the figures for the NDEA Fellows in the natural sciences who initially enrolled in non–Tier I programs. The completion rate with no allowance for transfers is 50 percent; when transfers are included, the completion rate jumps to 66 percent (the largest increase of this kind for the data shown in the table). One possible inference is that students in the natural sciences may have been particularly inclined to transfer to more highly rated

---

1956 (p. 43). For candidates holding a master's degree who were enrolled as doctoral students in the arts and sciences in these universities during the period September 1950 through December 1953 (the universe for the Tucker et al. study), they found that attrition rates in all fields were lowest within Stratum 1, appreciably higher in Stratum 2, and higher yet in Stratum 3. The differences were very substantial.

(and generally larger) programs, with better research facilities, in order to finish their studies.[16]

The results of this set of comparisons provide further reason to be concerned about the changing distribution of doctorates conferred, as described in Chapter Four. At the minimum, this evidence warns that programs outside the Research I category, which may not be well established, can experience lower completion rates as well as other problems associated with the arduous and costly process of building strong programs of graduate study.

STAGES OF ATTRITION

In the case of the Larger and Smaller university groups, it is possible to extend the analysis by identifying the point in the process of graduate education at which differences in attrition related to the scale of programs are most evident. The critical (distinguishing) stage is not, as one might perhaps have expected, dissertation writing. Rather, it is in the first year, and then in the rest of the pre-ABD stage of graduate study, that attrition is much greater in the Larger programs than in the Smaller programs. The differences are dramatic, within both the EHP and MP fields (Figure 8.5).

In the EHP fields, approximately 25 percent of the entering students in the Larger programs dropped out before the start of the second year of graduate study, and another 30 percent failed to reach ABD status by satisfying all requirements for the PhD except the dissertation—resulting in total pre-ABD attrition of about 55 percent. In contrast, only 18 percent of EHP students in the Smaller programs failed to achieve ABD status. The same pattern prevails in the MP fields, where pre-ABD attrition was 44 percent in the Larger programs compared to 10 percent in the Smaller programs.

Part of this marked difference in levels of pre-ABD attrition may be due to conscious decisions on the part of some Larger programs to use the early years of graduate study to weed out weaker students. The greater use of master's degree programs as initial hurdles to the PhD may serve the same purpose.[17] But it is also true that the introduction to graduate study may be a particularly vulnerable period for some potentially fine PhD candidates, who may be helped to persevere in supportive settings. Smaller programs may have been more successful than Larger programs in helping such students complete course

---

[16]The "no-transfers" data presented in Table 8.3 are defined differently for the NDEA Fellows than for the Woodrow Wilson Fellows, and the resulting inconsistency is of some consequence. The number of universities entered by the NDEA Fellows was so large and diverse as to rule out, on practical grounds, coding each institution individually. Rather, the institutions were assigned to one of three categories: Research I, Other Research/Doctorate, and Other. Transfers, then, were defined as students who entered an institution in one of these categories and earned a PhD in an institution in another of the three categories. Nearly 90 percent of the transfers defined in this way moved to Research I universities. The use in the NDEA case of this much cruder definition of transfers leads to overestimates of completion rates excluding transfers (applying the stricter "no-transfers" criterion used in the case of all other data sets).

[17]See Appendix A for a discussion of the problem of distinguishing "master's-only" candidates from PhD candidates who nonetheless had to enroll initially in a master's degree program. In collecting data from individual universities, considerable efforts were made to exclude from the entering cohorts students who were thought to be "master's-only" candidates.

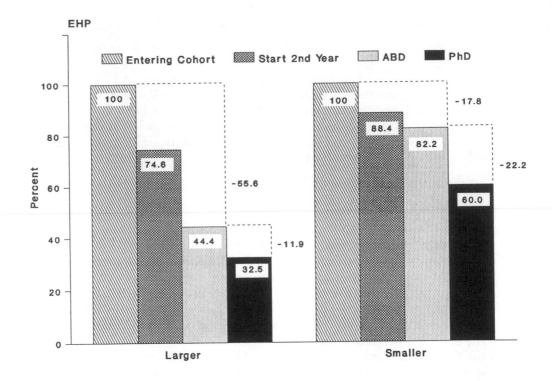

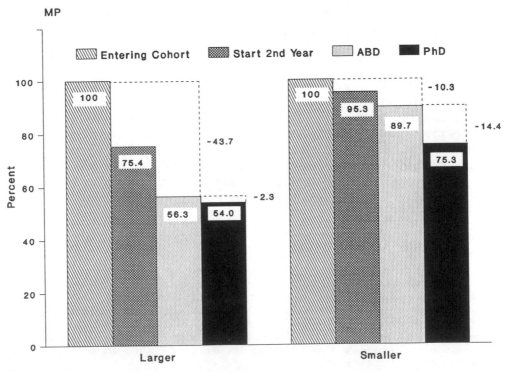

Figure 8.5
Attrition by Stage, Scale of Graduate Program, and Field of Study, 1972–1976 Entering Cohort

Source: Ten-University data set. Data are from Berkeley, Chicago, and Columbia (Larger programs), and Cornell, Harvard, Princeton, and Stanford (Smaller programs).

work, pass requirements, and so on. They may actually have been too successful in some cases, if one believes that a somewhat greater number of students should have been discouraged from pressing on with graduate study earlier in their student careers. Decisions to terminate graduate students are often hard for departments to make, and even clear decisions may sometimes be postponed because of a misplaced sense of kindness or simply a lack of courage. It is difficult to know how to strike balances of this kind, and ultimately there is no substitute for responsible judgment at the departmental level.

In any case, these data indicate that once ABD status has been achieved, the "survivors" complete dissertations and obtain doctorates in roughly the same relative numbers in Larger and Smaller programs. Although the absolute amount of attrition at this stage was greater in the Smaller programs (for instance, in the EHP fields, it was 22 percent of all entering students, compared to 12 percent in the Larger programs), the proportion of entering students who reached this stage was also much greater in these programs.

It is useful to think in terms of a conditional probability, defined as the percentage of all those who reached ABD status who subsequently earned the doctorate. This measure indicates that whatever combination of factors led to higher overall attrition in Larger programs, these factors operated at the pre-ABD stages of doctoral study (Table 8.4). Once the dissertation-writing stage was reached, the Smaller and Larger programs were comparable with respect to attrition in the EHP fields, and the Larger programs had lower attrition in the MP fields. The barriers to completion of the dissertation at the ABD stage of graduate study, which are especially serious in the EHP fields, seem to have afflicted Smaller programs and Larger programs alike.[18]

TIME-TO-DEGREE

Larger versus Smaller Comparisons

Time-to-degree is also clearly related to the scale of graduate programs. In our six fields, recipients of doctorates in the Larger programs took almost one full year longer to complete their work than their counterparts in the Smaller

TABLE 8.4
Conditional Probability of Obtaining PhD, Given ABD Status, by Scale of Graduate Program, 1972–1976 Entering Cohort (percent)

Fields	Larger	Smaller
EHP	73	73
MP	96	84

Source: Ten-University data set. Data are from Berkeley, Chicago, and Columbia (Larger programs), and Cornell, Harvard, Princeton, and Stanford (Smaller programs).

---

[18]Tucker, Gottlieb, and Pease (1964, 49–55) discuss stages of attrition at great length. It is difficult to compare their results directly with ours, however, because they limited their entering population to students holding a master's degree. Consequently, early attrition is removed from their data by the way in which entering cohorts are defined. Even so, they found ABD-stage attrition to be lower than their definition of pre-ABD attrition. They also found (as we did) that both total attrition and ABD attrition were lower in the natural sciences than in the humanities. The unique contribution of

programs. The differential is widest in the EHP fields, where median elapsed time-to-degree was 7.5 years at the Larger universities and 6.4 years at the Smaller universities (Figure 8.6).[19]

As in the case of completion rates, looking at only those recipients of doctorates who held national fellowships allows us to control for the possible effects of differences in the availability of financial aid and in quality of doctoral candidates. The findings are absolutely clear-cut: The differences in median elapsed time-to-degree between fellowship winners who attended Larger and Smaller programs (1.2 years for the Woodrow Wilson Fellows and 0.9 years for the Danforth Fellows) are very similar to the difference for all students in these same programs (compare Figures 8.6 and 8.7). It is evident that factors beyond

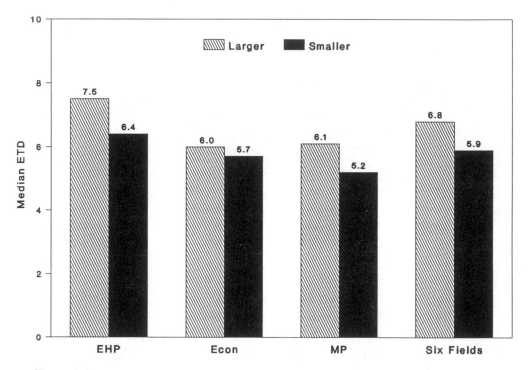

Figure 8.6
Median Elapsed Time-to-Degree by Scale of Graduate Program and Fields of Study, 1967–1976 Entering Cohort

Source: Ten-University data set. Data are from Berkeley, Chicago, and Columbia (Larger programs), and Cornell, Harvard, Princeton, and Stanford (Smaller programs). See Appendix G, Table G.8–1.

---

the Tucker et al. study is its estimates of stages of attrition seen in relation to "quality strata" (described in footnote 15). While they found that total attrition was lowest at their Stratum 1 universities, they also found that ABD attrition was highest among students in these universities. This is a puzzling finding, which they do not interpret.

[19]We will not present separate figures for men only and women only in this section because the patterns are much the same (Appendix G, Table G.8–9) in the fields for which there are enough observations to justify comparisons. If anything, the tendency for students at Larger universities to take longer than students at Smaller universities is more pronounced for women than for men in the EHP fields and less pronounced for women in mathematics and physics; however, small cell sizes make it hazardous to generalize outside the humanities.

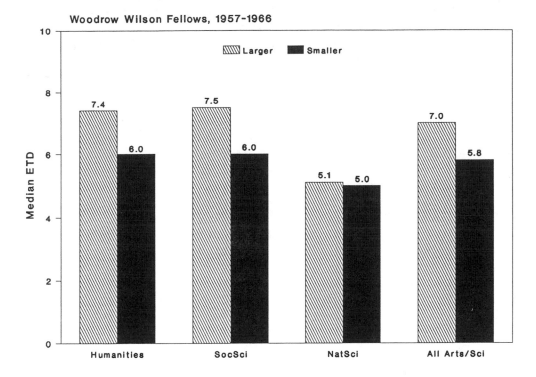

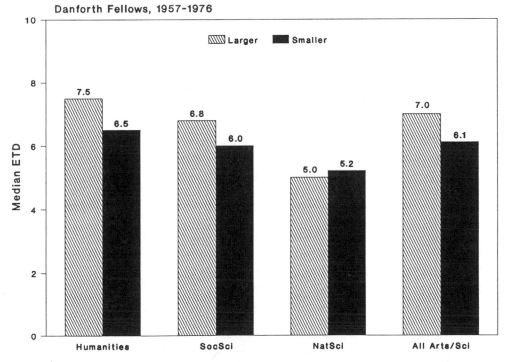

Figure 8.7
Median Elapsed Time-to-Degree of Woodrow Wilson and Danforth Fellows by Scale of Graduate Program and Broad Field, 1957–1976 Entering Cohorts
   Source: National Fellowship data set. See Appendix G, Table G.8–9.

the availability of fellowship assistance and the presence of carefully selected candidates are causing students at the Larger universities to take appreciably longer to complete their studies than students at the Smaller universities.

The congruent patterns are especially striking in the EHP fields and the humanities. Both the differences between the Larger and Smaller universities and the absolute levels of median time-to-degree fall within an exceedingly narrow band in these three separate data sets (compare Figure 8.6 and the two panels of Figure 8.7).

The MP fields represent the only cluster of fields in which the fellowship holders exhibit a pattern that is different from the pattern for all students. The difference in time-to-degree between Larger and Smaller programs that is so evident when we compare all students (6.1 years in the Larger programs versus 5.2 years in the Smaller programs) disappears when we look only at holders of national fellowships. The Woodrow Wilson and Danforth Fellows in mathematics and physics had a median time-to-degree ranging from 5.0 to 5.2 years regardless of whether they attended Larger or Smaller programs. This is almost precisely the same median time-to-degree found for all students in mathematics and physics at the Smaller universities—but a significantly lower time-to-degree than that for all students in these same fields at the Larger universities. This appears, then, to be one instance in which fellowship support and/or selection criteria may have affected time-to-degree.

Other Institutional Comparisons

The Doctorate Records File, the most comprehensive data set in existence, allows us to compute median elapsed time-to-degree for all recipients of doctorates in the 1967–1971 BA cohort. We were thus able to compare median time-to-degree at Research I universities with median time-to-degree at "All Other Research/Doctorate" institutions. Overall, doctoral recipients at Research I universities completed their degrees in half a year less (on average) than recipients at Other Research/Doctorate institutions (for the field-specific differentials, see Figure 8.8). We expect that students at Research I universities enjoyed, overall, more financial support than did their counterparts at Other Research/Doctorate institutions, and the Research I students may have had stronger academic preparation.[20]

It is also possible to use the data for the Woodrow Wilson Fellows to compare time-to-degree across quality tiers (excluding transfers). Averaging the results for the 1957–1961 and 1962–1966 cohorts yields results that are remarkably similar to those reported above. Woodrow Wilson Fellows in Tier I programs finished doctorates in 0.4 of a year less than the time required by fellows in the other tiers.[21] The difference by quality tier in the humanities is somewhat larger than the differences in the other broad sets of fields.

---

[20]Running these comparisons for women only (which is possible here because the cell sizes are so large) yields a pattern of results which is analogous in all respects to the results for men and women combined.

[21]These results were obtained by calculating an unweighted average of the median elapsed time-to-degree for each of the three broad fields (humanities, social sciences, and natural sciences), thereby not allowing the overall results to be affected by differences in the distribution of students across fields in the various tiers. Separate averages for Tiers II, III, and IV were combined (again calculating an unweighted average) to obtain a composite value for non–Tier I programs. We do not report time-to-degree results for the NDEA data because these fellowships were not always awarded to students just beginning graduate study.

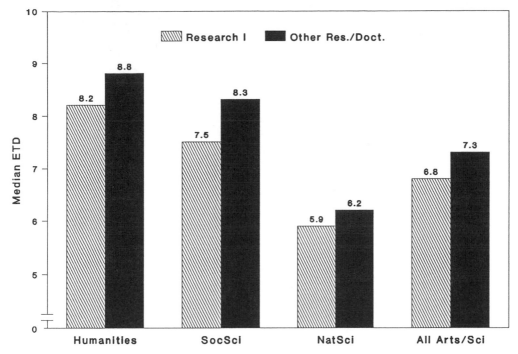

Figure 8.8
Median Elapsed Time-to-Degree by Type of Institution and Broad Field, All Doctorates, 1967–1976 Entering Cohort
Source: Special tabulations from Doctorate Records File.

Cumulative Completion Rates

The full extent of the differences in outcomes between the Larger and Smaller programs can be seen most clearly by examining cumulative completion rates, which combine information on time-to-degree and the number of entering students who ultimately complete doctoral studies. In the EHP fields (top panel of Figure 8.9), approximately 20 percent of entering students in the Smaller programs obtained doctorates within the first five years of graduate study, as compared with only about 7 percent in the Larger programs. The absolute size of this gap continues to widen steadily until eight years of graduate study have passed, when the cumulative completion rates are, respectively, 49 percent and 21 percent. Both curves then start to plateau, with the ultimate completion rates reaching 61 percent for Smaller programs and 33 percent for Larger programs.

Cumulative completion rates in the MP cluster of fields accelerate more rapidly at all universities, with almost 60 percent of entering students in the Smaller programs earning doctorates within six years, compared with 30 percent in the Larger programs. The absolute size of the gap in completion rates becomes smaller when the two curves plateau. Otherwise the MP relationship is very much the same as the relationship in the EHP fields (compare the top and bottom panels of Figure 8.9).

These curves summarize outcomes for students who entered graduate school between 1967 and 1976. To see if there have been changes in these relationships

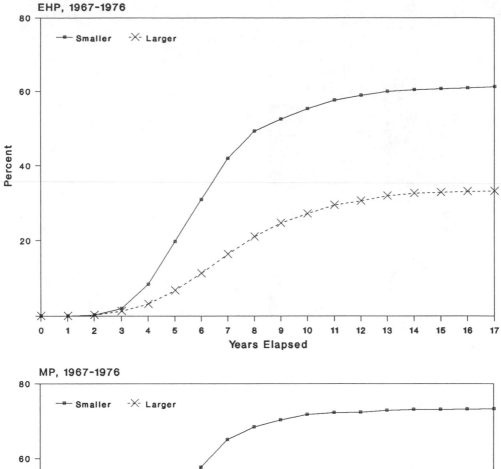

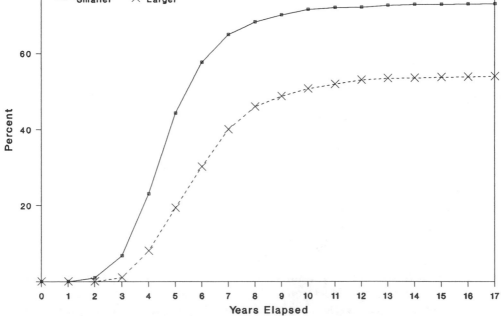

Figure 8.9
Cumulative Completion Rates by Scale of Graduate Program and Fields of Study,
1967–1976 Entering Cohort

Source: Ten-University data set. Data are from Berkeley, Chicago, and Columbia (Larger programs), and Cornell, Harvard, Princeton, and Stanford (Smaller programs).

over time, we have made analogous calculations for three successive five-year entering cohorts and summarized truncated completion rates after 4, 7, 12, and 17 years in Table 8.5. The differences in cumulative completion rates between the Smaller and Larger programs vary ever so slightly across cohorts, and the basic conclusion is that these differences have been both large and remarkably stable in both the EHP and MP clusters of fields over 15 years.[22] There is certainly no evidence that they are disappearing, or that they have been affected noticeably by changing conditions in academic labor markets.

TABLE 8.5
Cumulative Completion Rates by Scale of Graduate Program and Fields of Study, 1967–1981 Entering Cohorts (percent of entering cohort completing PhD within given period)

Fields	Years Elapsed	Scale	Entering Cohorts (cumulative %)		
			1967–1971	1972–1976	1977–1981
EHP	4	Smaller	11.2	5.5	3.4
	4	Larger	3.7	2.6	1.8
		Difference	7.5	2.9	1.6
	7	Smaller	46.7	37.1	35.6
	7	Larger	19.2	13.5	11.3
		Difference	27.5	23.6	24.3
	12	Smaller	63.4	54.5	—
	12	Larger	33.6	27.4	—
		Difference	29.8	27.1	—
	17	Smaller	66.1	—	—
	17	Larger	36.4	—	—
		Difference	29.7	—	—
MP	4	Smaller	20.3	25.8	14.4
	4	Larger	9.1	7.0	5.0
		Difference	11.2	18.8	9.4
	7	Smaller	62.6	67.3	61.5
	7	Larger	39.2	40.9	38.8
		Difference	23.4	26.4	22.7
	12	Smaller	73.2	71.4	—
	12	Larger	52.0	54.1	—
		Difference	21.2	17.3	—
	17	Smaller	74.9	—	—
	17	Larger	53.0	—	—
		Difference	21.9	—	—

Source: Same as Table 8.4.
Notes: These figures show the cumulative percentages of all entering students in each cohort who had earned doctorates by the number of years elapsed (4, 7, 12, or 17) since entry to graduate school. Dash indicates that truncation prevents presentation of data.

---

[22]The same conclusion holds for economics, which is not shown in the table.

The underlying forces must be strong and systemic, and a major task of Chapters Twelve and Thirteen is to provide a deeper understanding of the causes of such persistent differences in outcomes. First, however, we shall use the next chapter to introduce a new concept—the student-year cost of a doctorate—which is useful in summarizing all aspects of the analysis of differences in outcomes as they relate to fields of study, scale of graduate programs, and time periods.

CHAPTER NINE

Student-Year Cost and Its Components

THERE ARE many ways of thinking about the "effectiveness"—or, more crudely put, the "efficiency"—of doctoral programs. Any simple measure is subject to abuse and misinterpretation. Still, there is merit in seeking a way of distilling the various pieces of information about time invested in graduate study into a single composite measure that can be used to compare results across fields of study, universities, and periods of time. The building blocks of such a measure have been described in the previous three chapters, and our objective here is to provide a quantitative summary of the measurable outcomes of graduate study, expressed in the form of an estimate of the total amount of student time that has had to be invested (on average) in order to "produce" one PhD.

THE CONCEPT AND ITS LIMITATIONS

The basic concept is simple: We add up the total number of years invested in doctoral study by all members of an entering cohort of graduate students and then divide by the number of doctorates earned by the cohort.[1] Thus, student-year cost per doctoral degree received (SYC) can be expressed as:

$$SYC = \frac{\Sigma \text{ Student Years Invested}}{\text{Number of PhDs Earned}}.$$

This student-year cost measure builds on concepts already introduced in this study: the completion rate, stages of attrition, and time-to-degree.[2] It also incorporates estimates of the time invested by students who do not complete PhDs. Finally, it focuses attention on those elements in the process of graduate education that tend to increase student-year costs:

- Low completion rates;
- Long time-to-degree for those students who do earn doctorates; and
- Greater concentration of attrition in the later years of graduate study, rather than in the earlier years.

---

[1]We now know that we have reinvented "the Breneman wheel." Unbeknownst to us at the time we were devising this approach, an essentially identical methodology was suggested as a measure of "efficiency" by David Breneman (1970) in his PhD dissertation. Breneman wrote: "Thus, a crude measure of 'efficiency' is the ratio of degree output to the input of student time. An 'inefficient' department would be marked by an excessively long average time to degree and/or a high rate of attrition, particularly if the attrition typically occurs after students have spent several years in the program." Unfortunately (as noted below), lack of data prevented Breneman from applying this approach to the departments at Berkeley that he studied.

[2]In previous chapters, time-to-degree has usually been reported as a median number of years. Here we use the mean, which takes fuller account of the extraordinary investment of time made by outliers and is easier to incorporate in ordinary computations.

SYC is, of course, a very imperfect measure of the economic cost of graduate study. It overstates the opportunity costs incurred by students in two ways. First, it "charges" an entering cohort for all years that have elapsed following entry to graduate school, even though some of this time may have been taken off from study or devoted in part to teaching or other employment. Second, it fails to "credit" those members of the cohort who failed to obtain doctorates with any "output," even though individuals may have obtained a master's degree or benefited in countless other ways from graduate education.

Moreover, this measure fails to capture the broader, less measurable benefits generated by graduate study that accrue to other participants in the educational process. Graduate students contribute to the scholarship and research of faculty and other research personnel, as well as to the quality of the overall academic environment and thus to the education received by both undergraduates and other graduate students. These "joint products" of graduate education are usually thought to be especially important in the sciences, but they are also far from trivial in other fields of study.

At the same time, SYC understates the true economic cost of graduate study by ignoring entirely all elements of cost other than the investment of student time. In particular, universities incur heavy institutional costs in the form of hours of faculty teaching and supervision and expenditures on libraries and laboratories. Numerous studies have shown that institutional expenditures per student tend to be far higher at the graduate level than at the undergraduate level.[3]

Expenditures of institutional resources on graduate education vary widely by field of study, institution, and stage of graduate study. Larger graduate programs may benefit from greater economies of scale, since the costs of largely fixed assets (such as the library) are distributed over more students. Larger programs may also be able to economize to some extent on faculty time, since more students can attend the same course. But there may also be an offsetting "cost" of another kind in that individual students may receive less attention. This may help explain why (as we shall see later in the chapter) student-year cost per degree conferred tends to be appreciably higher in the larger programs.

We cannot, in any case, do more than note such complications and call attention to the limitations of SYC as a proxy for the net costs of graduate education seen in all relevant dimensions. Any attempt to specify the full range of costs and benefits associated with graduate study would require another (very ambitious) study. Our emphasis must remain on the opportunity costs represented by the investment of student time. As we document in the remainder of this chapter, these costs are hardly inconsequential.

---

[3]For example, in 1968 the Carnegie Commission on Higher Education proposed that the federal government make cost-of-education grants that were approximately five times larger per graduate student than per undergraduate to reflect differences in levels of cost (Carnegie Commission on Higher Education 1968, 30–31). For an excellent discussion of the complications involved in estimating the costs of graduate education, see Balderston (1974, 127–53). This study contains references to other studies and provides some sense of the rough range of the costs of graduate programs in various fields. James (1978) reviews data from a variety of sources and concludes that "graduate costs are at least three times [greater than] undergraduate costs, and the ratio becomes 1/6 if research is treated as an input into graduate education" (p. 179).

Surprisingly little is known about the amount of student time invested in graduate education, largely because the relevant data are hard to compile and generally unavailable. The most difficult information to assemble relates to the time spent by students who never receive degrees. What is needed is longitudinal data for each student, designed to capture year-to-year changes in status.[4]

The data collected at the university level for this study permit systematic analysis of the time invested by individual students, though some significant problems still exist. For students who left graduate school without a doctorate, we know only the interval within which they departed (for example, after the first year, before reaching ABD status, or after ABD status was achieved). The length of time spent at the stage in which attrition occurred remains unknown, and we have had to make estimates based on the experiences of other students in the same field, cohort, and university.[5]

DIFFERENCES BY FIELD OF STUDY

As the analysis in Chapter Seven implies, student-year cost varies substantially by field of study. The comparison between the quantitative sciences and the humanities emphasizes again the differences between these two groups of fields within the arts and sciences. At five universities for which detailed data are available, the student-year cost of a doctorate in English, history, and political science (EHP) was over 12 years for students in the 1972–1976 cohorts, whereas the comparable figure for mathematics and physics (MP) was fully one-third less—just over 8 years.[6]

Student-year costs in individual EHP fields fall within a fairly tight range, from a high of 13.8 years for political science to 11.4 years for English. The difference in SYCs between mathematics and physics is even narrower (8.5 and 8.2 years, respectively). The time investment needed to obtain a doctorate by a

---

[4]Breneman (1970) discusses data problems in detail in his doctoral dissertation. He also cites an important early study (Stark 1966) that uses data for individual students to calculate a measure of the time invested relative to the number of degrees awarded in four departments at Berkeley. Breneman himself was forced to use a much less precise approach—namely, an aggregate comparison between degrees awarded and enrollments at the departmental level—because longitudinal information for individuals was not available.

[5]The specific assumption used in our calculations is that the time spent by noncompleters during the interval at which they left graduate study was equal to 80 percent of the average time spent by completers at the same stage of graduate study (pre–second year, pre-ABD after first year, or post-ABD). Other assumptions have been tested, and the overall results are rather insensitive to even quite substantial differences in assumptions.

[6]These are five-university averages of SYCs (with SYC at each institution receiving an equal weight) in the EHP and MP fields for the 1972–1976 entering cohorts at Berkeley, Columbia, Cornell, Michigan, and Princeton. SYCs for each university, in each group of fields, were calculated by pooling the data for individual students. These five universities were chosen for this analysis because they were able to provide the most reliable data on stages of attrition across the main fields of study.

Students from the 1972–1976 entering cohorts reported as still enrolled as of the summer of 1989 (a total of 132 at the five universities) were treated as cases of attrition after the ABD stage, and assigned the average time-to-attrition of students in the same field, university, and cohort known to have left graduate school after having achieved ABD status. Two mutually offsetting biases of this assumption should be noted: (1) overestimation of student-year cost as some of the long-time "still-enrolled" students eventually earn degrees; and (2) underestimation of student-year cost as students spend additional years in the system with or without obtaining degrees. The net effect can be either an increase or a decrease in SYC.

cohort in economics (8.7 years on average) was much closer to the number of years required in the quantitative sciences than in the EHP fields. Also, the variance across individual graduate programs (the standard deviation of the SYC) was lower in economics than in any other field (Table 9.1).[7]

Student-year cost can be broken down into two main components: (1) time invested by those who obtained doctorates (SYC of completion); and (2) time invested by those who did not obtain doctorates (SYC of attrition). Both of these components contribute to the very large difference in SYC between the EHP and MP fields. However, while the EHP fields entailed heavier time costs of both kinds, the difference between the EHP and MP fields in the cost of attrition was far greater than the difference in the cost of completion. In fact, the cost of attrition per doctorate conferred was nearly 2.5 times greater in the EHP fields than in the MP fields—and accounted for fully 70 percent of the large overall difference in average student-year cost (Figure 9.1).

A disparity of this magnitude warrants close scrutiny. At what stages of graduate study were the costs of attrition concentrated, and where were the differences between the EHP and MP fields especially pronounced? Our data indicate that the costs of attrition were higher in the EHP fields than in the MP fields at every stage of graduate study, but that the differentials were by no means uniform (Figure 9.2).[8] In the EHP fields, post-ABD attrition accounted for

TABLE 9.1
Student-Year Cost by Field, 1972–1976 Entering Cohort
(years per degree)

Field	Five-University Average	Standard Deviation
English	11.4	4.4
History	13.3	1.8
Political Science	13.8	3.4
Economics	8.7	1.1
Mathematics	8.5	1.9
Physics	8.2	1.5

Source: Ten-University data set. Data are from Berkeley, Chicago, Cornell, Michigan, and Princeton.

Notes: In the field of mathematics, data for Chicago were unavailable. Field averages are unweighted means of the rates for each constituent university cohort.

---

[7] In each of these fields, there is, of course, a considerable dispersion of SYC figures among universities, as we show below (Figure 9.3).

[8] The basic equation for student-year cost can be thought of as the sum of the following components:

$$SYC = ETD^{Mean} + [TTA_1^{Mean} (N_1)/C] + [TTA_2^{Mean} (N_2)/C] + [TTA_3^{Mean} (N_3)/C],$$

where ETD^{Mean} is the mean time-to-degree for completers; TTA_1^{Mean} and N_1 specify the mean time-to-attrition and the absolute number of students who leave prior to the start of the second year; C is the number of completers; TTA_2^{Mean} and N_2 specify the time-to-attrition and the absolute number of students who leave after the start of the second year but prior to achieving ABD status; and TTA_3^{Mean} and N_3 specify the mean time-to-attrition and the absolute number of students who leave after achieving ABD status.

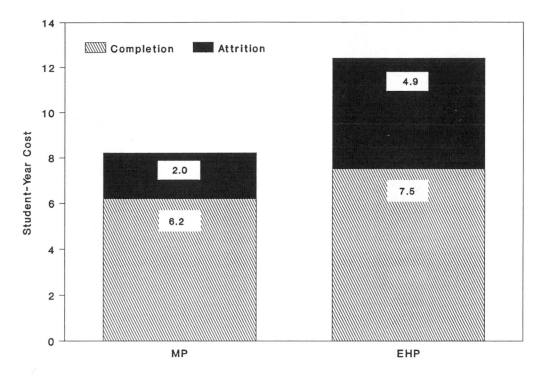

Figure 9.1
Components of Student-Year Cost by Fields of Study, 1972–1976 Entering Cohort
Source: Ten-University data set. Data are from Berkeley, Chicago, Cornell, Princeton, and Michigan.
Notes: These measures are the arithmetic average of the student-year cost values from the individual universities. See text for discussion of method of computation.

0.5 more student years than pre-ABD attrition. In the MP fields, on the other hand, the time cost of pre-ABD attrition was slightly greater than the time cost of post-ABD attrition (top panel of Figure 9.2).

Still more detailed examination of the pre-ABD stage suggests that, as one would have surmised, the student-year cost of attrition during the beginning stage of graduate study (prior to the second year) was notably small in both sets of fields. It accounted for just 0.4 years in the EHP fields and 0.2 years in the MP fields, in spite of the fact that 10 to 15 percent of all attrition in both sets of fields occurred at that stage (refer back to Figure 7.3). The implications for SYC of departures during (or at the end of) the first year are modest because "quick" attrition by definition consumes little student time. Attrition after the first year but prior to the achievement of ABD status accounted for most of the time cost at the pre-ABD stage and was far from negligible, especially in the EHP fields (1.8 years per degree conferred).

Examination of other components of SYC calls attention to an additional factor that has contributed to very high student-year cost in the EHP fields. Graduate students who reached ABD status but did not finish their degrees spent more time attaining ABD status than did their counterparts who went on to receive doctorates. Those who ultimately failed to earn doctorates spent an average of

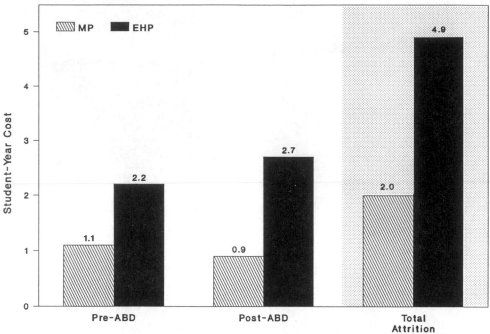

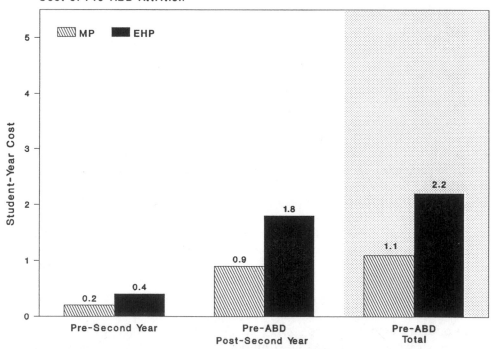

Figure 9.2
Attrition Component of Student-Year Cost by Stage and Fields of Study, 1972–1976
Entering Cohort

Source: Ten-University data set. Data are from Berkeley, Chicago, Cornell, Michigan, and Princeton.

Notes: These measures are the arithmetic average of the student-year cost values from the individual universities. See footnote 8 and text for discussion of method of computation.

3.6 years satisfying all requirements except the dissertation, whereas completers spent an average of 3.4 years at the pre-ABD stage.[9]

One central point emerges from this discussion: A large amount of "late" attrition has been more responsible than any other single factor for producing such high—unacceptably high, in our view—student-year costs in the EHP fields.

DIFFERENCES BY SCALE OF GRADUATE PROGRAM

While the overall level of student-year cost is unquestionably high in the EHP fields, there is also considerable variation among individual graduate programs. In particular, there is a definite relationship between scale of graduate program and SYC (Table 9.2). The two universities within this data set that had the largest graduate programs in the EHP fields, calibrated by sizes of entering cohorts (Berkeley and Chicago), both had a student-year cost in excess of 15 years per doctorate conferred. We have comparable data for four universities with smaller graduate programs; they had student-year costs ranging from a low of 8.7 years (Yale) to a high of 10.6 years (Cornell).[10]

TABLE 9.2
Student-Year Cost by Scale of Graduate Program, EHP Total,
1972–1976 Entering Cohort (years per degree)

University	No. Students Entering	SYC
Berkeley	820	15.9
Chicago	761	15.4
Michigan	407	10.3
Yale	382	8.7
Princeton	250	9.5
Cornell	226	10.6

Source: Ten-University data set.

[9]These figures are also for students in the 1972–1976 cohort in the EHP fields at the same five universities.

[10]Since the lack of some key data for certain universities prevented us from including in this analysis all of the universities in the Smaller and Larger groupings used in Chapter Eight, we do not capitalize "smaller" and "larger" in this discussion (thereby reserving the capitalized designations for the particular sets of universities listed in Chapter Eight).

Yale provided reliable data for the EHP fields, but no data for the MP fields, which is why Yale is included in these figures but not in the averages presented earlier. See Appendix G, Table G.9–1, for more detailed data. This basic pattern holds when we consider the more limited data available for some other universities within our Ten-University data set. A third university with large programs, Columbia, is characterized by low completion rates and long time-to-degree (see Chapter Eight) and therefore must also have had an exceptionally high SYC; however, reliable data related to stages of attrition are unavailable, and no precise calculation can be made. Similarly, the data on completion rates and time-to-degree reported earlier for Harvard suggest that student-year cost in the EHP fields at that university has probably been similar to the SYC figures for the two other universities with small programs (Cornell and Princeton), but here again we lack the information on stages of graduate study necessary for the calculation of SYC.

It is instructive to locate the sources of these very large differences in SYC between the larger and smaller graduate programs. The broadest distinction to be drawn is between the attrition component of SYC and the completion component. While both contributed to higher costs in the larger programs, the attrition component was much more important quantitatively (Table 9.3). The student-year cost of attrition was 3.9 years higher in the larger programs than in the smaller programs, and the attrition component therefore accounts for more than two-thirds of the overall difference of 5.7 years in SYC.

As noted in the previous chapter, the larger programs may have enrolled more first-year students, with the conscious objective of weeding out a significant fraction of the entering class prior to the dissertation stage of graduate work. Whatever the explanation, it is clear that the student-year cost associated with pre-ABD attrition was vastly different in the larger and smaller programs: 4.1 years per degree conferred versus 0.6 years. Thus, the weeding-out phenomenon could account for as much as 60 percent of the overall difference in student-year cost between the larger and smaller programs (or 3.5 years out of the total of 5.7 years).[11] The post-ABD costs of attrition were much less disparate: 3.2 years versus 2.8 years.

While greater attrition in both pre-ABD and post-ABD stages of graduate study was the most important contributor to the exceptionally high SYC totals for the larger programs, we should not lose sight of the significant role played by the completion component of SYC. Recipients of PhDs in the EHP fields in

TABLE 9.3
Components of Student-Year Cost by Scale of Graduate Program, EHP Total, 1972–1976 Entering Cohort (years per degree)

Component	Larger Programs	Smaller Programs	Difference
SYC of attrition			
Pre-ABD	4.1	0.6	3.5
Post-ABD	3.2	2.8	0.4
Subtotal	7.3	3.4	3.9
SYC of completion (ETD)	8.4	6.6	1.8
Total SYC	15.7	10.0	5.7

Source: Ten-University data set. Data are from Berkeley and Chicago (larger programs), and Cornell and Princeton (smaller programs). See Appendix G, Table G.9–1.

[11]Since a number of the students who leave without receiving the PhD do receive a master's degree, this is an instance in which the failure of our measure to give any "credit" for the master's degree may lead to an exaggeration of the true cost of the time invested in graduate study, seen in relation to all "outputs."

As we compare the cost of attrition at different stages (primarily pre- and post-ABD) across institutions and fields, it is important to note that programmatic requirements for ABD status differ within and across institutions, both in content and in timing. One model, which is common at large institutions, includes both a master's thesis (expected between the first and the second year) and a PhD qualifying exam (expected in the third year). A second model, which is more common within smaller programs, consists of one "general" examination, which usually occurs between the second and the third year.

the larger programs took almost two years longer (actually 1.8 years) to complete their degrees than their counterparts in the smaller programs,[12] and this disparity represents approximately one-third of the overall difference in student-year cost between the larger and smaller programs. Part of the explanation is the large tail of the elapsed time-to-degree (ETD) distribution in the EHP fields at Berkeley and Chicago, where 23 percent of the completers took 11 or more years to obtain the PhD (as compared with 5 percent in the smaller programs).[13]

In the MP fields, where the distribution of programs by scale is much less pronounced, there is no strong association between student-year cost and scale (Table 9.4).[14] Berkeley had by far the largest graduate programs in these fields (with entering cohorts in 1972–1976 more than three times as large as the entering cohorts at any of the other universities in this data set), and yet the SYC at Berkeley was not significantly different from the mean SYC for all graduate programs in the MP fields. The Princeton programs in the MP fields, which were only marginally smaller than the programs at Michigan and Cornell, had by far the lowest student-year cost (5.2 years).

The reference to this exceptionally low SYC in mathematics and physics leads directly to a more general point. There is a remarkable range of student-year cost figures when consideration is given to both field of study and individual institution (Figure 9.3). The number of years invested by all students per doctorate earned by the cohort has varied from a low of 5.0 years in mathematics at one university to a high of 20.1 years in political science at another university. Many of these differences appear to have more to do with the characteristics of particular departments than with systematic differences related to fields of study, larger versus smaller programs, or particular universities.

TABLE 9.4
Student-Year Cost by Scale of Graduate Program, MP Total, 1972–1976 Entering Cohort (years per degree)

University	No. Students Entering	SYC
Berkeley	573	9.2
Cornell	176	9.0
Michigan	160	9.3
Princeton	148	5.2

Source: Ten-University data set.

[12]This figure differs modestly from the roughly comparable figure given in Chapter Eight because it is a comparison of means, not medians, and there is some difference in the coverage of particular universities within the Ten-University data set.

[13]These very long completers were no doubt employed (probably even full-time) during at least the latter stages of work on their dissertations. The SYC measure overstates the true student-year cost in this situation since it implicitly assumes that students are always enrolled full-time. The location of these two larger programs in metropolitan areas may facilitate a combination of work-for-pay and work-on-dissertation that would be more difficult to accomplish in places such as Ithaca and Princeton. Larger programs in urban settings may feel more of a responsibility for graduate students who require this kind of flexibility.

[14]Chicago has been omitted from this table because circumstances made it impossible to provide data for mathematics.

Student-Year Cost	Field
Less than 5.5	Math (Princeton) Physics (Princeton)
Greater than 5.5, less than 8	Economics (Princeton) English (Michigan) English (Princeton)
Greater than 8, less than 9	Economics (Berkeley) Economics (Michigan) Math (Cornell) Physics (Berkeley) Physics (Chicago)
Greater than 9, less than 10	Economics (Cornell) English (Cornell) Math (Berkeley) Math (Michigan) Physics (Cornell) Physics (Michigan)
Greater than 10, less than 12.5	Economics (Chicago) History (Michigan) History (Princeton) Political Science (Cornell) Political Science (Princeton)
Greater than 12.5, less than 15	English (Chicago) History (Chicago) History (Cornell) Political Science (Berkeley) Political Science (Michigan)
Greater than 15	English (Berkeley) History (Berkeley) Political Science (Chicago)

Figure 9.3
Student-Year Cost by Field and University, 1972–1976 Entering Cohort
Source: Ten-University data set.

TRENDS

The level of SYC has risen substantially over time. A comparison of estimates for the 1962–1966 and 1972–1976 cohorts reveals increases of roughly 20 percent within the MP fields and 30 percent within the EHP fields (Figure 9.4). Almost all of the increase within MP occurred during the earlier part of this period (between the 1962–1966 and the 1967–1971 cohorts), whereas the larger part of the increase within EHP occurred later (between the 1967–1971 and the 1972–1976 cohorts).[15]

In general, the same pattern of increases occurred within the larger and smaller universities. Contributing to the overall increase in the student-year cost of a doctorate were both declining completion rates (increases in the cost of attrition) and increases in the time spent in graduate school by those who did complete PhDs (increases in the cost of completion). Particularly noteworthy is the magnitude of the increase in the cost of attrition within the EHP fields,

---

[15]These comparisons over time are based on estimates of SYC for two larger and two smaller universities (Berkeley and Chicago, and Cornell and Princeton, respectively) for which comparable data were available. The 1962–1966 figures exclude Princeton and have been aligned with the 1967–1971 figures for all four universities by correcting for the difference in the absolute level of SYC between Princeton and the other three universities, with the data for the 1967–1971 cohort used as the reference point.

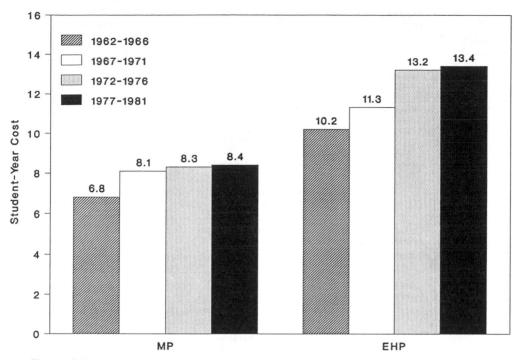

Figure 9.4
Student-Year Cost by Fields of Study, 1962–1981 Entering Cohorts
Source: Ten-University data set. Data are from Berkeley, Chicago, Cornell, and Princeton.
Notes: These measures are the arithmetic average of the student-year cost values from the individual universities. The math program at Chicago is not included in this figure (see footnote 14).

especially within the larger universities. In these universities, this component of SYC rose from 4.5 years per doctorate for the 1962–1966 cohort to 6.9 years for the 1972–1976 cohort (Table 9.5).

From the standpoint of policymakers, one of the most salient questions is whether SYC has continued to rise for more recent cohorts. Because of the long duration of graduate study, this question is hard to answer; and it is especially hard for those very groups in which the high level of SYC makes the question most pertinent (EHP students in the larger universities). No definitive answers can be given, but it is possible to make some provisional judgments by using the projection techniques described in Chapter Six.[16]

---

[16]Since many of the students in the 1977–1981 cohorts were still enrolled in 1989 (when these data were collected), comparisons with earlier cohorts can be made only by projecting ultimate completion rates and time-to-degree. Since a certain number of students in the 1972–1976 cohorts may also be expected to complete their degrees in years after 1989 (albeit a much smaller number than in the 1977–1981 cohorts), completion rates and time-to-degree were also projected for these cohorts. These SYC figures differ slightly from those presented earlier for the 1972–1976 cohorts because the earlier calculations were based on the assumption that all students reported as still enrolled after 12 to 17 years would never complete their degrees.

Projections were made by using a family of equations (the extreme value distributions) fitted to the data showing cumulative completion rates for years elapsed since entry to graduate school (see Chapter Six, especially footnote 32). While the fits are good, the nature of this process and the small number of universities for which data were available combine to caution against overinterpreting the results.

TABLE 9.5
Trends in Components of Student-Year Cost by Scale of Graduate Program and Fields of Study, 1962–1981 Entering Cohorts (years per degree)

	Cohort			
	1962–1966	*1967–1971*	*1972–1976*	*1977–1981*
EHP fields				
Larger				
Total SYC	12.9	13.8	16.0	16.7
Due to completion	8.5	8.2	9.1	9.2
Due to attrition	4.5	5.6	6.9	7.4
Smaller				
Total SYC		8.7	10.3	10.1
Due to completion		6.1	6.9	7.4
Due to attrition		2.6	3.4	2.7
MP fields				
Larger[a]				
Total SYC	7.7	8.9	9.1	9.0
Due to completion	6.5	6.9	7.2	7.4
Due to attrition	1.2	2.1	1.9	1.6
Smaller				
Total SYC		7.2	7.4	7.7
Due to completion		5.6	5.7	6.1
Due to attrition		1.7	1.8	1.6

Source: Same as Table 9.3.

Notes: See text for method of computation. Figures presented for the 1972–1976 and 1977–1981 cohorts are projections based on truncated data.

[a]Mathematics at Chicago is not included.

The main finding is that the projected SYC figures for the most recent cohorts (1977–1981) are approximately the same as the figures for the 1972–1976 cohorts. Generally speaking, this is true for both the EHP and MP groups of fields and (with some variations) for both the larger and smaller universities (Table 9.5).

Perhaps some comfort can be taken from the apparent halt in the upward trend in SYC evident in the experiences of previous cohorts. It is hard to be encouraged, however, by a situation in which the student-year cost of a doctorate appears to have become stuck at an exceedingly high level. Projecting student-year costs of 13.4 years per doctorate in the EHP fields and 8.4 years in the MP fields underscores the joint effects of low completion rates (including a considerable amount of "late" attrition) and the long duration of graduate study for many who do earn doctorates.

PART THREE

Policies and Program Design

CHAPTER TEN

Financial Support for Graduate Students

THE AVAILABILITY of financial support is often assumed to be *the* most important factor in encouraging the timely completion of the PhD—and its absence is widely believed to cause protracted periods of time to be devoted to frustrating (and often ultimately unsuccessful) efforts to obtain a PhD. Reports concerning the state of graduate education invariably cite the precipitous decline in federal funding of fellowships and traineeships as a major cause of the sharp contraction in graduate training that occurred in the 1970s and early 1980s. Looking to the future, and to an anticipated shortage of PhDs in the arts and sciences, they also regularly call for increased federal funding, with an emphasis on both new fellowship programs and the expansion of existing programs.[1]

Implicit in such discussions is the assumption that additional fellowship support will allow graduate students to finish their doctoral degrees more quickly and in greater numbers. Whether provided through federal or institutional initiatives, fellowships have long been thought to be the "best" form of financial support, and they are almost always awarded to those students thought to be most promising.

While these assumptions and attitudes seem plausible intuitively, their validity has not been demonstrated. Only a few studies have examined financial support data for complete cohorts of entering students in individual institutions, and broader sets of data have not existed.[2] As discussed in Chapter Five, our Ten-University data set—all of its limitations notwithstanding—provides a unique opportunity to examine the relationships between principal sources of support and completion rates and time-to-degree, both among universities and over time.

In order to explore these relationships, however, we must cross particularly treacherous terrain. It is difficult, first, to specify "financial support" with precision; the same student often receives multiple forms of support, sometimes even in the same academic term. Also, the great complexity and variety of patterns of financial aid employed by various graduate programs create additional problems in collecting and assembling reliable data in a consistent format. Finally, it is exceedingly difficult to disentangle completely the effects of different types of financial support from other variables (such as the perceived merit of

---

[1]See, for example, National Commission on Student Financial Assistance 1983; Bowen and Sosa 1989; and Association of American Universities 1990a.

[2]Previous studies include Stark (1966), Goldberg (1984), and Nerad and Cerny (1991). For a survey of financial support at the postbaccalaureate level, see Froomkin (1983).

To the best of our knowledge, the only source of national data across fields of study is the Doctorate Records File, with summary tabulations published in *Summary Reports* (various years). While useful as an indicator of broad national trends in patterns of support, these data do not permit comparisons of support available to those who successfully completed doctorates (the only students represented in this data set) with support provided to those who left graduate study without PhDs.

candidates). Failure to recognize these complications can lead to *over*interpretation of results—and to serious errors.

The kinds of summary statistics for groups of universities that we cited in previous chapters can be misleading since the relative importance of types of support and their timing vary markedly from institution to institution. Some universities offer many fellowships and few teaching assistantships (TAs), others offer large numbers of TAs, some offer TAs mainly to advanced students while others use TAs in the early years of graduate study, some expect large numbers of entering students to pay their own way, and so on—in dizzying variety. To permit informed interpretations of results under these variegated conditions, we adopt a different approach in this chapter and present data for individual universities.

Two general conclusions stand out:

- First, money plainly matters. Students forced to rely primarily on their own resources have had markedly higher attrition rates and longer time-to-degree than comparable students who received financial aid.
- Second, the *form* of financial support appears to make less difference than has commonly been supposed. Students in the English, history, and political science (EHP) fields supported mainly by fellowships have not had consistently higher completion rates than students who relied more heavily on teaching assistantships; on the contrary, teaching assistants have not infrequently had higher completion rates. Students with fellowships have tended to take somewhat less time to finish their degrees than students with TAs, but the differences in elapsed time-to-degree observed to date have been modest. These consistent patterns—if properly understood—do not negate the contributions that can be made by fellowship programs. But they do highlight fundamental questions concerning the structure of financial support, which we discuss in more detail below and in later chapters.

COMPLETION RATES

"Institutional" versus "Own Support"

The universities participating in this study were asked to classify graduate students by their "primary" (generally defined as "largest single") source of support.[3] We find a very definite pattern when we compare completion rates for students at each institution in the EHP fields whose primary source of support was "Institutional Support" (fellowships, provided from external or internal sources, or teaching assistantships), with completion rates for students who had to rely on "Own Support." Fifteen institution- and time-specific comparisons of this kind can be made (treating a comparison between groups of students with and without Institutional Support within a single university during a given five-year interval as one case—for example, students with and without Institutional Support in the EHP fields at Columbia in the 1972–1976 entering cohort).

---

[3]See Appendix A for a detailed explanation of data collection and Chapter Five for a discussion of trends in forms of support in the EHP fields. We focus here on the EHP fields because the number of graduate students supported primarily by their own resources in the sciences (and usually in economics as well) was too small in most cases to permit meaningful analysis.

In 14 of the 15 comparisons, completion rates were lower for students who relied primarily on their own resources than for students with institutional funding.[4]

In general, completion rates for Own Support students were approximately one-half to two-thirds as high as completion rates for institutionally supported students (Figure 10.1). And it must be remembered that students in the Own

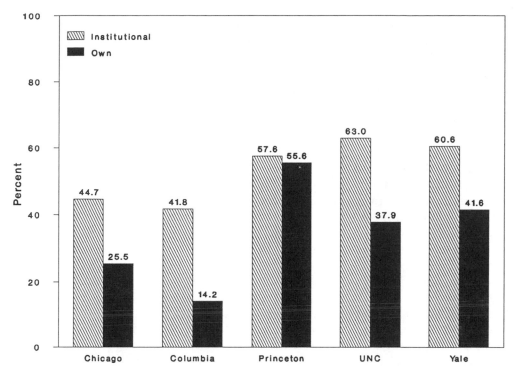

Figure 10.1
Minimum Completion Rates by Primary Source of Support, EHP Total, 1972–1976 Entering Cohort

Source: Ten-University data set. See Appendix G, Table G.10–1.

Notes: Institutional Support includes both students supported primarily through fellowships and students supported primarily through teaching assistantships.

---

[4]See Appendix G, Table G.10–1. We show completion rates for only those cells that contain at least 20 students. Thus, no completion rates are shown for Own Support students at Cornell because the number of students in this category was always between 10 and 16 per cohort. As Table G.10–1 indicates, many other cells contain well over 100 observations.

Princeton is something of an anomaly. It is the only institution where the disparity in completion rates between supported and nonsupported students was so small that it did not pass tests of statistical significance. The explanation requires an understanding of Princeton's financial aid and admission policies in the 1970s. Support was awarded on the basis of financial need, and students were admitted without Institutional Support only if it was clear that they had sufficient resources of their own (including loan funds provided by the university at low interest rates) to be able to finance full-time graduate study. Thus, in the Princeton case, there does not seem to have been a substantial difference in available resources between students receiving support from the university and those dependent on their own resources. In fact, those self-supported students who were relatively affluent may have had more resources at their disposal than students with modest amounts of university-provided assistance. Given these rather special circumstances, the high completion rate of self-supported students at Princeton can be seen as corroborating the basic relationship described here, rather than contradicting it.

Support category (as defined here) may have received some assistance from institutional sources. Students entirely dependent on resources of their own are presumably even less likely to complete doctorates. In another study, completion rates for such students in the EHP fields were found to be as low as 3 percent.[5]

An obvious hypothesis is that Institutional Support allowed students to concentrate more fully on their studies.[6] Most graduate students are financially independent of their parents and may even have families of their own to support. Without any financial aid, they generally have to find other employment, and the attendant obligations may prevent them from completing their degrees in a timely manner, if at all. For this reason, Own Support will often correlate with part-time student status (which, in turn, may remove eligibility for institutional funding). Studying on only a part-time basis surely reduces the probability of earning a doctorate.

The basic pattern described above holds when we look separately at the main stages of doctoral education and employ a somewhat different criterion for defining Institutional and Own Support.[7] The likelihood that a student will cross the first major hurdle in seeking the PhD and achieve ABD status is strongly associated with the provision of Institutional Support. Students who received either a fellowship or a teaching assistantship (or both) during their first two years of graduate study achieved ABD status in far higher proportions than students who did not receive support. In the 1972–1976 cohorts, the differences in these first-stage completion rates were 7 to 10 percentage points at Princeton and Yale, and 15 to 25 points at Chicago, Columbia, and UNC (top panel of Figure 10.2).[8]

It is not surprising that the presence of Institutional Support also increases the probability that students who have reached ABD status will subsequently complete dissertations and receive the PhD. The more noteworthy finding is that differences in final-stage completion rates are appreciably smaller in a number of instances than corresponding differences at the pre-ABD stage.

---

[5]Stark 1966, 26–27. This early study was based on data for students who entered the English, history, and political science departments at Berkeley in 1951, 1954, and 1957. Their completion rates were compared with completion rates for students in chemistry. This author's stark conclusion was that "students other than chemists probably aren't being flunked out, but are instead being slowly *starved out*" (emphasis in original).

[6]Solmon (1976, 133) reminds us that financial aid also serves other purposes. It adds to self-esteem by indicating that faculty believe a student is worthy of support. Also, some forms of financial aid, such as teaching and research assistantships, bring students into more frequent contact with faculty members.

[7]In this part of the analysis, those students who had either a fellowship or a teaching assistantship (or both) during the first or second year of graduate study are classified as having had Institutional Support during the pre-ABD stage of graduate study. Students who had neither of these forms of Institutional Support are placed in the Own Support category. Similarly, students who had either a fellowship or a teaching assistantship at any time after achieving ABD status are classified as having had Institutional Support during the dissertation stage; and students who had neither form of Institutional Support after achieving ABD status are classified as Own Support. No concept of "primary" support is invoked here, and some students classified as having received Institutional Support may have received relatively small sums of money from institutional sources and been heavily dependent on their own resources. Put another way, Own Support is now a very pure category, since it denotes the complete absence of *any* Institutional Support.

[8]See Appendix G, Table G.10–2 for additional first-stage completion rates, by type of support, for other cohorts. While the absolute figures vary by cohort, the basic relationship is the same.

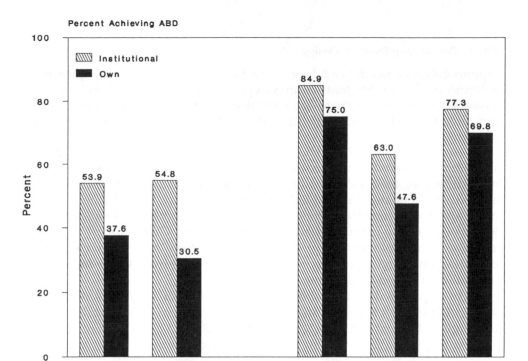

Percent Achieving ABD

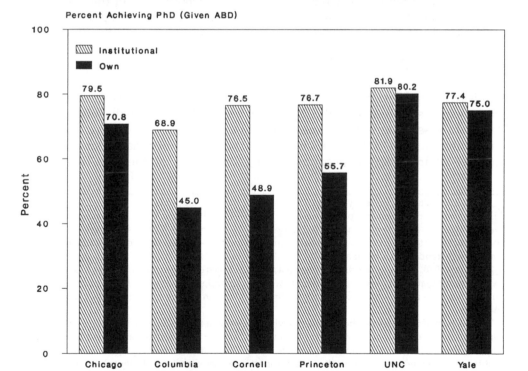

Percent Achieving PhD (Given ABD)

Figure 10.2
Minimum Completion Rates by Source of Support, University, and Stage of Graduate Study, EHP Total, 1972–1976 Entering Cohort

Source: Ten-University data set. See Appendix G, Tables G.10–2 and G.10–3.

Notes: Institutional Support includes students supported through either fellowships or teaching assistantships, or both. The top panel reflects source of support during the first two years of study; the bottom panel reflects source of support during the dissertation stage. See text for further definition of support categories.

Indeed, at UNC and Yale, they are so small that they fail to pass significance tests (Figure 10.2 and Appendix G, Tables G.10–2 and G.10–3).

The variations across universities are intriguing. At Chicago, attrition rates for Own Support students were high in the pre-ABD years but relatively low for those who cleared that hurdle, even if they were solely dependent on their own resources after achieving ABD status. Is it reasonable to suppose that at institutions characterized by considerable early attrition, the Own Support students who do reach the dissertation stage possess in unusually large measure the persistence needed to press on to obtain the PhD?[9]

The patterns at Cornell and Princeton offer a sharp contrast. At these two institutions, the ABD students with Institutional Support have gone on to finish their dissertations in much higher proportions than their peers who were dependent entirely on Own Support at this final stage of graduate study. There is much less early attrition at these universities, and it is possible that the real testing of dedication to the task—for students who must rely solely on their own resources—occurs at the dissertation stage.

The Vexing Issue of Student "Quality"

A valid criticism of the above interpretation of the consistent correlation between higher completion rates and the presence of Institutional Support is that it does not take into account the possibility of systematic differences in the average quality of those groups of students with and without Institutional Support. In other words, it is possible that students dependent on their own resources complete the PhD in smaller proportions because, academically, they are weaker students. One would expect that more of these students were "borderline" cases, who were admitted, but not supported financially, because their credentials did not bode as well for successful completion of the PhD program.

This line of reasoning could help explain the exceptionally large disparity— approximately a 2:1 ratio—in overall completion rates in the Larger programs (Berkeley, Chicago, Columbia) between students with institutional support and students dependent primarily on their own resources. Presumably the Larger programs take more chances in admissions, and then count on a competitive process of selection during the first year or two to narrow the pool of PhD candidates.

We attempted to obtain additional data that would permit proper analysis of cross-effects of this kind. GRE scores were available only for some students, however, and these data do not suggest a strong correlation between this very imperfect measure of quality and completion rates.[10] Qualitative differences between prospective students are notoriously difficult to measure, and we

---

[9]The limited data that are available for Berkeley (where financial-support data could be provided only for entering cohorts from 1978 forward) are broadly consistent with the pattern at Chicago.

[10]Among the three larger institutions, only Columbia was able to supply scores for as many as 60 percent of the entering students in the EHP fields in the 1972–1976 cohort. We aggregated the 522 scores that we had into two broad ranges: GRE-Verbal scores of 700 and over, and GRE-Verbal scores of 699 and below. There was no significant difference in minimum completion rates. Indeed, students with lower GRE-Verbal scores actually completed their doctorates in slightly greater proportions than students with higher scores (29 percent versus 25 percent). The absence of a statistically significant relationship in these data is consistent with findings based on much more elaborate research. See, for example, Dawes 1975; Rubin 1980; and Zwick 1991.

thought it might help to use a more direct measure—namely, the rankings assigned by graduate schools to students at the time of admission. These departmental rankings reflect both quantitative measures, such as GRE scores and undergraduate grades, as well as recommendations and other indicators thought by those making admission decisions to be relevant.

Rankings were available at three universities (Columbia, Princeton, and Yale). At Columbia and Yale, we found the expected simple correlation between quality and outcomes: Students ranked in the top half of those offered admission had higher completion rates than those ranked in the bottom half. (The rankings are too crude an index of quality to justify groupings more elaborate than "top half" and "bottom half.") At Princeton, on the other hand, there were no consistent differences in completion rates between those in the top and bottom halves of the distribution. Differences in the sizes of entering cohorts may help explain these results. Columbia, in particular, admits so many students that the range of qualifications must be broader than the range at a comparable university that enrolls very small cohorts.

The most revealing findings were obtained when we separated out those students ranked in the bottom half and then compared completion rates for those bottom-half students who had Institutional Support with completion rates for those dependent on Own Support. Those with Institutional Support consistently had higher completion rates than those who relied on Own Support. The conclusion is clear. Institutional Support continues to be correlated with completion rates after controlling for quality in this rough way. This basic pattern holds for overall completion rates, for first-stage (ABD) completion rates, and for dissertation-stage completion rates (calculated with only those students who had achieved ABD status included in the base).[11]

Of course, this is hardly a perfect test of the complex relationships involved, and some part of the association could well be due to further variations in quality *within* the bottom half—which may have been correlated with Institutional Support. Still, we interpret these findings as reinforcing the commonsense view that the availability of institutional funding definitely helps graduate students complete doctoral programs.

Another way of thinking about these interrelationships deserves mention. Among the highly select students admitted to these graduate programs, factors such as enthusiasm, commitment, sense of direction, and intellectual and emotional maturity are plainly important in determining whether a student will

---

[11]See Appendix G, Table G.10–4. Similar comparisons could not be made for students in the top half because almost all of them received Institutional Support. Moreover, many of these highly ranked students who did not receive funding from the university probably had either financial resources of their own or sources of external support.

Another type of comparison at Columbia is instructive. When we look only at students who were supported primarily through fellowships, we find that those ranked in the bottom half of the distribution had much *higher* completion rates than those ranked in the top half. This counterintuitive finding almost certainly reflects awards of fellowships *following* admission; that is, we suspect that those students in the bottom half who ultimately were recorded as having been supported primarily by fellowships were identified in the course of their graduate study as exceptionally promising. It is not surprising then, that this rather small number of bottom-half students chosen carefully on the basis of their actual performance in graduate school completed at higher rates than the larger number of top-half fellowship recipients, many of whom were no doubt chosen prior to admission. This pattern illustrates well the importance of looking carefully at the dynamics of graduate programs, and at the timing of decisions concerning various forms of financial support.

complete the PhD. While we cannot assess these attributes ourselves, we can assume that prestigious national fellowship programs attempted to take such factors into consideration in choosing their winners. Even this still-broader measure of perceived merit does not prove to be a very powerful predictor of either completion rates or time-to-degree—in spite of the simultaneous presence of generous financial support (Chapter Eleven).

There is one reliable set of national data germane to this discussion, but its coverage by field of study is limited. The National Science Foundation (NSF) carefully tracks applicants to the NSF fellowship program and groups them on the basis of panel ratings. We have worked with the records for three groups defined by such rankings and award status: members of Quality Group I, all of whom were awarded fellowships; members of Quality Group II who were awarded fellowships because of considerations such as geographic location and gender; and the other members of Quality Group II, who were *not* awarded fellowships.[12]

The NSF fields most comparable to our EHP fields are the "other social sciences," which include mainly political science, sociology, and anthropology—but not economics or psychology. When we compare completion rates for award winners in Quality Groups I and II (1972–1976 entering cohort), we find small differences that, surprisingly, favor the Group II awardees: The completion rates were 59 percent and 65 percent, respectively. This result suggests the absence of any pure "quality" effect, at least at this level of accomplishment. The more significant finding is that Quality Group II *non*awardees had an appreciably lower completion rate (51 percent) than either group of award winners. The most obvious inference is, again, that funding makes a difference—especially in fields in which non-NSF sources of institutional support are limited.[13]

In fields where institutional support is more readily available from non-NSF sources, we might expect a slightly different pattern of completion rates. Physics is a good reference point. In this field, the rank ordering of completion rates across the same three groups was identical with the ranking for "other social sciences"—but the drop-off in the completion rate among the Quality Group II nonawardees was much smaller (Table 10.1). The smaller difference in physics could well be due to the greater availability of other (non-NSF) sources of financial support in this field, as compared with the situation in "other social sciences."

TABLE 10.1
Minimum Completion Rates, NSF Quality Groups, 1972–1976 Cohort (percent)

	Quality Group		
	QG1-Awd	QG2-Awd	QG2-Non
Other social sciences	59.3	64.8	50.7
Physics	81.8	87.8	79.8

Source: National Fellowship data set.

Notes: "QG1-Awd" is Quality Group I awardees. "QG2-Awd" is Quality Group II awardees. "QG2-Non" is Quality Group II nonawardees.

---

[12]See Snyder (1988) for further discussion of Quality Groups.

[13]These completion rates are based on special tabulations prepared by NSF.

On the basis of these varied sets of data, we conclude that the relationship between the availability of institutional support and eventual completion rates would not be eliminated even if it were possible to employ more sophisticated tests controlling for cross-relationships with perceived merit. The evidence seems persuasive: The availability of financial support matters greatly. We turn now to an examination of differences in completion rates associated with the *form* in which institutional support is provided.

Fellowships versus Teaching Assistantships

Because fellowships provide at least some freedom from both financial concerns and time-consuming responsibilities associated with earning money, they have been thought to be the ideal form of support for graduate students—at least in the humanities. In the sciences, some argue that research assistantships can be more useful than fellowships. Research assistantships are, in any case, rarely available in the humanities. In these fields, teaching assistantships are the alternative mode of institutional support.[14]

Within the Ten-University data set (and the EHP fields), Cornell offers the best opportunity to compare outcomes for students with fellowship support to outcomes for students with teaching assistantships.[15] A mixed picture emerges when overall completion rates are compared for the two cohorts of Cornell students where the "primary support" criterion can be used to distinguish fellowship support from teaching-assistantship support (Figure 10.3 and Appendix G, Table G.10–5).[16] In the 1962–1966 cohort, fellowship recipients

---

[14]In this respect, mathematics is more like the humanities than it is like the sciences. The forthcoming report of the Committee on Doctoral and Postdoctoral Study in the Mathematical Sciences (1992) calls attention to the overdependence on teaching assistantships for financial support in the mathematical sciences. According to the data collected for this study, nearly 60 percent of full-time mathematics graduate students in doctorate-granting institutions were supported by teaching assistantships, as contrasted with a figure of 23 percent for science and engineering graduate students.

[15]The structure of financial support at the other universities limits the direct comparisons that can be made. During the years in question, Chicago, Princeton, and Yale had large numbers of students supported primarily by fellowships, but only insignificant numbers supported mainly by teaching assistantships. Berkeley, Columbia, and UNC, on the other hand, had large numbers supported by teaching assistantships but relatively few in the fellowship category. Some use can be made of data from Berkeley and Columbia, but it must be acknowledged that we are dependent mainly on observations from Cornell for this part of our analysis.

[16]Completion rates for the 1967–1971 and 1972–1976 cohorts are not shown in the figure (though they are given in Appendix G, Table G.10–5) because they may be biased. Use of the primary-support criterion can lead to biased estimates of overall completion rates if the probability of receiving one form of support or the other is itself a function of the stage of graduate study. For example, if fellowships are given mainly to first- and second-year students, and TAs are given mainly to dissertation-stage students, students supported primarily by teaching assistantships will almost certainly be seen to have had higher completion rates simply because more of them survived to the dissertation stage. In this hypothetical case, attrition at the pre-ABD stage will be concentrated among fellowship-holders purely as a consequence of the pattern of financial support. And in both the 1967–1971 and 1972–1976 cohorts, the ratio of fellowships to TAs at the first- and second-year stage was at least twice the corresponding ratio at the dissertation-stage.

Fortunately, this problem is not nearly as severe in the 1962–1966 and 1977–1981 cohorts at Cornell. In the 1962–1966 cohort, the difference in relative numbers of awards is both less pronounced and in the opposite direction (fellowships were relatively more common at the dissertation stage than they were during the first and second years); as a consequence, the "true" difference in completion rates between fellowship holders and TA holders must have been smaller

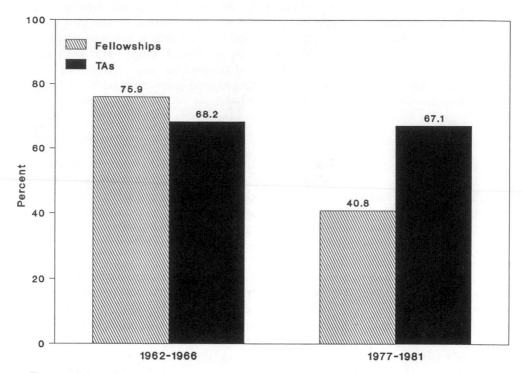

Figure 10.3
Minimum Completion Rates by Primary Source of Support at Cornell, EHP Total,
1962–1981 Entering Cohorts
Source: Ten-University data set. See Appendix G, Table G.10–5.

completed the PhD in larger numbers than holders of TAs. In the 1977–1981
cohort, on the other hand, the opposite relationship holds, and the difference
between the minimum completion rates for those supported primarily by
teaching assistantships (67 percent) and those supported primarily by fellowships (41 percent) is hardly trivial.

More information can be gleaned from the Cornell data by looking separately
at the two main stages of graduate study and grouping students into pure
categories that include those who had only one form of support or the other
(fellowships or TAs, but not both). These comparisons are free of the problem of
bias that restricts the reliability of the primary-support comparisons and can be
made for all cohorts.

The probability of completing the first stage of graduate study and achieving
ABD status (top panel of Figure 10.4) was about the same for fellowship holders
and holders of TAs in the two earliest cohorts. Starting with the 1972–1976
cohort, however, a definite pattern emerges. Students with TAs were appreciably more likely to complete this phase of graduate study than were students
supported by fellowships. The probability of earning a PhD, given the achieve-

---

in this cohort than the apparent difference shown in Figure 10.3. In the 1977–1981 cohort, the ratio
of fellowships to TAs was much more comparable in the two stages of graduate study, and there is
no reason to believe that the higher completion rate shown for holders of TAs is an artifact of the
pattern of financial support.

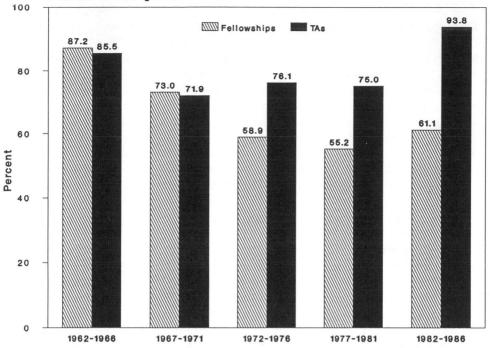

Percent Achieving ABD

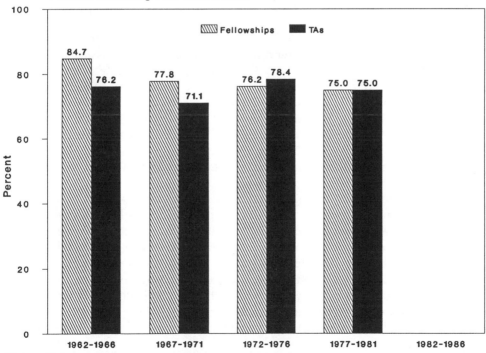

Percent Achieving PhD (Given ABD)

Figure 10.4
Minimum Completion Rates by Source of Support at Cornell, EHP Total, 1962–1986 Entering Cohorts

Source: Ten-University data set. See Appendix G, Table G.10–5.

Notes: The top panel reflects source of support during the first two years of study; the bottom panel reflects source of support during the dissertation stage. See text for further definition of support categories.

ment of ABD status, was slightly higher for fellowship holders than for TA holders in the early cohorts and then essentially the same in the 1972–1976 and 1977–1981 cohorts (bottom panel of Figure 10.4). These finer-grained data suggest that the higher overall completion rates for students supported primarily by TAs in the 1977–1981 cohort were due to differences in outcomes at the early stage of graduate study, not to differences at the dissertation stage.[17]

Seen in the context of the conventional wisdom concerning the virtues of fellowships, these findings may well be regarded by some as counterintuitive. In recent cohorts, at least, completion rates for students supported by teaching assistantships have not lagged behind completion rates for students supported by fellowships—indeed, students holding teaching assistantships reached ABD status in higher proportions than fellowship recipients and then went on to complete PhDs in roughly the same proportions as those holders of fellowships who had also achieved ABD status.

When considered in conjunction with the discussion in previous chapters, one possible interpretation deserves consideration. Teaching facilitates a structured engagement with one's colleagues (as well as one's students), and the sometimes-higher completion rates of students in the EHP fields who had served as teaching assistants can be seen as confirming the hypothesis that such interaction is an important, perhaps even vital, factor for many students in the successful completion of graduate study—or at least in achieving ABD status. Students holding only fellowships may have found it easier to become isolated or even "lost" in the bowels of vast research libraries and the complexities of subjects hard to unravel without collaborators and some modicum of structure.

The apparent strengthening of this pattern over time also deserves comment. Using the primary-support criterion (Figure 10.3), we saw that fellowship recipients in the 1962–1966 cohort finished at a higher rate than teaching assistants in that cohort, but that fellowship recipients in the 1977–1981 cohort finished at appreciably lower rates, relative to TA recipients. When we looked in more detail at trends in completion rates by stages, we found that the TA-"advantage" at the pre-ABD stage became consistently larger in each succeeding cohort; and at the dissertation stage, the advantage once enjoyed by fellowship holders in the earlier cohorts disappeared in the data for the later cohorts.

Changes in academic job markets may help explain this trend. During the 1960s, when confidence about academic job prospects was high, students may have needed relatively little encouragement to complete doctoral studies. In this environment, the usual kinds of fellowships may have been an effective form of support at both the pre-ABD and dissertation stages. As conditions in academic labor markets deteriorated and students became discouraged about their prospects, one would expect personal support and "engagement" with one's intended vocation to become much more important. Many students no doubt developed a real need for the kind of structured relationships with faculty that

---

[17]At UNC, we have usable data for EHP students in the 1967–1971 cohort, and there, too, students with TAs achieved ABD status in higher proportions than students with fellowships (83 percent versus 68 percent). This same pattern also exists in the data for recent cohorts at Columbia. At Berkeley, on the other hand, there was no appreciable difference in first-stage completion rates between fellowship holders and TA holders (see Appendix G, Table G.10–5).

An extensive study done at Northwestern found little evidence that students awarded fellowships in their first year consistently outperformed other students (Goldberg 1984).

teaching assistantships facilitated. Also, contact with undergraduate students may have served to reinforce prior commitments to teaching as a career (and thus to continuing pursuit of the PhD), in periods when many other omens were unfavorable.[18]

Another (noncompeting) hypothesis is based on the response of some faculty members and professional associations to the grim job prospects for academics in the 1970s. In some instances, graduate students were counseled to consider "alternative career choices," such as law and business.[19] It is possible that holders of fellowships were more mobile, from this standpoint, than students chosen by their departments for teaching assistantships. Many of those chosen to receive national fellowships, for example, were presumably broadly talented young people capable of pursuing many vocations.

Comparisons with the Sciences

In physics, the relationship between completion rates and sources of financial support is opposite to the one found in the EHP fields: Students supported primarily by fellowships completed the PhD at rates substantially higher than those supported primarily by teaching assistantships (Figure 10.5). Yet this two-way comparison tells only part of the story, since in the sciences research assistantships are a third major form of support. Overall, students supported primarily through research assistantships completed the PhD in higher proportions than students in any other support category.

The explanation for these relationships is straightforward and related directly to the comments made above about the need to bear in mind the patterns of financial support in various settings at different stages of graduate study. In two of the three universities included in this analysis (Berkeley and Cornell), research assistantships in physics were largely reserved for students who had "survived" to the dissertation stage of graduate work. They went almost exclusively to students who had surmounted earlier hurdles and who were thought to have something valuable to contribute to the research project providing the funding. In contrast, teaching assistantships were awarded mainly to pre-ABD students. In such situations, it is not surprising that students who were reported to have been supported *primarily* through teaching assistantships also had far lower completion rates than other students. If these pre-ABD teaching assistants had "stayed the course," they would have been recorded as having been supported primarily through research assistantships.[20]

---

[18]The "socializing" value of teaching assistantships is stressed in a recent study by Girves and Wemmerus (1988). On the basis of a detailed study of experience at Ohio State, they note that in "assistantship roles, a student is given the opportunity to apprentice in the academic profession. Students learn the norms and expectations of the department as they become part of the instructional or research team. Fellowship students . . . may miss out on this important socialization process and may become isolated and even alienated from the department" (p. 170).

[19]See, for example, Hellstrom 1979, 95–99. Professor Hellstrom served as Chairman of the Modern Language Association's Advisory Committee on the Job Market, and in this essay applauds the efforts of various regional groups to "initiate and sponsor conferences on alternative career choices." Hellstrom is outspoken, however, in voicing his own skepticism that administrators and faculty members in general will "face their responsibilities" in this matter. He notes all the pressures to maintain graduate enrollments, as well as the proliferation of new programs.

[20]We are indebted to Professor David Jackson of the Berkeley physics department and Professor David Castle of the Cornell physics department for help in understanding their respective graduate programs.

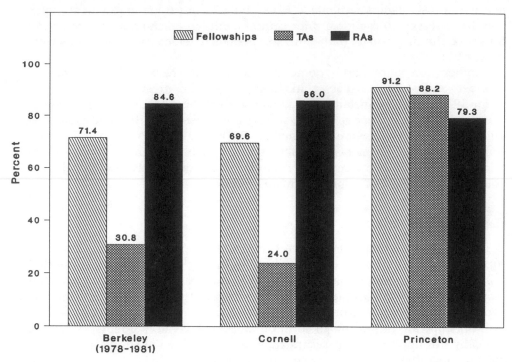

Figure 10.5
Minimum Completion Rates in Physics by Primary Source of Support and University,
1972–1976 Entering Cohort
Source: Ten-University data set.

The third university, Princeton, is a very different case because research
assistantships were often awarded to students in early stages of their graduate
study precisely to give them some immediate exposure to research. Nor were
teaching assistantships reserved for beginning students. In this institutional
context, completion rates for physics students correlate differently with type-of-
support than at the other two universities. Fellowship recipients, for instance,
had unusually high completion rates (over 90 percent). This is readily understandable when we recognize that, for many years, the Princeton physics
department went to great lengths to ensure that even the holders of the most
prestigious fellowships participated in laboratory research at early stages of their
careers in order to reduce the twin risks of isolation and lack of appreciation for
the nature of research at the graduate level.[21]

More generally, as noted earlier, holders of fellowships in physics have had
relatively high completion rates. In a field such as physics, structure is inherent
in requirements and the collaborative nature of most research, and teaching
assistantships are not needed to provide contact with faculty or the field. In this
context, with laboratory settings and group research projects already in place,
fellowship funding (or a research assistantship tied directly to the student's own
project) is likely to be most effective in promoting the expeditious completion of
the doctorate, since no time is taken from work on the student's own tasks. But

---

[21]Professor Samuel Treiman of the Princeton physics department was helpful in explaining the
special characteristics of his department's graduate program.

of course these forms of support do not provide experience in teaching, which also should be an integral part of graduate study for students who intend to pursue academic careers.[22]

In the EHP fields, the general pattern of financial support makes it less likely that students will fail to gain teaching experience, and teaching assistantships also provide socializing benefits that are achieved in other ways in the sciences. However, as we discuss below, the risk is that excessive reliance on teaching assistantships will delay completion of the doctorate indefinitely. Fellowship support can be especially critical in the final stages of graduate study, when students in the humanities and related fields need uninterrupted time to finish dissertations if they are to complete their degrees. The *timing* of various forms of graduate student support is itself of great importance.

TIME-TO-DEGREE

Having to rely on one's own resources not only reduces the likelihood that a PhD will eventually be obtained, it also normally entails longer time to the doctorate. The Ten-University data set supports this proposition and provides new information concerning magnitudes. Own Support students (using the primary support criterion) took about 1 full year longer than students with Institutional Support at Columbia, 0.9 of a year at UNC, 0.8 of a year at Yale, and 0.3 of a year at Berkeley and Princeton. These are comparisons of medians, and, viewed in the context of the life of a graduate student, may be read as either large or small numbers, depending on one's expectations. In general, they represent an extra 10 to 20 percent of the time required by the typical student to earn a doctorate.[23]

While teaching assistantships in the EHP fields facilitate involvement in one's field and encourage graduate students to complete their studies, the extra time required for preparation and teaching could lengthen significantly the time-to-degree. Again, experience at Cornell is the only reliable benchmark that can be used to estimate the magnitude of any such effect. In all cohorts after the 1962–1966 cohort, students at Cornell supported primarily by teaching assistantships took longer to earn doctorates than students supported primarily by

---

[22]Unfortunately, not all teaching assistantships in the sciences offer good preparation for teaching. While there is considerable variety in the duties assigned to teaching assistants in the humanities (ranging from stimulating participation in a course directed by a respected faculty member to more mundane supervision of language sections), they are likely to be involved in actual teaching or leading of discussion groups that broaden the student's understanding of the field. Teaching assistants in the sciences are more likely to perform less-stimulating tasks, such as grading problem sets and supervising laboratories. The wide range of tasks assigned to teaching assistants in all fields makes it harder to generalize about this group than about fellowship holders—who are generally required only to cash checks.

[23]The source is the Ten-University data set. A broadly similar conclusion was reached by Abedi and Benkin (1987) in their study of recipients of doctorates at UCLA, which was based on data from the Doctorate Records File. While the categories of financial support were limited to those available from this source, regression analysis led to the conclusion that "the most important variable in predicting the total time to doctorate for all UCLA doctorate recipients (1976–1985) was the source of support during graduate school" (p. 10). Mean time-to-degree for students dependent primarily on "Own Earnings" was 10.82 years, compared with 8.06 years for "Fellowships/Grants," and 7.68 for "On Campus Earnings" (Table 1, p. 9). Unfortunately, the categories do not allow calculation of separate figures for teaching assistants or for students in our particular fields of study.

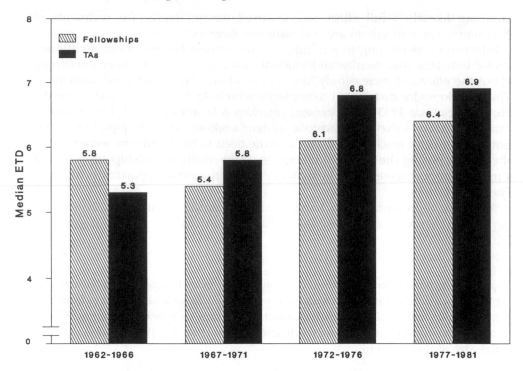

Figure 10.6
Elapsed Time-to-Degree by Primary Source of Support at Cornell, EHP Total, 1962–1981
Entering Cohorts
Source: Ten-University data set. See Appendix G, Table G.10–6.

fellowships. The difference was about half a year (Figure 10.6 and Appendix G, Table G.10–6).

The data on stages of graduate study at Cornell indicate that reliance on the TA-form of support has had a particularly strong effect on time-to-degree in the most recent cohorts, and that the effect has been most evident at the dissertation stage. In the 1977–1981 cohort, EHP students dependent on teaching assistantships spent an average (median) of 3.4 years after achieving ABD status before receiving their PhDs, as compared with a median of 2.9 years for students with fellowship support. Students in this cohort with TAs also spent two-tenths of a year longer to reach ABD status than students with fellowships.[24]

Moreover, we suspect that these very limited data understate, perhaps to a significant degree, the extent to which teaching assistantships can extend the period of time needed to obtain a doctorate in the EHP fields. As we saw earlier, the major increase in dependence on teaching assistantships occurred in the late 1970s and early 1980s at universities such as Berkeley and Yale, as well as Cornell (refer back to Figure 5.9), and these developments may not yet have had

---

[24]See Appendix G, Table G.10–6. The available data for Berkeley and Columbia are too limited to be helpful in assessing differences in time-to-degree.

anything like their full effect on measured time-to-degree for recipients of doctorates, some of whom are still pursuing degrees.[25]

Information pertaining to a number of universities beyond those mentioned above indicates that faculty and students alike have become very concerned about the effects of increasingly heavy dependence on teaching assistantships. The questionnaire distributed to students who held Mellon Fellowships in the Humanities from 1983 to the present provides relevant evidence. One question concerned factors that can lead to a student's taking longer to gain the PhD.[26] Employment as a teaching assistant and the need to hold odd jobs were cited as the factors posing the greatest difficulties. Conversely, fellowship support and summer support were overwhelmingly cited as the most important positive or "helpful" factors.

A faculty representative in English commented as follows in submitting a departmental proposal to the Mellon Foundation for strengthening graduate education:

> Normally our students are teaching not simply for years but for substantial amounts of time each year and in a great variety of courses. . . . The teaching changes from year to year and students find themselves making an enormous investment of time simply in reading and following the courses they teach. They find that the thesis is pushed to the edge of their concern, ...

A representative from another university, describing the situation in Romance Languages, wrote:

> Partly because teaching absorbs time not directly devoted to course work, and partly because graduate course work and exam preparation cannot readily be made research-oriented, Romance Languages students, like humanities students generally, do not have the advantage of their scientific colleagues of integrating closely their research with their graduate courses or teaching.

A faculty member in comparative literature at a third university commented:

> Figures indicate a negative correlation between teaching and progress toward degree, and although we have no departmental statistics on this point, our collective observation emphatically corroborates it. Add to that slowdown the university's four-year limit on graduate student teaching, and one has a paradigmatic case of the student who, in the fifth or sixth year—usually at some early stage in dissertation writing—must turn to other part-time (or full-time) employment, a circumstance that at best merely slows progress further and at worse causes the student to take a leave of absence or drop out.

---

[25]Subsequently, in the late 1980s, efforts were made at a number of universities to reduce reliance on TAs, in part because of widely shared concerns about their effects on the duration of graduate study. See, for example, the Prown Report at Yale (Prown and Committee 1989).

[26]See Appendix C for more information on this survey.

And one last comment along similar lines:

> Teaching—with its dual role of support and preparation for later jobs—is an important part of professional formation for most graduate students, but to realize its value demands both careful preparation of would-be teaching assistants and teaching loads not so large as to prevent progress toward the degree. Both the load at one time and the length of time spent teaching need to be moderate. Our students tend to be divided between those who teach too much (and are slowed) and those who teach too little (and lack adequate experience going on the job market). The quantity and form of financial aid thus constitute the single most decisive variable.

These examples could be multiplied many times. Excessive teaching leads to greater time-to-degree and eventually to some greater attrition. Multiple jobs inevitably increase already existing pressures. The variety of teaching assignments—and their lack of connection to research—makes for a more difficult situation in the humanities than in the sciences. The picture is generally one of considerable difficulty if not bleakness—even though virtually all students testify to their enjoyment of teaching itself. It is the "excess" that matters.

In concluding this chapter, we want to warn again against overinterpretation of results. The measures of different forms of support used here are very crude. They do not capture the *amounts* of support provided, nor do they reflect in any detail the sequence of forms of support, the degree of continuity of support provided, or (in most cases) the criteria used by departments to allocate available student-aid resources.

We do not doubt the most basic conclusion: Institutional assistance is of critical value in permitting students to complete their degrees, and in reasonable periods of time. Increasing the effectiveness of graduate education requires a willingness to support those students who cannot pursue a PhD without considerable financial assistance.

Some of the statistical associations summarized in this chapter may discourage unduly those who see the value of providing fellowships to graduate students— and may encourage a further proliferation of teaching assistantships. In our view (expanded in subsequent chapters), more teaching assistantships are not the solution to any of the problems facing graduate education, even as we strongly endorse the value of this form of support. (Nor is heavier reliance on teaching assistantships desirable, in our view, from the perspective of undergraduate education.)

The analysis of this chapter is sobering, however, in that it causes those of us who have been advocates of the fellowship form of support to avoid exaggerating its value *independent of the right supporting environment*. Physics provides a useful example of how well fellowship assistance can work under appropriate conditions. At every school for which data are available, physics students supported primarily by fellowships finished their degrees more rapidly than did those who relied more heavily on assistantships. But of course "structures" were generally already in place in these physics departments, and what students needed most were resources and the time to complete their work. In the absence of such conditions, fellowship support can be much less effective.

In the next chapter, we consider the results achieved by national fellowship programs instituted in earlier years, and that analysis corroborates this theme. Renewed efforts have to be made to find ways in which varied forms (and combinations)[27] of financial aid can be made to contribute more effectively to improved outcomes for students and institutions alike.

---

[27]A suggestive, though not conclusive, set of data pertains to students in the EHP fields who had *both* fellowship support and teaching assistantships. At Cornell, about one-third of all students held both fellowships and teaching assistantships in their first and second years. At Yale, about one-fifth of all students fell into this category. And at these two universities, the EHP students who had received both forms of institutional support reached ABD status with greater frequency than their compatriots who had only one form of support or the other. The *combination* may have been helpful precisely because the two forms offered complementary advantages.

CHAPTER ELEVEN

National Fellowship Programs

CONCERN AT the national level for the welfare of graduate education and graduate students almost invariably has been expressed through the development of fellowship programs, either publicly or privately financed. Such was the case during the 1960s, when a shortage of faculty and a more general concern about the adequacy of the nation's investment in higher education resulted in the creation and extension of a number of large-scale national fellowship programs. While some discussion of the results achieved by these programs has been incorporated into previous chapters, we have not as yet attempted to evaluate overall accomplishments (and shortcomings). That is the task of this chapter.

Consistent with the objectives of this study, we focus on two measurable outcomes of graduate study—completion rates and time-to-degree. We do not attempt to evaluate the success of various fellowship programs in achieving broader objectives, such as encouraging larger numbers of the most talented undergraduates to enroll in PhD programs, stimulating greater interest in teaching as a vocation, strengthening selected graduate institutions, increasing the geographical dispersion of PhD programs, and encouraging broader participation of women and minority groups in graduate study.

National fellowship programs unquestionably have accomplished a great deal—in service of broad policy objectives and at the level of the individual. It is less clear, however, that they have had as much of an effect on completion rates and time-to-degree as many would have expected. Data analyzed in this chapter demonstrate that completion rates have been surprisingly low (given the quality of the students chosen and the financial support provided), and that it has taken nearly as long for the recipients to complete their degrees as it has taken other graduate students.

This sobering conclusion is one of the most important findings to emerge from this research. It is buttressed by the general consistency of the evidence. Still, there are some instructive differences in outcomes among programs and over time. In addition, there have been pronounced differences in the outcomes for men and women recipients, which are discussed in the last part of the chapter.

PROGRAM TYPES

The seven national fellowship programs with which we are concerned in this chapter can be classified according to two primary characteristics:[1]

- Type of recipient—either an individual who wins a portable fellowship through a national competition, or an institution (which in turn makes awards to its own students); and

---

[1]The individual fellowship programs and the database constructed to evaluate these programs (the National Fellowship data set) are described in detail in Appendix B.

- Status of the graduate students who are to be supported—either entering students or advanced students.

The programs of the Danforth Foundation and the Woodrow Wilson National Fellowship Foundation (sometimes referred to, for present purposes, simply as the Woodrow Wilson Foundation) are of most direct relevance. First, they provided a significant number of fellowships in the humanities and social sciences (our fields of special interest) enough years ago to permit a meaningful analysis of outcomes. Second, they awarded fellowships to entering students through national competitions (thereby providing a quality check). Third, the fellowships they provided were portable (that is, individuals who won these fellowships could choose, within some limits, the graduate programs they wished to enter). And, last, many of the recipients elected to attend universities for which we have comparable data for other students.

The National Science Foundation (NSF) program has had many of these same characteristics, and it is a useful point of reference in studying the experiences of other portable fellowship programs even though most of its awards have been concentrated in the natural sciences and the quantitative social sciences. The Mellon Fellowships in the Humanities is another nationally competitive, portable fellowship program that is comparable in many respects, but it has been in existence only since 1983 and therefore offers only limited opportunities for comparisons.

The second broad category of national fellowship programs consists of those that made awards to institutions, and relied on the institutions to select individual recipients. Most of the National Defense Education Act (NDEA) Fellowships provided in the 1960s and early 1970s belong to this category, but the lack of records unfortunately makes it impossible to study intensively more than a single entering cohort (the 1962 cohort).[2] The institutionally based Ford Foundation program evolved from the (portable) Woodrow Wilson fellowship program in the 1960s, and the subsequent experience with this program of grants to universities is instructive, even though only secondary-source material is available for evaluation.

The Whiting fellowship program is an important variant of the institutionally based approach. It has provided fellowship funds to a selected group of universities, which in turn have made awards to highly qualified graduate students near the end of the dissertation stage of their work. The results achieved by this program of assistance to advanced students offer additional insights into mechanisms for encouraging the completion of doctoral studies.

PORTABLE FELLOWSHIP PROGRAMS

The Danforth and Woodrow Wilson Fellowship Programs

These two national fellowship programs shared a number of characteristics. Both programs:

- Were portable, in that few constraints were placed on the freedom of the individual fellow to choose a particular graduate program;

---

[2]A relatively small number of NDEA Fellowships were portable, but the lack of adequate records makes it impossible to study this group.

- Chose recipients through national competitions that assured a high degree of selectivity;
- Provided a generous stipend in addition to tuition;
- Made awards to students across a broad spectrum of fields in the arts and sciences;
- Sought to encourage students to pursue careers in teaching; and
- Were in operation during the latter half of the 1950s and early to mid-1960s (with the Danforth program continuing until 1976).

There were also important differences. First was the length of time for which financial support was guaranteed (four years or more for the Danforths versus one year for the Woodrow Wilsons). Second was scale (100+ Danforth awards per year, as compared with 900–1,000 Woodrow Wilsons in their peak years). Third was the effort made to create a sense of "community"; the Danforth program included conferences and other activities designed to reinforce the commitment of the fellows to teaching as a vocation, whereas the much larger Woodrow Wilson program was more anonymous and impersonal.[3]

The measurable outcomes achieved by the two programs differed considerably. In our six fields of study, the Danforth Fellows had significantly higher completion rates and slightly lower time-to-degree (Figure 11.1).[4]

The full explanation for the greater "success" of the Danforth program, as reflected in these two simple measures of outcomes, is no doubt complex. For example, detailed aspects of selection procedures could well have been important. Still, the differences shown in Figure 11.1 are not surprising, given the stronger assurance of continuing financial support by the Danforth Foundation and the greater effort by that program to provide individual attention and encouragement to students. These two factors undoubtedly helped to raise

---

[3]At its inception, the Danforth program aimed to attract graduate students who both aspired to an academic career and "recognize[d] the place of religion in their personal lives and the work of education" (Danforth Foundation 1956, 6). Although the explicit religious emphasis was dropped in the late 1950s, fellows continued to be chosen in part on the basis of personal qualities and commitments. In addition, the Danforth Foundation continued to invest in conferences, dinners, and other special activities intended to foster a sense of community. (See Appendix B for further discussion.)

[4]The difference in overall completion rates is easily significant at the 99 percent level of confidence.

All of the comparisons in the first part of this chapter are restricted to men only since data for all fellowship winners are influenced by the presence of significant numbers of women in the Woodrow Wilson program and their almost total absence from the Danforth program during the years included in this analysis. Outcomes for women differed markedly from outcomes for men (especially in the early years), and the experiences of women in the various fellowship programs are analyzed separately in the last section of this chapter.

Focusing on fellowship winners in the six fields of study permits us to compare these results with other sets of data. In addition, fellowship winners outside the six fields are distributed in ways that complicate rather than inform the analysis. For instance, sizable numbers of Danforth Fellows elected to study religion or philosophy, and sometimes to attend seminary as well as graduate school—with evident consequences for time-to-degree.

To ensure comparability, these comparisons are also restricted to the 1957–1961 and 1962–1966 cohorts (the only two cohorts with data for both fellowship programs). To obtain sufficiently large cell sizes for the Danforth Fellows, all of these comparisons use pooled data for the two cohorts; cell sizes are shown in Appendix G, Tables G.11–1 and G.11–2.

Finally, these data include transfers (that is, students who earned doctorates at any university, regardless of where they began graduate study, are counted as "completers"). Later in the discussion, we analyze outcomes excluding transfers.

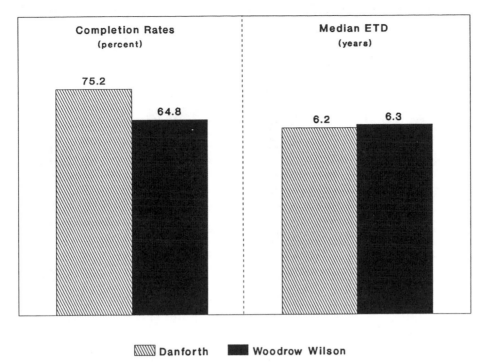

Figure 11.1
Minimum Completion Rates and Elapsed Time-to-Degree for Danforth and Woodrow
Wilson Fellows, Men Only, Six-Field Total, 1957–1966 Entering Cohorts
Source: National Fellowship data set.
Notes: Data include transfers. See Appendix G, Tables G.11–1 and G.11–2.

completion rates for the Danforth Fellows and reduce time-to-degree somewhat.[5]

Support for this interpretation is provided by additional comparisons that take
account of variations in outcomes associated with field of study and scale of
graduate program. While the difference in completion rates between Danforth
and Woodrow Wilson Fellows is modest in the mathematics and physics (MP)
fields, it is large in the English, history, and political science (EHP) fields (Figure
11.2).[6] Also, the "advantage" enjoyed by the Danforth over the Woodrow
Wilson Fellows in both completion rates and time-to-degree is much more
evident among those recipients who attended Larger programs than among
those who attended Smaller programs (Figure 11.3).[7]

---

[5]The figures for completion rates and time-to-degree reported here differ markedly from those
contained in two self-studies conducted by the Danforth and Woodrow Wilson programs in 1976 and
1977, respectively (Danforth Foundation 1976; and Woodrow Wilson National Fellowship Foundation 1977). Both of these studies are flawed by: (1) reliance on questionnaires without correcting for
biases introduced by the pattern of responses; and (2) data problems associated with the existence
of truncation.

The first of these two problems—uncritical acceptance of results based on the experiences of those
who chose to return the questionnaire—is by far the most serious. For example, the Danforth study
(p. 11) claims that 97 percent of the Danforth Fellows completed doctorates. The Woodrow Wilson
study shows a completion rate for U.S. men of 74.7 percent (p. 2), while also noting that many of
(continued)

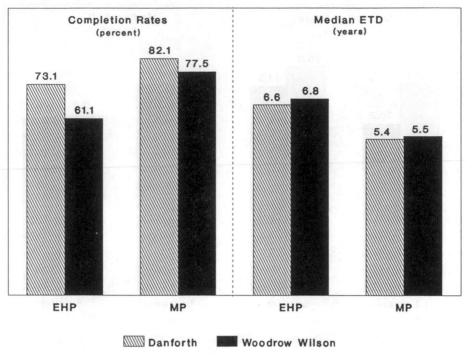

Figure 11.2
Minimum Completion Rates and Elapsed Time-to-Degree for Danforth and Woodrow Wilson Fellows by Broad Field, Men Only, 1957–1966 Entering Cohorts
Source: National Fellowship data set.
Notes: Data include transfers. See Appendix G, Tables G.11–1 and G.11–2.

Less multiyear fellowship support was available generally in the EHP fields and in the Larger programs both for Woodrow Wilson Fellows (who were dependent on their universities for support after the first year), as well as for other students. The assurance of multiyear support provided to the Danforth Fellows therefore must have been especially valuable to those in the EHP fields and to those in Larger programs. Similarly, the efforts made by the Danforth Foundation to stay in touch with its fellows may have made more difference to those outside the sciences and to those attending Larger programs, where anonymity was more likely to be a problem.

---

those not shown as completing expect to earn their degrees at some later time. These figures are a dramatic warning against reliance on a simple questionnaire approach. Professor Joseph Mooney (1968) conducted an independent study of the Woodrow Wilson fellowship program that was rigorous, analytical, and more accurate than the self-studies. Mooney's findings generally are consistent with those reported here.

[6]This difference in the EHP fields is significant at the 99 percent level of confidence; the difference in the MP fields is not statistically significant (Appendix G, Table G.11–1).

[7]The relatively small number of Danforth Fellows in these cohorts who attended the Larger programs (61) prevented even this large absolute difference in completion rates (14 percentage points) from producing a Z-value large enough to pass the test of statistical significance at the 95 percent level. This difference is significant, however, at the 89 percent level.

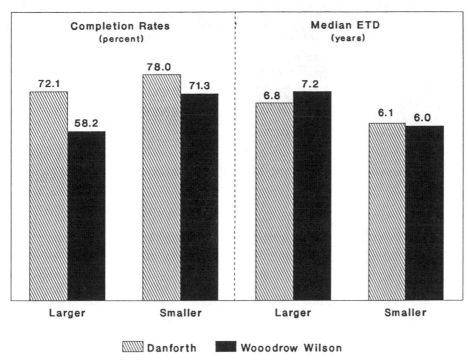

Figure 11.3
Minimum Completion Rates and Elapsed Time-to-Degree for Danforth and Woodrow Wilson Fellows by Scale of Graduate Program, Six-Field Total, Men Only, 1957–1966 Entering Cohorts

Source: National Fellowship data set.
Notes: Data include transfers. See Appendix G, Tables G.11–1 and G.11–2.

Conversely, in the sciences and in the Smaller programs more generally, the unique characteristics of the Danforth program apparently made less difference. Woodrow Wilson Fellows were likely to have been successful in gaining additional funding beyond the first year of study and thus would have gained financial support comparable to the Danforth Fellows. In addition, the community aspect of the Danforth program may not have been as vital, since some greater degree of collaboration with faculty and peers already provided a sense of belonging to an identifiable group.

It is relatively easy, then, to find convincing explanations for both the greater overall success of the Danforth program and for the specific "locations" at which it made the most difference. It is much less clear whether the *magnitude* of any of these differences in outcomes was commensurate with the greater investments of resources and time made by the Danforth Foundation as compared with those made by the Woodrow Wilson National Fellowship Foundation. In pondering this question, it should be noted that the advantages gained by extra investments in particular groups of graduate students should be expected to depend on the context—on the availability of other sources of support (financial and personal) and on the needs of students, which are affected by job market prospects among other things. From all these points of view, the late 1950s and early to mid-1960s were good times for graduate students, and one could argue that a "Danforthlike" program might have had a stronger differential impact in more stressful times. However, other evidence (noted below) concerning the results achieved by the Danforth program in the late 1960s and early 1970s casts serious doubt on this line of reasoning.

Another perspective on the effectiveness of these two portable fellowship programs is obtained by comparing the outcomes achieved by both Danforth and Woodrow Wilson Fellows with the outcomes for *all* graduate students pursuing PhDs in the same fields at the same universities in roughly the same periods. Some intriguing findings emerge:[8]

- For the six fields as a whole, these data offer no evidence that either the Danforth Fellows or the Woodrow Wilson Fellows did appreciably better than the entire population of graduate students attending the same universities in the same fields (Figure 11.4). In fact, the completion rate for the Woodrow Wilson Fellows was significantly *lower* than the all-student rate.[9]
- The lack of impact on completion rates is especially pronounced in the MP fields, where the rates for all graduate students were modestly *higher* than the rates for either Danforth or Woodrow Wilson Fellows. While these differences are so small as to be nonsignificant, it is surely hard to argue that the fellowship programs had any positive effect on completion rates for scientists. Median time-to-degree was shorter, however, for both groups of fellowship winners in the sciences (and especially for the Danforth Fellows attending the Larger programs).[10]
- There is only one cell in this matrix in which a fellowship program recorded a completion rate that was clearly higher than the rate for all (comparable) students. The Danforth Fellows *in the EHP fields* attending the *Larger*

---

[8]These comparisons *exclude* transfers, and the completion rates for the two fellowship programs shown here are therefore lower than those shown above, since all students who left their original programs are now counted as noncompleters, even though some received PhDs elsewhere. This exclusion is necessary to achieve comparability with the university data, which cannot capture the outcomes for students who transferred to other programs. The problem is further complicated by the fact that opportunities to transfer may have been greater for some of the national fellowship recipients (especially the Danforth Fellows) than for graduate students in general. The reason is that the Danforth Fellows could take their awards with them, whereas other graduate students would have had to apply anew for support, in competition with all seekers of financial aid. Comparisons of completion rates with and without transfers across fellowship programs support this hypothesis. The relative number of transfers (who eventually earned degrees elsewhere) is appreciably higher among Danforth Fellows than among Woodrow Wilson Fellows.

In comparing university data with fellowship-program data, the "transfer" bias may be offset by the choice of cohorts. The university data are available only for the 1967–1971 cohorts, whereas the fellowship-program data go back to 1957–1961. Since completion rates tended to drift downward over these years, this lack of perfect alignment of the data decreases the completion rates obtained from the university data (relative to the rates obtained from the fellowship data), just as the transfer phenomenon has the opposite effect.

[9]See Appendix G, Table G.11–3, for cell sizes and the Z-score. One possible explanation for the lower completion rate among Woodrow Wilson Fellows could be, ironically, the objective of the program itself: Woodrow Wilson Fellowships were awarded to entering students with the aim of *recruiting* students to graduate education. Consequently, in some cases, the fellowships may have acted as a "teaser," attracting to graduate school students who would not otherwise have considered the option and may have had a less strong commitment to graduate education.

[10]Appendix G, Tables G.11–3 and G.11–4. The differences in time-to-degree are not large enough, however, to be statistically significant.

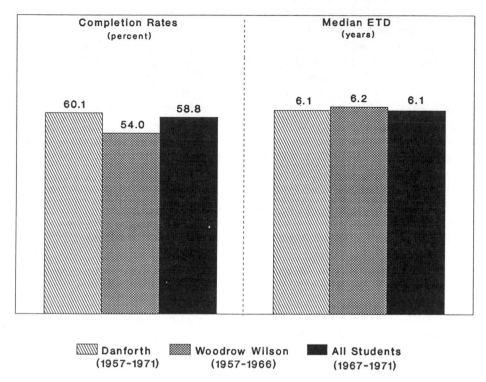

Figure 11.4
Minimum Completion Rates and Elapsed Time-to-Degree for Danforth and Woodrow Wilson Fellows and Ten-University Students, Men Only, Six-Field Total, 1957–1966 Entering Cohorts
Source: National Fellowship data set. See Appendix G, Tables G.11–3 and G.11–4.
Notes: Data do not include transfers.

programs had a completion rate of 52 percent (excluding transfers), as compared with a rate of 39 percent for all graduate students. Even so, the completion rate for Danforth Fellows in the EHP fields at the Larger universities was well below the corresponding completion rate for *all* graduate students in the EHP fields at the *Smaller* universities (67 percent).

In assessing the experiences of these fellowship programs, there is one final comparison to be made. For the Danforth program only, it is possible to examine trends in completion rates over time. Cell sizes are large enough to permit such comparisons only in the EHP fields, and only rough comparisons then, since the shifting numbers of transfer-recipients complicate the analysis. Still, the general picture is clear. As noted in Chapter Six, completion rates for Danforth Fellows declined steadily between the 1957–1961 and 1972–1976 cohorts—with an especially sharp drop occurring between the 1967–1971 and 1972–1976 cohorts.[11]

Several explanations can be offered. The effort to remain in close contact with individual fellows, and to encourage a sense of "fellowship" that went well

---

[11]Completion rates with transfers for Danforth Fellows in the EHP fields at all universities were 77 percent (1957–1961), 71 percent (1962–1966), 65 percent (1967–1971), and 54 percent (1972–1976). Completion rates excluding transfers followed the same general trajectory.

beyond receipt of financial assistance, was greater in the early years of the program than in the later years. This shift was a consequence of a complex series of changes in the leadership of the program, its scale, and external conditions (the attitudes of graduate students and labor market prospects).[12]

The number of new Danforth Fellows elected each year rose from an annual average of about 100 (1958 through 1963) to approximately 115 to 125 (1964 through 1974). While modest by many standards, the cumulative effect of even this much of an increase evidently made it more difficult for a small staff to stay in close touch with all of the Fellows. This experience serves as a warning against assuming too readily that apparently incremental changes in program size will have minimal effects.

The changing environment, and the climate on campuses, was almost surely an even more basic determinant. One person associated with the Danforth Foundation observed that, whereas the Fellows in the earlier years were clearly committed to the program, students chosen in the late 1960s and 1970s were often skeptical, questioning, and sometimes even antagonistic. "The Fellows were now fighting us," another observer commented. It is no coincidence that these were the years when there was much turmoil on campuses, and sometimes strong anti-establishment feelings. It would have been astonishing had these waves not washed over the Danforth program, as they washed over every other dimension of campus life.

Completion rates for graduate students in general declined at the same pace as completion rates for the Danforth Fellows (Chapter Six), in large part, we believe, because of the ever-more-discouraging state of the academic labor market. Grim job prospects appear to have discouraged many students from continuing with PhD programs—including, we suspect, a number of those with Danforth Fellowships or comparable financial aid. This is further evidence of how difficult it is for any national fellowship program to overcome major external forces affecting all students and institutions.

The Mellon Fellowship Program

The Mellon Fellowships in the Humanities program is similar to the Danforth and Woodrow Wilson programs, but its relatively young age permits the reporting of only preliminary results.

Begun in 1983, the Mellon program was designed to attract promising students to doctoral programs, with the stated assumption that these students would pursue careers in college or university teaching and scholarship. Eligible fields of study are restricted, however, to the humanities as traditionally defined. Like the Woodrow Wilson and Danforth Fellows, the Mellon Fellows are chosen through highly selective national competitions, and the fellowships are portable. The Mellon program is comparable in scale to the Danforth program (100 to 124 awards have been made per year), and it, too, provides generous multiyear support. Another similarity with the Danforth program is

---

[12]A symbolic (and real) "marker" of this change was the decision made in the mid-1960s to end the annual conferences held at Camp Miniwanca on Lake Michigan since the early days of the program, and to replace this event with a series of regional gatherings. Also, the first Executive Director, K. I. Brown (who retired in 1961), traveled extensively, having dinner with the fellows and talking with them. This practice was also discontinued in the later years of the program.

the effort made to foster and encourage a sense of collegiality and common purpose through personal communications with individual fellows and support of annual conferences organized by the Fellows.

Despite its attractive (Danforthlike) features, outcomes to date have not been what the leadership of the program had originally anticipated (Table 11.1). In the first cohort, 35 percent of the Fellows have received doctorates after eight years, and nearly one-quarter have resigned from the program. If half of those recorded as still enrolled eventually complete their degrees (which could prove to be an optimistic assumption), the eventual completion rate will be 56 percent. In the second cohort, the minimum completion rate is 31 percent after seven years, with a resignation rate of 17 percent. Here, too, an eventual completion rate on the order of 50+ percent seems likely.[13]

These projected completion rates for the Mellon Fellows are amazingly close to the rate of 54 percent in the EHP fields recorded by the last (1972–1976) cohort of Danforth Fellows. This is a somewhat discouraging finding, especially in view of a modest improvement in job prospects in the late 1980s compared to the 1970s. Job prospects dimmed again in the early 1990s because of the severe financial constraints under which most colleges and universities have been operating. While this may not be a long-term phenomenon, it is likely to deter at least some students from beginning and finishing doctorates during the early part of the decade.

It would be hazardous to speculate on median time-to-degree figures for these cohorts since so much depends on both how many of the "still-enrolled" students finish and how long it takes them. However, we can report that, of all Mellon Fellows in the 1983 and 1984 cohorts, only 8 percent earned doctorates within five years of the time of the award, and only 20 percent earned doctorates within six years. A comparison of these results with those achieved by the Danforth Fellows is not encouraging. Of all Danforth Fellows in the humanities (1957–1976 entering cohorts), 18 percent earned doctorates within five years and 28 percent earned doctorates within six years.

TABLE 11.1
Status of Recipients of Mellon Fellowships in the Humanities, 1983–1985 Entering Cohorts

	Number of Awards	Number of PhDs	% with PhD	Number Lost	% Lost
1983	94	33	35.1	22	23.4
1984	116	36	31.0	20	17.2
1985	116	13	11.2	23	19.8

Source: Tabulations provided by the Woodrow Wilson National Fellowship Foundation, as of August 1991.

---

[13]In the case of the third cohort, the most meaningful number at this juncture is the resignation rate, which is already 20 percent. As explained in Appendix C, an intensive effort was made to interview the "lost" (resigned) Mellon Fellows to learn more about why they had resigned and what they were now doing, and long interviews were conducted with almost half of them. Of this group, 40 percent were enrolled in other programs (mostly law); 51 percent were working full-time (mostly in business); and the remaining 9 percent could not be classified. Approximately three-quarters of these former fellows indicated that they had been dissatisfied with some aspect of graduate studies: teachers, advisors, academia, or the specific educational program being offered. Under 14 percent cited personal reasons, such as financial pressures and health.

The 1989 annual report prepared by the director of the Mellon program, Dr. Robert F. Goheen, expressed particular concern about how long it was taking fellows to complete their studies:

[A]s reported last year, we have had to become somewhat lenient about extending eligibility for dissertation support into the sixth year. There are simply too many factors either beyond an individual's control or that emerge as unusual requirements of a discipline—advisors on leave, illness, need to master two or more exotic languages, a required year of field research, etc.,—that arise to delay some of our ablest and most committed Fellows.

At the same time, I must record great disappointment at how slowly the Fellows of the first two cohorts have been moving to completion of the dissertation, attainment of the PhD, and on out into faculty positions. . . . [O]verall the rate of progress of these early Mellon Fellows to the PhD and out into full time faculty appointments runs far below our hopes and expectations.[14]

Taken together, these data and observations are an important reminder of how difficult it is, under present conditions, to achieve completion rates in the humanities of much over 50 percent and to prevent time-to-degree from continuing to rise (much less reduce it). It is evidence of this kind that has persuaded us of the importance of looking closely at the "internal" aspects of graduate programs (Chapters Twelve and Thirteen), and of designing new programs of assistance that may offer better prospects of encouraging systemic improvements in graduate education.

The National Science Foundation Fellowship Program

The National Science Foundation fellowship program was created in 1952. The selection process has always been very competitive, and the fellowships are generous. Until 1972, the awards were given at three levels (first-year awards, intermediate awards, and terminal-year awards), provided one or two years of support, and were renewable. In 1972, the period of the award was standardized at three years, and applicants were limited to students at or near the beginning of graduate study. This structure is still in existence today.

The National Science Foundation keeps excellent track of its Fellows. For the purposes of this study, existing NSF data have been reorganized to permit comparisons with the Ten-University data set and the data on other fellowship programs. Moreover, two careful studies have been made of the outcomes achieved by this program (which include measures beyond those we consider in this book, such as postgraduate activities and accomplishments).[15]

Completion rates for NSF Fellows have been remarkably high overall, even as they have varied by field (ranging, in the 1972–1976 cohort, from 67 percent in the social sciences to 92 percent in chemistry). Also, the NSF Fellows have had remarkably low time-to-degree. Unfortunately, it is difficult to compare the NSF outcomes with those achieved by other fellowship programs because of the marked differences in the fields of study in which most awards are made.

---

[14]Goheen 1989, 9–11.

[15]Harmon 1977; and Snyder 1988. See also the discussion in Chapter Ten of the differences in outcomes associated with NSF "Quality Groups," and between awardees and nonawardees within Quality Groups.

The most reliable comparison contrasts the results achieved by NSF and Woodrow Wilson Fellows in the 1962–1966 cohorts in the MP fields (men only). Somewhat surprisingly, the Woodrow Wilson Fellows appear to have had a slight, but not statistically significant, edge in completion rates (Figure 11.5). The more important point is that both groups of fellows completed the doctorate in very large numbers; it is rare to see any completion rates in the 75 to 80 percent range.[16]

Time-to-degree comparisons are especially interesting (right-hand side of Figure 11.5). Again, both Woodrow Wilson and NSF Fellows in the MP fields did very well; the NSF awardees earned their doctorates in an average of five years. For later cohorts in the MP fields, it is also possible to compare time-to-degree of NSF Fellows with time-to-degree of all graduate students in the eight-university group and for all graduate students receiving doctorates from U.S. universities. These comparisons highlight even more vividly the remarkably short time-to-degree achieved by NSF awardees, and the extent to which the NSF Fellows finished in a substantially shorter period of time than their contemporaries. There was a difference of three-quarters of a year between the median time-to-degree of the NSF winners (4.9 years) and the overall median for MP students in the eight-university group (5.6 years). And, as expected, the corresponding

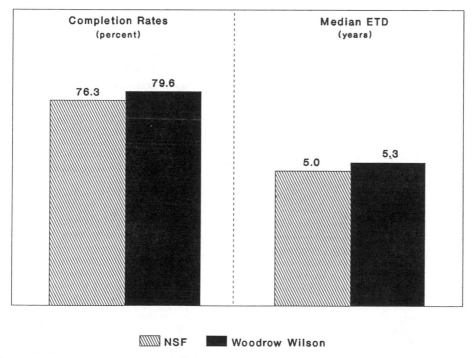

Figure 11.5
Minimum Completion Rates and Elapsed Time-to-Degree for NSF and Woodrow Wilson Fellows, Men Only, MP Total, 1962–1966 Entering Cohort
Source: National Fellowship data set.

---

[16]Completion rates for NSF Fellows in the MP fields dropped to 67 percent in the 1967–1971 cohort, but then recovered strongly to 80 percent in the 1972–1976 cohort.

difference is even greater (approximately 1.2 years) when NSF Fellows are compared with students receiving doctorates from all U.S. universities.[17]

This pattern of relative time-to-degree (NSFs first, then the eight-university group, and finally all recipients of doctorates at U.S. universities) is consistent across each of the individual five-year cohorts that have been grouped for this analysis. The pattern is all the more striking since, as we have seen earlier, time-to-degree is often unaffected, or affected very little, by such factors as type of financial aid and type of fellowship. Furthermore, this pattern cannot be attributed to any particular quality group, since time-to-degree appears to vary little among the quality-award tiers as defined by NSF (Appendix G, Table G.11–5).

The success of the NSF program in shortening time-to-degree may be due in large part to the rigorous nature of the selection process. Rather than relying purely on undergraduate performance as a measure of academic potential, NSF has attempted to determine graduate-level motivation and abilities as well. Applications consist of the usual GRE scores, undergraduate record, and faculty recommendations. In addition, however, each applicant is required to submit information on previous research experience as well as a study plan and research proposal for graduate-level work. The applications are evaluated by panels of scientists. This careful selection process requires a large commitment of time and effort not only by NSF but by the applicant as well, but it apparently helps to ensure that NSF winners, beyond being capable of graduate work, are sufficiently focused to permit expeditious progress toward the PhD.[18]

It is also possible that access to *fellowship* funds, as a distinct form of support, has accelerated progress of NSF students toward the PhD by relieving them of some duties they might otherwise have had to discharge as teaching assistants or research assistants. In the natural-science fields covered by the NSF program, the collegiality and socialization functions served by both kinds of assistantship are generally provided through such mechanisms as laboratory groups and collaborative research. In these settings, having some time entirely to one's self, as an NSF Fellowship ensures, may well permit students to complete their research more promptly.

The effects of the NSF fellowship program on completion rates are less clear. The earlier comparison with completion rates for Woodrow Wilson Fellows is of limited significance because it relies on data from so long ago (the 1962–1966 entering cohort). However, a comparison using data for the 1967–1976 cohorts

---

[17]Median elapsed time-to-degree for U.S. residents who earned doctorates at all U.S. universities in the MP fields was 6.1 years for the 1962–1966 and 1967–1971 cohorts and 6.2 years for the 1972–1976 cohort. (The source of these numbers is special tabulations from the Doctorate Records File prepared for this project by the National Research Council [NRC].)

[18]The emphasis given by the NSF to early consideration of research plans is of course much more practical in fields such as mathematics and physics than it would be in a subject such as English literature, where graduate students often confront entirely new approaches and frequently find it difficult, even after the initial years of graduate study, to define a research topic. (See Chapters Twelve and Thirteen, and Appendix F.) Mechanisms that work well in one field may not be readily transferred to other fields without significant modifications.

within the eight-university group is consistent with these earlier results in that, once again, there is no strong evidence that NSF Fellows had higher completion rates than other graduate students.[19]

These comparisons, rough as they are, suggest that the NSF program has had more of an impact on time-to-degree than it has had on completion rates within the MP fields. This finding is particularly interesting because it contrasts so sharply with the outcomes achieved by the other portable fellowship programs within the EHP fields. Those programs had hardly any perceptible impact on time-to-degree, and only modest effects on completion rates in specific settings.

INSTITUTIONALLY-BASED PROGRAMS

The three programs discussed in this section have in common a funding mechanism entirely different from the mechanisms used to make grants to individuals through portable fellowship programs. These institutionally-based programs made grants to universities, which in turn made awards to individual students enrolled at those universities. The similarities end there, however. One of the programs was federally funded and the other two were privately funded. The federally funded program was intended (among other things) to widen the geographic distribution of PhD programs. Both of the privately funded programs focused on small groups of leading graduate programs and sought to achieve highly specific objectives. In short, the three programs differ so fundamentally that each needs to be considered on its own terms.

The NDEA Program

As already noted (Chapter Three), the NDEA Title IV fellowship program was created by Congress in 1958 in response to the launching of Sputnik and the perception that there was an overwhelming shortage of well-qualified college teachers. The program had three basic objectives: (1) to increase the number of university teachers by assisting doctoral students preparing for academic careers; (2) to encourage the development and full utilization of the capacity of doctoral programs; and (3) to promote a wider geographic distribution of doctoral programs of good quality.

Awards were made to institutions, and once an institution's application had been approved by the Office of Education, the institution submitted the names of individual students to receive fellowships. Eligibility was restricted to U.S. citizens or permanent residents who intended to pursue academic careers, and financial support was provided for up to three years (tuition plus a stipend to cover living expenses). In addition, the institution received a cost-of-education grant of up to $2,500 per student. The number of new fellowships awarded

---

[19]This comparison cannot be made with precision because of our inability to treat transfers in a consistent way. The completion rate for NSF Fellows in the MP fields in the 1967–1976 cohorts was 74 percent, whereas the completion rate for the eight-university group in the same fields and cohorts was 65 percent. However, the NSF figures include transfers, while the university data exclude them. Since transfer-completers often represent more than 8 percent of an entering cohort, including transfers in the university data set could well raise that completion rate above the NSF rate.

annually began with 1,000 in 1959, and then continued at the level of 1,500 for the next five years. A period of rapid expansion followed, when the number of awards made annually increased to 3,000 in 1965, and 6,000 in 1966 and 1967; the number then returned to 3,000 for the duration of the program.[20]

Although the NDEA Title IV fellowship program ran from 1959 to 1973, it was possible to obtain data for only the 1962 cohort of Fellows. All other records (even the names of Fellows) apparently were either lost or destroyed. This is exceedingly unfortunate since this program made awards to many students who attended graduate programs not included in other data sets,[21] and it would have been useful to examine the outcomes for students in these programs in the late 1960s and early 1970s, when conditions in academic labor markets had changed so substantially.[22]

Out of necessity, then, we have focused our analysis on the 1,071 NDEA Fellows in arts and sciences fields who received awards in 1962. The principal finding is that completion rates by broad field were very similar to those for Woodrow Wilson Fellows who studied in the same fields and universities during the mid-1960s (Figure 11.6).[23]

This comparison is too limited in time and scope to support broad generalizations, but it does suggest that completion rates for cohorts in the mid-1960s were not affected substantially by the mechanism used to award fellowships. Students selected by their own universities completed their doctorates in approximately the same numbers as students chosen through national selection procedures.

---

[20]A detailed history of the program can be found in Lindquist (1971).

[21]In keeping with the stated intention of the program to correct for a perceived maldistribution of PhDs and PhD programs, awards were concentrated in areas of the country, such as the Southeast, where "doctoral programs were weakest." (Sharp, Sensenig, and Reid 1968, 4). Schools with new or expanding programs that applied for Title IV money received a large portion of the Title IV dollars. The effect of this policy is evident when, using the Tier analysis explained in Chapter Four, we find that NDEA Fellows were distributed almost evenly across the four quality tiers. In the case of six-field recipients of NDEA Fellowships in the 1962 cohort, the distribution was as follows: 26 percent in Tier I, 25 percent in Tier II, 31 percent in Tier III, and 19 percent in Tier IV. The Woodrow Wilson Fellows, in contrast, were concentrated heavily in Tier I (85 percent of those in the 1957–1966 cohorts). (These figures were calculated from the National Fellowship data set.)

[22]Moreover, the official studies of this fellowship program were also limited to the awards made in the early years of the program. These studies were carried out in two phases by the Bureau of Social Science Research, Inc., and submitted to the U.S. Office of Education (Sharp, Sensenig, and Reid 1968; and Holmstrom and Sharp 1970). The Phase I report (March 1968) examined the first four years of the fellowship program (1958 to 1962) and was based on data obtained directly from the Office of Education. One revealing finding was that in each cohort approximately 25 percent of the fellows resigned before completing tenure of the fellowship. The Phase II report (July 1970) was based on data obtained directly from NDEA Fellows through a mail survey questionnaire. This was an elaborate study, and many of the specific findings concerned issues outside the purview of this book. The results relevant to our work are roughly consistent with our own analysis of the 1962 cohort of NDEA Fellows.

[23]These comparisons include transfers and are limited to students in Tier I programs, since so few Woodrow Wilson Fellows chose to attend programs in other tiers. See Chapter Eight (Table 8.3 and Appendix G, Table G.8–8) for data showing differences in completion rates across tiers for NDEA Fellows.

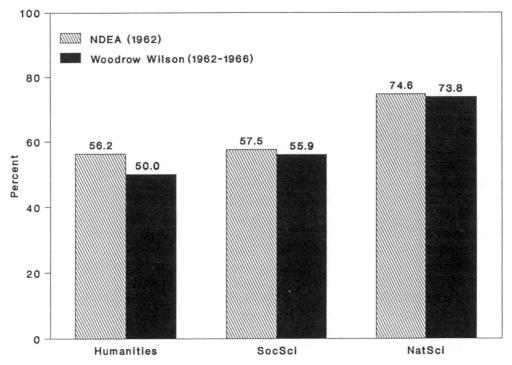

Figure 11.6
Minimum Completion Rates for Woodrow Wilson and NDEA Tier I Fellows by Broad Field, Men Only

Source: National Fellowship data set.

Notes: Data include transfers. The Woodrow Wilson data are for the 1962–1966 entering cohort and the NDEA data are for the 1962 entering cohort.

The Ford Foundation Program

In 1967, not quite ten years after the establishment of the NDEA Fellowships, the Ford Foundation instituted an ambitious program designed to do nothing less than reform graduate education. This program was a major departure from the provision of portable (Woodrow Wilson) fellowships which the Foundation had funded for the previous ten years. It was decided that less emphasis was needed on the *recruitment* of graduate students, which had been a primary purpose of the portable fellowship program, and that more emphasis was needed on improved *efficiency* of the programs themselves. The Foundation believed that reform would be achieved only through institutional efforts, and the new program provided grants to ten universities (Berkeley, Chicago, Michigan, Pennsylvania, Wisconsin, Cornell, Harvard, Princeton, Stanford, and Yale) that had enrolled large numbers of Woodrow Wilson Fellows.

Inspired by Berelson's (1960) landmark book, the Ford program was aimed at reducing inefficiency in the humanities and social sciences, largely through the establishment of a four-year norm for doctoral education (counting only years since initial enrollment, the measure of elapsed time-to-degree [ETD] used in this study). The clarity of this goal notwithstanding, the means through which it was to be achieved were much less well defined. The Foundation made only two stipulations: (1) that students supported by the grant not be identified as Ford Foundation Fellows; and (2) that stipends not exceed amounts provided for under the NDEA Title IV fellowship program.

The conditions may have been so loosely defined because of the philosophy concerning graduate student support that inspired the program. The general idea was that if students in the humanities and social sciences could be given financial support that was comparable to what was provided in the sciences, time-to-degree in the humanities and related fields would be shortened appreciably and would approximate the results achieved in the sciences. It was thought that providing students with the financial means to remain continuously enrolled as full-time students would reduce *total* elapsed time to the doctorate. Once a new four-year norm was established in the "strong centers" of graduate education, other institutions were expected to adopt it.

The program was by all accounts a failure in achieving its stated purpose—the conclusion reached by David Breneman following an intensive, and exceedingly insightful, evaluation of the program.[24] Breneman reviewed the original proposals submitted by each of the ten universities as well as annual reports and accompanying data. He also made use of supplementary data obtained from the Doctorate Records File and conducted site visits and campus interviews with presidents, deans, and faculty members to obtain additional information regarding the implementation of the program.

Breneman's analysis was limited to some extent by serious problems of availability of data and by his dependence on the PhD-year method of organizing the available information on time-to-degree (even though he recognized, in principle, the serious problems of bias that diminish the usefulness of this approach).[25] His conclusions are compelling nevertheless. They shed light not only on the overly optimistic projections, faulty assumptions, misunderstandings, and miscommunications that afflicted the Ford Foundation program, but also on the nature and process of graduate education itself. We refer the reader to the report and attempt here mainly to buttress Breneman's conclusions with more complete data than were available to him.

By what might appear to be a fortunate coincidence, our Ten-University data set includes eight of the ten institutions that received Ford Foundation support, and we are able to calculate time-to-degree in the EHP fields for six of these universities for the 1967–1971 cohorts.[26] As Figure 11.7 shows, and as Breneman

---

[24]Breneman 1977. James W. Armsey prepared a companion document which focused on the internal management of the program and is very helpful in understanding the problems that plagued the program from start to finish (Armsey 1977). The above discussion of the evolution of the Ford program and the following account of specific problems and findings is based almost entirely on these two sources (and mainly on Breneman's excellent study). The Ford Foundation deserves credit for having commissioned and made available these two highly critical studies.

[25]See Appendix D.

[26]The need to examine the data for the 1967–1971 cohorts—the entering classes affected most directly by the Ford program—prevents the inclusion of Michigan and Yale in the following summary statistics. Data for those two universities begin with the 1972–1976 cohort. As demonstrated in Chapter Seven, the EHP fields are a good proxy for the larger list of fields of study supported by the Ford Foundation.

(continued)

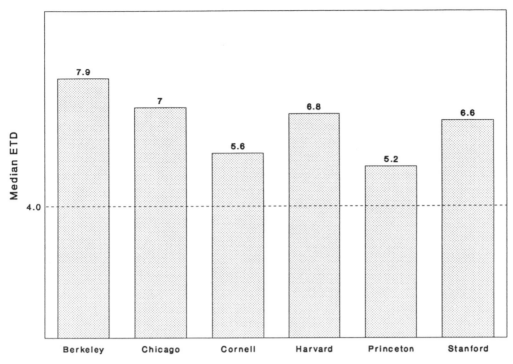

Figure 11.7
Median Time-to-Degree at Six Institutions Supported by the Ford Foundation Graduate
Program, Men Only, EHP Total, 1967–1971 Entering Cohort
Source: Ten-University data set.

reports, none of these universities came close to achieving the four-year norm
recommended by the Ford Foundation.[27]

Princeton had the lowest median ETD, 5.2 years in the EHP fields, but
Breneman concluded that the Ford Foundation grant to Princeton ironically
increased its median time-to-degree. In earlier years, graduate students at
Princeton had been allowed to register for only three years of full-time study.
The Ford Foundation grant led to a change in financial aid policies and allowed
students an extra year of graduate education on full fellowship. According to
Breneman, "the major effect of [the Ford program] was to further those forces
(increased specialization and professionalism) that had already undermined the
three-year concept." While faculty members offered a variety of explanations,
Breneman concludes: "[T]he fact remains that the major visible effect of the

The overlapping nature of these two sets of institutions is not actually a coincidence as much as
it is a consequence of following essentially the same principle in deciding on the universities to study
in depth (and to support). That is, the Ford Foundation chose its ten universities mainly on the basis
of the choices of graduate programs that were made by winners of the Woodrow Wilson portable
fellowships. We chose our ten universities largely on the basis of the choices of graduate programs
made by winners of the Mellon portable fellowships.

[27]Moreover, these data underestimate the gap between the four-year norm and the actual results
since they are for men only. If women had been included as well, the median time-to-degree would
have been even longer (see the last part of this chapter).

Ford grant at Princeton was an increase in the median elapsed time to degree."[28] This experience can also be interpreted as another instance in which a new "norm" (four years in this case) became a de facto "floor."

There is now general agreement that a four-year norm is neither realistic nor desirable as a goal in the humanities and social sciences, and a fairer test of the Ford program may be to ask whether time-to-degree was shortened at all during its lifetime. The limited data that are available indicate that time-to-degree did not fall by any significant amount relative to the experience of the previous five-year cohorts.[29] It must be recognized, however, that the external environment was changing rapidly (federal support for graduate education was falling and job prospects for academics were worsening). And it is certainly possible that time-to-degree would have lengthened even more had it not been for the Ford Foundation initiative.

Still, under the most generous interpretation, the Ford Foundation program did not succeed either in establishing a new norm for time-to-degree or in reforming graduate education. It did, however, lead to a number of definitive findings, such as this conclusion stated (and underlined) by Breneman: "*[These findings] should permanently put to rest the view that humanities and social science disciplines can become as efficient as the sciences in PhD production simply by providing them with equivalent amounts of graduate student financial support.*"[30]

One of the most peculiar aspects of the Ford program was its preoccupation with time-to-degree and its lack of interest in attrition. Breneman attributes this characteristic to the influence of Berelson's book. In any case, it is now clear to almost everyone that attrition is a serious problem, and most people would agree with this observation by Breneman: "In my view, the emphasis [on time-to-degree] was misplaced. Attrition, I believe, is a more serious problem . . . , and an opportunity was lost . . . to explore ways in which attrition could be reduced."[31]

The Whiting Fellowship Program

The last fellowship program for which we have collected a significant amount of data is the Whiting fellowship program. Beginning in 1972, the Whiting Foundation made grants to six universities—Bryn Mawr, Columbia, Harvard, Princeton, Stanford, and Yale. (Chicago was added in 1976.) The grants were intended to be used by the institutions to establish prestigious one-year fellowships for PhD candidates in the humanities during their final dissertation year. They were to be generous enough to liberate students from financial worries while they completed this final task.[32]

---

[28]Breneman 1977, 78–79.
[29]These comparisons can be made for three universities. Time-to-degree between 1962–1966 and 1967–1971 actually rose by one-tenth of a year for one (Berkeley), and it fell by one-tenth of a year and by three-tenths of a year for the other two (Chicago and Cornell, respectively).
[30]Breneman 1977, 49.
[31]*Ibid.*, 55.
[32]Mrs. Giles Whiting Foundation 1983.

Like the Ford program, the grants made by the Whiting Foundation have had a clear, albeit different, focus. Alone among all the fellowship programs discussed in this chapter, the Whiting Fellowships have been directed at the dissertation stage of graduate study. The universities receiving Whiting grants have awarded these fellowships to highly promising students who had already passed qualifying examinations and had proven themselves able scholars. This approach must have reduced, to some considerable extent, the odds that fellowship recipients would change their minds about pursuing a doctorate. Also, the decision to have these fellowships administered directly by individual universities rather than by external panels or committees, has meant, one would like to assume, that informed decisions could be made about the prospects of the awardees on the basis of the observation of sustained progress over a number of years.

The bulk of our data is for the 1972–1976 and 1977–1981 BA cohorts of Whiting Fellows. Since the objective of the fellowship is to provide financial support for graduate students who are likely to complete their dissertation within a year to 18 months, the cumulative completion rate seems the most instructive measure in evaluating success. For both of these cohorts, the cumulative completion rates followed similar patterns (Figure 11.8). Approximately 35 percent of the Whiting Fellows received the PhD within one year after receipt of the fellowship, and an additional 25 percent within two years (60 percent in all). Another 10 to 15

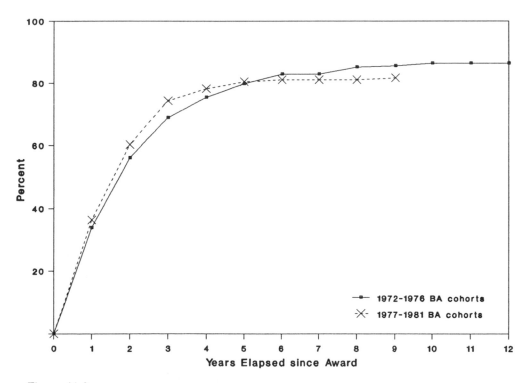

Figure 11.8
Cumulative Completion Rates for Whiting Fellows, Men Only, Humanities Only, 1972–1981 BA Cohorts
Source: National Fellowship data set.

percent finished in the third year after the award, and the incremental rate of completion then continued to decline. A plateau was reached at a cumulative completion rate of approximately 80 to 85 percent after four years following receipt of the award.[33]

This pattern has varied by scale of graduate program and type of university (Figure 11.9). The ultimate completion rate for these carefully chosen fellows has reached the 85 to 90 percent range at the Smaller programs. At the Larger programs, roughly the same proportion of fellows (about 35 percent) completed their PhDs after the first year. Thereafter, however, the increments in the cumulative completion rate slowed, and the completion rate eventually plateaued at approximately 75 to 80 percent. Part of the explanation may be that the Larger programs have had less fellowship funds available from other sources, and therefore may have been under more internal pressure to award Whitings to advanced students who were not as close to completing their degrees.

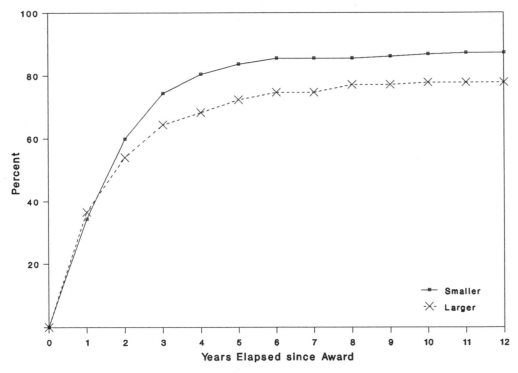

Figure 11.9
Cumulative Completion Rates for Whiting Fellows by Scale of Graduate Program, Men Only, Humanities Only, 1972–1981 BA Cohorts
Source: National Fellowship data set.

---

[33]This finding contradicts a conclusion contained in the Whiting Foundation's "Ten Year Report and Directory," which states that "95% [finished] within three years" (Mrs. Giles Whiting Foundation 1983, 7). We are unable to account fully for the discrepancy, except to note that our analysis encompasses far more Whiting Fellows than did the Whiting Foundation's own analysis (1,061 versus 598) and that 10 percent of the Whiting Fellows failed to return the questionnaire used to determine the percentages cited in the Whiting Foundation's report.

When completion rates for Whiting Fellows are compared with the conditional completion rates for *all* graduate students at the same universities who had reached ABD status (now limiting the analysis to students in English and history), completion rates for the Whitings are found to have been about 10 percentage points higher.[34] This much of an incremental "return" may be as much as one can expect at the final-stage of doctoral education. It can be seen as demonstrating the value of dissertation-stage fellowships awarded to students declared by their departments to be ready to complete their doctorates. At the same time, it is impossible to know how many of these same students would have completed their dissertations without Whiting Fellowships.

In any case, these results are an important guide for understanding what are reasonable prospects for completion of the dissertation. Even this highly select group of advanced graduate students required two years (with full financial support during at least one of these years) for a simple majority to complete their PhD. Furthermore, roughly 15 percent of these fellows never completed their degrees. These data challenge common assumptions about completion of the dissertation as graduate programs are now structured.

Dr. Goheen commented on this point in his 1989 annual report on the Mellon fellowship program:

> I have come to think that the traditional form of dissertation grant needs reconsideration. The experience of the Newcombe Fellowships, the Whiting Fellowships, and to some extent that of the former Woodrow Wilson Dissertation Fellowships all show that a single, supposedly terminal year of support aimed to lead directly to the PhD produces degree holders on that schedule much less often than not.[35]

Attrition at this late stage of graduate study is, in our view, unhealthy. It is a waste of human and institutional resources, and these findings suggest that, even under the most advantageous conditions, an increment of financial support is not sufficient, in and of itself, to result in a high (90+) percentage of graduate students clearing this final hurdle. We return in Chapter Thirteen to a much fuller discussion of this particularly vulnerable moment in graduate study and of what might be done, inside graduate programs, to help more graduate students complete their dissertations.

WOMEN PARTICIPANTS

In previous chapters, we presented a number of findings concerning completion rates and time-to-degree separately for men and women students. The objective was to ensure that seemingly general patterns were neither created nor obscured by patterns associated primarily with gender. We concluded that fundamental differences in outcomes related to field of study, scale of graduate programs, and type of financial support hold regardless of whether one is looking at the experiences of men and women separately or together. Thus far, however, we

---

[34]There are comparable data for three universities (Chicago, Princeton, and Yale). The average completion rate for the Whitings at these three universities (1972–1981 cohorts) was 85 percent. The comparable conditional completion rate (taking the number of students who had reached ABD status as the base) for students in English and history at these universities was 74 percent. (The sources of these figures are the National Fellowship data set and the Ten-University data set.)

[35]Goheen 1989, 12.

have not focused on the extent of differences in outcomes between men and women.

A comprehensive analysis of differences in outcomes achieved by men and women would require a far-ranging study of the demographic, socioeconomic, and other factors involved. While such an analysis would be very valuable, it is outside the scope of this study.[36] However, we can provide some findings based primarily on the National Fellowship data set (supplemented by the Ten-University data set, and by data from the Doctorate Records File for time-to-degree only).

Representation of Women

Women's participation in national fellowship programs has increased steadily over the last three decades (Table 11.2). In the late 1950s and early 1960s, women comprised roughly 20 to 30 percent of the Woodrow Wilson and NDEA

TABLE 11.2

Number and Percent of National Fellowships Awarded to Women, Various Cohorts and Programs

Fellowship Program	Cohorts						
	1957–1961	1962	1962–1966	1967–1971	1972–1976	1977–1981	1982–1986
Woodrow Wilson							
Number	1,081		1,515				
% of total	29.4%		32.8%				
NDEA							
Number		194					
% of total		18.1%					
Danforth							
Number			60	160	241		
% of total			10.6%	28.0%	45.6%		
NSF							
Number			274	385	562		
% of total			13.3%	17.5%	26.9%		
GFW[a]							
Number				85	52		
% of total				100.0%	100.0%		
Whiting							
Number				79	185	132	64
% of total				45.1%	44.8%	42.4%	42.1%
Mellon							
Number							395
% of total							50.3%

Source: National Fellowship data set.
[a]Graduate Fellowships for Women.

[36]While there has been much general discussion of opportunities for women in higher education, surprisingly little systematic research appears to have been directed to these questions. Perhaps the most comprehensive study is 15 years old (Solmon 1976), and was concerned specifically with issues of discrimination and affirmative action. (Solmon's study also contains an extensive bibliography of other early studies and sources of information.) For studies focused on baccalaureate origins of women PhDs, see Tidball and Kistiakowsky (1976) and Tidball (1986). For a recent study that focuses on three universities, see Zwick (1991). Of course, there are also a number of commentaries on the role of women in specific fields of study. See, for example, the forthcoming report on graduate

fellowship recipients. By the 1970s and 1980s, women were receiving 45 to 50 percent of the fellowships in programs that focused on the humanities. In the sciences, the trend is similar, but the percentages are much lower. In the NSF fellowship program, the percentage of fellowships awarded to women has increased steadily, rising from only 13 percent in the 1960s to about 27 percent in the 1970s and to 42 percent in 1991.

These numbers are quite consistent with data for all entering graduate students in universities within our Ten-University data set (Figure 11.10). In the EHP fields, the percentage of women has increased reasonably steadily from about 35 percent in the 1960s and early 1970s to 42 to 45 percent in the 1980s. In the MP fields, the corresponding increase has been from just under 10 percent to about 17 percent in 1986. The absolute numbers of women in mathematics and physics in these data sets are so small that (except for a few observations based on the Woodrow Wilson and NSF data), much of the rest of this analysis focuses on the humanities and the EHP fields.[37]

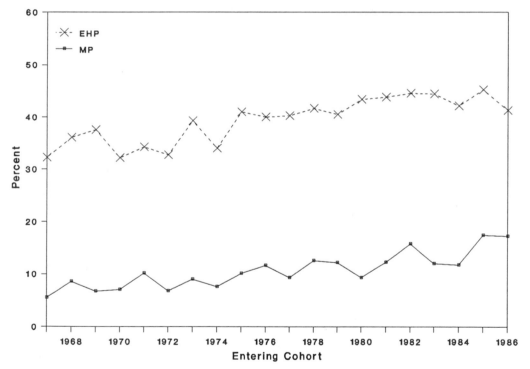

Figure 11.10
Women as Share of Total Entering Cohort, EHP and MP Totals, 1967–1986 Entering Cohorts

Source: Ten-University data set. Data are from Berkeley, Chicago, Columbia, Cornell, Harvard, Princeton, and Stanford.

---

education in mathematics (Committee on Doctoral and Postdoctoral Study in the Mathematical Sciences 1992).

[37]The data for women in the MP fields in the university data set have even less utility for purposes of analysis of outcomes than the overall figures on the graph suggest because the percentages are

Completion Rates

The Woodrow Wilson fellowship program offers by far the richest source of evidence on completion rates for women in the humanities in the late 1950s and early to mid-1960s. Between 1957 and 1966, almost 1,900 of these fellowships were awarded to women in the humanities. *Less than one-quarter of these women ever earned doctorates*—as compared with over 60 percent of their male counterparts. And the completion rate for the modest number of women recipients in the MP fields was lower yet—under 20 percent.[38]

The extremely low completion rates among the women were clearly recognized by the Woodrow Wilson National Fellowship Foundation. In its 1963–1964 Report, the Foundation described attrition among women fellows as a "cause for gloom." The report also noted with concern that "[o]ne-third of the men teaching began at, or have been promoted to, the rank of assistant professor while not quite one-sixteenth of the women were so employed. Three times as many women as men, with much the same training and at the same age, are appointed to the somewhat anomalous rank of lecturer." There was, however, no discussion in this report of ways to remedy the situation.[39]

Such high attrition was so discouraging that at least one foundation excluded women from consideration altogether. Women were eligible for Danforth Fellowships when they were first offered in 1951, but in 1955 a decision was made to limit the competitions to men on the ground that "[women's] attrition rates in graduate school were too high to warrant the investment of limited Foundation funds."[40]

Unfortunately, it is impossible to make definitive comparisons with our Ten-University data set because information for the early cohorts of students is so limited. Data are available for the 1962–1966 cohorts at three universities (Berkeley, Chicago, Columbia), and the completion rate for women in the EHP

---

dominated by the attendance of women at Berkeley. In most of these years, women students at Berkeley represented at least 40 percent of all women attending the seven universities in the MP fields.

[38]The actual completion rates were 24 percent in the humanities (22 percent in the EHP fields) and 19 percent in the MP fields. These rates include transfers. Excluding transfers (as is done in defining completion rates based on the Ten-University data set) drives these rates to still lower levels (18 percent for all the humanities, 17 percent in the EHP fields, and 16 percent in the MP fields). The source of these data is the National Fellowship data set.

[39]Woodrow Wilson National Fellowship Foundation 1964, 79–80.

[40] The Danforth competition was not reopened to women until 1965. In the same year, "almost in seeming penance," the Danforth Foundation began the program of Graduate Fellowships for Women (Danforth Foundation 1976, 3).

Unlike the Danforth program, the Woodrow Wilson fellowship program remained open to both men and women during all the years of its existence. However, an informal limit of 25 percent apparently was set on the number of awards that could go to women. In 1962, the regional chairmen voted to elect women in the coming competition "without any regard to the target of 25%" because "in some regions it may have prevented the election of outstanding women candidates" (Woodrow Wilson National Fellowship Foundation 1964, 58). Despite this decision, the percentage of women fellows never rose much above 30 percent (Weiss 1986, 10).

The eligibility of women for fellowship support was debated widely. One author described the issue this way: "It is said that so many things can happen to interfere with a woman's commitment to graduate study—marriage, pregnancy, moving away with her husband, and so on—that a man is a better bet for a long-range contribution to society. Although such practice seems unjust to the individual (since no one can predict which man or woman will complete the degree), many regard

fields at these universities was somewhat higher (37 percent) than the completion rates for women in the Woodrow Wilson fellowship program in the same cohort in similar fields (27 percent). However, there is still evidence of a large gap in completion rates between men and women in the Ten-University data set; the completion rate for men at these same universities in the same cohort in the same fields was 59 percent.[41]

The dramatic finding is the completion rate achieved by the Danforth Foundation after it reopened its competition to women in 1965. Women in the 1967–1971 cohort of Danforth Fellows (when they were first present in large enough numbers to permit meaningful comparisons) completed their doctorates at an unheard-of rate of 71 percent. This was a markedly higher completion rate than that achieved by their male contemporaries in the EHP fields, and it more than doubled the completion rate achieved by the previous (1962–1966) cohort of Woodrow Wilson women (Figure 11.11).

We know of no way to parse out credit among the many factors involved, but there is some evidence that the Danforth Foundation was particularly discrim-

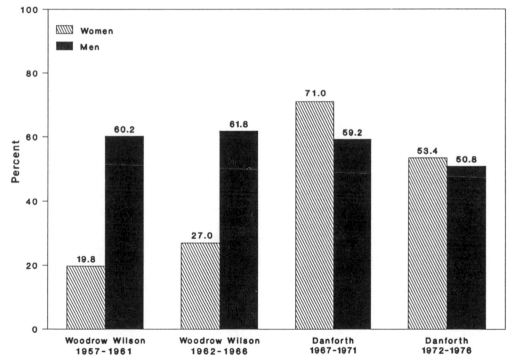

Figure 11.11
Minimum Completion Rates for Danforth and Woodrow Wilson Fellows by Gender, Humanities Only, 1957–1966 Entering Cohorts
Source: National Fellowship data set.

it as a more responsible use of graduate training resources" (Cross 1974, 42, as cited in Solmon 1976, 24).

[41]See Appendix G, Table G.11–6.

inating in its choice of women recipients in these years. Alice Rossi, a sociologist at the University of Massachusetts at Amherst who served on the Foundation's advisory committee on fellowships for women, has a "distinct memory" that reviewers of the applications tended to favor "sure bets," whom she characterizes as "women who had already completed well some phase of advanced education, and who had 'normal' personal biographies, i.e., still married but with small families, children in adolescence, not young preschoolers."[42]

It is improbable, however, that any selection procedure by itself could have produced such extraordinary completion rates. The societal context was, we believe, another major factor at work. During the mid- to late 1960s, women at the BA level began to move away from fields of study, such as education, that had traditionally attracted very large numbers of women. In 1958, nearly half of all BA degrees awarded to women were in education; by 1968, the percentage had fallen to 37 percent; in 1986, it was 13 percent. The humanities were the main "receiving" fields during the first phase of this movement away from the field of education. The percentage of BAs awarded to women in the humanities rose from 12 percent in 1958 to 18 percent in 1968 (the peak year).[43]

Thus, by the late 1960s, the pool of potential women graduate students in the humanities had increased markedly. Also, these were years when many women felt freer to postpone marriage and childbearing, and to assign a higher priority to planning careers for themselves. These conditions no doubt made it easier for the Danforth Foundation to identify highly qualified women candidates who were determined to earn a PhD.

In the 1972–1976 cohort of Danforth Fellows, women continued to complete their doctorates in larger numbers than men, but the gap narrowed appreciably (and nearly disappeared) as completion rates for women declined from their 1967–1971 level even more rapidly than completion rates for men. These were years in which there was a sharp drop in the interest of women in the humanities at the undergraduate level, and an offsetting upsurge of interest in business as well as other fields.[44] Women had more vocational choices, and this made it increasingly unlikely that—even in a program like the Danforth—completion rates for women would exceed completion rates for men.

Women in the EHP fields within our Ten-University data set had lower completion rates than men during these years, and the size of the gap remained more or less constant from 1968 through 1974 (Figure 11.12). The clarity and persistence of this pattern serve as at least implicit evidence of the importance of the extremely selective nature of the process by which the Danforth Foundation awarded fellowships to women in the mid- to late 1960s.

No completion rates can be given for fellowship recipients in the EHP fields after the 1972–1976 cohorts because the Danforth program ended and the Mellon

---

[42]Rossi 1990 (personal correspondence). Rossi goes on to cite an anecdote of a heated debate about the "deservedness" of one particular candidate who did not fit this mold but, after Rossi's insistence, was awarded the fellowship and eventually earned her degree.

Another person involved in the administration of the Danforth program confirmed (in a personal conversation) that women were screened "with the greatest care" during these years.

[43]Turner and Bowen 1990, 518–20. The original source of these data is *Earned Degrees Conferred Survey*, various years.

[44]Turner and Bowen 1990, 519–20. Again, the *Earned Degrees Conferred Survey* is the original source of the data.

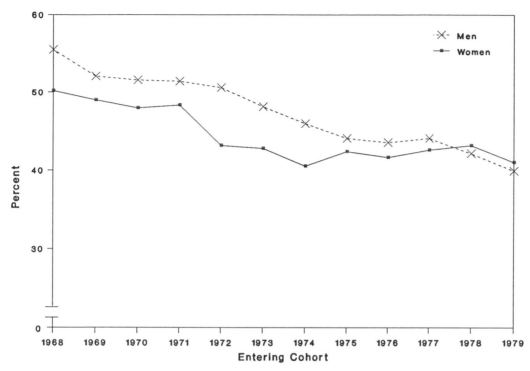

Figure 11.12
Minimum Completion Rates by Gender, EHP Total, 1968–1979 Entering Cohorts
Source: Same as Figure 11.10.

program did not start until 1983. However, we can conclude, on the basis of the Ten-University data set, that the gender gap in completion rates within universities closed in the late 1970s. If anything, completion rates for women in the EHP fields have exceeded completion rates for men in the most recent cohorts for which reliable data are available (Figure 11.12).

A somewhat surprising corollary is that this overall parity in completion rates conceals nontrivial differences between Larger and Smaller universities (Figure 11.13). In the late 1960s, completion rates for women in the EHP fields were roughly 85 percent of the men's rates in both Larger and Smaller universities. These ratios then began to diverge. By the late 1970s, completion rates for women in the Smaller universities had risen *above* the rates for the men. In the Larger universities, on the other hand, the completion rates for women had fallen 15 to 20 percent below the rates for the men. One can only speculate as to the factors at work. Perhaps the scale of the Larger programs made it harder to respond effectively to the complex circumstances that sometimes afflict women graduate students seeking to balance competing claims and pressures.

As noted earlier, there are still not enough women candidates for doctorates in mathematics and physics in our set of universities to permit an analysis of trends. The NSF data are more extensive, and they do demonstrate the same tendency toward convergence of completion rates for men and women that was noted in the EHP fields within the ten universities. It will suffice to present

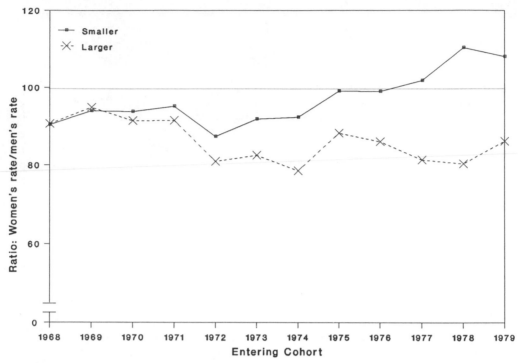

Figure 11.13
Women's Minimum Completion Rates as a Percentage of Men's Minimum Completion Rates by Scale of Graduate Program, EHP Total, 1968–1979 Entering Cohorts

Source: Ten-University data set. Data are from Berkeley, Chicago, and Columbia (Larger programs), and Cornell, Harvard, Princeton, and Stanford (Smaller programs).

summary statistics for all NSF recipients in the natural sciences in three successive five-year cohorts (Table 11.3). It is evident that a great deal of progress has been made in removing the disparity in completion rates that was so substantial in the mid-1960s. Of course, it must also be recognized that the absolute numbers of women recipients of NSF Fellowships (and of doctorates) remain very low in fields such as physics.

TABLE 11.3
Completion Rates by Gender, Recipients of NSF Fellowships, Natural Sciences Only, 1962–1976 Entering Cohorts

	Entering Cohorts		
Group	1962–1966	1967–1971	1972–1976
Men only	81.0	72.7	80.2
Women only	61.4	65.1	76.8
Women's rate/men's rate	75.8%	89.5%	95.8%

Source: National Fellowship data set.

Notes: Completion rates are weighted averages of the rates for the component fields of study (for example, mathematics, physics, life sciences, psychology).

Time-to-Degree

Time-to-degree has also varied systematically with gender, even though the patterns are somewhat complex when fields of study and various data sets are taken into account (Figures 11.14 and 11.15). Two main conclusions stand out:

- Women have taken longer than men to complete their doctorates. With a single important exception to be noted below, this simple proposition holds for the humanities and the sciences, for recipients of fellowships, for all students in the Ten-University data set, for faculty promoted to tenure within our faculty-promotion (FacPro) data set, and for recipients of doctorates at all universities.[45]
- For all recipients of doctorates (in both the humanities and the sciences), the gender gap in time-to-degree has diminished steadily, but it has not disappeared. In more restricted data sets (Danforth and Ten-University), differences in time-to-degree in the humanities appear to have stabilized at about half a year.

NSF Fellows in the natural sciences constitute the major exception to these generalizations (left-hand panel of Figure 11.15). For these students, there has been virtually no difference between men and women in time-to-degree in any cohort. Moreover, the absolute level of time-to-degree has been constant over time. For men and women alike, in all three of the five-year entering cohorts for which we have data, NSF Fellows have registered a median time-to-degree of almost exactly five years. Our interpretation of the extraordinary consistency of these figures is that they demonstrate the strong effects on *all* NSF Fellows of the NSF selection process (discussed above), the guarantee of generous financial support, and the characteristics of the fields themselves.[46]

Of all the other comparisons shown in Figures 11.14 and 11.15, only one shows essentially the same time-to-degree for men and women. Approximate parity was achieved in the 1967–1971 Danforth cohort, and it is not surprising that this is the same cohort in which women completed their degrees in such extraordinarily high numbers. We suspect that the unusual combination of factors that led to such high completion rates for these women also eliminated the difference in time-to-degree related to gender. It may be even more noteworthy, however, that the previous half-year differential quickly reestablished itself in the experiences of the 1972–1976 Danforth cohort. A differential of the same magnitude is also evident when we examine the EHP fields within the Ten-University data set.[47]

The stability of the gender differential for these highly selected groups of individuals stands in sharp contrast to the steady decrease in the gender gap for all recipients of doctorates in the humanities (bottom right-hand panel of Figure 11.14). In the 1962–1966 cohort, median time-to-degree was 1.6 years longer for

---

[45]When studying time-to-degree, it is possible (as it is not when studying completion rates) to make comparisons using national data from the Doctorate Records File.

[46]The influence of field of study is also reflected in the general tendency for differences in time-to-degree between men and women to be smaller in the sciences than in the humanities (compare Figures 11.14 and 11.15).

[47]The large difference in time-to-degree for men and women in the FacPro data set is attributable almost entirely to differences within the liberal arts colleges in this data set, not to differences within the universities (Appendix E).

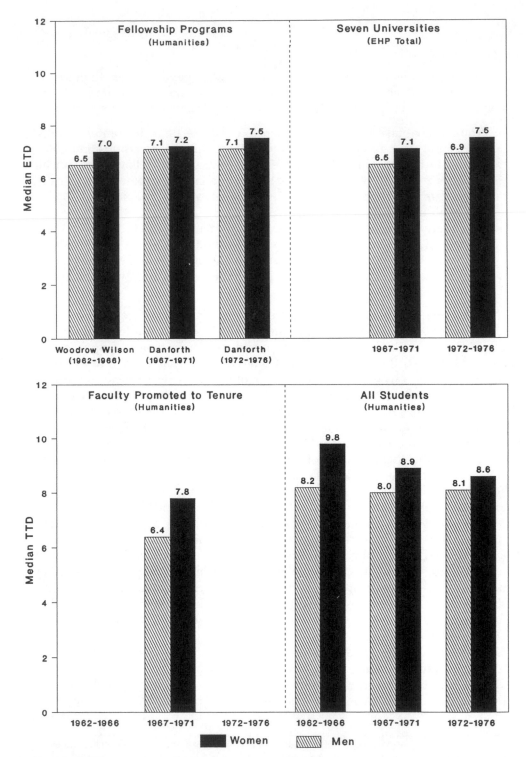

Figure 11.14
Median Time-to-Degree by Gender, Selected Data Sets, Humanities Only, 1962–1976
Entering Cohorts

Source: Fellowship data are from the National Fellowship data set; "Seven Universities" data are from the Ten-University data set (Berkeley, Chicago, Columbia, Cornell, Harvard, Princeton, and Stanford); faculty promotion data are from the FacPro data set; and "All Students" data are from special tabulations of the Doctorate Records File.

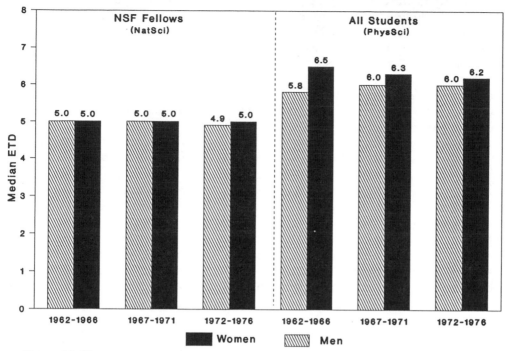

Figure 11.15
Median Time-to-Degree by Gender, Selected Data Sets, Sciences Only, 1962–1976 Entering Cohorts

Source: Fellowship data are from the National Fellowship data set, and "All Students" data are from special tabulations of the Doctorate Records File.

all women in the humanities than for all men, and we suspect that the explanation has to do with the circumstances prevailing in the mid- to late 1960s. In general, women received less financial aid than men (recall, for example, that women were not eligible for Danforth Fellowships then).[48] In addition, many no doubt had to juggle pursuit of the PhD with family responsibilities and (for that and other reasons) may have had to study on a part-time basis.

While conditions have surely improved in these respects, as attitudes and opportunities have changed, women in general still must surmount a wider range of obstacles than men. This may explain why the median time-to-degree figure for women remains higher than the figure for men in the most recent data available. And it also suggests that the remaining part of the gender gap in time-to-degree may prove highly resistant.

In concluding this discussion of national fellowship programs and related issues, we want to emphasize several points. First, we have been evaluating these programs *only* from the point of view of completion rates and time-to-degree, and while these are important indicators, they offer but one window on these programs and the broader purposes that they serve. Fellowships are intended to accomplish—and do accomplish—many more objectives than those

---

[48]Solmon 1976, 132ff.

related only to attrition or the duration of graduate study. It would be a serious error, in our judgment, to lose sight of other contributions.

To cite one example, the Woodrow Wilson program, despite its low completion rates, encouraged more women to become scholars. As one historian, Nancy Weiss, put it: "[The Woodrow Wilson program] . . . served as a progressive force in enlarging opportunities for women to pursue graduate education." At a time when there was little encouragement and close to no money for women who wanted to pursue graduate study, the Woodrow Wilson Fellowships probably helped many women in the 1950s and 1960s pave the way for future women scholars. On a more individual level, Weiss concludes that "[the Woodrow Wilson Fellowships] made a critical difference in shaping the self-images, opportunities, and professional aspirations of the women who received them." She goes on to cite numerous examples of women scholars who felt that the fellowship had played a critical role in their decision to pursue and complete graduate studies.[49]

A more general contribution made by the national fellowship programs has been to direct attention to the importance of graduate education. These programs have had major "announcement effects,"and without question have led a number of able young people to embark on academic careers. In addition, they have given faculty and administrators committed to graduate education a sense that others, outside academia, share their concerns.

Finally, these programs provided substantial amounts of tangible support when it was badly needed. No one should underestimate the value of that support in fields that require long training and in which the later professional rewards—in financial terms—are so modest compared with those provided by other professions. It may be the case that certain kinds of fellowship funding *alone* sometimes fail to achieve significant reductions in attrition or time-to-degree. But it is equally clear that without a reasonably satisfactory threshold level of funding, many students will neither undertake graduate study nor complete doctorates—especially if potential graduate students are already carrying large loans taken out to pay for college.

At the same time, the limited success achieved in reducing attrition and time-to-degree underscores the difficulties of effecting broad changes in graduate education by working mainly from "outside" the graduate programs themselves. Even the Ford Foundation initiative, which represented the strongest effort to bring about internal changes, demonstrated an insufficient understanding of the dynamics of graduate programs and of the key role played by departmental faculty in defining the context within which students pursue doctorates. It is to factors of this kind that we turn in the next two chapters. They are, we believe, as critical as adequate funding in improving the effectiveness of doctoral programs.

---

[49]Weiss 1986, 9.

Requirements and Program Content

THE THESIS of the next two chapters is a simple one: The ways in which universities and faculties define and conduct programs of graduate education matter enormously. While external factors such as the state of the academic labor market and the availability of national fellowships exert powerful influences of their own, their effects are mediated through departmental structures and informal modes of decisionmaking. A great deal, in other words, depends upon what happens "inside" particular fields of study, graduate programs, and universities.

Proving this proposition, and providing documentation that will stand the test of analysis, is difficult. At the same time, we have already noted much relevant evidence. For example, the demonstrable effect that program size has had upon attrition and time-to-degree implies that a bundle of factors contained in the concept of scale are of major consequence. These include: the faculty/student ratio (with its implications for advising students and monitoring performance); the number of courses, subfields, and options available to students (with the possibility that a wide array of choices may lead to more false starts); the potentially increased difficulty in very large programs of reaching a consensus concerning intellectual directions; and, in programs where there are so many students and faculty, the difficulties encountered by individuals in seeking to know one another well, or even to see one another on a regular basis.

In this chapter, we begin to explore this complex terrain by examining the general structure of graduate study in the English, history, and political science (EHP) fields as expressed in the official requirements for obtaining a doctorate. We also consider the effects that broad intellectual currents have had on the content of selected graduate curricula as reflected in specific course offerings. Then, in the next chapter, we consider how these and other factors have affected the progress of students in the EHP fields through the stages of graduate study, noting intervals in the process of studying for a doctorate that appear particularly hazardous (for example, the period immediately after qualifying examinations) and factors that seem either to impede or accelerate progress toward the PhD.[1]

The source materials used in these two chapters consist in part of the same kinds of data on attrition and time-to-degree used throughout this study. In

---

[1] We limit most of this discussion to the EHP fields and related areas within the humanities and social sciences because it would have been impractical to extend this kind of textured analysis to more than a few fields of study. The focus on the EHP fields reflects the special interests of the Andrew W. Mellon Foundation. It is not meant to imply that the same questions are unimportant in other fields within the humanities and social sciences, or within the sciences. (For a recent analysis of the field of mathematics that reflects the same general approach taken here and reaches many of the same conclusions, see the forthcoming study by the Committee on Doctoral and Postdoctoral Study in the Mathematical Sciences [1992]).

addition, however, we base our discussion on the following kinds of information:

- University catalogs and departmental brochures;
- Published reports by professional associations, such as the Modern Language Association;
- Discussions and debates in the literature concerning the character and directions of certain fields of study;
- Materials from institutional self-studies (including some student surveys and reports);
- Proposals to improve graduate education submitted to the Andrew W. Mellon Foundation by individual departments and universities;
- Interviews with faculty members at some of these same universities;
- Questionnaires distributed to all Mellon Fellows in the Humanities; and
- Observations by psychologists and therapists who have counseled PhD candidates.

Analyzing materials of this kind is inherently difficult. So many variables are at work—operating with varying effects in a range of university settings upon individuals in differing circumstances—that it is possible only to provide a synopsis of the major factors, indicating those which are mentioned most frequently and persuasively. What follows, therefore, is an interpretation of a diverse set of materials, which necessarily are used selectively.[2]

REQUIREMENTS FOR THE PHD

We begin with an examination of some changes over the last three decades in the basic structure of graduate programs in EHP fields at selected universities. While catalogs and other official publications are (understandably) often regarded as bland and uninformative, they constitute the primary source of information when seeking to determine whether stipulated requirements and timetables for the PhD have been modified significantly, and whether it is possible to identify systematic differences related to scale of graduate program.

Comparisons of Catalogs

During the 1960s, requirements for the PhD at smaller-scale universities were often defined centrally and printed at the front of catalogs. The stipulated time-to-degree was often stated clearly and was usually quite limited in duration. Language requirements were also generally explicit and offered few options. General examinations tended to be comprehensive, and the number of subfields available to students for intensive concentration was tightly constrained. Teaching assistantships were far from plentiful and were not emphasized either as part of graduate education or as a major source of financial support.

---

[2]There is an extensive body of literature on the internal processes of graduate education. One recent bibliography was prepared by Tinto (1991). We refer to a few of these studies in this chapter and the next, but we do not provide anything approaching a full review of this voluminous set of materials.

Two excerpts from the catalogs of universities with relatively small graduate programs are illustrative:

> The degree of Doctor of Philosophy (Ph.D.) is the highest degree . . . offered by the University. It is conferred for work of distinction in which the student displays powers of original scholarship. The minimum requirement for this degree is three full years of graduate study and research in residence. In many cases the student must spend more than three years. . . . No more than six years from the time a student begins graduate study will normally be allowed. . . .
>
> A reading knowledge of French and German is required. In special cases, . . . one of the required languages may be replaced by another. . . . *No student will be allowed to register for a third term in the Graduate School who has not passed at least one of the required foreign languages. No student will be allowed to register for a fifth term of graduate study who has not passed both.* . . .
>
> Typical patterns of support in different departments vary markedly. . . . Teaching is normally looked upon as a privilege reserved when possible for advanced students. (*Bulletin of Yale University, Graduate School, 1963–1964*, 18–19, 23)

> In order to qualify for the degree of Doctor of Philosophy, the candidate is required to pass the General Examination in his subject, present an acceptable dissertation, and pass the Final Public Oral Examination. Normally, it is necessary for a student to devote three years to graduate study in order to meet these requirements. . . .
>
> The General Examination is designed to ascertain the student's general knowledge of his subject, his acquaintance with scholarly methods of research, and his power of organizing and presenting his material. The examination is not restricted to the content of graduate courses but is comprehensive in character. . . .
>
> A number of part-time assistantships in instruction and research are available both to entering and continuing students, principally in the natural sciences and engineering. Occasionally there are assistantships available in the social science departments. . . . Only a few departments in the humanities offer assistantships. (Princeton University, *The Graduate Catalogue Announcement, 1963–1964*, 20–21, 26)

Somewhat different structures characterized mid-sized or large universities. Requirements and expectations—even in the 1960s—tended to be defined departmentally, with more options available and less explicit (or more generous) timetables stipulated. The 1964–65 catalog at Chicago, for example, lists degree requirements on a divisional basis, and a single brief paragraph summarizes the PhD guidelines.[3] French and German are singled out as the required languages, with substitutions possible, but the requirements are defined in terms that are comparatively factual ("a minimum of three full quarters of residence . . . the completion with satisfactory grades . . . the completion of an acceptable dissertation . . . "). Overall timetables for completion of the PhD are not given. Departmental statements are somewhat more elaborate, but still succinct, and students are invited to be directly in touch with the departmental office for additional information.[4] Columbia's catalogs are similar in certain respects. In most of the humanities and related social sciences, they do not indicate specific overall time-limits for the completion of doctoral degrees.

---

[3]University of Chicago, *Announcements, Graduate Programs in the Divisions, 1964–1965*, 109.

[4]University of Chicago, *Announcements, Graduate Programs in the Divisions, 1964–1965*; see pp. 123–24 for the English Department requirements.

Harvard represents an intermediate case. As at the larger universities, PhD requirements tended to be stipulated by departments; but as at the smaller universities, these requirements were generally quite structured and offered relatively few options. In English literature, for example, three languages were required (Latin or Greek, and two modern languages from the set of French, German, and Italian). Expectations concerning progression through the program were described as follows:

> An oral examination passed before the end of the student's second year in the PhD program, by which time all course and foreign language requirements must have been met. . . . The periods of concentration are:
>
>   a. English Literature, to 1500
>   b. English Literature, 1500–1660
>   c. English Literature, 1660–1800
>   d. English Literature, since 1800
>   e. American Literature, from the beginning to the present.
>
> One hour of the examination will be devoted to the literature and essential scholarship in the period of concentration, and one hour to literature outside that period. . . . The above program assumes that the total time required for proceeding to the PhD degree will be four years.
> (Harvard University, *Graduate School of Arts and Sciences, 1963–1964*, 3–4)

Noteworthy is the relative simplicity with which special fields are described (by historical period, in a neatly segmented progression). Also, there are clear time-lines (two years to the oral examination, four years for the entire program); and the oral examination is comprehensive (one hour on the special field and one hour on "everything else").

Basic distinctions in requirements and catalog styles between smaller and larger programs were generally sustained in the two decades after the 1960s, but several other important changes occurred. By the 1970s, departments—rather than the central administration—had become generally responsible for defining most requirements, even at the smaller universities. In addition, the number of special fields or subfields increased as part of the considerable expansion of course-offerings and numbers of faculty documented in Chapter Five.

Consequences of these developments can be detected even in departments that have remained comparatively structured and that show considerable continuity in their program definitions. For instance, the 1989–90 description of requirements in English at Harvard shows both a good deal of similarity to—and some significant differences from—the entry for the 1960s. In 1989–90, the catalog read (our emphasis):

> A reading knowledge of *two* languages is required, one ancient and one modern: either Latin or Greek and normally, French, German, Italian or Spanish. Other modern languages may be acceptable. . . .
> Each student is required to take a written comprehensive examination no later than the spring of the second year. This examination is in eight parts as follows: (1) English literature to 1500; (2) Renaissance (1500–1600); (3) Restoration and Eighteenth Century (1600–1800); (4) Nineteenth Century British and American Literature; (5) American Literature to 1900; (6) Twentieth Century English and American Literature; (7) History and Theory of Criticism; (8) History and Studies of the Language. Students may be

excused from three parts of the exam if they have completed course work as follows. . . .

Dissertation Qualifying Examination.—This is a two-hour oral examination which is to be taken by the end of the third year of graduate study. . . . The exam will normally be divided into two equal parts—one hour on the dissertation area and one hour general questioning. Special attention may be paid to areas of weakness on the written exam. . . .

The normal amount of time for the completion of the PhD program is six years. When a student has been in the program for eight years . . . without completing the dissertation, the student *may* be asked to withdraw, without prejudice, from the program.

(Harvard University, *Graduate School of Arts and Sciences, Graduate Studies in the Humanities, 1989–90*, 24–26)

There is no need to discuss in detail the changes from the mid-1960s to 1989–90. But attention should be paid to the reduction in the language requirement (from three to two), with a simultaneous increase in options; the expansion in the number of special fields (criticism and theory, plus language); the opportunity to "write off" up to three fields through course-work; and the lengthening of expected time-to-degree from four to six years, with an additional clause suggesting that up to eight years is potentially acceptable before a student *may* be asked to withdraw.

While no single set of modifications in any one department can be used as a reliable index of general patterns, these changes offer a reasonable guide to many of the shifts that occurred in EHP and related fields during the past quarter-century. For example, at one of the larger programs (English at Chicago), we find that during the 1960s the PhD requirements mention "fields of specialization" but do not enumerate them. The oral exam is based on a reading list "compiled by the student" and approved by the department, which consists of "seventy-five titles (whole works or major parts thereof), whose literary significance the student is prepared to defend, distributed fairly representationally among literary periods and kinds."[5]

If we then compare the statement of requirements for English at Chicago in 1989, we again find increased complexity:

In the first or second quarter of the second year of the PhD program (the first year of Research Residence as defined by the University's categories), students should plan to take the oral fields examination. Students must choose four fields from among the following list of fifteen: Old English; Middle English; Tudor; Stuart; Eighteenth Century; Romantic; Victorian; Earlier American; Later American; Modern British and American; Film and Popular Culture; History and Theory of Criticism; Linguistics; Stylistics and Language Theory; History and Theory of Genres. While the choice of fields should be sensitive to potential areas of dissertation research, the Department encourages students to express a breadth of interest by preparing fields in more than one literature or chronological period. . . .

The foreign language [requirement] for the PhD degree may be fulfilled in one of three ways: students may take reading examinations in two languages, normally French and German; they may take two courses in the literature of one language; or they may demonstrate competence in one language by translating without the use of

---

[5]University of Chicago, *Announcements, Graduate Programs in the Divisions, 1964–65*, 124.

a dictionary a text from the literature of that language and by writing an essay in English on the literary characteristics of the text.
(University of Chicago, *Announcements, Graduate Programs in the Divisions, 1989–90*, 174)

The changes in structure revealed by comparisons of selected programs in English can be retraced in other fields and institutions. In history, for example, there was a shift from a very considerable concentration on European and American courses in the 1960s to a more diversified set of offerings (including several non-Western subfields) in the late 1980s. Concomitantly, the number of special fields and options from which students could choose also expanded, as did the number of foreign language options. In general, stipulated time-to-degree figures (where specified) tended to move from four years in the 1960s, to five, six, or even seven years in the late 1980s, depending on the program and institution. In at least one case, there is a published expectation of "eight to nine years."

Also, expectations with respect to teaching assistantships altered unequivocally, from a somewhat skittish 1960s attitude ("occasionally," "a few," "teaching is a privilege") to nearly complete normalization. For example, the relevant part of the English department listing for Princeton in the 1989–90 catalog reads as follows: "The department offers many opportunities for teaching experience in conjunction with its large undergraduate program. All students are required to teach a minimum of three hours in one semester."[6] The analogous paragraph in the 1988–89 Yale Graduate School announcement applies to all programs in the Graduate School of Arts and Sciences: "At Yale, teaching and full-time graduate study are regarded as complementary, and teaching assistants remain registered as full-time students."[7]

Commentary on Main Developments

The examples of changes in stated requirements cited above are obviously selective. At the same time, many would recognize these trends as reasonably typical of a broad range of fields and institutions in the humanities and related social sciences. Consulting catalogs is a more complex exercise than it might first appear to be, and it can mislead unless one bears in mind several caveats. Often, for example, history department listings do not include large areas of non-Western history (or the history of the ancient world, or the history of science) that are the province of separate free-standing departments and programs. Similarly, English departmental listings may or may not include developments that have taken place in comparative literature or other interdisciplinary literary programs and centers.

But these qualifications only serve to underline a main point: In spite of the fact that the total number of graduate course-offerings is smaller now than at the peak period of approximately 1970, the number of subfields, ancillary fields, and interdisciplinary options has increased. This situation has created, in turn, another problem in graduate education. Because the number of full-time faculty is not materially different now than in the early 1970s, and because the range of academic subjects and special fields has grown so much, covering what is now considered to be the legitimate (indeed, expected) "universe of knowledge" has become a formidable task. Under such circumstances, students often have

---

[6] Princeton University, *Graduate School Announcement, 1989–90*, 101.
[7] Yale University, *Graduate School, Programs and Policies, 1988–89*, 7.

difficulty locating an adviser who knows in detail about a potential thesis field or topic, and faculty members may find themselves stretched in ways that are stimulating but not always manageable, as they try to respond to a wide range of student interests across a large span of fields.

A second major conclusion is that, just as programs and fields of knowledge have become more difficult to organize and manage, so, too, have formally stated expectations tended to slip. Sometimes the slippage is the result of a realistic attempt to deal with complexity by providing more options—which in turn are often harder to define sharply or limit rigorously. Sometimes, however, the slippage is a consequence of converging external and internal pressures that are less benign.

To illustrate, changes in published expectations concerning time-to-degree reflect, at least in part, the realities of the difficult job market for academics that has existed since the early 1970s. Also, students have had less financial aid, and therefore have had to teach more to support themselves. At the same time, there are more subtle internal explanations for some of these changes. Faculty members are often reluctant to place even more pressures and burdens upon doctoral candidates who are already highly uncertain about their prospects. As a consequence, more "incompletes" may be given in courses, more term papers may remain unfinished, more deadlines pass unnoticed. Busy faculty and anxious students find it easier—and in many ways more humane—to overlook what appear to be merely bureaucratic strictures and requirements, especially when the enforcement of such requirements requires considerable time, energy, and even uncheerful confrontations.

In larger programs, the tendency to accept such patterns of behavior is reinforced by the sheer difficulty of attempting to keep track of everything and everyone. In smaller programs, the very fact that students and faculty may know one another well can create a tendency on the part of the faculty to be exceptionally sympathetic and understanding, at a time when so many aspects of the external environment appear to be comparatively indifferent, uncertain, and even unfriendly.

In attempting to describe this situation as objectively as possible, it is difficult to avoid characterizing it. And it is not always easy to distinguish positive from negative developments. For example, if institutions had enforced strictly their four-year requirements concerning time-to-degree, that effort would almost certainly have led to even greater attrition in the 1970s and 1980s, given the state of the job market. If institutions had neglected the study of non-Western history (or politics, or languages and literature), our society would surely have been left with an even smaller supply of trained internationalists capable of understanding and working in an increasingly interdependent community of peoples and nations.

In these respects, much that has happened in graduate programs since the 1960s has been beneficial, indeed essential. At the same time, there has obviously been some loss of articulated coherence in the formal curriculum, some measurable loss of structure and control in program definition and management, and an increased sense of uncertainty about where to draw sensible boundary lines—or how much more can possibly be included in the formal curriculum. If one clear risk of drawing such boundaries is the potential exclusion of some important fields of knowledge, the risk of not drawing them is the almost inevitable attenuation of certain forms of clarity, of a sense of direction, and of certain forms of effectiveness.

CURRICULAR DEVELOPMENTS: SUBFIELDS

Examination of changes over the last 25 years in the content of the graduate curriculum within English, history, and political science provides a sharper sense of the extent and character of some of these broad trends. Counting the number of courses actually offered in individual subfields (not simply those listed in the catalog) provides at least an approximate sense of major shifts in emphasis, and that is the approach taken in this section. Looking closely at course descriptions (in the next section) yields additional information that is more finely grained. Finally, considering the intellectual state of quite broad areas of learning (see especially Appendix F, "Theory and Its Reverberations") helps fill out the picture—even as it remains a rudimentary sketch.

The following analysis of subfields is based on a detailed study of the curricula of nine EHP programs at five universities (Columbia, Cornell, Harvard, Princeton, Yale) from 1963–64 to 1989–90.[8] Data for course-offerings are presented in two-year clusters in order to smooth the erratic fluctuations that can occur in any single year. Four points in time have been chosen, corresponding approximately to the periods of rapid expansion (from the 1960s to 1970s), contraction (in the late 1970s), and then renewed growth (in the 1980s).

The Individual EHP Fields

ENGLISH

In the field of English, we have compiled course listings for four programs. All courses have been distributed among the following subfields: early-period courses (through 1800); offerings in nineteenth/twentieth–century literature; courses in American literature; and criticism/theory/genre courses.[9] In general,

---

[8]See Chapter Five for a discussion of these programs, including data on faculty size and numbers of courses offered. Information also was collected for some programs at other universities (including Pennsylvania and Stanford), but there was considerable variation in the scale of programs, in the range and number of subspecialties, and in the extent to which "the same" departments or programs at different universities include a similar configuration of allied fields. For example, some history departments include ancient history, plus some regional areas (Asia, the Middle East, etc.), plus the history of economics, or of science, as integral parts of their own curriculum and staffing. Others have separate departments for many or all of these related fields.

We became convinced that it was wiser to depend for statistical data on a fairly small set of institutions whose programs have been approximately the same size, and whose structure (including the number and type of subfields) has been roughly similar. To attempt to compare, for example, an English department that has maintained the same four or five principal subspecialties over a 25-year period with one that has shifted from virtually no specialties to more than a dozen produces data that are utterly discrepant in character.

[9]Comparative literature listings have been excluded from programs in English unless the courses were taught by faculty who were listed on the English department masthead, or unless the courses were integral parts of the English department's own program. This approach tends to understate—in some cases, very significantly—the amount of theory and criticism actually being taught in literary fields at the graduate level, since a considerable amount of theoretical work is offered in comparative literature programs.

More generally, the following guidelines have been followed in assigning courses to subfields. First, we followed the taxonomy of each program. In doubtful cases, we made our best judgment based on the course description. In this gray area, there is clearly room for debate, and others might well have arrived at different counts. The difficulties become most apparent when a course had both a chronological and a topical focus. Nonetheless, the preponderance of courses can be classified, at

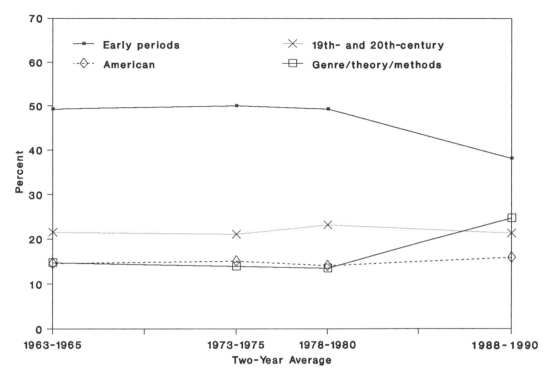

Figure 12.1
Distribution of Courses Offered in English by Subfield, Four-University Average,
1963–1990
Source: Authors' tabulations for Cornell, Harvard, Princeton, and Yale. See text and footnotes 6 and 7 for an explanation of methods.

the line of development is extremely clear (Figure 12.1). Courses in the earlier chronological fields have on average diminished in relative number, falling from 49 percent of all offerings in 1963–1965 to 38 percent in 1988–1990. American literary offerings and more recent literature (nineteenth/twentieth centuries) have remained remarkably stable in their percentage shares. The area of striking growth has been literary theory, criticism, and courses that deal with particular genres.

The total number of courses offered in literature is now larger (313 in 1988–1990 in these programs, as compared to 229 in 1963–1965). Therefore,

---

least in the programs under discussion. Of course, the substance of what is taught in many courses has inevitably changed, and the approach to the material has been modified. Still, "Tudor England," or "Urban Politics in America," or "Pre-Shakespearean Elizabethan Drama" can be readily distinguished from "Historiography" or "Theories of Fiction."

Within fields, some subfields have been aggregated. For instance, the four or five relatively small subheadings used by most English programs to describe offerings from the earliest period through the eighteenth century have been combined. Finally, a small number of courses, generally offered in the 1980s, have been excluded because they were sufficiently interdisciplinary or wide ranging in their coverage that they defied categorization.

If a department included a particular subfield (such as history of economics, history of science, or ancient history), but later dropped this area or transferred it elsewhere, all related courses were excluded for all periods.

although the aggregate percentage share of early-period courses has dropped from 49 percent to 38 percent since 1963–1965, the actual number of such courses has in fact grown slightly (from 110 to 116, or by about 5 percent). Within the early periods, the greatest general falloff has been in Old English, which was previously required, and in aspects of the medieval period. "Mainline" renaissance offerings (Shakespeare to Milton), by contrast, have held up very well.

The strong emergence of theory (in terms of formal course offerings) is clearly a phenomenon of the 1980s. A few graduate programs had invested quite substantially in theoretical work before that time, and some theoretical/critical courses were offered by virtually every program at least as early as the 1950s and early 1960s. But the most pronounced and broadly based shift in emphasis took place between 1978–1980 (33 courses representing 13 percent of all courses offered by our four programs) and 1988–1990 (79 courses, representing 25 percent). Moreover, as noted earlier, these figures undoubtedly underrepresent growth in the theory/criticism field because offerings in comparative literature and related fields are not counted.

Evaluating these changes is far from simple. For example, if one were starting in 1990 with an utterly clean slate, what would be the optimal balance among subfields? It is not clear that one would, for example, assign fully half of a program's courses to English literature before 1800, if the objective were also to give reasonable representation to three centuries of American prose and poetry, to the study of major genres that cut across time-periods, or to the two centuries of literature from Wordsworth through the post–World War II era. Whether 40 percent is a more appropriate figure for the earlier periods—or perhaps 60 percent—is certainly open to debate. Meanwhile, most observers would probably think that 75–80 percent of all course offerings devoted exclusively to the earlier periods—or only 25–30 percent—would represent proportional investments that were too extreme.

The question of "theory" is one to which we will return at a later point because it is obviously a significant issue—philosophical and largely epistemological in its essence—that has touched a number of fields within the humanities and related social sciences.

HISTORY

The pattern in history (Figure 12.2) is somewhat more complex, but some of the main contours are similar.[10] The percentage shares of courses dealing with the earlier periods have tapered off. Offerings in American history have fluctuated, but the net result over a quarter-century is a remarkably constant share of course offerings. The two growth areas have been non-Western history (up from just under 20 percent to about 25 percent) and historiography/theory/ methods (up from 7 percent to 12 percent).

Compared to English literature, there has been less of a decline in course offerings related to earlier periods—but, of course, the base percentage (especially for medieval/early modern) was much smaller to begin with. Similarly, although "methods" and "theory" have grown, the growth has been less

---

[10]These detailed data relate to just two graduate programs. Although this is a very small sample, briefer examination of several other graduate programs in history revealed developments that are similar in fundamental respects.

dramatic. Finally, we see the same tendency toward a more equal balance among subfields.

POLITICAL SCIENCE

Variations across individual programs tend to be greater in political science, simply because the number of subfields and methodological approaches offer considerable scope for specialization and differentiation. Some departments, for example, have become highly mathematical or statistical in orientation, and are strongly committed to the use of quantitative analysis. Others have retained stronger links to selected humanistic disciplines, such as moral philosophy, history, and constitutional law.

Nevertheless, some general patterns emerge (Figure 12.3). Comparative politics has continued to constitute a dominant part of the discipline. If anything, it has accounted for a slightly larger share of course offerings in recent years. International relations has also grown relative to other subfields. Many departments are doing less in American politics since peaks reached in the mid-1960s and early 1970s, when domestic issues (in civil rights and social programs more generally) were in sharp focus. At that time, American politics and international relations were approximately equal in shares of courses

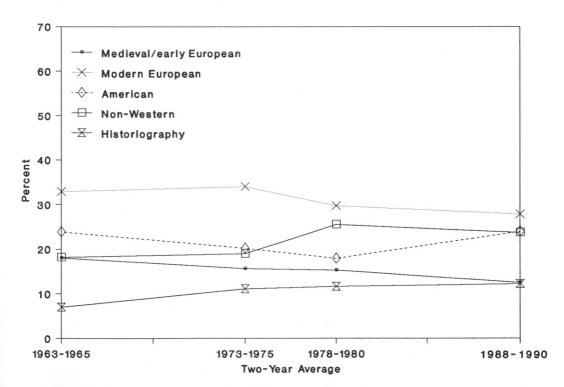

Figure 12.2
Distribution of Courses Offered in History by Subfield, Two-University Average, 1963–1990

Source: Authors' tabulations for Harvard and Princeton. See text and footnotes 6 and 7 for an explanation of methods.

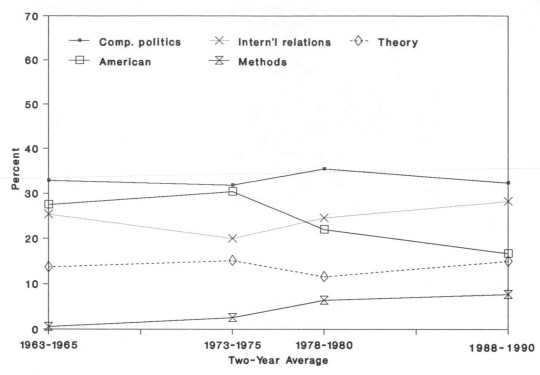

Figure 12.3
Distribution of Courses Offered in Political Science by Subfield, Three-University Average, 1963–1990

Source: Authors' tabulations for Columbia, Harvard, and Yale. See text and footnotes 6 and 7 for an explanation of methods.

offered. Since then, the lines have diverged sharply. There has been a shift in emphasis to the international sphere (buttressing, in some ways, the continuing interest in comparative politics), with a somewhat diminished concentration on exclusively American issues.

These rough breakdowns, however, mask several important developments. For example, many courses in both comparative politics and international relations now include a strong American component, and this is another instance of how traditional categories have altered. The emergent pattern is one in which the United States is studied less as an isolated political entity (though 15–20 percent of graduate courses retain this focus), and more as a nation (or political system), viewed in an international context.

Finally, the issue of theory and/or methodology presents itself differently in political science, as compared to English or history. The field of political theory, for instance, is of long-standing significance in political science. It is taught (at least in several of our selected EHP programs) with a considerable historical dimension and often focuses upon several landmark texts. In this sense, political theory has a very different character than the current conception of theory in literature. The fact that offerings in political theory have held up well in several of these programs since the early 1960s suggests a substantial degree of stability in one of the core areas of the discipline. While aspects of this subfield have undoubtedly been affected by modern and postmodern approaches, recent theoretical developments seem to have been integrated more successfully into the already-existing framework of this discipline, with less overt strain and divisiveness, than in other humanistic and social science fields, such as literature, history, art history, and anthropology.

One of the main methodological developments in political science has centered not so much upon modernist reconceptualizations of a philosophical kind as upon ways in which quantitative analysis should be considered an integral aspect of the field. Whether one studies electoral politics and voting behavior, the politics of cities and states, or the effectiveness of certain governmental programs, it is impossible to proceed very far without the capacity to collect and analyze systematically many kinds of information, including economic data, demographic statistics, and a wide variety of other materials. Not surprisingly, therefore, most political science departments now require their graduate students to develop at least some capacity to use quantitative tools. One result has been a steady rise in the number of courses in methods.

Common Tendencies

Drawing conclusions from this set of nine programs across three fields (at five universities) is obviously difficult. However, the statistical evidence presented here—and an informal sampling of other programs and institutions—suggest that a few broad developments have affected a number of graduate programs in the EHP fields.

First, some diminishment of courses offered in earlier historical periods has taken place. Anecdotal evidence from individual institutions and professors suggests that enrollments in those courses have also tended to fall.

Second, there has been a rise in the non-Western, international, and comparative dimensions of these fields. This has meant that work is almost inevitably more interdisciplinary in nature. In English and American literature, the analogue has been the inclusion of more literature from nontraditional sources within the context of English and American culture broadly defined (that is, African-American literature, Hispanic-American literature in its various manifestations, Native American texts, and Asian-American writers).

Third, there has been greater concentration on modern periods, beginning in the late eighteenth century and including a strong set of twentieth-century offerings. This shift has obviously been disconcerting to some, and programs will have to continue to work hard to consider what degree of balance they wish to sustain in their curricula.[11] Finally, it is clear that "theory"—or methodology,

---

[11]In assessing this development, it must be remembered that in the early 1960s, twentieth-century materials were (almost by definition) in much shorter supply than they are now, and even the Victorian period was relatively little studied—it was to some extent out of fashion, and to some extent still seemed very recent. We are now, however, at a point where the entire twentieth century is virtually behind us, and it is not surprising that our own perceptions of the past, and those of our students, are inevitably altered by this simple fact.

For students who will be between the ages of 18 and 28 during the next decade, the twentieth century is far less "contemporary" and far more "historical" than it appears to individuals whose life-spans have coincided with some considerable part of the century. This is no reason to neglect earlier periods—indeed, it can constitute a strong reason to pay extra attention to them. But if students are to understand the major figures, the large-scale national and international develop-

or criticism, or interpretation—has in the 1980s come to play a markedly more important role in the formal curriculum in all EHP fields than during the preceding eras. Although the specific theoretical or interpretive concerns vary from field to field, it is nonetheless clear that there now exists a far greater self-consciousness about methods, approaches, and the ways in which one defines (or discovers) knowledge.[12]

The effects of this set of developments on graduate education and graduate students have been considerable, we believe, and they are incorporated in the discussion near the end of this chapter as well as in Chapter Thirteen.

COURSE CONTENT

While the preceding analysis of subfields provides a general idea of some of the large-scale developments within the humanities, a sharper picture of changes in the intellectual definitions of these fields can be obtained by examining course descriptions over a 25-year period for a small sample of graduate programs.

History

We focus the first part of this discussion on courses offered in European history by one highly rated but small-scale department. By comparing courses listed in the catalogs for 1964–65, 1978–80 (a single catalog, even though it spans two academic years), and 1989–90, it is possible to identify major patterns quite distinctly.

There is some variety in stated methodological approach evident in the offerings listed in 1964–65 (top panel of Table 12.1). The majority of courses, however, are defined quite strictly in terms of recognizable time-periods or established eras: "The Tenth Century," "Early Modern Europe," " The Reformation," "The Renaissance and Counter Reformation," "The French Revolution," "The July Monarchy," "German History, 1862–1914," and "European Diplomacy, 1870–1914." Naturally, such general topics give instructors a wide latitude with respect to the materials studied and the approach to be adopted. Nonetheless, the landscape is a rather familiar chronological one that deals in categories created largely in the latter part of the nineteenth century or the early twentieth century.

---

ments, and the extraordinary episodes that have shaped and altered the world that they are inheriting, then substantial attention must also be given to the intellectual developments and other events that have taken place in the last two centuries.

[12]Many factors have combined to create the particular intellectual climate that has made theory and interpretation such central concerns in academic life. The 1980s have witnessed (as have analogous moments in earlier historical eras) a sustained preoccupation with central epistemological and hermeneutical questions. Some of these questions are related to social and political developments, such as the emergence of stronger feminist perspectives and non-Western views of the world. Others concern the extent to which we believe even the firmest factual knowledge relating to the natural world or human experience is ever more than highly provisional, hypothetical, or approximate.

Appendix F contains an extended commentary on the nature and significance of the recent discussion of "theory," as reflected in the writings of a number of scholars in such fields as English and anthropology.

TABLE 12.1
Course Descriptions in European History

1964–1965 Catalog

The Literature of Continental Medieval History
The World of the Divine Comedy
The Medieval Town
The Tenth Century
Medieval England and France: Politics and
    Constitution
Early Modern Europe—Readings and Discussion
Early Modern Europe—Research Seminar
The Reformation
The Renaissance and Counter-Reformation in Italy
The Left Wing of the Reformation and European
    Society
Introduction to the Source of Canon Law
Seminars in Medieval Canon Law

Seminar in the Reformation
The Historiography of Western Europe, 800–1900
Problems in Comparative European History
Problems in the Political and Social
    History of Europe (19th/20th C.)
The French Revolution
The July Monarchy
German History, 1862–1914
Topics in the History of Germany, 1914 to
    Present
Modern Italy
European Diplomacy, 1870–1914
European Diplomacy, 1914–1939
European Imperialism

1978–1980 Catalog

Italian and Northern Renaissance History
Problems in Medieval Economic and Social History
The Medieval Town
The World of the Divine Comedy
Civil and Canon Law in Medieval Europe
Medieval Social Problems
Proseminar in Medieval Studies
Studies in Medieval Thought: The Twelfth Century
Studies in Medieval Thought: The Augustinian
    Tradition
Intellectual History of the Middle Ages
The Papacy in the Middle Ages
Religion and Society, 1250–1650
Reformation Historiography
Reformation Europe: 1450–1650
Early Modern Europe
French Government and Society in the
    Ancient Regime, 1500–1789

European and English Intellectual History
European Cultural History, 1870–1914
German Social and Cultural History,
    1848–1914
Studies in the Urbanization of Europe
The Nineteenth Century French Revolutions
German History, ca. 1890–1945
Economics, Politics and Society in Germany,
    1848–1945
Fascism
European Diplomacy
Italian History Since 1848

General:
Psychology in History
Historical Demography
Psychological Methods in Historical Research
Sociology and History
Quantitative Methods of Historical Research

1989–1990 Catalog

Intellectual History of the Middle Ages
Studies in Medieval Intellectual History:
    The Late Middle Ages
Law and Society in Medieval Europe
Judaism, Christianity, and Islam to 1492
The Reform of Christian Culture, 1517–1618
From Medieval to Modern—Topics in the
    History of Europe, 1300–1500
The Reform of Christian Culture
Introduction of Early Modern Europe I:
    16th Century
Early Modern Spain, 1450–1716
Research Seminar, France 1789 to the Present
Topics in Modern French Social History
Topics in Modern German History
Research Seminar on Modern German
    History

Relations of the Great Powers since 1890
Britain and Germany in the 19th Century

General:
Modern Cultural History
Current Historiography
Research Seminars in Modern Historiography
Psychohistory
Aspects of Military and Strategic History
Agrarian Societies: Culture, Society, History
    and Development
Computer Methods for Historians
Theories of War and Peace in Europe
    and North America, 1750–1918
International Security: Historical and Political
    Science Approaches
The Historiography of the Family

Notes: The above listings do not include courses concentrating on British history or Russian history. Courses listed under the heading "general" are those that do not fit a geographic or chronological heading.

By 1978–80 (middle panel of Table 12.1), there had been a fairly marked shift toward social history, intellectual history, and a broader conception of how different aspects of society interact to produce what is termed cultural history. In addition, an entirely new set of methodological courses had been introduced, buttressing a more general transformation already under way. While there were still courses on "The World of the Divine Comedy," "The Medieval Town," "Early Modern Europe," and "European Diplomacy, 1917–1945," a significant change was in process. We now see "Medieval Social Problems," "Religion and Society, 1250–1650," and "Studies in the Urbanization of Europe." Historical studies had become more inclusive, more interdisciplinary, more focused upon the intersection of social, economic, and political (or religious) problems, more varied in their range of methodological approaches, and more complex in their implied definition of culture.

When we turn to the 1989–90 catalog (bottom panel of Table 12.1), it is more difficult to identify a single directional movement. Few, if any, of the 1964–65 titles are left. The Renaissance, the Counter-Reformation, Early Modern Europe, and Canon Law have all disappeared, not only as course offerings but even as governing conceptual categories in course titles. "Reformation Europe: 1500–1648" is perhaps the only clear titular link to the era of the mid-1960s, although terms such as "Medieval" and "Modern" do, of course, appear in various contexts. Many courses are defined more flexibly and are therefore susceptible to becoming either more specialized or simply more adaptable, depending on the inclinations of the instructor. These courses are usually headed "Topics in. . . ." Moreover, the cultural, comparative, and topical reach of at least several offerings is greater than in previous eras. Finally, there is a pronounced expansion in the number and variety of courses in historiography and theory.

This analysis of a single history program constitutes only the slenderest of threads from which to suspend an argument of any kind, much less a series of generalizations. But the intellectual currents just described do in fact tally quite closely with broad developments in the historical field, as plotted in our examination of statistical data on subfields and as measured against the kinds of changes apparent in the catalogs of other programs.

The field of historical studies has moved more into statistical or "cliometrical" types of analysis; social and cultural (including popular culture) topics of concern; categories of analysis borrowed from psychology, anthropology, and economics (to mention only three related fields); and structuralist as well as other recent theoretical approaches. All of these tendencies have, to a greater or lesser degree, altered the shape and substance of many curricula in programs throughout the country. They have often been accompanied by a reduction in the number of courses devoted to traditional forms of political history, the history of "elites" and of "high culture," and traditionally defined chronological periods.

Tension among these various approaches often runs high, and can be traced in any number of recent books, articles, and reviews.[13] While future develop-

---

[13] The bibliography is vast, but mention should be made of at least Gertrude Himmelfarb's *The New History and the Old* (Harvard University Press, 1987), and Lawrence Stone's review of this volume, "Resisting the New," in the *New York Review of Books*, December 17, 1987. In addition, volumes such as *The New Historicism*, edited by H. A. Veeser (Routledge, 1989), are useful surveys. Anthropological perspectives, such as *The Predicament of Culture* by James Clifford (Harvard University Press,

ments are difficult to predict, many of the newer methodologies seem by now to have been absorbed and are being used in a more eclectic way than when they were first introduced.[14]

English Literature

Broad intellectual currents similar to the kind that have influenced course offerings in history have also affected many graduate programs in other fields within the humanities. Still, considerable differences in patterns of development can be seen among high-quality programs within the same field. This point can be illustrated by comparing changes in course offerings in two different departments of English.[15]

In the case of the first department (A), a considerable degree of stability is evident in these listings for 1963–64 and 1989–90, though the substance of the courses, including the precise texts studied and the approach to them, is certainly not captured by mere titles. (To facilitate comparison of changes over

---

1988) are also helpful introductions to the debate. Other interesting perspectives are offered by Paul Otto Kristeller in his recent Haskins Lecture, "A Life of Learning" (ACLS pamphlet, April 26, 1990); Carl E. Schorske in "Expanding the Enlightenment Tradition" (Commencement Address, SUNY, Stonybrook, May 15, 1988); and Robert Connor in "The New Classical Humanities and the Old," published in the April–May 1985 issue of *The Classical Journal*. This list is readily expandable, and the bibliographies contained in these studies and papers can be used as a guide to further readings.

[14]The desire to strike a different balance in the study of history, and to widen the perspective offered by traditionally defined curricula, is not perhaps as new as many people often assume. Quite apart from the striking and powerful contributions of nineteenth-century cultural historians (such as Burckhardt), there were less conspicuous but not insignificant protestations from literary figures.

Even so comparatively understated a writer as Jane Austen parodied traditional historical writing, and was pleased to announce defiantly in one spoof that "there will be very few dates in this history." Meanwhile, one of her earliest witty heroines (in *Northanger Abbey*) allowed that she could "not be interested in" any "real solemn history. . . the quarrels of popes and kings, with wars or pestilences in every page; the men all good for nothing, and hardly any women at all."

Austen's irony is always complex, and these particular strictures (with their obvious exaggerations) should not be taken naively at face-value. But she was in her own way a superb social historian of everyday life—life in its mundane and frequently overlooked manifestations, life where the traditional substance of political or military or industrial/economic reality rarely intrudes. Women play a leading and assertive (if not necessarily triumphant) role. Country walks, long conversations, courtship, dances, and outings make up the fabric of life and history as they are actually lived by many (if not the majority of much less comfortable) people. In this sense, Austen focuses our attention on a segment of English society that lives outside the realm of history as presented in traditional curricula.

Later writers—George Eliot, Dickens, Trollope, Dreiser, and Joyce—presented readers with larger and more inclusive panoramic visions, but only rarely touched upon "the quarrels of popes and kings." It is difficult to believe that this vast body of increasingly "realistic" social history—in fictional form—did not ultimately have a powerful influence, at least subliminally, upon historians and others attempting to chronicle or capture the substance of human life as it has been lived.

This is not to suggest that literature and history are to be conflated, but merely to emphasize that it was not so large a step (or so sharp a shift in vision) for later-day historians to begin thinking about social and cultural history, or the history of everyday life, since fiction had in its own way already entered that domain.

[15]Again, the titles and descriptions are taken from courses *listed* (not necessarily given) in the years indicated. Since both programs are relatively small, however, the proportion of courses actually offered is quite high. Finally, it should be added that the courses listed are those identified as being exclusively or primarily for graduate students. Readers who wish to examine changes in courses offered in other programs or in other fields can turn directly to catalogs and departmental brochures.

TABLE 12.2
Course Descriptions in English Literature, Institution A

1963–1964	1989–1990
Introduction to Old English	—
Old English Poetry	Old English Poetry
Old Irish	Old Norse
Development of English Language (to 1400)	Linguistic Thought
Development of English Language (1400 to present)	Studies in the English Language: 1400 to present
Medieval Lyric and Dramatic Lit.	Special Studies in Medieval Lit.
Chaucer	Chaucer (1)
Medieval Romance	Chaucer (2)
Middle English Religious Lit.	Middle English Religious Lit.
Spenser	Spenser
Renaissance in England	Renaissance in England
Elizabethan Drama	Renaissance Drama
Jacobean and Caroline Drama	Special Studies in Ren. Drama
Shakespeare (1)	Shakespeare (1)
Shakespeare (2)	Shakespeare (2)
Milton	—
The Early 17th Century	The Early 17th Century
Literature of the Restoration	Literature of the Restoration
Restoration and 18th Century Drama	Restoration and 18th Century Drama
British and American Drama since 1820	—
The 18th Century (1st Half)	The 18th Century
The 18th Century (2nd Half)	—
Special Studies in the Augustan Period	Special Studies in the 18th Century
The Romantic Period	The Romantic Period
The Victorians	The Victorians
—	Special Studies in the 19th Century
American Literary Traditions	Foundations of an American Literary Tradition
Special Studies in American Authors	Special Studies in American Authors
American Poetry	American Poetry
The American Novel (1890 to present)	The American Novel
The Victorian Novel	The Victorian Novel
Studies in the English Novel	Studies in the English Novel
Poetics	Poetics
Criticism	Criticism
Rhetorical Theory and Its Place in English Criticism	—
Seminar in Historical Research	Seminar in Historical Research
Seminar in Historical Criticism	—
—	Afro-American Literature
—	Modern Drama
—	Selected Topics in Criticism
—	Problems in Literary Study
—	Literature and Society
—	Literature and Gender

time, the courses are aligned in Table 12.2 to make clear which ones have remained, which have been dropped, and which have been added.)

The effort to retain a fundamental chronological sequence, with some attention to all major periods and most major writers, is clear in both the 1963–64 and the 1989–90 lists. It is also clear where modest growth has occurred: Two new courses were added in special fields (Afro-American Literature and Gender Studies), as well as a small number of new courses in criticism, theory, and cultural studies. In general, however, remarkably little has changed in terms of the structure of the program and its general coverage.

The second program (B) presents a different picture. The precise listings from the 1960s are difficult to reconstruct and are not presented here. However, a comparison of 1974–75 with 1989–90 proves to be sufficiently—indeed, more powerfully—illuminating, since it shows how much change has occurred in a quite short time-span (Table 12.3).

Of the 34 courses listed in 1974–75 (which were generally designed in terms of chronological periods, established genres, or major authors), 13 have either identical or approximate analogues in 1989. Even in these cases, the courses sometimes tend to be more specialized ("George Eliot" instead of "Victorian Fiction"; "Wordsworth" instead of "Romantic Literature"), and some periods have virtually been dropped altogether (for example, the Restoration period, the eighteenth century, and nineteenth-century American fiction). Instead, there is now a strong emphasis on topics or themes ("Bodies and Machines," "Mourning, Melancholy and Hysteria"), a fairly strong representation of gender-related subjects, a modest core of Afro-American literary courses, and an obvious increase in the number of courses devoted to theoretical questions.

Perhaps most striking is the fact that in 1989–90, a smaller absolute number of courses was listed (29 versus 34), and yet the variety of subfields and topics had expanded considerably. In microcosm, this particular pattern of development shows quite dramatically what may occur when the intellectual substance of programs or fields continues to expand internally—with respect to new areas of knowledge or new approaches to be explored—while the teaching resources (and hence the number of courses) are no greater, and perhaps less, than were previously available.

From the perspective of the conduct of graduate education, perhaps the most salient point is that a student who wishes to chart a course through the curriculum just described obviously requires a good deal more guidance, and must make more complex methodological, topical, and other kinds of fundamental choices, than the student who enters a more traditional curriculum organized on an historical basis. Shall the student concentrate in theory and criticism, sacrificing a good deal of historical "coverage?" If so, *which* theoretical or critical approaches should be chosen? Are there sufficient courses in specialized areas to constitute a reasonably full and balanced program of study?

Several faculty members interviewed in the course of this study commented explicitly on the problems created for graduate students by these interconnected developments. One professor referred to "[a] frightening array of incompatible theories, methodologies and intellectual alternatives," and then added: "It takes more time to survey and understand the alternatives, and it also induces a kind of paralysis in students. . . ." Another faculty member described the problems

TABLE 12.3
Course Descriptions in English Literature, Institution B

1974–1975	1989–1990
Studies in the English Language	—
Readings in Old English	Old English
Beowulf	Beowulf
Middle English	—
Medieval Drama	—
Chaucer	Chaucer
—	Chaucer and the Courtly Tradition
Grammatical Analysis	—
Studies in the 16th Century	Authority and Experience in the Renaissance Epic
Studies in Elizabethan and Jacobean Drama	—
Studies in Shakespeare	Shakespeare
Studies in Milton	—
—	English and American 17th Century Prose
Restoration and 18th Century Drama	—
The English Novel in the 18th Century	—
Studies in Romantic Literature	Studies in Wordsworth
Studies in Victorian Prose	—
Studies in Victorian Poetry	Victorian Poetry
Studies in Victorian Fiction	George Eliot (Seminar)
Studies in Modern Fiction	—
Studies in Modern Poetry	Topics in Modernism
Studies in Modern Drama	—
The Political Novel in America	—
Studies in American Literature	—
Studies in 19th Century American Literature	The American Transcendental Movement
Studies in Modern American Poetry	—
Studies in Contemporary Literature	Post-Modern Fiction
Politics and Religion in America	—
Studies in American Culture	—
Studies in Dramatic Literature	—
Studies in Biography	—
Studies in Anglo-Irish Literature	—
Literary Criticism	—
The Teaching of English	—
Critical and Scholarly Perspectives (1)	—
Critical and Scholarly Perspectives (2)	—
—	The Archeology of Early Christian England and Ireland
—	Mourning, Melancholy and Hysteria
—	Writing
—	The Theater of Revolution: The Politics and Poetics of Spectacle
—	Writers of the Revolution
—	Gender in 19th Century America
—	Gothic and Gender
—	Bodies and Machines
—	Literature and Theory
—	Critical and Theoretical Perspectives on the Modernist Tradition
—	Marxism and Post-Colonial Discourse
—	Feminist Theory and Psychoanalysis
—	Literary Anti-Feminism
—	Avant-Garde Theory of Drama
—	Black Women Writers
—	Afro-American Lit. in Ante-Bellum America
—	The Harlem Renaissance

presented by students searching for a dissertation topic this way: "I have a theory, but not a subject"; or "I have a subject, but no theory."[16]

Dilemmas such as these, exacerbated in some instances by shifts in the content of fields and trends in intellectual currents, must be worked out (or not) in the context of departmental structures and processes. And it is to these more organizational aspects of graduate education that we now turn.

---

[16]In a recent study of differences in the duration of graduate study by discipline, Baird (1990, 380) concludes: "The differences in the mean duration of doctoral study across disciplines . . . suggest a rough correspondence to the clarity of the central paradigms within disciplines and the degree of agreement about those paradigms. For example, chemistry and biochemistry probably have relatively clear and agreed upon bodies of knowledge and procedures; disciplines such as French literature and art history may thrive on differences in definitions of content and interpretation."

Program Design, Oversight, and "Culture"

DOCTORAL PROGRAMS do not "run themselves." Much depends on the care with which they are designed and the expectations that are established concerning the character and quality of work to be done by those admitted. The degree of structure built into the system is also very important. Under this heading, we include the clarity with which guidelines concerning the completion of requirements are communicated, the firmness with which they are enforced (always allowing for the intelligent application of general rules to individual cases), and the extent to which the performance of students and faculty alike is monitored.

Perhaps most important of all is what Jonathan Cole, the Provost of Columbia and a distinguished sociologist, has called the "academic culture" of a department. He uses this phrase to include "the accepted model of working relationships between faculty and students" and has suggested that probably the most important element in lengthening time-to-degree at Columbia "has been an attitude of passivity and distance on the part of the faculty. The old Graduate Faculties were famous for their hauteur and their expectation that all initiative rested with the student. Not all of this was bad; graduate school is a place for adults, after all, and Columbia in particular was not and is not a paternalistic institution. But few would disagree that an attitude of laissez-faire was carried too far."[1]

This is certainly not to suggest that there is anything approaching a single template that can be used to assess program design and oversight. Arrangements that make excellent sense in one field, institutional context, or time period may be impractical or simply wrongheaded in other settings. Still, there is widespread agreement that some arrangements (and some "philosophies") work better than others. No one, to our knowledge, disputes the need for careful scrutiny of the internal workings of graduate programs if their effectiveness is to be improved.

There is the incontrovertible fact that completion rates and time-to-degree vary dramatically among programs that have many common attributes. For example, we have seen that the student-year cost of a doctorate varies considerably among PhD programs in the same field that are roughly equivalent in scale and rated quality. While job prospects and other external forces plainly affect completion rates and time-to-degree, so do policies and practices internal to departments and universities. No one interested in graduate education should be reluctant to look hard at them.

---

[1]These observations are taken from the proposal for improving graduate education submitted to the Andrew W. Mellon Foundation by Columbia University. A similar observation about the importance of intangible aspects of graduate programs was made by a distinguished economist, Kenneth Boulding: "What matters more than anything else in graduate education is the subculture of the department, and this may differ widely even within the same institution" (1978, 148).

STAGES OF GRADUATE STUDY

One of the characteristics of doctoral study is that it is less structured and less precisely orchestrated than either undergraduate education or graduate programs in professional fields, such as business, law, and medicine. Also, the "structure" that does exist often varies considerably by field of study and institution. These complications notwithstanding, three principal stages are common to almost all PhD programs.

The first comprises a period of formal course-work that usually lasts two or three years. The second is a less well-defined interim period in which other stipulated requirements (and usually some teaching assignments) are completed. This stage may involve passing a general examination or qualifying exam and satisfying foreign language requirements, as well as choosing a dissertation topic and, in some cases, submitting an approved prospectus. The last stage is one of intensive dissertation research and writing, including a final defense of the dissertation.

These three stages are to some extent artificial constructs, which ideally should function as parts of an integrated and continuous process. Nonetheless, they do correspond quite closely to the segmented nature of many PhD programs, particularly as these programs are perceived and experienced by the students themselves.

In this chapter, we will try to identify particular "moments," or transition-points, that affect most profoundly the ability of graduate students to complete their degrees in a timely way.[2] Both the data from the Ten-University data set and impressions gleaned from a large number of interviews and other materials pertinent to particular graduate programs persuade us that the most vexing problems are to be found in the stages of graduate study that follow the completion of course work. Moreover, a number of these problems experienced in the mid-to-later stages of graduate study have become ever more acute in recent years.[3]

ENTRY-LEVEL ATTRITION VERSUS LATER ATTRITION

First, however, explicit account should be taken of attrition that occurs soon after a student begins graduate study. A student's first encounter with graduate school is often a daunting experience. With its "professional" colorations, graduate study can represent a sharp contrast with undergraduate work. Much

---

[2]Cole and Singer (1989) have also published a most interesting paper in which they argue that "limited differences" in the early experiences of scientists, as they are being educated and trained, cumulate to have powerful effects on their productivity. What may seem to be small advantages at one point in a person's career create access to other advantages, which lead to further opportunities, and so on. This analysis underscores the importance of looking carefully at seemingly small problems encountered at every stage of doctoral education, and not minimizing their potential long-term consequences.

[3]As in Chapter Twelve, our conclusions in this chapter are based on a variety of sources of information and evidence, including a lengthy series of interviews with faculty members, institutional self-studies, and proposals to improve graduate education submitted to the Andrew W. Mellon Foundation. In addition, use is made of a questionnaire distributed to all recipients of Mellon Fellowships in the Humanities, as well as published reports and studies of a more general kind.

of the attrition that occurs during, or at the end of, the first year no doubt reflects decisions by students that graduate school, or one particular graduate school, was not a right choice. "Sorting" of this kind is, in some large measure, both inevitable and desirable—however it may be perceived at the time.

The sometimes "healthy" aspect of early attrition is readily illustrated by excerpts from letters of resignation submitted by three Mellon Fellows in the Humanities:

> I have decided to leave graduate school at the end of this semester to pursue a career in medicine. No one could have been more surprised at this decision than I was. . . . Over the last two years I have come to realize that I wish to center my work on people, not literary texts. . . .

> The decision [to resign the Mellon Fellowship] may seem sudden . . . but it is really only the final resolution of long-standing doubts. . . . It is no disenchantment with literature, no lowered estimate of the potential civilizing and moralizing influence of its study, that is responsible for my decision. But for a *career* in literary scholarship to be worthwhile, one needs a mind which soars easily, a mind to which broad and comprehensive perspectives come more or less naturally. I have (reluctantly, I must admit) come to the conclusion that—good grades and "academic praise" notwithstanding—my mind is not of that order. And to creep forever among details, laboriously climbing over clods like a beetle, at best working to swell the journals with mediocrity—how unsatisfying! . . . Amateur status is my proper status.

> At the beginning of last semester, I realized that I would much rather be living and working in China at this time than pursuing a PhD degree in the U.S. It is likely that I will return to school in the not-too-distant future, but for the moment, I am considering several job offers which will allow me to reside in Asia for one or two years.[4]

The character of a graduate program, and the philosophy of a department in determining how many students to admit (and how much winnowing to anticipate), will of course affect the amount of entry-level attrition. No less important is the skill of the department in identifying candidates with the requisite motivation, personal qualities, and intellectual capacity. Above some threshold of academic preparation and general intelligence, we suspect that success in graduate school depends in large measure on commitment, stamina, and the capacity to function under difficult conditions—qualities that are difficult to assess, especially in a student who has not yet enrolled.

In any case, these are old conundrums, and there is no evidence to suggest that any new developments, internal to graduate programs, have altered what transpires at this earliest stage of graduate study. The data on attrition prior to the start of the second year show a rather consistent pattern over time, with roughly 25 percent of entering students at larger programs failing to return for the second year and roughly 10 to 15 percent of students in smaller programs leaving at this stage of graduate study (Table 13.1).[5]

---

[4]The reasons given by these Mellon Fellows for deciding to leave graduate study illustrate well our discussion of healthy attrition. However, they are not representative of the opinion of other Mellon Fellows who left the program, the majority of whom expressed dissatisfaction with graduate study. This was often cited as the primary reason for leaving graduate school.

[5]Year-to-year data for individual graduate programs reveal that there was a mild upward "blip" in pre–second year attrition for cohorts entering during the mid-1970s. This presumably resulted from

TABLE 13.1
Attrition and Time Spent by Stage of Graduate Study and Scale of Program,
EHP Total, 1967–1981 Entering Cohorts

Stage of Graduate Study	Conditional Attrition Rate (%)			Time Spent (Average Number of Years)		
	1967–1971	1972–1976	1977–1981	1967–1971	1972–1976	1977–1981
Larger						
Pre–Second Year	22.9	25.7	27.4			
Other pre-ABD	34.9	39.2		4.2	4.1	
Post-ABD	23.1	27.0*		4.0	4.3	
Smaller						
Pre–Second Year	10.0	15.3	12.2			
Other pre-ABD	9.2	9.2	9.7	2.4	2.7	2.8
Post-ABD	23.0	28.3	30.0*	3.6	4.0	
Four-University average						
Pre–Second Year	19.8	23.3	23.4			
Other pre-ABD	27.9	31.6		3.3	3.4	
Post-ABD	24.0	28.0*		3.8	4.1	

Source: Ten-University data set. Data are from Berkeley and Chicago (Larger programs), and Cornell and Princeton (Smaller programs).

Notes: The "Four-University average" is for all four universities. "Conditional Attrition Rate" is the percentage of those who entered the stage who left graduate school without completing the stage; see text for further explanation. "Time Spent" is the average number of years spent at each stage by those who completed the stage. Cells have been left blank where truncation problems would have caused figures to be misleading. Figures marked with an asterisk are estimates, based on assumptions concerning the number of still-enrolled students who will eventually complete their doctorates.

From our perspective, the disturbing findings for both attrition and the amount of time invested are associated with later stages of graduate study. Post–first year attrition has drifted upward, as has the time spent in achieving ABD status (Table 13.1). The percentage of students who never earn PhDs, in spite of having achieved ABD status, has risen in both larger and smaller programs, as has the time spent at the dissertation stage by those who completed doctorates. The direction of change is unmistakable, and the absolute numbers are high enough to be grounds for serious concern.

Of all English, history, and political science (EHP) students in this set of larger and smaller programs who returned for a second year of graduate study, roughly 30 percent did not achieve ABD status. Of those who did achieve ABD status, more than 25 percent did not complete their dissertations and earn doctorates. Moreover, the time spent by those who did succeed in surmounting these various hurdles has increased—especially at the dissertation stage—from levels that were already high. The balance of this chapter is devoted to considering some of the reasons for this state of affairs.

---

the exceedingly discouraging job prospects for academics at that time. Entry-level attrition since then seems to have returned to levels characteristic of the late 1960s and early 1970s. The modest further increase shown in Table 13.1 for the 1977-1981 cohorts at the two larger universities included in this analysis is entirely a function of experience at one of these universities.

THE TRANSITION FROM COURSE WORK TO DISSERTATION PROSPECTUS

By virtually all accounts, the time between the end of graduate course work and the moment of energetic engagement with a promising dissertation topic has become an unusually difficult period for graduate students.

For students who must complete (or choose to complete) an MA thesis, one problem at this stage is a tendency to "overpolish" this particular piece of work. Part of the difficulty is that it is often hard for students to know just what is expected, and how much depends on the master's thesis. Another problem is uncertainty concerning the amount of time that should be spent preparing for "orals," "generals," or other qualifying examinations. Many faculty have noted a tendency for students to "overprepare," only to be disappointed when they are not given the opportunity to demonstrate on the examination more than some small part of what they have learned.[6]

Selecting A Dissertation Topic

A still more troublesome problem, and one mentioned more often than any other hurdle, is selecting an appropriate topic for a doctoral dissertation. It is not uncommon for students to spend between one and two years searching for the "right" topic and preparing a dissertation prospectus.[7] As part of a proposal to improve graduate education in political science, one director of graduate studies described the transition-point between course work and the dissertation as follows:

> It is extremely tempting for students in their third year to use the time to relax from the rigors of the first two years, finish up a seminar paper or a remaining skill requirement, and devote themselves to their teaching. It is easy to postpone the anxieties of proposal development from one day to the next, one month to the next, even one year to the next. . . .[8]

The reasons offered to explain this phenomenon vary considerably but are not necessarily inconsistent with one another. Several reports, as well as the testimony of individual faculty members, suggest that there is too little emphasis during the first two years on helping students to understand what it means to do independent research. In many cases, courses are simply a higher-level version of undergraduate work, with somewhat more ambitious "term-papers" to write.[9]

---

[6]Both of these problems are discussed in the recent Berkeley study of graduate education by Nerad and Cerny (1991, 4).

[7]*Ibid.*, p. 3.

[8]In citing materials such as this from proposals to the Andrew W. Mellon Foundation, we have not identified particular individuals and universities since most of these materials were not intended for publication.

[9]The interviews and reports that we have received contain many comments to this effect from faculty and students in the EHP fields. This is also a central conclusion of the recent self-study of graduate education in economics carried out by the Commission on Graduate Education in Economics: "Only 49% of graduate students responding to the [1988-89] COGEE survey thought core courses prepared them well or very well for dissertation work. By contrast, 75% of students in the 1977–78 cohort felt that way" (American Economics Association, 1991, 25). The accompanying report by Professor W. Lee Hansen, Executive Secretary of the Commission, contains supporting

At the same time, students learn to be skeptical of much received opinion during these years. They are taught to be analytic and critical, without necessarily acquiring the habits of mind and training to undertake more constructive and fruitful research and writing. The consequence can often be a rather sudden paralysis as students finish their courses and term-papers and are then confronted with the formidable task of identifying a significant dissertation topic. The same director of graduate studies cited earlier explains:

> Another source of the third-year diversion is inherent in developing the critical sensibility that is part of the process of becoming a disciplined professional. During the first two years, students are taught to be critical of the literature. The methodology used in existing studies is found to be inadequate. Findings are dismissed as trivial. Now the graduate students face the reality that they, too, must undertake a study that may be regarded by others as inadequate, defective, trivial . . . .

In some fields, the complexity and variety of recent theoretical approaches add new and occasionally insurmountable difficulties to an already complex task. According to one faculty member in an English department:

> The new and more varied objectives of research and writing have changed the very definition of literature, making the "canon" of what needs to be read as literature an ever-widening and outward-spiralling body of materials. Much is added, yet nothing—in a serious academic setting—can be rejected. . . . It is not surprising then, that in this time of transition, with its introduction of methods and agendas, in themselves complex, there is some measure of confusion among students: not "loss of direction," exactly, . . . but rather that sort of intellectual and procedural uncertainty which is bound to arise in frontier territory. The result can be, and frequently is, mental overload, with delays caused by prolonged preparation, unrealistically conceived dissertation projects, unwieldy drafts of dissertation prospectuses, and even at times severe cases of writer's block for which psychiatric counselling proves necessary.

In still other fields, the desirability (or the necessity) of undertaking a complicated interdisciplinary approach adds yet another dimension to the problem. Some disciplines require extensive fieldwork, and perhaps the mastering of two or more demanding languages.

Even more pervasively, there is the view (sometimes held more fervently by the student than by anyone else) that a dissertation should be a *magnum opus*—a work that is significant, certainly publishable, and preferably brilliant and original enough to be the foundation of one's future career. (We return later to a discussion of expectations concerning the dissertation, which, of course, affect the process of research and writing as well as the initial task of selecting a topic.) When several of these demands and expectations converge—Pelion heaped upon Ossa—the total effect can be intimidating.

---

data and this summary observation: "Both graduate students and faculty members reported that relatively little occurs during the first two years of graduate programs to develop in students the capacity to carry out independent research of the kind required to complete a PhD dissertation" (Hansen 1991, 38).

Student responses to surveys tend to bear out such impressions. The reasons given by one recipient of a Mellon Fellowship in the Humanities for leaving the program at a relatively late stage are not atypical:

> In literary studies, preparing oneself for the job market and doing research at the same time is made particularly difficult because of uncertainties about what sort of topics and approaches will be marketable in a few years time. . . . Students are encouraged to do interdisciplinary studies and adopt novel methods but they are still expected to apply for jobs which are organized by the old period divisions. . . .

More generally, among those factors which Mellon Fellows in the Humanities mentioned as hindering or slowing down their progress toward the PhD degree, the entries which received the largest percentage ratings (next to fellowship scarcity) are "Difficulty in Finding (Dissertation) Topic" and "Burn-Out." Nearly one-third of students in smaller programs checked the first of these factors as "slowing them down" either a great deal (11.9 percent) or a little (20.1 percent). In larger programs, the corresponding percentages were 10.4 and 39.6 percent. Between 40 and 50 percent of all students at both sets of universities said "burn-out" was the most salient factor.[10]

Hence, while many students and faculty see genuine excitement, challenge, and intellectual vitality in the new fields and methodologies, many are also concerned about the degree of uncertainty and indecision that has been created. One proposal from an English department included this observation: "The range of possible approaches to literary studies poses inevitable dangers; it can mean confusion for the student and fragmentation for the field itself." If even the choice of topic is delayed so long (well into the fourth year), what is the plausible expectation for completion?

The Nature of the Dissertation

Other factors affect the nature and pace of dissertation research once a topic has been chosen. Especially important is one already mentioned: expectations concerning the originality, scholarly depth, and significance of the dissertation.

This is hardly a new concern. Professor Jacob Viner, who always stressed the role of scholarship in graduate training, nonetheless warned against expecting too much from doctoral education itself—which he saw as only a stage in a lifelong pursuit of learning. In an essay written when graduate education was a much shorter process than it is today, Viner wryly observed:

> There is so much that needs to be known, and so little time in one's student days for learning it, that it is not a depreciation of the doctor's degree to regard it as merely marking the termination of one advanced stage in one's education, the last stage in which the responsibility is shared with others, to be followed by another stage lasting to the end of one's life in which one is intellectually wholly on one's own. The University of Avignon, in 1650, found itself faced by a candidate for the doctorate who had capacity but who had applied himself less closely to the pursuit of knowledge than to less exacting and more exciting extra-curricular activities. After some hesitation, it conferred the doctoral degree upon him with the notation *sub spe futuri studii*, which I am told can be translated as "in the hope of future study." May I suggest that our

---

[10]These data are from a survey of Mellon Fellows conducted in 1990. See Appendix C.

doctoral degrees should be granted, and accepted, in this spirit even when there is not occasion to spell it out in the letter of the parchment?[11]

Viner's protestations notwithstanding, testimony from various quarters suggests that expectations have risen since the early 1960s, and that academic pressures in this direction have been reinforced by external job-market conditions. To the extent that desirable jobs (or indeed any jobs) have been scarce in universities during the past 20 years, students and faculty alike have concluded that only the best-prepared and most-published graduate students are likely to succeed in the competition. That, in turn, has led many to conceive of the dissertation not as the first step in a long scholarly career, but as the significant, ground-breaking work that will secure a rewarding position at an institution that encourages scholarship as well as teaching.

Only last year, a Nobel-prize winner in economics, speaking about the state of graduate education, asked:

> Could it be that we overvalue a kind of spurious "originality" at the expense of "normal science?" I think so, but I am not sure . . . .

> It is getting less plausible to mine the same old data one more time. That seems to leave no option for the student who wants to make a mark except to invent a brand new idea and strike out in untraveled directions. That could be bad for students. . . and bad for the discipline.[12]

Support for this hypothesis concerning the nature of the dissertation can be found in comparatively objective measures and subjective impressions. Professor Theodore Ziolkowski, a scholar in Germanic Languages and Literature and Dean of the Graduate School at Princeton, has reported that the length of dissertations has continued to increase. Ziolkowski is persuaded that this is a serious part of the problem of lengthening time-to-degree, and he has proposed that "universities should impose a strict upper limit on theses and refuse to accept those that are too long."[13]

One encouraging sign is that concerns about the nature of the dissertation are receiving increasing attention. For example, a new policy statement by the

---

[11]Viner 1958, 370. The essay was written in 1950. Later in the essay, Viner comments on how the writing of books (not dissertations) can be viewed: "Rousseau once said, as reported by David Hume, that 'one half of a man's life is too little to write a book and the other half to correct it.' Rousseau must have meant a scholarly book, for he himself wrote many books, and never corrected any of them, as far as I have been able to discover" (p. 373).

[12]Solow 1990, 449.

[13]Ziolkowski 1990, 193. The recent AAU report, "Institutional Policies to Improve Doctoral Education," also calls attention to the excessive length of some dissertations (Association of American Universities, 1990b).

Evidence of a more indirect kind comes from the questionnaire sent to all Mellon Fellows in the Humanities. These students were asked whether "Time to Improve Publication Record" was a factor in slowing down progress toward the degree. Approximately 8 percent of the students in smaller programs replied that it was "a significant factor," and about 25 percent replied that it had slowed them down "a little." There were fewer responses to this question from students in larger programs. In smaller programs, with more favorable faculty-student ratios, it seems plausible to assume that careful advising, monitoring, and "placement" of individual students might also result in more attention to professional preparation and publication. In reviewing the proposals for support that came to the Andrew W. Mellon Foundation from graduate programs, it was striking to see how many of them included a request for travel and prepublication support to help students attend professional conferences, prepare papers, and make formal presentations at colloquia.

Council on Graduate Schools entitled "The Role and Nature of the Doctoral Dissertation," presents the following:

> The dissertation is the beginning of one's scholarly work, not its culmination. Dissertation research should provide students with hands-on, directed experience in the primary research methods of the discipline, and should prepare students for the type of research/scholarship that will be expected of them after they receive the PhD degree.[14]

The tone of this statement contrasts with that of an earlier (1968) statement by the Association of Graduate Schools and the Council of Graduate Schools:

> The Doctor of Philosophy degree . . . has become the mark of highest achievement in preparation for creative scholarship and research.
> . . . When the student completes research which is a significant contribution to knowledge, it is presented in clear and concise English as his dissertation.[15]

While it is always tempting to overinterpret such changes, it seems clear that the recent statement by the Council of Graduate Schools is closer to the spirit of the Avignon pronouncement quoted by Professor Viner than it is to the more ambitious goals (overly ambitious, in our view) stated in earlier years. A harder question has to do with the ultimate authority (influence?) of deans, as contrasted with faculty in departments.[16]

Other Factors Affecting Dissertation Research

Dissertation research in many of the EHP fields has also been complicated in another way. The expectation that students will do extended archival research or fieldwork abroad is now fully established, at least in fields such as history, art history, anthropology, and area studies. The days of the "library thesis" are not gone altogether, but research that relies extensively on secondary sources—or only on *published* primary sources—is almost certain to be regarded as inadequate in many humanistic fields. Although archival research or fieldwork always may have been seen as highly desirable, the shift seems to consist of movement from a nascent or selective expectation to a far more generalized one.

In certain fields—such as history—intensive archival work has simply become *de rigueur*. Moreover, as social, cultural, and other forms of history (often based on statistical analysis) have emerged, a far greater variety of sources has become relevant. Hence, the aspiring historian now needs more time to travel, to seek, to find, and then to analyze; and this implies more time spent abroad, more financial aid, and more potential for "losing one's way." Art historians, musicologists, and area-studies specialists face different but not dissimilar problems.

What all of this means (in terms of the structure of graduate education) is that there is now a special form of pressure on the early phase of dissertation work, not simply to identify a dissertation topic, but to do enough early fieldwork or

---

[14]Council of Graduate Schools 1991, 3.

[15]Association of Graduate Schools and Council of Graduate Schools 1968, 1, 10.

[16]See the earlier discussion of the disappointing results achieved by the Ford Foundation's program of institutional grants, which depended heavily on the capacity of provosts and deans to bring about change at the departmental level (Chapter Eleven).

archival research so that an informed decision can be made concerning the viability of a proposed topic. Does enough material exist? Can the subject be studied adequately in a reasonable amount of time? Are there unusual conditions (political, economic, or other) that might interfere with the continuity of research abroad? Are the foreign-language demands too formidable? These and other questions can be addressed if the student has an opportunity to spend two-to-four months abroad in his or her third (at latest, fourth) year, evaluating the situation before committing irrevocably to a single line of research.

The need for such exploratory work has been made clear by faculty, students, and institutional self-studies. At the same time, nearly everyone also points out the extremely difficult conditions—far more difficult than in earlier eras—that currently exist abroad. Archives, libraries, and other materials are not easily accessible in many countries, either because of government policy or because there are insufficient funds to maintain facilities and to keep them open on a regular basis. Sensitivities about publishing unflattering findings are a worry. Finally, because of the fall in value of the dollar as measured against many other currencies, it is extremely expensive for a student to spend lengthy periods of time abroad. The days of the impecunious, itinerant, cheerful student-scholar, traveling and living on virtually nothing, have essentially ended. Airfares, food-costs, housing, and virtually everything else is extraordinarily expensive.

Compounding this problem is the dearth of funds that can be used to support this particular type of research. One faculty member in the field of history drew attention to this problem in a departmental proposal to the Mellon Foundation:

> One of the most important uses of travel grants is almost never funded by outside sources: brief, preliminary trips to archives when students are in the early stages of developing their dissertation projects. By being able to define their topic in terms of documents that they have already seen, rather than just speculated about, students can use travel grants of this sort to design dissertations that are far more likely to be completed in the six-year time horizon . . . .

A faculty member from an anthropology department also emphasized this point:

> Most of our students cannot gather the necessary data for a thesis without obtaining either a substantial doctoral dissertation grant or coming under the umbrella of a faculty member with a project grant. Hence, an important stage at which more financial support would make a significant difference is in Phase 2, when preliminary research is being undertaken and the thesis prospectus and grant request refined . . . .

In addition to the initial stages of research abroad, another particularly difficult moment for many graduate students occurs immediately after their return from extended fieldwork or archival research. The problems that arise are the kind associated with any complex transition, such as finding a new apartment and adjusting to a new environment. In the case of graduate students, such difficulties can be magnified by the need to find financial resources. If a demanding teaching assistantship is the primary means of support, preparations for teaching only add to the number of tasks that may preclude even the initial effort to organize and begin to digest one's field-notes.

As an experienced dissertation supervisor in art history has observed (in another proposal submitted to the Mellon Foundation):

> The high incidence of interruption at this point in the production of the PhD appears to us the principal reason for a second and uncontrollable period of drift, the actual delay resulting from a pause to earn funds may be double the length of the pause, or more; for the loss of momentum is compounded *by the need to re-warm the dish, a dispiriting process in which the most natural casualty is a sense of urgency.* [emphasis added]

Representatives of several other programs—especially in art history, anthropology, history, and religion—have commented on the reentry issue, and all have suggested the need to take self-conscious and structured steps (including the provision of financial help) to prevent students from stumbling badly at this point in their work.

In summary, quite apart from broad curricular developments, several other factors have made the entire period from the end of courses to full engagement with dissertation research an especially difficult one. These include more complex expectations concerning the nature of fully professional (often cross-disciplinary, as well as highly specialized) research in several fields; more ambitious conceptions concerning the nature of the dissertation; and more challenging fieldwork and archival demands (combined with less funding for these purposes). Pressures have converged, transforming the second phase of PhD study into what one commentator has called a "black hole," into which many doctoral candidates simply disappear for extended periods of time, if not forever.

COMPLETION OF THE DISSERTATION

For those students who have identified a dissertation topic and done a good deal of research on it, what are the main barriers to completion? Since time spent in the post-ABD phase of graduate study appears to have increased, on average, by six months to one year in many disciplines,[17] it would be helpful to know what obstacles confront students who are fully engaged with their theses—and how these students can be helped to bring their dissertations to speedier conclusions.

Dissertation Advising

From all the evidence available, this is perhaps the most variable of all variables, because it depends so much upon individual personalities, styles, and expectations. Even with the best of intentions, and apparent mutual understanding, the entire dissertation process often goes awry because it is so deeply structured on a personal apprentice-model, with both the professor and the student being given very broad latitude. This model contrasts with common practice in the natural sciences.

---

[17]The data in Table 13.1 understate the change that has occurred because of the truncation problem. As more late (and later) finishers are included in the data, the average number of years spent in the post-ABD stage will rise for the 1972–1976 and 1977–1981 cohorts. The economics survey cited previously (American Economics Association 1991, 23–24) observes that median time-to-degree has increased by more than a year over the last two decades and "it is clear . . . that the increase is at the dissertation stage." Other data from individual departments, submitted as parts of proposals to the Mellon Foundation, suggest similar increases.

In humanistic fields, tales abound of professors who are impossible to satisfy—because they set unrealistic standards, or are determined to ensure that no conceivable avenue of research on the dissertation is left unexplored, or because they are persuaded that the dissertation has always been and should continue to be a protracted crucible-like experience. While such stories are undoubtedly exaggerated, they are surely not entirely without some foundation in fact.[18]

Interviews with faculty members at a number of the universities participating in this study revealed a wide range of attitudes and practices. At one extreme, some faculty are just "too busy" and give advising low priority. At the other extreme, many faculty seem to take it for granted that if they agree to act as a dissertation adviser, they will hold regular meetings with the student, set up a schedule, make certain from the beginning that the topic is feasible and researchable, request outlines and chapters at specified moments, and "see the student through." More common, however, was the attitude—unquestionably genuine—that "my door is always open," or "students who wish to see me can always count on the fact that I will make myself available." This approach works well with certain students, but it is obviously insufficient for the person who is uncertain, who feels unable or unwilling to confront an adviser before feeling "in control" of all the relevant materials, or who may even call once or twice and purely by chance not find the adviser available just at that moment.

In these cases, students do in fact often drift without guidance for considerable periods of time, while faculty members continue to operate on the presumption that their declared accessibility, and their genuine interest in students, are sufficient to make the process work. If a student fails to appear for weeks, or perhaps months, there may be no "call" sent out, no direct assertion of control undertaken by the faculty member. Meanwhile, the student may be lost in bibliographic or other thickets, and is almost bound to think that he or she cannot have a conversation with the adviser, because such an encounter will only reveal deep areas of ignorance or vulnerability. Months go by, the psychological barriers grow greater (on the student's part), and the adviser's door remains open but undarkened by the candidate's presence.

One approach to this set of problems is to urge graduate students to be realistic in their expectations concerning the help that they will receive from an adviser and to plan to work on their dissertations as "autonomous" individuals. Thus, David Sternberg offers the following advice:

[A]lthough one may pick a thesis topic with a particular professor's counsel, encouragement and approval (such approval is often required), one should *never* pick it because that faculty member is going to see one through the two-odd years of the project. The topic must be above "politics and personalities," stand alone on its own and the candidate's merits of researchability, contribution and originality.

---

[18]Writing in the 1950s, Carmichael recorded this story: "A Dean supervised a candidate's research and . . . kept the candidate revising and polishing for six years. After earning his degree, the candidate told his supervisor that the dissertation lacked a dedication which should have read: 'To [the Dean] without whose understanding, encouragement and criticism this dissertation would probably have been completed five years ago'" (Carmichael 1961, 50–51).

A more dramatic account is offered by Cude: "Theodore Streleski walked into the office of his thesis supervisor at Stanford University, and bludgeoned the professor to death with four blows to the head." Streleski is quoted as saying "'Stanford, with de Leeuw's help, took nineteen years of my life with impunity and I decided I would not let that pass'" (Cude 1987, 45).

. . . The candidate should write his dissertation with the bottom-line assumption that *nobody* is going to help him. Within that general guideline, recent successful candidates are better sources for advice and counsel than the graduate faculty . . . . (p. 58)

Another approach is to encourage faculty members to think of their responsibilities as advisers as constituting, in the words of R. W. Connell, "the most advanced level of teaching in our education system." Connell notes that:

The commonest complaint of PhD students is that they never get to talk to their supervisors. The commonest complaint of supervisors is that their PhD students never come to talk to them. I think it is up to the supervisor to bridge the gap. [At the same time, it has to be recognized that]. . . [s]upervisors also have rights, and competing obligations . . . [including] even a few shreds of life outside the department. These determine how quickly one can read drafts, and how much time one can give to devising bibliographies or reading new literature to keep up with the student. Supervisors have to draw lines to protect themselves as well as to give the student space to work independently.[19]

Still another approach involves attempting to alter fundamentally the "apprenticeship" model. Thus, a number of graduate programs have recently moved to "committee systems," in which the dissertation prospectus, the research-plan, and progression-steps are reviewed by a small group of faculty members who are committed to the plan and to the student. This approach helps to ensure that no one faculty member will have exclusive control over the process, and it also helps to ensure that the student feels responsible to a *set* of faculty members, who schedule actual meetings with him or her, at agreed-upon times along the way. The committee system will probably not work for all programs—and it has its own particular hazards. But it does seem to work well at several institutions, and it goes some distance toward ameliorating the "isolation" problem, the total exclusivity of the apprentice-pupil arrangement, and the tendency on the part of everyone to forget that the dissertation-phase should be thought of as something for which the faculty *as a whole* continues to have joint responsibility.[20]

Finally, it does seem to be the case that few programs (if any) maintain careful and continuous records concerning faculty performance in dissertation-advising, and that effectiveness in this sphere usually counts for very little in the evaluation of faculty members when annual salary increases or even promotions are taken into account. Whether a faculty member has many, few, or no dissertation advisees; whether the students ever complete their dissertations, or complete them in a reasonably timely way; whether the advising process has been structured well and has been reasonably satisfactory—there is little or no

---

[19]Connell 1985, 38–41. For an extensive discussion of adviser-advisee relationships seen from the perspective of developmental psychology, see Bargar and Mayo-Chamberlain (1983, 407–32).

[20]The need for shared responsibility in the advising of graduate students has been noted not only in humanistic fields, but in the more theoretical sciences where research also tends to be a rather solitary pursuit. In a forthcoming report on the state of graduate education in the mathematical sciences, considerable emphasis is placed on the need to have a graduate student's progress monitored by someone besides the thesis advisor. This report also notes that students who make little or no progress in their thesis research not only waste their own time, but sap the morale of other students as well (Committee on Doctoral and Postdoctoral Study in the Mathematical Sciences, 1992).

documentation on these and related matters in most programs. It seems odd at best that the culminating aspect of the doctoral program should be subject to so little serious evaluation and monitoring, and that faculty members should not be more accountable.

Combating the Problem of Isolation

In their analysis of factors affecting those students at Berkeley who took longer than the average amount of time to earn PhDs, Nerad and Cerny record this observation:

> Students in the humanities and social sciences wrote their dissertations in total isolation. They felt lost in the transition from what they called a "class-taking person" to a "book-writing person." During this period they completely withdrew from department activities. Most said, "No one on the faculty knows about my topic, so why should I meet with them." During the actual writing period they found it very difficult to work as a teaching assistant or at another unrelated on-or-off campus job.[21]

The characteristic mode of research in most humanistic and social science fields surely plays an important part in creating the peculiarly isolated and therefore difficult milieu in which EHP (and other) students undertake their dissertations. The distinction has often been made between the form of collaborative, laboratory-based research that doctoral students in the sciences ordinarily experience, and the solitary, peripatetic "archival" life that many humanists lead during their dissertation years. Indeed, there is a growing psychological literature that highlights this point, among many others. An unpublished PhD thesis by Joan Rodman notes "the collegial environment" that is established in most scientific laboratories, and which provides "common structures [that] develop the material for dissertation topics." But this context of "support and academic community contrasts with that of the social sciences and humanities in which students delay entry, have poorly defined career goals, and work in isolation on the dissertation."[22]

Many programs have recognized that some form of structured joint discussions among students and faculty during the dissertation years can be extremely valuable in creating an analogue to the "collaborative research model" that prevails in the sciences. Different vehicles have been tried, and no single format will suit all disciplines or all institutions. But the preliminary results from a variety of pilot projects are encouraging. Two graduate programs in English in our set of departmental proposals have described the kinds of initiatives that are already under way or in the planning stage:

> To create a new design for this final year and a half, we find ourselves with several mechanisms already in place. For example, we have graduate colloquia in each of the primary areas in which dissertations are done. These are a local staging area for students to read a chapter of their dissertation, to discuss each other's work, and to do so in the presence of faculty, and with faculty. In these colloquia they look at major current work in the field and, you might say, perceive themselves fundamentally as someone writing, someone doing a thesis rather than as teachers or assistants in a course.

· · · · · · · · · · · · · · ·

---

[21]Nerad and Cerny 1991, 4.
[22]Rodman 1986, 3–4.

The dissertation workshop has been designed to meet a number of specific needs in the context of the collective mentorship which we outlined . . . . Its primary purposes are to provide (1) structure, incentive, and support for graduate students to advance the writing of their dissertations as far as possible before initiating the search for an academic position in the fall of their fifth year; (2) a forum for the sharing of dissertation-related research or specific pilot studies between students and faculty; (3) a collective context for efforts to define emerging fields or methodological problems that would engage a broad range of faculty and students . . . .

Financial Support and Completion Fellowships

In focusing on the importance of so many, sometimes quite subtle, factors that define the setting in which graduate students seek to complete their dissertations, it would be a serious error to overlook one of the most basic considerations: funding. The recent report of the Council of Graduate Schools is abundantly clear on this point:

> Barriers to timely completion of the dissertation are myriad, but the one most frequently cited by faculty, students, and graduate administrators alike is lack of adequate financial support during the dissertation phase of the doctoral program, a problem that is especially vexing to students in the humanities and the social sciences.[23]

The same point has been made by virtually all the faculty and students in our sample: Without dissertation fellowships—preferably for a full year, and sometimes a year and a summer—designed to permit graduate students to concentrate totally on the task of writing their theses, and of bringing their work to a conclusion, the entire PhD process can be delayed inordinately. Students trying to support themselves by teaching or odd-jobs, while simultaneously trying to do intensive research and writing, are at an obvious disadvantage. Lack of assured support often creates not only immediate pressures to find ways to pay bills, but various forms of psychological stress as well.

For these reasons and others, many students become deeply involved in their roles as teaching assistants. They spend long hours in preparation for their classes, enjoy teaching, and come to know their students well, often functioning as excellent undergraduate advisers. In short, they are committed to what they are doing in the classroom and see this activity as integral to their future as faculty members. All of this is extremely encouraging—so long as a reasonable balance is maintained between early pre-doctoral involvement in teaching and the need to finish one's PhD. The enthusiasm and commitment of teaching assistants must be retained, but the extent of their teaching must, whenever feasible, be limited. Otherwise, dissertations may lag interminably, and the teaching assistants may become weary, discouraged, and even bitter.

The data presented in Chapters Ten and Eleven (especially for the Whiting Fellows) indicate that dissertation fellowships do help students complete this final hurdle of graduate study. The point to add here is that the mechanism through which such support is provided can be very important. Fellowships of this kind are likely to be most effective if they are offered on a competitive basis—and are available only to students who reach certain milestones within

---

[23]Council of Graduate Schools 1991, 17.

certain specified periods of time. Students and faculty alike need clearly defined goals and incentives. An application process that requires demonstrated progress on the thesis, and a realistic timetable for the completion of the dissertation, seem critical if financial support is to be used in ways that are genuinely productive and that motivate students and faculty to finish the task at hand.

THE NEED FOR EVALUATION AND MONITORING

In addition to whatever specific improvements can be made at all stages of study, we are persuaded that much can be gained from a more general awareness of the set of problems discussed here, and a commitment on the part of the faculty to systematic review of the effectiveness of the graduate program.

Students and institutions invest innumerable years, enormous energy, and massive amounts of financial resources in doctoral programs. Yet there is comparatively little accounting for what happens at many of the most critical junctures. In previous eras, when most programs were small and when candidates were relatively few, the individual apprentice-system was a plausible model. But given the totally new system that has evolved since the 1960s— particularly its heterogeneity, scale, comparative lack of funding, and decreased effectiveness in terms of completion rates and time-to-degree—the time for sensible modification seems overdue.

Many institutional self-analyses have been made, and some are highly instructive. Internal departmental reports, for example, provide a valuable insight into the dynamics of "program management." This is an excerpt from a report prepared by one of the larger history graduate programs:

> Examination of progress to degree by students in various cohorts from 1965 to present shows surprising consistency, within certain limits. . . . Roughly 55%–65% of each cohort completes second year requirements and takes the oral examination in their fields. And in years just after a major curricular revision, most take the oral by the end of the second year. Then there is a drift toward taking the examination in the third year. . . . It is noteworthy that now six years into the current curriculum, History is experiencing considerable pressure to allow orals in the third year, particularly in certain fields . . . .
>
> Where time-to-degree falls down is during completion of the dissertation—with the bulk of students (from those who do complete) finishing in 7–10 years. Better funding coupled with tighter enforcement of rules on timing seems to have streamlined progress toward the History PhD at the pre-dissertation stage since 1983. The Department is now seeking better funded teaching opportunities and dissertation-year fellowships to speed time-to-degree . . . .

This report shows the tendency of programs to oscillate, with periods of tightening followed by contrary pressures to relax the system. Some changes work well, but only for limited periods of time.

Other reports suggest that while some curricular revisions can be fruitful, some can be disastrous. In an effort to provide students with more options, for instance, one political science program decided to allow students to submit two research papers (in addition to an MA thesis) as an alternative to the ordinary PhD preliminary examination. These essays were to be "theoretically informed papers which differed significantly from each other and from the MA essay in substance, method and approach." Each of the papers required two faculty readers and all six readers had to be different individuals.

The results were only too predictable (at least in retrospect):

> Over time even larger numbers of students elected to write Option II papers rather than sit for the Option I Preliminary Examination; and despite Departmental rules which placed time limits on completion of the papers, in reality students, with support from many faculty, bogged down for years attempting to write definitive publishable pieces. . . . It was not uncommon to see seventh and eighth year students still not admitted to candidacy and still working on Option papers—which frequently ended up as dissertation chapters . . . . Prior to the curricular revision of 1987, internal self-studies in Political Science revealed *almost total attrition from entering cohorts of the late 1970s and early 1980s*. This crisis coupled with improved financial aid for graduate students, which mandated better evidence of progress toward degree completion, paved the way for the curricular reforms of 1987. [emphasis added]

The lessons to be drawn reinforce points already made. Major research papers tend to take on the dimensions of mini-dissertations, and the department in question, through the creation of its special option, essentially multiplied the number of publishable "dissertations" that students were obliged to write. Beyond that, the tendency to substitute papers for exams, and then to allow the deadline for papers to be indefinitely extended, is a constant hazard—at the undergraduate level as well as the graduate level. "Incompletes" become something close to the rule, rather than the exception. Finally, the slowness of programs to modify their systems in the face of even ruinous circumstances is all too apparent. In this case, it took several years, with *almost total attrition*, before the situation was addressed.

This experience illustrates dramatically one of the points to which we would assign greatest emphasis. There must be much closer, more systematic, monitoring of the progress of graduate students at the program level. If continuous monitoring, record-keeping, and evaluation had been in place, the situation described above would not have been able to go on so long without corrective action.

A related problem is the lack of rigorous enforcement of rules, goals, and guidelines that have been established. One example—drawn from the experience of a leading department of political science—follows:

> Our data show the number of students who had held a successful thesis conference at various points in time after they have passed the general examination. In the past four years only thirteen students of eighty-one have held a conference within one year, the goal that the Department has in mind . . . . Only nineteen of the students have held a conference within the eighteen month time period that is the Department's officially stated expectation.

Situations such as these may arise because of a simple lack of record-keeping, or a reluctance to be too "hard" on students who are already seen as burdened in various ways. More fundamentally, the absence of strong enforcement of departmental norms may stem from the lack of a structure that can be relied on to do the work involved and, perhaps, from the lack of a strong tradition of accountability.

The general implication is the need for faculty to accept collective responsibility for the results achieved by their graduate programs. The course of study needs to be well-defined, with sensible but firm expectations and deadlines at every major point along the way. Most of all, there should be a clear acknowledgement that the faculty members have a joint obligation to run a *program*—a coherent, structured entity—for which they should feel accountable.

Of course, this is all easier said than done. One inherent complication is that graduate studies must accommodate personal idiosyncrasies and complex "rhythms" in ways that make the process profoundly different from undergraduate education or professional school education. Yet these genuine differences are often too readily cited by faculty and students alike as justification for programs that are so loosely structured (and sometimes so large) that they are intrinsically incapable of functioning well.

The force of the testimony and evidence cited above leads us to underscore again the initial presumption of the chapter: The design, oversight, evaluation, and careful monitoring of graduate programs make an enormous difference to the quality of the educational experience, the morale and progress of students, and the extent to which human and financial resources are used effectively.

Recommendations

THIS STUDY has been motivated from the first by a desire to find ways in which the effectiveness of doctoral programs might be improved, but we nonetheless decided at an early stage to concentrate on describing current realities and examining factors affecting measurable outcomes. The need for basic analysis was too great, in our judgment, to permit any other emphasis. When it comes to stating specific policy recommendations, therefore, we find ourselves somewhat reticent.

Our analysis of government programs and foundation initiatives has been limited to those most directly relevant to graduate education within the arts and sciences. Within the academic world, we have looked carefully at only a small number of graduate programs (mainly in the humanities and related social sciences), located within a clearly unrepresentative group of universities. Thus, this body of research does not lead to recommendations on a wide range of issues that must be considered in formulating policy. Nor does our comparative advantage lie in offering that kind of advice. Rather, we have tried to provide an analytical and empirical framework that might serve, at the minimum, as a kind of "reality check" in evaluating policy recommendations.

The following discussion of policymaking in graduate education is best regarded, then, as a general commentary, based not only on the findings of this study, but also on consideration of many of these topics over a number of years. We begin with some basic propositions concerning the funding of graduate education, then discuss the role of the federal government and foundations, and end with a longer discussion of the implications of this study for policies and practices within universities.

GENERAL PROPOSITIONS

The measurable outcomes of graduate education are influenced strongly by the external setting, and especially by conditions in job markets. Favorable labor markets in academia encourage undergraduates to embark on graduate study, and they also encourage students already enrolled in graduate programs to complete their PhDs without undue delay. In addition, the state of the academic labor market influences decisions by public and private benefactors to invest more or less heavily in graduate education. Job prospects also affect the ways in which faculty and administrators conduct graduate programs: how they make admissions decisions, what amounts and forms of financial aid they offer, how hard they press graduate students to finish, and what priority they attach to curricular reform. The magnitude of such effects can be readily exaggerated, however, given the understandable tendency to attribute disappointing outcomes to external factors, such as the job market, that are outside the control of the individual and the institution.

Two other sets of factors—the availability of financial support for graduate students and the internal characteristics of graduate programs—affect completion rates and time-to-degree directly. They interact in complex ways, and any attempt to decide which of the two is ultimately more important is largely beside the point. These interactions can be highly productive (if, for example, financial aid awards are used to create incentives for students to meet specified requirements within defined time periods), but they also can have negative effects. For example, the greatly increased reliance during the 1970s and early 1980s on teaching assistantships, which has had long-lasting effects on many graduate programs in the humanities and related social sciences, was driven in large part by funding shortfalls.

Levels of Funding

Providing sufficient financial assistance to doctoral candidates is especially important in the arts and sciences because the reward structure of the vocations chosen by many PhDs limits severely the amount of self-financing that can be expected. Also, graduate students are generally regarded as independent of their parents, which limits reliance on family support. Nonetheless, the National Research Council reports that of all doctorate recipients in all fields in 1989, 48 percent relied primarily on personal resources (including spouse's earnings); another 35 percent relied primarily on university funding; 12 percent depended primarily on federal sources of support; and the remaining 5 percent relied primarily on other sources.[1] In the humanities, the percentages relying primarily on personal resources and on university resources were higher yet; in the physical sciences, however, only 18 percent used primarily personal resources (Figure 14.1).[2]

For all of their limitations, these data indicate clearly both the differences in the basic structure of financial support between broad fields and the critical roles played at the present time by personal resources and university funding. To expect students to cover more of the costs of graduate education out of personal resources, would be to put at risk both the number and quality of candidates for doctorates.[3] Such an approach would also make it even more difficult to include

---

[1] *Summary Report 1989*, Table 11. These figures are for U.S. citizens only. Notes to this table state: "A recipient's 'primary' source of support is the source with the largest reported percentage. 'Personal' includes loans as well as own earnings and contributions from the spouse/family. . . . Percentages . . . are based on the number of PhDs with known primary support" (p. 26). Of course, many of these students were almost certainly studying part-time during many of the years that they pursued doctorates—and they may well have been studying part-time because they did not have access to institutional support. If the analysis were limited to full-time students, the percentage dependent on personal resources would have been somewhat lower.

[2] In some groups of fields not shown in this figure, students relied even more heavily on personal resources than they did in the humanities. In the field of education, for example, 74 percent of doctoral recipients relied primarily on personal resources.

[3] Looking at these data, one might think that it would be possible to shift more of the financing load in the physical sciences to self-support. In our view, however, this would be ill-advised. Generally, better-paying alternatives are open to these students, who also have greater difficulty pursuing doctorates on a part-time basis. Of course, the opportunity costs (income foregone by studying rather than pursuing employment opportunities) borne by graduate students in any field constitute such a large component of the true cost to the student that even those receiving generous financial

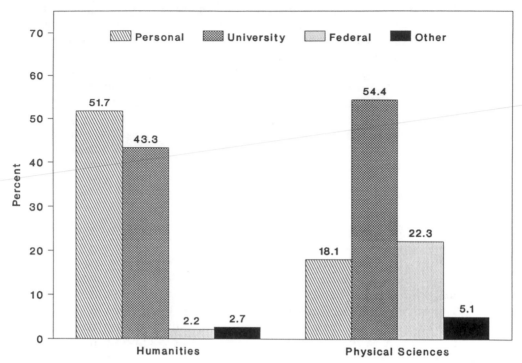

Figure 14.1
Primary Sources of Support, Humanities and Physical Sciences, National Data, 1989
Source: *Summary Report 1989*, Table 11, p. 26.
Notes: Data are for U.S. citizens only.

within the professoriate any significant representation of minority groups or, indeed, any significant number of individuals from families of modest means. The potential effects on the character and quality of teaching within the nation's entire educational system—and the subsequent effects on so many aspects of national life—are strong reminders of the need to maintain effective programs of financial aid at the graduate level.

The *form* and *timing* of financial support are very important, but discussions of (for instance) the merits of fellowships versus teaching assistantships at various stages of graduate study should not obscure the overriding need for adequate overall levels of support. All of the problems we have discussed would be exacerbated if financial support were reduced. Additional funds, judiciously deployed, are needed to improve the effectiveness of doctoral study—in a period when well-functioning graduate programs will have especially important contributions to make.

Graduate education should not be seen as a "poor cousin" of either undergraduate education (which always has a stronger alumni/ae constituency) or research (which is more visible, and which often attracts outside funding more

---

assistance contribute handsomely to the costs of their education. At the same time, tuition charged at the graduate level covers such a small fraction of the *institutional* costs of graduate study that universities also contribute substantially, even when the student or an outside donor pays "full" tuition.

readily). Hard as it will be, especially under straitened financial conditions, educational institutions must continue to invest significant amounts of their own unrestricted funds in the support of graduate students. But not even the most determined effort to assign graduate education a high priority will permit adequate funding from institutional sources alone. Costs are too high, and competing priorities are too compelling. External funders must help much more generously, we believe, than they do at present.

Pluralistic Sources of Funding

The arguments in favor of pluralistic sources of funding are both pragmatic and conceptual. Diversification of any portfolio normally reduces risk, and there is ample evidence to indicate the dangers of becoming too dependent on any single source of funding. The risks are not merely financial. Dominant donors, private and public, can have too much influence on the shape of programs. The experience of the United Kingdom in recent years offers more dramatic evidence of the difficulties posed for all concerned—those responsible for making grants and those responsible for receiving and administering them—when one source of funding is all-important.[4]

Another advantage of multiple sources of funding is that they permit, at least in principle, some specialization of function: Different patrons may be particularly well-suited to provide certain kinds of support. While monolithic organizational structures may be capable of achieving higher levels of coordination, they are likely to impose unhealthy degrees of uniformity on educational programs that are highly varied and complex. One of the strengths of higher education in this country is precisely the fact that different institutions serve different purposes, have different characteristics, and operate at different levels of cost. Messy as it may seem—and as it often is in reality—this "system" has definite advantages, and the existence of multiple sources of funding surely facilitates the existence of a wider variety of programs and institutions than would exist otherwise.

These rather abstract propositions may be illustrated by considering some of the roles played by the federal government, foundations, and universities in supporting graduate education.

THE FEDERAL GOVERNMENT

The federal responsibility for providing significant assistance to graduate education and research (particularly in the sciences) remains well accepted in this

---

[4]See, for example, the debate over the decision of the Economic and Social Research Council (ESRC) to "blacklist" institutions with very low submission (completion) rates (Young, Fogarty, and McRae 1987). The criticisms of the ESRC's policy have included a challenge to the statistical reliability of the measure used to determine ineligibility for government funding—which serves as a reminder of the dangers inherent in relying on simple (too simple) quantitative indices in formulating policy (Colombo and Morrison 1988).

More generally, the decisions by Oxford, Cambridge, and other British universities to be more aggressive in seeking private funds reflect some of these concerns, as well as an overriding need for more resources. For an earlier discussion of the case for multiple sources of funding, using Britain as a case study, see Bowen (1964, especially p. 7).

country.[5] That central fact is more striking than ever in light of the tendency in recent years for the federal government to relinquish other responsibilities that it had accepted previously.

The rationale is clear-cut: A strong system of graduate education is thought to benefit not only the individuals being educated, but the nation at large. There are "spillover" benefits that affect this country's capacity to innovate, to compete successfully in the world economy, to pursue its political and military objectives, and (many of us would argue) to be a country with a stimulating intellectual life, a set of shared values that includes respect for the individual, an appreciation of the arts and culture, and a capacity for democratic self-government. Because of its place at the apex of the higher-education system, doctoral education affects the character and quality of teaching at the college level and (less directly) at all other levels. While the multiple benefits of this country's system of doctoral education defy precise measurement, they seem to be widely appreciated and understood.[6]

Of the many federal programs that support graduate studies, the NSF fellowship program is perhaps the best known and, by all accounts, the most successful.[7] Its characteristics illustrate several ways in which well-designed federal programs can be particularly effective:

- First, the portable feature of the NSF Fellowships has permitted the ablest students to enroll in the strongest programs without the need for judgments about quality to be reached through a political process.
- Second, the careful selection procedures followed by the NSF, using national panels of scientists, have both reinforced the standing of the program and attracted highly qualified students with real commitments to graduate education. Investing in "process" can yield high returns.
- Third, the continuity of the program—multiyear support for recipients and confidence on the part of students and universities that the program would not suddenly be terminated or radically reconfigured—have made it a source of stability in settings in which there is too much uncertainty.
- Fourth, and perhaps most important of all, the NSF program illustrates that well-designed federal programs can have high visibility and therefore strong "announcement effects"—signaling to prospective graduate students, in particular, the importance that the nation as a whole attaches to doctoral education. Because of its visibility and stature, and the message that it conveys, we suspect that the NSF fellowship program has served to encourage many nonrecipients to pursue PhDs.

---

[5]For example, the overall budget for the National Science Foundation (NSF) has increased from $171 million in 1989 to $204 million in 1990 to $322 million in 1991 and $390 million in 1992 (proposed). See *Budget of the United States Government: Fiscal Year 1992* (Office of Management and Budget 1991). The history of federal support for graduate education dates mainly from World War II. For a brief review, with references to other sources, see Association of American Universities (1990a, 15–18).

[6]Benefits extend well beyond the boundaries of the states in which doctorate-granting institutions are located, in part because recipients of doctorates are so mobile. This is one reason why responsibility for graduate education has been seen to rest primarily at the federal level. States support doctoral education mainly indirectly, through their general support of those doctorate-granting institutions in their states for which they have primary fiscal responsibility.

[7]Outstanding students have been attracted to doctoral programs, completion rates have been relatively high, time-to-degree has been relatively low, and many recipients have had successful careers (see Chapter Ten).

The NSF model is best seen as one component of a long-term strategy for supporting graduate education, and it is encouraging that other governmental agencies have similar fellowship programs.[8] Some variant of this model has obvious appeal as a mechanism to support doctoral candidates in the humanities and related social sciences (those not covered by the NSF program), and the Javits fellowship program was created with this objective in mind. Modest in scale (about one-fifth the funding level of the NSF program in 1989), and still to develop as sharp a focus as the NSF program, this program is too new to evaluate properly; it is, nonetheless, a potentially valuable instrument of national policy. Unfortunately, however, the future of even this small program now seems threatened.[9]

Whatever the precise vehicle chosen, the humanities, no less than the sciences, need a well-respected "capstone" fellowship program—with status, continuity, and therefore the capacity to demonstrate a visible national commitment to scholarship and teaching in these essential fields of study. Such a program should operate on a larger scale than the Javits program, and it must be seen as more than the product of temporary interest. It should be seen as analogous to the NSF program, designed to have long-lasting consequences.[10]

If it had strong support from both the executive and legislative branches, the existing Javits program in the Department of Education could evolve into such a program. Another organizational option to consider would be to locate such a program under the National Endowment for the Humanities (NEH). That would be one way of ending the dispute over whether graduate education in the humanities, as in the sciences, deserves national support on a long-term basis. The parallelism with the NSF program is appealing.

In thinking about the structure of a continuing program of portable fellowships in the humanities, consideration should be given, however, to modifying at least one significant feature of the NSF model—namely, the guarantee of three or more years of fellowship support to students yet to embark on graduate work.

---

[8]For example, the National Defense Science and Engineering Graduate Fellowships (Association of American Universities 1990a, Appendix).

[9]Without wishing to become enmeshed in the current debate over reauthorization of Title IX of the Higher Education Act, we want to express our agreement with those who have opposed the administration's proposal to combine the Javits program (and the Harris program, discussed below) with the newer Graduate Assistance in Areas of National Need program. To eliminate any fellowship funding designed specifically for the humanities would send entirely the wrong signal, in our judgment, to prospective graduate students. Also, in light of the record of allocation of funds under the Graduate Assistance in Areas of National Need program, it is easy to understand the skepticism of many as to whether the humanities and related social sciences would fare well under that banner. According to a recent story in the *Chronicle of Higher Education* (Jaschik 1991, A15), five departments in the field of foreign languages (currently the only eligible field within the humanities) had received awards as of April 1, 1991, as compared with 180 in the sciences and engineering. In addition, there is the issue of whether the portability of the Javits Fellowships would be lost under the proposed merger of programs—presumably it would.

The Truman program represents another model (Myers 1991, A29ff). It is a federal program that makes awards to undergraduates interested in public service for use during senior year in college and then for graduate study. The distinctive aspect of this type of program is that its awards are funded from interest earned on its own Congressionally created endowment. This funding mechanism provides more assurance of continuity than annual appropriations, but of course also requires a larger initial appropriation to establish the endowment.

[10]At present, the Mellon Fellowships in the Humanities offer more awards to PhD candidates in the humanities than any government program. This is an anomalous situation, since no private foundation should be expected to play such a role on a continuing basis.

The findings reported in this study cause us to question whether guaranteed multiyear fellowship awards in these fields are the most appropriate form of support. In particular, the higher attrition rates in the humanities, even for holders of prestigious national fellowships, raise questions about the desirability of betting so heavily on students yet to enter graduate school. We believe that modifications in the structure of these graduate programs (as suggested in the latter part of the chapter) can lead to higher completion rates, but it might be wisest to wait for clear progress along these lines before committing so many resources to multiyear fellowships.

A more promising approach at this juncture might be to offer a larger number of generous entry-level awards, initially providing just one-year of support, which could then be combined with supplementary *fellowship* funding (as distinct from more general, cost-of-education grants) for discretionary use in the same field by those institutions chosen by the recipients. This approach would provide the strong announcement effect needed, and would encourage able students to begin graduate study, without presuming to predict with high confidence which students will ultimately finish their studies. It would also give those universities attracting these students the flexible funds needed to create incentives for larger numbers of graduate students (including those who won the entry-level awards) to make timely progress toward the doctorate.[11]

The research reported in this study also underscores the special need for fellowship support in the humanities at the dissertation stage of graduate study. More fellowships of this kind, made available on a competitive basis, would encourage larger numbers of the ablest graduate students to complete their doctorates. Fellowships targeted at the dissertation stage of graduate study represent a well-documented, long-term need. Experience with similar programs administered by private foundations demonstrates the effectiveness of this approach. What is needed now is a larger, more ambitious program.[12]

A program of this kind would seem to be an especially appropriate mechanism for federal support of doctoral education in the humanities. In general, the federal government has a comparative advantage in administering programs of reasonably large scale, which can attract a broad range of applicants, and which

---

[11]Many other variants are, of course, possible. Supplementary funding might not accompany fellowship winners automatically. Universities that attracted entry-level winners of these fellowships could be invited to apply—and compete for—supplementary funding of the training-grant variety. This would be a more complicated approach, but it would stimulate careful thinking about the most effective use of the supplementary funds. In effect, a portable program would be linked to a program of institutional support.

This provisional recommendation represents a departure from the thinking that guided illustrative recommendations made in an earlier study (Bowen and Sosa 1989, 181–86). Those earlier recommendations did not distinguish the humanities from the sciences and were made without the benefit of the data reported here. They simply followed the NSF model, including the recommendation of guaranteed multiyear fellowship support.

[12]Two major dissertation fellowship programs in the humanities are the Newcombe Fellowships and dissertation awards sponsored by the Whiting Foundation. The Newcombe program is administered by the Woodrow Wilson National Fellowship Foundation and makes about 40 portable one-year awards each year (information supplied by Judith Pinch, who administers the program, in a personal communication). A total of between 50 and 70 Whiting Fellowships have been awarded each year by the seven universities chosen by the Whiting Foundation to participate in this program (see Appendix B). The American Council on Learned Societies and the Social Science Research Council also award limited numbers of dissertation fellowships through area studies programs.

can be structured and administered in a consistent and straightforward way. If such a program were to be inaugurated under the sponsorship of the National Endowment for the Humanities (one obvious organizational home), it would enable the Endowment to identify itself more strongly with the scholarship of future faculty of high quality as well as with the scholarship of individuals already holding doctorates.

The federal government also has a special responsibility, we believe, for leading the effort to encourage larger numbers of minority students to earn doctorates in the arts and sciences. The extremely disappointing record to date speaks for itself (see Chapter Two). More fellowship assistance, in company with other efforts directed at undergraduate students, is essential if progress is to be made. Corporations, foundations, and universities are active in this area, and they provide similar kinds of assistance. But this is surely one instance where the broader consequences—educational, social, and political—of failing to move aggressively to correct past deficiencies justify special efforts at the national level. The Harris Fellowships have embodied this principle (especially in the field of public service), and it is easy to understand why strong objections have been raised to the recent proposal that this program, like the Javits program, be merged into the Graduate Assistance in Areas of National Need program of the Department of Education.[13]

A broader issue concerns the extent to which governmental programs of assistance to graduate students should rely mainly on the mechanism of portable awards. There has long been a tension between the principle of portability and the desire to support a variety of institutions directly. The National Defense Education Act (NDEA) program of the 1960s, which we have discussed at several places in this study (see Chapters Three, Four, and Eleven, and Appendix B), represented a major effort to affect the geographical distribution of graduate programs. Working in an entirely different field, and pursuing a separate set of objectives, the National Institutes of Health have long had a large-scale program of institutional grants that support student traineeships. The Foreign Language and Area Studies Program of the Department of Education has made grants to specific institutions and programs, which in turn have assisted graduate students. Most recently (1986), the program of Graduate Assistance in Areas of National Need was established within the Department of Education.

Institutionally targeted programs can serve a wider range of objectives than portable fellowship programs, and there is merit in both approaches. The major risk with institutionally targeted programs, in our view, is that allocation decisions will be made on the basis of criteria that are insufficiently attuned to sustainable educational priorities, defined in national terms. The NDEA program of the 1960s may have succeeded too well in stimulating the creation of new doctoral programs in many regions of the country and in encouraging the further development of programs that have remained below critical mass. The analysis in Chapter Four implies that, at this juncture, there is more than

---

[13]The same principle has been recognized in programs of the National Science Foundation and the National Institutes of Health. We are on record elsewhere as proponents of the policy of permitting financial assistance to be provided on a targeted basis to students from underrepresented minority groups (Bowen and Rudenstine 1991).

adequate capacity in the overall system of doctoral education in the arts and sciences.[14]

The challenge today is to encourage strong programs to operate more effectively. It would be unfortunate if additional incentives were created for the further proliferation of very small programs or even for spreading too thinly resources that are already extremely limited. Effective program management is needed at the level of the overall system of graduate education, as well as within individual institutions.[15]

States also play a role in controlling the number of doctorate-granting programs if they choose to exercise licensing (or program approval) authority. California, Missouri, and New York are three states that have worked to discourage what they have seen as tendencies by institutions to add doctoral programs (or to sustain them) in the absence of a need for them, or in situations in which the requisite institutional resources seemed to be lacking.[16] Not surprisingly, ambitions to strengthen offerings in graduate education often yield grudgingly to what faculty and others can see as interference in academic matters by bureaucrats. While understanding such feelings, we believe that there is value, in principle, to restraints of this kind, given the difficulty that many institutions have had in resisting pressures to create new programs and in closing programs that have not succeeded in achieving stated objectives. In practice, the wisdom of state regulation in this area depends on the criteria invoked and the quality of the decisionmaking process.

A very different concern, applicable to all governmental programs, is that funds provided by the federal government will simply displace funds that otherwise might have been provided by universities themselves. Recent work by Ronald Ehrenberg and his colleagues provides some evidence that displacement effects are quite small. Working with a simple behavioral model, and using data

---

[14]One of the strongest statements against proliferation of graduate programs was made more than a decade ago by the chairman of the English department at the University of Florida, who also served at the time as chairman of the MLA Advisory Committee on the Job Market (Hellstrom 1979, 97).

[15]The risk in heavy reliance on portable programs is just the opposite: that they will concentrate resources too heavily on a small group of high-status institutions. In the 1950s and early 1960s, there was more reason to be concerned that portable fellowships would help students who attended only a small number of prestigious graduate programs concentrated in the Northeast and in California. The subsequent development of strong graduate programs throughout the country (in part as a result of government programs, such as the NDEA), which is documented in Chapter Four, reduces the need to be as concerned about this aspect of the problem of allocation of funds. In addition, these concerns can be addressed by putting absolute limits on the number of awards that can be used at any one institution (a limitation on the degree of portability that has been adopted by some private foundation fellowship programs). Of course, it is important to remember that portable programs are intended to permit the ablest students from all over the country to choose for themselves the graduate programs that will serve them best.

[16]In Missouri, Governor Christopher Bond is reported to have called for creation of "an academic common market" in the region in order to limit the number of doctoral programs needed in each state. The problem of an excessive number of doctoral programs has been of concern in New York State for over 20 years (New York State Board of Regents 1973). See National Board on Graduate Education (1975, especially p. 18) for a general discussion of efforts at the state level. A recent report by the California Postsecondary Education Commission (1985, 70) observed: "In several disciplines, the University of California offers more doctoral programs than necessary to accommodate student demand or the needs of society for doctorates in those disciplines. . . . Some doctoral programs have produced so few graduates during the past five years that their viability is questionable." The Commission recommended consolidation of doctoral programs in several disciplines (mostly in the humanities and social sciences).

for the sciences generated by the NSF, they estimate that increasing the number of students supported by external funds by 100 will decrease the number supported by institutional funds by about 18.[17] Many foundations, concerned with this same issue, have become adept at structuring grants so as to preclude any serious possibility of displacement. In short, this is a problem that can be solved much more readily than many of the other difficulties confronting efforts to improve graduate education.

FOUNDATION SUPPORT

There is a considerable history of foundation involvement with graduate education, and it has been as varied as the foundations themselves. This nonuniformity of approach is, in our view, entirely appropriate. The case for pluralistic sources of support applies within the foundation world as well as between foundations and other classes of patrons.

Each foundation is accountable to its own trustees, and their particular beliefs and points of view will, of course, influence programs, as will the predilections of officers and staff members. No one would claim that foundations are removed from "politics," in the large sense of the term. Precisely because they are so individualistic, foundations can address a wider range of issues and endorse a wider range of approaches than most governmental entities. They may be less subject to conventional consensus politics than are government agencies—but we certainly do not suggest that foundations are at all immune from the tendency to follow current trends. Indeed, as a group, they may be *more* subject to that tendency than many other funding sources.

Ideally, foundations will develop prototype programs that do not require the infrastructure or the funding appropriate at the federal level. Foundations are generally better equipped to enter particular niches than entities responsible to broader constituencies, and it should be easier for them to change directions. If a foundation succeeds in developing a particularly effective program, related directly to a pressing national need, the program then might be adopted by others, and perhaps put on a more permanent footing by the government itself. In this respect, the roles of foundations and government agencies should be highly complementary.

The success of foundation initiatives in any field depends on a reasonable degree of expertise. This consideration alone argues for some specialization of function among the larger foundations.[18] The success of the Sloan Foundation's fellowships in support of postdoctoral fellows and young faculty members in mathematics and the sciences is surely due in part to that foundation's history of interest in those fields, the presence of well-trained staff, and that founda-

---

[17]Ehrenberg, Rees, and Brewer 1991. The authors go on to note that "since some of the institutional funds that are 'saved' may be redirected to support graduate students in the humanities and other fields not represented in the data, the total effect of such a policy change is probably somewhat smaller." Ehrenberg's estimate is surprisingly consistent with the guess in an earlier study (Bowen and Sosa 1989, 185) that "the net effect of . . . new fellowships would be to increase the number of graduate students by 75 percent of the number of new awards."

[18]Corporate support of doctoral education also illustrates the principle of concentrating efforts in areas in which a funding organization has both a particular interest and some special competence. For these reasons, corporate support should be expected to be especially important in the sciences and engineering.

tion's capacity to recruit outstanding academics to participate in the selection of fellows. The Ford Foundation's support of graduate and postgraduate opportunities for minority students serves as another example of a foundation's persistent engagement with a critical area of need. Ford has had sufficient experience in the area to develop the needed expertise, and it has also commissioned professional evaluations of its programs.[19]

Careful assessment is critical if the prototype function of foundation programs is to enjoy credibility. And it must be acknowledged that even the most determined and most objective efforts at evaluation have often been disappointing. Both Breneman's review of the Ford Foundation's early program of institutional grants intended to reduce time-to-degree (discussed at length in Chapter Eleven) and the later Arce-Manning review of the Ford Foundation's fellowship programs for minority students illustrate all too well how hard it is to evaluate a program after-the-fact. After recounting the heroic efforts made to locate the 2,306 recipients of Ford Foundation fellowships for minorities awarded between 1970 and 1981, Arce and Manning state candidly:

> One serious problem . . . was the failure to build into the administration of the program a provision for long term evaluation. . . . Any future programs should give particular attention to the need for evaluation research during the initial conception of the program, in its data collection and retention, and in its maintenance of records.[20]

In addition to being able to target support to particular fields of study and particular population groups, foundations have the capacity to be somewhat more "interventionist" than government agencies. In part this is because they have the luxury of working with smaller groups of institutions and adopting a quasi–case study approach. For example, foundations can collaborate with

---

[19]For a history of the Ford Foundation's programs for minorities in graduate education, see Arce and Manning (1984, Chapter 2). For a review of Ford's postdoctoral fellowships for minorities, see Marrett and Sharp (1985).

[20]Arce and Manning (1984, 24). After determined efforts, 82 percent of the recipients were located, of whom approximately 75 percent completed a survey instrument. Thus, usable responses were obtained from just over 60 percent of the recipients, making it difficult to interpret the completion rates (Table V–10b).

The general comments by Arce and Manning about the difficulties of evaluating these programs echo the more plaintive tone of an earlier report designed to evaluate the NDEA program: "We feel that evaluation studies . . . are becoming increasingly expensive, difficult and time-consuming to carry out because of inadequate respondent addresses, difficulties and delays in obtaining data from some universities and, in some cases, respondent uncooperativeness. Future student programs . . . should carry a stipulation alerting recipients to the possibility of future research and evaluation efforts and provide for periodic updating of addresses. Further, comparison groups or institutional data which may be requested for evaluation should be identified at the time fellowship programs are first funded" (Holmstrom and Sharp 1970, 8). One is reminded of the difficulties encountered by the Danforth Foundation and the Woodrow Wilson National Fellowship Foundation in surveying their awardees (see Chapter Eleven).

The more general problem is the lack of reference points caused by the absence of national, longitudinal data of the kind needed for these purposes. Malaney classified 94 articles that appeared in academic journals from 1976 to 1987, and found that only one of them was able to aggregate data in ways that made comparisons possible across institutions (Malaney 1987, 28). The recently established Center for Research in Graduate Education at the University of Rochester is attempting to address this problem, but it is too early to judge its success.

universities in seeking to incorporate into graduate curricula better methods of preparing graduate students to teach.

A further example of this approach, which we know in the greatest detail, follows directly from the findings reported in this study. Largely as a result of this research, the Mellon Foundation has embarked on a new institutionally based program that is designed to assist a small number of graduate institutions achieve systemic improvements in doctoral programs in the humanities. A key feature of this program is that it is departmentally oriented and encompasses explicit goals developed by the participating departments. The need for full engagement of faculty at the departmental level is one of the main lessons to be derived from the Ford Foundation's earlier program of institutional support, which was relatively unstructured and relied on contacts with provosts and deans (see Chapter Eleven).

In this new program, proposals have been tailored to address specific problems identified by the faculty (and sometimes by committees of graduate students) in particular departments, with the objective of improving outcomes for *all* entering students, not just for those who happen to receive support through these departmental grants. Foundation dollars will be used strategically by departments to provide (for example) summer stipends following the completion of qualifying examinations within a certain time period, assistance while preparing dissertation outlines, and fellowship support at the dissertation stage for those students who have made sufficient progress to justify confidence that they will be able to finish their work expeditiously.[21]

In company with a new program of portable entry-level fellowships to be awarded through national competitions, this program will replace the current Mellon Fellowships in the Humanities. The existing program has relied too heavily, we now believe, on guaranteed multiyear packages of support for entering students. The difficulty with portable, multiyear fellowships in the humanities is not just that the evidence to date fails to justify betting so heavily on students yet to begin graduate study. Seen from the perspective of a foundation convinced of the need to encourage fundamental changes in the structure of graduate programs, awarding fellowships of this kind provides insufficient incentives. To create appropriate incentives for students as well as changes in the structure of graduate programs, departments require flexible funds that they can allocate in timely ways to the most deserving students—and the provision of such funds by the Foundation needs to be conditioned on the commitment of departments to a set of specific actions that it has proposed to achieve stated goals. Portable multiyear fellowships do not provide either the flexible funding or the commitment to well-conceived improvements in programs needed to achieve better outcomes.[22]

---

[21]A fuller description of this program, including the criteria used to choose the participating universities, is available from the Andrew W. Mellon Foundation. We are painfully aware of the limited resources we are able to commit to this important but expensive undertaking and (because of the need to concentrate resources if they are to have the desired impact) the limited number of departments and institutions that therefore can be included. We would like to broaden the reach of the program at least modestly over time if resources permit. Also, if the results are good enough, we hope that other funders will want to support related projects at other universities.

[22]Pelikan (1983, 77) has argued that portable fellowships will themselves provide sufficient incentives to improve programs (since departments must compete to attract the winners). The

Of course, it remains to be seen whether this new program of institutional support—avowedly more interventionist—will help the participating departments to raise completion rates, reduce time-to-degree, and simultaneously improve the quality of the education offered. In keeping with the advice we have given others, we are committed to maintaining full records from the start, and to developing a database that will permit reliable comparisons of outcomes for new cohorts with outcomes achieved in the past. Success or failure will depend heavily on what happens within the affected departments, and we now conclude this chapter—and the book—by discussing more generally some of the recommendations for graduate programs that grow out of this study.

UNIVERSITY PROGRAMS

The healthy variety of graduate programs and curricula means that recommendations must allow a great deal of room for exceptions and the odd case. What works well in one context may be utterly inappropriate in another setting. The suggestions that follow are relevant mainly for programs in the humanities and related social sciences and are intended to stimulate further discussion.[23]

Program Size and Content

We are doubtful that there is any such thing as an optimal size for graduate programs. It seems clear, nonetheless, that programs can be too small to be effective, and the data presented in Chapter Four suggest that this is a serious issue. New PhD programs should be created only under the most unusual (and compelling) circumstances, and a strong case can be made for reexamining the justification for some existing programs.[24]

The evidence in Chapter Eight raises the related question of whether some programs also may have become too large. At the minimum, graduate programs and graduate deans should consider carefully how many graduate students can be taught properly. Apart from the quality of the pool of applicants, attention

---

evidence to date does not support that hypothesis. Portable fellowships have not led to the general "overhaul" of graduate education that Pelikan advocated. Leading departments have been able to attract recipients of such fellowships without making major changes in their programs. Information is imperfect, it is difficult for students to transfer if they are disappointed with their initial choice of graduate program, and the incentives to improve have not been strong enough.

[23]The general tenor of these recommendations has much in common with the proposals for *Institutional Policies to Improve Doctoral Education* presented by the Association of American Universities (AAU) and the Association of Graduate Schools (AGS) in a recent report (Association of American Universities 1990b). We take this as encouraging evidence that our thinking is not wildly at variance with the ideas of those with direct responsibility for particular graduate programs. The AAU-AGS report also indicates the seriousness with which this entire subject is viewed by the university community at large.

The recommendations in this section are based heavily on the discussion in Chapters Twelve and Thirteen. We will use cross-references only when evidence was presented in some other chapter.

[24]Lest anyone doubt the seriousness with which this suggestion is made, or suspect that it is made in ignorance of the potential consequences for deans and provosts, we note here the wounds incurred many years ago as a result of a decision to "suspend" a graduate program in Slavic languages and literatures at Princeton. The rationale for this decision is recorded in Bowen et al. (1972). We recall vividly the anguish caused by that decision and as a result are all the more aware of how hard it is (much too hard, we believe) to come to such conclusions.

must be paid to the limited amount of financial support available and the ability (and willingness) of faculty to supervise large numbers of students.

Program content is at least as sensitive a question as scale of program. It would be far too much to say that graduate curricula are largely an aggregation of what individual faculty members choose to teach, and when they choose to teach. Several programs we have examined are in fact very well constructed and monitored. However, it is not always clear that sufficient thought has been given to what would constitute comprehensive intellectual training for graduate students in the field in question. Indeed, some programs appear to be mainly the product of the intellectual inclinations of individual faculty members.

Active debates in recent years over intellectual directions within certain fields in the humanities and social sciences undoubtedly have complicated the task of shaping a curriculum. As new theoretical approaches and new topics or subject areas are explored, careful attention must be given to the structure of graduate curricula so that students are given not only opportunities to specialize, but also an introduction to their fields that has a significant degree of both coherence and comprehensiveness. Graduate students in fields with more settled methodologies and more constrained boundaries may find it easier to move steadily toward completion of the PhD than their counterparts in fields undergoing more rapid change.[25] Ferment that is intellectual and substantive is hardly to be discouraged, and graduate students should not be overly protected from it. But it should be recognized that their need for guidance may be even greater in such contexts.

There is also a more general point. While the argument for integrating faculty research interests and faculty teaching are stronger at the graduate level than at the undergraduate level, it is worth pondering whether there should be so close an interlock between these two activities as now seems to be the case. There are real arguments for considering the structure of a graduate curriculum as something that should have its own intellectual integrity, to which faculty should more willingly adapt when considering the assignment of teaching duties. Such an approach will not make departmental discussions easier, but it might be a healthy counterweight to patterns that conceive of the curriculum as growing principally out of the particular interests and points of view of individual faculty members.

Norms and Structure

Graduate programs of all sizes and orientations share a need for organizational clarity and well-understood expectations. Mistakes have been made in the past by advocating unrealistic norms for completion of the PhD and ignoring the issue of attrition altogether.

In the discussion that follows, we concentrate on factors that affect the pacing and continuity of graduate study, with an emphasis on reducing time-to-degree. While less is said about attrition, the two problems are so intertwined that steps taken to shorten the duration of graduate study should also increase the number

---

[25]Evidence to this effect is contained in a recent study of the social sciences in Britain, where it is reported: "Economists, psychologists and human geographers perhaps found a more ready coalescence of research interests around some limited themes or issues than did sociologists or political scientists" (Young, Fogarty, and McRae 1987, 35).

who finish. Separate mention should be made, however, of the need to confront directly the *timing* of attrition.

Early attrition is much to be preferred to late attrition, and the saddest, and most costly, experiences involve students who hang on and on, never to earn a doctorate. All interests are served by not delaying judgments concerning the fit between a student's interests and capabilities and the requirements of a particular doctoral program. A regularized system of evaluation, at known intervals, should reduce the large amount of late attrition, thereby lowering the costs of doctoral education and simultaneously sparing students the agonies and indignities of prolonged graduate study that simply trails off into other pursuits.

With regard to time-to-degree, we do not want to propose goals that will never be met. But norms are needed, and we are persuaded that there is merit in thinking in terms of a basic six-year program for the English, history, and political science (EHP) fields. Graduate students in such fields as economics, mathematics, and physics have shown that a shorter time period can work well, and a five-year norm would seem appropriate for them (four years in some situations).[26]

While there is nothing magical about a six-year plan for the humanities, we believe that such a model comes closest—in the light of our own research and other studies—to a norm that is realistic, potentially affordable, and consistent with educational results of high quality. Obviously, some students will complete their degrees in four or five years, and we have no interest in suggesting that such students delay their progress. Others (especially in language-intensive or interdisciplinary fields) may require up to seven years of study, and we have no desire to propose the imposition of mechanical deadlines that might impair qualitative results.

We do know, however, that virtually *all* the pressures at the doctoral level have a tendency to elongate doctoral study. Virtually every program and every discipline has quite legitimate concerns about special problems and difficulties that should be taken into account, and these concerns almost invariably lead to the conclusion that "an extra year or more is essential." There is no simple way to respond to, or refute, such concerns. They are genuine and grow out of a desire to help students, as well as to maintain high quality. But results obtained from the Ten-University database demonstrate that many excellent programs in a variety of fields and institutions have been able to manage six-year programs with real success, at a level of quality that is incontestable. Hence, it is reasonable to view with some skepticism proposals that argue for a different normative model.[27]

Some students will always take longer than others, and an occasional late finisher will be extraordinarily brilliant. Often, these are the anecdotal cases that are cited in defense of lengthy and highly flexible PhD programs. But *norms* for an entire system of graduate education should not be based on the unusual,

---

[26]The remainder of this discussion focuses mainly on the humanities and related social sciences, since it is in those fields that the twin problems of attrition and time-to-degree are most pronounced.

[27]The results obtained from our study of faculty promoted to tenure at a set of liberal arts colleges and universities provide strong support for this conclusion (Appendix E). Departments regularly promote to tenure young colleagues who finished their doctorates in fewer years than the norm for graduate students in the department recommending the promotion. This kind of evidence illustrates what economists sometimes call "revealed preference." It is the most powerful kind of evidence.

spectacular case. The right procedure, we believe, is not to modify the norm, but to ensure some degree of flexibility so that programs are capable of responding intelligently to truly special circumstances. Otherwise, the well-documented tendency for doctoral studies to be subject to considerable drift is likely to be reinforced.

To be effective, a norm of this kind must be based on an underlying structure that supports it. Without wanting to go into excessive detail, we suggest:

- Seeking ways to encourage students to begin to engage the reality of serious dissertation-related research during their first and second years, so that the transition from traditional course-work to intensive original research is less abrupt and paralyzing for many students.
- Designing the general (or qualifying) examination so that it retains substantial breadth, but also leads students to concentrate, in at least one component, on topics that are clearly related to the student's emerging special field and a potential dissertation topic.
- Discouraging students from postponing this examination, by making clear what is (and is not) required, and gearing funding incentives to the timely completion of this basic requirement.
- Seeking ways in which language (or other special) requirements can be fulfilled early in the process, so that students cannot—for example—register for their next phase of study until such requirements have been met.
- Establishing procedures that encourage students to make clear progress in defining thesis topics within stipulated time-frames. For example, it may be advisable to consider making the dissertation-prospectus a component of the general examination, with the requirement that it be completed no later than the autumn or winter of a student's third year of study.
- Helping students with summer grants or short-term funding during the early phase of dissertation work, so that necessary fieldwork, archival research, or other important preliminary tasks can be undertaken.
- Finding mechanisms that help students at the dissertation stage to maintain momentum. An initial draft of some portion of the thesis might be scheduled for submission within (for example) 12 months following the prospectus. Any such timetable is purely illustrative. The point is that unless the entire process of dissertation research and writing is given some clear structure and there is in place a set of guidelines that are consistently monitored and enforced, there is little prospect of responding adequately to the feeling of drift to which many students and faculty have testified.
- Facilitating a greater sense of collegiality as research and writing proceed. Dissertation workshops or colloquia can be helpful devices in structuring opportunities for students and faculty to meet together to discuss approaches to research, to the dissertation, and to the actual work-in-progress of individual students. Students in the colloquium can be scheduled to present reports on the current state of their research and to submit drafts of dissertation chapters for review and discussion by the group. The result can be a collaborative forum that is in some ways analogous to settings in the sciences that seem to work well.[28]

---

[28]There are important differences between mathematics and the sciences in this respect. The forthcoming report of the Committee on Doctoral and Postdoctoral Training in the Mathematical

- Formulating guidelines for the *completion* of the thesis. Consideration should be given to what benefits, privileges, and services can continue to be extended to graduate students who have not met such guidelines and who do not appear to be actively engaged with their work or in regular contact with advisers.

One last point about structure concerns the number of separate hurdles to be cleared. In general, it seems advisable to minimize the number of major hurdles, since each one creates new anxieties and new possibilities for postponement, and to be as clear as possible about the nature of each hurdle. A structure need not be complex to be effective.

Faculty Advising

Another critical element in the design of graduate programs is effective advising—which can itself be a major component of "structure." As mentioned in Chapter Thirteen, some programs have shifted from the concept of a single adviser to that of a small committee. Students may feel more comfortable with a group than with a single adviser. The faculty members who constitute the committee can reinforce one another's sense of responsibility to the student and to an ordered process—all of which may be more problematic if an individual faculty member and an individual graduate student are left entirely to themselves.

It would be difficult to overemphasize the need for regular, scheduled meetings between students and dissertation advisers (or committees) throughout the process, with clear expectations about a work schedule and a timetable for completion of drafts. Faculty must take the initiative in creating and managing this process or structure. Otherwise, many students will drift, or simply be lost.

Faculty advisers (and departments) also need to be more scrupulous in helping students who will not succeed to learn this hard fact sooner. Our interviews revealed more than a little embarrassment about such cases on the part of faculty, who either paid insufficient attention or simply lacked the heart to deliver a painful message at an earlier stage in the process.

Faculty members should be evaluated with respect to their performance as advisers (especially dissertation advisers). How many PhD candidates has a faculty member been advising? How long has each advisee been at work on the dissertation? How many dissertations have been completed, and how many are still incomplete after the passage of several years? How much hard evidence of progress is in hand? When was each advisee seen last? It is difficult to think of responsibilities that are more important than dissertation advising, and the case for careful, and sensitive, evaluation seems compelling.

Sciences (1992) discusses the problem of isolation in mathematics in much the same terms that the phenomenon is discussed in the humanities. The Committee recommends that efforts be made to cluster faculty in research areas, so that graduate students will be helped to form groups that function well both intellectually and socially.

The British study of the social sciences (Young, Fogarty, and McRae 1987, 35ff.) contains an even stronger endorsement of the importance of fostering "collegiality," or at least "aspirations to collegiality," through workshops. This study also stresses the importance of having both "reasonable numbers of graduate students and a clear sense of shared research interests."

The Form and Pacing of Financial Support

Whatever the structure of the program, however effective the advising, an adequate overall level of financial support is essential to achieving reasonably high completion rates and reasonably low time-to-degree. Institutions that are more affluent clearly have an advantage in this respect, and part (but clearly not all) of the higher completion rates and shorter time-to-degree achieved by the Smaller programs may be attributed to the fact that they also have had at their disposal greater financial-aid resources per student. The availability of financial support has to influence the goals that a program can set for itself. Excessive reliance on income from unrelated employment and a corresponding need to study part-time take an inevitable toll.

It is also true that the packaging, pacing, and precise allocation of financial aid resources can be as important—especially in a time of economic stringency—as the amount of aid available. There is a critical relationship between the components of program design discussed above and the specific ways in which scarce financial aid resources are distributed to students.

For example, multiyear guarantees of fellowship support (particularly when front-loaded) may be very effective in the competition to attract excellent graduate students at the time of admission. But if that approach means that students in general cannot expect to receive any (or only very little) fellowship assistance at a later point, or support to help with summer study, or assistance to undertake serious archival research or fieldwork in the early stages of the dissertation, or cannot expect to receive dissertation-completion grants—then one may have inadvertently created a system in which candidates are given sufficient incentives to *begin* doctoral work, but far too little means to complete the program.[29]

There is much to be said for basing financial aid awards, after the first year of graduate study, on careful reviews of performance. More generally, the allocation of financial aid funds should be related to the particular educational rhythm of the program. For example, students might be eligible for early dissertation-research awards for preliminary archival or fieldwork exploration, but only on the basis of a well-prepared and approved proposal, submitted within a specified time-period (that is, during the third year of residence, and no later than the autumn of the fourth year). Students could be declared eligible to apply for dissertation-completion grants only if they were in a position to submit for review a draft of some substantial portion of the thesis, together with a plausible work-plan for its completion. Such applications might be submitted no later than the spring of the fifth year, and funds might only be awarded to those students judged to be in a position to finish no later (for instance) than the summer following the sixth year.

Guidelines obviously need to vary by program and university, but certain general principles apply broadly. Different forms of aid would be designed to

---

[29]This is a specific example of situations in which the apparent advantages of greater competition among educational institutions may have perverse effects when an assessment of final results is made. A more widely publicized example is the recent decision by the Justice Department that apparently prevents the continuation of collaborative efforts to base financial aid at the undergraduate level solely on need; see the commentary by Paul Gray, chairman of the Massachusetts Institute of Technology (*New York Times*, July 22, 1991, A15).

help students at specified moments in their studies. Clear timetables for applications would be established, perhaps based on an approximate six-year path to the PhD. Such timetables would serve as a healthy incentive for students and faculty alike to work in a purposeful way on realistic projects. Moreover, even if only a portion of students won competitive awards, the availability of the awards, and the competitive process itself, could have a positive effect on the way in which all students approached the dissertation.

Teaching assistantships should be an integral part of graduate training—as well as one source of financial support. It is highly desirable, in our view, for students to gain teaching experience under good supervision. But it is just as important that students be limited in the amount of teaching they are permitted to do. Ideally, two years of part-time teaching might be the norm, with three years an absolute limit. Initial encounters with teaching, and with eager and appreciative students, can be very rewarding for graduate students and can reinforce commitments to graduate study and an academic career. But teaching can also be highly seductive. Students can use teaching responsibilities as an excuse for not getting on with the hard, more solitary tasks of defining and completing a dissertation, and a certain amount of institutional protection against easy temptations may be required.

Monitoring, Reporting, and Accountability

Graduate programs stand in need of self-conscious self-evaluation on a continuous basis. It might well be a wise investment to expect one person in each program of any significant size to keep track of the progress of every graduate student (including meetings with advisers, requirements fulfilled, extent and type of financial aid awarded, and number of terms in service as a teaching assistant). Longitudinal records of this kind, updated every academic term, would allow faculty, directors of graduate studies, and deans to know how students are faring, and would enable programs to monitor attrition rates, time-to-degree, and relevant aspects of faculty performance. If results were seen to be unsatisfactory, programs could take stock and make adjustments more expeditiously than at present. Difficult as this process may be, especially when budgets are tight and there is little logistical support, faculty simply must be in a position to know what happens to graduate students entrusted to the care of a program or department.[30]

A related need is for renewed attention to the accuracy and adequacy of materials routinely made available to candidates for admission. In the 1960s, it was not unusual for graduate catalogs to list precisely what courses would be given in the forthcoming year, and by which faculty member. Also, some indication was often given of which faculty members would be on leave. These catalogs were generally written in a clear expository style, and the format was such that an interested student was guided by both the lucidity of the presentation and explicit detail.

---

[30]The universities participating in the Mellon Foundation program of institutional support outlined above have agreed on the characteristics of a record-keeping system that will permit these kinds of analyses to be made within individual institutions and (on a comparable basis) across departments, institutions, and time periods.

Today, many catalogs consist of a minimum of prose, a long list of numbered course-titles without description, many entries that state "instructor to be announced," and no indication of which faculty members will be on leave, or when, or for how long. To a student attempting to choose and plan intelligently, it is important to know which courses are likely to be offered and whether faculty in whom the student has a strong interest are likely to be at the university during the student's terms of residence. Granted that forward planning (and the timing of sabbaticals) is more difficult now than in the 1960s, it seems reasonable to expect departments to design at least a two-year plan that would be tolerably comprehensive.[31]

A more ambitious proposal would involve regular publication of the norms established by each graduate program for time-to-degree as part of a broader effort to increase the amount of relevant information available to doctoral candidates. Publication of such norms might be accompanied by recent statistics concerning the program's actual performance with respect to time-to-degree and attrition. Recent recommendations on institutional policy published by the AAU and the Association of Graduate Schools are consonant with these suggestions and are stated in even firmer tones: "Departments should . . . gather and make available data on actual performance and should adopt procedures to bring actual and expected standards into accord; if a program's announced time-to-degree is four years and the actual lapsed time is seven years, the program has created false advertising that undermines student performance and faculty expectations."[32]

There is a perverse similarity between proposals for greater disclosure of outcomes for graduate students and proposals for greater disclosure of graduation rates for undergraduate athletes in revenue-producing sports in American universities.[33] While the prototypical PhD candidate might be thought to have little in common with the 260-pound nose-tackle, those concerned about the welfare of each group assume that: (1) better information concerning normal outcomes should enable prospective athletes and prospective graduate students to make more informed choices of schools to attend, and (2) the need to produce such data, and make them publicly available, could stimulate greater efforts by universities to improve both graduation rates and the completion of dissertations.

Time-Limited Doctorates: A British Proposal

At the conclusion of a study of ways to improve doctoral education in the social sciences in Britain (with special attention given to the need to increase the

---

[31]A good deal of information that previously appeared in catalogs can now be obtained directly from programs by candidates who are applying for admission. Some of these materials are very thorough, but they can also be too limited in their coverage. For example, as some fields become more cross-disciplinary, students may need comprehensive information about cognate programs in other departments.

[32]Association of American Universities 1990b, 16. An OECD (1989) study reports the imposition of a requirement in the United Kingdom that "the Research Councils publish regularly statistics by university showing the proportions of the students they support who submit their dissertations within four years" (p. 50).

[33]The National Collegiate Athletic Association first required institutions to report completion rates for students in athletic programs in 1990. This commitment was subsequently reaffirmed by the Knight Commission Report (*Chronicle of Higher Education*, March 27, 1991, A33 and A36).

number of graduate students who submit doctoral theses within a specified number of years), the authors propose the establishment of a new option for graduate students: enrollment in a doctoral program of *time-limited* study.[34] It is recognized that there is a wide diversity of expectations among faculty concerning the dissertation, and no one can imagine that these differences will be resolved readily. But perhaps there is merit, it is argued, in testing the quality of dissertations produced by doctoral candidates who elect to participate in programs designed explicitly to require that doctorates be completed within some set number of years.

Faculty in some fields of study might have more confidence in the value of such an experiment than faculty in other fields, and it should be remembered that these authors were assessing the social sciences, not the humanities. There is no need, in any case, to be doctrinaire in approaching this question. But perhaps our British colleagues are correct in suggesting that in at least some fields, good scholarship (and good training) would be obtained under such constraints. The assessment of results would have to depend on time-to-degree (which would be appreciably shorter by dint of program specification), on completion rates (which should be higher), and on whether the quality of the research represented by the dissertation convinced others that the student deserved what the authors of this proposal call *parity of esteem*.

This proposal is not without analogues. It is reminiscent of the seemingly harsh norms for completion of the PhD enunciated by determined deans in the past and of regulations promulgated at some universities more recently that deny continuing registration to students who fail to earn doctorates within a prescribed time frame. The idea of a time-limited doctorate is very different, however, from recurring suggestions that separate doctorates be established for individuals who see themselves as potential teachers but not as potential scholars.[35]

We have no convincing ideas as to how an experiment with a time-limited doctoral program might be launched (including how strong candidates and leading departments might be induced to participate), and we continue to be skeptical about the viability of any two-track proposal. Perhaps this proposal is best regarded as an alternative to ponder if other efforts to improve outcomes fail.

We realize that many of the suggestions made above may seem unduly regimental and insensitive to the problems of individual students and the circumstances of particular programs. We would regret any such interpretation and would be unhappy if our intentions were misread. We start from the proposition that quality of accomplishment matters more than anything else. But we also have come to recognize that graduate education is costly in human

---

[34]Young, Fogarty, and McRae 1987, 61ff. A four-year limit is suggested, but of course this must be understood in the context of the British system of doctoral education, which involves much less course work than the U.S. system. Also, British graduate programs build on a higher degree of specialization at the BA level than U.S. programs.

[35]For commentaries on this long-running debate, see Berelson (1960, 44–92, 248–51), and a subsequent Carnegie Council study (Dressel and Thompson 1977). In a recent publication focused on faculty scholarship, Ernest Boyer restates reasons for opposing the Doctor of Arts degree (Boyer 1990, especially pp. 68ff.).

terms—in years and years of study, which result too often in dashed hopes and deep resentments formed "in pursuit of the PhD." It is surely possible to develop arrangements whereby entering cohorts of students in the EHP fields do not have to invest (collectively) 10 to 15 student years for every doctorate earned. Graduate education consumes very scarce institutional resources, and we do not believe that faculty or students engaged in the process would want to exempt it from sensible scrutiny based on evidence of results achieved.

It is clear that some graduate programs have operated far more effectively than others, thereby demonstrating that it is possible to achieve appreciably better outcomes without sacrificing either a legitimate concern for individual students or an overriding commitment to high quality. Also encouraging is the clear interest of many faculty members and administrators in addressing what they recognize to be long-standing problems. Leadership must come from within the universities, but faculty members and deans will need help—more flexible resources for student aid than have been available in recent years and strong institutional support for policies and procedures that will inevitably arouse opposition.

The potential rewards are very great. The low completion rates and long time-to-degree that often prevail now mean that even modest improvements would increase markedly the number of recipients of doctorates. In our view, working to improve the effectiveness of current programs is by far the most sensible way to begin to prepare for the faculty staffing problems that are anticipated by the end of the decade. In many situations, a combination of increased external support and strong internal efforts to improve program design and program management should make it possible to achieve substantial increases in the number of doctorates conferred without significant increases in the sizes of entering cohorts.

Visible improvements in outcomes can also be expected to have other positive effects, including making graduate study more attractive to the most able undergraduates and more satisfying to those already pursuing the PhD. While the lot of many graduate students will never be an entirely cheerful one, clearer paths can be provided and many irritants can be removed. Travails notwithstanding, graduate education can be enormously rewarding to students as well as of great value to the society. It is, at its best, an exhilarating enterprise.

The Ten-University Data Set

FOR REASONS explained in Chapter One, we undertook to collect detailed data on cohorts of entering students from ten individual universities. A principal objective was to permit careful analysis of completion rates and time-to-degree, with individual students classified by field of study, university, and year of entry. We were interested not only in calculating overall completion rates and time-to-degree, but also in measuring attrition and time spent at specific stages of graduate study. Also, we wanted to be able to relate these outcomes of graduate study to other variables such as gender, form of financial support, and (where possible) measures of the perceived quality of students.

DATA AND PROCEDURES

While our data vary somewhat by institution because of differences in record-keeping, degree requirements, and definitions of variables, the collection and coding of the data were standardized to a considerable extent by employing a single coding scheme, which was developed after close consultation with representatives of the participating universities. The standard format used in collecting data is reproduced at the end of this appendix. In addition, each university was asked to send a narrative describing specific assumptions that had been made in the process of assembling data. Also, one of our collaborators, Julie Ann Sosa, took special responsibility for working directly with the individuals at the participating universities who were collecting data so that we could provide consistent answers to frequently asked questions.

Universities Included

The ten universities that provided data were: the University of California at Berkeley (Berkeley), the University of Chicago (Chicago), Columbia University, Cornell University, Harvard University, the University of Michigan at Ann Arbor (Michigan), Princeton University, Stanford University, the University of North Carolina at Chapel Hill (UNC), and Yale University.

Fields of Study

Data were collected for six specific fields of study: English, history, economics, political science, mathematics, and physics/astronomy. In the main, fields of study were defined quite consistently across universities, but there were some (relatively minor) differences in definitions of boundaries, which are noted in the following comments on individual university data sets. Our general practice was to adopt whatever definitions of field were customary at the university in question.

Definition of Entering Cohorts

Entering cohorts comprise all entering PhD candidates who started graduate study in the given calendar year; since most students enrolled initially in the fall of the year, this means that data for, say, 1972, generally refer to students who began graduate study in the academic year 1972–73. (Some institutions indicated the precise month in which students enrolled.)

Distinguishing PhD candidates from students who entered graduate school intending only to earn a master's degree was a particularly vexing problem. Obviously, the latter group should not be counted as having failed to complete programs simply because they did not earn a PhD—which, after all, had never been their goal.[1] Our objective was to include in the Ten-University data set only presumptive PhD candidates, and our approach was to ask each graduate school to make this determination as best it could. The universities were asked to send records only for those entering students who were regarded at the time of entry as interested in obtaining a PhD, even though it was understood that in certain programs students would formally become candidates for the PhD only after satisfying certain requirements (including, in some cases, receipt of the MA).

Fortunately, this problem of distinguishing MA-only candidates from likely PhD candidates did not exist in the majority of programs included in this study, since most of these programs either admit only PhD candidates or distinguish at admission those on the MA track from those on the PhD track. Some ambiguities were never resolved satisfactorily (see, for instance, the discussion below of students in English at Chicago), but most universities that had this problem, such as Columbia, seem to have been successful in segregating the records of those entering students who were interested from the beginning in obtaining the PhD.

Treatment of Transfers

In general, the data set includes students who transferred into our six fields of study from either another university or from another graduate program at the same institution. Some of these students arrived with MAs (in either the field of the PhD or a different field), and some with no advanced degrees. As the data format indicates, we tried to obtain such information when it was available. For these transfers, the year of entry to graduate school was defined as the year in which they began graduate study in the PhD field.

In calculating completion rates (and, therefore, attrition), students were treated as noncompleters if they failed to obtain a PhD at the university in question and in their PhD field by 1988 (in a very few cases, the spring of 1989). Thus, completion rates based on the Ten-University data set understate system-wide completion rates in that they do not allow for the fact that some students who dropped out of the programs examined here subsequently earned doctorates at other institutions, either in the same field of study or in a different field.

---

[1]Breneman (1970, 7ff.) was very aware of this problem. He wrote: "Since we are examining only PhD degree programs, we need to exclude terminal MA enrollments from our data. However, the two programs are often so thoroughly integrated that they cannot be meaningfully separated. In some departments, all students, regardless of terminal degree aspiration, are required to enroll initially in the MA program. . . . Finally, some students really may not know which degree they will ultimately want when first enrolling, while in some circumstances students may have reason to disguise their true intentions. . . . Thus, the quest for a 'true' enrollment series that includes all PhD candidates and excludes terminal MA candidates is hopeless; in order to proceed, intelligent compromises must be made." Breneman may have been especially sensitized to this problem because he was working solely with data for Berkeley, where it can be especially difficult to distinguish the two groups of students.

Also, some students known to have dropped out may ultimately return to complete their degrees; "attrition" is not necessarily a permanent state.

Some of the students who left one of the graduate programs included in the Ten-University data set may even reappear in the data set (and be recorded for a second time as an entering student) if they transferred to another institution within the Ten-University group. We were unable to track such students across institutions and had simply to record them as not having completed the program in which they enrolled initially. (For some special exceptions to our general rules regarding transfers, see the sections on Berkeley, Harvard, and Yale in the discussion of individual university data sets.) In the case of the National Fellowship data set (described in Appendix B), we were able to take account of transfers in calculating completion rates.

Stages of Graduate Study

In the interest of facilitating study of attrition at various stages along the path toward the PhD, we asked a number of questions concerning the status of students and their success in passing various hurdles within specified periods of time. Specifically, we asked universities to tell us whether entering students enrolled in a second year of graduate study, and how long it took students to attain ABD status. The second-year question proved to be somewhat problematic for Berkeley and UNC, where some students who received the PhD and some who achieved ABD status were reported to have not enrolled in the second year. To correct such anomalies, we changed the response to the second-year question.

If students were reported to have reached the ABD stage (recognizing that this milestone is defined differently in different fields of study within the same university, as well as in different universities), we asked the universities for the year in which the students were advanced to candidacy. Data about such critically important hurdles were difficult to collect, but we obtained reasonably reliable information from six schools: Berkeley, Chicago, Cornell, Princeton, UNC, and Yale. If information was missing on status by stage of study, we included the other data that were available in our calculation of basic completion rates and time-to-degree. The data on attrition and time spent by stage of graduate study were critical in permitting the calculation of the measure of student-year cost of obtaining a PhD (described in Chapter Nine). Information of this kind on progress toward the PhD by defined stages of graduate study is one of the special features of this data set.

Financial Support

A considerable effort was made to collect information concerning the broad types of financial support provided at various stages of graduate study, with special attention paid to fellowships and teaching assistantships. Students were coded as having received "significant" fellowship support if they received an award that paid for more than half of the estimated cost of tuition, room, and board. Our summary question about the student's primary form of support (over the first six years of graduate study, since that is when the data are most reliable) proved to be the most difficult for the institutions to answer. Schools generally used their own judgment or very simple calculations to arrive at a response.

Merit

We asked, separately, for students' scores on the verbal and math sections of the GRE. These data were difficult to collect, were generally available only for subsets of students, and often were available for only the most recent cohorts. In some instances, percentiles alone were recorded, in which case we calculated scale scores, using conversion tables from the Educational Testing Services in Princeton, New Jersey. We did not analyze the GRE scores in fine detail; rather, we compared the outcomes of students with scores of 700 or above to those of students with scores below 700. To get at issues pertaining to student quality, we also asked for departmental rankings of students at the time of their admission, and we asked whether the student held an honorific fellowship during the dissertation phase of study.

Time Period Covered

Each institution was asked to provide, if possible, data going back to the 1962 entering cohort and extending through the 1986 entering cohort. To obtain large enough cell sizes to permit certain kinds of comparisons, we aggregated some of the data by five-year cohorts (1962–1966, 1967–1971, 1972–1976, 1977–1981, and 1982–1986). In other parts of the analysis, we constructed time series based on data for individual years.

The decision to seek data over such a long time period was based on our general interest in studying trends and on our more specific interest in examining relationships between outcomes and shifting conditions in academic labor markets, as well as changes over time in the relationship between outcomes and the availability of funding for graduate study, gender, and other variables. Also, the long duration of graduate study argues strongly for collecting data over as long a period as possible.

Berkeley, Cornell, and Chicago are the three universities that were most successful in providing data going back to the 1962 cohort. It was difficult for a number of universities to provide as much historical data as would have been desirable, and some were able to provide demographic information (including data on outcomes) but not data on financial aid for certain years. Table A.1 indicates the coverage of the Ten-University data set by institution and by time period.

Consistency of Data

An extensive set of diagnostics and frequency checks allowed us to identify some inconsistencies in the data. We adopted a series of assumptions to ensure that ambiguous cases and observations with missing information would be excluded from the system file used for the analysis. Cases in which the institution lacked information concerning the gender of the student were included in the totals, even though they could not be included in the separate tabulations shown for men and women. Since we focused our analysis on U.S. citizens and permanent residents, we excluded from the main part of the analysis non-U.S. residents and observations lacking citizenship information.

We also excluded from our analysis observations with numbers for time-to-degree, or for components of time-to-degree, that were implausible. More specifically, we excluded records when time-to-degree was a negative number,

TABLE A.1
Coverage of Ten-University Data Set by Institution and Cohort

Institution	Cohorts				
	1962–1966	1967–1971	1972–1976	1977–1981	1982–1986
Demographic					
Berkeley	x	x	x	x	x
Chicago	x	x	x	x	x
Columbia		x	x	x	x
Cornell	x	x	x	x	x
Harvard		x	x	x	x
Michigan			x	x	x
Princeton		x	x	x	x
Stanford	x	x	x	x	x
UNC		x	x	x	x
Yale			x	x	x
Financial					
Berkeley				x	x
Chicago	x	x	x	x	x
Columbia		x	x	x	x
Cornell	x	x	x	x	x
Harvard					
Michigan				x	x
Princeton		x	x	x	x
Stanford				x	x
UNC		x	x	x	x
Yale			x	x	
Merit					
Berkeley					
Chicago	x	x	x	x	x
Columbia		x	x	x	x
Cornell	x	x	x	x	x
Harvard					
Michigan					
Princeton		x	x	x	x
Stanford					x
UNC					
Yale			x	x	

Notes: Demographic and financial data for UNC begin in 1968, not 1967. Financial data for Berkeley begin in 1978, not 1977. Financial data for Michigan begin in 1978, not 1977. For all schools except Cornell, data on the perceived "merits" of students are said to exist when GRE scores are reported.

when time-to-degree was less than two years, and when time from entry to graduate school to ABD status was less than one year.

Taken together, these assumptions excluded approximately 5,000 records (roughly 12 percent of all observations originally submitted) from the raw data file.

Institutional Data Collection

One institution, Berkeley, found the data collection task relatively simple because their data were already in machine-readable form. Others found the task more formidable; Columbia, for example, first had to find individual student folders (most of which were scattered in the basements of different departments), then had to create a computer database, and finally had to keypunch all of the information. A recurring problem was that certain information was available in one office (say, the registrar's office), and other data were in other offices (such as departmental offices or the office of the graduate dean). The desirability of centralized control over graduate school records is one indisputable lesson of this entire project. It took approximately one year to collect all of the data and assemble the approximately 41,000 individual records ✓ originally submitted (of which 35,671 were eventually used) that make up our Ten-University data set.

Code numbers were assigned by universities to individual student records, and our staff cleaned and analyzed the data in that form. Anonymity of individuals was protected. Idiosyncrasies in the data for each institution are described below.

INDIVIDUAL UNIVERSITY DATA SETS

Berkeley

The graduate school at Berkeley has been concerned about the progress of its graduate students for some time. As a result, its extensive data set is in machine-readable form, and producing the information that was required for our analysis of demographics was relatively straightforward. Berkeley was able to provide complete demographic data, including the information on stages of graduate study required for the calculation of the student-year cost of a PhD, going back as far as 1962. Berkeley provided us with reliable information for 9,224 student records.

Information about financial support and merit was not in machine-readable form, however, and it had to be keypunched from the individual folders of students kept by departments. It was feasible to collect these data only for the 1978–1981 entering cohorts.

DEMOGRAPHICS
The field of study breakdowns are slightly broader at Berkeley than at other universities: English includes comparative literature; economics includes agricultural and research economics; mathematics includes applied mathematics; and physics includes astronomy. Also, completion rates indicate whether students who were registered at any time in any of our six fields of study received a PhD from Berkeley in one of these six fields. In other words, the completion rates include students who transferred within Berkeley within our six fields. For this reason, reported completion rates at Berkeley may be slightly higher, other things equal, than at other universities.

Berkeley provided attrition data by stage of graduate study. The second-year question was interpreted as asking if the student enrolled in a second year of graduate study in the second calendar year after entry; when we found inconsistencies that occurred because people who went on to receive PhDs or achieve ABD status took a year off, we corrected the response. Students are admitted to candidacy at Berkeley when they pass their qualifying exams. This was used as a proxy for ABD status. Students were considered to be working toward ABD status—and not treated as dropouts—if they were registered within the last two years.

FINANCIAL SUPPORT

Students were considered to have received fellowship support if they held a fellowship for at least two semesters during their first two years or if they held a fellowship at any time during the dissertation stage of their studies. A full teaching assistantship (TA) was considered to be at least one half-time appointment before admission to candidacy and at least two half-time appointments thereafter.

MERIT

Departmental rankings were unavailable, and GRE scores were incomplete.

Chicago

The data collection effort at Chicago began in the registrar's office, which maintains a database containing basic demographic information about all students. It is believed to be very reliable for entering cohorts after 1970, and a good starting point for entering cohorts from the 1960s onward.

To supplement this information, it was necessary to coordinate the efforts of several deans and the registrar, and to search actual student files, transcripts, and annual matriculation lists kept at the departmental level. The data for physics were believed to pose some special difficulties, because that department was unable to fill in gaps in the registrar's database. An even more serious problem affected mathematics, since a fire had eradicated essential data. The fragmentary data remaining could not be evaluated, and we decided against presenting any data for mathematics at Chicago. All of these problems notwithstanding, Chicago provided 6,073 usable observations, beginning with the 1962 entering cohort.

DEMOGRAPHICS

The problem of distinguishing master's candidates from PhD candidates was particularly intractable at Chicago in English, where the norm has been to admit all students to a master's program. To avoid inadvertently including master's students among entering PhD candidates, a decision was made to include only students who completed the master's phase of the program and were then admitted to the PhD program. For this reason, early attrition in this department may be understated and eventual completion rates somewhat overstated, as compared with what they would have been had it been possible to distinguish master's and PhD candidates more precisely.

The ABD stage at Chicago is defined as admission to candidacy, which occurs when a dissertation proposal is accepted. When data for year of admission to candidacy were missing, normal patterns within the department were used to estimate the date. For example, in 85 percent of cases in economics, admission to candidacy occurred in either the same year or the year prior to the awarding of the PhD.

FINANCIAL SUPPORT

Some of this information was missing, particularly in the early cohorts. If students reported any fellowship assistance during the first two years, they were reported as having had significant support. If support during the dissertation stage was obtained, it was assumed to have been based on merit. Until recently, there have not been significant opportunities for graduate students in the humanities and social sciences to receive TAs at Chicago, so when data were missing from the records, Chicago routinely responded negatively to the TA question in the four relevant fields of study.

MERIT

GRE scores were unavailable until the early 1980s.

Columbia

Columbia had perhaps the most difficult data-gathering task. The number of records in its data set was the second largest; yet it had to start from the beginning (essentially) and assemble a database from individual student files. It had to rely on a number of different sources and data collection methods. Student admission folders, stored for decades in the basement of Low Library, identified the population under study. These numbers were checked against computerized records kept by the registrar going back to 1965. All financial aid information except for two years was entered by hand from the graduate school records. After all corrections were made, 5,494 student records from Columbia were used in this analysis.

DEMOGRAPHICS

Data were provided for entering cohorts starting in 1962, but because of various problems we used data beginning in 1967. The number of entrants for the 1970–1974 cohorts classified as U.S. residents had to be modified because nearly half of the observations for these years lacked citizenship information. We addressed this problem by estimating percentages based on citizenship data from the neighboring cohorts, and then distributing the unclassified observations accordingly.

Columbia was unable to provide reliable attrition data by stage of graduate study. Consequently, no student-year cost calculations were made for Columbia.

FINANCIAL SUPPORT

No financial aid data were available prior to 1970. Since only a relatively small proportion of students at Columbia receive fellowship support, students who received any fellowship support were coded as having received significant support. To be classified as a teaching assistant, a student was required to have taught a class or discussion section; responsibility for grading and reading papers was not counted.

MERIT

The GRE was not required for admission before 1970, and a number of students are still admitted without GRE scores, so this component of the data set is incomplete.

Cornell

Cornell does not have a central database, but it does have a graduate dean who has kept a meticulous record of all graduate students by hand, in binders, over a long tenure. Her data were supplemented by financial support data kept separately, in "the orchard." As a result, once the Cornell numbers were entered into a computer, they were very clean. The Cornell data set—particularly for demographic information—is complete and extremely reliable. Cornell supplied 3,143 usable records, starting with the 1962 cohort.

DEMOGRAPHICS
Cornell provided us with detailed data for attrition by stages of graduate study, and is one of the main sources of data used in making calculations of the student-year cost of a PhD for all cohorts. The ABD stage at Cornell was defined as admission to candidacy, which occurs when the student passes qualifying exam "A."

FINANCIAL SUPPORT
Cornell provided reliable data for all cohorts. When it was difficult to answer the question concerning the primary source of support, the following assumptions were made: For the 1962–1975 entering cohorts, whenever a student was supported the same number of years by TAs and fellowships, the student was classified as a teaching assistant, since most fellowship holders taught part-time; for the 1976–1989 entering cohorts, whenever a student was supported the same number of years by TAs and fellowships, the student was coded as a fellowship holder because most teaching assistants had summer fellowships.

MERIT
Only limited numbers of GRE scores were available. Departmental rankings and information concerning honorific dissertation fellowships were entirely unavailable. Cornell subsequently supplied information on applicant pools and numbers of matriculants, which were combined with GRE data in the analysis of student quality (see Chapter Ten).

Harvard

There is no central database at Harvard, and data collection for this project required that we use a variety of sources, starting with departmental dockets kept by the admissions and financial aid offices and then supplementing these with alumni/ae records, commencement programs, and sources at the registrar's office. The master list of students was then checked with the individual departments, and modifications were made. There were 1,911 usable records from Harvard for entering cohorts beginning in 1967.

DEMOGRAPHICS
Harvard provided reliable data from which it was possible to calculate completion rates and registered time-to-degree (RTD), rather than elapsed time-to-degree (ETD) (see Chapter Six for definitions of these terms). Since the year of entry was unknown for students in the earliest entering cohorts, it had to be calculated by subtracting a "G-year" number (which represents the

number of years a student was registered) from the year of PhD or the last year of candidacy. While Harvard's time-to-degree measurements are slightly lower than they would have been if regular data on ETD had been available, the difference can be assumed to be small.

Also, students who transferred into any of our six fields of study from other fields of study at Harvard were excluded from the database; they are believed to represent about 2 percent of the total. At Harvard, history excludes American civilization, and economics excludes decision sciences and business economics, two programs run in conjunction with the Harvard Business School.

Harvard was unable to provide reliable data for attrition by stage of graduate study.

FINANCIAL SUPPORT AND MERIT
These data were unavailable.

Michigan

In order to identify the students to be included in this study, Michigan worked from a variety of sources, including its computerized Student Characteristics Database, graduate school admission files, "active" student files, degree files, "purged" record files, and data prepared annually for the NRC's Doctorate Records File. Fellowship and graduate assistantship data were added later. Reliable information was provided for 2,266 students, starting with the 1972 entering cohort.

FINANCIAL SUPPORT
Reliable data are available from 1978. A full TA was defined as the student's holding at least a 25 percent appointment. Since the graduate school keeps a record only of fall/winter appointments (TAs held from May to August are not included in the data set), and since "combined" appointments (which include TAs, research assistantships, and/or staff assistantships) could not be disaggregated, the number of TAs is understated. In order to answer the question on the primary source of support, the graduate school used a total cost variable based on its own research. If "own support" covered more than half of total expenses, it was designated as the primary source of support. Otherwise, the largest single component (fellowship, research assistantship, or TA) of the outside support was reported to be the primary source of support.

MERIT
Only partial data on GRE scores were available. Departmental ranking at time of admission was not available for any cohort. Michigan does not keep a record of honorific fellowships awarded to its graduate students by outside organizations, but it was able to report whether the student won one of the graduate school's own predoctoral fellowships.

Princeton

Princeton's central database is well ordered and complete, but not computerized. It consists of a set of looseleaf notebooks kept by the graduate school, which contain most of the demographic and financial aid information for all entering graduate students. Students' names are organized alphabetically by cohort within departments, and their progress through graduate study can be traced across rows in the binders. Rank at time of admission is the only piece of information kept separately. Princeton provided usable records for 2,146 students who entered the graduate school in our six fields starting in 1967.

DEMOGRAPHICS

Among all of the universities included in this data set, Princeton has had the strictest limitation on the number of years that a student may be registered. Status as an enrolled student officially lapses after four or five years of enrollment, and students are officially considered inactive after seven years. As a result, decisions about whether students were still pursuing the PhD after this number of years had to be made on an individual basis in consultation with the respective departments. Princeton assumed that the student had dropped out if 10 years had elapsed after entry to graduate school and there was no additional information from the department. In contrast to the convention followed by most universities, students who transferred from their original field to another PhD program at Princeton, even if it was outside the six fields, were retained in the data set. A very small number of students fell into this category.

Princeton provided data on attrition by stage of graduate study for nearly all students. The ABD stage was considered to be reached when the student passed the General Examination.

FINANCIAL SUPPORT

Significant fellowship support was defined as support that covered at least the cost of tuition. Since few students at Princeton hold a full TA for more than one term, a full TA was defined as at least six contact hours of teaching in one semester. The question on the primary source of support was, again, difficult, and Princeton often assumed that the general pattern of responses applied in cases where information was missing. Since teaching assistants rarely held full TAs, the primary source of support for most students in the humanities and social sciences was fellowships, and for students in the sciences, it was teaching or research assistantships or outside fellowships.

MERIT

There are no GRE scores available for students in the 1967–1971 entering cohort, but there are reliable GRE scores for the later cohorts. Information about departmental rank at time of admission was provided.

Stanford

Stanford assembled data from a variety of sources. Data prior to 1980 came from the central computer file and from the files of the Office of Graduate Studies. Several departments provided supplementary information from departmental files for the earliest years. As a result, data collection begins with 1962 for English, history, and physics; data for the other three fields begins in 1967. For the most recent cohorts, information came entirely from the central student computer file. When student names were missing from the computer file, they were checked by the registrar's office by use of transcripts. Stanford provided 2,927 usable student records.

DEMOGRAPHICS
We were unable to obtain reliable data for attrition by stage of graduate study at Stanford.

FINANCIAL SUPPORT
Data are available only from 1972. The central computer file does not contain information about loans.

MERIT
Reliable data on merit are available only from 1972. Data on departmental ranking at time of admission are not available, and approximately half of the GRE scores are missing for the 1977–1981 cohort.

University of North Carolina

UNC has a computerized database in the registrar's office which contains information about fields of study, gender, citizenship, year of entry, enrollment/ PhD award status, and, in most cases, GRE scores. However, it was necessary to go back to the actual student folders kept by individual departments and to financial aid office records to collect information about attrition by stages of graduate study and financial support. Records kept by the English, history, and economics departments were the most reliable; in contrast, information for the political science department was the most disorganized. UNC provided 1,836 records for cohorts from 1968 to 1986.

DEMOGRAPHICS
UNC was able to provide data by stage of graduate study. Students who entered the MA/PhD program were not considered to be enrolled in the second year in the PhD program until after they had received the MA; we corrected internal assumptions of this kind when they were inconsistent with the approach followed by the other institutions included in the Ten-University database. The ABD stage at UNC is reached when the student has passed a written exam, passed a preliminary oral exam, and satisfied any foreign language requirements for the PhD. It should be noted that in some departments considerable progress is made on the dissertation before the ABD requirements are fulfilled. In mathematics, for example, completion of the language requirement is often delayed until weeks or even days before the PhD is completed. When there was missing information, the date at which the student applied for PhD candidacy was used as a proxy.

FINANCIAL SUPPORT
Financial aid awards were coded as fellowships if they required no service at all by the student in return for the award. Full TAs were defined as quarter-time positions that required the assistant to work 10 hours per week and paid more than half of the estimated annual cost of a year of graduate study (see the

discussion in the first part of this appendix for the definition of "significant" support). A few graduate assistantships and research assistantships were included with the TAs if they fulfilled the criteria stated above. In our six fields of study, UNC students are generally not allowed to be teaching assistants for more than 10 semesters.

MERIT

Data on departmental ranking at time of admission were not available. Some GRE scores were available.

Yale

While information was available in machine-readable form in the registrar's office at Yale, it was difficult to assemble this information because students appear (and reappear) for every year in which they are enrolled. The actual student folders for the names on the list had to be obtained from the archives. Final transcripts and financial aid cards also had to be collected separately for every student on the registrar's list.

It was impossible in a few cases to find all of the records; in others, the only existing information was the final transcript. In the end, Yale provided 651 records, beginning with the 1972 cohort. However, these data cover students in only three of our six fields of study: English, history, and political science.

DEMOGRAPHICS

English does not include American literature, and in a few cases includes students who were enrolled jointly in a JD program at Yale. When students transferred from relevant programs in the arts and sciences into one of the three fields reported, the year of entry was coded as the year of transfer, rather than the year of initial entry to graduate study at Yale. Since this underestimates time-to-degree as measured at the other universities, we also collected data showing how many years of work before this starting date were accepted as credits toward the Yale PhD, and then modified the records accordingly.

Yale was able to provide data by stage of graduate study. The ABD stage at Yale is reached when the dissertation prospectus is formally accepted by the department; thus, students were coded as having reached the ABD stage if there was a prospectus title and date of submission on record. This is a more rigorous criterion than those used by most other graduate programs, and therefore the ABD stage at Yale may be reached slightly later than at other universities.

FINANCIAL SUPPORT

Fellowship awards were coded as being significant if they covered at least half of all expenses (including tuition and living expenses). A full TA during the first or second year of graduate study was defined as the student's having taught 10 hours or more each week for at least one semester. A full TA during the dissertation phase was defined as the student's having taught for two semesters during the fourth year or beyond, or starting in the third year for students with advanced credit. Students who received aid in the form of fellowships generally held the awards for three years; they were coded as having had fellowship support as their primary source of support. Other students generally received half-tuition and made up the rest of their expenses through teaching and their own resources; they were coded as using their own resources as the primary source of support.

MERIT

Partial information on GRE scores was available, but otherwise there were no data on the perceived merits of individual students.

Ten-University Coding Instructions

A.W. Mellon Foundation: Bowen/Sosa   November 17, 1989

GRADUATE STUDENT STUDY: REVISED FORMAT FOR COLLECTING
DATA FROM PARTICIPATING UNIVERSITIES

Notes:

(1) If possible, please provide data on an ASCII (no label) tape.

(2) If a particular question cannot be answered (either for an individual or for all individuals within a university), simply leave the relevant column(s) blank.

(3) Specific column numbers (widths and locations) are suggested to facilitate subsequent merging of data. If these suggestions are inappropriate in certain institutional contexts, please explain what alternative column numbers are used.

---

1. Name (identification number to be assigned to each individual by the University):
   1 . . . to x
   [columns 1–4]

2. University:
   1 = Univ. of California at Berkeley
   2 = Chicago
   3 = Columbia
   4 = Cornell
   5 = Michigan
   6 = Princeton
   7 = Stanford
   8 = Harvard
   9 = Indiana
   10 = Johns Hopkins
   11 = University of North Carolina (Chapel Hill)
   12 = MIT
   13 = Pennsylvania
   14 = Wisconsin
   15 = Yale
   16 = All Other
   [cols. 5–6]

3. Field (Department):
   1 = English and American Literature
   2 = History
   3 = Economics

4 = Political Science
5 = Mathematics
6 = Physics
[cols. 7–8]

4. Gender:
   1 = Male
   2 = Female
   [col. 9]

5. Citizenship:
   1 = U.S. citizen or non-citizen who is a permanent resident of the U.S.
   2 = All others
   [col. 10]

6. Year of entry to Graduate School:
   62 = 1962, etc. . . . to 1986
   [cols. 11–12]

7. Month of entry to Graduate School (if readily available):
   1 = Jan
   2 = Feb
   3 = Mr
   4 = Ap
   5 = May
   6 = June
   7 = July
   8 = Aug
   9 = Sept
   10 = Oct
   11 = Nov
   12 = Dec
   [cols. 13–14]

8. Was the Ph.D. degree obtained:
   1 = Yes
   2 = Student still enrolled in Ph.D. program
   3 = No (student no longer pursuing Ph.D.)
   [col. 15]

9. Year of receipt of Ph.D.:
   66 = 1966, etc. . . . to 1989
   [cols. 16–17]

10. Month of receipt of Ph.D. (if readily available):
    1 = Jan
    2 = Feb
    3 = Mr
    4 = Ap
    5 = May
    6 = June
    7 = July
    8 = Aug

9 = Sept
10 = Oct
11 = Nov
12 = Dec
[cols. 18–19]

11. Did student complete all requirements for Ph.D. except dissertation (i.e., pass qualifying examination, preliminary examination, orals, or otherwise admitted to candidacy for Ph.D.):
1 = Yes
2 = Still attempting to satisfy these requirements
3 = No (student no longer pursuing degree)
[col. 20]

12. Year of completion of all requirements for Ph.D. except dissertation:
64 = 1964, etc . . . to 1989
[cols. 21–22]

13. Was student enrolled in Ph.D. program at start of second year of graduate study:
1 = Yes
2 = No
[col. 23]

14. What was student's score on Verbal GRE:
650 = 650 score, etc. . .
[cols. 24–26]

15. What was student's score on Math GRE:
650 = 650 score, etc. . .
[cols. 27–29]

16. Departmental ranking at time of admission (if available):
1 = Ranked in top half of students offered admission
2 = Ranked in bottom half of students offered admission
[col. 30]

17. Did student win honorific fellowship at dissertation stage (competitive national fellowship such as Whiting or internal fellowship awarded on merit):
1 = Yes
2 = No
[col. 31]

18. Did student have significant fellowship support during either of the first two years of graduate study:
1 = Yes
2 = No
[col. 32]

19. Did student have significant fellowship support during the dissertation phase of graduate study:
    1 = Yes
    2 = No
    [col. 33]

20. Did student have a "full" teaching assistantship during half or more of the first year of graduate study:
    1 = Yes
    2 = No
    [col. 34]

21. Did student have a "full" teaching assistantship during half or more of the second year of graduate study:
    1 = Yes
    2 = No
    [col. 35]

22. Did student have a "full" teaching assistantship during at least one year during dissertation phase of study:
    1 = Yes
    2 = No
    [col. 36]

23. What was student's "primary" source of support during graduate study:
    1 = Fellowships
    2 = Teaching Assistantships
    3 = Research Assistantships
    4 = Own/family resources
    [col. 37]

The National Fellowship Data Set

DATA FROM national fellowship programs permit direct comparisons of outcomes (completion rates and time-to-degree) across fellowship programs, controlling for differences in field of study, university attended, gender, and time period. When used in conjunction with the Ten-University data set, the National Fellowship data set also permits comparisons of outcomes for fellowship winners with outcomes for all graduate students in the same fields at the same universities during the same time period. Time-to-degree for fellowship winners can also be compared with time-to-degree for all graduate students through the use of the Doctorate Records File.

The National Fellowship data set is used throughout the second and third parts of the study and is especially relevant to the discussions of financial support and perceived merit (see Chapter Ten) and the effectiveness of various types of national fellowship programs (see Chapter Eleven).

DATA AND PROCEDURES

Coverage

Records of 13,904 individual recipients of national fellowships were assembled through a complex two-stage approach, described below. These are students who were awarded national fellowships through programs run under the auspices of the Woodrow Wilson National Fellowship Foundation, the Danforth Foundation (including the Danforth Fellowships, the Kent Fellowships, and the Graduate Fellowships for Women), the National Science Foundation (NSF), the U.S. Office of Education (National Defense Education Act [NDEA] Fellowships), the Whiting Foundation, and the Andrew W. Mellon Foundation. Use has also been made of David Breneman's review of the Ford Foundation's program of institutional support.[1]

Since the focus of this book is the arts and sciences, the universe of winners of national fellowships under the programs listed above was purged of the records of those individuals who were pursuing other fields of study. This procedure had the greatest effect on the NDEA population, since NDEA Fellowships were designed to be used in the widest range of fields.

Assembling Demographic Data

The first step in building this database was to obtain lists of winners of fellowships from each of the sponsors. Ideally, these lists, when combined with

---

[1]Breneman 1977. This roster of national fellowship programs is only partial. It was not practical to study a larger number, and we were unable to consider, for example, the experiences of the American Association of University Women, Jacob Javits, Charlotte W. Newcombe, and Spencer fellowship programs.

other sources of data, included information on year of award (and sometimes year of BA and year of entry to graduate school), field of study, university at which graduate study was undertaken, and gender. In the main, it was necessary for our staff to code raw data provided by the various sponsors of fellowship programs. A standardized coding form was used to achieve as much consistency as possible across fellowship programs, and also maximum consistency with the format of the data collected in the Ten-University data set. The standard coding format used is reproduced at the end of this appendix. Procedures followed in obtaining data for individual fellowship programs are described below.

Determining Outcomes

The NSF, alone among national fellowship programs of long standing, has tracked carefully the outcomes for all fellows included in its program. With a very few exceptions, noted below, accurate calculations of completion rates and time-to-degree could not be made for recipients of other awards solely on the basis of information in their files.

The second stage of this data collection effort thus required finding a reliable way to identify those students within each fellowship program who had completed doctorates in various years. The first effort at solving this problem involved the use of the Dissertation Abstracts file maintained by University Microfilms International (UMI). This database contains the titles and abstracts of more than 1 million dissertations written since 1861, as well as the institutions at which they were written. Using DIALOG (the commercial on-line service), we undertook to match the names of the winners of national fellowships with authors of dissertations recorded on the Dissertation Abstracts file. The year of completion of the dissertation was used as a proxy for the year of completion of the PhD.

To achieve a more complete—and more reliable—record of outcomes, we subsequently asked the National Research Council (NRC) to match the name of each of our fellowship winners against the Doctorate Records File (DRF), which contains basic demographic information for every individual who has received a PhD in the United States since 1920. All the relevant demographic information that we had collected from the files of the individual fellowship programs (including not just names, but also field of study, BA institution, PhD institution entered, gender, and year of fellowship award) was used to establish a scoring system to determine the likelihood that an apparent match between a name in our fellowship file and a name in the DRF was a correct match. Individual matches were made by NRC staff on a case-by-case basis, taking into consideration such factors as the size of the BA institution and the student's surname. If a case was ambiguous, a match was not claimed. As a consequence of the care with which this process was carried out, the NRC staff were confident about the reliability of their matches.

There was a reasonably high level of general agreement between the results based on the UMI and NRC (DRF) matching processes, which was reassuring. The findings reported in this study are based on the (more complete) DRF matches, but the initial UMI effort was also useful because it confirmed that the general approach was sensible. We saw that it was possible to merge these kinds of data sets and, for the first time, to calculate completion rates for winners of various national fellowship programs in a reliable and consistent way.

Organizing and Cleaning the Data

The precise year of entry to graduate school and the year of BA were known for only some of the fellowship winners. As a general rule, the year of fellowship award was used as a proxy for both the year of BA and the year of entry to graduate school. (The Whiting program required a different approach, as explained below.) This procedure results in a modest downward bias in the total time-to-degree (TTD) estimates that we derive from the National Fellowship data set (that is, our estimates are slightly lower than the "true" values), since some students won national awards in years following receipt of the BA.[2]

Certain assumptions had to be made to eliminate cases that seemed problematic from the data set and to ensure as much consistency as possible. In order to avoid ambiguity and instances of missing information, we excluded the small number of observations that showed TTDs of less than two years. In the case of Whiting Fellowships, we excluded observations showing the year of receipt of PhD to be the same as the year of award. We also excluded observations that lacked information concerning field and gender, since these two variables are important to much of this analysis. Taken together, these assumptions resulted in the elimination of about 2 percent of all observations from the raw data files.

INDIVIDUAL FELLOWSHIP PROGRAMS

The following profiles of individual fellowship programs are presented in the order in which the programs were established.

Woodrow Wilson Fellowship Program

The Woodrow Wilson fellowship program was created in 1945 and expanded with the help of gifts from the Carnegie Corporation, the Rockefeller Foundation, and the Association of Graduate Schools to support approximately 200 graduate students annually in the arts and sciences. By 1957, however, these grants had run out, and the Ford Foundation assumed responsibility for the program until it ended, as a nationally competitive portable fellowship program, in 1966. (As explained below, it was replaced in 1967 by a major program of institutional support, through which the Ford Foundation provided money to ten universities which had enrolled the largest numbers of Woodrow Wilson Fellows.)

When the Ford Foundation assumed control of the original Woodrow Wilson fellowship program in 1957, it increased the number of fellowships offered each year from about 200 to about 1,000. Students were nominated by their undergraduate institutions, and their names were submitted to regional committees. Each region of the country had a quota of awards, which, in turn, was dependent on the percentage of BAs awarded in the region in fields of study in

---

[2]On the other hand, this procedure results in a modest *upward* bias in our estimates of elapsed time-to-degree (years between entry to graduate school and completion of the PhD), since some award winners deferred entry to graduate school. Here again the evidence that is available suggests that the bias is small.

which the Woodrow Wilson Fellowships were offered. Regional committees made 70 percent of the selections; alternates chosen at the regional level were passed on to the national committee, which then selected the remaining 30 percent of the fellows. This dual selection process was intended to ensure that each region of the country was represented and that areas rich in academic talent were not underrepresented. About one-fifth of all nominees were awarded fellowships.

According to a Woodrow Wilson National Fellowship Foundation survey, between 1945 and 1977, 41 percent of the fellowships were given in the social sciences, 39 percent in the humanities, and 20 percent in mathematics and the science fields. Students in professional fields were not eligible for the fellowships. Fellows were also required to be U.S. citizens or in the process of becoming U.S. citizens. A group of 12 Research I universities enrolled more than half of the Woodrow Wilson Fellows between 1945 and 1977.

The Woodrow Wilson awards paid for tuition for the first year of graduate study only, and also provided a stipend in the first year of approximately $1,500. From 1957 on, the Foundation also provided a $2,000 cost-of-education grant per fellow to the PhD institution. Some institutions used this money to provide a second year of support to their Woodrow Wilson Fellows. From 1962 to 1972, approximately 1,600 one-year dissertation fellowships were offered. Until 1967, only Woodrow Wilson Fellows were eligible to compete for these awards. The number of dissertation awards was then increased, and the pool of eligible candidates was extended beyond those who had held Woodrow Wilson Fellowships in their first year. We did not collect separate data for the dissertation fellows.

The records of this program are maintained in the offices of the Woodrow Wilson National Fellowship Foundation, which today administers a number of other fellowship programs (including the Mellon Fellowships in the Humanities, described below). Staff at the foundation provided a list of Woodrow Wilson award winners and other demographic data, which we coded and entered into the National Fellowship database. Recipients who entered a university outside the U.S. were excluded from the data set. We collected reliable data for 8,298 Woodrow Wilson Fellows in the 1958–1966 cohorts.

An official study commissioned by the Woodrow Wilson National Fellowship Foundation (1977) asked many relevant questions about this program. However, this study appears to have been flawed in design, since it overstates completion rates and understates TTD. The essential difficulty with the study is that it relied on a mail survey, which yielded a relatively low—and almost surely nonrepresentative—response.[3]

Danforth Foundation Fellowship Programs

The Danforth Foundation supported three different fellowship programs between 1951 and 1980: the Danforth Fellowships, the Graduate Fellowships for Women, and the Kent Fellowships. All the Danforth Foundation fellowship programs were extremely generous, providing support for five years of graduate

---

[3]Woodrow Wilson National Fellowship Foundation 1977.

study. They were all administered in the same way, but the criteria for selection were obviously different.

The only published study of these programs known to us is *The Danforth and Kent Fellowships: A Quinquennial Review*.[4] Some of the results reported in this study are misleading, however (see Chapter Eleven). The essential difficulty is that this study, like the Woodrow Wilson National Fellowship Foundation study referred to above, relied on a mail survey of fellows that yielded an unrepresentative return.

Additional information concerning these programs was obtained from Lillie Mae Marquis, who was responsible for administering the Danforth program over its many years and who remembers an extraordinary number of fellows.

No computerized records are available, but basic demographic data for all fellows were obtained from the files and then coded and entered into the National Fellowship database by our staff. We were able to collect complete information on 2,686 fellows.

DANFORTH FELLOWSHIPS

Created in 1951, the Danforth fellowship program was "intended to be different, to be more than merely a source of money distributed anonymously through monthly checks."[5] The fellowships were portable five-year awards covering tuition costs and a living stipend, and they were given only to students beginning their graduate study in the arts and sciences. More than half of all the Danforth Fellowships were awarded in the humanities; another 25 percent were given in the social sciences, 10 percent in the natural sciences, and 5 percent in mathematics. The stated purpose of the program was to use both meanings of the term *fellowship*: one denoting a form of financial grant to graduate students; the other, "a group sharing similar interests and experiences on equal terms in a congenial atmosphere."

The "fellowship of the fellowships," as it was called, was promoted in a variety of ways. The program was closely administered, and there was an emphasis on interaction between fellows and with faculty at regional and national conferences. In the beginning, fellows were required to attend a national conference every year. As the number of fellows in the program increased, attendance at these conferences became too large, and the requirement was changed to attendance at the national conference only during the first and second years. After that, they were urged to attend annual regional conferences. Later, a "final year" conference was created for fellows completing their study. Fellows were also required to submit two reports every year describing their progress toward the PhD. In addition, departmental heads were required to send reports to the Danforth Foundation reporting fellows' progress toward the PhD.

The Danforth program was intended to "aid men of proved ability and leadership who recognize the place of religion in their personal lives and the work of education, and are seriously searching for religious maturity within the Christian tradition." While the religious emphasis of the program had been reduced by the early 1960s, fellows continued to be chosen for personality traits

[4]Danforth Foundation 1976.

[5]Danforth Foundation 1976, 5. The other quotations in the next few pages used to describe features of the Danforth program are from this same source (pp. 2, 3, 5, and 6).

and ethical or religious values, as well as for academic ability. Fellows were also required to sign a statement indicating an intention to use their PhDs to go into college or university teaching or administration.

Women were originally eligible for Danforths when the program was created, but in 1955 they were disqualified on the ground that "their attrition rates in graduate school were too high to warrant the investment of limited Foundation funds." The wives of Danforth fellows, however, were eligible for stipends to study during this time. The fellowship competition was formally reopened to women in 1965. Because of all these changes, we chose to exclude women altogether from our universe of Danforth Fellows prior to 1965.

Although there were only about 50 fellows in the earliest cohorts, the number in each annual cohort had grown to more than 100 by the late 1950s and early 1960s. Institutions were allowed to nominate between two and five students, and approximately 2,500 applications were received by the Danforth Foundation each year. Applicants nominated by their undergraduate institutions subsequently had to go through an extensive national selection process, which included interviews.

We have data for male Danforth Fellows in the 1958–1976 cohorts and for female Danforth Fellows in the 1965–1976 cohorts. The total number of male and female Danforth Fellows included in this study was 2,054.

GRADUATE FELLOWSHIPS FOR WOMEN

According to a published study by the Danforth Foundation, "almost in seeming penance," the Graduate Fellowships for Women were added to the Danforth program in 1965. They were intended to provide opportunities for mature women to resume graduate studies. The data set is very limited, however, and we have data for just 168 students in the 1967–1976 cohorts.

KENT FELLOWSHIPS

The Kent Fellowship program was created in 1923 under the auspices of the National Council on Religion in Higher Education. By 1962, the council could no longer sustain the fellowship program, and the Danforth Foundation assumed responsibility for program support and administration in that year.

While the Danforths were only available to students just starting graduate study, the Kents were also awarded to students who had completed their first year of graduate study and had the endorsement of a faculty member. More than 80 percent of all Kents were given in the humanities and social sciences; indeed, the humanities alone accounted for almost 70 percent of the total. We have data for 464 students in the 1957–1976 cohorts of Kent Fellows.

National Science Foundation Fellowship Program

The NSF fellowship program was created in 1952. While the bulk of awards since then have been given in engineering and the physical sciences, including math, chemistry, physics/astronomy, and earth sciences, nearly one-third to one-half of the awards have been given in the life sciences, psychology, and the social sciences, including economics, political science, anthropology, and sociology. As the number of applicants in these other fields has increased over time, so, too, has the number of awards conferred.

Until 1972, three different kinds of fellowships were given: (1) first-year awards; (2) intermediate awards; and (3) terminal awards for one or two years, with the possibility of renewal. As a result, the duration of awards ranged from a few months to five years, and a little more than half of the fellows held their awards for three years or more. In 1972, the fellowship term was standardized at three years, and awards were made only to students at or near the beginning of graduate study.

The fellowships are awarded to U.S. citizens and permanent residents, and the selection process is highly competitive. For 1990–1991, 850 new awards were made. The amount of the stipend was $12,900, and fellows received a cost-of-education allowance up to $6,000 toward tuition and required fees.

Information about NSF Fellows is collected by the NRC in a cumulative index. This index was merged with the data files associated with the Survey of Earned Doctorates (SED) and Survey of Doctorate Recipients (SDR), and special tabulations were run for the 1962–1976 cohorts, using the three different data sets. The NSF provided various tabulations and cross-tabulations, rather than individual records.

These tabulations include information about the undergraduate institutions of applicants, the graduate institutions of fellows, truncated completion rates, time-to-degree, and early professional activities. These data have been organized by field of study and gender for three groups of individuals: NSF Fellows rated (by panels) as Quality Group 1; NSF Fellows rated as Quality Group 2; and nonawardees also rated as Quality Group 2 (who were considered to be of comparable ability but did not receive the award for reasons pertaining to such distributional objectives as region, field, gender, and race). Because of this unique feature of the data set (the inclusion of a control for student quality at the time of admission to graduate school), it has been possible to study the difference between student quality effects (Quality Group 1 awardees versus Quality Group 2 awardees) and award effects (Quality Group 2 awardees versus Quality Group 2 nonawardees).

Several published studies contain information about the backgrounds of applicants and their success in obtaining awards.[6]

National Defense Education Act Fellowship Program

The NDEA Title IV fellowship program was created by Congress in 1958 in response to the Soviet launching of Sputnik and the perception of an overwhelming shortage of well-qualified college teachers. The Title IV fellowship program had three basic objectives: (1) to increase the number of university teachers by assisting doctoral students preparing for academic careers; (2) to encourage the development and full utilization of the capacity of doctoral programs; and (3) to promote a wider geographic distribution of doctoral programs of good quality.

The scale of the Title IV program changed significantly over time. The number of new fellowships awarded annually began with 1,000 in 1959, and then continued at 1,500 for the next five years. A period of rapid expansion followed, when the number of awards made annually increased to 3,000 in 1965 and then

---

[6]Harmon 1977; and Snyder 1988.

to 6,000 in 1966 and in 1967. The number then returned to 3,000 for the balance of the program's life.

The NDEA fellowship program provided up to three years of financial support, and it was open only to U.S. citizens or permanent residents who intended to pursue academic careers. Awards were made to institutions, and since one of the stated intentions of the Title IV program was to correct for a perceived maldistribution of PhDs and PhD programs, awards were especially concentrated in areas of the country, such as the Southeast, where "doctoral programs were weakest."[7] Schools with new or expanding programs that applied for Title IV money received a large portion of the Title IV dollars. Once an institution's application had been approved by the Office of Education, individual students were nominated to receive these fellowships by the institution.

The award paid for tuition, and each fellow received a stipend of $2,000 for the first academic year, $2,200 for the second, and $2,400 for the third. An allowance for dependents was also given. In addition, the fellow's institution received a cost-of-education grant of up to $2,500 per student.

Though the NDEA Title IV fellowship program ran from 1959 to 1973, an extensive search through the archives of the Department of Education and the Library of Congress resulted in the recovery of only one directory of fellows, for 1962, with addresses, fields of study, and PhD institutions. Consequently, we have had to limit our analysis to this single cohort. After deleting the records of those fellows studying in fields outside the arts and sciences, we were left with 1,071 fellows in arts-and-sciences fields. The available demographic data for these fellows was coded and entered into the National Fellowship database.

The NDEA Fellows attended a much larger pool of institutions than did the students in the other fellowship programs in our study. To reflect this diversity, we employed two additional sets of codes in classifying institutions attended by NDEA Fellows (Carnegie categories and the "Quality Tiers" described in Chapter Four).

Ford Foundation Institutional Fellowship Program

At least in part in response to the discussion stimulated by Bernard Berelson's (1960) landmark book, the Ford Foundation decided in 1966–1967 to phase out support for the Woodrow Wilson fellowship program and to allocate approximately the same amount of annual fellowship support directly to ten universities as part of a program to reform graduate education in the humanities and social sciences. Whereas recruitment was viewed by the foundation as the major need in the late 1950s and early 1960s, improved efficiency in graduate education was seen as the highest priority for the late 1960s and early 1970s. The new Ford Foundation program continued until 1974.

Most of our information about this program comes from David Breneman's report to the Ford Foundation, *Efficiency in Graduate Education: An Attempted Reform*, and a companion document by James Armsey describing the manage-

---

[7]Sharp, Sensenig, and Reid 1968, 4. For other evaluations of the NDEA program, see Holmstrom and Sharp (1970); and Lindquist (1971).

ment of the program.[8] No records exist of individuals supported through this program, and, as noted below, one stipulation was that none of them be identified as Ford Fellows. Breneman's study is a critical analysis, which contains extensive summary data on time-to-degree by field of study and institution. The study also includes more limited data on completion rates.

The ten universities that participated in this program were selected by the Ford Foundation and asked to submit proposals. In general, they were the institutions that had enrolled the most Woodrow Wilson Fellows under the previous program. While there was a general understanding that the purpose of these institutional grants was to institutionalize a four-year norm for attainment of the PhD and to improve the preparation of college teachers, each university was given substantial flexibility in pursuing these goals. There were only two stipulations: that the supported students not be identified as Ford Fellows and that their stipends not exceed amounts paid under the NDEA Title IV program. As a result, the terms of the fellowship varied from campus to campus.

Whiting Institutional Fellowship Program

The Whiting fellowship program began in 1972 with grants from the Whiting Foundation to six universities (Bryn Mawr, Columbia, Harvard, Princeton, Stanford, and Yale); the University of Chicago was added to the program in 1976. These institutional grants were intended to be used to establish fellowships for PhD candidates in the humanities in the final stages of dissertation writing. The awards were intended to be generous enough to set the Whitings apart as the "premier fellowship in the humanities granted by each participating institution."[9]

Grants are made by the foundation to the seven participating institutions, which are responsible for the bulk of the program's administration and for selection of Whiting Fellows on their own campuses. The size of the fellowship stipends is set by the individual institutions, but for 1990–1991 the Whiting Foundation required that it be fixed at not less than $12,000. Most of the institutions have a similar selection procedure, and decisions are made on the basis of merit, without regard for financial need.

The fellowships were intended for candidates thinking seriously about careers in academia "who are reasonably expected to complete their dissertation within a year to 18 months following receipt of the award." Nearly 80 percent of Whiting Fellows have been in the following humanities fields: history, English, foreign languages and literature, art, art history and archaeology, and philosophy.

An average of between 50 and 70 fellowships have been awarded each year, though the numbers were slightly larger between 1977 and 1981. Data for the Whiting Fellows are maintained by the Whiting Foundation; some additional information needed for this study had to be obtained from the seven participating universities.

Since the Whiting Fellowship is a dissertation-stage award, it was necessary

---

[8]Breneman 1977; and Armsey 1977.

[9]Whiting Foundation 1983. The other quotation below is from this same source (the 10-year report on the program).

for the purposes of most of our analysis (that is, the calculation of time-to-degree) to reorganize Whiting award cohorts according to their year of entry to graduate school. The data were also organized according to year of award to permit analysis of the length of time between receipt of award and completion of dissertation.

After coding and cleaning the data, information on 1,063 Whiting Fellows named between 1973 and 1989 was included in the National Fellowship database.

The Mellon Fellowships in the Humanities

The Mellon fellowship program was begun in 1983 to attract promising students to doctoral programs in the humanities. Mellon Fellowships can be used only in the traditional humanities disciplines and cannot be used, for example, for the study of creative and performing arts. Too little time has elapsed since the creation of the program to permit the calculation of reliable completion rates and time-to-degree. Most of the fellows are still enrolled in graduate programs. However, the first seven cohorts of Mellon Fellows were asked to complete an extensive questionnaire, which asked about the fellows' experiences in graduate school and (where relevant) the reasons why fellows had chosen to leave the program. (This study is described fully in Appendix C, which also includes copies of the questionnaires.)

The Mellon Fellowships provide two years of support at the start of graduate study, with the option of a third year of support during the dissertation phase. In addition to covering the cost of tuition and standard fees, the fellowship provides students with a stipend ($11,000 in 1989–1990) for living expenses. During the second year, the graduate school is expected to pay a third of the tuition and fees. During the final dissertation year, fellows who have performed with distinction are eligible for stipends. This support is not normally available to fellows beyond their fifth year of graduate study unless there are extenuating circumstances.

Students nominated by faculty at their undergraduate institutions advance to a regional selection committee, which in turn makes recommendations to a national committee. Approximately 10 percent of active candidates receive awards. These fellowships are portable and can be used at any graduate school in the United States or Canada, but a maximum of ten Mellon Fellows are allowed to attend any university, and only three may be enrolled in the same department.

National Fellowship Coding Instructions

February 2, 1990

REVISED CODING INSTRUCTIONS FOR ALL DATA

1. Name (identification number to be assinged by coder, ignore current numbers)
   1 . . . . to x
   [columns 1–5]

2. University entered, or where resident at time of award:

   a. For all fellows except NDEA:
   1 = Univ. of California at Berkeley
   2 = Chicago
   3 = Columbia
   4 = Cornell
   5 = Michigan
   6 = Princeton
   7 = Stanford
   8 = Harvard
   9 = Indiana
   10 = Johns Hopkins
   11 = University of North Carolina (Chapel Hill)
   12 = MIT
   13 = Pennsylvania
   14 = Wisconsin
   15 = Yale
   16 = All others

   b. For NDEA fellows, the following classification:
   1 = Research 1 university
   2 = Other Research/Doctorate (Research 2 + Doctorate 1 + Doctorate 2)
   3 = All Other
   [cols. 6–7]

3. Field (department): (for Woodrow Wilson and NDEA, codes run from 1 to 9. For the Whiting, Danforth, Kent and Graduate Fellowships for Women, the codes run from 1 to 19.)
   1 = English
   2 = History
   3 = Economics
   4 = Political Science
   5 = Mathematics
   6 = Physics
   7 = Other Humanities for WWF and NDEAs; DON'T USE for Whitings, Danforths, Kents and GFWs

8 = Other Social Sciences
9 = Other Natural Sciences (incl. Psychology)
10 = Foreign Languages and Literatures
11 = Art, Art History, Archaeology
12 = Philosophy
13 = Comparative Literature
14 = Classics
15 = Music
16 = American Studies
17 = Religion
18 = Linguistics
19 = Other Humanities (defined exclusive of above fields)
[cols. 8–9]

4. Gender:
   1 = Male
   2 = Female
   3 = Ambiguous
   [col. 10]

5. Year of Receipt of Fellowship:
   73 = 1973–74, etc. to 88 = 1988–89
   [cols. 11–12]

6. Did individual receive Ph.D. per DIALOG? Not available for Whiting.
   1 = Yes
   2 = No
   [col. 13]

7. Year of Ph.D. for those coded 1 in Col. 13:
   74 = 1974–75, etc.
   [cols. 14–15]

8. University at which Ph.D. was received: Not available for NDEA. See variable 15 below.
   1 = Univ. of California at Berkeley
   2 = Chicago
   3 = Columbia
   4 = Cornell
   5 = Michigan
   6 = Princeton
   7 = Stanford
   8 = Harvard
   9 = Indiana
   10 = Johns Hopkins
   11 = University of North Carolina (Chapel Hill)
   12 = MIT
   13 = Pennsylvania
   14 = Wisconsin
   15 = Yale

16 = All others (This is likely to be Bryn Mawr for Whiting fellowships since the fellowship was offered to entering students only at selected institutions. If the student transferred, this can refer to other institutions.)

[cols. 16–17]

9. Last names of the students:
[cols. 18–47]

10. First names of the students:
[cols. 48–77]

11. Undergraduate Institution attended, when available: (Only available for Woodrow Wilson and Whiting)
[cols. 78–112]

12. Type of fellowship:
1 = Woodrow Wilson
2 = NDEA
3 = Whiting
4 = Danforth
5 = Kent
6 = Graduate Fellowships for Women
[col. 113]

13. Year of B.A. Degree: Whiting only
77 = 1977, etc.
[col. 112–115]

14. Year of entry into graduate school: Whiting only
77 = 1977, etc.
[col. 116–117]

End of Record for Woodrow Wilson and Whiting

15. Transferred, is degree-granting institution different from the graduate institution entered? NDEA only
1 = Yes
2 = No
[col. 118]

16. Roose-Anderson rating of department: NDEA only
1 = Top ranking (2.0–3.0)
2 = Middle ranking (1.5–1.9)
3 = Low ranking (0.8–1.4)
4 = Unranked and all other
[col. 119]

17. GRE score - verbal: Available only for Danforth, Kent, and Graduate Fellowships for Women
[col. 120–122]

18. GRE score - quantitative: Available only for Danforth, Kent, and Graduate Fellowships for Women

   [col. 123–125]

*End of record for Danforth, Kent, and Graduate
Fellowships for Women*

Survey of Mellon Fellows in the Humanities

As ONE part of our study of national fellowship programs, we undertook a detailed analysis of the Mellon Fellowships in the Humanities. This fellowship program, which is administered by the Woodrow Wilson National Fellowship Foundation and directed by Dr. Robert F. Goheen, is relatively new. The first entering cohort began graduate study in 1983, and statistics on time-to-degree and completion rates are therefore incomplete. However, the program does provide an opportunity to review the recent experiences of a group of carefully selected graduate students, and in this way to investigate some of the more qualitative aspects of graduate education.

General information about the Mellon Fellowships in the Humanities is included in Appendix B, and Chapters Eleven, Twelve, and Thirteen include comments on the outcomes of the program to date as well as information obtained from the two questionnaires described below (and reproduced at the end of this appendix).

ADMINISTRATION OF PRIMARY QUESTIONNAIRE

The primary questionnaire[1] was mailed in February 1990 to all 798 individuals who had participated in the Mellon fellowship program by that time. A second mailing was made in April. Altogether, 635 responses were received, for a response rate of 79.6 percent.

The first part of the primary questionnaire was concerned with each student's graduate career. Questions covered enrollment status each year, sources of financial support and loan obligations, interruptions of graduate study and the reasons for them, progress toward the PhD, time required to reach various "milestones," and factors encouraging and inhibiting progress toward the PhD.

The second part of this questionnaire concerned experiences as a teaching assistant and preparation for undergraduate teaching. Students were asked about the existence, extent, and effectiveness of training for undergraduate teaching provided through departmental programs, centers, courses, summer programs, and informal guidance from faculty.

ADMINISTRATION OF SUPPLEMENTARY QUESTIONNAIRE

The supplementary questionnaire[2] was intended to collect more detailed data on the experiences of fellows who had resigned from the program ("lost" fellows).

---

[1] This questionnaire was designed by Carolyn Makinson, Program Associate for Population at the Andrew W. Mellon Foundation. Assistance in design of the questionnaire and data entry was provided by Joyce Lopuh of the Office of Population Research (OPR) at Princeton University. Mark Van Landingham, a graduate student at OPR, performed many of the statistical tabulations and analyses.

[2] This questionnaire was designed primarily by Dan Cullen, Vice President of Mathtech, Inc. (formerly Mathematica, Inc.), a consulting firm based in Princeton, New Jersey.

It was administered through phone interviews during May, June, and July of 1990. These interviews were conducted by employees of Mathtech, Inc., and student employees of the Andrew W. Mellon Foundation.

Of the 76 fellows who had resigned from the program, the interviewers were able to reach and interview 37. No one contacted declined to be interviewed. The 39 fellows who were not interviewed were unreachable despite extensive efforts to find them (including contacting departments where graduate study was undertaken and parents).

The supplementary questionnaire asked about academic and nonacademic activities since leaving the program, reasons for leaving, the value of the program to these students, and suggestions for improving it. The fellows were provided with choices for their answers to some questions, but many questions were open ended. Qualitative responses were encouraged.

Primary Questionnaire for Mellon Fellows

GRADUATE CAREERS

AND

TEACHING PREPARATION

OF

MELLON FELLOWS

GRADUATE CAREER

First of all, we would like to know about your status as a graduate student in the Humanities since you first began formal graduate study.

1. In what calendar year did you first start graduate school?

    Please write in year

    (13-14) | 19 □□

---

2. In the following table, we wish to collect information on whether or not you were studying, for each academic year since you first started graduate school. The column entitled Year 1 in the table is your first year of graduate school. *Please circle ONE number in each column* up to and including the year in which you gained the Ph.D. *Circle number '4' or '5'* for the year AFTER you gained the Ph.D. or terminated graduate study for good. (Treat enrollment in absentia as graduate study.)

ACADEMIC YEAR

STATUS	Year 1 (15)	Year 2 (16)	Year 3 (17)	Year 4 (18)	Year 5 (19)	Year 6 (20)	Year 7 (21)
Graduate student during <u>entire</u> academic year	1	1	1	1	1	1	1
Graduate student part of the year, unenrolled part of the year	2	2	2	2	2	2	2
Not enrolled during the <u>entire</u> academic year	3	3	3	3	3	3	3
ALREADY GAINED PH.D.	4	4	4	4	4	4	4
TERMINATED GRADUATE STUDY PRIOR TO PH.D.	5	5	5	5	5	5	5

1

3. Still thinking about the time since you first started graduate school, we would like to know the sources from which you received financial support during each academic year, whether you were enrolled or not (do not include summer employment). *Please circle number '1' for all sources which applied to you in any given academic year* up to and including the year in which you gained the Ph.D. or terminated graduate study for good.

ACADEMIC YEAR

SOURCE OF SUPPORT

	Year 1 (22-29)	Year 2 (30-37)	Year 3 (38-45)	Year 4 (46-53)	Year 5 (54-61)	Year 6 (62-69)	Year 7 (70-77)
Mellon fellowship support	1	1	1	1	1	1	1
Other fellowship without duties	1	1	1	1	1	1	1
Fellowship involving assistantship duties	1	1	1	1	1	1	1
Teaching or research assistantship in your department or a related department (not as part of a fellowship package)	1	1	1	1	1	1	1
Other employment on campus	1	1	1	1	1	1	1
Employment off campus	1	1	1	1	1	1	1
Loans (non-family)	1	1	1	1	1	1	1
Savings or family support including family loans	1	1	1	1	1	1	1

---

4. We would like to know about the loan obligations (excluding family loans) which students take on before and during graduate school.

   a. What was the total amount of your loan obligation at the time you first started graduate school?

   (78-83)

   Please enter the amount in dollars $ [ ][ ][ ][ ][ ][ ] .00

   b. What was your loan obligation at the time you gained the Ph.D. or terminated graduate study for good (or your current loan obligation, if you are still in the process of obtaining the Ph.D.)?

   (84-89)

   Please enter the amount in dollars $ [ ][ ][ ][ ][ ][ ] .00

2

325

5. How many <u>completed</u> quarters or semesters had you spent <u>enrolled</u> in graduate school by the beginning of February 1990? Count time spent at <u>all</u> institutions and in <u>all</u> programs since you first started graduate school. Include enrollment in absentia, but not breaks away from study.

Please enter a number for semesters and quarters. (If all enrollment has been quarters, please enter '00' for semesters. If all enrollment has been semesters, please enter '00' for quarters.)

(90-91)

SEMESTERS ☐☐

(92-93)

QUARTERS ☐☐

6. a. Have you ever interrupted graduate study for any period? (Do not include study or research away from the home campus as an interruption.)

Please circle one number

(94)

Yes 1 *Answer b & c below*
No 2 *Skip to Q.7*

b. How many times have you interrupted graduate study?

Please write in number of times

(95)

☐

c. Listed below are several reasons which sometimes lead to students interrupting graduate study. For each interruption (number of times written in at 6b), *please enter in the "REASONS" box the number* for the <u>main</u> reason (and secondary reason, if any) which led to the interruption. *Please enter in the "PERIOD" box the time in months and years* before you resumed graduate study. (If you have not returned to graduate school, please write '7's in the YEARS and MONTHS boxes.)

Reasons for dropping out	CODE NUMBER
Ill health	01
Financial difficulties	02
Got married	03
Divorce/marital problems	04
Obligations to own children/childbirth	05
Obligations to parents	06
Dissatisfied with program	07
Wanted a break from graduate school/studying	08
Was offered a job I wanted to do	09
Advised by univ. to take leave	10
Other reason *(write in below)*	11

'OTHER' REASON

		REASONS		PERIOD	
		Main Reason	Secondary Reason	Years	Months
_____	First Time Dropped out	☐☐	☐☐	☐☐ ☐☐ (96-103)
_____	Second time	☐☐	☐☐	☐☐ ☐☐ (104-111)
_____	Third time	☐☐	☐☐	☐☐ ☐☐ (112-119)

3

7. a. Have you passed all requirements for the Ph.D., <u>including</u> the dissertation and the final oral examination?

Please circle one number   (120)

Yes 1 *Skip to Q.8*

No   2 *Answer b below*

  b. Have you passed all the requirements for the Ph.D., <u>other than</u> the dissertation and the final oral examination?

Please circle one number   (121)

Yes 1 *Answer c & d below*

No   2 *Skip to d below*

  c. From the time you first entered graduate school, how much time elapsed until you passed all requirements except the dissertation?

Please write in the years and months   Years Months

(122-125)

☐☐ ☐☐

  d. Have you/had you begun work on the dissertation?

Please circle one number   (126)

Yes 1 *Answer e below*

No   2 *Skip to Q.13*

  e. Has/had the prospectus or the plan of work for your dissertation been approved either formally or informally by the designated authority (advisor, committee, etc.)?

Please circle one number   (127)

Yes 1 *Answer f below*

No   2 *Skip to Q.13*

  f. Do you expect to pass <u>all</u> requirements for the Ph.D., including the dissertation and the final oral examination, within the next 24 months?

Please circle one number   (128)

Yes 1 *Answer g below*

No   2 *Skip to Q.9*

  g. Do you expect to pass <u>all</u> requirements for the Ph.D., including the dissertation and the final oral examination, within the next 12 months?

Please circle one number   (129)

Yes 1 *Skip to Q.9*

No   2 *Skip to Q.9*

4

8. a. From the time you first entered graduate school, how much time elapsed until you passed all requirements except the dissertation?

Please write in the years and months

Years Months

(130-133)

b. How much time elapsed from the time you passed all pre-dissertation requirements, until you completed the dissertation and passed the final oral examination?

Please write in the years and months

Years Months

(134-137)

Please <u>skip</u> Questions 9 - 12 if the plan of work for your dissertation has <u>not</u> been approved.

9. We would like to know about the guidance which you have had for your dissertation research.

a. Have you taken a research methods seminar?

Please circle one number   (138)

Yes 1 *Answer b & c below*

No   2 *Skip to c below*

b. How would you rate the value of the research methods seminar to your dissertation research?

Please circle one number   (139)

Very helpful   1

Somewhat helpful   2

Not helpful   3

c. Apart from any research methods seminars, how well have your graduate courses and seminars prepared you for dissertation research?

Please circle one number   (140)

Very useful preparation 1

Somewhat useful   2

Not useful   3

5

328

10. a. Did you choose your dissertation topic entirely on your own or was your advisor involved in the decision?

Please circle *one* number only　　　(141)

Entirely my own choice　　1

Mainly my own choice, but my　　2
advisor was involved

Mainly my advisor's choice,　　3
although I had some say

Assigned by my advisor　　4

b. Is your dissertation part of a faculty member's research project?

Please circle one number　　　(142)

Yes　1

No　2

---

11. Listed below are various factors which can help a student gain the Ph.D. in good time. For each factor, *please circle the one number which best describes the effect it had on the time it took you* (or is now taking you) to gain the Ph.D. (Factors which can make a student take longer are addressed in Q.12.)

	Helped me gain the Ph.D. a lot sooner	Helped me gain the Ph.D. a little sooner	Made no difference/ did not apply to me	
Academic-year financial support from the University	1	2	3	(143)
Financial support from the Mellon Fellowship	1	2	3	(144)
Other academic-year fellowship support	1	2	3	(145)
Summer support	1	2	3	(146)
Guidance from faculty on coursework	1	2	3	(147)
Advice from faculty on choosing a dissertation topic	1	2	3	(148)
Guidance from faculty on dissertation research	1	2	3	(149)
Encouragement/moral support from faculty	1	2	3	(150)

6

329

12. Listed below are factors which can lead to a student taking longer to gain the Ph.D. For each factor, *please circle the one number which best describes the effect it had on the time* it took you (or is now taking you) to gain the Ph.D.

	Slowed me down a lot	Slowed me down a little	Made no difference/ did not apply to me	
Departmental indifference to time to degree	1	2	3	(151)
Dissertation advisor left the university	1	2	3	(152)
Dissertation advisor present but inaccessible	1	2	3	(153)
Dissertation advisor did not encourage prompt completion of dissertation	1	2	3	(154)
Compulsory service as Teaching Assistant (TA)	1	2	3	(155)
Taking jobs because needed money (including non-compulsory TA-ing)	1	2	3	(156)
Lack of summer support	1	2	3	(157)
Lack of funds for research	1	2	3	(158)
Difficulty fixing on final dissertation topic	1	2	3	(159)
Major shift in discipline or field of concentration in mid-course	1	2	3	(160)
Research materials not available	1	2	3	(161)
Inadequate preparation in foreign languages	1	2	3	(162)
Inadequate preparation in statistics/computing	1	2	3	(163)
Conscious decision to take time to develop or improve publication record before entering job market	1	2	3	(164)
Burn-out/lack of self-motivation	1	2	3	(165)
Personal problems unrelated to study	1	2	3	(166)

7

330

13. a. How long does it normally take for a graduate student in your department/program to complete all requirements for the Ph.D. other than the dissertation?

Please circle one number (167)

Less than one year	1
One year, less than two years	2
Two years, less than three years	3
Three years, less than four years	4
Four years or more	5

b. How long did it/will it take you?

Please circle one number (168)

Less than one year	1
One year, less than two years	2
Two years, less than three years	3
Three years, less than four years	4
Four years or more	5
Terminated graduate study for good before completing requirements	6

c. Recognizing that course requirements serve a purpose, do you think the requirements of your department are...

Please circle one number (169)

...insufficient	1
...about right	2
...or excessive?	3

14. In the current semester or quarter, how many hours a week on average do you spend on your graduate studies? (If you are not currently enrolled, please enter '997'.)

(170-172)

Please write in hours

15. What <u>one</u> change do you think universities or other institutions could make to help someone like you gain the Ph.D. more quickly, without sacrificing the quality of the degree?

Please write in <u>briefly</u> the <u>one</u> change you would <u>most</u> like to see.

OFFICE
CODING
(173-174)

8

331

TEACHING PREPARATION

Now we would like to ask some questions about your experience as a Teaching Assistant (TA) and the training you received to help you become a TA. We shall be inquiring consecutively about: departmental programs (Q.17), a center (Q.18) or course (Q.19) provided by your university outside your department, including summer programs (Q.20), and informal guidance received from individual professors (Q.21).

16. a. Have you ever been a TA or instructor since you began graduate school?

Please circle one number　　　　　　　(175)

Yes　1　*Answer b & c below*

No　　2　*Skip to Q.23*

b. How many quarters or semesters have you been a TA or instructor? (Count current quarter/semester if you are currently a TA.)

Please enter a number for semesters and quarters. (If all TA-ing has been quarters, please enter '00' for semesters. If all TA-ing has been semesters, please enter '00' for quarters.)

(176-177)

SEMESTERS　☐☐

(178-179)

QUARTERS　☐☐

c. For how many different courses have you been a TA or instructor?

(180-181)

Please write in number　☐☐

DEPARTMENTAL TA-TRAINING PROGRAM

17. a. Does your <u>department</u> have a formal program to train students to be TAs?

Please circle one number　　　　　(182)

Yes　　　　　　　　1　*Answer b below*

No　　　　　　　　2　*Skip to Q.18*

Not in my time　　　3　*Skip to Q.18*

b. Did you take part/are you taking part in the program?

Please circle one number　　　　(183)

Yes　1　*Answer c - e below*

No　　2　*Skip to Q.18*

c. Is/was teaching in the program carried out...

Please circle one number　　　　(184)

...entirely by regular faculty　　1

...mainly by regular faculty　　　2
but with some involvement of
experienced TAs

...mainly by experienced TAs　　3
but with some involvement
of regular faculty

...or entirely by experienced TAs?　4

d. How would you rate the value of the departmental training program to your teaching?

Please circle one number　　　　(185)

Very helpful　　　　1

Somewhat helpful　　2

Not much use　　　　3

Too early to say　　4

9

e. Do you feel the time demands of the departmental training program are/were...

> *Please circle one number* (186)
>
> ...insufficient   1
>
> ...about right   2
>
> ...or excessive?   3

INSTITUTIONAL TA-TRAINING SERVICES

18. a. Does your university or graduate school have a center available to help graduate students prepare to be effective teachers?

> *Please circle one number* (187)
>
> Yes   1 *Answer b & c below*
>
> No   2 *Skip to Q.19*
>
> Not in my time   3 *Skip to Q.19*

b. Is use of the center entirely voluntary?

> *Please circle one number* (188)
>
> Yes 1
>
> No   2

c. Have you used it?

> *Please circle one number* (189)
>
> Yes 1 *Answer d below*
>
> No   2 *Skip to Q.20*

d. Does the center offer a formal program of instruction?

> *Please circle one number* (190)
>
> Yes 1 *Answer e & f below*
>
> No   2 *Skip to h below*

e. Is the formal program required for beginning TAs?

> *Please circle one number* (191)
>
> Yes 1
>
> No   2

f. Have you used/are you using the formal program of instruction?

> *Please circle one number* (192)
>
> Yes 1 *Answer g & h below*
>
> No   2 *Skip to h below*

g. How would you rate the value of the formal program to your teaching?

> *Please circle one number* (193)
>
> Very helpful   1
>
> Somewhat helpful 2
>
> Not much help   3
>
> Too early to say   4

h. Does the center offer videotaping?

> *Please circle one number* (194)
>
> Yes 1 *Answer i & j below*
>
> No   2 *Skip to j below*

10

i. Have you used the videotape service?

        Please circle one number   (195)

                                      Yes 1

                                      No   2

j. Does the center offer personal coaching?

        Please circle one number   (196)

                                      Yes 1 *Answer k & l below*

                                      No   2 *Skip to l below*

k. Have you ever received personal coaching from the center?

        Please circle one number   (197)

                                      Yes 1

                                      No   2

l. How would you rate the offerings of the center overall in preparing you to be an effective teacher?

        Please circle one number   (198)

            Very helpful   1

            Somewhat helpful 2   *Skip to Q.20*

            Not much help   3

            Too early to say   4

---

19. Even though there is no university training center, does your university or graduate school offer a course or courses during the academic year to train students to be TAs?

        Please circle one number   (199)

            Yes   1

            No   2

            Not in my time   3

SUMMER PROGRAM FOR NEW TAs

20. a. Does your graduate school offer a summer program for new TAs?

        Please circle one number   (200)

            Yes   1 *Answer b & c below*

            No   2 *Skip to Q.21*

            Not in my time   3 *Skip to Q.21*

b. Is the summer program...

        Please circle one number   (201)

            ...voluntary   1

            ...or compulsory? 2

c. Have you attended the summer program?

        Please circle one number   (202)

                                      Yes 1 *Answer d below*

                                    No   2 *Skip to Q.21*

11

d. How would you rate the value of the summer program to your teaching?

Please circle one number   (203)

Very helpful	1
Somewhat helpful	2
Not much help	3
Too early to say	4

FACULTY GUIDANCE ON TA-ING

21. a. Moving now to informal guidance on teaching provided by individual professors in your department, have you received such guidance?

             Please circle one number   (204)

                 Yes   1   *Answer b - d below*

                 No   2   *Skip to d below*

    b. Did the guidance you received/are receiving include...

             Please circle one number for each item

	Yes	No	
...advance discussion of the curriculum?	1	2	(205)
...advance discussion of the readings?	1	2	(206)
...supervision of grading?	1	2	(207)
...evaluation of one or more teaching sessions?	1	2	(208)
...informal discussions?	1	2	(209)

    c. How would you rate the value of this guidance to your teaching?

             Please circle one number   (210)

Very helpful	1
Somewhat helpful	2
Not much help	3
Too early to say	4

    d. In your judgement, are/were most professors in your department willing to offer this kind of guidance or is/was it only given by a few individuals?

             Please circle one number   (211)

Most	1
Only a few or none	2

---

22. What <u>one</u> change do you think your department or institution could make to better prepare someone like you to be a TA?

Please write in <u>briefly</u> the <u>one</u> change you would <u>most</u> like to see.

_____

_____

_____

_____

_____

12

23. *Please write in:*

Age in Years
(214-215)

Your age at last birthday

Date you filled in the questionnaire

(216-219)

Month   Day

90

PLEASE CHECK THROUGH THE QUESTIONNAIRE TO MAKE SURE YOU HAVE NOT MISSED ANY QUESTIONS.

THANK YOU VERY MUCH FOR YOUR HELP.

13

336

Supplementary Questionnaire for Mellon Fellows

April 25, 1990

GRADUATE CAREERS

AND

TEACHING PREPARATION

OF

MELLON FELLOWS

OFFICE CODING	
Serial Number	(1-3)
University	(4-5)
Department/ Program	(6-7)
Year of Award	(8-9)
F/H	(10)
Group	(11)
M/F	(12)

INTRODUCTION AND CONFIRMATION OF STATUS

Hello. May I speak to **<name of Mellon Fellow>**. [*If the respondent is not available, determine when and where he/she can be reached. When the individual is reached, continue:*]

This is **<interviewer's name>** calling on behalf of the Mellon Foundation.

According to the records I have, you were awarded a Mellon Fellowship on **<start date>** and subsequently you left the program. Is this correct? [*If the respondent disagrees with this, record the information below. If the respondent believes that he or she is still in the program, tell him that you will check further and will get back to him. Otherwise, continue.*]

As you know, the Mellon Fellowship Program is designed to help talented individuals obtain a Ph.D. degree in the humanities and to enter college teaching as a career. The Mellon Foundation is currently reviewing this program to increase its effectiveness and value. As part of this effort, a questionnaire was recently distributed to past and present participants in the Mellon Fellowship program about their activities in this area.

We are conducting a brief follow-up telephone survey with Fellows whose participation in the program ended *prior* to the award of a Ph.D. degree in the humanities. The records I have indicate that you are in this category. [*If the respondent disagrees, record the information below and tell him that you will check further and will get back to him. Otherwise, continue.*]

1

PARTICIPATION REQUEST

Your spending the time to answer a few questions about your participation would be very helpful for us. It should take between 10 and 15 minutes to answer these questions. In general the questions will concern your participation in the Mellon Fellowship program, how it helped or hindered your academic progress, what choices you made about your subsequent academic activities and career decisions, and how you think the Fellowship program could be improved. Your answers will be kept in strict confidence within the Mellon Foundation.

[**Only** *if the respondent protests about the confidentiality, read the following and check the appropriate answer below.*] I can remove your name from the answer sheets so that no one can identity your answers. Would that be satisfactory?

[*In any case, complete the following participation report:*]

_____	1.	Did not request confidentiality
_____	2.	Requested confidentiality
_____	3.	Declined to participate because of confidentiality concerns
_____	4.	Declined to participate for other reasons:

_____

_____

CONFIRMATION OF END-DATE

As background information for your answers, could you tell me when you left the Mellon Fellowship Program. This would be when you left the graduate program for which the Mellon Foundation was providing assistance. It might have been coincident with the last funding that you received or subsequent to that time if you continued your studies in the same program for a while longer.

_____ Year that respondent left program

2

338

ACADEMIC ACTIVITIES SINCE LEAVING THE MELLON FELLOWSHIP PROGRAM

1. Have you continued or do you intend to continue any academic studies since you left the program? [*Check one.*]

    _____ 1. Yes
    _____ 2. No [*Skip to question 5.*]

2. What is your current academic status? [*Read the following list and check one.*]

    _____ 1. Am currently enrolled?
    _____ 2. Have completed studies?
    _____ 3. Have temporarily suspended studies *with definite* plans to re-enroll?
    _____ 4. Or have suspended studies *without definite* plans to re-enroll?

3. What degree or degrees, if any, have you received or do you expect to receive beyond your first BA degree? What are the fields and the awarding universities? When did you or would you expect to receive the degrees? [*Fill in the following table for all degrees.*]

Degree	Field	University	Year

4. On the following five level scale, how valuable was your study as a Mellon Fellow to this *subsequent academic study* that we've been discussing? [*Read the following list and check one.*]

    _____ 1. Essential
    _____ 2. Very valuable
    _____ 3. Valuable
    _____ 4. Not much value
    _____ 5. No value at all

3

339

NON-ACADEMIC ACTIVITIES SINCE LEAVING THE FELLOWSHIP PROGRAM

5. What are your current activities? If you are engaged in different activities over the course of a week or a year, please tell us about any which involve 20% or more of your time. [*If there are multiple activities:*] What percent of your time are you involved in each activity?

Activity: _____   Percent of time: _____

_____   _____

_____   _____

_____   _____

_____   _____

_____   _____

Interviewer: Check the appropriate activities based on the above or probe further to determine the appropriate entries:

_____	1.	Academic studies
_____	2.	Teaching - college level
_____	3.	Teaching - pre-college level
_____	4.	Academic administration - college level
_____	5.	Academic administration - pre-college level
_____	6.	Government employment - elected
_____	7.	Government employment - hired
_____	8.	Not-for-profit employment
_____	9.	Other employment - legal
_____	10.	Other employment - medicine
_____	11.	Other employment - journalism
_____	12.	Other employment - business
_____	13.	Other employment - self-employed - consulting
_____	14.	Other employment - self-employed - creative writing
_____	15.	Other employment - other
_____	16.	Neither employed nor studying - leisure
_____	17.	Neither employed nor studying - raising a family
_____	18.	Neither employed nor studying - disability
_____	19.	Neither employed nor studying - other

4

6. On the following five level scale, how valuable was your study as a Mellon Fellow to these *current activities* that we've been discussing? [*Read the following list and check one.*]

    _____ 1. Essential
    _____ 2. Very valuable
    _____ 3. Valuable
    _____ 4. Not much value
    _____ 5. No value at all

7. Regarding your career choices, on a scale of 0 to 10 where 0 means "definitely will *not* chose" and 10 means "definitely *will* chose", how likely do you think you are to make college level teaching your principal career?

    _____   Likelihood from 0 (will not chose) to 10 (will chose).

5

VALUE OF MELLON FELLOWSHIP PROGRAM

8. We would now like to talk about the overall value of the Mellon Foundation program. Why did you leave the Mellon Fellowship program?

Reasons for leaving: _____

_____

_____

_____

Interviewer: Check the appropriate activities based on the above or probe further to determine the appropriate entries:

1. Left academic study - dissatisfaction with institution:

    _____ 1a. Dissatisfied with teachers
    _____ 1b. Dissatisfied with advisors (general or dissertation)
    _____ 1c. Dissatisfied with academia (politics, structure, etc.)
    _____ 1d. Dissatisfied with education being provided

2. Left academic study - dissatisfaction with studies:

    _____ 2a. Dissatisfied with field as a career
    _____ 2b. Dissatisfied with research as a career
    _____ 2c. Dissatisfied with teaching as a career
    _____ 2d. Dissatisfied with narrowness of specialization

3. Left academic study - career interests changed:

    _____ 3e. Decided other opportunities would be more fulfilling
    _____ 3f. Found that abilities different from mine were needed

4. Left academic study - compelled to leave:

    _____ 4g. Could not afford to continue studies
    _____ 4h. Personal reasons (children, own or others illness, etc.)
    _____ 4i. University asked or suggested withdrawal or termination

5. Changed status so no longer qualified for fellowship:

    _____ 5j. Changed university or field of academic study
    _____ 5k. Interrupted studies

6. Obtained other financial resources in same field of study & university:

    _____ 6l. Dropped from the Mellon program altogether
    _____ 6m. Changed to Honorary Mellon Fellow status

6

9. Considering all of its effects on your academic studies, your current activities, and your career, how valuable has your study to date as a Mellon Fellow been? Has it been: [*Read the following list and check one:*]

    _____   1.   Essential
    _____   2.   Very valuable
    _____   3.   Valuable
    _____   4.   Not much value
    _____   5.   No value at all

SUGGESTIONS

10. If a program were going to make three years of funding available to a graduate student, how would you allocate that support among the various years of study? Specifically, would you please rank the following five periods according to how valuable support is in each of those periods. [*Read list. Then ask, "Which is the most valuable period for support," and enter a "1" by that period. Repeat the process asking , "Which is the second (third, etc.) most valuable period for support," and enter a "2" ("3", etc.) by the corresponding period.*]

    _____   1.   In the first year of graduate study
    _____   2.   In the second year of graduate study
    _____   3.   In subsequent years but before dissertation is begun
    _____   4.   During the first year of work on the dissertation
    _____   5.   In subsequent years while writing the dissertation

11. For an individual like yourself who does not complete the program, what is the best time to terminate those studies? Based on your experience, for example, would it have been wiser in retrospective for you to have stopped the program earlier or not to have started the program at all?

    _____   1.   No - *Skip to question 13*
    _____   2.   Yes

7

343

12. When do you think it would have been best for you to have stopped? Why then?

Time and reasons: _____

_____

_____

_____

_____

13. If you had it to do over again, would you apply for a Mellon Fellowship?

_____ 1. Yes
_____ 2. No

Interviewer: If you don't think the previous responses fully explain this answer, ask the following:

Why?

Reasons: _____

_____

_____

_____

_____

8

CHECK FOR UNRETURNED QUESTIONNAIRES

14. If you have any additional suggestions or comments, please give us a call. The number is **609-924-9424**. Please ask for **Kate Ryan,** the administrative assistant for the Mellon Foundation.

    We may have a few follow-on questions. We hope you won't mind if we call you back again at some later time.

15. [*Interviewer: Ask this question if the respondent has not returned the original question:*] I have one last item that will just take a minute to cover. The Mellon Foundation sent you a written questionnaire in the mail around **<date>**, and we have not received it back yet. Did you receive that questionnaire?

    _____ 1. No [*Skip to Question 18.*]

    _____ 2. Yes [*Continue.*]

16. [*If "yes":*] Do you still have it or should we send you another copy?

    _____ 1. Send another [*Skip to Question 18, second sentence and confirm address.*]
    _____ 2. Still has [Continue.]

17. [*If "still has":*] The Mellon Foundation would greatly appreciate your completing and returning the questionnaire. It's very important for the Foundation to obtain everyone's responses.

    [*Skip to Question 19.*]

18. [*Otherwise:*] I'd like to send you another copy since it's important for the Foundation to obtain everyone's responses.

    Let me confirm your address. [*Read* **<address>**. *If not correct, ask for the correct address and enter it below.*]

    Address: _____

    _____

    _____

9

19. I'd like to thank you very much for your help and time in answering the questions this morning/afternoon/evening. Your answers will be very helpful to us.

Interviewer: The following space is provided for any extended comments provided by the respondent or any observations you may have about the interview. (Your comments must be differentiated from those of the respondent.)

Question number	Who? I=Interviewer R=Respondent	Comments
___	___	_____
___	___	_____
___	___	_____
___	___	_____
___	___	_____
___	___	_____
___	___	_____
___	___	_____
___	___	_____
___	___	_____
___	___	_____
___	___	_____
___	___	_____
___	___	_____
___	___	_____

10

Measuring Time to the Doctorate: Reinterpretation of the Evidence

William G. Bowen*, Graham Lord†, and Julie Ann Sosa*

Communicated by Ansley J. Coale, October 19, 1990 (received for review September 30, 1990)

ABSTRACT

There has been increasing concern that the length of time it takes to earn a doctorate in this country has increased dramatically over the last 20 years. The regularly cited evidence— organized by the year in which recipients of doctorates were awarded their degrees—is seriously misleading, however. The application of stable population theory to the problem suggests that the steady fall in the sizes of entering cohorts to graduate school has inflated both the measure of the absolute level of median time to degree and the increase in time to degree. When the same underlying data are reorganized by the year in which recipients of doctorates received their baccalaureate, the statistical bias is eliminated, and the median total time to degree in the humanities is shown to have risen 15–20% rather than the reported 40%.

FOR AT least 30 years, students, faculty members, and policymakers have been concerned about the length of time it takes to earn a doctorate (1–3). Recently, this problem has received new emphasis, largely because of what appears to have been a dramatic increase in the total time to degree (TTD) over the last 20 years. Data collected by the National Research Council indicate that median years from the Bachelor of Arts (B.A.) to the Doctor of Philosophy (Ph.D.) for all doctorate recipients in all fields at U.S. universities increased from a low of 7.9 in 1970 to 10.5 in 1988. The reported increase for recipients who were U.S. residents receiving doctorates was even more pronounced. In the humanities, the median TTD for U.S. residents receiving doctorates appears to have increased faster yet—by nearly 40%, from 9.0 years in 1972 to 12.4 in 1988 (Fig.

*Andrew W. Mellon Foundation, 140 East 62nd Street, New York, NY 10021; and †Mathtech (Mathematica) Inc., Princeton, NJ 08540.

Reprinted from *Proceedings of the National Academy of Sciences USA* 88 (February 1991): 713–17. Reprinted in accordance with the copyright policy of the National Academy of Sciences.

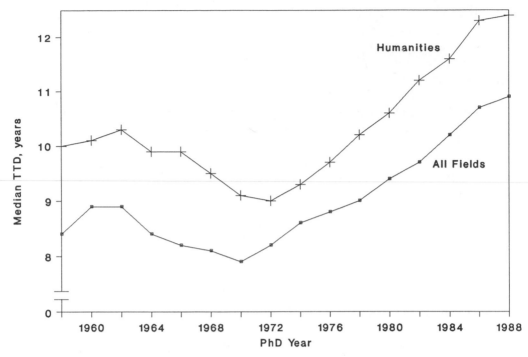

Figure D.1
Median Years to Doctorate, U.S. Residents, Ph.D.-Year Cohorts

D.1).[1] Not surprisingly, commentators in the popular press and elsewhere have seized on these findings and issued new calls for reform of graduate education (5–7).

We find ourselves in the peculiar position of applauding the desire to shorten TTD while rejecting the interpretation of the evidence used to suggest that it has increased dramatically. The regularly cited evidence is derived from data for cohorts of students grouped by the year in which they were awarded doctorates. For example, 12.4 years is the median TTD for all graduate students in the humanities who received doctorates in 1988 and therefore includes students

---

[1]The figures in the text and Fig. D.1 (and all other data in this paper unless otherwise indicated) are from special tabulations provided by the National Research Council from its "Survey of Earned Doctorates." Similar data have been published in ref. 4 and in earlier reports. These figures are for TTD, which is a gross measure of the number of years elapsed between earning a baccalaureate and a doctorate. The same trend is reported for a net measure of time lapse, "registered time to degree." The essential points apply to both of these measures; for the sake of simplicity, we generally refer only to TTD.

We have shown the data for the humanities as well as for all fields in part because working with a specific subject area minimizes the problems associated with the changing composition of degrees awarded. There has been a net shift of students over the last decade from fields with long durations (such as education and the humanities) to fields with shorter durations (such as the physical sciences and the life sciences); thus, taking account of changes in composition not only fails to explain the apparent increase in median TTD for all fields but also implies an even greater increase. "Direct standardization" of the all-field medians for composition by field in 1978 raises the median for 1988 by almost a full year—from 10.5 to 11.4. In the remainder of this paper, we focus on TTD in the humanities.

from many different entering cohorts—some who earned B.A. degrees as long ago as, say, 1972, some from the late 1970s, and some as recently as 1984. We demonstrate in the next section that this Ph.D.-year method of aggregation produces a highly misleading picture of trends in median TTD under the unusual conditions that have prevailed in American graduate education since World War II.

We then regroup the same underlying data by the year in which recipients of doctorates received their B.A. degrees. This B.A.-year method of aggregation (technical problems of its own notwithstanding) is free of the potential statistical bias that afflicts the Ph.D.-year method and is preferable in any event. Statistics for B.A.-year cohorts answer more directly the questions most relevant to students and policymakers: How much time does a typical B.A. recipient spend pursuing a doctorate? By how much has TTD actually risen? Using the B.A.-year approach, we estimate that the reported Ph.D.-year median for 1988 overstates the time a typical humanities graduate student spends earning a doctorate by as much as 2 years and that TTD in the humanities has risen 15–20% since 1972, not almost 40%.

SOURCES OF BIAS

Superficially, the case for concluding that TTD has risen dramatically since about 1970 seems abundantly clear, and it is easy to see why so many authors (including two of us; ref. 8) have taken the time series data depicted in Fig. D.1 at face value. This is, however, a serious error. The steepness of the apparent "trend" and the exaggeration of the absolute level of median TTD are largely statistical artifacts, created by the use of the Ph.D.-year method of aggregation during a period when there was a marked decline in the number of doctorates conferred per B.A.-year cohort. These twin problems are illustrated in Table D.1, which shows the time path of the simulated changes in median TTD for Ph.D.-year cohorts induced by a decline in the number of doctorates per B.A.-year cohort. This table is built on the key assumptions that the distribution of TTD for each B.A. cohort is absolutely constant over time (with the same percentages of recipients in each cohort earning degrees in 4 years or less, in 5 years, in 6 years, and so on), and therefore that median TTD is also constant. This assumption allows us to isolate the shifts in median TTD (for Ph.D.-year cohorts) caused by changes in the rate of growth of entry cohorts. To make this example realistic, we have used the actual distribution of TTD for the 1968 B.A.-year cohort in the humanities. (The exact shape of this distribution is shown in Fig. D.2 as the 0% growth-rate line. Substituting an alternative TTD distribution leads to results very similar to those reported below.)

The top rows in the table (years T-5 through T=0) show the stable conditions that result when there has been both an unchanging TTD distribution and a 0% growth rate in the number of doctorates per B.A.-year cohort over prior years.[2] The number of recipients of doctorates in each B.A.-year cohort is assumed to be fixed at 1000; the number of recipients of doctorates in each Ph.D.-year cohort also will be 1000 because of the assumption of a 0% growth rate; the median TTD for B.A.-year cohorts is always 9.15, given the assumption of an unchanging

---

[2]Twenty years is required to reach a new equilibrium (achieve stability) given the 1968 B.A.-year TTD distribution assumed here, with some students taking this long to earn their doctorates.

TABLE D.1
Simulated Effects of Moving from a 0% Growth Rate to a −4% per Year Growth Rate

| | Recipients | | Median TTD | |
Year	B.A.-year	Ph.D.-year	B.A.-year	Ph.D.-year
T-5	1000	1000	9.15	9.15
T-4	1000	1000	9.15	9.15
T-3	1000	1000	9.15	9.15
T-2	1000	1000	9.15	9.15
T-1	1000	1000	9.15	9.15
T=0	1000	1000	9.15	9.15
1	960	1000	9.15	9.15
2	922	1000	9.15	9.15
3	885	1000	9.15	9.15
4	849	998	9.15	9.17
5	815	993	9.15	9.19
6	783	984	9.15	9.23
7	751	971	9.15	9.30
8	721	955	9.15	9.38
9	693	936	9.15	9.47
10	665	913	9.15	9.56
11	638	890	9.15	9.65
12	613	864	9.15	9.72
13	588	837	9.15	9.77
14	565	810	9.15	9.82
15	542	782	9.15	9.86
16	520	754	9.15	9.88
17	500	726	9.15	9.90
18	480	698	9.15	9.91
19	460	670	9.15	9.91
20	442	644	9.15	9.92
21	424	618	9.15	9.92
22	407	593	9.15	9.92
23	391	569	9.15	9.92

Notes: The B.A.-year TTD distribution is assumed to be constant at the 1968 values for the humanities. (See 0% growth-rate line on Fig. D.2.)

TTD distribution; and the median TTD for Ph.D.-year cohorts also will be stable at 9.15. This base-case simulation shows that there is no bias in either the level of median TTD or the trend in TTD for students grouped by Ph.D.-year cohort so long as the number of doctorates produced by each B.A.-year cohort is constant.

If the growth rate for the number of recipients in B.A.-year cohorts shifts to −4% per year (which is a conservative estimate of what occurred during the late 1960s and 1970s), the number of Ph.D. recipients in the next B.A. cohort falls immediately, but the number of Ph.D.-year recipients is not affected until year 4, when the fastest completers among the smaller B.A.-year cohorts begin to appear in the Ph.D.-year distribution. Median TTD for the Ph.D.-year cohorts simultaneously shifts upward slightly.

This process goes forward, with decreasing numbers of Ph.D.-year recipients and increasing Ph.D.-year medians, until a new equilibrium is reached (after 20

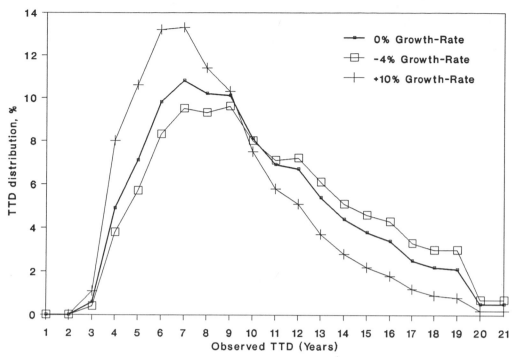

Figure D.2
Shifts in TTD Distributions, Humanities, Ph.D.-Year Cohorts

years), when the median TTD stabilizes at 9.92. This new median will remain constant so long as the number of B.A.-year recipients declines by −4% per year. The accompanying distribution of (stable) TTD is shown in Fig. D.2 as the −4% growth-rate line. The rightward shift in the Ph.D.-year TTD distribution (from the 0% growth-rate line) is evident.

The shift toward longer observed TTD results, in effect, from the inability of the successively smaller B.A.-year cohorts to replace fully the number of "fast" recipients from previous (larger) B.A.-year cohorts. In demographic parlance, the population is "aging," and that is why the observed median TTD for Ph.D.-year cohorts increases even though the median TTD for successive B.A.-year cohorts is unchanged. The situation is analogous to a life-table model in which the average age at death rises in spite of constant age-specific death rates because declining birth rates result in a shift in the age distribution of the population.[3]

This example illustrates the concepts involved, but it fails to explain fully why the reported upward trend in median TTD has been so exaggerated. The shift in the number of B.A. recipients that actually occurred during the 20 years was from a strongly positive growth rate to a negative growth rate, not just from a 0 growth rate to a negative growth rate. Table D.2 completes this part of the analysis by replacing the 0% growth rate with a positive 10% per year growth rate (the approximate rate of increase in the number of Ph.D. degrees per

TABLE D.2
Simulated Effects of Moving from a 0% Growth Rate to a −4% per Year Growth Rate

| Year | Recipients | | Median TTD | |
	B.A.-year	Ph.D.-year	B.A.-year	Ph.D.-year
T-21	135	102	9.15	9.15
T-20	149	102	9.15	9.12
T-19	164	103	9.15	9.06
T-18	180	106	9.15	8.94
T-17	198	110	9.15	8.75
T-16	218	115	9.15	8.50
T-15	239	122	9.15	8.31
T-14	263	130	9.15	8.17
T-13	290	140	9.15	8.06
T-12	319	151	9.15	7.99
T-11	350	164	9.15	7.93
T-10	385	179	9.15	7.89
T-9	424	196	9.15	7.87
T-8	466	215	9.15	7.85
T-7	513	236	9.15	7.84
T-6	564	259	9.15	7.84
T-5	621	285	9.15	7.84
T-4	683	314	9.15	7.83
T-3	751	345	9.15	7.83
T-2	826	379	9.15	7.83
T-1	909	417	9.15	7.83
T=0	1000	459	9.15	7.83
1	960	505	9.15	7.83
2	922	556	9.15	7.83
3	885	610	9.15	7.84
4	849	664	9.15	7.89
5	815	713	9.15	7.99
6	783	754	9.15	8.16
7	751	785	9.15	8.37
8	721	807	9.15	8.64
9	692	819	9.15	8.87
10	665	823	9.15	9.07
11	638	822	9.15	9.25
12	613	814	9.15	9.39
13	588	802	9.15	9.52
14	565	786	9.15	9.64
15	542	767	9.15	9.74
16	520	745	9.15	9.81
17	500	721	9.15	9.86
18	480	696	9.15	9.90
19	460	670	9.15	9.91
20	442	644	9.15	9.92

Note: The B.A.-year TTD distribution is assumed to be constant at the 1968 values for the humanities.

B.A.-year cohort in the immediate post-World War II years). The underlying TTD distribution for all B.A.-year cohorts remains fixed at its 1968 parameters.

The top 21 rows of Table D.2 show how median TTD for Ph.D.-year cohorts decreases from 9.15 when the growth rate was 0% to 7.83 when a new equilibrium is achieved (with a +10% per year growth rate). This strongly positive rate produces a spurious downward trend in median TTD and also a biased equilibrium level (now too low). The entire Ph.D.-year TTD distribution has shifted sharply to the left (+10 growth-rate line on Fig. D.2) because of the heavier weight in these distributions of the much larger number of fast finishers.

The bottom section of Table D.2 shows the effects of a subsequent shift from a +10% growth rate to a −4% growth rate. In contrast to the situation depicted in Table D.1, the number of Ph.D.-year recipients continues to increase well after the time when the number of B.A.-year recipients declines (because of the continuing contribution of the larger B.A.-year cohorts during the period of 10 percent growth), and the spurious upward trend in median TTD for Ph.D.-year cohorts is much steeper.

The extent of the shifts in the Ph.D.-year TTD distributions can be seen readily when we group some of the intervals and present the "equilibrium" medians together (Table D.3). The same TTD distribution for B.A.-year cohorts is seen to generate radically different Ph.D.-year distributions (with, for example, the percentage of all recipients taking 14 years or more rising from 10.0 at a +10% growth rate to 24.9 at a −4% rate). These perturbations are large by any reckoning, and the magnitude of the associated changes in median TTD demonstrates why statistical bias can be such a serious problem.

TRENDS FOR B.A.-YEAR COHORTS

It is impossible to present a definitive picture of the actual trend in either the number of Ph.D. recipients or median TTD for each B.A.-year cohort up to the present. It is only when all members of a cohort entering graduate school are dead that truly definitive measures of numbers of recipients and TTD can be

TABLE D.3
Percent Shifts in TTD Distributions of Ph.D.-Year Cohorts, by Growth Rate for Doctoral Recipients in B.A.-Year Cohorts

TTD, yr	*Growth Rates for BA-Year Cohorts*		
	+10%/yr	0%/yr	−4%/yr
0–4	9.1 %	5.5 %	4.3 %
5–7	37.1	27.7	23.5
8–10	29.1	28.4	26.9
11–13	14.7	19.0	20.4
14–16	6.7	11.6	14.1
17+	3.3	7.8	10.8
Median Years	7.83	9.15	9.92

Note: The B.A.-year TTD distribution is assumed to be constant at the 1968 values for the humanities. These are stable ("equilibrium") distributions for Ph.D.-year cohorts associated with each specified growth rate. See Fig. D.2 for the individual year distributions.

obtained. If carried up to the present, observed median TTD for B.A.-year cohorts would have significant biases. They would trend down even when the "true" median was constant or rising because reported medians exclude members of recent B.A.-year cohorts who will obtain doctorates in more years than have elapsed at the time median TTD is measured. Similarly, the number of recipients of doctorates in recent B.A.-year cohorts would be understated because only fast finishers would be counted.

Given the long duration of graduate study and the need to have statistics that are current, there is no perfect solution to this problem. However, distortion can be minimized and reasonable estimates of trends obtained by calculating truncated measures for B.A.-year cohorts which, in effect, cut off the tails of the distributions for all B.A.-year cohorts after a specified number of years (e.g., 10, 12, or 16 years). Truncated measures permit fair comparisons over time so long as there is no major change in the relationship between the (excluded) tail of the distribution and the main part. There are well-known techniques ("event history analysis" or "survival analysis") that could be used to address this problem. However, our main points can be made by using the simpler approach of truncation.

Number of Recipients

The direct relevance of the particular growth rates analyzed above is seen when we plot (Fig. D.3) the number of Ph.D. recipients in the humanities who belonged to B.A.-year cohorts between 1958 and 1976, using truncated series showing the number of recipients who earned degrees in 16 years or less and in 12 years or less. (These cohorts were of course the sources of large numbers of graduates who finished doctorates during the period when median TTD for Ph.D.-year cohorts is reported to have risen so markedly.) The presence of two distinct "regimes" is striking. Between 1958 and 1964, the number of recipients of doctorates in the humanities per B.A.-year cohort increased steadily and rapidly—at an average annual rate of more than 10%. The trend then reversed abruptly, and the number of recipients per B.A.-year cohort declined at an average annual rate of more than 4%.[4]

Thus, the extent of statistical bias associated with the use of the Ph.D.-year method can be estimated for this period by calculating the change in median TTD associated with moving from a regime in which the number of Ph.D. recipients per B.A.-year cohort had been growing steadily at a rate of 10% per year to a regime in which this number suddenly declines 4% per year. If we allow the −4% growth rate to operate for 16 years (the number of years used to calculate the reported increase in median TTD by the Ph.D.-year method), the resulting shift is from a median TTD of 7.83 to a new median of 9.74—an apparent increase of just over 24% (Table D.2).[5]

---

[4]These growth rates have been rounded downward so as not to exaggerate the changes that occurred; they are based on the 16-year truncated data set, which we believe to be the most reliable indicator of trends in number of recipients. Annualized growth rates were calculated by taking the geometric means of the actual annual growth rates between 1958 and 1964 and between 1964 and 1972; the rates obtained in this way are +10.85% and −4.91%, respectively.

[5]Data obtained from our larger study of individual universities support the assumption that the downward trend in recipients per B.A.-year cohort extended well beyond 1972 (the last year for which we have national data). The number of graduate students entering Ph.D. programs in

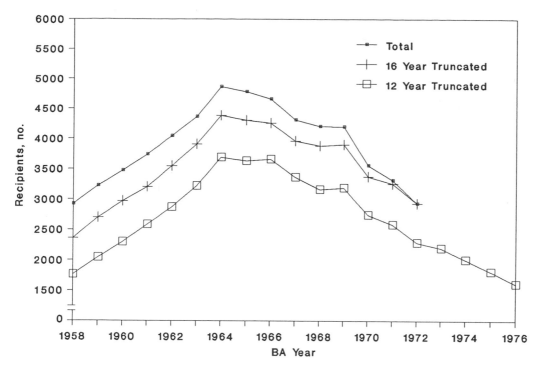

Figure D.3
Number of U.S. Ph.D. Recipients, Humanities, B.A.-Year Cohorts

To reiterate a central point: when we are studying trends in median TTD for Ph.D.-year cohorts, it is the pronounced shift from one growth rate to a very different growth rate that causes statistical distortion. The period since the late 1960s is unique in the history of American graduate education in that the number of recipients of doctorates declined for a number of years. Prior to this time, the number of doctorates awarded appears to have increased steadily at an average rate of something like 7% per year for more than four decades (with only World War II interrupting the pattern) (10). Because of the long-term steadiness of the rate of expansion in these earlier periods, data aggregated by Ph.D. year can be used to study trends in TTD prior to the mid-1960s without worrying about large-scale distortion. However, the levels of median TTD reported historically will almost all be biased downward because of the positive growth rate.

MEDIAN TTD

The last piece of the puzzle consists of the actual data on TTD grouped by B.A.-year cohorts. Special tabulations provided by the National Research

---

English, history, and political science at seven leading universities declined an average of more than 30% between 1972 and 1981; moreover, completion rates declined somewhat and median TTD rose at least modestly, leading to the conclusion that the number of recipients of doctorates per B.A.-year cohort declined even more rapidly than the number of entrants.

Council permitted us to regroup the same underlying national data to test the hypothesis that the trend in median TTD for B.A.-year cohorts should be much flatter than the trend for Ph.D.-year cohorts shown in Fig. D.1. The results are consistent with what one would have expected to find on the basis of the preceding analysis (Fig. D.4). The medians for the distributions truncated at 10 and 12 years increase at average annual rates of 0.88% and 1.12% between 1966 and 1980 and between 1966 and 1978, respectively, and we suspect that these estimates are, if anything, high.[6]

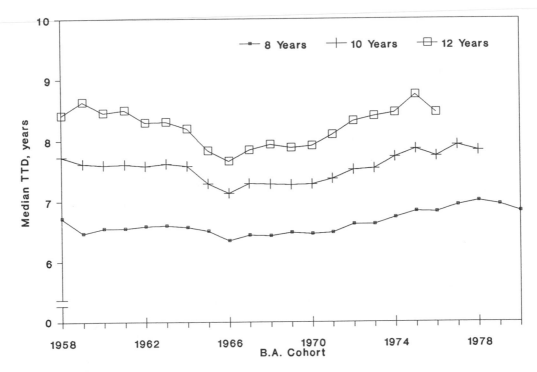

Figure D.4
Truncated Median TTD, Humanities, B.A.-Year Cohorts

---

[6]These rates of increase were calculated by fitting regression lines to the logarithms of the TTD figures. Increases in TTD appear to have been moderating in the most recent years. For example, the provisional Ph.D.-year median for all doctorates in all fields for 1989 is 10.5 years (the same median reported for 1988).

The trough in median TTD for B.A.-year cohorts in 1966, which is evident no matter which truncation is studied, cannot be the result of some anomaly in data collection (a natural suspicion) because the TTD data for these B.A.-year cohorts were collected over the many different years when these students received doctorates. Rather, we suspect that the dip in TTD between 1960 and 1966 was the product of a number of factors: the vigorous effort to reduce TTD that followed the publication of Berelson's book in 1960 (1), the more generous fellowship support made available in the mid-1960s, and the very favorable job markets for those who received doctorates. We believe that the sharp upturn in TTD that immediately followed was due in large part to changes in draft deferments and other events associated with the Vietnam War and not merely to a reversal of some of the factors mentioned above.

Given the need to work with truncated series, it would be especially unwise to invest these rates with specious precision. Roughly speaking, they translate into increases of between 15% and 20% over a 16-year period. This is hardly a negligible increase in median TTD, but it is also very different from a 38% increase (the 16-year figure for the Ph.D.-year data shown in Fig. D.1). The claims of consistency are satisfied by adding the estimate of the effect of statistical bias obtained above (+24%) to a rough mid-point of these estimates of the actual increase in median TTD (say +18%) and comparing the total (+42%) to the observed increase in median TTD for Ph.D.-year cohorts (+38%).[7]

In short, the same conclusion is reached whether we look at the problem from the perspective of the potential statistical bias involved in the Ph.D.-year method of aggregation or from the perspective of trends for the B.A.-year cohorts. Both approaches suggest strongly that the trend in the observed medians for Ph.D.-year cohorts exaggerates the "true" increase in TTD, which appears to have been one-third to one-half the size of the reported increase.

CONCLUDING REMARKS

Our intention in this paper has not been to criticize the National Research Council for the way it collects and publishes data on TTD. The Doctorate Records File is an extraordinarily rich (and reliable) source of information, and it is hard to envision any practical alternative to obtaining information from recipients of doctorates in the years in which they earn their degrees. The obvious lesson is that the method of organizing data can affect markedly the interpretation of apparent findings, and the results described here are an unusually good illustration of a particular source of statistical bias.[8]

An unfortunate consequence of this methodological problem is that some students may have been discouraged from pursuing doctorates in the humanities because they were led to believe that median TTD was as much as 2 years longer than it really is. The reality is bad enough, without any exaggeration of

---

[7]This is not a perfect comparison because the completion time distribution may not be constant over time. Also, the 38% increase was obtained simply by dividing the 1988 median by the 1972 median, rather than by fitting a regression line to the logarithms of the values. If we use the logarithmic method, the observed increase in Ph.D.-year TTD rises from 38% to 41%.

Data on trends in TTD that we have assembled for individual universities provide additional support for these findings. Preliminary evidence indicates only modest increases in median TTD in the humanities between the B.A.-year cohorts of 1967–1971 and 1972–1976. Aggregating these data by Ph.D. year rather than by B.A. year yields more pronounced upward trends—what one would expect, given the changes in the sizes of entry cohorts (which parallel the national changes).

[8]What is perhaps more surprising is the lack, to the best of our knowledge, of published discussions of this instance of what is clearly a generic problem. Special mention should be made, however, of David Breneman, who referred directly to this problem in an internal, unpublished study of the Ford Foundation's doctoral dissertation program prepared in July 1977 (D. Breneman, personal communication). Breneman also credits W. Lee Hansen and Judith S. Craig with having called attention earlier to the two ways of aggregating TTD data, but they did not recognize (W.L. Hansen and J.S. Craig, personal communication), as Breneman did, the associated problem of statistical distortion. We, too, were innocent of this complication until we were forced, by the way we had structured our larger study of graduate education, to reconcile TTD data organized by year of B.A. with TTD data organized by year of Ph.D. Ansley Coale suggested the relevance of population theory when we asked for help with our empirical puzzle (A. Coale, personal communication).

level and steepness of trend. For policymakers in graduate education, the danger is that the problem of TTD, serious as it is, will be overstated relative to other major problems. For example, we are convinced that attrition in the arts and sciences—the percentage of entering cohorts who never receive doctorates—has been both underestimated and too often ignored. Once again, a large part of the explanation has to do with data collection. There are no national data on completion rates, because such data can be collected only if determined efforts are made to follow the careers of all entrants to a graduate program, including those who drop out. This is exceedingly hard to do, but it is essential if the overall effectiveness of graduate education is to be assessed adequately.

APPENDIX

We have shown in the text how a change in the size of successive cohorts of B.A.-year recipients of Ph.D.s can bias the median when we use the Ph.D.-year method of grouping (Tables 1 and 2). The magnitude of the shifts in median TTD for Ph.D.-year cohorts is also determined by the shape of the completion-time distribution, which is assumed to be constant over time. The expression we develop below is valid for means but can be used to approximate the result for medians.

Assuming that the population has attained stability, then

$$\frac{dm}{dr} = - Var(T) \qquad [1]$$

where m is the mean TTD for the Ph.D.-year cohort; $Var(T)$ is the variance of the distribution of TTD for each B.A.-year cohort, assumed to be constant over time; and r is the growth rate for the B.A.-year cohorts.

To establish this equation, which applies to instantaneous small changes of r, we first define T to be a random variable that denotes the time in years from baccalaureate to the award of the doctorate and $g(t)$ to be its probability density. That is, $g(t)dt$ gives the probability an individual will finish the Ph.D. between t and $t + dt$ years. Hence, the mean at graduation in the stable population with growth rate r is given by:

$$m = \frac{\int te^{-rt}g(t)dt}{\int e^{-rt}g(t)dt}. \qquad [2]$$

The lower and upper limits of both integrals are 0 and ∞.

To see the effect of a change in the mean with respect to a change in the variable r, we first take logarithms and then differentiate:

$$\ln m = \ln \int te^{-rt}g(t)dt - \ln \int e^{-rt}g(t)dt. \qquad [3]$$

Therefore,

$$\frac{dm}{mdr} = -\frac{\int t^2 e^{-rt} g(t)dt}{m\int e^{-rt} g(t)dt} + m$$

$$= -\frac{E(T^2)}{m} + m \qquad [4]$$

where $E(T^2)$ denotes the second moment of the random variable T about the origin. We obtain Eq. 1 when we substitute the second moment by the variance of T, $Var(T)$, plus the mean squared.

To illustrate this formula, let us consider the humanities 1968 completion-time distribution we have used in the text. Its variance is equal to 16.005 years^2. When we substitute this value in the equation, we get an expected shift of 2.10 years for a change in growth rate from 10% to -4%. The simulation of Table D.2 shows the actual shift to be $9.92 - 7.83$—i.e., 2.09 years.

We thank A. Coale, N. Goldman, C. Makinson, D. Quackenbush, N. Rudenstine, K. Sochi, S. Turner, and M. Witte for their help.

REFERENCES

1. Berelson, B. (1960) *Graduate Education in the United States* (McGraw-Hill, New York), pp. 156–185.
2. Harmon, L. R. (1978) *A Century of Doctorates* (National Academy Press, Washington, DC), pp. 54-58.
3. Tuckman, H., Coyle, S. & Bae, Y. (1990) *On Time to the Doctorate* (National Academy Press, Washington, DC), pp. 107–111.
4. National Research Council (1989) *Summary Report, 1988* (National Academy Press, Washington, DC), pp. 21–24.
5. Evangelauf, J., *The Chronicle of Higher Education* (March 15, 1989), p. 1.
6. *The New York Times* (May 3, 1989), p. 1.
7. Ziolkowski, T. (1990) *Am. Scholar* 59(2), Spring, pp. 177–195.
8. Bowen, W.G. & Sosa, J.A. (1989) *Prospects for Faculty in the Arts and Sciences* (Princeton University Press, Princeton, NJ), pp. 163–166.
9. Coale, A. J. (1972) *The Growth and Structure of Human Populations: A Mathematical Investigation* (Princeton University Press, Princeton, NJ).
10. Harmon, L. R. (1978) *A Century of Doctorates* (National Academy Press, Washington, DC), p. 6.

Time-to-Degree and Faculty Promotion: A Study of Faculty Promoted to Tenure at Four Universities and Three Colleges, 1980–81 to 1989–90

As part of our investigation of graduate education in the United States, we undertook a small-scale study of faculty promoted to tenure. The primary objective was to determine whether there was a significant difference in total time-to-degree (TTD), defined as year of PhD minus year of BA, between faculty promoted to tenure at a set of highly selective institutions and graduate students in general. Another objective was to examine differences in TTD within this special universe of high-achieving faculty members related to field of study, gender, and type of institution (defined here as university versus liberal arts college). Finally, we wanted to see if differences in TTD by field of study were offset (at least in part) by subsequent differences in the time lapse between receipt of the PhD and promotion to tenure.

THE POPULATION STUDIED

The database for this study includes all arts-and-sciences faculty promoted to tenure between 1980–81 and 1989–90 at four research universities (Columbia, Michigan, Princeton, and Stanford) and three liberal arts colleges (Smith, Swarthmore, and Williams).[1] These institutions are broadly representative of their respective sectors of higher education. In addition, they illustrate differences within their sectors that are related, for example, to fields in which they have special academic strength, the length of time they have been coeducational, and—among the universities—geographical location.

While the hurdle of promotion to tenure no doubt varies within this universe, both by field of study and by institution, it is a high hurdle at all seven of these colleges and universities. From the standpoint of this study, that is their most salient common characteristic.

As a measure of quality, promotion to tenure at an institution with high standards has the virtue of being relatively free from at least some of the inevitable errors of judgment that affect decisions to recruit assistant professors (as well as, *a fortiori*, decisions to award fellowships to graduate students). Thus, working with this set of recently promoted faculty members permits a close examination of time-to-degree for an identifiable group of doctoral recipients of high talent.

Each of the seven institutions provided a list of all individuals promoted to tenure between 1980–81 and 1989–90, along with the department in which the individual was promoted (the field of study), year of promotion, year of BA, and year of PhD. Some of the institutions also volunteered additional information,

---

[1]This is sometimes referred to in the text as the "FacPro" data set.

including year of entry to graduate study and the institution awarding the PhD degree. We excluded from the raw data set a small number of individuals who did not have PhDs or had been appointed directly into tenured positions. We also excluded those individuals whose files lacked key pieces of information or whose fields were outside the scope of this study (most notably, engineering).

There are 443 individuals in the data set. Of these, approximately two-thirds were at one of the four universities, and approximately one-third were at one of the three colleges. The full array of promotions, classified by field of study, by gender, and by type of institution, is presented in Table E.1 so that cell sizes can be considered in interpreting results.

Table E.2 shows the distribution of promotions by broad field. About 40 percent of all promotions within both the colleges and the universities were in

TABLE E.1

Cell Sizes: Faculty Promoted to Tenure by Field, Type of Institution, and Gender, 1980–81 to 1989–90

	Four Universities			Three Colleges			Total		
Field	Men	Women	All	Men	Women	All	Men	Women	All
English	12	11	23	7	9	16	19	20	39
History	16	8	24	7	4	11	23	12	35
Other Humanities	52	20	72	14	21	35	66	41	107
Total Humanities	80	39	119	28	34	62	108	73	181
Econ	17	0	17	16	3	19	33	3	36
PolSci	12	8	20	5	1	6	17	9	26
Other SocSci	13	10	23	7	6	13	20	16	36
Total SocSci	42	18	60	28	10	38	70	28	98
Total Hum/SocSci	122	57	179	56	44	100	178	101	279
Math	10	0	10	4	3	7	14	3	17
Physics	15	0	15	3	1	4	18	1	19
Other NatSci	75	22	97	24	7	31	99	29	128
Total NatSci	100	22	122	31	11	42	131	33	164
All Arts/Sci	222	79	301	87	55	142	309	134	443

Source: FacPro data set; see accompanying text for description.

TABLE E.2

Distribution of Faculty Promotions by Broad Field and Type of Institution, 1980–81 to 1989–90 (percent)

Field	Four Universities	Three Colleges	Total
Humanities	40%	44%	41%
SocSci	20	27	22
NatSci	41	30	37

Source: FacPro data set.

the humanities (including history), despite the general decline in interest in the humanities documented in various studies. There were relatively more promotions within the sciences (including psychology) than within the social sciences, and this differential was much larger for the universities than for the colleges.

The share of promotions awarded to women in the various fields of study varied by type of institution (Table E.3). For example, women accounted for 26 percent of all promotions in the four universities and 39 percent in the three colleges. However, this calculation includes Smith, a women's college, which has a higher overall percentage of women faculty members than any of the other institutions in this study. If Smith were excluded, and the data for colleges were limited to Williams and Swarthmore, the differential favoring the promotion of women in the colleges as contrasted with the universities would be diminished but by no means eliminated. Women accounted for 35 percent of all promotions in the two remaining colleges.[2]

MEDIAN TIME-TO-DEGREE

The outcome analyzed here is total time-to-degree, and the answer to our principal question is clear. TTD was appreciably shorter among faculty members promoted to tenure at these colleges and universities than among all recipients of doctorates in the arts and sciences (Table E.4). On average, the median TTD for this group of faculty was roughly 80 percent of the median for doctoral recipients as a group.

Still, the length of time that it took the typical tenured faculty member to receive a doctorate was by no means negligible: over five years from receipt of BA in the sciences and almost seven years in the humanities and social sciences. This finding warns against embracing exaggerated notions of how quickly even the ablest individuals can be expected to complete their doctorates.

TABLE E.3
Women's Share of Faculty Promotions by Broad Field and Type of Institution, 1980–81 to 1989–90 (percent)

Field	Four Universities	Three Colleges	Two Coed Colleges[a]	Total
Humanities	33%	55%	54%	40%
SocSci	30	26	10	29
NatSci	18	26	28	20
All fields	26	39	35	30

Source: FacPro data set.
[a]Williams and Swarthmore only.

[2]The absolute numbers of women promoted to tenure are also noteworthy. If we exclude Smith, there were no women among the 45 faculty members promoted to tenure in economics and physics at the remaining six institutions. In mathematics, no women were promoted within the universities, compared to 10 men (Table E.1).

TABLE E.4
Median Time-to-Degree among Faculty Promoted to Tenure and All Doctorate
Recipients by Broad Field, 1967–1971 BA Cohorts (number of years)

Field	Faculty Promoted to Tenure	All Doctorate Recipients
SocSci	6.8	8.5
NatSci	5.2	7.0[a]
All Arts/Sci	6.1	7.6

Source: FacPro data set and special tabulations from Doctorate Records File.

Notes: "All Doctorate Recipients" are recipients of doctorates in the arts and sciences who earned their BAs between 1967 and 1971. While the faculty members in our study received their BAs in varying years, their median five-year cohort was 1967–1971.

[a]Unweighted average of physical sciences, biological sciences, and psychology.

TABLE E.5
Median Time-to-Degree among Faculty Promoted to Tenure by Field, Type
of Institution, and Gender, 1967–1971 BA Cohorts (number of years)

Field	Four Universities			Three Colleges			Total		
	Men	Women	All	Men	Women	All	Men	Women	All
English	4.8	6.1	5.1	5.7	11.0	7.1	5.1	6.3	5.4
History	7.7	9.5	8.2	7.7	10.5	8.1	7.7	9.5	8.2
Other Humanities	6.7	7.8	7.1	6.3	7.7	6.8	6.5	7.8	7.0
Total Humanities	6.3	7.4	6.8	6.4	8.2	7.2	6.4	7.8	7.0
Econ	4.6	—	4.6	7.0	13.0	8.0	5.1	13.0	5.3
PolSci	7.5	7.0	7.1	7.0	—	7.5	7.3	7.1	7.2
Other SocSci	6.0	8.0	6.4	9.0	8.0	8.3	6.5	8.0	7.3
Total SocSci	5.3	7.3	5.8	7.3	11.5	7.9	6.1	7.8	6.8
Total Hum/SocSci	6.0	7.4	6.5	6.8	8.3	7.4	6.3	7.8	6.9
Math	4.2	—	4.1	4.5	6.0	5.0	4.3	6.0	4.3
Physics	5.4	—	5.4	7.0	—	7.5	5.5	—	6.1
Other NatSci	5.2	5.3	5.2	5.4	6.6	5.6	5.2	5.6	5.3
Total NatSci	5.1	5.3	5.1	5.3	6.6	5.6	5.1	5.7	5.2
All Arts/Sci	5.4	6.8	5.7	6.3	7.9	6.9	5.7	7.3	6.1

Source: FacPro data set.

Notes: Dash indicates empty cell or cell with fewer than three members. While the faculty members in our study received their BAs in varying years, their median five-year cohort was 1967–1971.

In designing this study, we expected TTD to vary not only according to field of study, but also by gender and between colleges and universities. As shown in Table E.5, this three-way analysis yields a highly systematic pattern of associations:

- Scientists consistently completed their degrees in less time than did faculty in the humanities and social sciences. The differences in medians are largest among women faculty members in the universities (2.1 years) and smallest among men faculty members in these same universities (0.9 years).

- While men and women scientists within the four universities finished in almost the same length of time, women took appreciably longer than men to obtain their degrees in the humanities and social sciences within the four universities and in all fields within the three colleges.
- TTD varies significantly within broad fields. Within the humanities, faculty who were promoted in English had a consistently shorter time-to-degree than did faculty promoted in history. This relationship holds for every comparison by gender and type of institution shown in the table except for women faculty in the three colleges; the anomaly is the high median TTD for women in English within these colleges. Overall, the difference in median TTD is—surprisingly—almost three years.
- Within the social sciences, faculty promoted in economics took appreciably less time to earn their degrees than did faculty in political science (5.3 years, as compared to 7.2 years overall). However, this large difference is due entirely to results within the universities, where the economists (who were, as we noted earlier, all male) had a median time-to-degree of just 4.6 years. In general, median TTD for faculty in political science is just below the corresponding median in history.
- As one might have expected, mathematicians finished their degrees more rapidly than other scientists—presumably because of the absence of laboratory work. In general, the physicists took somewhat longer than the other scientists. While faculty in engineering were excluded from the body of this study, median TTD for faculty promoted to tenure in engineering at two universities was computed, and their median TTD (5.4 years) is only slightly higher than the median for all of the sciences within the four universities (5.1 years).
- Focusing on university-college differences, we found that median TTD for male faculty members who were promoted to tenure was nearly the same within both sets of institutions in both the humanities (6.3 years within the universities; 6.4 years within the colleges) and the natural sciences (5.1 years within the universities; 5.3 years within the colleges). This result, however, stands in contrast to the general tendency for TTD to be shorter among the university faculty than among the college faculty. This is particularly true for women faculty.
- Median TTD for women faculty promoted to tenure in all fields within all seven of these institutions was 1.6 years longer than median TTD for the comparable group of men. Only a small part of this overall difference is due to the relatively small number of women promoted in the sciences. Within the humanities and social sciences, median TTD for women was, respectively, 1.4 and 1.3 years longer than median TTD for men. These gender-related differences appear to be significantly greater than the differences by gender reported for all recipients of doctorates by the National Research Council.
- There appears to be a rather persistent negative correlation between median TTD and the perceived competitive strength of a particular department in a particular university. In general, the greater the presumed ability of a department to compete for top candidates for appointment, the lower the TTD for those promoted to tenure in the department. This conclusion is based in part on inspection of the detailed TTD figures for particular departments within individual colleges and universities (which are not

reproduced in this appendix). This pattern offers additional support for the general proposition that student quality is related to time-to-degree.

DISTRIBUTION OF TTD BY INTERVALS

In addition to calculating medians, we calculated cumulative percentages of faculty who completed their degrees in four years or less, in six years or less, in eight years or less, and in ten years or less. The results for all seven institutions are presented in Table E.6. Concentrating on the ends of the distribution, we found the following relationships:

- Overall, one-fifth of all faculty promoted to tenure within all seven institutions included in this study finished their PhDs within four years of receiving their BAs. Nearly 60 percent of the mathematicians finished this quickly, as did roughly one-quarter of all faculty members (men and women) in English, economics, physics, and other sciences. Generally speaking, the probability of finishing in four years or less was about twice as high for faculty in the universities as for those in the colleges. It was also about twice as high among men as among women.
- The striking difference between English and history that was evident in the medians is even clearer in the cumulative percentages. Whereas 72 percent of faculty in English completed their doctorates within six years of the BA, only 20 percent of faculty in history received their degrees this quickly. The field closest to history in this respect is political science, in which 35 percent of these faculty finished their degrees in six years or less.

TABLE E.6
Cumulative Distribution of Time-to-Degree among Faculty Promoted to Tenure by Field and Gender, 1967–1971 BA Cohorts (percent)

Field	All				Men				Women			
	4 Years or Less	5–6 Years	7–8 Years	9–10 Years	4 Years or Less	5–6 Years	7–8 Years	9–10 Years	4 Years or Less	5–6 Years	7–8 Years	9–10 Years
English	25.6	71.8	82.1	84.6	26.3	89.5	94.7	100.0	25.0	55.0	70.0	70.0
History	8.6	20.0	60.0	80.0	13.0	30.4	69.6	82.6	0.0	0.0	41.7	75.0
Other Humanities	8.4	41.1	71.0	80.4	7.6	50.0	77.3	84.8	9.8	26.8	61.0	73.2
Total Humanities	12.2	43.6	71.3	81.2	12.0	52.8	78.7	87.0	12.3	30.1	60.3	72.6
Econ	25.0	61.1	72.2	88.9	27.3	66.7	78.8	97.0	—	—	—	—
PolSci	3.8	34.6	80.8	92.3	5.9	41.2	76.5	88.2	0.0	22.2	88.9	100.0
Other SocSci	13.9	38.9	66.7	83.3	15.0	50.0	70.0	85.0	12.5	25.0	62.5	81.3
Total SocSci	15.3	45.9	72.4	87.8	18.6	55.7	75.7	91.4	7.1	21.4	64.3	78.6
Total Hum/SocSci	13.3	44.4	71.7	83.5	14.6	53.9	77.5	88.8	10.9	27.7	61.4	74.3
Math	58.8	88.2	94.1	94.1	64.3	92.9	100.0	100.0	33.3	66.7	66.7	66.7
Physics	26.3	68.4	94.7	94.7	27.8	72.2	100.0	100.0	—	—	—	—
Other NatSci	27.3	74.2	92.2	99.2	29.3	75.8	92.9	99.0	20.7	69.0	89.7	100.0
Total NatSci	30.5	75.0	92.7	98.2	32.8	77.1	94.7	99.2	21.2	66.7	84.8	93.9
All Arts/Sci	19.6	55.8	79.5	88.9	22.3	63.8	84.8	93.2	13.4	37.3	67.2	79.1

Source and Notes: Same as Table E.5.

- Approximately 81 percent of faculty promoted to tenure within the humanities had a TTD that was lower than the median for all recipients of doctorates in the humanities. The corresponding figures in the social sciences and the natural sciences are 72 percent and 87 percent, respectively.
- At the long end of the distribution, we found that 21 percent of all the faculty included in this study received their PhDs nine years or more after receiving their BAs and that 11 percent took eleven years or more.[3]
- We were able to look more closely at the histories of faculty members who took eleven years or more to finish the PhD in two of the universities participating in this study, and we found that relatively long delays in starting PhD programs often accounted for the high TTD. Elapsed time-to-degree (ETD), defined as year of PhD minus year of entrance to PhD program, was eleven years or more for only about one-third of these individuals.

TIME-TO-PROMOTION

While the focus of this study was primarily time-to-degree, it was also possible to examine a related proposition having to do with time-to-promotion. Several

TABLE E.7
Median Time-to-Promotion by Field, Type of Institution, and Gender, 1967–1971 BA Cohorts (number of years)

Field	Four Universities			Three Colleges			Total		
	Men	Women	All	Men	Women	All	Men	Women	All
English	7.7	8.0	7.8	8.0	8.0	8.0	7.8	8.0	7.9
History	7.4	8.8	7.9	8.3	8.5	8.4	7.7	8.7	8.0
Other Humanities	8.0	8.3	8.1	8.0	7.6	7.8	8.0	7.9	8.0
Total Humanities	7.8	8.3	8.0	8.1	7.7	7.9	7.9	8.0	7.9
Econ	6.3	—	6.3	9.0	7.8	8.8	7.6	7.8	7.6
PolSci	7.8	7.5	7.7	6.8	—	6.5	7.5	7.6	7.4
Other SocSci	8.7	8.5	8.6	7.3	7.5	7.4	8.2	8.1	8.2
Total SocSci	7.4	8.1	7.6	7.9	7.5	7.8	7.6	7.9	7.7
Total Hum/SocSci	7.6	8.2	7.8	8.0	7.7	7.9	7.7	8.0	7.8
Math	6.3	—	6.3	10.0	9.0	9.6	7.4	9.0	7.6
Physics	8.7	—	8.7	10.0	—	9.0	8.9	—	8.8
Other NatSci	8.3	8.7	8.4	9.5	9.3	9.5	8.6	8.8	8.6
Total NatSci	8.1	8.7	8.2	9.7	9.0	9.5	8.5	8.8	8.5
All Arts/Sci	7.8	8.3	7.9	8.4	7.9	8.2	8.0	8.1	8.0

Source: FacPro data set.
Notes: Dash indicates empty cell or cell with fewer than three members. Median time-to-promotion measures the time between receipt of the BA and promotion to tenure. While the faculty members in our study received their BAs in varying years, their median five-year cohort was 1967–1971.

---

[3] Only 10 percent of women promoted to tenure within the universities took eleven years or more from BA to PhD, compared to 36 percent of women promoted in the colleges.

colleagues have suggested that the shorter TTD in the sciences, compared with the humanities and social sciences, is somewhat misleading as a measure of the duration of "training" in that young scientists are more likely than their counterparts in other fields to hold postdoctoral appointments. We have no direct measure of the frequency or duration of postdoctoral appointments among the faculty included in this study, but it is possible to calculate the median time between receipt of PhD and promotion to tenure.

Time between receipt of PhD and promotion to tenure was in fact longer for scientists than for humanists and social scientists (Table E.7). This was true for both male and female faculty members in both the universities and the colleges. Within the universities, the difference between the median for faculty in the sciences and that for faculty in the humanities and social sciences was 0.5 years for both men and women; therefore, this difference offsets something like half of the corresponding difference in median TTD for the men and one-quarter for the women.

Theory and Its Reverberations

In Chapter Twelve, we reviewed some of the ways in which selected English, history, and political science (EHP) graduate programs have changed since the 1960s, as well as some of the ways in which others have retained a quite persistent image and substance. Given this variety, generalizations are bound to be misleading. The current situation in many humanistic and social science fields is such that observers in search of material to criticize or parody can find ample evidence to support the proposition that everything is in disarray. Alternatively, others are in an equally strong position to assert (with considerable evidence) that a large number of programs have not changed dramatically over time, and that many of the most highly rated have remained quite focused, structured, and eclectic in methodology.

Nonetheless, the very fact that the curricula of two major programs in English literature could differ as much as those examined in Chapter Twelve indicates that the humanities and related disciplines have been in a period of deep transformation and division, born of profound intellectual self-scrutiny and philosophical questioning. While these issues are far too complex for summary treatment, they deserve at least some further discussion because they bear directly upon the substance of so much education in the arts and sciences.

What follows is an effort to describe (in an inevitably limited way) the current state of "theory" in selected humanistic and related social-science fields as depicted by several scholars and commentators. It is not our purpose to judge whether the existing state is cause for jubilation or alarm (and both exclamatory modes are abundantly represented in the literature). Rather, we are primarily concerned to indicate some of the main tendencies that define the present situation.

In one sense, that situation is vividly enough described in the titles of many recent volumes: Hans Belting's *The End of the History of Art?*, Terry Eagleton's *Criticism and Ideology*, Clifford Geertz's *Works and Lives: The Anthropologist as Author*, Alvin Kernan's *The Death of Literature*, Frederick Jameson's *The Prison House of Language*, Gertrude Himmelfarb's *The New History and the Old*, James Clifford's *The Predicament of Culture*—and so on. Behind some of these works lie the writings of a number of continental theorists and critics: Walter Benjamin, Theodor Adorno, Claude Levi-Strauss, Barthes, Foucault, Lacan, Derrida, and others. And beyond those just mentioned there are earlier philosophers as different and yet transformative as Nietzsche and Wittgenstein, linguistic theorists such as Saussure, earlier Marxist literary critics such as Lukacs, and a substantial number of feminist writers and theorists.

Because there has been a succession of highly visible theoretical movements or points of view since at least the 1960s, and because there are any number of competing theories even now, it is impossible to provide a single explanation of the current situation. At the same time, many current theories take their initial point of departure from a set of intellectual premises that one can identify, and these are perhaps best expressed by some of the writers already mentioned. The following quotations offer a modest introduction to at least part of the terrain that is being explored:

> In contrast to the nineteenth century view of life as a mighty conflict, the twentieth century has been increasingly dominated by a conception of reality as a created system . . . . We make up our universe, that is, from our own particular point of view, and it would look quite different from other points of view, no one of which has priority over others. . . . Language, according to Saussure, is a formal structure or set of rules within which at any given time a word or concept derives its meaning not by referring to a fixed reality but from its place in the system, in relationship, that is, to the other parts of the system. The same concept underlies the characteristic social sciences of our time, anthropology and sociology, which see the different human societies they study as so many codes, systems for living, constructed by men to arrange in some kind of coherent order all the things and activities the system chooses to include. . . . [Man's] business is no longer to seek and represent some absolute truth, but to live within and perfect the system in which he participates, recognizing that it is only one of many ways of organizing the world.
>
> (Alvin Kernan, *The Imaginary Library: An Essay on Literature and Society* [Princeton University Press, 1982], 168)

> The title of this session ["Analysis, Narrative, and the Structure of the Past"], which would, a generation ago or even more recently, have signified an item of consensus, now denotes an area of conflict. To put it simply, the past has no structure, at least not in any sense of a separate, objective, "given" reality, independent of our contemplation, patiently awaiting our discovery of it. Rather, the past is increasingly conceived as the malleable outcome of a set of transactions—dialogic, perhaps, or contestatory—in which meaning issues from the convergence of event, imagination, and our modes of discourse. . . . The documents and documentary traces in which individual and social life is embedded are never merely neutral records. . . .
>
> The 19th century dream of scientific precision, whether in literary or historical analysis, has given way to an acceptance of shared limits. Absolute standards of judgment have been challenged by the idea that norms are themselves the construction of communities; "truth" represents the protocols, conventions, and beliefs that prevail in a specific society at a specific moment.
>
> Like all upheavals, the collapse of boundaries between, e.g., the "factual" and "fictional," between the "documentary" and the "imagined," between the metaphorical and the conceptual, is unsettling. . . .
>
> (Peter Conn, "Narrative in the Making of History," in *Viewpoints* [ACLS, 1989], 26–27)

> One of the major assumptions upon which anthropological writing rested until only yesterday, that its subjects and its audiences were not only separable but morally disconnected, that the first were to be described but not addressed, the second informed but not implicated, has fairly well dissolved. The world has its compartments still, but the passages between them are much more numerous and much less well secured. . . .
>
> Indeed the very right to write—to write ethnographically—seems at risk. The entrance of once colonized or castaway peoples (wearing their own masks, speaking their own lines) onto the stage of the global economy, international high politics, and world culture has made the claim of the anthropologist to be a tribunal of the unheard,

a representor of the unseen, a kenner of the misconstrued, increasingly difficult to sustain. Malinowski's happy "Eureka!" when first coming upon the Trobrianders— "Feeling of ownership: It is I who will describe them"—sounds in a world of OPEC, ASEAN, *Things Fall Apart* . . . not merely presumptuous, but outright comic. . . .

All of this is made the more dire, leading to distracted cries of slight and crisis by the fact that at the same time, the moral foundations of ethnography have been shaken by decolonization . . . , its epistemological foundations have been shaken by a general loss of faith in received stories about the nature of representation. . . . What is the evidence? How was it collected? What does it show? How do words attach to the world, texts to experience, works to lives . . . ?

(Clifford Geertz, *Works and Lives: The Anthropologist as Author* [Stanford University Press, 1988], 132–135)

The cluster of related concepts that reveal themselves in these passages—concepts derived from the separate fields of literature, history, and anthropology, with allusions to physics, linguistics, sociology, and other disciplines—defines in at least an approximate way the "epistemological crisis" that has been fostered by the emergence of competing theories and has simultaneously given rise to yet more theories. Again and again, we encounter the same fundamental idea: Individuals and particular cultures shape various definitions of reality, in contrast to the notion that reality is something objective, waiting to be discovered.

As a consequence, the very process of description can become a dubious one. Does the author *describe*, or is he or she creating, imagining, constructing? Are there secure identifiable facts, or only interpretations? Are some interpretations more accurate than others? Can those who carry the burden—through some form of historical inheritance—of a colonial-imperialist identity presume to understand or speak for (or intrude upon) those who have been previously dominated or marginalized? How can one know and understand experience that these others (or the "Other") have undergone? Even if one believes one knows, how does one finally know that one ever really knows?

It is precisely at this point that, for many writers, epistemological doubt can give way to demoralization and intellectual paralysis, or to ideological assertiveness and conflict, or to efforts aimed at finding some new common ground. In curricular terms, the debate often centers upon questions related to the traditional canon, or to the values of Western civilization in contrast to those of other traditions. Shall we, for example, diminish the number of established major texts or major authors in order to make room for previously subordinated voices and traditions—whether feminist, ethnic, political, or religious in nature? What constitutes a significant text: one that has had an important influence on traditions—especially Western traditions—reaching into the deep past, or perhaps one that speaks with power to realms of experience untouched by works in the traditional canon? Or both? Why should the varieties of human experience, the history, and the forms of aesthetic expression of previously subordinate or marginal groups be viewed as less important or compelling than those of dominant groups? To what extent are appeals to quality and standards of judgment helpful in answering such questions? What criteria of quality are relevant, and how are they to be applied? By whom?

Once these and other questions have been raised, it is clear why "theory" can assume so important a role in academic and intellectual affairs. If one is unsure or uncertain about fundamental matters, then the best one may be able to do is to explore alternative hypotheses or theories. Moreover, if uncertainty and doubt persist for a considerable time, then the potential for a very great number of alternative and rival theories will almost certainly increase.

While these problems may be especially apparent at the present time, it may be helpful to recall that our predicament is hardly unique. Fundamental transformations took place during the Renaissance and Reformation eras in Western Europe. An analogous reordering occurred in the latter part of the Enlightenment era, with the movement into what we have come to call the Romantic period. Finally, the crisis in the later Victorian age—stimulated by advanced Biblical scholarship, by Darwin's theories, by Marx's analysis of social and economic structures, and by other significant developments—clearly created a major divide between the later part of the nineteenth century and modern civilization. Moreover, all of these earlier changes had deep educational implications, and led to highly divisive debates.

While our own situation may seem equally or even more fragmented, and less amenable to accommodation than several earlier crises, it is useful to remember the very powerful "shaking of the foundations" at other moments in the past. Both the nature of the current debate and its particular form of fragmentation are outlined more sharply in the following quotation:

> The present situation in the study of literature at least, and in the United States at least, is characterized by what I have elsewhere called the almost universal triumph of theory. . . .
>
> I mean what is evident on every side, not only the development of a large number of powerful repeating theoretical discourses, each with its somewhat barbarous code name, hermeneutic, phenomenological, Lacanian, feminist, reader response, Marxism, Foucauldian, structuralist, semiotic, deconstructionist, new historicist, cultural-critical, and so on, but also the immense proliferation of courses, curricula, books, handbooks, dissertations, essays, lectures, new journals, symposia, study groups, centers, and institutes all overtly concerned with theory or what are called cultural studies. . . . What needs to be stressed here is the large number of competing theories and their incoherence. They cannot be synthesized into some one grand all-inclusive theory of literature.
>
> The victory of theory has transformed the world of literary study from what it was when I entered it 40 years ago. In those happy days we mostly studied primary works, in the context of literary history, with some overt attention in our teaching to the basic presupposition of the so-called new criticism . . . . Now it seems to be necessary to be acquainted with a large number of incompatible theories, each claiming exclusive allegiance. I sometimes feel sorry for my students who must read and be tested on all of these things for which I was not held accountable.
>
> (J. Hillis Miller, "Humanistic Research," in *The Humanities in the University: Strategies for the 1990's*, American Council of Learned Societies Occasional Paper no. 6 [ACLS, April 1988], 25–26)

Miller's observations are interesting for several reasons. First, they do indeed point to the amount of incoherence and conflict in the intellectual fields with which we are concerned. They also make it quite clear that, while these conflicts mirror and have an undoubted effect upon important tensions in the larger world outside academia, they are also quite academic in nature, and have achieved something of the character of a scholastic debate that is beginning to show some signs of breaking under the strain of its own weight. Indeed, the fact that Professor Miller—a very able theorist himself—can so easily survey the field with such detachment and obvious irony suggests how close things may be to the point where prolonged and unresolved conflict can finally lead to weariness and even boredom, resulting eventually in a new and unpredictable shift of direction.

One disconcerting aspect of the present situation is that the strongly asserted claims and the rhetoric of much recent theory have provoked—not always deeper and more philosophically thoughtful responses—but (perhaps not surprisingly) a similar rhetoric by antagonists. Armageddon looms large in the minds of many writers, who often become increasingly preoccupied with differences, rather than with the effort to clarify arguments and positions in an attempt to achieve a sharper understanding of the real intellectual issues.

Nevertheless, there are several recent signs, from a number of quarters, suggesting that some individuals and groups are now focusing on the question of how to present and absorb or integrate—insofar as possible—some of the different perspectives and modes of analysis now available. There have been some discernible shiftings of positions, and some proposals to seek a form of truce that would leave room for further exploration and debate, but would do so within a more precisely articulated framework.

There is not space here to discuss these recent developments in detail (nor should one suggest that they represent a broad consensus rather than a set of signals, or straws in the wind). One might cite, however, Stanley Fish's (1989) article "Being Interdisciplinary Is So Very Hard to Do," in which he underlines the fairly straightforward point that scholars and critics who wish to dissolve traditional disciplines of knowledge on the grounds that such disciplines are socially or culturally "constructed" may well be correct in their premise. At the same time, Fish goes on to make the equally basic point that any new "interdisciplinary" (or other) curricular structure can scarcely then make the claim that it is somehow free from contingency, cultural conditioning, or ideology. As Fish suggests: "Typically the members of . . . [a] new discipline represent themselves as anti-disciplinary, but in fact, as Daniel Schon points out, they will constitute a 'new breed' of 'counter-professionals/experts' " (pp. 20–21).

Fish's conclusion is candidly based on his own personal interests and preferences rather than on an effort to be more generally prescriptive:

> For my own part . . . I find the imperialistic success of literary studies heartening and the emergence of cultural studies as a field of its own, exhilarating. It is just that my pleasures at these developments have nothing to do with the larger claims—claims of liberation, freedom, openness—often made for them. The American mind, like any other, will always be closed, and the only question is whether we find the form of closure it currently assumes acceptable to our current urgencies.
> (Stanley Fish, "Being Interdisciplinary Is So Very Hard to Do," *Profession* [MLA], 1989, 21)

Fish's piece ends on a relativist and highly personal note—all categories of knowledge are constructed, and the main question is whether the current ones interest us and respond to our urgencies. But there is, of course, the continuing question of who "we" are, and whose urgencies are at stake—quite apart from whether one accepts the initial premise concerning the purely constructionist view of truth and of intellectual modes of inquiry. The article makes the point that new interdisciplinarians and proponents of openness, judged by certain premises, have no firmer epistemological ground to stand upon than their predecessors. Fish, however, goes further than at least one dominant version of constructionist theory would require or posit: For it is certainly possible to argue that within the conventions of a given cultural system, one can make the case for distinctions, or better (or worse) choices, or more (or less) accurate analyses of conditions and behavior. In this sense, the differences between various alternatives need not be merely a matter of personal pleasure or preference, but can be based upon values and beliefs intrinsic to the society in question.

Of course there will almost inevitably be competing values and shifting beliefs—with accompanying tensions—in any culture. But that fact in itself does not force one to accept the position of radical skepticism and of choice based upon purely personal "exhilaration," as suggested by Fish. Even if one is skeptical about "ultimate" or transcendent truths (whether there are absolutes outside or beyond the bounds of particular cultural systems), one may still believe that alternatives or choices *within* a given system can be illuminated by debate, argument, and analysis consistent with the values and forms of discourse intrinsic to that system.

In addition to Fish's point of view, there are, of course, others: Some see the current ferment as exciting, stimulating, and an indication that fields of knowledge are in an appropriately robust phase, which should be celebrated. Others, such as Gerald Graff, have suggested that one way to rationalize the current situation is to accept its lack of consensus, but to make that very dissonance a more explicit part of the curriculum. One would then have a curriculum in which conflicting interpretations and theories were taught explicitly, and were negotiated in the open; such a situation would "not be a retreat from literature but a way of helping students make sense of it" (Graff 1988).

Looking further afield, there are those who believe that the fundamental epistemological points are never likely to be resolved, and who argue therefore in favor of what might be termed a trial-and-error evolutionary process—a careful sifting of new methods of analysis, a gradual assimilation of those aspects that seem more substantive and compelling (terms that are, of course, also open to debate), until one ultimately reaches some future situation in which a more limited and tested set of approaches have become (at least for some period of time) generally established and more broadly accepted. This position is philosophically untidy, and far too vague for observers who see epistemological or ideological issues as absolutely critical to the matter at hand. At the same time, it would not be difficult to make a strong case for the view that (at least in certain humanistic and related social science fields) this evolutionary/assimilationist approach, punctuated by moments of rapid change at critical moments, represents quite accurately the way in which university curricula have been generated for a very long period of time. The results rarely, if ever, meet the test of critics who have more lucid paradigmatic models in mind, but they do often accommodate a quite healthy diversity of views and substantive materials— something which can render both students and faculty a very considerable intellectual service.

Finally, there are scholars and critics who are much more dubious about the contingent/constructionist premises that underlie so much theory. A recent article by John Searle (1990) in the *New York Review of Books* questions directly the view that "most authorities" in major fields of learning have deserted the idea that important forms of empirical knowledge are testable, are verifiable, and represent a reasonable approximation of objective reality. Searle rests much of his case on work in the sciences, but makes some thoughtful (if inevitably inconclusive) points with respect to other fields. Other writers would, of course, go much further than Searle in arguing more definitively for a set of identifiable absolute or transcendent truths as the standard against which one can then proceed to evaluate categories of knowledge, and assess what should (or should not) be part of the formal curriculum.

Such positions can claim a special coherence or consistency, but they, too, must inevitably confront and resolve difficult metaphysical or religious issues: *Which* set of transcendent values should guide us, among the varieties postulated by innumerable religious thinkers and philosophers across the world's many cultures? Indeed, even within the *same* broad religious or philosophical tradition there have been fierce debates—including of course the original Renaissance debate in Western Europe about whether classical authors and ancient classical civilization should be taught in Christian institutions of learning, given the very different moral and other values that classical texts embody (whether Homer, Catullus, Aristophanes, Plato, Thucydides, Aristotle, Plautus, or Sappho). Establishing the legitimacy of classical learning in the face of strict Puritan values was far from easy, and appeared to many to represent a more cataclysmic philosophical and educational change than any shift we are currently witnessing.

Indeed, throughout most of the nineteenth century (quite apart from the twentieth), the dilemma concerning what could be taught or studied—without running the risk of subverting established morality or theology—continued to be the subject of acrimonious debate, which often had deeply damaging human and intellectual consequences. Anyone who rereads Cardinal Newman's *Loss and Gain*, Santayana's *Character and Opinion in the United States*, or the letters and other documents relating to critical moments in the lives of Theodore Parker, Charles Eliot Norton, Thomas Huxley, Arthur Hugh Clough, William James, Leslie Stephen, and Matthew Arnold can hardly escape the fact that "honest doubt" and epistemological uncertainty—if not paralysis—had by then struck deeply into that zone where "education" and "belief" are pressed together in what are often discomfortable ways.

One forgets too easily, perhaps, that the pillar of Boston and Cambridge Brahmin society, Charles Eliot Norton, was nearly denied a professorship at Harvard because of his agnosticism. And one may perhaps fall back too readily on Arnold's reassuring phrase about the need to study "the best that has been thought and said" without remembering that this phrase is only part of a sentence that lays an equal stress on the need to open up and enlighten the parochial, sectarian, narrowly religious England that Arnold saw all around him, so that "the free play of mind" could be introduced as a liberating (as well as rational) energetic force. Arnold desired to introduce Hellenism as a counterbalance to conceptions of education and morality that were—in his view—far too rigid in their "Hebraic" outlook, and far too materialistic in their conception of life.

Indeed, Arnold himself had substantial difficulty finding satisfactory criteria to define "the best," and it would be difficult to claim that his own formulations were based on anything genuinely philosophical or religious, rather than upon his own fine taste, his well-attuned literary ear and eye, his profound human experience, and his familiarity with the tradition of European (but scarcely any other) letters. Terms such as "high seriousness" do not, in the end, take us very far—especially when they lead Arnold himself to exclude figures such as Chaucer from the pantheon of the very greatest English poets, not to mention Donne, Marvell, Pope, and others.

One may admire Arnold greatly, but to believe that he offers clear guidance either to "truth" or to a philosophically grounded curriculum is to overlook even his own expressed doubts concerning the larger situation in which he found himself: "And we are here as on a darkling plain,/ Swept by confused alarms of struggle and flight,/ Where ignorant armies clash by night." These lines are certainly not the last word on Arnold—there is none. But to forget his sense of deep pathos and doubt—"Wandering between two worlds, one dead,/The other powerless to be born"—is to forget very much indeed.

In concluding this discussion, it may be useful to return to an anthropological and a literary text, since it is difficult to imagine disciplines in which the confrontation between the observer and the observed is more likely to be problematic from the point of view of interpreting human behavior and human utterances, in all their ambiguity and otherness. Interestingly enough, two excellent scholars have recently written on this subject in a way that accepts—with qualifications—much that recent theory has made vivid, but they have also called with some confidence for a renewed effort to negotiate the perceived differences between subject and object, reader and text, interpreter or describer and the external cultural and other structures that invite understanding and explication.

For Clifford Geertz, part of the way toward a solution is to begin by accepting the fact that our descriptive modes are indeed rhetorical: That is, in describing or writing, we necessarily use language as a means of expressing truths as we see them, but we use language also as a persuasive instrument, which is inevitably artful, constructed, and not at all the utterly neutral or transparent medium that some might wish it (or believe it) to be. There is nothing novel or shocking about this point. It surely expresses a self-consciousness about the relation of linguistic expression and truth-saying that has at least something in common (however modified by later theory) with views expressed by some classical as well as Renaissance and later rhetoricians.

In any event, the recognition that writing may be consciously or unconsciously biased in its effort to persuade, or that it may be limited in its capacity to describe aspects of the perceived world as fully and richly as one might wish, does not lead Geertz either to epistemological paralysis, literary "silence," or a confident view that one can somehow overcome these limitations in the quest to discover and utter absolute truths. It leads him, instead, to insist on the fact that one can—through intellectual effort, deep familiarity, and trained insight—come to know a great deal about the nature and behavior of some other individuals and some cultures.

However different such individuals and cultures may be from oneself, they are not (for Geertz) totally alien and beyond the reach of informed and trained human understanding. Since language is an imperfect medium, it can never capture—any more, and perhaps rather less, than the human mind—the full substance of what has been observed. In this sense, language is a limiting but far from completely imprisoning medium, which one must use consciously as an art-form—an art-form (perhaps very crudely analogous to certain modes of painting) capable of rendering reasonable approximations of what one has seen and learned with the help of intelligence, experience, and imagination. It may well be that such approximations only yield us knowledge of behavior and societies that are themselves culturally "constructed": In effect, there is no window upon metaphysical reality beyond or above the particular social patterns at hand. But the patterns themselves are at least not unyielding.

Reasonable approximations of this kind are in need of constant reexamination and revision, but that fact does not vitiate their qualified, yet still precious, truth-value. As Geertz notes:

> The strange idea that reality has an idiom in which it prefers to be described, that its very nature demands we talk about it without fuss—a spade is a spade, a rose is a rose—leads on to the even stranger idea that, if literalism is lost, so is fact.
>
> This cannot be right, or else almost all the writings discussed in this book, major and minor alike (as well as virtually all the ethnographics now appearing), would have to be held as lacking reference to anything real. . . .
>
> [The ethnographic] task is still to demonstrate again, in different times and with different means, that accounts of how others live can carry conviction. . . . This capacity to persuade readers . . . that what they are reading is an authentic account by someone personally acquainted with how life proceeds in some place, at some time, among some group, is the basis upon which anything else ethnography seeks to do —analyze, explain, amuse, disconcert, celebrate, edify, excuse, astonish, subvert— finally rests. . . . [It is] the *fons et origo* of whatever power anthropology has to convince anyone of anything—not theory, not method, not even the aura of the professorial chair, consequential as this last may be.
> (Clifford Geertz, *Works and Lives: The Anthropologist as Author* [Stanford University Press, 1988], 140–44)

The complex form of artful mediation that Geertz describes is different from, but not utterly dissimilar to, what some literary critics have been recently suggesting. J. Hillis Miller—to quote him once again—has recently written:

> Literary theory . . . is of little or no use unless it is "applied," used. Theory must be active, productive. What theory performs is, or ought to be, new readings, in the broadest sense of the word. . . .
>
> But what I mean by "new readings" must not be misunderstood. I do not mean "new" in the sense of "determined by a new historical situation or political climate," nor do I mean "new" in the sense of determined by new theoretical presuppositions, nor do I mean "new" in the sense of a certain vulgar form of reader response criticism or vulgar misunderstanding of poststructural criticism which generally takes such criticism to presuppose that the reader is free to make the text mean anything he or she wants it to mean. My conviction is that any valid reading is authorized only by the text read, the words on the page. This means that though theory may facilitate genuine reading, there is always a dissymmetry between theory and reading. This might be formulated by saying that reading is more likely to be the disconfirmation or severe modification of theory than its triumphant validation. What happens when we read happens by a necessity that displays the sovereign power of the text read over the reader. That sovereignty lies in the way the text in question gives readers access to meanings otherwise inaccessible. But these are likely to be almost inexhaustibly complex. . . . This means that each genuine act of reading is to some degree new,

inaugural, even if we are reading something we have read, taught, or written about dozens of times before. The new reading uncovers hitherto unidentified aspects of the meanings to which the text in question gives the reader access.

(J. Hillis Miller, "Humanistic Research," in *The Humanities in the University: Strategies for the 1990's*, American Council of Learned Societies Occasional Paper no. 6 [ACLS, 1988], 29–30)

Once again, one sees (as in Geertz) a conviction that the object to be studied has its own reality—a sovereign power—greater than any theory, and indeed greater than any single mind, interpreter, or interpretation. There are "inexhaustible" meanings, but that does not imply they are necessarily contradictory or illusory or arbitrary. One presses more deeply, one learns more—even as one learns more about another human being or a particular place—without ultimately exhausting the complexity of what is being studied. Yet our continuous probing, and our articulation of perceptive (if partial) approximations of what is "out there"—that process of probing, adjusting, and exploring is one that, in the minds of many scholars and critics, can still be carried on with conviction.

It would be inaccurate to suggest that Geertz and Miller have identical views, or that they represent an emergent consensus concerning the role of theory at the present time. Many critics would clearly deny that texts have a "sovereign power," and others would be far more skeptical than either Geertz or Miller about our capacity to understand patterns of behavior, patterns of culture, or patterns of meaning in texts. While one can certainly challenge radical skepticism of this latter kind, few people currently believe that one can offer a persuasive refutation, in rational or logical terms, to the various forms of deep philosophical skepticism that have been part of the Western tradition for a very long time. In this sense, current theoretical debates may indeed be fundamentally unresolvable—although perhaps no more (or less) unresolvable than analogous debates in previous historical periods.

Additional Tables

Chapter Two

TABLE G.2–1
Number of Doctorates Conferred by Citizenship and Field, Selected Years

Field	Citizenship	1958	1972	1984	1988
English	U.S. Res.	322	1,316	667	626
	Non-U.S. Res.	11	54	66	91
	Total	333	1,370	733	717
History	U.S. Res.	302	1,124	563	520
	Non-U.S. Res.	15	62	54	83
	Total	317	1,186	617	603
PolSci	U.S. Res.	185	800	542	426
	Non-U.S. Res.	26	111	153	208
	Total	211	911	695	634
Math	U.S. Res.	214	1,095	443	386
	Non-U.S. Res.	24	186	255	363
	Total	238	1,281	698	749
Physics	U.S. Res.	453	1,403	775	784
	Non-U.S. Res.	44	231	305	518
	Total	497	1,634	1,080	1,302
Econ	U.S. Res.	275	711	512	485
	Non-U.S. Res.	57	183	282	368
	Total	332	894	794	853
Six-Fields	U.S. Res.	1,751	6,449	3,502	3,227
	Non-U.S. Res.	177	827	1,115	1,631
	Total	1,928	7,276	4,617	4,858
All Fields	U.S. Res.	8,001	29,572	25,251	24,891
	Non-U.S. Res.	772	3,469	6,086	8,589
	Total	8,773	33,041	31,337	33,480

Source: Special tabulations from Doctorate Records File.
Notes: Values for non-U.S. residents were obtained by subtracting those for U.S. residents from the total; this is equivalent to classifying all "unknowns" as non-U.S. residents.

TABLE G.2–2
Number of Doctorates Conferred by Field and Racial/Ethnic Group, U.S. Residents
Only, 1988

Field	White	Black	Hispanic	Asian	Total[a]
English/AmLit	571	26	6	12	615
History	471	9	15	14	509
PolSci/Policy	357	29	10	13	409
Subtotal: EHP	1,399	64	31	39	1,533
Econ	397	15	12	49	473
Math	331	3	4	33	371
Physics/Astron	669	12	14	52	747
Subtotal: Six-Fields	2,796	94	61	173	3,124
ComputerSci	265	2	2	44	313
Chemistry	1,253	21	48	85	1,407
EarthSci	495	3	8	15	521
Engineering	1,651	31	63	332	2,077
BiologicalSci	2,954	48	76	170	3,248
Health/AgriSci	1,192	55	33	62	1,342
Psych	2,421	100	93	47	2,661
SocSci/Other[b]	786	51	33	34	904
Hum/Other[c]	1,591	53	91	43	1,778
Business	581	19	9	65	674
Prof/Other[d]	693	66	16	32	807
Education	4,646	408	159	130	5,343
Other/Unspecified	29	0	1	1	31
Total	21,353	951	693	1,233	24,230

Source: Data for Six-Fields are from special tabulations of the Doctorate Records File. Data for other
fields are from *Summary Report 1988*, Appendix A, Table 1A.

[a]Does not include Native Americans or PhD recipients who did not answer the questions related
to race and ethnicity.

[b]Includes all social sciences except economics, political science, and psychology.

[c]Includes all humanities except English, American literature, and history.

[d]Includes all professional fields except business: for example, communications, library science,
social work, and theology.

TABLE G.2–3

Numbers of BAs and PhDs by Field and Racial/Ethnic Group, U.S. Residents Only

	White		Black		Hispanic		Asian		Total	
Field	BA	PhD	BA	PhD	BA	PhD	BA	PhD	BA	PhD
English/AmLit		571		26		6		12		615
Hum/Other		1,591		53		91		43		1,778
Letters	36,315		1,980		694		460		39,449	
ForeignLang	8,614		293		909		210		10,026	
Subtotal: Humanities	44,929	2,162	2,273	79	1,603	97	670	55	49,475	2,393
History		471		9		15		14		509
PolSci/Policy		357		29		10		13		409
Econ		397		15		12		49		473
SocSci/Other		786		51		33		34		904
SocSci	85,535		8,129		2,888		1,645		98,197	
Subtotal: SocSci	85,535	2,011	8,129	104	2,888	70	1,645	110	98,197	2,295
Physics		669		12		14		52		747
ComputerSci		265		2		2		44		313
Chemistry		1,253		21		48		85		1,407
EarthSci		495		3		8		15		521
PhysSci	21,246		906		405		596		23,153	
Subtotal: PhysSci	21,246	2,682	906	38	405	72	596	196	23,153	2,988
Psych	34,701	2,421	3,308	100	1,305	93	839	47	40,153	2,661
Math	9,445	331	584	3	185	4	391	33	10,605	371
BiologicalSci	37,276	2,954	2,269	48	1,144	76	1,489	170	42,178	3,248
Engineering	60,848	1,651	2,449	31	1,433	63	3,066	332	67,796	2,077
Education	93,724	4,646	9,494	408	2,847	159	723	130	106,788	5,343
Business	174,198	581	13,400	19	4,114	9	3,943	65	195,655	674
Other	245,417	1,914	17,861	121	5,908	50	5,432	95	274,618	2,180
Total	807,319	21,353	60,673	951	21,832	693	18,794	1,233	908,618	24,230

Sources: BA data are from the *Digest of Education Statistics* (1988) and reflect BAs awarded in the 1980–81 academic year (excluding American Indians and non-resident aliens). PhD data are from *Summary Report 1988*, Appendix A, Table 1A, and reflect PhDs conferred in 1988.

TABLE G.2–4
Number of Doctorates Conferred by Field and Racial/Ethnic Group, U.S. Residents
Only, 1988 and 1982

Year and Group	English/ AmLit	History	PolSci	Econ	Math	Physics	EHP	Six- Fields	Human- ities	All Fields
1988										
White	571	471	357	397	331	669	1,399	2,796	2,633	21,353
Black	26	9	29	15	3	12	64	94	88	951
Hispanic	6	15	10	12	4	14	31	61	112	693
Asian	12	14	13	49	33	52	39	173	69	1,233
Total	615	509	409	473	371	747	1,533	3,124	2,902	24,230
1982										
White	652	558	435	420	436	644	1,645	3,145	2,769	22,062
Black	23	27	45	18	6	11	95	130	103	1,133
Hispanic	9	9	15	14	6	9	33	62	132	612
Asian	11	8	15	38	32	43	34	147	55	1,000
Total	695	602	510	490	480	707	1,807	3,484	3,059	24,807

Source: Special tabulations from Doctorate Records File.

Chapter Three

Explanation of Methods

The basic equation used to apportion the change in the number of doctorates between any two points in time is

$$\Delta D_6 = (B + \Delta B) * (f + \Delta f) * (p + \Delta p) - (B * f * p).$$

Thus, the direct effects of changes in particular variables can be measured as follows:

ΔBfp = Change in number of doctorates due to change in the size of the pool of BA recipients;

ΔfBp = Change in number of doctorates due to change in BA field choice; and

ΔpBf = Change in number of doctorates due to change in the proclivity of BA recipients to obtain a PhD.

The remaining terms are cross-effects, as they reflect the combined effects of several adjustments. These terms are summarized as ΣX, which is defined as follows:

$$\Sigma X = B\Delta p\Delta f + \Delta Bfp + \Delta B\Delta pf + \Delta B\Delta p\Delta f.$$

The data used in this calculation are shown in Table G.3–1. Table G.3–2 shows periodic differences and the direct effects of changes in B, f, and p on the number of PhDs awarded. These figures were calculated using pooled data for the six fields. The basic results reported here hold when the calculations are made on a field-specific basis. The share of BA recipients began to decline somewhat earlier in physics and mathematics than in the other four fields.

TABLE G.3–1
Six-Field Share of BAs and Doctorates Conferred by Gender, 1954–1976 BA Cohorts

	Total BAs (B)	Field Preference (f)	Six-Field BAs	Six-Field PhDs (D_6)	Share BAs Receiving PhD (p)
Men and Women					
1954	267,880	0.150	40,053	1,628	0.0406
1956	287,944	0.153	44,195	1,961	0.0444
1958	340,871	0.156	53,343	2,665	0.0500
1960	370,015	0.175	64,887	3,704	0.0571
1962	379,783	0.205	78,015	4,608	0.0591
1964	459,270	0.224	102,888	5,660	0.0550
1966	524,117	0.228	119,619	5,272	0.0441
1968	636,863	0.232	148,030	4,104	0.0277
1970	798,070	0.221	176,109	3,557	0.0202
1972	894,110	0.192	171,433	3,010	0.0176
1974	954,376	0.162	154,956	2,612	0.0169
1976	934,443	0.135	126,185	2,394	0.0190
Men					
1954	163,587	0.159	25,998	1,541	0.059
1956	177,293	0.162	28,708	1,798	0.063
1958	219,167	0.163	35,721	2,427	0.068
1960	231,739	0.183	42,306	3,341	0.079
1962	225,633	0.217	49,068	4,135	0.084
1964	262,027	0.239	62,677	4,974	0.079
1966	301,051	0.240	72,300	4,595	0.064
1968	359,747	0.245	87,966	3,297	0.037
1970	453,605	0.233	105,529	2,884	0.027
1972	503,631	0.205	103,052	2,373	0.023
1974	530,907	0.179	94,993	2,072	0.022
1976	508,549	0.152	77,475	1,887	0.024
Women					
1954	104,293	0.135	14,055	87	0.006
1956	110,651	0.140	15,487	163	0.011
1958	121,704	0.145	17,622	238	0.014
1960	138,276	0.163	22,581	363	0.016
1962	154,118	0.188	28,947	473	0.016
1964	197,243	0.204	40,211	686	0.017
1966	223,066	0.212	47,319	677	0.014
1968	277,116	0.217	60,064	807	0.013
1970	344,465	0.205	70,580	673	0.010
1972	390,479	0.175	68,381	637	0.009
1974	423,469	0.142	59,963	540	0.009
1976	425,894	0.114	48,710	507	0.010

Sources: BA data are from *Earned Degrees Conferred Survey*. PhD data are from special tabulations of the Doctorate Records File, organized by BA cohort.

TABLE G.3-2
Changes in Six-Field Shares of BAs and PhDs Conferred by Gender, 1954–1976 BA Cohorts

	Change in BA Pool (ΔB)	Change in Six-Field Share (Δf)	Change in PhD-Proclivity (Δp)	Total Change (ΔD)	Change Due to B (ΔBfp)	Change Due to f (ΔfBp)	Change Due to p (ΔpBf)	Sum Cross-Effects (ΣX)
Men and Women								
1954–1956	20,064	0.004	0.004	333	121.94	43.19	149.21	18.67
1956–1958	52,927	0.003	0.006	704	360.45	38.40	246.97	58.18
1958–1960	29,144	0.019	0.007	1,039	227.85	321.40	380.02	109.72
1960–1962	9,768	0.030	0.002	904	97.78	634.86	128.59	42.78
1962–1964	79,487	0.019	−0.004	1,052	964.44	417.35	−316.30	−13.49
Subtotal 1954–1964				4,032	1,772.46	1,455.20	588.50	215.85
1964–1966	64,847	0.004	−0.011	−388	799.17	106.23	−1,125.39	−168.01
1966–1968	112,746	0.004	−0.016	−1,168	1,134.09	97.17	−1,955.67	−443.59
1968–1970	161,207	−0.012	−0.008	−547	1,038.83	−207.77	−1,114.13	−263.93
Subtotal 1964–1970				−2,103	2,972.09	−4.38	−4,195.19	−875.52
1970–1972	96,040	−0.029	−0.003	−547	428.05	−466.37	−464.90	−43.78
1972–1974	60,266	−0.029	−0.001	−398	202.88	−461.11	−120.26	−19.52
1974–1976	−19,933	−0.027	0.002	−218	−54.55	−439.60	327.85	−51.69
Subtotal 1970–1976				−1,163	576.38	−1,367.08	−257.31	−114.99
Men								
1954–1956	13,706	0.003	0.003	257	129.11	29.08	87.27	11.53
1956–1958	41,874	0.001	0.005	629	424.66	11.78	152.51	40.04
1958–1960	12,572	0.020	0.011	914	139.22	291.47	393.97	89.35
1960–1962	−6,106	0.035	0.005	794	−88.03	638.87	224.16	19.00
1962–1964	36,394	0.022	−0.005	839	666.96	413.22	−241.00	−0.19
Subtotal 1954–1964				3,433	1,271.93	1,384.44	616.91	159.73

384

TABLE G.3–2
Continued

	Change in BA Pool (ΔB)	Change in Six-Field Share (Δf)	Change in PhD-Proclivity (Δp)	Total Change (ΔD)	Change Due to B (ΔBfp)	Change Due to f (ΔfBp)	Change Due to p (ΔpBf)	Sum Cross-Effects (ΣX)
1964-1966	39,024	0.001	-0.016	-379	740.78	19.92	-990.59	-149.12
1966-1968	58,696	0.004	-0.026	-1,298	895.89	83.48	-1,885.17	-392.20
1968-1970	93,858	-0.012	-0.010	-413	860.19	-160.14	-892.98	-220.07
Subtotal 1964–1970				-2,090	2,496.86	-56.73	-3,768.73	-761.39
1970-1972	50,026	-0.028	-0.004	-511	318.06	-347.44	-453.96	-27.66
1972-1974	27,276	-0.026	-0.001	-301	128.52	-297.96	-125.22	-6.34
1974-1976	-22,358	-0.027	0.003	-185	-87.26	-307.81	241.67	-31.60
Subtotal 1970–1976				-997	359.32	-953.21	-337.50	-65.61
Women								
1954-1956	6,358	0.005	0.004	76	5.30	3.36	60.93	6.41
1956-1958	11,053	0.005	0.003	75	16.28	5.63	46.17	6.93
1958-1960	16,572	0.019	0.003	125	32.41	30.43	45.28	16.89
1960-1962	15,842	0.025	0.000	110	41.59	54.50	5.98	7.93
1962-1964	43,125	0.016	0.001	213	132.35	40.40	20.84	19.41
Subtotal 1954–1964				599	227.94	134.31	179.19	57.57
1964-1966	25,823	0.008	-0.003	-9	89.81	27.81	-110.70	-15.93
1966-1968	54,050	0.005	-0.001	130	164.04	14.73	-41.24	-7.54
1968-1970	67,349	-0.012	-0.004	-134	196.13	-44.12	-234.27	-51.74
Subtotal 1964–1970				-13	449.98	-1.57	-386.21	-75.20
1970-1972	46,014	-0.030	0.000	-36	89.90	-97.80	-15.52	-12.58
1972-1974	32,990	-0.034	0.000	-97	53.82	-121.93	-21.19	-7.69
1974-1976	2,425	-0.027	0.001	-33	3.09	-103.84	84.13	-16.38
Subtotal 1970–1976				-166	146.81	-323.57	47.42	-36.66

Source: Table G.3–1.

385

Chapter Four

TABLE G.4–1
Number of Doctorate–Granting Programs by Field and Quality Tier, 1958, 1972, and 1988

Field and Year	Quality Tier				
	I	II	III	IV	Total
English					
1958	25	12	14	9	60
1972	29	26	31	38	124
1988	29	25	30	48	132
All years	29	26	31	65	151
History					
1958	25	12	13	11	61
1972	25	24	31	38	118
1988	25	22	30	47	124
All years	25	24	33	82	164
PolSci					
1958	18	13	8	8	47
1972	21	22	22	26	91
1988	21	23	24	47	115
All years	21	24	25	73	143
Econ					
1958	16	13	17	11	57
1972	19	20	35	34	108
1988	19	22	35	43	119
All years	19	22	36	65	142
Math					
1958	23	18	14	5	60
1972	26	28	42	43	139
1988	25	28	41	43	137
All years	26	28	44	79	177
Physics					
1958	26	20	20	4	70
1972	30	26	46	43	145
1988	31	26	48	50	155
All years	31	26	48	82	187
Six-Fields					
1958	133	88	86	48	355
1972	150	146	207	222	725
1988	150	146	208	278	782
All years	151	150	217	446	964

Source: Special tabulations from Doctorate Records File.
Notes: "All years" refers to the total number of programs awarding degrees between 1958 and 1988.

TABLE G.4–2
Number of Doctorates Conferred by Field and Quality Tier, 1958, 1972, and 1988

Field and Year	Quality Tier				Total
	I	II	III	IV	
English					
1958	235	42	41	15	333
1972	700	232	283	155	1,370
1988	300	140	120	157	717
History					
1958	221	32	33	31	317
1972	595	240	214	137	1,186
1988	293	110	95	105	603
PolSci					
1958	115	42	17	37	211
1972	420	220	163	108	911
1988	220	151	105	158	634
Econ					
1958	179	80	54	19	332
1972	382	184	205	123	894
1988	309	192	222	130	853
Math					
1958	153	42	35	8	238
1972	571	274	268	168	1,281
1988	333	163	150	103	749
Physics					
1958	310	115	62	10	497
1972	831	307	351	145	1,634
1988	678	253	239	132	1,302
Six-Fields					
1958	1,213	353	242	120	1,928
1972	3,499	1,457	1,484	836	7,276
1988	2,133	1,009	931	785	4,858

Source: Special tabulations from Doctorate Records File.

TABLE G.4-3
Number of Doctorates Conferred by Field, Established and New Programs, and Quality Tier, 1958–1988

Field	Quality Tier	1958	1960	1962	1964	1966	1968	1970	1972	1974	1976	1978	1980	1982	1984	1986	1988	Total 1958–1988
English																		
Established	I	235	269	304	368	422	527	572	649	605	521	422	379	299	271	265	267	6,375
	II	42	38	35	47	73	108	107	136	137	129	105	91	82	78	66	76	1,350
	III	41	33	59	63	60	113	123	141	149	108	86	82	68	63	54	52	1,295
	IV	15	18	30	9	32	23	42	57	53	49	47	46	41	26	29	28	545
	Total	333	358	428	487	587	771	844	983	944	807	660	598	490	438	414	423	9,565
New	I	0	5	7	12	15	28	38	51	53	49	66	37	39	42	38	33	513
	II	0	12	11	10	22	44	64	96	115	106	93	71	57	64	59	64	888
	III	0	8	12	11	34	55	83	142	129	114	90	90	69	68	79	68	1,052
	IV	0	3	5	8	13	32	69	98	128	138	116	156	115	121	129	129	1,260
	Total	0	28	35	41	84	159	254	387	425	407	365	354	280	295	305	294	3,713
History																		
Established	I	221	252	248	327	371	407	596	595	578	527	428	376	353	280	294	293	6,146
	II	32	36	42	58	79	89	152	153	159	128	88	66	66	63	44	54	1,309
	III	33	28	39	65	70	77	106	127	99	80	62	53	37	41	28	44	989
	IV	31	23	18	27	40	61	46	67	64	49	36	25	27	18	26	17	575
	Total	317	339	347	477	560	634	900	942	900	784	614	520	483	402	392	408	9,019
New	I	0	0	0	0	0	0	0	0	0	0	0	0	0	0	0	0	0
	II	0	5	5	16	21	31	59	87	85	77	67	50	60	58	42	56	719
	III	0	12	7	20	33	34	60	87	95	102	56	78	66	57	52	51	810
	IV	0	8	7	17	31	42	72	70	106	132	115	97	83	100	77	88	1,045
	Total	0	25	19	53	85	107	191	244	286	311	238	225	209	215	171	195	2,574

Field	Quality Tier	1958	1960	1962	1964	1966	1968	1970	1972	1974	1976	1978	1980	1982	1984	1986	1988	Total 1958–1988
Math																		
Established	I	153	187	229	328	407	473	551	543	492	437	346	323	303	274	321	314	5,681
	II	42	42	68	113	106	144	235	186	196	150	142	117	123	112	122	114	2,012
	III	35	29	39	74	86	97	101	126	106	76	65	47	50	59	55	64	1,109
	IV	8	9	11	7	11	24	27	27	27	13	11	10	10	10	10	4	219
	Total	238	267	347	522	610	738	914	882	821	676	564	497	486	455	508	496	9,021
New	I	0	2	4	6	13	16	16	28	45	25	20	20	19	28	23	19	284
	II	0	11	13	20	59	66	89	88	60	53	46	46	36	49	51	49	736
	III	0	7	15	25	67	89	107	142	140	114	110	89	85	86	77	86	1,239
	IV	0	4	9	15	20	62	99	141	145	135	98	92	94	80	70	99	1,163
	Total	0	24	41	66	159	233	311	399	390	327	274	247	234	243	221	253	3,422
Physics																		
Established	I	310	332	479	495	596	739	788	771	630	553	547	497	489	530	634	619	9,009
	II	115	114	111	157	186	266	287	260	233	224	142	152	140	171	177	180	2,915
	III	62	52	75	113	129	165	206	198	123	105	94	79	93	81	77	113	1,765
	IV	10	13	13	13	16	17	27	13	12	6	9	11	11	7	6	7	191
	Total	497	511	678	778	927	1,187	1,308	1,242	998	888	792	739	733	789	894	919	13,880
New	I	0	3	1	12	25	55	53	60	44	59	45	40	51	51	47	59	605
	II	0	0	1	5	22	26	41	47	36	61	37	45	42	49	55	73	540
	III	0	14	16	32	51	95	129	153	119	105	101	81	105	109	107	126	1,343
	IV	0	2	14	39	36	73	124	132	142	124	92	78	83	82	84	125	1,230
	Total	0	19	32	88	134	249	347	392	341	349	275	244	281	291	293	383	3,718

TABLE G.4–3
Continued

Field	Quality Tier	1958	1960	1962	1964	1966	1968	1970	1972	1974	1976	1978	1980	1982	1984	1986	1988	Total 1958–1988
PolSci																		
Established	I	115	144	152	175	185	271	258	397	340	304	259	201	182	163	178	196	3,520
	II	42	44	58	66	98	112	156	164	195	182	153	144	151	149	113	107	1,934
	III	17	7	11	10	20	24	26	61	58	54	41	41	34	36	41	40	521
	IV	37	36	31	39	41	76	62	67	64	71	54	48	33	39	34	31	763
	Total	211	231	252	290	344	483	502	689	657	611	507	434	400	387	366	374	6,738
New	I	0	0	5	4	6	16	16	23	19	23	26	16	23	15	25	24	241
	II	0	3	7	14	13	20	26	56	53	66	60	51	42	62	64	44	581
	III	0	0	6	18	22	37	61	102	101	92	116	107	103	96	88	65	1,014
	IV	0	4	8	11	23	24	31	41	79	95	142	122	141	135	116	127	1,099
	Total	0	7	26	47	64	97	134	222	252	276	344	296	309	308	293	260	2,935
Econ																		
Established	I	179	173	188	231	259	314	336	362	316	302	328	285	289	283	315	288	4,448
	II	80	102	114	119	154	160	179	157	154	140	119	118	113	115	132	129	2,085
	III	54	45	62	92	108	105	132	120	135	152	94	113	112	112	111	125	1,672
	IV	19	12	18	33	24	26	36	51	40	30	26	31	26	34	34	21	461
	Total	332	332	382	475	545	605	683	690	645	624	567	547	540	544	592	563	8,666
New	I	0	1	5	4	8	11	25	20	18	17	18	17	13	15	11	21	204
	II	0	6	3	10	7	21	19	27	26	60	32	54	54	56	65	63	503
	III	0	10	14	25	31	43	60	85	85	88	106	69	75	93	88	97	969
	IV	0	3	14	13	36	67	66	72	79	96	78	80	79	86	104	109	982
	Total	0	20	36	52	82	142	170	204	208	261	234	220	221	250	268	290	2,658

TABLE G.4-3
Continued

Field	Quality Tier	1958	1960	1962	1964	1966	1968	1970	1972	1974	1976	1978	1980	1982	1984	1986	1988	Total 1958–1988
Six-Fields																		
Established	I	1,213	1,357	1,600	1,924	2,240	2,731	3,101	3,317	2,961	2,644	2,330	2,061	1,915	1,801	2,007	1,977	35,179
	II	353	376	428	560	696	879	1,116	1,056	1,074	953	749	688	675	688	654	660	11,605
	III	242	194	285	417	473	581	694	773	670	575	442	415	394	392	366	438	7,351
	IV	120	111	121	128	164	227	240	282	260	218	183	171	148	134	139	108	2,754
	Total	1,928	2,038	2,434	3,029	3,573	4,418	5,151	5,428	4,965	4,390	3,704	3,335	3,132	3,015	3,166	3,183	56,889
New	I	0	11	22	38	67	126	148	182	179	173	175	130	145	151	144	156	1,847
	II	0	37	40	75	144	208	298	401	375	423	335	317	291	338	336	349	3,967
	III	0	51	70	131	238	353	500	711	669	615	579	514	503	509	491	493	6,427
	IV	0	24	57	103	159	300	461	554	679	720	641	625	595	604	580	677	6,779
	Total	0	123	189	347	608	987	1,407	1,848	1,902	1,931	1,730	1,586	1,534	1,602	1,551	1,675	19,020

Source: Special tabulations from Doctorate Records file.

Notes: Established programs are defined as those that awarded at least one doctorate in the field in question in 1958. New programs are defined as those that awarded at least one doctorate in the field in question in some year after 1958, but no degrees in 1958.

TABLE G.4–4
Number of Doctorate-Granting Programs and Doctorates Conferred by Field and Size
of Program, 1958, 1972, and 1988

Field and Year	Number of:		Doctorates Conferred by:	
	Very Small Programs	Small Programs	Very Small Programs	Small Programs
English				
1958	3	16	6	41
1972	16	55	63	311
1988	11	60	29	189
History				
1958	8	26	23	58
1972	29	71	82	376
1988	31	77	47	190
PolSci				
1958	3	16	4	31
1972	17	42	49	186
1988	30	61	51	144
Econ				
1958	4	12	4	24
1972	17	36	49	147
1988	20	44	37	110
Math				
1958	8	13	15	23
1972	40	76	136	373
1988	37	75	60	172
Physics				
1958	5	13	12	33
1972	35	65	112	306
1988	40	74	76	201
Six-Fields				
1958	31	96	64	210
1972	154	345	491	1,699
1988	169	391	300	1,006

Source: Special tabulations from Doctorate Records File.
Notes: Very small programs are defined as those that conferred fewer than two doctoral degrees, on average, in the 1980s. Small programs are defined as those that conferred fewer than four doctoral degrees, on average, in the 1980s.

TABLE G.4-5
Degree-Granting Activity of Programs by Field and Quality Tier, 1958–1988

Field	Quality Tier	Number of Programs			Distribution of 1988 "Inactive Programs" by Last Year in Which PhD Was Awarded														
		All Years Total[a]	1988 Only Total[b]	1988 Only Inactive[c]	1986	1984	1982	1980	1978	1976	1974	1972	1970	1968	1966	1964	1962	1960	1958
English	I	29	29	0															
	II	26	25	1	1														
	III	31	30	1	1														
	IV	65	48	17	6	2	2	3	1	1		1	1						
History	I	25	25	0															
	II	24	22	2	1	1													
	III	33	30	3	2	1													
	IV	82	47	35	8	7	8	2	3	2	1		1	1		1		1	
PolSci	I	21	21	0															
	II	24	23	1	1														
	III	25	24	1	1														
	IV	73	47	26	11	5	3	1	3		1	1		1					
Econ	I	19	19	0															
	II	22	22	0															
	III	36	35	1	1														
	IV	65	43	22	4	5	2	1	4	3			2	1					
Math	I	26	25	1	1														
	II	28	28	0															
	III	44	41	3	1	2													
	IV	79	43	36	16	5	4	3	2	2	1	1		1					1
Physics	I	31	31	0															
	II	26	26	0															
	III	48	48	0															
	IV	82	50	32	4	5	10	5	2		2	1	1	1			1		
Six-Fields	I	151	150	1	1														
	II	150	146	4	3	1													
	III	217	208	9	6	3													
	IV	446	278	168	49	29	29	15	15	8	5	4	5	5	0	1	1	1	1
	Total	964	782	182	59	33	29	15	15	8	5	4	5	5	0	1	1	1	1

Source: Special tabulations from Doctorate Records File.
[a]Total number of programs that granted a doctorate in any year from 1958 through 1988.
[b]Total number of programs that granted a doctorate in 1988.
[c]Total number of programs that did not grant a doctorate in 1988.

TABLE G.4–6
Programs Reaching Critical Mass by Field, Quality Tier, and New and Established
Programs, 1958–1988

		Programs Averaging More Than:				All PhD Programs
		Three PhDs per Year		Two PhDs per Year		
Field	Quality Tier	N	% of All PhD Programs	N	% of All PhD Programs	N
English						
All	Total	104	68.9	127	84.1	151
	Tier IV	23	35.4	42	64.6	65
New	Total	48	52.7	67	73.6	91
	Tier IV	18	32.1	33	58.9	56
History						
All	Total	83	50.6	107	65.2	164
	Tier IV	13	15.9	28	34.1	82
New	Total	27	26.2	51	49.5	103
	Tier IV	7	9.9	22	31.0	71
PolSci						
All	Total	73	51.0	92	64.3	143
	Tier IV	16	21.9	27	37.0	73
New	Total	33	34.4	48	50.0	96
	Tier IV	12	18.5	22	33.8	65
Econ						
All	Total	88	62.0	105	73.9	142
	Tier IV	16	24.6	29	44.6	65
New	Total	38	44.7	51	60.0	85
	Tier IV	12	22.2	21	38.9	54
Math						
All	Total	98	55.4	118	66.7	177
	Tier IV	15	19.0	28	35.4	79
New	Total	42	35.9	59	50.4	117
	Tier IV	12	16.2	24	32.4	74
Physics						
All	Total	107	57.2	126	67.4	187
	Tier IV	14	17.1	25	30.5	82
New	Total	42	35.9	57	48.7	117
	Tier IV	12	15.4	22	28.2	78
Six-Fields						
All	Total	552	57.3	675	70.0	964
	Tier IV	108	24.2	178	39.9	446
New	Total	230	37.8	333	54.7	609
	Tier IV	73	18.3	144	36.2	398

Source: Special tabulations from Doctorate Records File.
Notes: The average number of doctorates per year is calculated over the program's life span, defined as the number of years between the year in which the first degree was conferred (1958 or later) and the year in which the most recent degree was conferred (1988 or earlier).

Chapter Five

TABLE G.5–1
Number of Courses Offered and Number of Faculty, Selected Programs, EHP Fields, 1963–1990

	1963–1965	1973–1975	1978–1980	1988–1990
No. courses offered				
English (4)	233	296	258	281
History (3)	333	439	388	342
PolSci (4)	325	501	478	516
Total EHP (11)	891	1,236	1,124	1,139
No. faculty teaching				
English (4)	154	206	184	215
History (3)	196	215	221	205
PolSci (2)	114	144	158	159
Total EHP (9)	464	565	563	579
No. masthead faculty				
Total EHP (12)	869	1,104	1,006	1,181
	Index: 1963–1965 = 100			
No. courses offered				
English (4)	100	127	111	121
History (3)	100	132	117	103
PolSci (4)	100	154	147	159
Total EHP (11)	100	139	126	128
No. faculty teaching				
English (4)	100	134	119	140
History (3)	100	110	113	105
PolSci (2)	100	126	139	139
Total EHP (9)	100	122	121	125
No. masthead faculty				
Total EHP (12)	100	127	116	136

Source: Authors' tabulations. See text, especially notes 1 and 2 in Chapter Five for method of tabulation.

Notes: Figures in parentheses are numbers of graduate programs included in the analysis. The four programs in English are Cornell, Harvard, Princeton, and Yale; the three programs in history are Harvard, Princeton, and Yale; the four programs in political science are Columbia, Harvard, Princeton, and Yale. Each interval is the sum of two academic years (for example, 1963–1965 is the sum of 1963–1964 and 1964–1965).

TABLE G.5–2
Number of Entering Graduate Students by University, EHP Total, 1962–1990

Year	Berkeley	Chicago	Columbia	Cornell	Harvard[a]	Princeton	Stanford	Yale[a,b]	Five University Total	Five University Index[c] 1964 = 100
1962	159		342	30			113			
1963	209		292	50			130			
1964	234	227	397	55			99			100
1965	251	241	331	49			98			
1966	184	215	179	63			90			
1967	218	176	257	92	69	55	65	102	575	100
1968	219	218	207	85	90	52	69	107	541	94
1969	249	166	288	77	92	79	79	117	653	114
1970	239	164	205	68	75	46	73	89	483	84
1971	205	197	211	47	84	51	68	86	479	83
1972	179	190	219	64	85	54	39	110	532	93
1973	181	156	278	46	81	72	49	116	593	103
1974	177	179	248	42	82	36	56	68	476	83
1975	198	156	204	59	60	65	53	82	470	82
1976	157	148	247	40	73	41	47	67	468	81
1977	112	114	213	44	53	61	48	55	426	74
1978	146	130	262	45	54	39	46	47	447	78
1979	116	124	247	43	58	37	41	48	433	75
1980	128	111	208	44	46	49	40	42	389	68
1981	127	115	187	49	59	38	45	40	373	65
1982	105	85	201	40	60	49	46	45	395	69
1983	154	99	207	31	61	43	39	51	392	68
1984	140	109	189	51	61	38	47	56	395	69
1985	90	161	218	39	62	37	27	61	417	73
1986	89	148	212	40	57	37	39	66	412	72
1987	100	115	162	50	55	42	40	60	369	64
1988	84	135	183	48	68	44	48	73	416	72
1989	112	142	180	49	64	51	53	63	407	71
1990	102		192	42	74	41	57	71	420	73

Source: Ten-University data set for years through 1984; direct inquiry was used to obtain information for years from 1985 through 1990. Five University Sum and Five University Index are based on data from Columbia, Cornell, Harvard, Princeton, and Yale.

[a]Data for the years 1982–1984 were not available and interpolation has been used to obtain the values presented in the table.

[b]Data for the years 1967–1971 were not available at Yale, and values have been imputed using the assumption that the ratio of students at Yale to students at Cornell, Harvard, and Princeton was the same during these years as it was during 1972–1976.

[c]For the purpose of presentation in the text and figures we assume that the 1964 value is equal to the 1967 value.

TABLE G.5–3
Number of Doctorates Conferred and Graduate Enrollment Index, EHP Fields,
Five-University Total, 1958–1986

Year	English	History	PolSci	Total EHP	PhD Index (1964 = 100)	Graduate Class Size[a]	Graduate Enrollment Index[b] (1964 = 100)
1958	78	93	49	220	73		
1960	94	97	69	260	86		
1962	87	84	67	238	79		
1964	106	129	67	302	100	439	100
1966	117	135	85	337	112	456	104
1968	167	132	118	417	138	479	109
1970	135	166	102	403	133	443	101
1972	145	149	138	432	143	482	110
1974	136	172	109	417	138	447	102
1976	106	140	100	346	115	407	93
1978	85	117	96	298	99	373	85
1980	76	103	71	250	83	320	73
1982	52	99	75	226	75	311	71
1984	62	79	60	201	67	298	68
1986	60	84	71	215	71	314	71

Source: Special tabulations from Doctorate Records File for Columbia, Cornell, Harvard, Princeton, and Yale.

[a]Graduate Class Size is the average of the number of doctorates conferred (Total EHP) and the number of entering students (Five University Sum in Table G.5–2) for the five universities.

[b]Graduate Enrollment Index is Graduate Class Size indexed at 1964 = 100.

TABLE G.5–4
Number of BAs Conferred and Undergraduate Enrollment Index, 1964–1988

	BA Degrees Conferred						Under-graduate Class Size[a] (All Fields)	Under-graduate Class Size[b] (EHP only)	Under-graduate Enrollment Index[c] (1964 = 100)
Year	Columbia	Cornell	Harvard	Princeton	Yale	Five University Total			
1964	1,298	1,561	1,155	750	936	5,700	6,040	1,872	100
1966	1,298	1,958	1,495	721	908	6,380	6,599	2,046	109
1968	1,257	2,080	1,710	770	1,000	6,817	6,288	1,949	104
1970	1,273	1,390	1,425	730	940	5,758	6,028	1,869	100
1972	1,172	1,604	1,539	828	1,155	6,298	6,182	1,916	102
1974	1,155	1,616	1,122	936	1,237	6,066	6,442	1,997	107
1976	1,226	1,653	1,618	1,065	1,255	6,817	6,878	2,132	114
1978	1,256	1,654	1,694	1,082	1,252	6,938	6,931	2,148	115
1980	1,204	1,702	1,688	1,029	1,300	6,923	7,062	2,189	117
1982	1,354	1,794	1,758	1,044	1,250	7,200	7,219	2,238	120
1984	1,375	1,828	1,679	1,110	1,245	7,237	7,193	2,230	119
1986	1,357	1,693	1,717	1,067	1,314	7,148	7,357	2,281	122
1988	1,357	1,899	1,862	1,094	1,353	7,565			

Source: Earned Degrees Conferred surveys.

Notes: Data for Columbia in the years 1964 and 1988 are estimated using 1966 and 1986 values.

[a]Undergraduate Class Size (All Fields) is the average of the total BAs conferred in year t and the total BAs conferred in year t + 2. This is equivalent to averaging the sophomore and senior classes, assuming constant attrition from each class.

[b]Undergraduate Class Size (EHP only) is obtained by multiplying Undergraduate Class Size (All Fields) by 0.31, the average share of degrees awarded in EHP fields at these five universities.

[c]Undergraduate Enrollment Index is Undergraduate Class Size indexed at 1964 = 100.

TABLE G.5–5
Level of Enrollment and Number of Faculty, Five-University Total, 1974–1989
(Index: 1974 = 100)

Year	Undergraduate Enrollment Index	Graduate Enrollment Index	Weighted Enrollment Index	Masthead Faculty Index[a]
1974	100	100	100	100
1976	107	91	102	
1978	108	83	100	
1979				91
1980	110	72	98	
1982	112	70	99	
1984	112	67	98	
1986	114	70	101	
1988				
1989				107

Source: Appendix Tables G.5–1 to G.5–4. Data are for Columbia, Cornell, Harvard, Princeton, and Yale.

Notes: Weighted Enrollment Index is the weighted sum of Undergraduate Class Size (EHP only) from Table G.5–4 and Graduate Class Size from Table G.5–3 with the graduate component given twice the weight as the undergraduate component and indexed at 1974 = 100.

[a]Values for Masthead Faculty are for two-year intervals such as 1973–1975.

Chapter Six

TABLE G.6–1
Components of Time-to-Degree, All Fields, 1960–1989 PhD Cohorts

Year	Medians				Means		
	TTD	RTD	TTD/RTD	RTD/TTD	TTD	ETD	RTD
1960	8.6	5.2	3.4	60.5%			
1964	8.2	5.4	2.8	65.9%			
1967	7.2	5.2	1.9	73.0%	8.19	7.34	5.63
1968	8.1	5.3	2.8	65.4%			
1972	8.2	5.8	2.4	70.7%			
1976	8.6	6.0	2.6	69.8%			
1978	8.9	6.1	2.8	68.5%			
1980	9.3	6.3	3.0	67.7%			
1984	10.0	6.8	3.2	68.0%			
1986	8.7	6.6	2.1	75.6%	9.84	8.66	7.02
1988	10.5	6.9	3.6	65.7%			
1989	10.5	6.9	3.6	65.7%			

Sources: Doctorate Records File, as reported in *Summary Reports* for the respective years, Table 2. Data for 1960 and 1964 represent two-year spans, 1958–1960 and 1964–1966, respectively, as reported in *Summary Reports* for 1958–1966. Data for 1967 and 1986 are from Tuckman 1990, Appendix Tables 1, 2.1, 2.2, 2.3, 2.4.

Notes: "All fields" (except for 1967 and 1986) comprise the universe of fields represented in the Doctorate Records File. For 1967 and 1986, "All fields" includes the following eleven fields: chemistry, physics/astronomy, earth/atmospheric/marine sciences, math/computer sciences, engineering, agricultural sciences, biosciences, health sciences, psychology, economics, and social sciences. TTD = Total Time-to-Degree; RTD = Registered Time-to-Degree (Years in School); and ETD = Elapsed Time-to-Degree.

Chapter Seven

TABLE G.7-1
Minimum Completion Rates (Rescaled) by Field, Selected Data Sets and Entering Cohorts (percent)

Field	Eight Universities		NSF Fellows			NDEA Fellows	Danforth Fellows			Woodrow Wilson Fellows	
	1967–1971	1972–1976	1962–1966	1967–1971	1972–1976	1962	1962–1966	1967–1971	1972–1976	1957–1961	1962–1966
NatSci											
Math	58.5	60.4	59.1	57.4	62.5	59.4	57.7	63.9	58.7	57.4	60.6
Physics	70.2	68.7	63.2	64.4	65.6	73.7	74.9	73.6	71.9	75.3	74.8
Other NatSci						64.4	63.8	62.6	65.3	64.0	62.3
Chemistry			74.1	73.4	66.3						
EarthSci			68.9	68.7	61.9						
LifeSci			67.7	70.5	65.4						
Psych			65.9	71.8	66.5						
Total NatSci	64.9	64.9	64.9	64.9	64.9	64.9	64.9	64.9	64.9	64.9	64.9
SocSci											
Econ	57.0	59.2	58.6	69.6	70.6	60.9	54.2	39.3	62.8	54.3	59.9
PolSci	53.4	48.2				51.7	56.1	49.0	47.9	46.2	43.9
Other SocSci			65.2	60.1	47.5	64.5	60.8	50.9	53.8	48.8	44.9
Total SocSci	55.0	53.2	62.3	63.6	54.4	59.0	56.9	48.2	53.1	49.0	48.5
Humanities											
English	55.0	46.3				51.5	54.5	52.6	47.2	39.2	41.5
History	51.1	43.3				50.8	58.8	62.2	48.5	50.2	51.3
Other Humanities						50.0				48.2	44.5
ForeignLang/Lit							64.1	52.8	48.0		
Philosophy							63.3	56.1	47.2		
Religion							54.9	50.0	47.6		
Other							49.9	44.1	39.5		
Total Humanities	53.0	44.8				50.7	57.2	52.9	45.7	44.8	44.3

Sources: Eight-university cohorts—Ten-University data set (Berkeley, Chicago, Columbia, Cornell, Harvard, Princeton, Stanford, and UNC); NSF, NDEA, Danforth, and Woodrow Wilson cohorts—National Fellowship data set.

Notes: Fellowship data include transfers. Foreign Languages and literatures include comparative literature. Values are rescaled with the completion rate of Total NatSci (really mathematics and physics combined) for eight universities in the 1967–1976 interval used as a reference point. This is the same reference point used in the tables and figures in the text.

TABLE G.7-2
Median Elapsed Time-to-Degree by Field, Selected Data Sets and Entering Cohorts (number of years)

Field	Eight Universities		NSF Fellows			NDEA Fellows	Danforth Fellows			Woodrow Wilson Fellows	
	1967–1971	1972–1976	1962–1966	1967–1971	1972–1976	1962	1962–1966	1967–1971	1972–1976	1957–1961	1962–1966
NatSci											
Math	5.1	5.3	4.4	4.6	4.3	4.9	5.3	6.0	5.8	5.3	5.2
Physics	6.2	6.0	5.2	5.4	5.1	5.4	5.4	6.0	5.4	6.0	5.5
Other NatSci						5.2	5.2	5.8	6.6	4.9	5.2
Chemistry			4.9	5.0	4.8						
EarthSci			5.1	5.8	5.4						
LifeSci			5.2	5.2	5.4						
Psych			5.0	4.8	4.2						
Total NatSci						5.2	5.3	5.9	6.3	5.3	5.3
SocSci											
Econ	5.6	5.9	5.3	4.7	4.5	5.2	6.1	6.3	5.5	5.6	5.6
PolSci	6.8	7.1				6.7	6.8	7.0	7.1	6.5	6.8
Other SocSci			5.4	6.4	6.3	5.7	5.6	6.3	7.7	7.1	7.2
Total SocSci						5.7	6.2	6.6	7.0	6.5	6.4
Humanities											
English	6.4	6.6				6.2	6.3	6.6	8.6	7.3	6.4
History	7.2	7.7				5.5	6.9	7.3	7.0	7.2	7.0
Other Humanities						6.5				7.2	6.4
ForeignLang/Lit							6.3	7.4	6.8		
Philosophy							6.4	6.5	5.4		
Religion							9.6	9.8	8.5		
Other							7.0	7.3	8.1		
Total Humanities						6.3	6.9	7.1	7.3	7.2	6.6

Sources: Eight-University cohorts—Ten-University data set (Berkeley, Chicago, Columbia, Cornell, Harvard, Princeton, Stanford, and UNC); NSF, NDEA, Danforth, and Woodrow Wilson cohorts—National Fellowship data set.

Notes: Fellowship data include transfers. Foreign languages and literatures include comparative literature.

Chapter Eight

TABLE G.8–1
Comparisons by Scale of Graduate Program, University Data, 1967–1981 Entering Cohorts

	Number of Entering Students							
	1967–1971		1972–1976		Total: 1967–1976		1977–1981	
Field	Larger	Smaller	Larger	Smaller	Larger	Smaller	Larger	Smaller
English	367	111	328	80	695	191	261	68
History	373	133	307	97	680	230	218	72
PolSci	229	80	222	81	451	161	173	62
Econ	163	79	160	83	323	162	149	76
Math	190	60	162	50	352	110	115	39
Physics	188	108	145	98	333	206	131	96
EHP	968	323	856	258	1,824	581	652	201
MP	378	168	307	148	685	316	246	135
Six-Fields	1,509	570	1,323	488	2,832	1,058	1,047	412

	Minimum Completion Rates							
	1967–1971		1972–1976		Average: 1967–1976		1977–1981	
Field	Larger	Smaller	Larger	Smaller	Larger	Smaller	Larger	Smaller
English	38.3	69.2	29.0	58.6	33.7	63.9	21.1	64.6
History	35.1	63.9	28.9	53.1	32.0	58.5	21.7	42.5
PolSci	36.9	65.3	31.9	57.3	34.4	61.3	22.0	49.2
Econ	43.6	65.7	46.7	64.0	45.2	64.9	40.6	60.9
Math	46.4	71.9	50.8	67.5	48.6	69.7	45.2	60.7
Physics	59.7	78.1	59.1	75.5	59.4	76.8	59.9	75.4
EHP	36.8	66.1	29.9	56.3	33.4	61.2	21.6	52.1
MP	53.1	75.0	55.0	71.5	54.1	73.3	52.6	68.0
Six-Fields	43.4	69.0	41.1	62.7	42.3	65.9	35.1	58.9

	Elapsed Time-to-Degree (years)							
	1967–1971		1972–1976		Average: 1967–1976		1977–1981	
Field	Larger	Smaller	Larger	Smaller	Larger	Smaller	Larger	Smaller
English	7.1	5.4	7.2	5.9	7.2	5.7	7.5	6.6
History	7.7	6.8	8.1	7.0	7.9	6.9	7.1	6.9
PolSci	7.1	6.6	7.9	6.8	7.5	6.7	7.8	7.0
Econ	5.9	5.5	6.1	5.8	6.0	5.7	6.2	5.9
Math	5.5	4.9	6.0	4.6	5.8	4.8	6.1	5.1
Physics	6.6	5.9	6.5	5.5	6.6	5.7	6.6	5.8
EHP	7.3	6.2	7.7	6.6	7.5	6.4	7.4	6.8
MP	6.0	5.4	6.2	5.0	6.1	5.2	6.4	5.5
Six-Fields	6.6	5.8	7.0	5.9	6.8	5.9	6.9	6.2

Source: Ten-University data set.
Notes: Larger includes Berkeley, Chicago, and Columbia; Smaller includes Cornell, Harvard, Princeton, and Stanford. Completion rates and elapsed time-to-degree for 1967–1976 are unweighted means of the individual cohorts.

TABLE G.8–2
Comparisons by Scale of Graduate Program, University Data, Men Only, 1967–1981
Entering Cohorts

	Number of Entering Students							
	1967–1971		1972–1976		Total: 1967–1976		1977–1981	
Field	Larger	Smaller	Larger	Smaller	Larger	Smaller	Larger	Smaller
English	182	68	162	49	344	117	118	34
History	250	100	190	67	440	167	137	45
PolSci	170	66	157	62	327	128	119	42
Econ	142	69	132	70	274	139	106	59
Math	170	55	139	47	309	102	101	33
Physics	178	104	136	92	314	196	121	86
EHP	601	234	510	179	1,111	413	374	122
MP	348	159	275	139	623	298	222	118
Six-Fields	1,091	462	916	387	2,007	849	702	299

	Minimum Completion Rates							
	1967–1971		1972–1976		Average: 1967–1976		1977–1981	
Field	Larger	Smaller	Larger	Smaller	Larger	Smaller	Larger	Smaller
English	41.0	69.3	30.3	60.9	35.7	65.1	23.3	61.9
History	37.4	68.0	31.9	56.2	34.7	62.1	21.7	37.4
PolSci	37.0	64.9	32.8	56.5	34.9	60.7	24.5	54.2
Econ	44.2	65.6	49.9	64.2	47.1	64.9	42.4	62.5
Math	46.8	71.1	53.2	67.4	50.0	69.3	48.8	60.0
Physics	59.4	79.3	59.7	76.1	59.6	77.7	59.7	76.0
EHP	38.5	67.4	31.7	57.9	35.1	62.7	23.2	51.2
MP	53.1	75.2	56.5	71.8	54.8	73.5	54.3	68.0
Six-Fields	44.3	69.7	43.0	63.5	43.7	66.6	36.7	58.7

	Elapsed Time-to-Degree (years)							
	1967–1971		1972–1976		Average: 1967-1976		1977–1981	
Field	Smaller	Larger	Smaller	Larger	Smaller	Larger	Smaller	Larger
English	6.8	5.3	6.7	5.7	6.8	5.5	7.5	6.5
History	7.7	6.5	8.0	7.1	7.9	6.8	7.2	7.0
PolSci	7.1	6.4	7.7	6.6	7.4	6.5	7.7	6.7
Econ	5.9	5.4	6.0	5.7	6.0	5.6	6.2	5.9
Math	5.4	4.8	5.9	4.5	5.7	4.7	6.1	5.1
Physics	6.6	5.9	6.5	5.5	6.6	5.7	6.5	5.8
EHP	7.3	6.2	7.7	6.6	7.5	6.4	7.5	6.7
MP	6.0	5.4	6.2	5.0	6.1	5.2	6.3	5.4
Six-Fields	6.6	5.8	7.0	5.9	6.8	5.9	6.9	6.2

Source: Ten-University data set.
Notes: Larger includes Berkeley, Chicago, and Columbia; Smaller includes Cornell, Harvard, Princeton, and Stanford. Completion rates and elapsed time-to-degree for 1967–1976 are unweighted means of the individual cohorts.

TABLE G.8–3

Comparisons by Scale of Graduate Program, University Data, Women Only, 1967–1981
Entering Cohorts

| | Number of Entering Students | | | | | | | |
| | 1967–1971 | | 1972–1976 | | Total: 1967–1976 | | 1977–1981 | |
Field	Larger	Smaller	Larger	Smaller	Larger	Smaller	Larger	Smaller
English	184	43	163	31	347	74	143	34
History	120	33	114	30	234	63	81	27
PolSci	58	14	62	18	120	32	55	19
Econ	21	10	28	13	49	23	43	17
Math	20	6	23	3	43	9	14	6
Physics	9	4	9	6	18	10	10	11
EHP	362	90	340	79	702	169	278	80
MP	29	11	32	9	61	20	24	17
Six-Fields	412	110	400	109	812	219	345	113

| | Minimum Completion Rates | | | | | | | |
| | 1967–1971 | | 1972–1976 | | Average: 1967–1976 | | 1977–1981 | |
Field	Larger	Smaller	Larger	Smaller	Larger	Smaller	Larger	Smaller
English	35.8	68.0	27.8	54.8	31.8	61.4	19.0	66.6
History	29.7	49.1	24.1	45.5	26.9	47.3	21.3	50.6
PolSci	37.8	66.7	29.9	59.6	33.9	63.2	17.0	41.8
Econ	38.8	65.1	29.8	70.5	34.3	67.8	37.8	55.9
Math	59.6	78.0	37.9	65.0	48.8	71.5	22.7	62.9
Physics	78.2	51.4	51.6	63.6	64.9	57.5	59.7	69.6
EHP	34.4	60.9	27.3	53.3	30.9	57.1	19.1	53.0
MP	68.9	64.7	44.7	64.3	56.8	64.5	41.2	66.3
Six-Fields	46.7	62.9	33.5	59.8	40.1	61.4	29.6	57.9

| | Elapsed Time-to-Degree (years) | | | | | | | |
| | 1967–1971 | | 1972–1976 | | Average: 1967–1976 | | 1977–1981 | |
Field	Larger	Smaller	Larger	Smaller	Larger	Smaller	Larger	Smaller
English	7.5	5.7	8.0	6.4	7.8	6.1	7.9	6.7
History	8.0	7.6	8.7	6.9	8.4	7.3	6.9	6.7
PolSci	7.0	7.2	8.3	7.4	7.7	7.3	7.5	7.7
Econ	6.6	5.7	6.7	6.3	6.7	6.0	6.2	5.8
Math	6.1	5.1	5.5	4.6	5.8	4.9	7.2	5.7
Physics	7.9	7.8	5.8	6.3	6.9	7.1	7.4	5.9
EHP	7.5	6.8	8.3	6.9	7.9	6.9	7.4	7.0
MP	7.0	6.4	5.6	5.4	6.3	5.9	7.3	5.8
Six-Fields	7.2	6.5	7.1	6.3	7.2	6.4	7.2	6.4

Source: Ten-University data set.

Notes: Larger includes Berkeley, Chicago, and Columbia; Smaller includes Cornell, Harvard, Princeton, and Stanford. Completion rates and elapsed time-to-degree for 1967–1976 are unweighted means of the individual cohorts.

TABLE G.8-4
Comparisons by Scale of Graduate Program, Fellowship Data, 1957–1976 Entering Cohorts

Number of Awardees

Fellowship Program	EHP		Total Humanities		Total SocSci		Total NatSci		All Fields	
	Larger	Smaller	Larger	Smaller	Larger	Smaller	Larger	Smaller	Larger	Smaller
Danforth										
1957–1961	16	59	16	111	8	30	12	25	36	166
1962–1966	31	102	39	175	14	39	10	50	63	264
1967–1971	35	97	51	165	17	36	12	38	80	239
1972–1976	21	68	41	123	21	33	11	25	73	181
Total	103	326	147	574	60	138	45	138	252	850
Woodrow Wilson										
1957–1961	458	585	527	827	204	252	126	234	857	1,313
1962–1966	490	839	649	1,265	202	359	97	231	948	1,855
Total	948	1,424	1,176	2,092	406	611	223	465	1,805	3,168

Minimum Completion Rates: No Transfers

Fellowship Program	EHP		Total Humanities		Total SocSci		Total NatSci		All Fields	
	Larger	Smaller	Larger	Smaller	Larger	Smaller	Larger	Smaller	Larger	Smaller
Danforth										
1957–1961	43.8	69.5	62.5	61.3	37.5	76.7	50.0	76.0	52.8	66.3
1962–1966	45.2	63.7	33.3	58.3	71.4	69.2	40.0	72.0	42.9	62.5
1967–1971	54.3	66.0	47.1	61.2	52.9	55.6	41.7	73.7	47.5	62.3
1972–1976	33.3	54.4	39.0	48.0	57.1	57.6	63.6	80.0	47.9	54.1
Total	44.2	63.4	45.5	57.2	54.7	64.8	48.8	75.4	47.8	61.3
Z-score	−3.22		−2.49		−1.09		−2.55		−3.48	
Woodrow Wilson										
1957–1961	24.7	43.4	22.4	43.8	30.4	52.8	51.6	58.1	28.6	48.1
1962–1966	34.3	53.0	32.4	49.8	36.1	56.0	51.5	70.6	35.1	53.6
Total	29.5	48.2	27.4	46.8	33.3	54.4	51.6	64.4	31.9	50.9
Z-score	−11.83		−14.86		−7.77		−2.73		−16.01	

405

TABLE G.8-4
Continued

Minimum Completion Rates: With Transfers

Fellowship Program	EHP		Total Humanities		Total SocSci		Total NatSci		All Fields	
	Larger	*Smaller*	*Larger*	*Smaller*	*Larger*	*Smaller*	*Larger*	*Smaller*	*Larger*	*Smaller*
Danforth										
1957–1961	62.5	76.3	81.3	76.6	50.0	80.0	91.7	84.0	77.8	78.3
1962–1966	67.7	76.5	61.5	74.5	85.7	74.4	70.0	78.0	68.3	75.4
1967–1971	68.6	73.2	62.7	71.5	64.7	61.1	66.7	84.2	63.8	72.0
1972–1976	47.6	58.8	48.8	54.5	61.9	66.7	63.6	84.0	54.8	60.8
Total	61.6	71.2	63.6	69.3	65.6	70.6	73.0	82.6	66.2	71.6
Z-score	−1.28		−0.93		−0.47		−0.72		−1.10	
Woodrow Wilson										
1957–1961	39.1	54.9	38.5	56.2	41.7	61.1	69.0	68.8	43.8	59.4
1962–1966	44.7	60.7	43.9	58.1	44.6	62.4	74.2	78.8	47.2	61.5
Total	41.9	57.8	41.2	57.2	43.2	61.8	71.6	73.8	45.5	60.5
Z-score	−7.71		−9.02		−5.63		−0.37		−9.67	

Source: National Fellowship data set.

Notes: Larger includes Berkeley, Chicago, and Columbia; Smaller includes Cornell, Harvard, Princeton, Stanford, and Yale. Note that Yale is in the Smaller category here, but not in the Ten-University data set. These are "pooled" data; that is, the figures for EHP for each cohort are for all students in the three fields; they are not averages of the separate rates for each constituent field. Similarly, the figures for Larger and Smaller groups of graduate programs are for all students in these programs; they are not averages of the rates for each constituent program. The "Total" figures are unweighted means for each cohort. Weighting by cell size does not change the results appreciably.

TABLE G.8-5
Comparisons by Scale of Graduate Program, Fellowship Data, Men Only, 1957–1976 Entering Cohorts

Number of Awardees

Fellowship Program	EHP		Total Humanities		Total SocSci		Total NatSci		All Fields	
	Larger	Smaller	Larger	Smaller	Larger	Smaller	Larger	Smaller	Larger	Smaller
Danforth										
1957–1961	16	59	16	111	8	30	12	25	36	166
1962–1966	27	88	30	156	13	35	9	46	52	237
1967–1971	25	66	35	105	11	29	11	32	57	166
1972–1976	8	43	17	76	8	20	9	14	34	110
Total	76	256	98	448	40	114	41	117	179	679
Woodrow Wilson										
1957–1961	285	443	327	618	137	207	102	190	566	1,015
1962–1966	320	632	395	915	150	281	79	191	624	1,387
Total	605	1,075	722	1,533	287	488	181	381	1,190	2,402

Minimum Completion Rates: No Transfers

Fellowship Program	EHP		Total Humanities		Total SocSci		Total NatSci		All Fields	
	Larger	Smaller	Larger	Smaller	Larger	Smaller	Larger	Smaller	Larger	Smaller
Danforth										
1957–1961	43.8	69.5	62.5	61.3	37.5	76.7	50.0	76.0	52.8	66.3
1962–1966	48.1	65.9	40.0	58.3	69.2	74.3	44.4	78.3	48.1	64.6
1967–1971	60.0	66.7	48.6	59.0	72.7	48.3	45.5	78.1	52.6	60.8
1972–1976	12.5	58.1	35.3	50.0	62.5	55.0	77.8	92.9	52.9	56.4
Total	41.1	65.1	46.6	57.2	60.5	63.6	54.4	81.3	51.6	62.0
Z-score	−3.55		−1.83		−0.27		−2.23		−2.19	
Woodrow Wilson										
1957–1961	35.1	52.8	31.8	53.2	41.6	61.8	58.8	67.4	39.0	57.6
1962–1966	45.0	61.2	43.0	58.1	42.7	66.9	57.0	78.5	44.7	62.7
Total	40.1	57.0	37.4	55.7	42.2	64.4	57.9	73.0	41.9	60.2
Z-score	−6.98		−8.96		−5.73		−2.57		−10.29	

TABLE G.8-5
Continued

Minimum Completion Rates: With Transfers

Fellowship Program	EHP		Total Humanities		Total SocSci		Total NatSci		All Fields	
	Larger	Smaller	Larger	Smaller	Larger	Smaller	Larger	Smaller	Larger	Smaller
Danforth										
1957–1961	62.5	76.3	81.3	76.6	50.0	80.0	91.7	84.0	77.8	78.3
1962–1966	70.4	79.5	63.3	76.3	84.6	80.0	77.8	84.8	71.2	78.5
1967–1971	72.0	71.2	60.0	68.6	72.7	51.7	72.7	90.6	64.9	64.9
1972–1976	25.0	62.8	41.2	56.6	75.0	70.0	77.8	92.9	58.8	63.6
Total	57.5	72.5	61.5	69.5	70.6	70.4	80.0	88.1	68.2	71.3
Z-score	−1.78		−1.11		0.01		−0.53		−0.54	
Woodrow Wilson										
1957–1961	52.3	65.7	51.7	67.5	52.6	70.5	78.4	80.0	56.7	70.4
1962–1966	56.9	69.9	57.5	67.7	52.7	73.0	82.3	85.9	59.5	71.2
Total	54.6	67.8	54.6	67.6	52.7	71.8	80.4	83.0	58.1	70.8
Z-score	−4.27		−4.74		−4.18		−0.35		−5.59	

Source: National Fellowship data set.

Notes: Larger includes Berkeley, Chicago, and Columbia; Smaller includes Cornell, Harvard, Princeton, Stanford, and Yale. Note that Yale is in the Smaller category here, but not in the Ten-University data set. These are "pooled" data; that is, the figures for EHP for each cohort are for all students in the three fields; they are not averages of the separate rates for each constituent field. Similarly, the figures for Larger and Smaller groups of graduate programs are for all students in these programs; they are not averages of the rates for each constituent program. The "Total" figures are unweighted means for each cohort. Weighting by cell size does not change the results appreciably.

TABLE G.8-6

Comparisons by Scale of Graduate Program, Fellowship Data, Women Only, 1957–1976 Entering Cohorts

Number of Awardees

Fellowship Program	EHP Larger	EHP Smaller	Total Humanities Larger	Total Humanities Smaller	Total SocSci Larger	Total SocSci Smaller	Total NatSci Larger	Total NatSci Smaller	All Fields Larger	All Fields Smaller
Danforth										
1962–1966	4	14	9	19	1	4	1	4	11	27
1967–1971	10	31	16	60	6	7	1	6	23	73
1972–1976	13	25	24	47	13	13	2	11	39	71
Total	27	70	49	126	20	24	4	21	73	171
Woodrow Wilson										
1957–1961	173	142	200	209	67	45	24	44	291	298
1962–1966	170	207	254	350	52	78	18	40	324	468
Total	343	349	454	559	119	123	42	84	615	766

Minimum Completion Rates: No Transfers

Fellowship Program	EHP Larger	EHP Smaller	Total Humanities Larger	Total Humanities Smaller	Total SocSci Larger	Total SocSci Smaller	Total NatSci Larger	Total NatSci Smaller	All Fields Larger	All Fields Smaller
Danforth										
1962–1966	25.0	50.0	11.1	57.9	100.0	25.0	0.0	0.0	18.2	44.4
1967–1971	40.0	64.5	43.8	65.0	16.7	85.7	0.0	50.0	34.8	65.8
1972–1976	46.2	48.0	41.7	44.7	53.8	61.5	0.0	63.6	43.6	50.7
Total	37.1	54.2	32.2	55.9	56.8	57.4	0.0	37.9	32.2	53.6
Z-score	−1.68		−3.31		−0.03		—		−3.69	
Woodrow Wilson										
1957–1961	7.5	14.1	7.0	15.8	7.5	11.1	20.8	18.2	8.2	15.4
1962–1966	14.1	28.0	15.7	28.0	17.3	16.7	27.8	32.5	16.7	26.5
Total	10.8	21.1	11.4	21.9	12.4	13.9	24.3	25.4	12.5	21.0
Z-score	−8.94		−10.59		−0.89		−0.22		−9.72	

TABLE G.8-6
Continued

Minimum Completion Rates: With Transfers

Fellowship Program	EHP		Total Humanities		Total SocSci		Total NatSci		All Fields	
	Larger	Smaller	Larger	Smaller	Larger	Smaller	Larger	Smaller	Larger	Smaller
Danforth										
1962–1966	50.0	57.1	55.6	63.2	100.0	25.0	0.0	0.0	54.5	48.1
1967–1971	60.0	77.4	68.8	76.7	50.0	100.0	0.0	50.0	60.9	76.7
1972–1976	61.5	52.0	54.2	51.1	53.8	61.5	0.0	72.7	51.3	56.3
Total	57.2	62.2	59.5	63.7	67.9	62.2	0.0	40.9	55.6	60.4
Z-score	−0.37		−0.40		0.29		—		−0.59	
Woodrow Wilson										
1957–1961	17.3	21.1	17.0	23.0	19.4	17.8	29.2	20.5	18.6	21.8
1962–1966	21.8	32.4	22.8	33.1	21.2	24.4	38.9	45.0	23.5	32.7
Total	19.6	26.8	19.9	28.1	20.3	21.1	34.1	32.8	21.1	27.3
Z-score	−4.14		−5.46		−0.30		0.21		−4.78	

Source: National Fellowship data set.

Notes: Larger includes Berkeley, Chicago, and Columbia; Smaller includes Cornell, Harvard, Princeton, Stanford, and Yale. Note that Yale is in the Smaller category here, but not in the Ten-University data set. These are "pooled" data; that is, the figures for EHP for each cohort are for all students in the three fields; they are not averages of the separate rates for each constituent field. Similarly, the figures for Larger and Smaller groups of graduate programs are for all students in these programs; they are not averages of the rates for each constituent program. The "Total" figures are unweighted means for each cohort. Weighting by cell size does not change the results appreciably.

TABLE G.8–7
Research I and Other Research/Doctorate Comparisons, NDEA Data, 1962 Cohort

| | Number of Awardees | | | | | | | |
| | Total Humanities | | Total SocSci | | Total NatSci | | All Arts/Sci | |
	Res I	OthRD	Res I	OthRD	Res I	OthRD	Res I	OthRD
Men and women	204	170	150	104	155	249	509	523
Men only	150	128	126	97	137	212	413	437
Women only	54	42	24	7	18	37	96	86

| | Minimum Completion Rates: No Transfers | | | | | | | |
| | Total Humanities | | Total SocSci | | Total NatSci | | All Arts/Sci | |
	Res I	OthRD	Res I	OthRD	Res I	OthRD	Res I	OthRD
Men and women	54.9	34.1	56.0	49.0	70.3	49.0	59.9	44.2
Men only	62.0	37.5	61.9	50.5	75.9	55.2	66.6	49.0
Women only	35.2	23.8	25.0	28.6	27.8	13.5	31.3	19.8

| | Minimum Completion Rates: With Transfers | | | | | | | |
| | Total Humanities | | Total SocSci | | Total NatSci | | All Arts/Sci | |
	Res I	OthRD	Res I	OthRD	Res I	OthRD	Res I	OthRD
Men and women	56.4	48.8	58.7	64.4	74.2	62.2	62.5	58.3
Men only	64.0	55.5	65.1	64.9	80.3	69.8	69.7	64.5
Women only	35.2	28.6	25.0	57.1	27.8	18.9	31.3	26.7

Source: National Fellowship data set.

Notes: Research I (Res I) and Other Research/Doctorate (OthRD) categories are based on the Carnegie classifications of institutions of higher education (Carnegie Foundation for the Advancement of Teaching 1987b). The Other Research/Doctorate category consists of institutions classified Research II, Doctorate I, and Doctorate II under the Carnegie system.

TABLE G.8–8
Minimum Completion Rates of Woodrow Wilson and NDEA Fellows by Quality Tier,
1957–1966 Entering Cohorts

	Minimum Completion Rates: No Transfers Quality Tier				
Program and Cohort	I	II	III	IV	II–IV
Woodrow Wilson, 1957–1961					
Humanities	35.0	25.9	31.8	30.5	28.9
SocSci	42.1	37.0	42.9	42.6	40.2
NatSci	58.0	46.5	57.9	56.3	51.2
Three-field average	45.0	36.5	44.2	43.1	40.1
All students	40.7	34.4	40.1	38.5	37.1
Woodrow Wilson, 1962–1966					
Humanities	41.3	33.9	42.9	27.6	34.8
SocSci	49.1	35.5	29.4	31.4	33.1
NatSci	62.7	55.4	45.5	53.8	52.7
Three-field average	51.0	41.6	39.3	37.6	40.2
All students	45.7	38.5	41.6	31.1	37.3
NDEA, 1962					
Humanities	47.4	39.2	44.8	46.8	42.9
SocSci	56.2	53.3	49.1	52.9	51.9
NatSci	71.4	50.6	51.7	47.1	50.0
Three-field average	58.3	47.7	48.5	48.9	48.3
All students	53.3	47.2	49.2	48.0	48.2

	Minimum Completion Rates: With Transfers Quality Tier				
Program and Cohort	I	II	III	IV	II–IV
Woodrow Wilson, 1957–1961					
Humanities	47.9	35.4	37.5	39.0	36.9
SocSci	51.4	44.4	47.6	51.0	42.5
NatSci	70.1	49.3	63.2	56.2	54.4
Three-field average	56.5	43.0	49.4	48.7	44.6
All students	52.8	41.5	45.6	45.9	43.7
Woodrow Wilson, 1962–1966					
Humanities	50.0	40.5	43.9	37.9	40.8
SocSci	55.9	40.3	41.2	37.3	39.2
NatSci	73.8	62.5	50.0	61.5	59.3
Three-field average	59.9	47.8	45.0	45.6	46.4
All students	54.4	44.8	44.5	39.7	43.4
NDEA, 1962					
Humanities	56.2	51.0	50.0	48.9	50.2
SocSci	57.5	63.4	59.7	64.7	62.4
NatSci	74.6	68.8	66.5	63.0	65.9
Three-field average	62.8	61.1	58.7	58.9	59.5
All students	60.8	60.2	60.5	60.0	60.3

Source: National Fellowship data set.
Notes: Quality Tiers are defined in Chapter Four. "All students" is the overall completion rate for students in the tier, regardless of the field of study. "Three-field average" is the average completion rate for the three broad fields, with each field receiving an equal weight.

Table G.8–9

Elapsed Time-to-Degree by Gender, Broad Field, and Scale of Graduate Program, Fellowship Data, 1957–1976 Entering Cohorts (number of years)

	Men and Women									
	EHP		Total Humanities		Total SocSci		Total NatSci		All Arts/Sci	
Fellowship Program	Larger	Smaller	Larger	Smaller	Larger	Smaller	Larger	Smaller	Larger	Smaller
Danforth										
1957–1961	6.9	6.4	7.1	7.3	7.0	5.2	4.5	5.0	6.6	6.4
1962–1966	6.8	6.1	7.3	6.2	6.2	5.9	4.0	5.1	6.6	5.9
1967–1971	6.6	6.3	7.3	6.2	6.3	6.8	5.3	5.2	6.9	6.1
1972–1976	9.8	6.6	8.3	6.1	7.5	6.2	6.3	5.5	7.7	6.0
Total	7.5	6.4	7.5	6.5	6.8	6.0	5.0	5.2	7.0	6.1
Woodrow Wilson										
1957–1961	7.0	6.1	7.2	6.2	6.9	5.9	5.2	4.8	6.6	5.8
1962–1966	7.7	6.1	7.6	6.0	8.1	6.1	5.0	5.2	7.3	5.8
Total	7.4	6.1	7.4	6.1	7.5	6.0	5.1	5.0	7.0	5.8

	Men Only									
	EHP		Total Humanities		Total SocSci		Total NatSci		All Arts/Sci	
Fellowship Program	Larger	Smaller	Larger	Smaller	Larger	Smaller	Larger	Smaller	Larger	Smaller
Danforth										
1957–1961	6.9	6.4	7.1	7.3	7.0	5.2	4.5	5.0	6.6	6.4
1962–1966	6.7	6.0	7.5	6.1	6.0	5.8	4.0	5.1	6.6	5.8
1967–1971	6.7	6.5	7.3	6.2	6.5	6.9	5.3	5.2	7.0	6.0
1972–1976	5.0	6.2	7.5	5.9	6.3	5.9	6.3	5.3	6.5	5.8
Total	6.3	6.3	7.4	6.4	6.5	6.0	5.0	5.2	6.7	6.0
Woodrow Wilson										
1957–1961	7.0	6.0	7.2	6.1	6.7	5.8	5.2	4.7	6.6	5.7
1962–1966	7.6	6.1	7.4	5.9	7.8	6.0	4.9	5.1	7.1	5.8
Total	7.3	6.1	7.3	6.0	7.3	5.9	5.1	4.9	6.9	5.8

	Women Only									
	EHP		Total Humanities		Total SocSci		Total NatSci		All Arts/Sci	
Fellowship Program	Larger	Smaller	Larger	Smaller	Larger	Smaller	Larger	Smaller	Larger	Smaller
Danforth										
1962–1966	7.0	9.0	4.0	8.0	7.0	7.0	—	—	4.5	7.5
1967–1971	5.5	5.5	7.0	6.3	4.0	6.5	—	5.0	5.5	6.3
1972–1976	10.0	7.0	9.5	6.4	8.3	6.8	—	6.7	9.0	6.6
Total	7.5	7.2	6.8	6.9	6.4	6.8	—	5.9	6.3	6.8
Woodrow Wilson										
1957–1961	7.3	7.5	7.5	7.0	8.8	7.3	5.0	5.5	7.1	6.8
1962–1966	8.1	6.2	8.3	6.1	9.0	6.7	6.0	5.8	8.2	6.1
Total	7.7	6.9	7.9	6.6	8.9	7.0	5.5	5.7	7.7	6.5

Source: National Fellowship data set.

Notes: Larger includes Berkeley, Chicago, and Columbia; Smaller includes Cornell, Harvard, Princeton, Stanford and Yale. Note that Yale is in the Smaller category here, but not in the Ten-University data set. These are "pooled" data; that is, the figures for EHP for each cohort are for all fellowship recipients in the three fields; they are not averages of the separate rates for each constituent field. Similarly, the figures for Larger and Smaller groups of graduate programs are for all fellowship recipients in these programs; they are not averages of the rates for each constituent program. The "All Arts/Sci" figures are unweighted means for each cohort. Weighting by cell size does not change the results appreciably. Dash indicates less than 20 observations.

Chapter Nine

TABLE G.9–1
Components of Student-Year Cost by University and Fields of Study, 1972–1976 Entering Cohort

	No. Entering Students	No. PhDs	Total SYC (years)	SYC Due to Completion (years)	SYC Due to Attrition (years)		
					Pre-2nd Year	Post-2nd Year, Pre-ABD	Post-ABD
EHP fields							
Berkeley	820	279	15.93	8.80	0.54	3.05	3.55
Chicago	761	227	15.43	8.00	0.77	3.85	2.81
Larger average	791	253	15.68	8.40	0.65	3.45	3.18
Princeton	250	138	9.48	6.40	0.21	0.17	2.69
Cornell	226	113	10.63	6.80	0.25	0.64	2.93
Smaller average	238	126	10.05	6.60	0.23	0.41	2.81
Michigan	407	218	10.25	7.30	0.18	1.14	1.63
Yale	382	214	8.74	6.10	0.19	0.62	1.82
MP fields							
Berkeley	573	292	9.24	6.60	0.25	1.99	0.40
Chicago	117	59	8.40	7.30	0.53	0.57	0.00
Princeton	148	120	5.17	4.50	0.04	0.05	0.59
Cornell	176	102	9.04	6.20	0.12	0.51	2.21
Michigan	160	84	9.33	6.60	0.24	1.41	1.08
Economics							
Berkeley	177	108	8.62	6.30	0.16	1.13	1.04
Chicago	182	76	10.34	6.50	0.53	2.26	1.05
Princeton	75	49	7.00	5.20	0.13	0.04	1.63
Cornell	54	30	9.28	6.30	0.13	0.81	2.03
Michigan	131	70	8.41	6.30	0.29	0.84	0.98

Source: Ten-University data set.

Notes: EHP and MP values are pooled data for all students in major field group at each university. Data for Chicago are for physics only.

Chapter Ten

Table G.10–1
Minimum Completion Rates by Primary Source of Support and University, EHP Total, Various Entering Cohorts

	Completion Rate (%)		Cell Size	
	Institutional Support	Own Support	Institutional Support	Own Support
Berkeley				
1978–1981	40.4	19.0	146	295
Chicago				
1962–1966	59.7	27.9	372	506
1967–1971	54.0	26.2	389	442
1972–1976	44.7	25.5	219	502
1977–1981	36.0	13.8	178	312
Columbia				
1972–1976	41.8	14.2	366	619
1977–1981	23.3	10.5	335	544
Cornell				
1962–1966	72.5	—	204	12
1967–1971	53.0	—	313	10
1972–1976	50.5	—	214	12
1977–1981	53.0	—	183	16
Princeton				
1967–1971	57.1	58.3	229	24
1972–1976	57.6	55.6	170	72
1977–1981	57.1	53.7	147	41
UNC				
1967–1971	75.7	67.1	103	158
1972–1976	63.0	37.9	92	195
1977–1981	52.9	25.3	153	99
Yale				
1972–1976	60.6	41.6	277	89
1977–1981	51.7	41.9	149	31

Source: Ten-University data set.

Notes: In this table, "Institutional Support" means that primary source of support was either a fellowship or a teaching assistantship. Dash indicates less than 20 observations.

Table G.10–2
Percentage Achieving ABD Status by Source of Support in First or Second Year
and University, EHP Total, Various Entering Cohorts

	% Achieving ABD		Cell Size	
	Institutional Support	Own Support	Institutional Support	Own Support
Berkeley				
1978–1981	80.2	36.7	182	256
1982–1986	60.1	31.7	341	240
Chicago				
1962–1966	68.9	36.5	379	501
1967–1971	66.3	38.2	410	422
1972–1976	53.9	37.6	228	495
1977–1981	51.3	25.7	193	300
1982–1986	51.0	16.8	245	191
Columbia				
1972–1976	54.8	30.5	420	568
1977–1981	51.1	27.3	427	454
1982–1986	39.2	10.7	477	336
Cornell				
1962–1966	88.3	—	206	10
1967–1971	76.9	—	321	2
1972–1976	72.4	—	217	9
1977–1981	74.6	—	189	10
1982–1986	78.0	—	168	8
Princeton				
1967–1971	90.0	78.3	231	23
1972–1976	84.9	75.0	172	72
1977–1981	85.1	80.9	141	47
1982–1986	87.5	—	152	16
UNC				
1967–1971	79.4	79.1	131	129
1972–1976	63.0	47.6	162	124
1977–1981	67.0	48.1	179	77
1982–1986	53.8	30.4	160	69
Yale				
1972–1976	77.3	69.8	308	43
1977–1981	72.1	—	165	6

Source: Ten-University data set.
Notes: In this table, "Institutional Support" means that source of support was a fellowship or a teaching assistantship or both. Dash indicates less than 20 observations.

TABLE G.10–3

Percentage Obtaining PhD Given ABD Status, by Source of Support in Dissertation Year and University, EHP Total, Various Entering Cohorts

	% Receiving PhD, Given ABD		Cell Size	
	Institutional Support	Own Support	Institutional Support	Own Support
Berkeley				
1978–1981	44.1	61.4	145	88
Chicago				
1962–1966	85.1	79.2	161	283
1967–1971	85.2	70.8	169	264
1972–1976	79.5	70.8	83	226
1977–1981	64.8	59.5	54	121
Columbia				
1972–1976	68.9	45.0	254	149
1977–1981	48.1	27.2	206	136
Cornell				
1962–1966	85.2	68.8	155	32
1967–1971	75.5	36.4	204	44
1972–1976	76.5	48.9	119	45
1977–1981	79.6	43.8	113	32
Princeton				
1967–1971	78.4	56.1	185	41
1972–1976	76.7	55.7	129	70
1977–1981	72.6	53.3	113	45
UNC				
1967–1971	86.5	90.5	111	105
1972–1976	81.9	80.2	72	91
1977–1981	69.0	64.4	113	45
Yale				
1972–1976	77.4	75.0	77	56
1977–1981	75.9	—	76	8

Source: Ten-University data set.

Notes: In this table, "Institutional Support" means that source of support was a fellowship or a teaching assistantship or both. Dash indicates less than 20 observations.

TABLE G.10–4
Minimum Completion Rates by Stage, Source of Support, and University, EHP Total,
Various Entering Cohorts

	Primary Support		% Reaching ABD Status		% Receiving PhD, Given ABD	
	Institutional Support	Own Support	Institutional Support	Own Support	Institutional Support	Own Support
Columbia						
1972–1976	60.5	11.7	69.5	30.5	67.6	40.8
1977–1981	16.7	7.7	72.2	27.3	47.0	21.4
Princeton						
1967–1971	71.7	56.7	94.4	—	81.8	—
1972–1976	50.0	50.0	83.9	70.7	75.6	55.3
1977–1981	58.8	—	83.0	80.0	86.0	55.2
Yale						
1972–1976	52.6	39.4	70.3	63.9	72.9	77.1
1977–1981	38.2	33.3	65.2	—	64.1	—

Source: Ten-University data set.

Notes: Data include only students who were ranked in the bottom half of their entering cohorts (see text). "Institutional Support" under the Primary Support heading means that a fellowship was the primary source of support (teaching assistantships were almost never the primary source of support). "Institutional Support" under the other headings means that the student had either a fellowship or a teaching assistantship or both during the stage of graduate education in question. Dash indicates less than 20 observations.

TABLE G.10–5

Cell Sizes and Minimum Completion Rates by Stage and University, Fellowship versus TA, EHP Total, Various Entering Cohorts

	Primary Support		Year 1 or 2		Dissertation Stage	
	FLSP	TA	FLSP-2	TA-2	FLSP-D	TA-D
	Cell Size (N)					
Berkeley						
1978–1981			88	51	65	37
1982–1986			99	138	na	na
Columbia						
1972–1976			387	—	131	43
1977–1981			366	30	85	43
1982–1986			320	26	na	na
Cornell						
1962–1966	116	88	86	69	98	21
1967–1971	246	67	230	32	117	38
1972–1976	115	99	95	46	42	51
1977–1981	98	85	58	52	36	40
1982–1986	na	na	54	32	na	na
	Minimum Completion Rate (%)					
Berkeley						
1978–1981			78.4	70.6	38.5	48.6
1982–1986			51.5	53.6	na	na
Columbia						
1972–1976			52.5	—	68.7	44.2
1977–1981			46.4	73.3	47.1	37.2
1982–1986			29.4	46.2	na	na
Cornell						
1962–1966	75.9	68.2	87.2	85.5	84.7	76.2
1967–1971	52.0	56.7	73.0	71.9	77.8	71.1
1972–1976	43.5	58.6	58.9	76.1	76.2	78.4
1977–1981	40.8	67.1	55.2	75.0	75.0	75.0
1982–1986	na	na	61.1	93.8	na	na

Source: Ten-University data set.

Notes: "Primary" refers to students who had the specified primary source of support; "FLSP" refers to students mainly supported by fellowships; and "TA" refers to students mainly supported by teaching assistantships. "Year 1 or 2" refers to students who had the specified source of support in the first or second year. "Dissertation Stage" refers to students who had the specified source of support in the dissertation year. Completion rates for the primary support category are measured as the number of PhD recipients divided by the number of entrants; rates for the ABD category reflect the number of students reaching ABD status in each support category divided by the number of entering students; and rates for the dissertation category are the number of students who completed the PhD in the support category divided by the number receiving dissertation support. Dash indicates less than 20 observations. "Na" indicates calculations would be misleading because of truncation.

TABLE G.10–6
Median Time-to-Degree by Stage and University, Fellowship versus TA, EHP Total,
Various Entering Cohorts

| | To Degree | | To ABD Status | | From ABD Status to PhD | |
			Elapsed Time (years):			
	FLSP	*TA*	*FLSP-2*	*TA-2*	*FLSP-D*	*TA-D*
Berkeley						
1978–1981			3.9	3.4	4.0	—
1982–1986			3.3	3.5	na	na
Columbia						
1972–1976			3.3	—	4.9	—
1977–1981			3.3	3.2	4.1	—
1982–1986			3.6	—	na	na
Cornell						
1962–1966	5.8	5.3	2.8	2.8	2.9	—
1967–1971	5.4	5.8	2.6	2.3	2.5	2.6
1972–1976	6.1	6.8	3.2	2.9	3.2	3.2
1977–1981	6.4	6.9	3.3	3.5	2.9	3.4
1982–1986	na	na	2.8	2.7	na	na

Source: Ten-University data set.

Notes: Source of support for time-to-degree is primary support. "Na" indicates calculations would be misleading because of truncation. Dash indicates less than 20 observations.

Chapter Eleven

TABLE G.11–1
Minimum Completion Rates (with transfers) by Scale of Graduate Program, Danforth and Woodrow Wilson Fellows, Men Only, 1957–1966 Entering Cohorts

	EHP Only		MP Only		Six-Fields	
	Number	*MCRT*	*Number*	*MCRT*	*Number*	*MCRT*
All universities						
Danforth	301	73.1	117	82.1	459	75.2
Woodrow Wilson	2,536	61.1	663	77.5	3,554	64.8
Difference		12.0		4.6		10.4
Z-score		2.95		0.58		3.00
Larger						
Danforth	43	67.4	16	—	61	72.1
Woodrow Wilson	605	54.7	124	76.6	782	58.2
Difference		12.7		—		13.9
Z-score		1.33		—		1.61
Smaller						
Danforth	147	78.2	48	83.3	214	78.0
Woodrow Wilson	1,075	68.2	238	83.2	1,469	71.3
Difference		10.0		0.1		6.7
Z-score		1.56		0.01		1.23

Source: National Fellowship data set.

Notes: "All universities" are all universities attended by fellowship winners, including "Larger," "Smaller," and other institutions. "Larger universities" are Berkeley, Chicago, and Columbia. "Smaller universities" are Cornell, Harvard, Princeton, Stanford, and Yale. "MCRT" indicates minimum completion rate with transfers. Dash indicates less than 20 observations in the cell.

TABLE G.11–2
Median Time-to-Degree (with transfers) by Scale of Graduate Program, Danforth
and Woodrow Wilson Fellows, Men Only, 1957–1966 Entering Cohorts

	EHP Only	MP Only	Six-Fields
All universities			
Danforth	6.6	5.4	6.2
Woodrow Wilson	6.8	5.5	6.3
Larger			
Danforth	7.1	5.5	6.8
Woodrow Wilson	7.6	6.0	7.2
Smaller			
Danforth	6.4	5.3	6.1
Woodrow Wilson	6.3	5.2	6.0

Source and notes: Same as Table G.11–1.

TABLE G.11–3
Minimum Completion Rates (no transfers) by Scale of Graduate Program, Danforth
and Woodrow Wilson Fellows and University Data, Men Only, 1957–1971 Entering
Cohorts

	EHP Only		MP Only		Six-Fields	
	Number	MCR	Number	MCR	Number	MCR
All universities						
Danforth (1957–1971)	233	61.2	79	59.3	332	60.1
Woodrow Wilson (1957–1966)	1,430	51.2	327	63.4	1,937	54.0
Seven universities (1967–1971)	2,738	55.0	1,680	65.7	5,120	58.8
Z-score						
Danforth/Seven universities		1.56		−0.89		0.39
Woodrow Wilson/Seven universities		−2.18		−0.60		−3.21
Larger						
Danforth (1957–1971)	68	51.5	22	36.4	92	47.8
Woodrow Wilson (1957–1966)	605	40.3	124	50.0	782	41.8
Seven universities (1967–1971)	1,804	38.5	1,044	53.1	3,273	44.3
Z-score						
Danforth/Seven universities		2.36		−1.76		0.72
Woodrow Wilson/Seven universities		0.97		−0.63		−1.46
Smaller						
Danforth (1957–1971)	212	67.0	67	73.1	302	67.5
Woodrow Wilson (1957–1966)	1,075	57.8	238	71.4	1,469	61.3
Seven universities (1967–1971)	934	67.4	636	75.2	1,847	69.7
Z-score						
Danforth/Seven universities		−0.08		−0.22		−0.52
Woodrow Wilson/Seven universities		−3.44		−0.68		−3.68

Sources: Ten-University and National Fellowship data sets.
Notes: "All universities" values are weighted averages of "Larger" and "Smaller" totals with these
subtotals weighted by the number of universities in each subset. "Larger universities" are Berkeley,
Chicago, and Columbia. "Smaller universities" are Cornell, Harvard, Princeton, and Stanford. Yale
is included as well for Danforth and Woodrow Wilson data, but not for university data. "Larger" and
"Smaller" university data are calculated as simple unweighted averages of fields and institutions.
"Larger" and "Smaller" fellowship data are pooled.

TABLE G.11–4

Median Time-to-Degree (no transfers) by Scale of Graduate Program, Danforth and Woodrow Wilson Fellows and University Data, Men Only, 1957–1971 Entering Cohorts

	EHP Only	MP Only	Six-Fields
All universities			
Danforth (1957–1971)	6.4	4.8	6.1
Woodrow Wilson (1957–1966)	6.6	5.2	6.2
Seven universities (1967–1971)	6.6	5.6	6.1
Larger			
Danforth (1957–1971)	6.8	4.2	6.4
Woodrow Wilson (1957–1966)	7.3	5.4	6.8
Seven universities (1967–1971)	7.2	5.9	6.6
Smaller			
Danforth (1957–1971)	6.2	5.1	5.9
Woodrow Wilson (1957–1966)	6.1	5.1	5.8
Seven universities (1967–1971)	6.1	5.3	5.7

Sources and notes: Same as Table G.11–3.

TABLE G.11–5
NSF Fellows by Quality Group and Field, Men Only, 1962–1976 Entering Cohorts

					Field				
	Math	Physics	Chem	EarthSci	LifeSci	Psych	Econ	Other SocSci	Total
1962–1966									
Cell size									
QG1-Award	210	147	104	26	79	28	28	34	656
QG2-Award	308	281	199	38	165	58	40	48	1,137
QG2-Non Award	35	21	8	7	28	2	9	27	137
MCR[a] (%)									
QG1-Award	74.8	78.9	92.3	88.5	89.9	89.3	75.0	85.3	82.0
QG2-Award	67.5	85.8	88.4	81.6	85.5	77.6	75.0	75.0	79.9
QG2-Non Award	57.1	66.7	—	—	53.6	—	—	44.4	56.9
Median ETD (yrs)									
QG1-Award	4.4	5.1	4.9	5.2	5.1	5.0	5.2	5.4	4.9
QG2-Award	4.7	5.5	4.8	5.1	5.2	4.5	5.8	6.0	5.1
QG2-Non Award	4.5	5.5	—	—	5.3	—	—	6.2	5.3
1967–1971									
Cell size									
QG1-Award	343	191	141	24	145	33	50	56	983
QG2-Award	172	143	126	43	145	45	71	82	827
QG2-Non Award	95	73	43	18	62	10	18	37	356
MCR[a] (%)									
QG1-Award	67.9	74.3	85.1	79.2	82.8	81.8	80.0	67.9	75.2
QG2-Award	51.7	72.7	81.7	69.8	72.4	80.0	67.6	61.0	68.3
QG2-Non Award	48.4	76.7	62.8	44.4	64.5	90.0	61.1	45.9	60.1
Median ETD (yrs)									
QG1-Award	4.6	5.3	5.0	5.7	5.3	4.6	4.6	6.0	5.0
QG2-Award	4.7	5.5	4.8	6.0	5.3	4.9	5.3	6.2	5.3
QG2-Non Award	4.9	6.2	5.1	5.1	5.3	4.4	5.7	6.4	5.4
1972–1976									
Cell size									
QG1-Award	156	105	81	47	232	72	66	123	882
QG2-Award	113	72	69	44	161	54	39	90	642
QG2-Non Award	161	106	83	51	238	68	72	105	884
MCR[a] (%)									
QG1-Award	78.8	81.9	82.7	72.3	83.6	80.6	86.4	56.9	78.1
QG2-Award	74.3	87.5	89.9	63.6	80.1	72.2	79.5	71.1	77.9
QG2-Non Award	64.6	80.2	83.1	56.9	71.4	76.5	77.8	49.5	69.8
Median ETD (yrs)									
QG1-Award	4.3	5.1	4.7	5.3	5.5	4.2	4.4	5.8	5.0
QG2-Award	4.4	5.1	4.7	5.1	5.1	4.4	5.1	6.7	4.9
QG2-Non Award	4.7	5.3	4.3	5.3	5.2	4.9	5.2	6.3	5.1

Source: Special tabulations from the National Science Foundation.

Notes: For definitions of Quality Group (QG) categories see note to Table 10.1. Dash indicates less than 20 observations in the cell.

[a]Minimum Completion Rate.

TABLE G.11–6
Minimum Completion Rates and Elapsed Time-to-Degree by Gender, EHP Total,
1962–1981 Entering Cohorts

	Men Only			
	1962–1966	*1967–1971*	*1972–1976*	*1977–1981*
3-Universities:				
Cell Size	1,418	1,407	1,124	732
MCR	59.2	46.1	40.5	32.8
ETD	6.9	6.8	7.2	na
8-Universities:				
Cell Size		2,954	2,453	1,760
MCR		56.3	46.1	39.3
ETD		6.6	7.0	na
Larger:				
Cell Size		1,804	1,529	1,121
MCR		38.5	31.7	23.2
ETD		7.2	7.4	na
Smaller:				
Cell Size		934	956	603
MCR		67.4	57.9	51.2
ETD		6.1	6.4	na

	Women Only			
	1962–1966	*1967–1971*	*1972–1976*	*1977–1981*
3-Universities:				
Cell Size	606	807	683	542
MCR	37.0	38.6	33.7	32.2
ETD	7.8	7.3	8.0	na
8-Universities:				
Cell Size		1,547	1,468	1,279
MCR		51.6	41.4	37.6
ETD		7.3	7.5	na
Larger:				
Cell Size		1,086	1,360	835
MCR		34.4	27.3	19.1
ETD		7.5	8.3	na
Smaller:				
Cell Size		359	456	391
MCR		60.9	53.3	53.0
ETD		6.8	6.9	na

Source: Ten-University data set.

Notes: "Three-Universities" includes Berkeley, Chicago, and Columbia. "8-Universities" includes
Berkeley, Chicago, Columbia, Cornell, Harvard, Princeton, Stanford, and UNC. "Larger" includes
Berkeley, Chicago, and Columbia. "Smaller" includes Cornell, Harvard, Princeton, and Stanford.
"Na" indicates calculations would be misleading because of truncation.

Definitions of Frequently Used Terms

COHORTS

BA Cohort: Data organized by year in which individuals received the BA.

Entering Cohort: Data organized by the year in which individuals began doctoral study in the program cited; when used with the National Fellowship data set (excepting the Whiting Fellows), this is synonymous with the year in which individuals received the fellowship award.

PhD Cohort: Data organized by year in which individuals received the PhD.

COMPLETION RATES

Minimum Completion Rate (MCR): The percentage of an entering cohort that earned the PhD by a given year.

Truncated Completion Rate (TCR): The percentage of an entering cohort that earned the PhD within a specified number of years.

Cumulative Completion Rates (CCR): The percentages of an entering cohort that earned the PhD within x years, $x + 1$ years, and so on.

DATA SETS

Ten-University data set: Described in detail in Appendix A; contains information on time-to-degree, stages of attrition, and completion rates, as well as other descriptive data, for graduate students at University of California (Berkeley), University of Chicago, Cornell University, Columbia University, Harvard University, University of Michigan, Princeton University, Stanford University, University of North Carolina (Chapel Hill), and Yale University.

National Fellowship data set: Described in detail in Appendix B; contains information on time-to-degree and completion rates, as well as other descriptive data, for recipients of Woodrow Wilson, Danforth, Mellon, NSF, NDEA, and Whiting fellowships.

FacPro: Described in detail in Appendix C; contains information on time-to-degree, as well as other descriptive data, for faculty promoted to tenure during the 1980s at three colleges and four universities.

Doctorate Records File: The compilation of information on individuals who received doctorates from U.S. universities from 1920 to the present; based on the annual *Survey of Earned Doctorates* and maintained by the National Research Council's Office of Scientific and Engineering Personnel.

FIELDS OF STUDY

Six-Fields: English, history, economics, political science, mathematics, and physics/astronomy.

EHP: English, history, and political science.

MP: Mathematics and physics/astronomy.

426

FINANCIAL SUPPORT

Primary (source of support): Largest single source of support during graduate study (fellowship, teaching assistantship, research assistantship, or own support); defined for each university in Appendix A.

ORGANIZATIONAL ABBREVIATIONS

AAU: American Association of Universities.
CGS: Council on Graduate Schools.
COFHE: Consortium on Financing Higher Education.
NDEA: National Defense Education Act.
NEH: National Endowment for the Humanities.
NRC: National Research Council.
NSF: National Science Foundation.

SCALE OF GRADUATE PROGRAM

Larger: Defined by size of entering cohorts; universities classified as having Larger programs are University of California (Berkeley), University of Chicago, and Columbia University.
Smaller: Defined by size of entering cohorts; universities classified as having Smaller programs are Cornell University, Princeton University, Harvard University, and Stanford University.

STAGES OF ATTRITION

Pre–Second Year: Students leaving graduate study before enrolling in the second year of graduate study.
Other Pre-ABD: Students leaving graduate study after the start of the second year, but before finishing all requirements prior to the dissertation.
ABD ("All But Dissertation"): Students leaving graduate study without receiving a PhD after finishing all requirements except the dissertation.

STUDENT-YEAR COST

Student-Year Cost (SYC): Total number of years invested in doctoral study by all members of an entering cohort divided by the number of doctorates earned by the cohort.

TIME-TO-DEGREE

Total Time-to-Degree (TTD): Number of years between the awarding of the BA and the awarding of the PhD.
Elapsed Time-to-Degree (ETD): Number of years between entry to graduate school and the awarding of the PhD.
Registered Time-to-Degree (RTD): Number of years that a student was actually registered before receiving a PhD.

References Cited

Abedi, J., and E. Benkin. 1987. "The Effects of Students, Academic, Financial and Demographic Variables on Time to Doctorate." *Research in Higher Education* 17:3–14.

Adelman, Clifford. 1984. "The Standardized Test Scores of College Graduates, 1964–1982." National Institute of Education.

American Economics Association. 1991. *Report of the Commission on Graduate Education in Economics*. Madison, Wisc.: University of Wisconsin.

Angrist, Joshua David. 1989. "Econometric Analysis of the Vietnam Era Draft Lottery." PhD diss., Princeton.

———. 1990. "Lifetime Earnings and the Vietnam Era Draft Lottery." *American Economic Review* 80(3):313–36.

Arce, Carlos H., and Winton H. Manning. 1984. "Minorities in Academic Careers: The Experience of Ford Foundation Fellows." Report to the Ford Foundation.

Armsey, James W. 1977. "The Anatomy of a Major Program: A Report to the Ford Foundation on Efforts to Reform Graduate Education in the United States." Report to the Ford Foundation.

Association of American Universities. 1990a. *The Ph.D. Shortage: The Federal Role*. Washington, D.C.: Association of American Universities.

———. 1990b. Washington, D.C.: *Institutional Policies to Improve Doctoral Education*. Association of American Universities.

Association of Graduate Schools. 1976. "The Research Doctorate in the United States." Washington, D.C.: Association of Graduate Schools.

Association of Graduate Schools and Council of Graduate Schools. 1964. *The Doctor of Philosophy Degree*. Washington, D.C.: The Association of Graduate Schools and The Council of Graduate Schools.

Baird, Leonard L. 1990. "Diciplines and Doctorates: The Relationships between Program Characteristics and the Duration of Doctoral Study." *Research in Higher Education* 31(4):369–85.

Balderston, Frederick E. 1974. "Difficulties in Cost Analysis of Graduate Education." In *Federal Policy Alternatives toward Graduate Education*. Washington, D.C.: National Board on Graduate Education.

Bargar, Robert R., and Jane Mayo-Chamberlain. 1983. "Advisor and Advisee Issues in Doctoral Education." *Journal of Higher Education* 54(4):407–32.

Baskir, L., and W. Strauss. 1978. *Chance and Circumstance*. New York: Knopf.

Benkin, Ellen M. 1984. "Where Have All the Doctoral Students Gone? A Study of Doctoral Attrition at UCLA." PhD diss., University of California, Los Angeles.

Berelson, Bernard. 1960. *Graduate Education in the United States*. New York: McGraw Hill.

Berger, Joseph. 1989. "Slow Pace toward Doctorates Prompts Fears of Unfilled Jobs." *New York Times*, May 3, 1.

Blackwell, James E. 1990. "Current Issues Affecting Blacks and Hispanics in the Educational Pipeline." In *U.S. Race Relations in the 1980s and 1990s: Challenges and Alternatives*, ed. Gail E. Thomas. New York: Hemisphere.

Boulding, Kenneth E. 1980. "Graduate Education as Ritual and Substance." In *The Philosophy and Future of Graduate Education*, ed. William K. Frankena. Ann Arbor: University of Michigan Press.

Bowen, Howard R., and Jack H. Schuster. 1986. *American Professors: A National Resource Imperiled*. New York: Oxford University Press.

Bowen, William G. 1964. *Economic Aspects of Education*. Research Report no. 104. Princeton: Economics Department, Industrial Relations Section, Princeton University.

Bowen, William G., Paul Benacerraf, Thomas Davis, William Lewis, Linda Morse, and

Carl Schafer. 1972. *Budgeting and Resource Allocation at Princeton University*. A report of a Demonstration Project supported by the Ford Foundation.

Bowen, William G., Graham Lord, and Julie Ann Sosa. 1991. "Measuring Time to the Doctorate." *Proceedings of the National Academy of Sciences* 88(3):713–17.

Bowen, William G., and Neil L. Rudenstine. 1991. "Colleges Must Have the Flexibility to Designate Financial Aid for Members of Minority Groups." *Chronicle of Higher Education*, January 9, B1, B3.

Bowen, William G., and Julie Ann Sosa. 1989. *Prospects for Faculty in the Arts and Sciences*. Princeton: Princeton University Press.

Bowen, William G., Sarah E. Turner, and Marcia L. Witte. 1992. "The B.A.-Ph.D. Nexus." *Journal of Higher Education* (January-February): 65–86.

Boyer, Ernest L. 1990. *Scholarship Reconsidered: Priorities of the Professioriate*. Special Report. Princeton: The Carnegie Foundation for the Advancement of Teaching.

Breneman, David W. 1970. "The Ph.D. Production Process: A Study of Departmental Behavior." PhD diss., University of California, Berkeley.

———. 1975. *Graduate School Adjustments to the "New Depression" in Higher Education*. Technical Report no. 3. National Board on Graduate Education. Washington, D.C.: National Academy of Sciences.

———. 1977. "Efficiency in Graduate Education: An Attempted Reform. A Report to the Ford Foundation." Brookings Institution.

California State Postsecondary Education Commission. 1985. "Graduate Education in California: Trends and Issues. Commission Report." Sacramento.

Carmichael, Oliver C. 1961. *Graduate Education: A Critique and a Program*. New York: Harper and Brothers.

Carnegie Commission on Higher Education. 1968. *Quality and Equality: New Levels of Federal Responsibility for Higher Education*. Special report and recommendations by the Commission. Hightstown, N.J.: McGraw Hill Book Company.

———. 1973. *Priorities for Action: Final Report of the Carnegie Commission on Higher Education*. Hightstown, N.J.: McGraw Hill Book Company.

Carnegie Foundation for the Advancement of Teaching. 1987a. "Foreign Students: A Valuable Link." *Change* 19 (July–August): 39–43.

———. 1987b. *A Classification of Institutions of Higher Education*. 1987. ed. Carnegie Foundation Technical Report. Princeton: Carnegie Foundation for the Advancement of Teaching.

Cartter, Allan M. 1966. *An Assessment of Quality in Graduate Education*. Washington, D.C.: American Council on Education.

———. 1974. "The Academic Labor Market." In *Higher Education and the Labor Market*, ed. M.S. Gordon. New York: McGraw Hill. Pp. 281–307.

———. 1976. *Ph.D.'s and the Academic Labor Market*. The Carnegie Commission on Higher Education. New York: McGraw Hill.

Casarett, Alison P. 1988. "Annual Statistical Report of the Graduate School, Cornell University: 1987–1988."

"The Changing Shape of Post-Graduate Education." 1987. *OECD Observer* 146(June–July): 13–15.

Cheit, Earl F. 1971. *The New Depression in Higher Education: A Study of Financial Conditions at 4 Colleges and Universities*. New York: McGraw Hill.

Cipra, Barry. 1991. "Math Ph.D.'s: Bleak Picture." *Science* 252(April): 252–53.

Clewell, Beatriz Chu. 1987. *Retention of Black and Hispanic Doctoral Students*. Princeton: Educational Testing Service.

Clifford, James. 1988. *The Predicament of Culture: Twentieth-Century Ethnography Literature and Art*. Cambridge: Harvard University Press.

Coale, A. J. 1972. *The Growth and Structure of Human Populations: A Mathematical Investigation*. Princeton: Princeton University Press.

Coale, A. J., and D. R. McNeil. 1972. "The Distribution by Age of the Frequency of First

Marriage in a Female Cohort." *Journal of the American Statistical Association* 67(December): 340.

Cohen, Sheldon S. 1974. *A History of Colonial Education: 1607–1776*. New York: Wiley.

Cole, Jonathan. 1979. *Fair Science*. New York: Free Press.

Cole, Jonathan R., and Burton Singer. 1989. "A Theory of Limited Differences: Explaining the Productivity Puzzle in Science." Mimeo. Not for quotation. Unpublished draft.

Colombo, Richard A., and Donald G. Morrison. 1988. "Blacklisting Social Science Departments with Poor Ph.D. Submission Rates." *Management Science* 34(6): 696.

Columbia University. 1990. "Producing Doctorates in the Humanities and Social Sciences at Columbia University." Report submitted to the Andrew W. Mellon Foundation.

Committee on Doctoral and Postdoctoral Study in the Mathematical Sciences. 1992. "Educating Mathematical Scientists: Doctoral and Postdoctoral Study in the United States." Forthcoming. Commissioned by the Board of Mathematical Sciences, National Research Council. Washington, D.C.: National Academy of Sciences.

Conn, Peter. 1989. "Narrative in the Making of History." In *Viewpoints*. Excerpts from American Council of Learned Societies Conference on the Humanities in the 1990's. Washington, D.C.: American Council of Learned Societies.

Connell, R. W. 1985. "How to Supervise a Ph.D." *Vestes* 28(2):38–42.

Connor, Robert. 1985. "The New Classical Humanities and the Old." *The Classical Journal*, April–May.

Consortium on Financing Higher Education. 1990. "Graduation Rates at COFHE Institutions." Report.

Cornell University. 1990. Proposal for Support of Graduate Students in the Humanities and Related Social Sciences. Submitted to the Andrew W. Mellon Foundation.

Council of Graduate Schools. 1991. *The Role and Nature of the Doctoral Dissertation*. Washington, D.C.: Council of Graduate Schools.

Cross, K. P. 1974. "The Woman Student." In *Women in Higher Education*, ed. W. T. Purness and A. Graham. Washington, D.C.: American Council on Education.

Cude, Wilfred. 1987. *The Ph.D. Trap*. Nova Scotia, Canada: Medicine Label Press.

———. 1989. "Graduate Education Is in Trouble." *Challenge* 32(5):59–63.

The Danforth Foundation. 1956. *The Program of Danforth Graduate Fellows: Some Questions and Answers*. St. Louis, Mo.: The Danforth Foundation.

———. 1976. *The Danforth and Kent Fellowships: A Quinquennial Review*. St. Louis, Mo.: Danforth Foundation.

Dawes, R. M. 1975. "Graduate Admissions Variables and Future Success." *Science* 187:721–23.

Decker, Robert L. 1973. "Success and Attrition Characteristics in Graduate Studies." *Journal of Economic Education* 4(2):130–37.

DePalma, Anthony. 1990. "Graduate Schools Fill with Foreigners." *New York Times*, November 11, 1.

Digest of Education Statistics. *See* U.S. Department of Education.

Doctorate Records File. *See* National Research Council. 1990.

Dressel, Paul L., and Mary Magdala Thompson. 1977. *A Degree for College Teachers: The Doctor of Arts*. A technical report for the Carnegie Council on Policy Studies in Higher Education. New York: Carnegie Council Foundation for the Advancement of Teaching.

Earned Degrees Conferred Survey. *See* U.S. Department of Education.

Ehrenberg, Ronald G. 1991. "Academic Labor Supply." In *Economic Challenges in Higher Education*, ed. Charles Clotfelter, Ronald Ehrenberg, Malcolm Getz, and John Siegfried. Chicago: University of Chicago Press. February 1991 draft. Forthcoming.

Ehrenberg, Ronald G., Daniel I. Rees, and Dominic J. Brewer. 1991. "How Would Universities Respond to Increased Federal Support for Graduate Students?" Unpublished paper. Cornell University. October 3.

Evangelauf, Jean. 1989. "Lengthening of Time to Earn a Doctorate Causes Concern." *Chronicle of Higher Education*, March 15, 13–14.

Fish, Stanley. 1989. "Being Interdisciplinary Is So Very Hard to Do." *Profession*. (Modern Language Association of America).

Frankena, William K., ed. 1980. *The Philosophy and Future of Graduate Education: Papers and Commentaries Delivered at the International Conference on the Philosophy of Graduate Education at the University of Michigan, April 13–15, 1978.* Ann Arbor: University of Michigan Press.

Freeman, Richard B. 1971. *The Market for College-Trained Manpower: A Study in the Economics of Career Choice.* Cambridge: Harvard University Press.

———. 1975a. "Supply and Salary Adjustments to the Changing Science Manpower Market: Physics, 1948–1973." *American Economic Review*, March, 27–39.

———. 1975b. "Overinvestment in College Training?" *Journal of Human Resources* 10:287–311.

Freeman, Richard B., and D. W. Breneman. 1974. "Forecasting the Ph.D. Labor Market: Pitfalls for Policy." Technical Report no. 3. National Board on Graduate Education. Washington, D.C.: National Academy of Sciences.

Froomkin, Joseph. 1983. *Support of Graduate and Professional Students.* Washington, D.C.: National Association on Student Financial Assistance.

Geertz, Clifford. 1988. *Works and Lives: The Anthropologist as Author.* Stanford, Calif.: Stanford University Press.

Gillingham, Lisa, Joseph J. Seneca, and Michael K. Taussig. 1991. "The Determinants of Progress to the Doctoral Degree." *Research in Higher Education* (32)4:449–468.

Girves, J. E., and V. Wemmerus. 1988. "Developing Models of Graduate Student Degree Progress." *Journal of Higher Education* 59:163–89.

Goheen, Robert F. 1989. "Mellon Fellowships in the Humanities: 1988–89 Annual Report." Princeton: The Woodrow Wilson National Fellowship Foundation.

Goldberg, Frank. 1984. "A Study of the Efficiency of the Fellowship Selection Process at a Major Research University." Paper presented at the Annual Meeting of the Association for the Study of Higher Education, Chicago, Ill., March 12–14.

Graff, Gerald. 1988. "Conflicts over the Curriculum Are Here to Stay; They Should Be Made Educationally Productive." *Chronicle of Higher Education*, February 17, A48.

Grassmuck, Karen. 1991. "Colleges Discover the Human Toll as They Struggle to Cut Work Forces." *Chronicle of Higher Education,* July 10, 1, 25, 28.

Gray, Paul E. 1991. "Measure Need, Not Money." *New York Times,* July 22, A15.

Hansen, W. Lee. 1986. "Changes in Faculty Salaries." In *American Professors: A National Resource Inperiled*, ed. Howard R. Bowen and Jack H. Schuster. New York: Oxford University Press.

———. 1991. *The Education and Training of Economics Doctorates: Major Findings of the American Economic Association's Commission on Graduate Education in Economics.* Madison, Wisc.: Commission on Graduate Education in Economics, University of Wisconsin.

Harmon, Lindsey. 1977. *Career Achievement of NSF Graduate Fellows: The Awardees of 1952–72.* Washington, D.C.: National Research Council.

———. 1978. *A Century of Doctorates: Data Analysis of Growth and Change.* Report for the National Research Council. Washington, D.C.: National Academy Press.

Hartnett, Rodney. 1987. "Has There Been a Graduate Student Brain Drain in the Arts and Sciences?" *Journal of Higher Education* 58:562–85.

Harvard University. 1963. *Graduate School of Arts and Sciences, Graduate Studies in the Humanities.*

Harvard University Graduate School of Arts and Sciences. 1990. "Graduate Support Grant Proposal to the Mellon Foundation." Submitted to the Andrew W. Mellon Foundation.

Hellstrom, Ward. 1979. "Academic Responsibility and the Job Market." *Association of Departments of English Bulletin*, no. 62:95–99.

Hettmansperger, T. P. 1984. "Two-Sample Inference Based on One-Sample Sign Statistics." *Applied Statistics* 33(1):45–51.

Himmelfarb, Gertrude. 1987. *The New History and the Old*. Cambridge: Harvard University Press (Belknap Press).

Hirschorn, Michael W. 1988. "Doctorates Earned by Blacks Decline 26.5 Pct. in Decade." *Chronicle of Higher Education*, February 3, 1.

Holden, Constance, 1991. "Do We Need More PhDs, or Is Fewer Really Better?" *Science*, March 1.

Holmstrom, Engin I., and Laure M. Sharp. 1970. *Study of NDEA Title IV Fellowship Program, Phase II*. Washington, D.C.: Bureau of Social Science Research.

Hughes, Raymond M. 1925. *A Study of Graduate Schools of America*. Oxford, Ohio: Miami University Press.

Institute of International Education. 1989. *Open Doors*. New York: IIE. Pp. 7–15.

James, Estelle. 1978. "Product Mix and Cost Disaggregation: A Reinterpretation of the Economics of Higher Education." *Journal of Human Resources* 13(2):157ff.

Jaschik, Scott. 1991. "Bush Proposal to Merge Popular Programs for Graduate Students Sparks Controversy." *Chronicle of Higher Education*, June 26, 15, 18.

Jaynes, Gerald, and Robin Williams, eds. 1989. *A Common Destiny: Blacks in American Society*. Washington, D.C.: National Academy Press.

Jones, L. V., G. Lindzey, and P. E. Coggeshall, eds. 1982. *An Assessment of Research— Doctorate Programs in the United States*. 5 vols. Washington, D.C.: National Academy Press.

Keniston, Hayward. 1959. *Graduate Study and Research in the Arts and Sciences at the University of Pennsylvania*. Philadelphia: University of Pennsylvania Press.

Kernan, Alvin B. 1982. *The Imaginary Library: An Essay on Literature and Society*. Princeton: Princeton University Press.

"Knight Commission Tells Presidents to Use Their Power to Reform the 'Fundamental Premises' of College Sports." 1991. *Chronicle of Higher Education*, March 27, A1, A33.

Kohler, Robert E. 1990. "The Ph.D. Machine: Building on the Collegiate Base." *ISIS* 81:638–62.

Kristeller, Paul Otto. 1990. *A Life of Learning*. Haskins Lecture, American Council of Learned Societies, April 26. Washington, D.C.: ACLS.

Levin, Sharon G., and Paula E. Stephan. 1991. "Research Productivity over the Life Cycle: Evidence for Academic Scientists." *American Economic Review* 81(1).

Lindquist, Clarence B. 1971. *NDEA Title IV Fellowships for College Teaching*. Washington, D.C.: U.S. Department of Health, Education and Welfare.

Loeb, Jane, and Franklin Duff. 1974. "Graduate Student Cohort Data for Individual Advising and Resource Allocation." *Research in Higher Education* 2:325–40.

Lomperis, Ana Maria. 1992. "The Demographic Transformation of American Doctoral Education." *Research in Labor Economics* 13 (forthcoming).

Magner, Denise K. 1989. "Decline in Doctorates Earned by Black and White Men Persists, Study Finds; Foreign Students and U.S. Women Fill Gaps." *Chronicle of Higher Education*, March 1, A11.

Malaney, Gary D. 1987. "A Decade of Research on Graduate Students: A Review of the Literature in Academic Journals." ASHE Annual Meeting Paper. Paper presented at the Annual Meeting of the Association for the Study of Higher Education, Baltimore, Md., November 21–24.

Marmion, H. 1968. *Selective Service: Conflict and Compromise*. New York: Wiley.

Marrett, Cora B., and Laure Sharp. 1985. "Postdoctoral Fellowships for Minorities Program: Outcomes Study." Unpublished manuscript.

Mayhew, Lewis B. 1970. *Graduate and Professional Education, 1980: A Survey of Institutional Plans*. New York: McGraw Hill.

Meyers, Christopher. 1991. "Federally Endowed Fellowship Programs Viewed as Models." *Chronicle of Higher Education* 38(September 11).

Meyerson, M. 1975. "After a Decade of the Levelers in Higher Education: Reinforcing Quality While Maintaining Mass Education." *Daedalus* 104(1):304–21.

Miller, J. Hillis. 1988. "Humanistic Research." In *The Humanities in the University: Strategies for the 1990's.* American Council of Learned Societies Occasional Paper no. 6. Washington, D.C.: ACLS. Pp. 25–30.

Mooney, Carolyn J. 1990a. "Universities Awarded Record Number of Doctorates Last Year; Foreign Students Thought to Account for Much of the Increase." *Chronicle of Higher Education* 36(April): A1, 11, 18.

———. 1990b. "Faculty Job Market Slowly Improving, Evidence Indicates." *Chronicle of Higher Education* 36(April): A1, 14–15.

Mooney, Joseph D. 1968. "Attrition among Ph.D. Candidates: An Analysis of a Cohort of Recent Woodrow Wilson Fellows," *Journal of Human Resources* 3(1):47–62.

Mrs. Giles Whiting Foundation. 1983. *Mrs. Giles Whiting Foundation and The Whiting Fellowships in the Humanities, Ten Year Report and Directory of Fellows, 1973–74 to 1982–86.* New York: Mrs. Giles Whiting Foundation.

National Board on Graduate Education. 1975. *Federal Policy Alternatives toward Graduate Education.* Washington, D.C.: National Academy of Sciences.

———. 1975. *Outlook and Opportunities for Graduate Education.* Washington, D.C.: National Board on Graduate Education.

National Commission on Student Financial Assistance. 1983. *Signs of Trouble and Erosion: A Report on Graduate Education in America.* Final Report. Washington, D.C.: National Commission on Student Financial Assistance.

National Research Council. Annual. *Summary Report: Doctorate Recipients from United States Universities.* Washington, D.C.: National Academy Press.

———. 1990. Survey of Earned Doctorates, conducted by the National Research Council and sponsored by five federal agencies (NSF, NIH, NEH, USDA, and ED).

National Science Foundation. 1965–1971. *Graduate Student Support and Manpower Resources in Graduate Science Education.* Annual. Washington, D.C.: National Academy Press.

———. 1977. *Graduate Science Education: Student Support and Postdoctorals. Detailed Statistical Tables.* Annual 1972–1977.

Naylor, Paul D., and Timothy R. Sanford. 1982. "Intrainstitutional Analysis of Student Retention across Student Levels." *College and University* 57(2):143–59.

Nerad, Maresi, and J. Cerny. 1991. "From Facts to Actions Expanding the Educational Role of the Graduate Division." *Communicator* (Council of Graduate Schools, Washington, D.C.) Special Edition (May).

New York State Board of Regents. Commission on Doctoral Education. 1973. *Meeting the Needs of Doctoral Education in New York State. A Report with Recommendations.* Albany, N.Y.: New York State Education Department.

Organization for Economic Cooperation and Development. 1989. *Post Graduate Education in the 1980's.* Paris: OECD.

Ott, Mary Diederich, Theodore S. Markewich, and Nancy L. Ochsner. 1984. "Logit Analysis of Graduate Student Retention." *Research in Higher Education* 21:4.

Pelikan, Jaroslav. 1983. *Scholarship and Its Survival: Questions on the Idea of Graduate Education.* Princeton: Carnegie Foundation for the Advancement of Teaching.

Pinch, Judith. 1991. Personal communication, August 8.

Pogrow, Stanley. 1978. "Program Characteristics and the Use of Student Data to Predict Attrition from Doctoral Programs." *College Student Journal* 12(4):348–53.

Porter, Oscar F. 1989. "Undergraduate Completion and Persistence at Four-Year Colleges and Universities." National Institute of Independent Colleges and Universities.

Princeton University. 1963. *The Graduate Catalogue Announcement, 1963–1964.*

Princeton University Graduate School. 1990. "Proposal to the Mellon Foundation for a Grant to Support Education in the Humanities and Social Sciences."

Proposals to the Andrew W. Mellon Foundation to Improve Graduate Education. 1990. Submitted to the Andrew W. Mellon Foundation by the following universities: University of California, Berkeley; University of Chicago; Columbia University; Cornell University; Harvard University; University of Michigan; University of Pennsylvania;

Princeton University; Stanford University; Yale University. *See also* individual institutions.

Prown, Jules, and Committee. 1989. "Report of the Ad Hoc Committee on Teaching in Yale College." Yale University, April 25.

Pulliam, John D. 1976. *History of Education in America*. Columbus, Ohio: Merrill Publishing Company.

Ringer, Fritz K. 1979. *Education and Society in Modern Europe*. Bloomington, Ind.: Indiana University Press.

Rodman, Joan. 1986. "Object Relations and Separation Anxiety. Factors in Finishing a Dissertation." PhD diss., International College.

Roose, Kenneth D. 1971. "Fifty Top Rated Institutions: Their Role in Graduate Education." *The Research Reporter* (Center for Research and Development in Higher Education, Berkeley, Calif.) 4:1.

Roose, Kenneth D., and Charles J. Andersen. 1970. *A Rating of Graduate Programs*. Washington, D.C.: American Council on Education.

Rosenhaupt, Hans. 1958. "Financial Support for Graduate Students." In *Graduate Students: Experience at Columbia University, 1940–1956*, ed. Hans Rosenhaupt. New York: Columbia University Press.

Rossi, Alice S. 1990. Letter to author, July 12, 1990.

Rossi, Alice S., and Ann Calderwood. 1973. *Academic Women on the Move*. New York: Russell Sage Foundation.

Rubin, D. B. 1980. "Using Empirical Bayes Techniques in the Law School Validity Studies." *Journal of the American Statistical Association* 75:801–16.

Rudd, Ernest. 1985. *A New Look at Post Graduate Failure*. Sponsored by Society for Research into Higher Education. Guildford, U.K.: NFER and Nelson.

Santayana, George. 1922. *Character and Opinion in the United States: With Reminiscences of William James and Josiah Royce and Academic Life in America*. New York: Scribner.

Schorske, Carl E. 1988. "Expanding the Enlightenment Tradition." Commencement address, State University of New York, Stonybrook, May 15.

Scientific Manpower Commission and Council of Graduate Schools. 1989. "The Impact of the Draft on Graduate Schools in 1968–69."

Searle, John. 1990. "The Storm over the University." *New York Review of Books*, December 6.

Shapiro, Harold T. 1990. Speech given before the National Academy of Engineering, December 6, 1990.

Schapiro, Morton O., Michael P. O'Malley, and Larry H. Litten. 1991. "Progression to Graduate School from the 'Elite' Colleges and Universities: Understanding the Past and Influencing the Future." *Economics of Education Review* 10(3).

Sharp, Laure M., Barton Sensenig, and Lenore Reid. 1968. *Study of NDEA Title IV Fellowship Program, Phase I*. Washington, D.C.: Bureau of Social Science Research.

Singer, A. 1989. "The Effect of the Vietnam War on Numbers of Medical School Applicants." *Academic Medicine*, October, 567–73.

Smith, Bruce L. R., and Joseph J. Karlesky, eds. 1978. *The State of Academic Science*. New Rochelle, N.Y.: Change Magazine Press.

Snyder, Joan. 1988. *Early Career Achievements of National Science Foundation Graduate Fellows, 1967–1976*. Office of Scientific and Engineering Personnel, Washington, D.C.: National Research Council.

Snyder, Robert G. 1985. "Some Indicators of the Condition of Graduate Education in the Sciences." In *The State of Graduate Education*, ed. Bruce L. R. Smith. Brookings Dialogues on Public Policy Series. Washington, D.C.: Brookings Institution.

Solmon, L. C. 1976. *Male and Female Graduate Students: The Question of Equal Opportunity*. New York: Praeger.

Solow, Robert M. 1990. "Discussion: Educating and Training New Economics Ph.D.'s: How Good a Job Are We Doing?" *American Economic Review* 80(2): 437–50.

Stanford University. 1990. "Proposal to the Andrew W. Mellon Foundation from Stanford University." Submitted to the Andrew W. Mellon Foundation, New York.

Stark, Rodney. 1966. "Graduate Study at Berkeley: An Assessment of Attrition and Duration." Survey Research Center, University of California, Berkeley.

Stern, Frederick Preston. 1985. "The Effects of Separation Individualization Conflicts on Length of Time to Complete the Dissertation." PhD diss., CUNY.

Stone, Lawrence. 1987. "Resisting the New." *New York Review of Books*, December 17.

Summary Report. See National Research Council.

Tidball, M. E. 1980. "Women's Colleges and Women Achievers Revisited." *Signs: Journal of Women in Culture and Society* 5(3):504–17.

———. 1986. "Baccalaureate Origins of Recent Natural Science Doctorates." *Journal of Higher Education* 57(6):606–20.

Tidball, M. E., and V. Kistiakowsky. 1976. "Baccalaureate Origins of American Scientists and Scholars." *Science* 193(August): 646–52.

Tinto, Vincent. 1991. "Toward a Theory of Graduate Persistence." Draft of paper presented at the annual meeting of the American Research Association, Chicago, April.

Tucker, Allan, David Gottlieb, and John Pease. 1964. *Attrition of Graduate Students at the Ph.D. Level in the Traditional Arts and Sciences.* Publication no. 8. East Lansing, Mich.: Michigan State University, Office of Research Development and the Graduate School.

Tuckman, Howard, Susan Coyle, and Yupin Bae. 1990. *On Time to the Doctorate.* Washington, D.C.: National Academy Press.

Turner, S. E., and W. G. Bowen. 1990. "The 'Flight from the Arts and Sciences': Trends in Degrees Conferred." *Science* 250 (October 26).

UNESCO. *See* United Nations Educational Scientific and Cultural Organization.

United Nations Educational Scientific and Cultural Organization. 1989. *Statistical Yearbook.* Paris: UNESCO.

University of California, Berkeley. 1990. "Grant to Reduce Time-to Doctoral Degree in Selected Humanities Departments." Proposal submitted to the Andrew W. Mellon Foundation, New York.

University of Chicago. 1964. *Graduate Programs, Announcements, 1964–65.*

———. 1990. "A Proposal to Improve Graduate Education at the University of Chicago." Submitted to the Andrew W. Mellon Foundation, New York.

University of Michigan. 1990. "Proposal from the University of Michigan to the Andrew W. Mellon Foundation for Dissertation Fellowships in the Humanities and Social Sciences." Submitted to the Andrew W. Mellon Foundation, New York.

University of Pennsylvania. 1990. "Proposal to the Andrew W. Mellon Foundation in Support of Selected Graduate Programs of the School of Arts and Sciences." Submitted to the Andrew W. Mellon Foundation, New York.

U.S. Bureau of the Census. 1980. *1980 Census, Public Use Micro Data Samples.* Extract from .1% U.S. sample. Washington, D.C.: Government Printing Office.

———. 1986. *1980 Census of Population and Housing: Current Population Reports.* Series P–20, no. 429. Washington, D.C.: Government Printing Office.

———. 1990. *1980 Census of Population and Housing. Current Population Reports.* Series P–20. Washington, D.C.: Government Printing Office.

U.S. Congress. Senate. Committee on Labor and Human Resources. Subcommittee on Education, Arts and Humanities. 1991. *Hearings on the Reauthorization of the Higher Education Act: Recommendations for Graduate and Professional Education.* Testimony by Theodore Ziolkowski. 102d Cong., 1st sess., May 17, 1991.

U.S. Department of Education. 1986–1991. *Digest of Education Statistics.* Washington, D.C.: Government Printing Office.

———. National Center for Education Statistics. Various years. *Earned Degrees Conferred; Projections of Education Statistics to 2000.* Washington, D.C.: Government Printing Office.

U.S. Department of Health, Education and Welfare. 1973. "Report on Higher Education:

The Federal Role-Graduate Education." Report of the Task Force, F. Newman, Chm. Washington, D.C.: Government Printing Office.

U.S. Office of Management and Budget. 1990. *Budget of the United States Government, Fiscal Year 1991.* Washington, D.C.: Government Printing Office.

———. 1991. *Budget of the United States Government, Fiscal Year 1992.* Washington, D.C.: Government Printing Office.

U.S. Selective Service System. 1984. *A Short History of the Selective Service System.* Washington, D.C.: Government Printing Office.

Veeser, H. Aram, ed. 1989. *The New Historicism.* New York: Routledge.

Veysey, Laurence R. 1965. *The Emergence of the American University.* Chicago: University of Chicago Press.

Viner, Jacob. 1958. *The Long View and the Short.* Glencoe, Ill.: Free Press.

Webster, David S. 1983. "America's Highest Ranked Graduate Schools, 1925–1982." *Change* 15(4):14–24.

Weiss, Nancy J. 1986. "Women and Woodrow Wilson Fellowships." *Journal of the National Association for Women Deans, Administrators, and Counselors,* Spring, 9–13.

Whiting Foundation. *See* Mrs. Giles Whiting Foundation.

Widnall, Sheila E. 1988. "AAAS Presidential Lecture: Voices from the Pipeline." *Science* 241(4874):1740–45.

Wilson, Kenneth M. 1965. *Of Time and the Doctorate Report of an Inquiry into the Duration of Doctoral Study.* Atlanta: Southern Regional Education Board.

Wolfle, Dael. 1978. "Forces Affecting the Research Role of Universities." In *The State of Academic Science,* vol. 3, ed. Bruce L. R. Smith and Joseph J. Karesky. New York: Change Magazine Press.

Woodrow Wilson National Fellowship Foundation. 1964. *Woodrow Wilson National Fellowship Foundation Report for 1963–1964.* Woodrow Wilson National Fellowship Foundation.

———. 1977. "Where Are They Now? A Survey of Woodrow Wilson Fellows and Woodrow Wilson Dissertation Fellows Elected between 1945 and 1971." Woodrow Wilson National Fellowship Foundation.

Yale University. 1963. *Bulletin of Yale University, Graduate School, 1963–64.*

———. 1990. "A Proposal to the Andrew W. Mellon Foundation for Graduate Education at Yale University." Submitted to the Andrew W. Mellon Foundation, New York.

Young, Ken, Michael P. Fogarty, and Susan McRae. 1987. *The Management of Doctoral Studies in the Social Sciences.* Occasional Paper no. 36. London: Policy Studies Institute.

Ziolkowski, Theodore. 1990. "The Ph.D. Squid." *American Scholar* 59(2):177–95.

Zwick, Rebecca. 1991. "An Analysis of Graduate School Careers in Three Universities: Differences in Attainment Patterns across Academic Programs and Demographic Groups." GRE Board, Educational Testing Service, Princeton, N.J.

Zwick, Rebecca, and H. I. Braun. 1988. "Methods for Analyzing the Attainment of Graduate School Milestones: A Case Study." GRE Board Professional Report no. 86–3P, Educational Testing Service, Princeton, N.J.

Index[1]

Abedi, J., 191n.23
academic labor market, 2–3, 10, 23, 41, 45,
    46–48, 53–55, 86, 109–111, 188, 204
    and non-U.S. doctoral recipients, 32
Adelman, Clifford, 24n.10
African-Americans, 37–40
American Council of Learned Societies,
    274n.12
American Economics Association, 254n.9,
    260n.17
Angrist, Joshua D., 47n.11
Arce, Carlos H., 278
Armsey, James W., 212n.24
arts and sciences
    and shift to applied and professional
        fields, 23, 26, 41, 45, 53–54,
        110
    focus of this study, 4
Asian-Americans, 37–40
Association of American Universities, 1n.2,
    19, 119n.31, 177n.1, 257n.13,
    273n.8, 280n.28, 287
Association of Graduate Schools, 119n.31,
    258, 280n.23, 287
attrition. *see also* completion rates
    and previous studies, 107–108
    and student-year cost, 167–170
    at various stages of graduate study, 111–
        113, 128–129, 251–253

BA-cohorts. *see* methodology
BA-PhD nexus, 41–55
Baird, Leonard, 249n.16
Balderston, Frederick E., 79n.19, 164n.3
Bargar, Robert, 262n.20
Barzun, Jacques, 107n.7
Baskir, L., 49n.14
Benkin, Ellen M., 107n.4, 112n.19, 191n.23
Berelson, Bernard, 1, 20n.3, 57n.2, 63n.7,
    107–108, 111n.16, 114, 119n.31,
    211, 214, 253n.30, 253n.31, 288n.35
Berger, Joseph, 115n.24
Blackwell, James E., 37n.26
Bond, Christopher, Governor, 276n.16
Boulding, Kenneth, 250n.1
Bowen, Howard R., 46n.6
Bowen, William G., 2n.5, 23n.9, 41, 47n.7,
    47n.10, 48n.12, 56n.1, 116n.26,

177n.1, 222n.43, 222n.44, 271n.4,
    274n.11, 275n.13, 277n.17, 280n.24
Boyer, Ernest, 288n.35
Breneman, David W., 56n.1, 59n.4, 67n.12,
    108n.8, 127n.7, 165n.4, 212,
    214n.28, 214n.30, 278
Brewer, Donald, 277n.17
British system of doctoral education, 288n.34
Bureau of Social Science Research, 210n.22

Calderwood, Ann, 32n.20
California, state of, 276
California Postsecondary Education Commis-
    sion, 276n.16
Cambridge University, 271n.4
Carmichael, Oliver C., 1n.3, 261n.18
Carnegie Classification System, 56n.1
Carnegie Commission on Higher Education,
    1n.3, 164n.3
Carnegie Foundation for the Advancement of
    Teaching, 32n.19
Cartter, Allan, 48, 55, 63n.7, 111n.15
Casarett, Alison P., 92n.16
Castle, David, 189n.20
Center for Research in Graduate Education,
    University of Rochester, 278n.20
Cerny, J., 107n.4, 128n.10, 177n.2, 254n.6, 263
Cheit, Earl F., 91n.14
Cipra, Barry, 2n.6
citizenship
    focus of this study, 4
    foreign interest in U.S. education, 32n.18
    non-U.S. doctorate recipients, 1, 26n.13,
        28–32, 34
    by field, 28–31
Clewell, Beatriz Chu, 37n.26
Clifford, James, 244n.11
Coale, Ansley, 117n.27, 120n.32
Cohen, Sheldon, 19n.1
Cole, Jonathan R., 32n.20, 250, 251n.2
Colombo, Richard A., 271n.4
Commission on Graduate Education in Eco-
    nomics, 254n.9
Committee on Doctoral and Postdoctoral
    Study in the Mathematical Sci-
    ences, 185n.14, 218n.36, 229n.1,
    262n.20, 283n.28
completion rates
    and academic labor market, 109–111

---

[1]Includes only material in Chapters One through Fourteen. Preface and Appendices are not indexed.